Creating America

A History of the United States

1877 to the 21st Century

McDOUGAL LITTELL

Zitkala-Ša
Native American author

Franklin D. Roosevelt
Thirty-second president of
the United States

Jane Addams
Progressive era social reformer

Maya Lin
Designer of the Vietnam
Veterans Memorial

Cesar Chavez
Labor and civil rights leader

Amelia Earhart
Aviator; first woman to fly solo
across the Atlantic Ocean

Barbara Jordan
Congressional representative
from Texas

Colin Powell
U.S. Secretary of State

Dr. Martin Luther King, Jr.
Civil rights leader

Creating America

A History of the United States

1877 to the 21st Century

Jesus Garcia

Donna M. Ogle

C. Frederick Risinger

Joyce Stevos

Ronald W. Reagan
Fortieth president of the
United States

McDougal Littell
A DIVISION OF HOUGHTON MIFFLIN COMPANY

Senior Consultants

Jesus Garcia is Professor of Social Studies at the University of Nevada at Las Vegas. A former social studies teacher, Dr. Garcia has co-authored many books and articles on subjects that range from teaching social studies in elementary school to seeking diversity in education. Dr. Garcia will serve as President of the National Council for the Social Studies in 2004–2005.

Donna M. Ogle is Professor of Reading and Language Arts at National-Louis University in Evanston, Illinois, and is a specialist in reading in the content areas with an interest in social studies. She is past president of the International Reading Association. A former social studies teacher, Dr. Ogle is also Director of a Goals 2000 grant for Reading and Thinking in the Content Areas for four Chicago high schools. She developed the K-W-L reading strategy that is so widely used in schools.

C. Frederick Risinger is Director of Professional Development and Coordinator for Social Studies Education at Indiana University. He is past president of the National Council for the Social Studies. Mr. Risinger also served on the coordinating committee for the National History Standards Project. He writes a monthly column on technology in the social studies classroom for *Social Education.*

Joyce Stevos recently retired from 36 years of service to the Providence, Rhode Island, Public Schools. For 15 of those years, she was the social studies area supervisor and developed programs on Holocaust studies, the Armenian genocide, character education, voter education, and government and law. Currently, she is a Ph.D. candidate in education focusing on how youth develop a citizen identity.

Copyright © 2005 by McDougal Littell, a division of Houghton Mifflin Company. All rights reserved.

Maps on pages A1–A39 © Rand McNally & Company. All rights reserved.

Acknowledgments begin on page R77.

ISBN 0-618-37684-4

Printed in the United States of America
4 5 6 7 8 9 – DWO – 07 06 05

Consultants and Reviewers

Content Consultants
The content consultants reviewed the manuscript for historical depth and accuracy and for clarity of presentation.

Roger Beck
Department of History
Eastern Illinois University
Charleston, Illinois

David Farber
Department of History
University of New Mexico
Albuquerque, New Mexico

Cheryl Johnson-Odim
Department of History
Loyola University
Chicago, Illinois

Joseph Kett
Department of History
University of Virginia
Charlottesville, Virginia

Jack N. Rakove
Department of History
Stanford University
Stanford, California

Virginia Stewart
Department of History
University of North Carolina,
   Wilmington
Wilmington, North Carolina

Christopher Waldrep
Department of History
Eastern Illinois University
Charleston, Illinois

Nancy Woloch
Department of History
Barnard College
New York, New York

Multicultural Advisory Board
The multicultural advisers reviewed the manuscript for appropriate historical content.

Betty Dean
Social Studies Consultant
Pearland, Texas

Tyrone C. Howard
College of Education
The Ohio State University
Columbus, Ohio

Jose C. Moya
Department of History
University of California
   at Los Angeles
Los Angeles, California

Pat Payne
Office of Multicultural Education
Indianapolis Public Schools
Indianapolis, Indiana

Betto Ramirez
Former Teacher, La Joya, Texas
Social Studies Consultant
Mission, Texas

Jon Reyhner
Department of Education
Northern Arizona University
Flagstaff, Arizona

Ronald Young
Department of History
Georgia Southern University
Statesboro, Georgia

Consultants and Reviewers

Teacher Consultants

The following educators contributed activity options for the Pupil's Edition and teaching ideas and activities for the Teacher's Edition.

Paul C. Beavers
J. T. Moore Middle School
Nashville, Tennessee

Holly West Brewer
Buena Vista Paideia Magnet School
Nashville, Tennessee

Ron Campana
Social Studies Consultant
New York, New York

Patricia B. Carlson
Swanson Middle School
Arlington, Virginia

Ann Cotton
Ft. Worth Independent School
    District
Ft. Worth, Texas

Kelly Ellis
Hamilton Junior High School
Cypress, Texas

James Grimes
Middlesex County Vocational–
Technical High School
Woodbridge, New Jersey

Brent Heath
De Anza Middle School
Ontario, California

Suzanne Hidalgo
Serrano Middle School
Highland, California

Barbara Kennedy
Sylvan Middle School
Citrus Heights, California

Pamela Kniffin
Navasota Junior High School
Navasota, Texas

Tammy Leiber
Navasota Junior High School
Navasota, Texas

Lori Lesslie
Cedar Bluff Middle School
Knoxville, Tennessee

Bill McKee
Brockport Central School
Brockport, New York

Brian McKenzie
Dr. Charles R. Drew Science
    Magnet School
Buffalo, New York

W. W. Bear Mills
Goddard Junior High School
Midland, Texas

Lindy Poling
Millbrook High School
Raleigh, North Carolina

Jean Price
T. H. Rogers Middle School
Houston, Texas

Meg Robbins
Wilbraham Middle School
Wilbraham, Massachusetts

Philip Rodriguez
McNair Middle School
San Antonio, Texas

Leslie Schubert
Parkland School
McHenry, Illinois

Robert Sisko
Carteret Middle School
Carteret, New Jersey

Marci Smith
Hurst-Euless-Bedford Independent
    School District
Bedford, Texas

James Sorenson
Chippewa Middle School
Des Plaines, Illinois

Nicholas G. Sysock
Carteret Middle School
Carteret, New Jersey

Lisa Williams
Lamberton Middle School
Carlisle, Pennsylvania

Michael Yell
Hudson Middle School
Hudson, Wisconsin

Teacher Panels

The following educators provided ongoing review during the development of prototypes, the table of contents, and key components of the program.

Bill Albright
Wilson Southern Junior High School
Sinking Spring, Pennsylvania

Henry Assetto
Gordon Middle School
Coatesville, Pennsylvania

James Berry
Kennedy Middle School
Grand Prairie, Texas

Ralph Burnley
Roosevelt Middle School
Philadelphia, Pennsylvania

Mary Ann Canamar
Garner Middle School
San Antonio, Texas

Zoe Carter
San Jacinto Junior High School
Midland, Texas

Stephen Cicero
Butler Area Junior High School
Butler, Pennsylvania

Charles Crescenzi
Dover Intermediate School
Dover, Pennsylvania

Sharon McDonald
Cook Junior High School
Houston, Texas

Phil Mifsud
Roosevelt Middle School
Erie, Pennsylvania

Joel Mumma
Centerville Middle School
Lancaster, Pennsylvania

September Olson
Richardson Middle School
El Paso, Texas

Donald Roberts
Frick International Studies Academy
Pittsburgh, Pennsylvania

Mary Rogers
Brookside Intermediate School
Friendswood, Texas

Lucy Sanchez
John F. Kennedy High School
San Antonio, Texas

Steve Seale
Hamilton Middle School
Houston, Texas

Yolanda Villalobos
Dallas Independent School District
Dallas, Texas

Diane Williams
Hill-Freedman Middle School
Philadelphia, Pennsylvania

Lisa Williams
Lamberton Middle School
Carlisle, Pennsylvania

Student Board

The following students reviewed pages for the textbook.

Adam Backhaus
Parkland School
McHenry, Illinois

Ben Barney
Hamilton Junior High School
Cypress, Texas

Amanda Berrier
Lamberton Middle School
Carlisle, Pennsylvania

Debra Hurwitz
T. H. Rogers Middle School
Houston, Texas

Reginald Jones
Dr. Charles R. Drew Science
  Magnet School
Buffalo, New York

Brendon Keinath
Wilbraham Middle School
Wilbraham, Massachusetts

Daniel MacDonald
Carteret Middle School
Carteret, New Jersey

Cameron Mote
Serrano Middle School
Highland, California

Kim Nguyen
Sylvan Middle School
Citrus Heights, California

Arianna G. Noriega
De Anza Middle School
Ontario, California

Nicholas Tofilon
Burlington Middle School
Burlington, Wisconsin

Emmanuel Zepeda
Haven Middle School
Evanston, Illinois

Pomeiock tribe member

Boston

24

Emma Holmes

Seven African-American congressmen during Reconstruction

ix

UNIT 2

America Transformed 1860 – 1914

x Immigrants approaching Ellis Island

Queen Liliuokalani

Tensions at Home and Abroad 1954 – PRESENT

UNIT

5

President John F. Kennedy

Buzz Aldrin

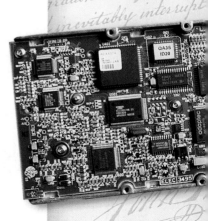

xiii

Features

CITIZENSHIP TODAY

Economics *in* History

America's HERITAGE

AMERICA'S HISTORY MAKERS

daily *life*

Features

HISTORY through ART

Now and then

Connections TO

STRANGE but True

Voices from the Past

A VOICE FROM THE PAST

Is it possible . . . that nine millions of men can make effective progress in economic lines if they are deprived of political rights? . . . If history and reason give any distinct answer to these questions, it is an emphatic *No.*

W. E. B. Du Bois,
The Souls of Black Folk

Voices from the Past

Visual Primary Sources for Assessment

Historical Maps

Charts and Graphs

The Effects of the War

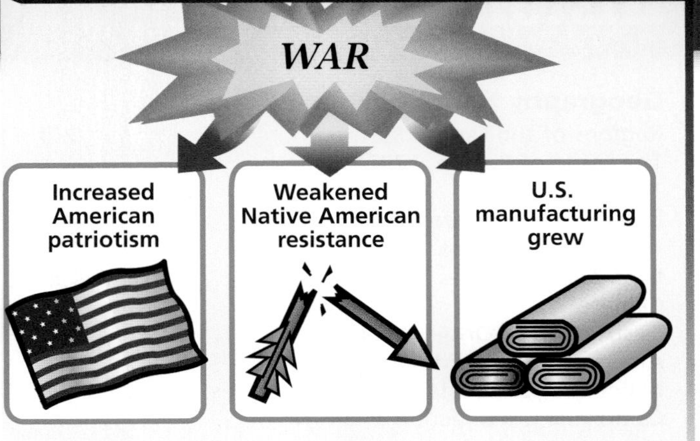

WAR
Increased American patriotism
Weakened Native American resistance
U.S. manufacturing grew

Charts

Graphs

CONNECTIONS TO MATH

Military Deaths in the American Revolution

Number of deaths*
30,000
25,000
20,000
15,000
10,000
5,000
0
British
Hessians
Americans
American Deaths
10,000 died in camp (of starvation, exposure, or disease)
8,500 died in British prisons
7,200 died in battle

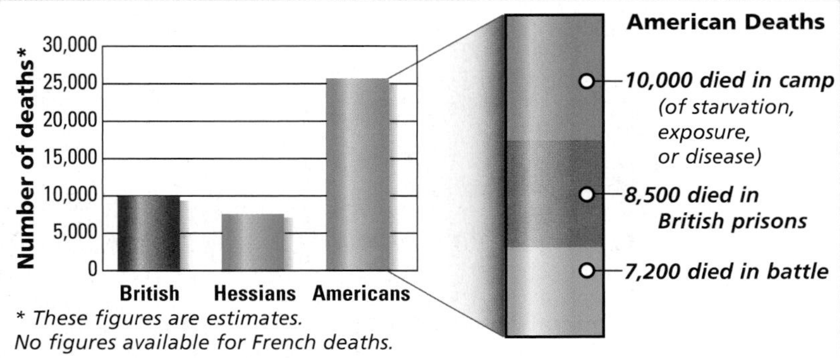

* *These figures are estimates.*
No figures available for French deaths.

Sources: *World Book Encyclopedia; An Outline History of the American Revolution*

Time Lines and Infographics

Time Lines

Infographics

How an Automobile Assembly Line Works

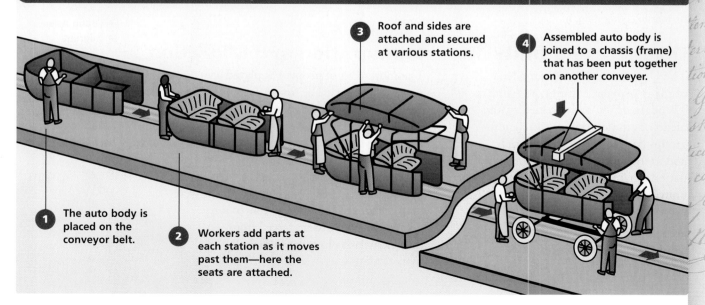

1 The auto body is placed on the conveyor belt.

2 Workers add parts at each station as it moves past them—here the seats are attached.

3 Roof and sides are attached and secured at various stations.

4 Assembled auto body is joined to a chassis (frame) that has been put together on another conveyer.

Imagine life in Jamestown, America's first permanent English settlement. The nation we inhabit now is a much different place than it was then, more than three centuries ago. Yet there are repeating themes—ideas and issues—in American history that tie the past and present together. This book focuses on nine significant themes in U.S. history. Understanding these themes will help you to make sense of American history.

Democratic Ideals

From the day they declared themselves citizens of a new nation, Americans have built their society around the principles of democracy. In a democracy, power lies with the people, and every individual enjoys basic rights that cannot be taken away. Throughout the nation's history, however, some Americans—mainly women and minorities—have had to struggle to gain their full rights. Still, the ideals of democracy remain the guiding principles of this land.

What right or freedom do you consider the most important? Why?

Citizenship

The citizens of the United States enjoy rights and freedoms found in very few other places in the world. Yet Americans know that with such freedoms come responsibilities and duties. Whether they stand in line to vote or spend a weekend to clean up a local river, Americans recognize that citizen participation is what keeps a democracy strong.

How do citizens that you know contribute to your community?

Dr. Martin Luther King, Jr.

Impact of the Individual

The history of the United States is the story not only of governments and laws but of individuals. Indeed, individuals have made the United States what it is today through their extraordinary achievements. American history provides a variety of examples of the impact of the individual on society in both the United States and the world.

Name several individuals who have an impact on American society today. What impact do they have?

A young Asian immigrant

Diversity and Unity

The United States has been a land of many peoples, cultures, and faiths. Throughout the nation's history, this blend of ethnic, racial, and religious groups has helped to create a rich and uniquely American culture. The nation's many different peoples are united in their belief in American values and ideals.

What things do you enjoy that came to the United States from other cultures?

Immigration and Migration

The movement of people has played a vital role in American history. The first Americans migrated from Asia thousands of years ago. Millions more have immigrated in the past five centuries. Even within the United States, large numbers of people have migrated to different regions of the country. However, movements to and within the United States have not always been voluntary. Africans were brought against their will to this country. Native Americans were forced from their homelands in order to make room for European settlers.

Why do you think people continue to immigrate to the United States?

Expansion

When the United States declared its independence from Great Britain, it was only a collection of states along the Atlantic Ocean. But the new country would not remain that way for long. Many Americans shared a sense of curiosity, adventure, and a strong belief that their destiny was to expand all the way to the Pacific Ocean. Driven by this belief, they pushed westward. Americans' efforts to increase the size of their nation is a recurring theme in early U.S. history.

Where do you predict that the exploration of space—the final frontier—will lead?

Poster for Buffalo Bill's Wild West show

America and the World

As the power and prestige of the United States have grown, the nation has played a much more active role in world affairs. Indeed, throughout the 20th century, the United States focused much of its energy on events beyond its borders. The nation fought in two world wars and tried to promote democracy, peace, and economic growth around the globe. As one of the world's political and economic leaders, the United States will continue to be a key player in world affairs throughout the new century.

What do you think the role of the United States in the world should be today?

Science and Technology

Americans have always been quick to embrace inventions and new ways of doing things. After all, this country was settled by people who turned away from old ways and tried new ones. In the past two centuries, new inventions, new technologies, and scientific breakthroughs have transformed the United States—and will continue to do so in the new century.

What recent inventions or innovations affect your life?

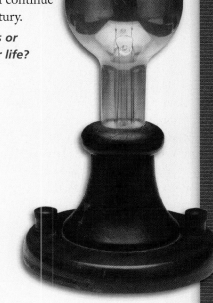

Economics in History

Economics has had a powerful impact on the course of U.S. history. For example, the desire for wealth led thousands to join the California Gold Rush in 1849. The nation as a whole has grown wealthy, thanks to its abundant resources and the hard work of its citizens. An important economic issue, however, has been how to make sure that all people have opportunities to share fully in the nation's wealth. This issue will continue to be important in the 21st century.

What do you think are the most exciting economic opportunities for Americans today?

Thomas Edison's first light bulb

This section of the textbook helps you develop and practice the skills you need to study history and to take standardized tests. Part 1, **Strategies for Studying History,** takes you through the features of the textbook and offers suggestions on how to use these features to improve your reading and study skills.

Part 2, **Test-Taking Strategies and Practice,** offers specific strategies for tackling many of the items you'll find on a standardized test. It gives tips for answering multiple-choice, constructed-response, extended-response, and document-based questions. In addition, it offers guidelines for analyzing primary and secondary sources, maps, political cartoons, charts, graphs, and time lines. Each strategy is followed by a set of questions you can use for practice.

CONTENTS

Part 1: Strategies for Studying History

Reading is the central skill in the effective study of history or any other subject. You can improve your reading skills by using helpful techniques and through practice. The better your reading skills, the more you'll remember what you read. Below you'll find several strategies that involve built-in features of *Creating America*. Careful use of these strategies will help you learn and understand history more effectively.

Preview Chapters Before You Read

Each chapter begins with a two-page chapter opener and a one-page **Setting the Stage** feature. Study the materials to help you get ready to read.

1 Read the chapter and section titles and study the chapter-opening visual. Look for clues that indicate what will be covered in the chapter.

2 Preview the time line. Note the years that the chapter covers. What important events took place during this time period?

3 Study the **Interact with History** feature. Experience what it was like to live in the past by answering **What Do You Think?** questions.

4 Read the **Setting the Stage** feature (see page S3). **What Do You Want to Know?** and **Read and Take Notes** will help focus your reading.

1

CHAPTER **5**

Growth in the West 1860–1900

Section 1 **Miners, Ranchers, and Cowhands**
Section 2 **Native Americans Fight to Survive**
Section 3 **Life in the West**
Section 4 **Farming and Populism**

Life in the West was hard and dangerous, as this Charles M. Russell painting of cowhands shows.

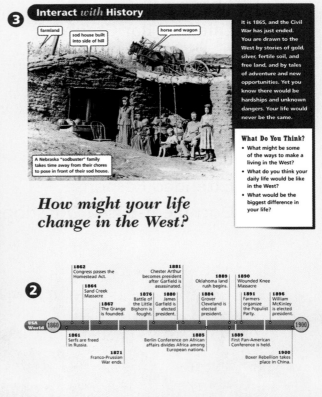

3 Interact *with* History

farmland   sod house built into side of hill   horse and wagon

A Nebraska "sodbuster" family takes time away from their chores to pose in front of their sod house.

How might your life change in the West?

It is 1865, and the Civil War has just ended. You are drawn to the West by stories of gold, silver, fertile soil, and free land, and by tales of adventure and new opportunities. Yet you know there would be hardships and unknown dangers. Your life would never be the same.

What Do You Think?
- What might be some of the ways to make a living in the West?
- What do you think your daily life would be like in the West?
- What would be the biggest difference in your life?

1862 Congress passes the Homestead Act.
1864 Sand Creek Massacre
1867 The Grange is founded.
1876 Battle of the Little Bighorn is fought.
1880 James Garfield is elected president.
1881 Chester Arthur becomes president after Garfield is assassinated.
1884 Grover Cleveland is elected president.
1889 Oklahoma land rush begins.
1890 Wounded Knee Massacre
1891 Farmers organize the Populist Party.
1896 William McKinley is elected president.

2

USA World   1860   1900

1861 Serfs are freed in Russia.
1871 Franco-Prussian War ends.
1885 Berlin Conference on African affairs divides Africa among European nations.
1889 First Pan-American Conference is held.
1900 Boxer Rebellion takes place in China.

Preview Sections Before You Read

Each chapter consists of three, four, or five sections. These sections focus on shorter periods of time or on particular historical themes. Use the section openers to help you prepare to read.

5 Study the sentences under the headings **Main Idea** and **Why It Matters Now.** These tell you what's important in the material that you're about to read.

6 Preview the **Terms & Names** list. This will give you an idea of the issues and personalities you will read about in the section.

7 Read **One American's Story** and **A Voice from the Past.** These provide one individual's view of an important issue of the time.

8 Notice how the section is divided into smaller chunks, each with a red headline. These headlines give you a quick outline of the section.

TERMS & NAMES
frontier
Great Plains
boomtown
long drive
vaquero
vigilante

4

Chapter **5** SETTING THE STAGE

BEFORE YOU READ

Preview the Theme
Diversity and Unity As Chapter 5 explains, hundreds of thousands of men, women, and children packed up their belongings and went to the West after the Civil War. Most were looking for new opportunities and land of their own; some were seeking freedom or adventure. Their arrival led to conflict with the Native Americans, who were the first occupants of the area.

What Do You Know?
What do you think about when you hear terms like *cowboy* and *Wild West*? What do you already know about the people, places, and events in the West in the last half of the 19th century?

THINK ABOUT
• what you have learned about the West from books, movies, and television
• what happens when different cultures clash

The West

What Do You Want to Know?
What details do you need to help you understand the settling of the West? Make a list of those details in your notebook before you read the chapter.

READ AND TAKE NOTES

Reading Strategy: Finding Main Ideas To make it easier for you to understand what you read, learn to find the main idea of each paragraph, topic heading, and section. Remember that the supporting details help to explain the main ideas. On the chart below, write down the main ideas about the many diverse people who settled the West.

S See Skillbuilder Handbook, page R5.

Cowhands/Ranchers · Miners · Native Americans · Many diverse people settled the West! · African Americans · Women · Mexican Americans · Farmers

1 Miners, Ranchers, and Cowhands

TERMS & NAMES
frontier
Great Plains
boomtown
long drive
vaquero
vigilante

6

5

MAIN IDEA	WHY IT MATTERS NOW
Miners, ranchers, and cowhands settled in the West seeking economic opportunities.	The mining and cattle industries that developed then still contribute to American economic growth.

7 **ONE AMERICAN'S STORY**
Nat Love was born a slave in Tennessee in 1854. After the Civil War, he was one of thousands of African Americans who left the South and went west. In 1869, Love headed for Dodge City, Kansas. He was 15 and now free.

Love's horse taming skills landed him a job as a cowhand. For 20 years, he took part in the cattle drives that brought Texas cattle to Kansas stockyards. He became well known for his expert horsemanship and his rodeo riding and roping. In his 1907 autobiography, Love offered a lively but exaggerated account of his life. He told how he braved hailstorms, fought wild animals, and held off human attackers.

A VOICE FROM THE PAST
I carry the marks of fourteen bullet wounds on different parts of my body, most any one of which would be sufficient to kill an ordinary man. . . . Horses were shot from under me, men killed around me, but always I escaped with a trifling wound at the worst.
Nat Love, *The Life and Adventures of Nat Love*

As you will read in this section, few cowhands led lives as exciting as that described by Nat Love, but they all helped to open a new chapter in the history of the American West.

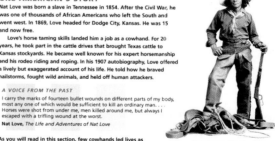
Nat Love was an African-American cowhand who became a rodeo star.

8 **Geography and Population of the West**
In the mid-1800s, towns such as St. Joseph and Independence, Missouri, were jumping-off places for settlers going west. They were the last cities and towns before the frontier. The **frontier** was the unsettled or sparsely settled area of the country occupied largely by Native Americans.

Many white settlers thought of the **Great Plains**—the area from the Missouri River to the Rocky Mountains—as empty. (See map on page 156.) Few had been attracted to its rolling plains, dry plateaus, and deserts. However, west of the Rockies, on the Pacific Coast, settlers had followed miners streaming into California after the 1849 gold rush. By 1850, California had gained statehood. Oregon followed in 1859.

What Do You Want to Know?
What details do you need to help you understand the settling of the West? Make a list of those details in your notebook before you read the chapter.

Use Active Reading Strategies As You Read

Now you're ready to read the chapter. Read one section at a time, from beginning to end.

1 Ask and answer questions as you read. Look for the **Reading History** questions in the margin. Answering these will show whether you understand what you've just read.

2 Try to visualize the people, places, and events you read about. Studying the pictures and any illustrated features will help you do this.

3 Read to build your vocabulary. Use the marginal **Vocabulary** notes to find the meaning of unfamiliar terms.

4 Look for the story behind the events. Read **Background** notes in the margin for additional information on people, places, events, and ideas.

---

*Reading***History**

D. Analyzing Causes What caused the decline of cattle ranching on the open range?

McCoy's plan turned cattle ranching into a very profitable business. Cattle fed on the open range for a year or two and cost the rancher nothing. Ranchers then hired cowhands to round up the cattle and take them to Abilene. There they were sold for as much as ten times their original price. The success of the Abilene stockyards spurred the growth of other Kansas cow towns, including Wichita and Dodge City. The cattle drives to cow towns along the railways were called the **long drives.**

Over time, cowhands followed specific trails across the plains. The first was the Chisholm Trail, which stretched from San Antonio, Texas, to Abilene, Kansas. It was named for Jesse Chisholm, a trader who marked the northern part of the route. From 1867 to 1884, about four million cattle were driven to market on this trail. As cattle raising became more profitable, ranching spread north across the plains from Texas to Montana.

*Reading***History**

C. Reading a Map Use the map on page 179 to locate the Chisholm Trail.

Vaqueros and Cowhands

The first cowhands, or *vaqueros*, as they were known in Spanish, came from Mexico with the Spaniards in the 1500s. They settled in the Southwest. The *vaqueros* helped Spanish, and later Mexican, ranchers manage their herds. From the *vaquero*, the American cowhand learned to rope and ride. Cowhands also adapted the saddle, spurs, lariat (which they used to rope a calf or steer), and chaps of the *vaqueros*.

About one in three cowhands in the West was either Mexican or African-American. Many Mexican cowhands were descendants of the *vaqueros*. Some African-American cowhands were former slaves. They came west at the end of Reconstruction because the enactment of Black Codes in the South put restrictions on their freedom. Also among the cowhands were a large number of former Confederate and Union soldiers.

Background
Chaps, from the Spanish word *chaperejos*, were seatless leather pants worn over trousers to protect legs from scrub brush, snakes, and cactus.

4

The "Wild West"

At first, the rapidly growing cow towns had no local governments. There were no law officers to handle the fights that broke out as cowhands drank and gambled after a long drive. A more serious threat to law and order came from "con men." These swindlers saw new towns as places to get rich quick by cheating others.

Vocabulary
con man: a person who cheats victims by first gaining their confidence

3

daily *life*

LIFE OF A COWHAND: THE ROUNDUP

During some parts of the year, the cowhand's life was downright dull. While cattle grazed on the open range, cowhands sat around the ranch, repairing their gear and doing odd jobs. The pace quickened at roundup time in the spring and fall.

For several weeks, 150 to 250 cowhands from nearby ranches rode hundreds of miles locating cattle. Cowhands from each ranch collected their cattle, removed sick or weak animals, and branded new calves. Then the cowhands were ready for the long drive. A roundup by *vaqueros* is shown in this painting by James Walker.

2

Some Union and Confederate veterans were led to crime by hard feelings left over from the Civil War. Outlaws like John Wesley Hardin, "Billy the Kid," and Jesse and Frank James made crime a way of life. Some women became outlaws, too. Belle Starr, better known as the Bandit Queen, was a legendary horse thief.

For protection, citizens formed vigilante groups. **Vigilantes** were people who took the law into their own hands. They caught suspected criminals and punished them without a trial. Vigilante justice often consisted of hanging suspects from the nearest tree or shooting them on the spot. As towns became more settled, citizens elected a local sheriff or asked the federal government for a marshal. These law officers would arrest lawbreakers and hold them in jail until the time of trial.

2

Bandit Queen Belle Starr sits atop a horse she just might have stolen.

End of the Long Drives

For about 20 years, the cattle industry boomed. As the railroads extended farther west and south into Texas, the long drives grew shorter. The future looked bright. But by 1886, several developments had brought the cattle boom to an end. First, the price of beef dropped sharply as the supply increased in the early 1880s. It fell from more than $30 a head to $7. Then came the newly invented barbed wire. As more settlers moved to the Great Plains to farm or raise sheep, they fenced in their lands with barbed wire. The open range disappeared, and cattle could no longer pass freely over the trails. Finally, in the harsh winter of 1886–1887, thousands of cattle on the northern Plains froze to death. Many ranchers were put out of business.

Meanwhile, as the mining and cattle industries were developing, the Native Americans of the Great Plains were being pushed off their land, as you will read in the next section.

*Reading***History**

D. Analyzing Causes What caused the decline of cattle ranching on the open range?

Section 1 Assessment

1. Terms & Names	2. Taking Notes	3. Main Ideas	4. Critical Thinking
Explain the significance of: • frontier • Great Plains • boomtown • long drive • *vaquero* • vigilante	Use a diagram to review the rise and fall of the cattle industry. cattle industry peaks	**a.** What economic opportunities drew large numbers of people to the West beginning in the 1860s? **b.** How did the transcontinental railroad spur Western settlement? **c.** What did cowhands learn from the *vaqueros*?	**Evaluating** Could cattle ranchers have stopped the decline of the cattle industry that occurred in the late 1880s? **THINK ABOUT** • economic causes • impact of weather • changing settlement patterns

ACTIVITY OPTIONS
LANGUAGE ARTS
MUSIC

Do research on a legendary figure of the West such as Wyatt Earp, "Calamity Jane," or Nat Love. Then write a **biographical sketch** or **song** about the person.

Vocabulary
con man: a person who cheats victims by first gaining their confidence

Background
Chaps, from the Spanish word *chaperejos,* were seatless leather pants worn over trousers to protect legs from scrub brush, snakes, and cactus.

Review and Summarize What You Have Read

When you finish reading a section, review and summarize what you've read. If necessary, go back and reread information that was not clear the first time through.

5 Reread the red headlines for a quick summary of the major points covered in the section.

6 Study any charts, graphs, and maps in the section. These visual materials usually provide a condensed version of information in the section.

7 Review the pictures and note how they relate to the section content.

8 Complete all the questions in the **Section Assessment**. This will help you think critically about what you have just read.

The buffalo was central to the life of Plains tribes. Its meat became the chief food in their diet, while its skins served as portable shelters called tepees. Plains women turned buffalo hides into clothing, shoes, and blankets and used buffalo chips (dried manure) as cooking fuel. Bones and horns became tools and bowls. Over time, many Plains tribes developed a nomadic way of life tied to buffalo hunting.

Vocabulary
nomadic:
wandering from place to place

A Clash of Cultures **5**

When the federal government first forced Native American tribes of the Southeast to move west of the Mississippi in the 1830s, it settled them in Indian Territory. This territory was a huge area that included almost all of the land between the Missouri River and Oregon Territory. Most treaties made by the government with Native Americans promised that this land would remain theirs "as long as Grass grows or water runs."

Reading **History**

A. Analyzing Causes What was the major source of conflict between white settlers and Native Americans?

Unfortunately, these treaty promises would be broken. Government policy was based on the belief that white settlers were not interested in the Plains. The land was considered too dry for farming. However, as wagon trains bound for Oregon and California crossed the Great Plains in the 1850s, some pioneers saw possibilities for farming and ranching on its grasslands. Soon white settlers moved onto the prairies.

These settlers pressured the federal government for more land. They also wanted protection from Native Americans in the area. In 1851, the government responded by calling the Sioux, Cheyenne, Arapaho, and

6

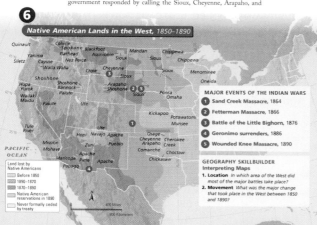

Native American Lands in the West, 1850–1890

MAJOR EVENTS OF THE INDIAN WARS
1. Sand Creek Massacre, 1864
2. Fetterman Massacre, 1866
3. Battle of the Little Bighorn, 1876
4. Geronimo surrenders, 1886
5. Wounded Knee Massacre, 1890

GEOGRAPHY SKILLBUILDER
Interpreting Maps
1. **Location** In which area of the West did most of the major battles take place?
2. **Movement** What was the major change that took place in the West between 1850 and 1890?

The Dawes Act Fails

Some white Americans had been calling for better treatment of Native Americans for years. In 1881, Helen Hunt Jackson published *A Century of Dishonor*, which listed the failures of the federal government's policies toward Native Americans. About the same time, Sarah Winnemucca, a Paiute reformer, lectured in the East about the injustices of reservation life.

Reading **History**

E. Analyzing Points of View Why did reformers support assimilation?

Many well-meaning reformers felt that assimilation was the only way for Native Americans to survive. Assimilation meant adopting the culture of the people around them. Reformers wanted to make Native Americans like whites—to "Americanize" them.

The **Dawes Act**, passed in 1887, was intended to encourage Native Americans to give up their traditional ways and become farmers. The act divided reservations into individual plots of land for each family. The government sold leftover land to white settlers. The government also sent many Native American children to special boarding schools where they were taught white culture. In "One American's Story," you read about the effort to Americanize Buffalo Bird Woman. But these attempts to Americanize the children still did not make them part of white society.

In the end, the Dawes Act did little to benefit Native Americans. Not all of them wanted to be farmers. Those who did lacked the tools, training, and money to be successful. Over time, many sold their land for a fraction of its real value to white land promoters or settlers.

The situation of Native Americans at the end of the 1800s was tragic. Their lands had been taken and their culture treated with contempt. Not until decades later would the federal government recognize the importance of their way of life. In the next section, you will read about some of the people who settled on Native American lands.

INDIAN LAND FOR SALE

GET A HOME
OF
YOUR OWN

PERFECT TITLE
POSSESSION
WITHIN
THIRTY DAYS

EASY PAYMENTS

FINE LANDS IN THE WEST
IRRIGATED   GRAZING   AGRICULTURAL
DRY FARMING

WALTER L. FISHER.   ROBERT G. VAL

7

This poster advertised the sale of Native American lands to white settlers.

8 Section **2** Assessment

1. Terms & Names	2. Taking Notes	3. Main Ideas	4. Critical Thinking
Explain the significance of: • reservation • Sand Creek Massacre • Sitting Bull • George A. Custer • Battle of the Little Bighorn • Wounded Knee Massacre • Dawes Act	Use a chart to compare the life of Plains people before and after the arrival of white settlers.	**a.** How did federal government policy toward Native Americans change as white settlers moved to the West? **b.** How did the destruction of the buffalo affect Plains peoples? **c.** Why was Wounded Knee a turning point in relations between Native Americans and the government?	**Recognizing Effects** How were the effects of the Dawes Act different from what was intended? **THINK ABOUT** • goals of the act • impact on the land use, culture, and independence of the Plains peoples

	Before	After
Meeting survival needs		
Customs		
Land use		

ACTIVITY OPTIONS
TECHNOLOGY
SPEECH

Research the life of a Native American leader discussed in this section. Create that person's **Web** page or give a **speech** from this person's perspective.

Part 2: Test-Taking Strategies and Practice

Improve your test-taking skills by practicing the strategies discussed in this section. Read the tips on the left-hand page. Then apply them to the practice items on the right-hand page.

Multiple Choice

A multiple-choice question consists of a stem and a set of choices. The stem is usually in the form of a question or an incomplete sentence. One of the choices correctly answers the question or completes the sentence.

1 Read the stem carefully and try to answer the question or complete the sentence without looking at the choices.

2 Pay close attention to key words in the stem. They may direct you toward the correct answer.

3 Read each choice with the stem. Don't jump to conclusions about the correct answer until you've read all of the choices.

4 Think carefully about questions that include *All of the above* among the choices.

5 After reading all of the choices, eliminate any that you know are incorrect.

6 Use modifiers to help narrow your choice.

7 Look for the best answer among the remaining choices.

answers: 1 (C), 2 (D), 3 (B)

---

stem

1 1. At the beginning of the Revolution, most **2** Americans were

Most is a key word here. Replacing it with *all* or *some* changes the sentence and calls for a different answer.

3 choices
- **A.** united in support of the war.
- **B.** Patriots who wanted independence from Great Britain.
- **C.** against a war with Great Britain.
- **D.** Loyalists who supported the British point of view.

2. Which of the following weapons were first used effectively during World War I?
- **A.** airplanes
- **B.** machine guns
- **C.** tanks
- **D.** all of the above

4 If you select this answer, be sure that all of the choices are correct.

3. In June 1945, Germany was divided into four zones controlled by
- **A.** Great Britain, France, the United States, and Japan.
- **B.** Great Britain, France, the United States, and the Soviet Union.
- **C.** the Allied Powers.
- **D.** all of the countries of Europe.

5 You can eliminate **A** if you remember that the Allies were still at war with Japan in June 1945.

6 Absolute words, such as *all, never, always, every,* and *only,* often signal an incorrect choice.

7 Either **B** or **C** could be correct. The Allied Powers did control Germany after World War II. However, Great Britain, France, the United States, and the Soviet Union controlled the four zones. Therefore, **B** is the best answer.

Directions: Read the following questions and choose the *best* answer from the four choices.

1. New inventions that helped open the Great Plains to farming included

    A. the steel windmill.

    B. barbed wire.

    C. the spring-tooth harrow.

    D. All of the above

2. Which of the following statements about the Constitution of the United States is *not* true?

    A. The Constitution provides for the election of a chief executive to serve for a term of four years.

    B. The Constitution establishes a bicameral legislature composed of the House of Representatives and the Senate.

    C. The Constitution gives the Senate the power to determine the constitutionality of laws passed by the Congress and state legislatures.

    D. The Constitution provides for change through an amendment process.

3. This song stanza refers to what U.S. event?
    "Here comes the dust-storm
      Watch the sky turn blue.
      You better git out quick
      Or it will smother you."

    A. The Dust Bowl migration to the West

    B. Summer migrant workers heading North

    C. The California gold rush

    D. Yellow fever outbreaks of the 1800s

4. In 1950, the United Nations Security Council voted to intervene after an act of aggression by which one of the following countries?

    A. Libya

    B. Great Britain

    C. North Korea

    D. The People's Republic of China

Song stanza: The Charles L. Todd and Robert Sonkin Migrant Worker Collection, 1940–1941, Library of Congress, American Folklife Center

Primary Sources

Primary sources are materials written or made by people who took part in or witnessed historical events. Letters, diaries, speeches, newspaper articles, and autobiographies are all primary sources. So, too, are legal documents, such as wills, deeds, and court cases.

1 Look at the source line and identify the author or authors. Consider why they are interested in the topic and what knowledge they may bring to the issue.

2 Skim the document to form an idea of what it is about. Look for topic sentences to help you preview the main ideas. (The justices are writing about voting rights.)

3 Note special punctuation. Ellipses indicate that words or sentences have been removed from the original passage. Brackets indicate words that were not in the original.

4 Carefully read the passage. Identify any facts the author presents and try to distinguish those from the author's opinion. If there are two viewpoints presented, compare and contrast them. Check to see if both are based on the same facts.

5 Before rereading the passage, skim the questions to identify the information you need to find.

The following paragraphs are taken from the majority and dissenting opinions of the Supreme Court case *Reynolds* v. *Sims* (1964).

2 The right to vote freely for the candidate of one's choice is of the essence of a democratic society, and any restrictions on that right strike at the heart of representative government. . . . We hold that, as a basic constitutional standard, the Equal Protection Clause [of the Fourteenth Amendment] requires that the seats in . . . a . . . state **3** legislature must be apportioned on a population basis.

1 —from the majority opinion written by Chief Justice Earl Warren

> Note that the two justices disagree about the meaning of the Constitution
>
> **4**

Finally, these decisions give support to a current mistaken view of the Constitution and . . . this Court. This view, in a nutshell, is that every major social ill in this country can find its cure in some constitutional "principle," and that this Court should "take the lead" in promoting reform when other branches of government fail to act.

4 For when, in the name of constitutional interpretation, the Court adds something to the Constitution that was deliberately excluded from it, the Court in reality substitutes its view of what should be so for the amending process.

1 —from the dissenting opinion written by Justice John Marshall Harlan

1. How did Chief Justice Warren view the Equal Protection Clause?

  A. as a basic constitutional standard that requires representation in state legislatures to be based on population

  B. as an unnecessary addition to the Fourteenth Amendment

  C. as a substitution for the amending process required by the Constitution

  D. as a restriction on the right to vote freely for the candidate of one's choice in a democratic society

5

2. Based on his dissenting opinion, Justice Harlan can be described as a strong defender of

  A. social reformers.

  B. strict constitutional interpretation.

  C. constitutional reform.

  D. governments based on republicanism.

answers: 1 (A), 2 (B)

Directions: Use this passage, taken from a letter on conservation written by President Theodore Roosevelt, and your knowledge of U.S. history to answer questions 1 through 3.

In the east, the States are now painfully, and at great expense, endeavoring to undo the effects of their former shortsighted policy in throwing away their forest lands. Congress has before it bills to establish by purchase great forest reserves in the White Mountains and the Southern Appalachians, and the only argument against the bills is that of their great expense. New York and Pennsylvania are now, late in the day, endeavoring themselves to protect the forests which guard the headwaters of their streams. Michigan and Wisconsin have already had their good timber stript from their forests by the great lumber companies. But the western States, far more fortunate than their eastern sisters in this regard, can now reserve their forests for the good of all their citizens, without expense, if they choose to show the requisite foresight.

—President Theodore Roosevelt, in a private letter in 1907

1. According to President Roosevelt, forests not yet damaged by timber companies could be set aside at no expense in the

   A. Midwest.

   B. East.

   C. South.

   D. West.

2. You can tell from this letter that President Roosevelt

   A. favored changing forests to farmland.

   B. was a good president.

   C. supported environmental protection.

   D. was an owner of a large lumber company.

3. Which one of the following statements from the letter is most strictly a fact?

   A. "Congress has before it bills to establish by purchase great forest reserves in the White Mountains. . . ."

   B. "New York and Pennsylvania are now, late in the day, endeavoring themselves to protect the forests. . . . "

   C. ". . . States are now painfully, and at great expense, endeavoring to undo the effects of . . . throwing away their forest lands."

   D. "But the western States, far more fortunate than their eastern sisters . . . can now reserve their forests. . . ."

Secondary Sources

Secondary sources are descriptions or interpretations of historical events made by people who were not at those events. The most common types of written secondary sources are history books, encyclopedias, and biographies. A secondary source often combines information from several primary sources.

① Read titles to preview what the passage is about.

② Look for topic sentences. These, too, will help you preview the content of the passage.

③ As you read, use context clues to help you understand difficult or unfamiliar words. (You can tell from the description of the battle in the previous sentences that the word *fiasco* must mean something like "disaster," "failure," or "blunder.")

④ As you read, ask and answer questions that come to mind. You might ask: Why would the Washington raid embarrass and anger Americans? Why did the Washington raid achieve little?

⑤ Before rereading the passage, skim the questions to identify the information you need to find.

❶ The British Offensive

❷ Ironically, Britain's most spectacular success began as a diversion from [its main] offensive [in the North]. A British army that had come up from Bermuda entered Chesapeake Bay and on August 24, 1814, met a larger American force . . . at Bladensburg, Maryland. The Battle of Bladensburg deteriorated into the "Bladensburg Races" as the American troops fled, virtually without firing a shot. The British then descended on Washington, D.C. Madison, who had witnessed the **❸** Bladensburg fiasco, fled into the Virginia hills. His wife, Dolley, loaded her silver, a bed, and a portrait of George Washington onto her carriage before joining him. British troops ate the supper prepared for the Madisons and then burned the presidential mansion **❹** and other public buildings in the capital. Beyond embarrassing and angering Americans, the Washington raid accomplished little, for after a failed attack on Baltimore, the British broke off the operation.

—Paul S. Boyer, et al., *The Enduring Vision*

❺ 1. Why do you think the authors refer to the Battle of Bladensburg as a "fiasco"?

A. because the American forces fled almost without a fight

B. because President Madison had to flee the White House

C. because it allowed the British to attack Washington, D.C.

D. because it was a famous victory for the British forces

2. What, according to the authors, did the British raid on Washington, D.C., accomplish?

A. It paved the way for the British capture of Baltimore.

B. It burned down all the public buildings in the city.

> Remember to be wary of choices that contain absolutes, such as *all*, *every*, or *only*.

C. It helped the British offensive in the North.

D. It embarrassed and angered many Americans.

answers: 1 (A), 2 (D)

Directions: Use this passage and your knowledge of U.S. history to answer questions 1 through 4.

Space Technology: Artificial Satellites

On October 4, 1957, the first artificial space satellite, *Sputnik 1*, was successfully launched by the Soviet Union. About four months later, the United States launched *Explorer 1*. Now, less than 50 years later, more than 2,000 satellites are orbiting the earth. They track weather patterns, control air traffic, and link the continents in a vast communications network. One satellite system, the Global Positioning System (GPS), can pinpoint locations on the earth. The GPS's series of 24 satellites, called Navstars, beam signals to the earth. Anyone with a GPS receiver can use these signals to determine his or her exact location. The GPS was originally developed to help military forces know exactly where they were on the earth's surface. Today, hikers, explorers, sailors, and drivers use GPS devices to determine location.

1. The United States launched its first satellite in

   A. 1956.
   B. 1957.
   C. 1958.
   D. 1959.

2. Why was the GPS first developed?

   A. to track weather patterns
   B. to find lost hikers
   C. to set up a worldwide communications network
   D. to help military forces find their exact location

3. The GPS is an example of a technological development that

   A. is only of use to military forces.
   B. has many peacetime uses.
   C. is too expensive for any group to use.
   D. is based on faulty scientific knowledge.

4. Which of these statements is *best* supported by the passage?

   A. Navstars are the best air traffic control system available.
   B. The United States and the Soviet Union cooperated in launching satellites in the 1950s.
   C. Artificial satellites threaten the space environment.
   D. People have used artificial satellites to improve life conditions.

Political Cartoons

Political cartoons are drawings that express views on political issues of the day. Cartoonists use symbols and such artistic styles as caricature—exaggerating a person's physical features—to get their message across.

❶ Identify the subject of the cartoon. Titles and captions often indicate the subject matter.

❷ Identify the main characters in the cartoon. Here, the main character is Horace Greeley, a candidate in the 1872 presidential election.

❸ Note the symbols—ideas or images that stand for something else—used in the cartoon.

❹ Study labels and other written information in the cartoon.

❺ Analyze the point of view. How cartoonists use caricature often indicates how they feel. The exaggeration of Greeley's physical appearance—short and overweight—makes him appear comical.

❻ Interpret the cartoonist's message.

The cartoonist shows Tammany Hall, New York's Democratic political machine, as a tiger. Uncle Sam, a symbol for the United States, is shown looking on.

The writing on the wall suggests that Tammany Hall wants reform. The "Whitewash" label on the bucket suggests that the tiger's true, corrupt, stripes are just being covered up.

Thomas Nast, *Harper's Weekly*, August 31, 1872

❶ **"What are you going to do about it, if 'Old Honesty' lets him loose again?"**

1. Based on the cartoon, what do you think was Horace Greeley's major issue in the 1872 presidential campaign?

   A. political reform
   B. states' rights
   C. abolition
   D. temperance

2. Which one of the following statements do you think *best* represents the cartoonist's point of view?

   A. Horace Greeley is an honest man.
   B. Tammany Hall supports political reform.
   C. Tammany Hall, regardless of Greeley's view, is still corrupt.
   D. Horace Greeley, like most Tammany politicians, is corrupt.

answers: 1 (A), 2 (C)

Directions: Use the cartoon and your knowledge of U.S. history to answer questions 1 through 3.

Rollin Kirby, *New York World*, 1917

"That's my fight, too!"

1. The cartoon character is a symbol of

    A. Americans opposed to war.

    B. the president of the United States.

    C. old soldiers retired from the United States Army.

    D. the United States as a whole.

2. The "fight" in the cartoon caption refers to

    A. the War of 1812.

    B. World War II in Europe.

    C. World War II in the Pacific.

    D. World War I in Europe.

3. The cartoonist's point of view is *best* described by which of the following statements?

    A. The United States believes it has an obligation to join in this foreign war.

    B. Uncle Sam is too old and too late for every battle.

    C. The United States should stay out of other countries' wars.

    D. A country should equip its soldiers with the best weapons and other supplies.

Charts

Charts present information in a visual form. History textbooks use several types of charts, including tables, flow charts, Venn diagrams, and infographics. The type of chart most commonly found in standardized tests is the table. It organizes information in columns and rows for easy viewing.

1 Read the title and identify the broad subject of the chart.

2 Read the column and row headings and any other labels. This will provide more details about the subject of the chart.

3 Compare and contrast the information from column to column and row to row.

4 Try to draw conclusions from the information in the chart. Ask yourself: What trends does the chart show?

5 Read the questions and then study the chart again.

Review difficult or unfamiliar words. Here, the term *nativity* means "place of birth."

1 United States Population by Region and Nativity, 1890–1920

	1890	1900	1910	1920
Northeast				
Total Population	17,407,000	21,047,000	25,869,000	29,662,000
% Native Born	78	77	74	77
% Foreign Born	22	23	26	23
North Central				
Total Population	22,410,000	26,333,000	29,889,000	34,020,000
% Native Born	82	84	84	86
% Foreign Born	18	16	16	14
South				
Total Population	20,028,000	24,524,000	29,389,000	33,126,000
% Native Born	97	98	97	97
% Foreign Born	3	2	3	3
West				
Total Population	3,134,000	4,309,000	7,082,000	9,214,000
% Native Born	76	79	79	82
% Foreign Born	24	21	21	18

Source: *Historical Statistics of the United States*

Compare changes in population over time and contrast statistics among regions. **3**

5 1. The two regions with the highest percentage of foreign-born inhabitants are the

A. Northeast and the West.
B. West and the South.
C. South and the North Central.
D. North Central and the Northeast.

2. When did immigration to the Northeast peak?

A. between 1910 and 1920
B. before 1900
C. between 1900 and 1910
D. after 1920

answers: 1 (A), 2 (C)

Directions: Use the chart and your knowledge of U.S. history to answer questions 1 through 4.

Voting in the Presidential Elections: 1968 to 2000 (Population 18 and Older)

Year	Number of People Who Voted (in millions)	Number of People Registered But Not Voting (in millions)	Percentage of Registered Voters Who Voted
1968	79.0	7.6	91.2
1972	85.8	12.7	87.1
1976	86.7	11.1	88.7
1980	93.1	12.0	88.6
1984	101.9	14.2	87.7
1988	102.2	16.4	86.2
1992	113.9	12.7	90.0
1996	105.0	22.6	82.3
2000	110.8	18.7	85.5

Source: U.S. Census Bureau

1. According to the chart, in which year did the largest percentage of registered voters actually vote?

   A. 1968

   B. 1976

   C. 1992

   D. 2000

2. Presidential elections are held in the United States every

   A. two years.

   B. three years.

   C. four years.

   D. five years.

3. Which statement about the number of people who voted in the presidential elections from 1968 to 2000 is true?

   A. More people voted in 2000 than in any other year.

   B. The number of people who voted increased every year since 1968.

   C. More people voted in 1992 than in any other year.

   D. The number of people who voted decreased every year since 1968.

4. From 1968 to 2000, the percentage of registered voters voting

   A. steadily increased.

   B. did not change at all.

   C. varied from year to year, but generally increased.

   D. varied from year to year, but generally decreased.

Line and Bar Graphs

Graphs show statistics in a visual form. Line graphs are particularly useful for showing changes over time. Bar graphs make it easy to compare numbers or sets of numbers.

1 Read the title and identify the broad subject of the graph.

2 Study the labels on the vertical and horizontal axes to see the kinds of information presented in the graph. Note the intervals between amounts and between dates. This will help you read the graph more efficiently.

3 Look at the source line and evaluate the reliability of the information in the graph. Government statistics on education tend to be reliable.

4 Study the information in the graph and note any trends.

5 Draw conclusions and make generalizations based on these trends.

6 Read the questions carefully, and then study the graph again.

1 **High School Graduates, 1880–1920**

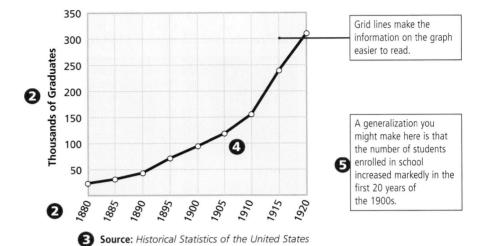

Grid lines make the information on the graph easier to read.

A generalization you might make here is that the number of students enrolled in school increased markedly in the first 20 years of the 1900s.

3 Source: *Historical Statistics of the United States*

6 1. How many students graduated from high school in 1905?

　A. exactly 100,000

　B. about 125,000

　C. about 150,000

　D. exactly 175,000

1 **Public Secondary School Enrollment, 1880–1920**

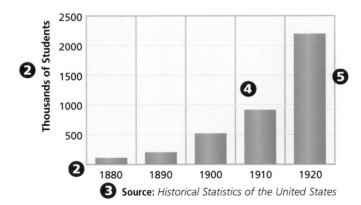

3 Source: *Historical Statistics of the United States*

6 2. Which one of the following sentences do you think *best* describes the trend shown in the bar graph?

　A. The number of students enrolled steadily increased.

　B. The number of students enrolled showed little change.

　C. The number of students enrolled rose and fell.

　D. The number of students enrolled steadily decreased.

answers: 1 (B), 2 (A)

S16

PRACTICE

For more test practice online . . .

TEST PRACTICE
CLASSZONE.COM

STRATEGIES FOR TAKING STANDARDIZED TESTS

Directions: Use the graphs and your knowledge of U.S. history to answer questions 1 through 4.

Motor Vehicle Registrations, 1930–1960

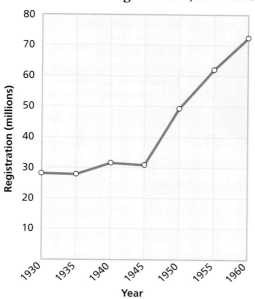

Source: *Historical Statistics of the United States*

Number of People Supplied with Food Per United States Farmer, 1930–1970

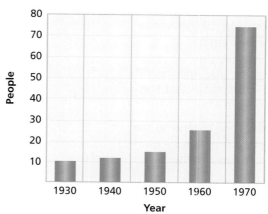

Source: U.S. Department of Agriculture

1. In which time periods did motor-vehicle registrations decline?

   A. 1930 to 1935 and 1935 to 1940

   B. 1930 to 1935 and 1940 to 1945

   C. 1935 to 1940 and 1940 to 1945

   D. 1935 to 1940 and 1945 to 1950

2. Which one of the following would be another good title for this graph?

   A. The American Love Affair with the Automobile

   B. Industrial Decline After World War II

   C. The Automobile Industry During the Great Depression

   D. Automobiles Through the Ages

3. The greatest increase in farmer productivity occurred between

   A. 1930 and 1940.

   B. 1940 and 1950.

   C. 1950 and 1960.

   D. 1960 and 1970.

4. Which is the *best* reason for the increase in farmer productivity?

   A. government policies alone

   B. technology and improved farming practices

   C. an increase in labor hours due to daylight saving time

   D. severe droughts in other areas of the world

Pie Graphs

A pie, or circle, graph shows relationships among the parts of a whole. These parts look like slices of a pie. The size of each slice is proportional to the percentage of the whole that it represents.

1 Read the title and identify the broad subject of the pie graph.

2 Look at the legend to see what each of the slices of the pie represents.

3 Read the source line and note the origin of the data shown in the pie graph.

4 Compare the slices of the pie and try to make generalizations and draw conclusions from your comparisons.

5 Read the questions carefully and review difficult or unfamiliar terms.

6 Eliminate choices that you know are wrong.

1 **The Popular Vote in the 1924 Presidential Election**

Sometimes the information in the legend is shown as labels around the outside of the pie graph.

2

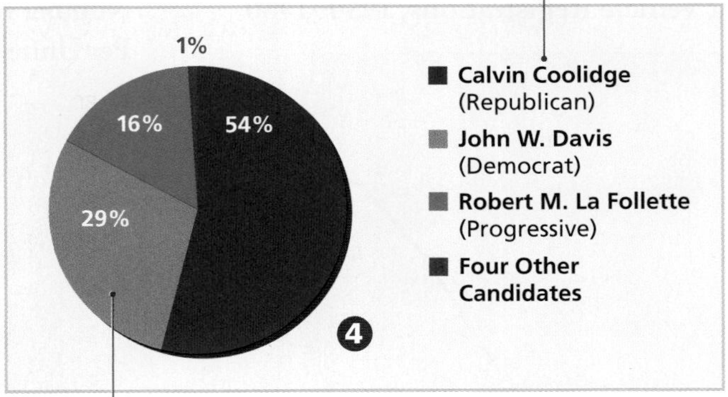

1%
16% 54%
29%

- Calvin Coolidge (Republican)
- John W. Davis (Democrat)
- Robert M. La Follette (Progressive)
- Four Other Candidates

4

3 Source: *Historical Statistics of the United States*

Remember that pie graphs show proportions, or percentages, of the whole, not absolute quantities.

1. In the 1924 presidential election, Calvin Coolidge won

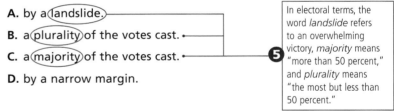

   A. by a landslide.
   B. a plurality of the votes cast.
   C. a majority of the votes cast.
   D. by a narrow margin.

In electoral terms, the word *landslide* refers to an overwhelming victory, *majority* means "more than 50 percent," and *plurality* means "the most but less than 50 percent."

5

2. Which party's candidate won the second largest share of the popular vote?

   A. the Democratic Party
   B. the Other Party
   C. the Progressive Party
   D. the Republican Party

You can eliminate **B** because there is no political party named "Other."

6

answers: 1 (C), 2 (A)

Directions: Use the pie graphs and your knowledge of U.S. history to answer questions 1 through 4.

Distribution of Workers in the United States, 1850 and 1900

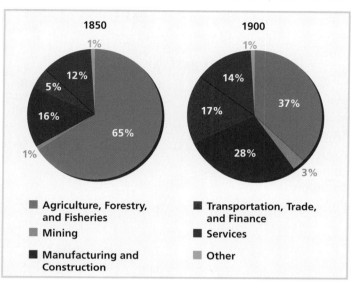

Source: *Historical Statistics of the United States*

1. In 1850, most people worked in

   A. agriculture, forestry, and fisheries.

   B. mining.

   C. services.

   D. transportation, trade, and finance.

2. In 1900, more people worked in manufacturing and construction than in

   A. agriculture, forestry, and fisheries.

   B. mining and agriculture, forestry, and fisheries combined.

   C. services and transportation, trade, and finance combined.

   D. transportation, trade, and finance.

3. Which occupation category showed an increase between 1850 and 1900?

   A. manufacturing and construction

   B. services

   C. transportation, trade, and finance

   D. all of the above

4. What helped to bring about the changes reflected in the two pie graphs?

   A. the passage of new immigration laws

   B. the growth of industry

   C. the decline of world agricultural markets

   D. all of the above

Political Maps

Political maps show countries and the political divisions within countries—states, for example. They also show the location of major cities. In addition, political maps often show physical features, such as rivers, seas, oceans, and mountain ranges.

1 Read the title to determine the subject and purpose of the map.

2 Read the labels on the map. This will reveal information about the map's subject and purpose.

3 Study the legend to find the meaning of symbols used on the map.

4 Look at the lines of latitude and longitude. This grid makes locating places much easier.

5 Use the compass rose or the North arrow to determine directions on the map.

6 Use the scale to estimate the distances between places shown on the map.

7 Read the questions, and then carefully study the map to determine the answers.

answers: 1 (C), 2 (D)

1 Alaska: Political

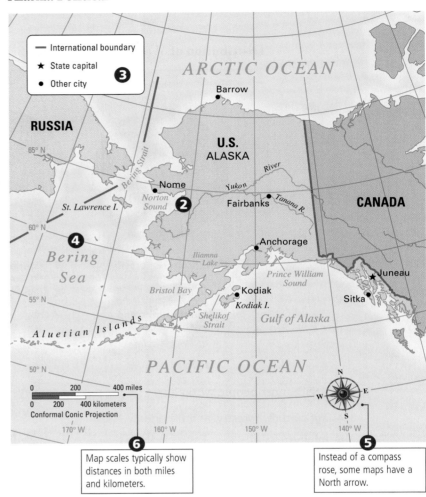

Map scales typically show distances in both miles and kilometers.

Instead of a compass rose, some maps have a North arrow.

7 **1.** Which one of the following cities is located closest to 65° N 150° W?

A. Anchorage

B. Barrow

C. Fairbanks

D. Nome

2. If you took an airplane trip from Juneau to Anchorage, in which general direction would you be traveling?

A. north

B. south

C. east

D. west

Directions: Use the map and your knowledge of U.S. history to answer questions 1 through 4.

San Francisco Bay Area

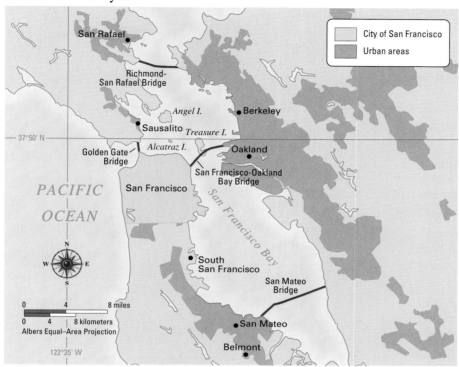

1. Which one of the following describes the location of Sausalito?

   A. north of 37° 50′ N latitude

   B. east of 122° 35′ W longitude

   C. west of Berkeley

   D. all of the above

2. About how far is San Rafael from San Mateo?

   A. 15 miles

   B. 30 miles

   C. 60 miles

   D. 120 miles

3. Which location would figure prominently in a history of immigration to the United States?

   A. Angel Island

   B. Golden Gate Bridge

   C. Treasure Island

   D. Belmont

4. Which one of the following place names does *not* reflect California's Spanish heritage?

   A. San Rafael

   B. Sausalito

   C. Alcatraz

   D. Oakland

Thematic Maps

A thematic map, or special-purpose map, focuses on a particular topic. The location of baseball parks, a country's natural resources, election results, and major battles in a war are all topics you might see illustrated on a thematic map.

1 Read the title to determine the subject and purpose of the map.

2 Examine the labels on the map to find more information about the map's subject and purpose.

3 Study the legend to find the meaning of the symbols and colors used on the map.

4 Look at the colors and symbols on the map and try to identify patterns.

5 Read the questions and then carefully study the map to determine the answers.

1 Americans on the Move, 1970s

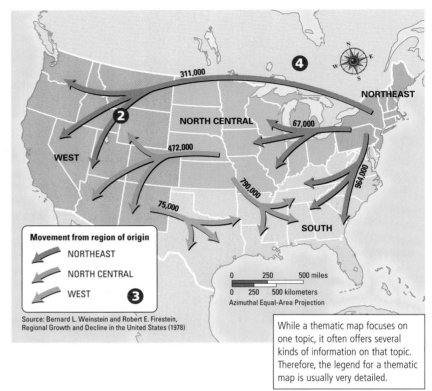

Movement from region of origin

NORTHEAST

NORTH CENTRAL

WEST **3**

Source: Bernard L. Weinstein and Robert E. Firestein, Regional Growth and Decline in the United States (1978)

While a thematic map focuses on one topic, it often offers several kinds of information on that topic. Therefore, the legend for a thematic map is usually very detailed.

5 1. Which region made the greatest gain in population because of people moving from one part of the country to another?

A. the South

B. the West

C. the North Central

D. the Northeast

2. The region that lost the most population from migration was the

A. North Central.

B. South.

C. Northeast.

D. West.

answers: 1 (A), 2 (C)

Directions: Use the map and your knowledge of U.S. history to answer questions 1 through 4.

U.S. School Segregation, 1952

Source: Pauli Murray, *States' Laws on Race and Color*

Legend:
- Segregation required
- Segregation permitted
- Segregation prohibited
- No specific legislation, or local option

1. In what region of the United States was segregation in schools most widespread?

    A. the Northeast

    B. the Midwest

    C. the South

    D. the West

2. In which of the following western states was segregation in schools prohibited?

    A. Arizona

    B. California

    C. Oregon

    D. Washington

3. What was the name given to laws passed by various states to separate the races?

    A. apartheid

    B. Jim Crow

    C. affirmative action

    D. emancipation

4. Which U.S. Supreme Court case struck down segregation in schools as unconstitutional?

    A. *Brown* v. *Board of Education*

    B. *Plessy* v. *Ferguson*

    C. *Hazelwood School District* v. *Kuhlmeier*

    D. *Williams* v. *Mississippi*

Time Lines

A time line is a type of chart that lists events in the order in which they occurred. In other words, time lines are a visual method of showing what happened when.

1 Read the title to discover the subject of the time line.

2 Identify the time period covered by the time line by noting the earliest and latest dates shown. On vertical time lines, the earliest date is shown at the top. On horizontal time lines, it is on the far left.

3 Read the events and their dates in sequence. Notice the intervals between events.

4 Use your knowledge of history to develop a fuller picture of the events listed in the time line. For example, place the events in a broader context by considering what was happening elsewhere in the world.

5 Note how events are related to one another. Look particularly for cause-effect relationships.

6 Use the information you have gathered from the above strategies to answer the questions.

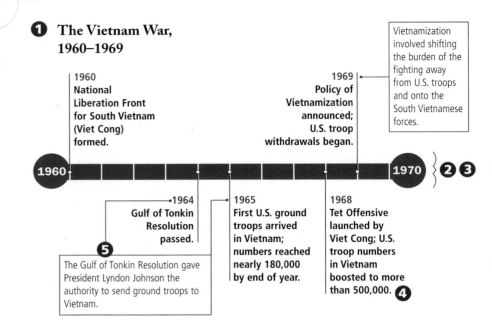

1 The Vietnam War, 1960–1969

1960
National Liberation Front for South Vietnam (Viet Cong) formed.

1969
Policy of Vietnamization announced; U.S. troop withdrawals began.

Vietnamization involved shifting the burden of the fighting away from U.S. troops and onto the South Vietnamese forces.

1960 — **1970** **2 3**

1964
Gulf of Tonkin Resolution passed.

5 The Gulf of Tonkin Resolution gave President Lyndon Johnson the authority to send ground troops to Vietnam.

1965
First U.S. ground troops arrived in Vietnam; numbers reached nearly 180,000 by end of year.

1968
Tet Offensive launched by Viet Cong; U.S. troop numbers in Vietnam boosted to more than 500,000. **4**

6 1. In what year was U.S. troop strength boosted to more than 500,000?

A. 1964

B. 1965

C. 1968

D. 1969

2. What event led to a reduction of U.S. troop strength in Vietnam?

A. passage of the Gulf of Tonkin Resolution

B. announcement of the policy of Vietnamization

C. launch of the Tet Offensive

D. formation of the Viet Cong

answers: 1 (C), 2 (B)

Directions: Use the time line and your knowledge of U.S. history to answer questions 1 through 3.

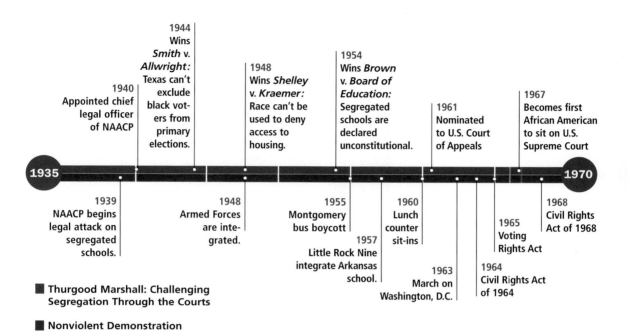

1940
Appointed chief legal officer of NAACP

1944
Wins *Smith* v. *Allwright:* Texas can't exclude black voters from primary elections.

1948
Wins *Shelley* v. *Kraemer:* Race can't be used to deny access to housing.

1954
Wins *Brown* v. *Board of Education:* Segregated schools are declared unconstitutional.

1961
Nominated to U.S. Court of Appeals

1967
Becomes first African American to sit on U.S. Supreme Court

1935 —————————————————————— 1970

1939
NAACP begins legal attack on segregated schools.

1948
Armed Forces are integrated.

1955
Montgomery bus boycott

1957
Little Rock Nine integrate Arkansas school.

1960
Lunch counter sit-ins

1963
March on Washington, D.C.

1964
Civil Rights Act of 1964

1965
Voting Rights Act

1968
Civil Rights Act of 1968

■ **Thurgood Marshall: Challenging Segregation Through the Courts**

■ **Nonviolent Demonstration and Legislative Action**

1. In what year did the NAACP achieve a major victory in its goal to desegregate schools throughout the United States?

A. 1939

B. 1944

C. 1954

D. 1964

2. How many years after *Brown* v. *Board of Education* did Arkansas integrate a public school?

A. three years

B. five years

C. seven years

D. ten years

3. Thurgood Marshall was known as "Mr. Civil Rights" because he was

A. a lawyer who successfully argued to end legal segregation in voting, housing, and education.

B. the chief legal officer of the NAACP beginning in the late 1930s.

C. the first African American appointed to the Supreme Court.

D. an African-American lawyer and judge before the civil rights acts were passed.

Constructed Response

Constructed-response questions focus on various kinds of documents. Each document usually is accompanied by a series of questions. These questions call for short answers that, for the most part, can be found directly in the document. Some answers, however, require knowledge of the subject or time period addressed in the document.

1 Read the title of the document to discover the subject addressed in the questions.

2 Study and analyze the document. Take notes on what you see.

3 Read the questions and then study the document again to locate the answers.

4 Carefully write your answers. Unless the directions say otherwise, your answers need not be complete sentences.

1 **Joseph Glidden's Patent**

2 Constructed-response questions use a wide range of documents, including short passages, cartoons, charts, graphs, maps, time lines, posters, and other visual materials. This is a copy of a legal document called a patent.

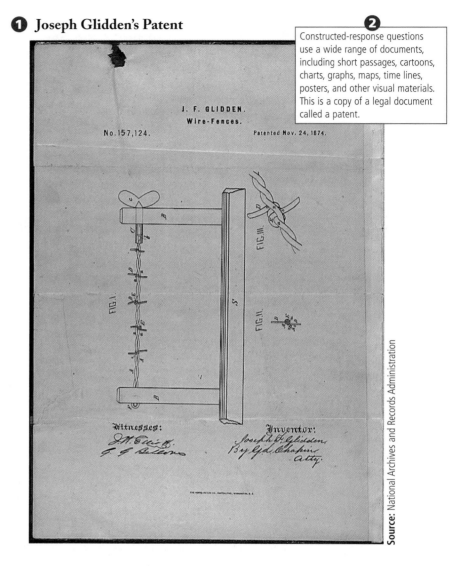

J. F. GLIDDEN.
Wire-Fences.
No. 157,124.   Patented Nov. 24, 1874.

Source: National Archives and Records Administration

3 **1.** What invention is illustrated on this patent?
4 *barbed wire fence*

2. What suggests that this is a legal document?
It is signed by witnesses and an attorney.

3. What other developments had a major impact on farming on the plains in the 1800s?
steel plows, reapers, threshers, dry farming

Directions: Use the photograph and your knowledge of U.S. history to answer questions 1 through 3. Your answers need not be complete sentences.

Exercise Desert Rock: Six Miles from Ground Zero

Troops of the Battalion Combat Team, U.S. Army 11th Airborne Division. Yucca Flats, Nevada, November 1, 1951.

Source: National Archives and Records Administration

1. Who is pictured in the photograph?

2. What are the soldiers in the photograph looking at?

3. What major nonmilitary global conflict caused the United States to conduct tests like "Exercise Desert Rock"?

Extended Response

Extended-response questions, like constructed-response questions, usually focus on one kind of document. However, they are more complex and require more time to complete than typical short-answer constructed-response questions. Some extended-response questions ask you to present information from the document in a different form. Others require you to apply your knowledge of history to information contained in the document.

❶ Read the title of the document to get an idea of the subject.

❷ Study and analyze the document. Take notes on your ideas.

❸ Carefully read the extended-response questions.

❹ If the question calls for a graph or some other kind of diagram, make a rough sketch on scrap paper first. Then make a final copy of your drawing on the answer sheet.

❺ If the question requires a written response, jot down ideas in outline form. Use this outline to write your answer.

❶ **Carbon Dioxide Output of Average U.S. Single-Family Home**

Source	Pounds of Carbon Dioxide per Year
Space Heating	10,132
Air Conditioning	2,609
Water Heating	3,618
Refrigerator, Freezer	3,429
Cooking	935
Other Appliances	6,337
Lighting	2,460
Automobile	20,960

❷ (marker beside Refrigerator, Freezer row)

Source: Rocky Mountain Institute, 1999

❸ **1.** Use the information in the chart to create a bar graph showing the annual carbon dioxide output of the average American single-family home.

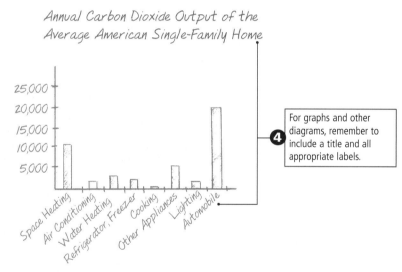

For graphs and other diagrams, remember to include a title and all appropriate labels. **❹**

❸ **2.** Write a short essay discussing the steps that the typical American family could take to reduce its carbon dioxide output.

❺ **Sample Response** The best essays will point out that families could reduce their carbon dioxide output by reducing their use of appliances and vehicles. Walking, carpooling, and taking public transportation would greatly reduce carbon dioxide output. So, too, would setting thermostats at a reasonable level to cut the use of heaters and air conditioners. Finally, replacing old appliances with newer, more efficient ones also would cut carbon dioxide emissions.

Directions: Use the chart and your knowledge of U.S. history to answer questions 1 through 3.

First Amendment Rights: the Five Basic Freedoms

Freedom of Religion	People have the right to practice the religion of their choice.
Freedom of Speech	People have the right to state their ideas.
Freedom of the Press	People have the right to publish their ideas.
Freedom of Assembly	People have the right to meet peacefully in groups.
Freedom to Petition	People have the right to petition the government.

1. Does the First Amendment guarantee your right to practice any religion you like?

2. You write a letter to the mayor asking for a stop sign to be placed at an intersection near your school. Which of the five basic freedoms are you exercising? If you publish your letter in the newspaper, which freedoms are you exercising?

3. Write an essay explaining how two of the First Amendment freedoms are related.

Document-Based Questions

A document-based question focuses on several documents—both visual and written. These documents often are accompanied by short-answer questions. You then use the answers to these questions and information from the documents to write an essay on a specified subject.

1 Carefully read the "Historical Context" to get an indication of the issue addressed in the question.

2 Note the action words used in the "Task" section. These words tell you exactly what the essay question requires.

3 Study and analyze each document. Think about how the documents are connected to the essay question. Take notes on your ideas.

4 Read and answer each of the document-specific questions.

Introduction

1 **Historical Context:** After the United States entered World War II, many men left their jobs to join the military. Millions of women stepped in to take their place in factories and offices.

2 **Task:** (Discuss) how life for women in the U.S. changed during World War II and (note) the gains that women made in the field of employment.

Part 1: Short Answer

Study each document carefully and answer the questions that follow.

3 **Document 1: Working Women During World War II**

Source: National Archives and Records Administration

4 How does this image of women workers differ from the traditionally accepted image of the time?

This image shows a woman in the nontraditional role of a factory worker. It also shows the woman as self-confident and physically strong.

Document 2: Women in the U.S. Work Force, 1940–1946

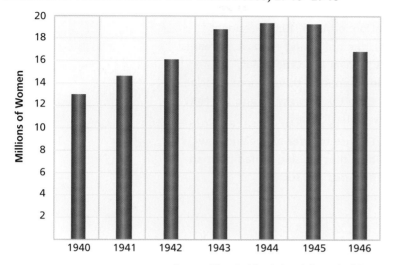

Source: *Historical Statistics of the United States*

What trends in women's employment does this graph show?

The graph shows a marked increase during the war years with a decrease after the war's end.

Document 3: The Future of Women's Work

Despite the surge of women into heavy industry, markedly larger numbers of new women entrants into the wartime work force took up clerical and service jobs, . . . and there women's gains proved far more durable. The number of women factory operatives plummeted at war's end. . . . By 1947 the proportion of working women in blue-collar occupations was actually smaller than it had been at the war's outset. . . . The future of women's work lay not in the wartime heavy industries, . . . but in the [growing] service occupations, which within a decade of the war's conclusion eclipsed factory work as the nation's principal source of employment.

— David M. Kennedy, *Freedom from Fear*

In what jobs did women make the most long-lasting gains?

clerical and service jobs

5 Part 2: Essay

Using information from the documents, your answers to the questions in Part 1, and your knowledge of U.S. history, write an essay that discusses how life for women changed during World War II and notes the gains that women made in employment. **6**

5 Carefully read the essay question. Then write an outline for your essay.

6 Write your essay. Be sure that it has an introductory paragraph that introduces your argument, main body paragraphs that explain it, and a concluding paragraph that restates your position. In your essay, include extracts or details from specific documents to support your ideas. Add other supporting facts or details that you know from your study of American history.

Sample Response The best essays will point out that the greatest change for American women during World War II was that many entered the work force for the first time (Documents 2 and 3) and that many took jobs that were not traditionally held by women (Document 1). Essays also should note that while many women took jobs traditionally held by men, more entered clerical and service jobs (Document 3). And while the number of women in industrial jobs declined after the war, the number in service jobs grew (Document 3).

Introduction

Historical Context: Upon his inauguration in March 1933, President Franklin D. Roosevelt told the nation, "the only thing we have to fear is fear itself." The country feared for its survival from the Great Depression. President Roosevelt would respond to this economic, social, and political crisis with his New Deal. Both the Depression and the New Deal would have lasting effects on the United States.

Task: Explain the New Deal program. Be sure to refer to specific New Deal legislation and its goals. Discuss how that legislation had both an immediate and a long-lasting impact on American society.

Part 1: Short Answer

Study each document carefully and answer the questions that follow.

Document 1: Machining in the Civilian Conservation Corps

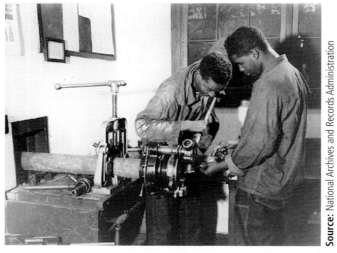

Source: National Archives and Records Administration

Young men between the ages of 17 and 23 were paid $30 a month to build lookout towers, plant trees, and engage in other conservation projects. These two men are working on machinery used at their CCC work camp.

How were these two young men helping themselves and their country by joining the Civilian Conservation Corps?

Adapted from document-based questions written by Bill McKee, Brockport Central School, Brockport, New York; and Brian McKenzie, Dr. Charles R. Drew Science Magnet School, Buffalo, New York.

S32

Document 2: National Old-Age Security

On January 31, 1940, the first monthly retirement check was issued to Ida May Fuller of Ludlow, Vermont, in the amount of $22.54. Miss Fuller, a legal secretary, retired in November 1939. She started collecting benefits in January 1940 at age 65 and lived to be 100 years old, dying in 1975. During her lifetime she collected a total of $22,888.92.
—Social Security Administration

What is the card shown in the picture, and how does it relate to Ida May Fuller's retirement checks?

Document 3: Major New Deal Programs

Year	Program	Accomplishments
1933	FERA (Federal Emergency Relief Administration)	Federal money for relief projects
1933	PWA (Public Works Administration)	Jobs building highways, bridges, etc.
1933	AAA (Agricultural Adjustment Administration)	Aid to farms
1933	TVA (Tennessee Valley Authority)	Tennessee Valley development plan
1933	CCC (Civilian Conservation Corps)	Conservation work for young men
1933	FDIC (Federal Deposit Insurance Corporation)	Deposits in insured banks protected
1933	NRA (National Recovery Administration)	Industry, prices, and wages regulated
1935	WPA (Works Progress Administration)	Jobs created by national works programs
1935	REA (Rural Electrification Administration)	Electricity brought to rural areas
1935	NYA (National Youth Administration)	Youth job and education programs
1935	Wagner Act	Labor unions protected
1935	Social Security Act	Unemployment insurance and retirement benefits

What are two ways the New Deal programs helped the government provide relief, recovery, and reform in response to the Depression?

Part 2: Essay

Using information from the documents, your answers to the questions in Part 1, and your knowledge of U.S. history, write an essay that explains the New Deal program. Be sure to refer to specific New Deal legislation and its goals. Discuss how that legislation had both an immediate and a long-lasting impact on American society.

The Landscape of America

The best place to begin your study of American history is with the geography of America. Geography is more than the study of the land and people. It also involves the relationship between people and their environment.

The United States is part of the North American continent. The United States ranks third in both total area and population in the world. It is filled with an incredible variety of physical features, natural resources, climatic conditions, and people. This handbook will help you to learn about these factors and to understand how they affected the development of the United States.

A timber company collects logs in the Northwest.

NORTHWEST

WEST

SOUTHWEST

0   500 Miles
0   1,000 Kilometers

0   100 Miles
0   200 Kilometers

A cowboy drives cattle in the West.

TABLE OF CONTENTS

A combine harvests wheat in the Midwest.

Fishers haul their catch toward shore in the Northeast.

NORTHEAST

MIDWEST

SOUTHEAST

N

0   500 Miles

0   1,000 Kilometers

Oranges are big business in the Southeast.

Themes of Geography

One useful way to think about geography is in terms of major themes or ideas. These pages examine the five major themes of geography and show how they apply to Boston, Massachusetts. Recognizing and understanding these themes will help you to understand all the different aspects of geography.

Location

"Where am I?" Your answer to this question is your *location*. One way to answer it is to use *absolute* location. That means you'll use the coordinates of longitude and latitude to give your answer (see page 8). For example, if you're in Boston, its absolute location is approximately 42° north latitude and 71° west longitude.

Like most people, however, you'll probably use *relative* location to answer the question. Relative location describes where a certain area is in relation to another area. For example, Boston lies in the northeast corner of the United States, next to the Atlantic Ocean.

THINKING ABOUT GEOGRAPHY What is the relative location of your school?

Boston is located on the shores of the Atlantic Ocean.

Place

"What is Boston like?" *Place* can help you answer this question. Place refers to the physical and human factors that make one area different from another. Physical characteristics are natural features, such as physical setting, plants, animals, and weather. For example, Boston sits on a hilly peninsula.

Human characteristics include cultural diversity and the things people have made—including language, the arts, and architecture. For instance, Boston includes African Americans, as well as people of Irish, Italian, Chinese, and Hispanic ancestry.

THINKING ABOUT GEOGRAPHY What physical and human characteristics make where you live unique?

Boston has grown and changed since this 1722 map.

Region

Geographers can't easily study the whole world at one time. So they break the world into regions. A *region* can be as large as a continent or as small as a neighborhood. A region has certain shared characteristics that set it apart. These characteristics might include political division, climate, language, or religion. Boston is part of the northeast region. It shares a climate—continental temperate—with the cities of New York and Philadelphia.

THINKING ABOUT GEOGRAPHY What characteristics does your city or town share with nearby cities or towns?

Airplanes from Boston's Logan International Airport move people and ideas around the globe.

People shop, eat, and interact at Boston's famous Quincy Market.

Movement

Movement refers to the shifting of people, goods, and ideas from one place to another. People constantly move in search of better places to live, and they trade goods with one another over great distances. Movement also causes ideas to travel from place to place. In recent years, technology has quickened the movement of ideas and goods.

Boston became known as the *Cradle of Liberty* because of the movement of ideas. The concepts of freedom and self-government that developed in Boston spread to the other colonies and helped to start the American Revolution.

THINKING ABOUT GEOGRAPHY What are some of the different ways you spread information and ideas?

Human-Environment Interaction

Human-environment interaction refers to ways people interact with their environment, such as building a dam, cutting down a tree, or even sitting in the sun.

In Boston, human-environment interaction occurred when officials filled in swampy areas to make the city larger. In other ways, the environment has forced people to act. For example, people have had to invent ways to protect themselves from extreme weather and natural disasters.

THINKING ABOUT GEOGRAPHY What are ways that people in your city or town have changed their environment?

Themes of Geography Assessment

1. Main Ideas

a. What is the relative location of your home?

b. What are three characteristics of the region in which you live?

c. What are at least three ways in which you have recently interacted with the environment?

2. Critical Thinking

Forming and Supporting Opinions Which aspect of geography described in these themes do you think has most affected your life? Explain.

THINK ABOUT

• ways that you interact with your environment

• how you travel from place to place

Map Basics

Geographers use many different types of maps, and these maps all have a variety of features. The map on the next page gives you information on a historical event—the War of 1812. But you can use it to learn about different parts of a map, too.

Types of Maps

Physical maps Physical maps show mountains, hills, plains, rivers, lakes, oceans, and other physical features of an area.

Political maps Political maps show political units, such as countries, states, provinces, counties, districts, and towns. Each unit is normally shaded a different color, represented by a symbol, or shown with a different typeface.

Historical maps Historical maps illustrate such things as economic activity, migrations, battles, and changing national boundaries.

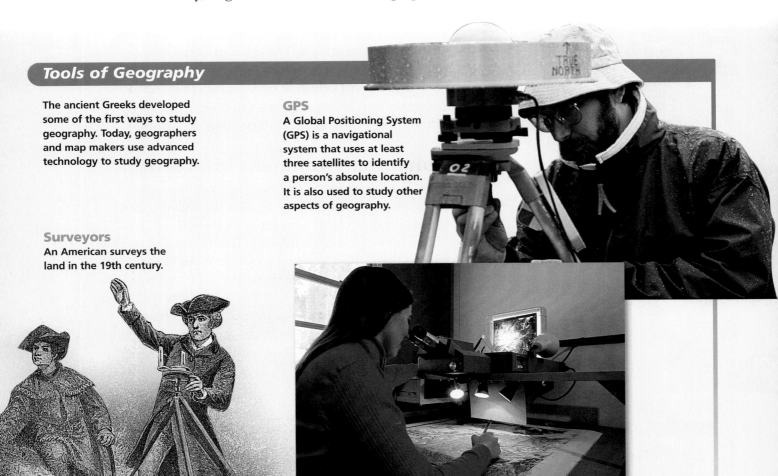

Tools of Geography

The ancient Greeks developed some of the first ways to study geography. Today, geographers and map makers use advanced technology to study geography.

GPS
A Global Positioning System (GPS) is a navigational system that uses at least three satellites to identify a person's absolute location. It is also used to study other aspects of geography.

Surveyors
An American surveys the land in the 19th century.

Computers
Computers can create electronic maps in which geographers can quickly add or remove features that keep the map current. Computers can also be used to monitor environmental problems such as deforestation and global warming.

Reading a Map

A **Lines** Lines indicate political boundaries, roads and highways, human movement, and rivers and other waterways.

B **Symbols** Symbols represent such items as capital cities, battle sites, or economic activities.

C **Labels** Labels are words or phrases that explain various items or activities on a map.

D **Compass Rose** A compass rose shows which way the directions north (N), south (S), east (E), and west (W) point on the map.

E **Scale** A scale shows the ratio between a unit of length on the map and a unit of distance on the earth. A typical one-inch scale indicates the number of miles and kilometers that length represents on the map.

F **Colors** Colors show a variety of information on a map, such as population density or the physical growth of a country.

G **Legend or Key** A legend or key lists and explains the symbols, lines, and colors on a map.

H **Lines of Longitude** These are imaginary, north-south lines that run around the globe.
Lines of Latitude These are imaginary, east-west lines that run around the globe. Together, latitude and longitude lines form a grid on a map or globe to indicate an area's absolute location.

The War of 1812

Legend:
← American forces
← British forces
✳ American victory
✳ British victory
🏛 Fort

Longitude Lines (Meridians)

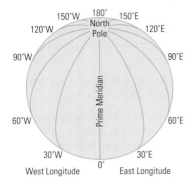

Latitude Lines (Parallels)

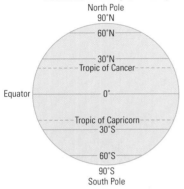

Northern Hemisphere

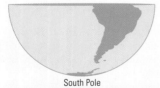

Southern Hemisphere

Longitude lines

- are imaginary lines that run north to south around the globe and are known as meridians
- show the distance in degrees east or west of the prime meridian

The prime meridian is a longitude line that runs from the North Pole to the South Pole. It passes through Greenwich, England, and measures 0° longitude.

Latitude lines

- are imaginary lines that run east to west around the globe and are known as parallels
- show distance in degrees north or south of the equator

The equator is a latitude line that circles the earth halfway between the North and South poles. It measures 0° latitude.

The tropics of Cancer and Capricorn are parallels that form the boundaries of the Tropics, a region that stays warm all year.

Latitude and longitude lines appear together on a map and allow you to pinpoint the absolute location of cities and other geographic features. You express this location through coordinates of intersecting lines. These are measured in degrees.

Hemisphere

Hemisphere is a term for half the globe. The globe can be divided into Northern and Southern hemispheres (separated by the equator) or into Eastern and Western hemispheres. The United States is located in the Northern and Western hemispheres.

Projections

A projection is a way of showing the curved surface of the earth on a flat map. Flat maps cannot show the size, shape, and direction of a globe all at once with total accuracy. As a result, all projections distort some aspect of the earth's surface. Some maps distort distances, while other maps distort angles. On the next page are four projections.

Mercator Projection

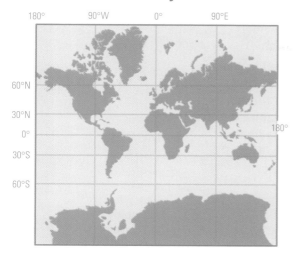

The Mercator projection shows most of the continents as they look on a globe. However, the projection stretches out the lands near the North and South poles. The Mercator is used for all kinds of navigation.

Azimuthal Projection

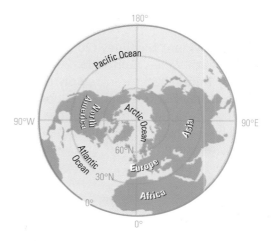

An azimuthal projection shows the earth so that a straight line from the central point to any other point on the map gives the shortest distance between the two points. Size and shape of the continents are also distorted.

Homolosine Projection

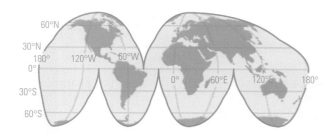

This projection shows the accurate shapes and sizes of the landmasses, but distances on the map are not correct.

Robinson Projection

Textbook maps commonly use the Robinson projection. It shows the entire earth with nearly the true sizes and shapes of the continents and oceans. However, the shapes of the landforms near the poles appear flat.

Map Basics Assessment

1. Main Ideas

a. What is the longitude and latitude of your city or town?

b. What information is provided by the legend on the map on page 7?

c. What is a projection? Compare and contrast Antarctica on the Mercator and the Robinson projections.

2. Critical Thinking

Making Inferences Why do you think latitude and longitude are so important to sailors?

THINK ABOUT
• the landmarks you use to find your way around
• the landmarks available to sailors on the ocean

Physical Geography of the United States

From the heights of Mount McKinley (20,320 feet above sea level) in Alaska to the depths of Death Valley, California (282 feet below sea level), the geography of the United States is incredibly diverse. In between these extremes lie such varied features and conditions as scorching Arizona deserts, lush Oregon forests, freezing Vermont winters, and sunny Florida beaches. Physical geography involves all the natural features on the earth. This includes the land, resources, climate, and vegetation.

Flowers and brush cover the Coral Pink Sand Dunes in southern Utah.

Land

Separated from much of the world by two oceans, the United States covers 3,717,796 square miles and spans the entire width of North America. To the west, Hawaii stretches the United States into the Pacific Ocean. To the north, Alaska extends the United States to the Arctic Circle. On the U.S. mainland, a huge central plain separates large mountains in the West and low mountains in the East. Plains make up almost half of the country, while mountains and plateaus make up a quarter each.

An abundance of lakes—Alaska alone has three million—and rivers also dot the landscape. Twenty percent of the United States is farmed, providing the country with a steady food supply. Urban areas cover only about two percent of the nation. Refer to the map on the next page for a complete look at the U.S. landscape.

THINKING ABOUT GEOGRAPHY What is the land like around your city or state?

Oil drilled from Alaska helps power the nation's planes, trains, cars, and factories.

Resources

The United States has a variety of natural resources. Vast amounts of coal, oil, and natural gas lie underneath American soil. Valuable deposits of lead, zinc, uranium, gold, and silver also exist. These resources have helped the United States become the world's leading industrial nation—producing nearly 21 percent of the world's goods and services.

These resources have also helped the United States become both the world's largest producer of energy (natural gas, oil, coal, nuclear power, and electricity) and the world's largest consumer of it. Other natural resources include the Great Lakes, which are shared with Canada. They contain about 20 percent of the world's total supply of fresh surface water. Refer to the map on the next page to examine the nation's natural resources.

THINKING ABOUT GEOGRAPHY What are the different natural resources that you and your family use in your daily lives?

Land and Resources

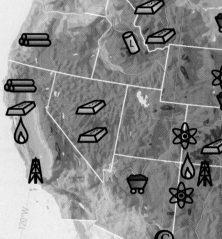

Miners extract such minerals as gold, silver, and copper from the Rocky Mountains.

N

| 0 | 250 Miles |
| 0 | 500 Kilometers |

PACIFIC
OCEAN

ATLANTIC
OCEAN

The Appalachians are among the earth's oldest mountains.

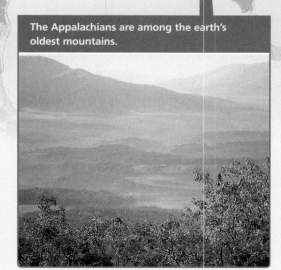

Aluminum	Lumber
Coal	Natural gas
Copper	Oil
Gold	Silver
Iron ore	Uranium
Lead	Zinc

Elevation Key

Feet		Meters
13,120		4,000
9,840		3,000
6,560		2,000
3,280		1,000
1,640		500
656		200
0		0
Below sea level		

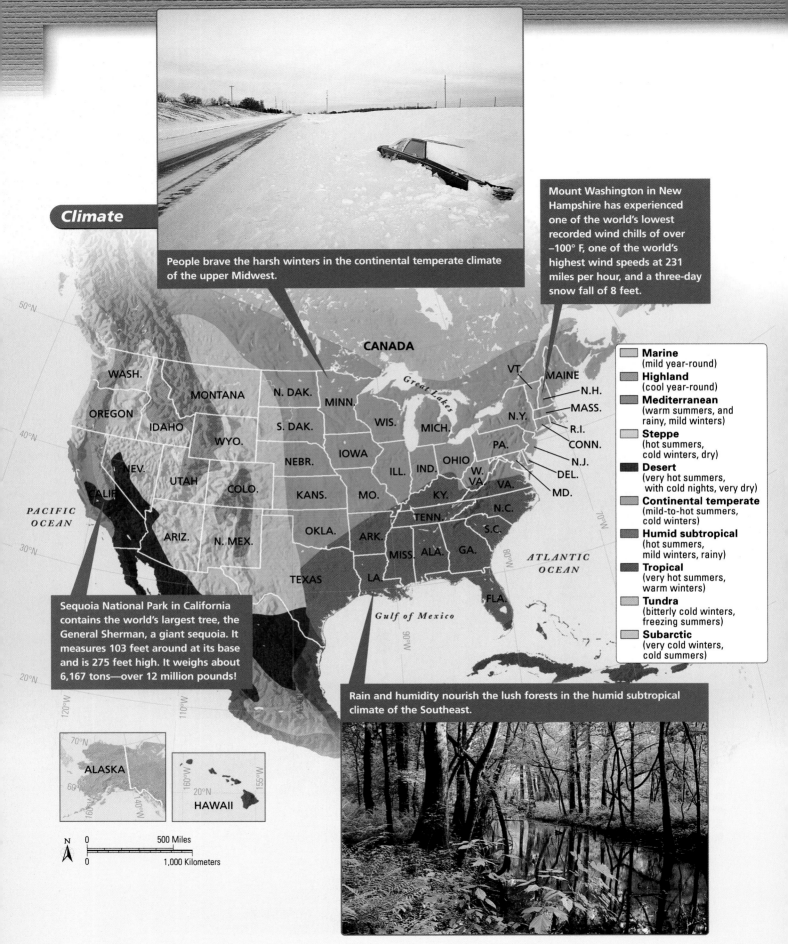

Climate

People brave the harsh winters in the continental temperate climate of the upper Midwest.

Mount Washington in New Hampshire has experienced one of the world's lowest recorded wind chills of over −100° F, one of the world's highest wind speeds at 231 miles per hour, and a three-day snow fall of 8 feet.

Marine
(mild year-round)

Highland
(cool year-round)

Mediterranean
(warm summers, and rainy, mild winters)

Steppe
(hot summers, cold winters, dry)

Desert
(very hot summers, with cold nights, very dry)

Continental temperate
(mild-to-hot summers, cold winters)

Humid subtropical
(hot summers, mild winters, rainy)

Tropical
(very hot summers, warm winters)

Tundra
(bitterly cold winters, freezing summers)

Subarctic
(very cold winters, cold summers)

CANADA

WASH.
OREGON
MONTANA
IDAHO
N. DAK.
MINN.
WYO.
S. DAK.
WIS.
MICH.
NEV.
UTAH
IOWA
NEBR.
ILL. IND. OHIO
CALIF.
COLO.
KANS.
MO.
KY.
W. VA.
PA.
N.Y.
VT. MAINE
N.H.
MASS.
R.I.
CONN.
N.J.
DEL.
VA.
MD.
ARIZ.
N. MEX.
OKLA.
ARK.
TENN.
N.C.
S.C.
TEXAS
LA.
MISS. ALA. GA.
FLA.

Great Lakes

PACIFIC OCEAN

ATLANTIC OCEAN

Gulf of Mexico

50°N
40°N
30°N
20°N

120°W
110°W
100°W
90°W
80°W
70°W

Sequoia National Park in California contains the world's largest tree, the General Sherman, a giant sequoia. It measures 103 feet around at its base and is 275 feet high. It weighs about 6,167 tons—over 12 million pounds!

Rain and humidity nourish the lush forests in the humid subtropical climate of the Southeast.

ALASKA
HAWAII

70°N
60°N
160°W
140°W
160°W
20°N
155°W

N

0   500 Miles
0   1,000 Kilometers

Climate

The United States contains a variety of climates. For example, the mean temperature in January in Miami, Florida, is 67° F, while it is 11° F in Minneapolis, Minnesota. Most of the United States experiences a continental climate, or distinct change of seasons. Some regional climatic differences include hot and humid summers in the Southeast versus hot and dry summers in the Southwest. Harsh winters and heavy snow can blanket parts of the Midwest, the Northeast, and the higher elevations of the West and Northwest. Refer to the map on the previous page to see the nation's climatic regions.

Human activities have affected the climate, too. For example, pollution from cars and factories can affect local weather conditions and may be contributing to a dangerous rise in the earth's temperature.

THINKING ABOUT GEOGRAPHY How would you describe the climate where you live?

Tourists and residents bask in the sunshine of Waikiki Beach in Hawaii.

Vegetation

Between 20,000 and 25,000 species and subspecies of plants and vegetation grow in the United States—including over 1,000 different kinds of trees. Climate often dictates the type of vegetation found in a region. For instance, cold autumns in the Northeast contribute to the brilliantly colored autumn leaves. Rain nourishes the forests in the Northwest and Southeast. The central plains, where rainfall is less heavy, are covered by grass. Cactus plants thrive in the dry southwestern deserts.

Along with natural vegetation, climate dictates the nation's variety of planted crops. For example, temperate weather in the Midwest helps wheat to grow, while warm weather nourishes citrus fruit in Florida and California.

THINKING ABOUT GEOGRAPHY What kinds of trees or plants grow in your region?

This mountainside burns with the autumn foliage of New Hampshire.

Physical Geography Assessment

1. Main Ideas

a. What are the different aspects of physical geography?

b. Which state contains the largest variety of climates?

c. What two states contain most of the country's oil resources?

2. Critical Thinking

Drawing Conclusions What do you think are the advantages of living in a country with diverse physical geography?

THINK ABOUT

• the different resources available in your region
• the variety of recreational activities in your region

Geographic Dictionary

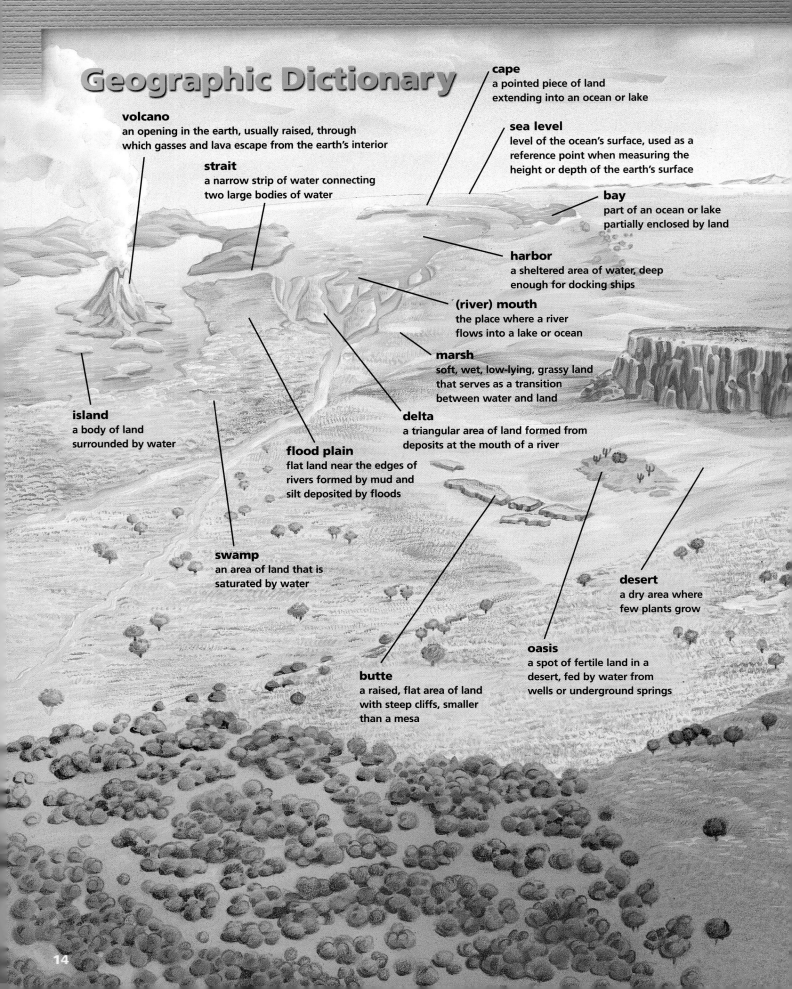

cape
a pointed piece of land extending into an ocean or lake

sea level
level of the ocean's surface, used as a reference point when measuring the height or depth of the earth's surface

bay
part of an ocean or lake partially enclosed by land

volcano
an opening in the earth, usually raised, through which gasses and lava escape from the earth's interior

strait
a narrow strip of water connecting two large bodies of water

harbor
a sheltered area of water, deep enough for docking ships

(river) mouth
the place where a river flows into a lake or ocean

marsh
soft, wet, low-lying, grassy land that serves as a transition between water and land

island
a body of land surrounded by water

delta
a triangular area of land formed from deposits at the mouth of a river

flood plain
flat land near the edges of rivers formed by mud and silt deposited by floods

swamp
an area of land that is saturated by water

desert
a dry area where few plants grow

oasis
a spot of fertile land in a desert, fed by water from wells or underground springs

butte
a raised, flat area of land with steep cliffs, smaller than a mesa

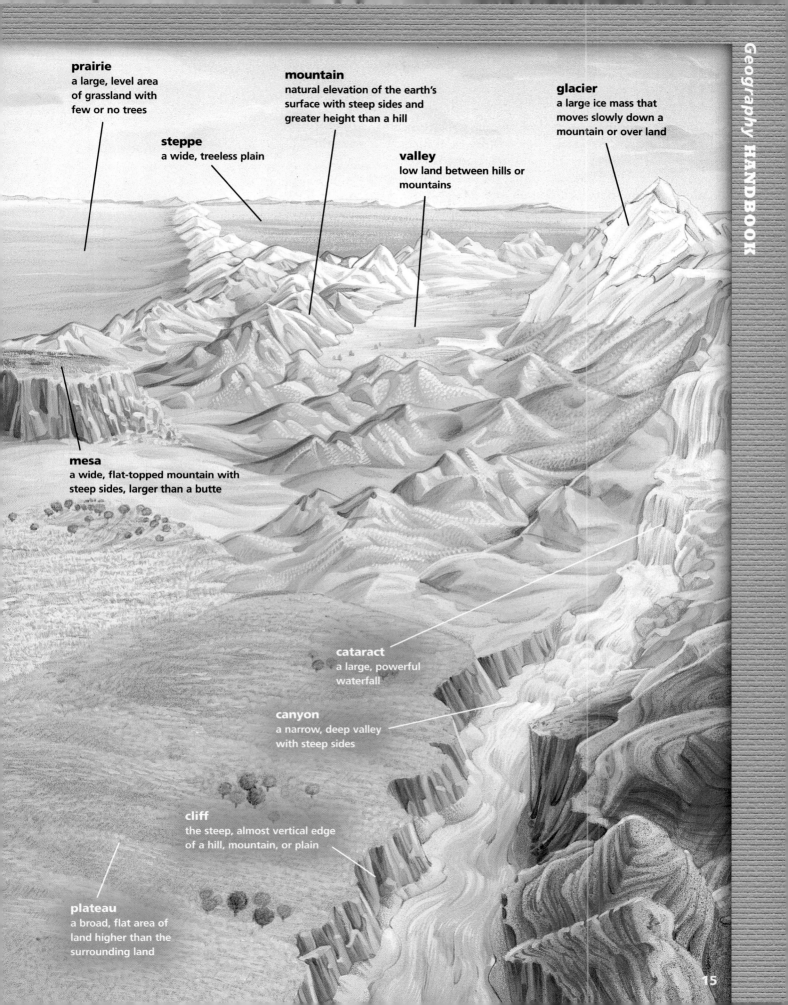

prairie
a large, level area of grassland with few or no trees

mountain
natural elevation of the earth's surface with steep sides and greater height than a hill

glacier
a large ice mass that moves slowly down a mountain or over land

steppe
a wide, treeless plain

valley
low land between hills or mountains

mesa
a wide, flat-topped mountain with steep sides, larger than a butte

cataract
a large, powerful waterfall

canyon
a narrow, deep valley with steep sides

cliff
the steep, almost vertical edge of a hill, mountain, or plain

plateau
a broad, flat area of land higher than the surrounding land

Human Geography of the United States

Human geography focuses on people's relationships with each other and the surrounding environment. It includes two main themes of geography: human-environment interaction and movement. The following pages will help you to better understand the link between people and geography.

Humans Adapt to Their Surroundings

Humans have always adapted to their environment. For example, in North America, many Native American tribes burned forest patches to create grazing area to attract animals and to clear area for farmland. In addition, Americans have adapted to their environment by building numerous dams, bridges, and tunnels. More recently, scientists and engineers have been developing building materials that will better withstand the earthquakes that occasionally strike California.

THINKING ABOUT GEOGRAPHY What are some of the ways in which you interact with your environment on a daily basis?

Early Americans of the Southwest protected themselves from the weather by building cliff dwellings.

The Hoover Dam, located on the Colorado River between Arizona and Nevada, provides electricity for Arizona, Nevada, and Southern California.

An oil spill from the ship *Exxon Valdez* harmed wildlife, such as this bird, in Prince William Sound, Alaska, in 1989.

Humans Affect the Environment

When humans interact with the environment, sometimes nature suffers. In the United States, for example, major oil leaks or spills occur each year—fouling shorelines and harming wildlife. Building suburbs and strip malls has also destroyed forests, farmland, and valuable wetlands.

THINKING ABOUT GEOGRAPHY What are some of the environmental problems in your city or town?

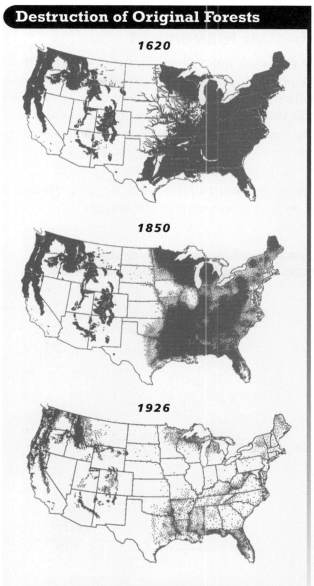

Destruction of Original Forests

1620

1850

1926

These maps show that, over the years, human beings have nearly cut down all the original forests in the United States. Each dot represents 25,000 acres.

Children plant trees along a Chicago expressway.

Preserving and Restoring

Americans—as well as people all over the world—have been working hard to balance economic progress with conservation. For example, car companies in the United States and around the world are working to develop pollution-free vehicles. In 1994, the average American family of four recycled around 1,100 pounds of waste. And, in the 1990s, Americans have planted more than two million acres of new trees each year.

THINKING ABOUT GEOGRAPHY What are some of the ways in which you help the environment?

Human Movement

In prehistoric times, people roamed the earth in search of food. Today in the United States, people move from place to place for many different reasons. Among them are cost of living, job availability, and climate. Since the 1970s, many Americans—as well as many new immigrants—moved to the Sunbelt. This region runs through the southern United States from Virginia to California. Between 1950 and 1990, that region's population soared from 52 million to 118 million.

THINKING ABOUT GEOGRAPHY Has your family ever moved? If so, what were some of the reasons?

This map shows human movement in the 1970s. The information below explains some of the results of this movement in the 1990s.

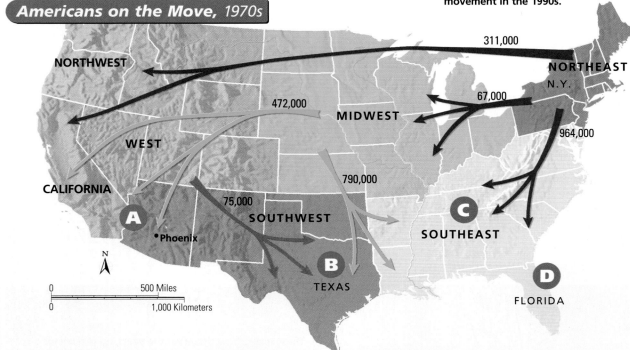

Americans on the Move, 1970s

NORTHWEST

NORTHEAST
N.Y.

311,000

472,000

67,000

964,000

MIDWEST

WEST

790,000

CALIFORNIA

75,000

A

●Phoenix

SOUTHWEST

SOUTHEAST

C

N

0 — 500 Miles
0 — 1,000 Kilometers

B

TEXAS

D

FLORIDA

A By 1996, the Phoenix-Mesa metropolitan area reached a population of 2.75 million, more than the number of people living in the entire state in 1980.

B Between 1990 and 1994, Texas overtook New York as the nation's second most populous state, behind California.

C One of the nation's fastest growing areas was the Southeast, where population growth ranged from six to nine percent between 1990 and 1994. Jobs grew in the area by 14 percent.

D Florida's population is growing so much that it could become as populous as New York state by around 2020.

New home developments cover the desert in Las Vegas, Nevada.

In the late 19th century, millions of immigrants arrived on the shores of the United States.

The Sears Tower overlooks Chinatown in Chicago.

Humans Spread Ideas and Information

Throughout U.S. history, people from all over the world have come to the United States. They have brought with them food, music, language, technology, and other aspects of their culture. As a result, the United States is one of the most culturally rich and diverse nations in the world. Look around your town or city. You'll probably notice different people, languages, and foods.

Today, the spreading of ideas and customs does not rely solely on human movement. Technology—from the Internet to television to satellites—spreads ideas and information throughout the world faster than ever. This has created an ever-growing, interconnected world. As the 21st century opens, human geography will continue to play a key role in shaping the United States and the world.

THINKING ABOUT GEOGRAPHY How have computers and the Internet affected your life?

Human Geography Assessment

1. Main Ideas

a. What are some of the ways that people have helped to restore the environment?

b. What are some of the ways that residents of your region have successfully modified their landscape?

c. What are some of the reasons that people move from place to place?

2. Critical Thinking

Recognizing Effects In what ways has technology helped bring people in the world together?

THINK ABOUT

- the different ways in which people communicate today
- the speed in which people today can communicate over long distances

GEOGRAPHY HANDBOOK ASSESSMENT

TERMS

Briefly explain the significance of each of the following.

1. physical map
2. political map
3. longitude
4. latitude
5. hemisphere
6. projection
7. flood plain
8. sea level
9. human geography
10. human movement

REVIEW QUESTIONS

Themes of Geography (pages 4–5)

1. What is the difference between *absolute* location and *relative* location?
2. What is meant by the theme of place?
3. What are the themes of movement and human-environment interaction?

Map Basics (pages 6–9)

4. What do you think are some of the benefits of using technology to study geography?
5. What are the three major kinds of maps?
6. What are latitude and longitude lines?

Physical Geography (pages 10–13)

7. How have the natural resources in the United States helped its economic development?
8. What are the different climates within the United States?

Human Geography (pages 16–19)

9. How is human geography different from physical geography?
10. What aspects of human geography might cause people to move?

CRITICAL THINKING

1. **Forming and Supporting Opinions** Which of the five themes of geography do you think has had the most impact on history? Why?
2. **Analyzing Causes** How do the climate and natural resources of an area affect its economy?
3. **Drawing Conclusions** How have computers helped geographers make more accurate maps?
4. **Making Inferences** Why do you think the Mercator projection is used for all types of navigation?
5. **Recognizing Effects** How does a diverse landscape help or hurt the economy of an area?

GEOGRAPHY SKILLS

1. INTERPRETING MAPS: Movement

Basic Map Elements

a. What region of the United States is shown?
b. Compare the number of teams on the 1987 map and the 2000 map. How many more teams are on the 2000 map?

Interpreting the Map

c. What geographic theme(s) is most responsible for the increase in sports teams in this region?
d. According to the map, which sport enjoyed the biggest surge in popularity in this region?

Major League Sports in Southeast Cities

1987

2000

Baseball (MLB)
Hockey (NHL)
Men's Basketball (NBA)
Women's Basketball (WNBA)
Football (NFL)
Soccer (MLS)

GEOGRAPHY SKILLS

2. INTERPRETING MAPS: Region

Study the map and then answer the questions.

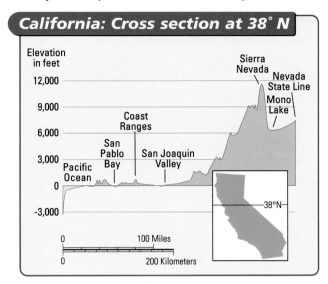

California: Cross section at 38° N

Basic Map Elements

a. What are the different landforms on the map?

Interpreting the Map

b. What is the level of the San Joaquin Valley? How many miles does it take to get from there to the highest point in California at the 38th parallel?

3. INTERPRETING PRIMARY SOURCES

In 1803, President Thomas Jefferson appointed Meriwether Lewis to explore the lands of the Louisiana Purchase. Jefferson gave him these instructions:

> The object of your mission is to explore the Missouri river . . . by its course & communication with the waters of the Pacific Ocean, may offer the most direct & practicable water communication across this continent, for the purposes of commerce. . . .
>
> Other objects worthy of notice will be the soil & face of the country, its growth & vegetable productions . . . the mineral productions of every kind. . . . climate as characterized by the thermometer . . . the dates at which particular plants put forth or lose their flowers, or leaf, times of appearance of particular birds, reptiles, or insects.
>
> **Thomas Jefferson,** quoted in *The Journals of Lewis and Clark*

a. What was Jefferson expecting to find in the West?

b. Why might the president want to know about the land's soil and vegetable production?

c. What aspect of human geography might be of interest to the president?

ALTERNATIVE ASSESSMENT

1. INTERDISCIPLINARY ACTIVITY: Math

Plotting Latitude and Longitude On a piece of graph paper, sketch a map of the United States. Be sure to draw in state boundaries, too. Then, using an atlas as a reference, draw and mark the latitude and longitude lines that cross the nation at five degree intervals. Plot the estimated longitude and latitude location of your city or town. Determine at which degrees the lines intersect where you live. Repeat this exercise for at least five different places you have visited or would like to visit within the United States.

2. COOPERATIVE LEARNING ACTIVITY

Making a Map How well do you know the neighborhood around your school? Form groups of three to four students. Then work together to draw a map of the neighborhood around your school. Include:

- streets
- residences
- stores
- geographic features
- important landmarks

The map should be accurate but not too cluttered with unnecessary details. Compare your group's map with those of the other groups in the class.

3. TECHNOLOGY ACTIVITY

Writing Directions Several Internet sites provide detailed maps of the United States. They also provide driving directions to most places in the country.

- Locate one of these map sites on the Internet.
- Think of a place in the United States that you would like to visit.
- Work with the computer to find the best route for reaching it.

Write out clear directions as well as the total mileage of your trip. Also, note the type of map it is and the features it highlights.

For more important geography sites . . .

INTERNET ACTIVITY
CLASSZONE.COM

4. HISTORY PORTFOLIO

Review your alternative assessment activities. Use comments made by your teacher or classmates to improve your work.

Additional Test Practice, pp. S1–S33

TEST PRACTICE
CLASSZONE.COM

Colonization and the Early Republic

The ruins of the Anasazi Cliff Palace, in modern-day Colorado, stand as a reminder of the Native American societies that existed before the arrival of Europeans.

"The story of my people and the story of this place are one single story."

—*Taos Pueblo man*

REVIEW CHAPTER

1

Colonization to Revolution

Beginnings—1783

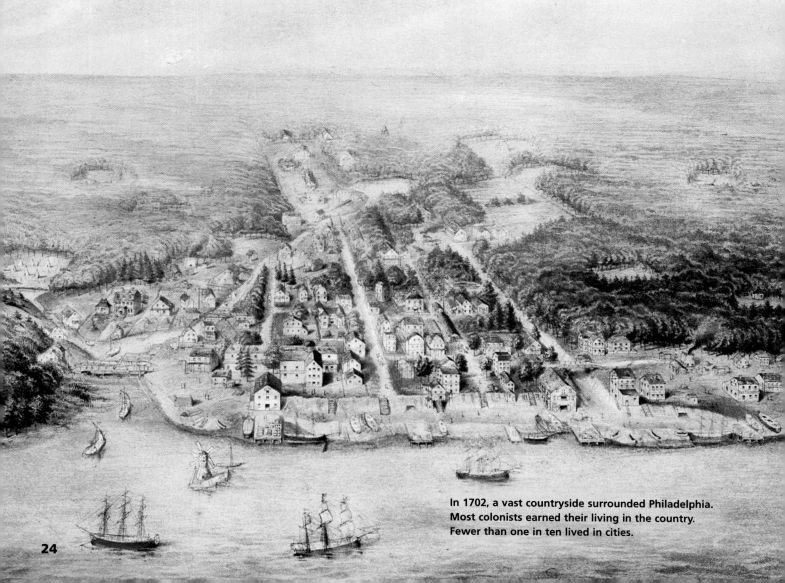

In 1702, a vast countryside surrounded Philadelphia. Most colonists earned their living in the country. Fewer than one in ten lived in cities.

Interact *with* History

Boston

Boston was the largest colonial city until the mid-1700s.

American colonies depended on trade.

Many craftspeople, such as this shoemaker, made a living in cities.

It is between 1600 and 1750 when you arrive in an American colony. After nearly a month of ocean travel, you are thrilled to see land. As you leave the ship, you wonder where you will live and how you will earn a living.

What Do You Think?

- In what year do you arrive?
- Will you choose to live where other people from your homeland live?
- How did you make a living in your old country? Will this influence your choice?

Would you settle on a farm or in a town?

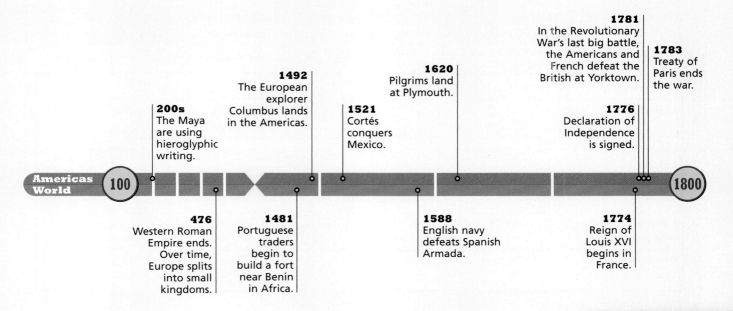

200s
The Maya are using hieroglyphic writing.

1492
The European explorer Columbus lands in the Americas.

1521
Cortés conquers Mexico.

1620
Pilgrims land at Plymouth.

1776
Declaration of Independence is signed.

1781
In the Revolutionary War's last big battle, the Americans and French defeat the British at Yorktown.

1783
Treaty of Paris ends the war.

Americas
World

100

1800

476
Western Roman Empire ends. Over time, Europe splits into small kingdoms.

1481
Portuguese traders begin to build a fort near Benin in Africa.

1588
English navy defeats Spanish Armada.

1774
Reign of Louis XVI begins in France.

BEFORE YOU READ

Previewing the Theme

Immigration and Migration From the 15th century to the 18th century, millions of people came to the Americas from other continents. Chapter 1 discusses why people came to the Americas and the effects of these migrations, including the creation of the United States.

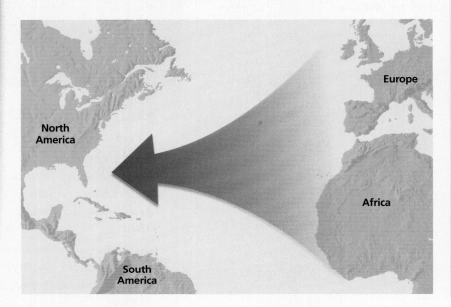

What Do You Know?

What comes to mind when someone uses the word *colonist?* Why do you think people colonized different territories?

THINK ABOUT
• what you've learned about colonists from movies, school, or your parents
• reasons that people travel throughout the world today

What Do You Want to Know?

What questions do you have about the colonization of the Americas? Write those questions in your notebook before you read the chapter.

READ AND TAKE NOTES

Reading Strategy: Taking Notes To help you remember what you read, take notes about the events and ideas discussed in the chapter. Taking notes means writing down important information.

The chart below lists the major events and ideas covered in the chapter. Use the chart to take notes about these important events and ideas.

 See Skillbuilder Handbook, page R3.

Event/Idea	Notes
Exploration	
Establishing Colonies	
Slavery in the Americas	
Colonial Conflict with Britain	
Revolutionary War	

TERMS & NAMES
Christopher
  Columbus
conquistador
missions
Columbian
  Exchange
slavery

MAIN IDEA	WHY IT MATTERS NOW
Native American, European, and African cultures came together in the Americas.	Native American, African, and European cultures shaped modern American culture.

ONE AMERICAN'S STORY

Solveig Turpin must climb cliffs and dodge cactus spines to do her work. She searches caves and cliffs for paintings that ancient people left on rock walls. One painting that Turpin found shows a nine-foot-long red panther. She believes it shows a religious leader who turned himself into an animal.

A VOICE FROM THE PAST

This is the Shaman [religious leader] who transforms into the largest and most powerful animal here. . . . I like to call [the shamans] supramen because they were over everything.

Solveig Turpin, quoted in *In Search of Ancient North America*

Solveig Turpin wears a shirt displaying the rock paintings of ancient peoples as she discusses her work.

   Archaeologists make theories about the past based on what they learn from artifacts, objects that humans made. They give clues about how ancient people lived. This section discusses the first Americans and the other people who came to America.

The First Americans

Scientists think that the first peoples migrated, or moved, to the Americas from Asia. But scientists disagree about how and when this move took place. During the last ice age, ancient people may have crossed a land bridge that joined Asia and North America. Some scientists who hold this theory believe the earliest Americans arrived 12,000 years ago. Other scientists believe humans came to the Americas about 30,000 years ago. These scientists believe that people came by many routes, over thousands of years.

   Over the centuries, many societies developed. From 1200 to 400 B.C., the Olmec people thrived along the Gulf of Mexico. They set up trade routes and built cities. From A.D. 250 to 900, the Maya society developed in southern Mexico and Guatemala. In what is now central Mexico, the Aztecs built a great empire in the 1400s and early 1500s. In the eastern part of what is now the United States lived several groups of people called Mound Builders who built large earthen structures. The last group of Mound Builders, the Mississippians, lived from A.D. 800 to 1700.

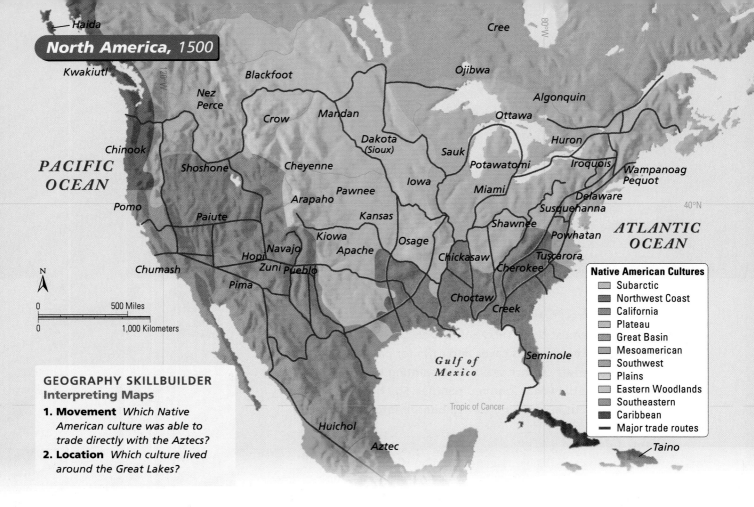

North America, 1500

Haida
Cree
Kwakiutl
Blackfoot
Ojibwa
Nez Perce
Algonquin
Crow
Mandan
Ottawa
Chinook
Dakota (Sioux)
Huron
PACIFIC OCEAN
Shoshone
Cheyenne
Sauk
Iroquois
Potawatomi
Wampanoag
Pomo
Pawnee
Iowa
Miami
Pequot
Arapaho
Delaware
Paiute
Kansas
Susquehanna
40°N
Kiowa
Osage
Shawnee
Powhatan
ATLANTIC OCEAN
Navajo
Apache
Chickasaw
Tuscarora
Hopi
Zuni Pueblo
Cherokee
Chumash
Pima
Choctaw
Creek
N
0   500 Miles
0   1,000 Kilometers
Gulf of Mexico
Seminole

GEOGRAPHY SKILLBUILDER
Interpreting Maps
1. **Movement** *Which Native American culture was able to trade directly with the Aztecs?*
2. **Location** *Which culture lived around the Great Lakes?*

Huichol
Aztec
Tropic of Cancer
Taino

Native American Cultures
- Subarctic
- Northwest Coast
- California
- Plateau
- Great Basin
- Mesoamerican
- Southwest
- Plains
- Eastern Woodlands
- Southeastern
- Caribbean
- Major trade routes

By 1500, the peoples of North America had divided into hundreds of cultural groups, speaking 2,000 languages. Their ways of life varied greatly. In the north, the Aleut and the Inuit hunted sea mammals. Many of the peoples of the Great Plains tracked bison.

The dwellings of various Native American groups also differed. The Pueblo of the American Southwest lived in many-storied houses of adobe—dried mud bricks. In the Eastern Woodlands, the Iroquois lived in 300-foot-long houses.

Societies of West Africa

Complex societies also developed in West Africa. From the 700s to the mid-1000s, the kingdom of **Ghana** prospered by controlling the trade of gold and salt. By the 1200s, the kingdom of Mali had taken over most of Ghana's territory. Mali became West Africa's most powerful state. Its wealth also came from control of the gold-salt trade. Eventually, Mali's power decreased. The Songhai (SAWNG•HY) people broke away from its control. In 1464, they began their own empire.

Reading **History**
A. Finding Main Ideas Why did Ghana prosper?

Societies of Europe

After the fall of the Roman Empire, Europeans searched for stability. Europeans turned to feudalism to protect themselves. Feudalism is a system in which a king allows lords to use lands that belong to him. In return, the lords owe the king military service and protection for the people living on the land.

Reading**History**
B. Identifying
Problems
What problems
were Europeans
trying to solve
with feudalism?

By the 1000s, feudalism had brought more stability to society. As the economy grew, many serfs ran away to towns and found work. Because so many serfs left the farms, feudalism began to weaken. Then, beginning in 1347, the bubonic plague swept across Europe. It killed about one-fourth of the population and reduced the number of workers. Lords competed for the laborers who survived, so they began to pay wages. As feudal lords lost power, kings grew stronger.

During the 1300s, many Europeans began to question long-held beliefs. This questioning led to the Renaissance. Lasting from the 1300s to about 1600, the Renaissance was a time of increased interest in learning. During the Renaissance, trade grew. European merchants wanted to expand trade and sought new trade routes.

European Exploration

As part of the search for new sea routes, the Portuguese explorer Bartolomeu Dias (DEE•uhs) reached the southern tip of Africa in 1488. Ten years later, another Portuguese explorer, Vasco da Gama, followed Dias's route. He continued north along the east coast of Africa. Then he sailed east across the Indian Ocean to India. He had found an all-water route to Asia. Spain and other European rivals wanted to take part in the profitable trade with Asia. They began to look for their own water routes to Asia.

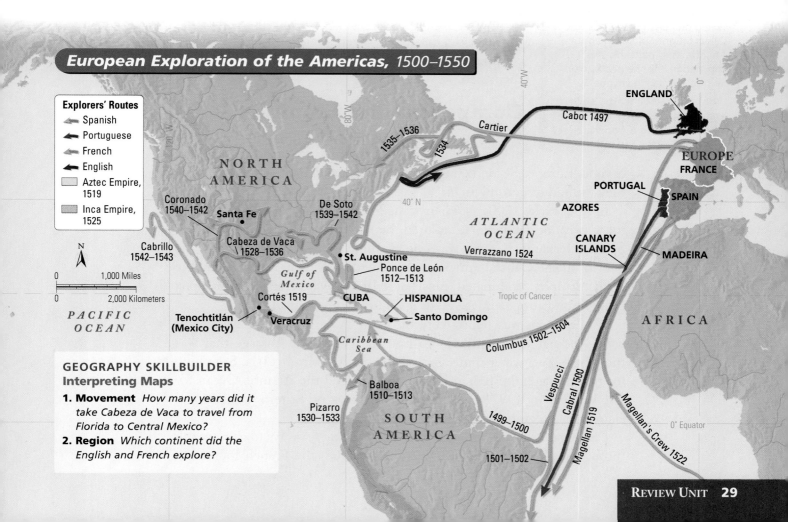

European Exploration of the Americas, 1500–1550

Explorers' Routes
- Spanish
- Portuguese
- French
- English
- Aztec Empire, 1519
- Inca Empire, 1525

Cabot 1497
Cartier
1535–1536
1534
Verrazzano 1524
Columbus 1502–1504
Vespucci
Cabral 1500
Magellan 1519
Magellan's Crew 1522
1499–1500
1501–1502

ENGLAND
EUROPE
FRANCE
PORTUGAL
SPAIN
AZORES
CANARY ISLANDS
MADEIRA
AFRICA

NORTH AMERICA
Coronado 1540–1542
Santa Fe
Cabrillo 1542–1543
Cabeza de Vaca 1528–1536
De Soto 1539–1542
St. Augustine
Ponce de León 1512–1513
CUBA
HISPANIOLA
Santo Domingo
Tropic of Cancer
ATLANTIC OCEAN
40° N

Cortés 1519
Tenochtitlán (Mexico City)
Veracruz
Gulf of Mexico
Caribbean Sea

PACIFIC OCEAN

N

0   1,000 Miles
0   2,000 Kilometers

Balboa 1510–1513
Pizarro 1530–1533
SOUTH AMERICA
0° Equator

GEOGRAPHY SKILLBUILDER
Interpreting Maps
1. **Movement** How many years did it take Cabeza de Vaca to travel from Florida to Central Mexico?
2. **Region** Which continent did the English and French explore?

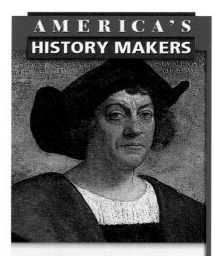

CHRISTOPHER COLUMBUS
1451–1506

Christopher Columbus's son Ferdinand wrote that his father "took to the sea at the age of 14 and followed it ever after."

Columbus's early voyages nearly cost him his life. When he was 25, pirates off the coast of Portugal sank his ship. Columbus survived by grabbing a floating oar and swimming to shore.

But he also learned a lot from sailing on Portuguese ships. The sailors taught Columbus about Atlantic wind patterns. This knowledge later helped him on his history-making voyage.

What character traits, shown in Columbus's early life, might have made him a good leader?

Meanwhile, an Italian sailor named **Christopher Columbus** thought he knew a faster way to reach Asia. Instead of sailing around Africa and then east, Columbus decided to sail west across the Atlantic.

In 1492, King Ferdinand and Queen Isabella of Spain agreed to back Columbus. Preparing to sail, Columbus assembled his ships—the *Niña*, the *Pinta*, and the *Santa María*.

After almost 10 weeks at sea, the ships landed on a Caribbean island. Columbus incorrectly believed that he had reached the Indies, islands in Southeast Asia. The islanders who greeted Columbus and his men were Taino (TY•noh) people, but Columbus mistakenly called them Indians. For three months, Columbus visited several Caribbean islands. After finding gold and precious objects on one of these islands, Columbus became convinced that he had reached Asia. In 1493, he sailed back to Spain. Neither Columbus nor the Spanish rulers suspected that he had landed near continents entirely unknown to Europeans.

Columbus made three more voyages to the Americas but never brought back the treasures he had promised Spain's rulers. But in time, the geographic knowledge Columbus brought back changed European views of the world. Europeans were eager to see if these continents that they had just learned about could make them rich.

*Reading***History**

C. Making Inferences Why do you think Ferdinand and Isabella backed Columbus's voyage?

Competition for Empire

European countries had three main goals during the age of exploration. First, they wanted to spread Christianity beyond Europe. Second, they wanted to expand their empires. Third, they wanted to become rich.

In the early 1500s, soldiers called ***conquistadors***, (kahn•KWIHS•tuh•dawrz) or conquerors, explored the Americas and claimed them for Spain. Hernando Cortés was one of these *conquistadors*. In 1519, he landed on the Central American coast with 508 men. At the time, the Aztec Empire dominated most of Mexico. Weakened by smallpox brought by Europeans, the Aztecs fell to Cortés in 1521.

While Spain was taking control of the Americas, other Europeans were sending out expeditions to find the Northwest Passage that was thought to be a water route through North America to Asia. Searching for this passage, the Italian John Cabot crossed the Atlantic Ocean for the English in 1497. He landed in the area of eastern Canada and claimed the region for England.

France and the Netherlands were also looking for ways to gain wealth through exploration and colonization. In 1608, the French founded a fur-trading post at Quebec. At the same time the Dutch were building a colony called New Netherland. It was located along the Hudson River.

By 1700, the Spanish Empire controlled much of the Americas. In the Spanish colonies, the Catholic Church built **missions,** settlements that included a church, a town, and farmlands. The goal of the missions was to convert Native Americans to Christianity. The Spanish also forced Native Americans to work on plantations, large farms that raised cash crops. The plantations thrived, but many Native Americans died.

The arrival of Europeans in the Americas began a movement of plants, animals, and diseases between the Eastern and Western hemispheres. This movement of living things between hemispheres is called the **Columbian Exchange.** When Europeans came to America, they brought with them germs that caused diseases such as smallpox. Native Americans had no immunity to them. As a result, millions of Native Americans died.

By 1600, **slavery,** the practice of holding a person in bondage for labor, was established in the Americas. Because Native Americans quickly died from overwork and disease, the Spanish and Portuguese enslaved Africans to provide labor. European slave traders shipped Africans to the Americas. On the coast of Africa, local kings gathered captives from inland. The local kings then traded these captives to slave traders for European goods.

The forced removal of people from Africa is called the African Diaspora. Before the slave trade ended in the late 1800s, about 12 million Africans had been enslaved and shipped to the Americas. Of these, perhaps 2 million died during the voyage across the Atlantic, called the middle passage. Once the enslaved Africans arrived in the colonies, they were sold at auction. Most were forced to work in farms or mines. They were also fed and housed poorly. By the 1700s, all the American colonies of European countries had African slaves.

*Reading***History**

D. Making Inferences What might have happened if Native Americans had been immune to European diseases?

The diagram above shows how slave traders packed enslaved Africans onto slave ships for the middle passage.

Section 1 Assessment

1. Terms & Names

Explain the significance of:
- Christopher Columbus
- *conquistador*
- missions
- Columbian Exchange
- slavery

2. Taking Notes

Use a chart like the one below to list ancient cultures of North America and their locations.

Ancient Culture	Location

3. Main Ideas

a. By what land bridge did some ancient people migrate to North America?

b. How did the West African kingdom of Ghana prosper?

c. What were the three main goals of European voyages of exploration?

4. Critical Thinking

Making Inferences What were the effects of the Columbian Exchange?

THINK ABOUT
- disease
- food
- livestock

ACTIVITY OPTIONS

ART

MATH

Research some aspect of the slave trade, such as the middle passage or the number of people enslaved. Paint a **picture** or draw a **graph** to show what you learned.

2 The English Colonies

TERMS & NAMES
Jamestown
House of Burgesses
Pilgrims
Mayflower
  Compact
Puritans
triangular trade
French and Indian
  War
Treaty of Paris

MAIN IDEA	WHY IT MATTERS NOW
Britain established a group of diverse colonies in North America.	The United States grew out of the British colonies in North America.

ONE AMERICAN'S STORY

John White traveled with the first English expedition to Roanoke, an island off North Carolina, in 1585. White sailed back to England in 1586 and then returned to Roanoke as governor the next year, bringing with him more than 100 settlers. White's daughter Elinor gave birth to a baby girl, Virginia Dare, during their stay. John White described the event.

A VOICE FROM THE PAST

On August 18 a daughter was born to Elinor, . . . wife of Ananias Dare. . . . The child was christened on the following Sunday and was named Virginia because she was the first Christian born in Virginia.

John White, *The New World*

Drawing by John White of an old man of the Pomeiock tribe.

In 1587, White sailed back to England to get supplies. White did not return to Roanoke until 1590. To his shock and grief, the colonists he left behind had all disappeared. The only clues to their fate were the letters *CRO* carved in a tree and the word *Croatoan* carved in a doorpost. White never discovered the fate of his family and the other colonists. In this section, you will learn why English settlers such as White came to America despite such dangers.

Jamestown

England tried to start several American colonies. Before 1607, all of them failed. Then in 1607, the Virginia Company of London financed the **Jamestown** colony near Chesapeake Bay. It became the first permanent English settlement in the Americas.

The Jamestown colonists faced hardship. Even though 800 more English settlers arrived in 1609, only 60 colonists were still alive by 1610. In 1612, the colonists learned to grow tobacco and began to earn profits for the Virginia Company.

Indentured servants, people who sold their labor to the person who paid their passage to the colony, began to arrive. After working for several years, they were free to farm or take up a trade. In addition to these workers, African servants were first brought to Jamestown in 1619.

The Virginia colonists became annoyed at the strict rule of the governor, who represented the Virginia Company in London. To provide more local control, the company created the **House of Burgesses** in 1619. It became the first representative assembly in the American colonies.

New England Colonies

In the early 1600s, a religious group called the Separatists wanted to separate from the Church of England. The **Pilgrims** were a Separatist group. To escape harsh treatment from the king, they sailed to America.

Their ship, the *Mayflower*, arrived off the Massachusetts coast in 1620. The men aboard the *Mayflower* signed an agreement called the **Mayflower Compact**. In it, they vowed to obey laws agreed upon for the good of the colony. The Mayflower Compact helped establish the idea of self-government.

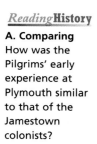

Reading History

A. Comparing How was the Pilgrims' early experience at Plymouth similar to that of the Jamestown colonists?

Like the early settlers at Jamestown, the Pilgrims faced hardship. Half the group had died by spring. However, the Pilgrims developed friendly relations with the Native Americans, who showed them how to survive in their new environment.

Between about 1630 and 1640, a religious group called the **Puritans** left England. The Puritans wanted to reform, or "purify," the Church of England. About 1,000 Puritans arrived in America in 1630.

The growing population of colonists led to conflict with Native Americans. In 1675–1676, the colonists won a brutal war against the Wampanoag tribe. The colonists took control of more Native American land.

Middle and Southern Colonies

The Middle Colonies included New York, New Jersey, Pennsylvania, and Delaware. They were located between New England to the north

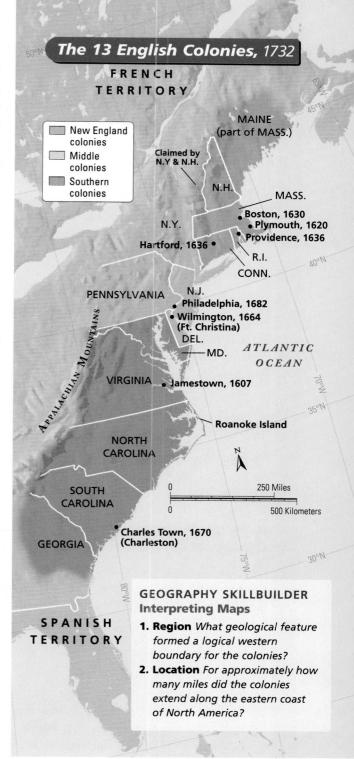

The 13 English Colonies, 1732

FRENCH TERRITORY

New England colonies

Middle colonies

Southern colonies

MAINE (part of MASS.)

Claimed by N.Y & N.H.

N.H.

N.Y.

MASS.
Boston, 1630
Plymouth, 1620
Providence, 1636

Hartford, 1636

R.I.

CONN.

PENNSYLVANIA

N.J.
Philadelphia, 1682
Wilmington, 1664 (Ft. Christina)

DEL.

MD.

APPALACHIAN MOUNTAINS

VIRGINIA
Jamestown, 1607

ATLANTIC OCEAN

Roanoke Island

NORTH CAROLINA

SOUTH CAROLINA

Charles Town, 1670 (Charleston)

GEORGIA

SPANISH TERRITORY

0   250 Miles

0   500 Kilometers

50°N
45°N
40°N
35°N
30°N
55°W
70°W
75°W
80°W

GEOGRAPHY SKILLBUILDER
Interpreting Maps

1. **Region** What geological feature formed a logical western boundary for the colonies?
2. **Location** For approximately how many miles did the colonies extend along the eastern coast of North America?

and the Chesapeake region to the south. Religious freedom attracted many groups, including Catholics, Quakers, and Jews, to these colonies.

In 1624, Dutch settlers financed by the Dutch West India Company founded the colony of New Netherland. New Netherland included the Hudson River valley, Long Island, and the land along the Delaware River. In 1664, the English took control of the colony from the Dutch. They renamed the colony New York.

In 1681, England's King Charles II gave William Penn a large piece of land in America. That territory came to be called Pennsylvania. Penn was a Quaker. He used this land to create a colony where Quakers could live according to their beliefs. They welcomed different religions and ethnic groups. Penn especially wanted the Native Americans to be treated fairly.

In addition to Virginia, more Southern Colonies were established. Lord Baltimore established Maryland in 1632 for Roman Catholics fleeing persecution in England. In 1663, Carolina was founded. Carolina's colonists needed laborers to grow rice and indigo. The English settlers encouraged the use of enslaved Africans. In 1732, James Oglethorpe founded Georgia as a refuge for debtors.

Colonial Economies

In New England, most farmers practiced subsistence farming. That is, they produced just enough food for themselves and sometimes a little extra to trade in town. Other New Englanders earned their living by fishing.

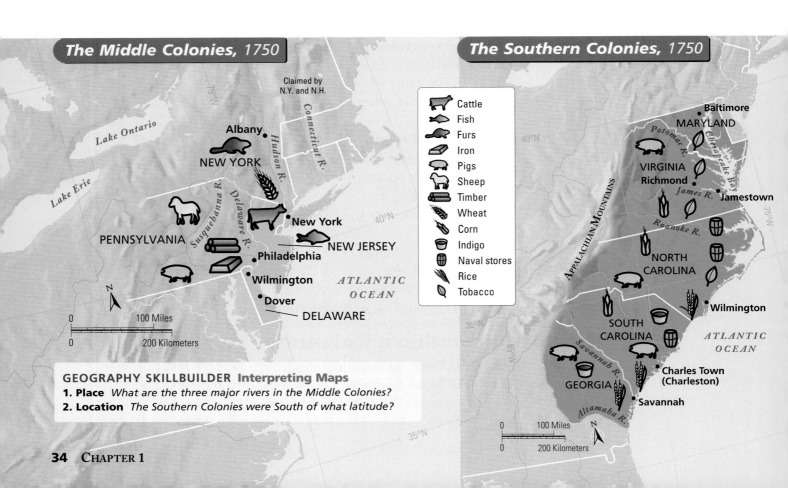

The Middle Colonies, 1750

The Southern Colonies, 1750

Claimed by N.Y. and N.H.

Lake Ontario
Lake Erie
Albany
NEW YORK
Connecticut R.
Hudson R.
PENNSYLVANIA
Susquehanna R.
Delaware R.
New York
NEW JERSEY
Philadelphia
Wilmington
Dover
DELAWARE
ATLANTIC OCEAN

Cattle
Fish
Furs
Iron
Pigs
Sheep
Timber
Wheat
Corn
Indigo
Naval stores
Rice
Tobacco

Baltimore
MARYLAND
Potomac R.
Chesapeake Bay
VIRGINIA
Richmond
James R.
Jamestown
Roanoke R.
APPALACHIAN MOUNTAINS
NORTH CAROLINA
Wilmington
SOUTH CAROLINA
ATLANTIC OCEAN
Savannah R.
Charles Town (Charleston)
GEORGIA
Savannah
Altamaha R.

0   100 Miles
0   200 Kilometers

N

0   100 Miles
0   200 Kilometers

N

GEOGRAPHY SKILLBUILDER Interpreting Maps
1. **Place** What are the three major rivers in the Middle Colonies?
2. **Location** The Southern Colonies were South of what latitude?

Reading History

B. Reading a Graph Ask and answer a question about the geographic pattern of changes in the slave population.

The Middle Colonies had a longer growing season than New England and a soil rich enough to grow cash crops. These crops were sold for money. The South's soil and long growing season were ideal for plantation crops, such as rice, indigo, and tobacco. During the 1600s, Southern planters turned to enslaved Africans for labor.

Many colonial merchants participated in the **triangular trade.** This type of trade had a route with three stops. For example, a ship might leave New England with a cargo of rum and iron. In Africa, the captain traded his cargo for slaves. Slaves then endured the middle passage to the West Indies, where they were exchanged for sugar and molasses. Traders took the sugar and molasses back to New England. There, the colonists used the molasses to make rum, and the pattern started over.

By 1750, over 235,000 enslaved Africans were in America. About 7 percent of these people lived in the Middle Colonies and around 85 percent lived in the Southern Colonies. On Southern plantations, enslaved persons performed exhausting work. If slaves did not appear to be working hard, they were often whipped. Slaves resisted slavery in many ways. They sometimes worked slowly, damaged goods, or purposely carried out orders the wrong way. At times, slaves became so angry and frustrated by their loss of freedom that they ran away. Others rebelled.

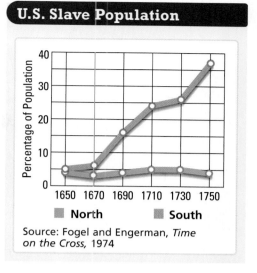

U.S. Slave Population

Source: Fogel and Engerman, *Time on the Cross,* 1974

Reading History

C. Finding Main Ideas How did enslaved Africans resist slavery?

Roots of Representative Government

American colonists expected certain rights that came from living under an English government. These "rights of Englishmen" had developed over centuries. In 1215, a group of English noblemen forced King John to accept the Magna Carta (Great Charter). This document guaranteed important rights to noblemen and freemen. Over time, the rights the Magna Carta listed were granted to all English people.

One of the most important English rights was the right to elect representatives to government. Parliament, England's chief lawmaking body, was the colonists' model for representative government.

English colonists formed their own representative assemblies. Even so, England had authority over them. In the late 1600s, King James II appointed Edmund Andros as governor of New England. Andros angered the colonists by ending their representative assemblies.

In 1688, James, a Catholic, fled England when Protestants offered the throne to his Protestant daughter, Mary, and her husband, William of Orange. This change of leadership was called England's Glorious Revolution. William and Mary agreed to uphold the English Bill of Rights. This was an agreement to respect the rights of English citizens and of Parliament. The American colonists were quick to claim these rights.

The New England colonists regained some amount of self-government.

This 1903 painting by Edward Deming shows an attack on British forces in 1755.

But they still had a governor appointed by the crown. The governor could strike down laws passed by the colonial assembly, but the assembly was responsible for the governor's salary. If he blocked the assembly, the assembly might refuse to pay him.

The French and Indian War

By the late 1600s, France claimed territory from the Appalachian Mountains to the Rocky Mountains. The English competed with the French in the region over the fur trade. The Huron and Algonquin peoples were allied with the French. The Iroquois were allied with the English. When British fur traders moved into the west in the 1750s, the French and their Native American allies destroyed a British trading post. The English colonists tried to reestablish an outpost in the region but were again defeated by the French and their allies. This started the **French and Indian War** (1754–1763).

The British took control of Canada in 1760, but the British and French continued fighting in other parts of the world for almost three more years. Finally, Britain won the war. By the **Treaty of Paris,** Britain claimed all of North America east of the Mississippi River. The treaty ended French power in North America.

*Reading*History

D. Recognizing Effects How did the fur trade lead to the French and Indian War?

Section 2 Assessment

1. Terms & Names

Explain the significance of:
• Jamestown
• House of Burgesses
• Pilgrims
• Mayflower Compact
• Puritans
• triangular trade
• French and Indian War
• Treaty of Paris

2. Taking Notes

Review the section and find four events to place on a time line that shows how the English colonies developed.

English Colonies Develop

1607 — | — | — | — | 1763

Which event do you think is the most important? Why?

3. Main Ideas

a. What is the Mayflower Compact?

b. What effect did the Glorious Revolution of 1688 have on the colonies?

c. What was the result of the French and Indian War?

4. Critical Thinking

Summarizing
How did the triangular trade work?

THINK ABOUT
• trade
• raw products
• finished goods

ACTIVITY OPTIONS

You need indentured servants to work on your plantation. Draw a **poster** or write an **advertisement** that will attract people to your plantation.

③ The American Revolution

TERMS & NAMES
George Washington
Declaration of Independence
Thomas Jefferson
Loyalists
Patriots
Treaty of Paris of 1783

MAIN IDEA
The American colonists fought to gain independence from Britain.

WHY IT MATTERS NOW
The American Revolution created the United States of America.

ONE AMERICAN'S STORY

James Otis, Jr., a young Massachusetts lawyer, was angry about Britain's lack of respect for colonial rights. For example, Britain allowed customs officials to use search warrants to enter any home or business to look for smuggled goods. Otis believed these searches were illegal.

Otis took up a case against the government that involved these search warrants. In court in February 1761, Otis spoke with great emotion for five hours about the search warrant and its use.

> *A VOICE FROM THE PAST*
>
> It appears to me the worst instrument of arbitrary power, the most destructive of English liberty and the fundamental principles of law, that was ever found in an English law-book.
>
> **James Otis, Jr.,** quoted in *James Otis: The Pre-Revolutionist* by J. C. Ridpath

Spectators listened in amazement. One of them, a young lawyer named John Adams, later wrote of Otis's performance: "Then and there, in the old Council Chamber, the child Independence was born." In this section, you will read more about the early protests against Britain's policies in America.

James Otis, Jr., argues in court against illegal search warrants in 1761.

Tighter British Control

Great Britain gained territory and faced large debts after the French and Indian War. To better govern America and pay off its debts, Parliament passed new laws and taxes. In 1764, they passed the Sugar Act, which taxed sugar and other products shipped to the colonies. Colonial leaders claimed that Parliament had no right to tax the colonies, since the colonists were not represented in Parliament

In 1765, Parliament passed the Stamp Act. This law required all legal and commercial documents to carry an official stamp showing that a tax had been paid. Colonial leaders protested. Colonial assemblies and newspapers took up the cry, "No taxation without representation!" Colonial merchants organized a boycott of British goods. A boycott is a refusal to buy. Parliament finally repealed the Stamp Act in 1766.

Bostonians Paying the Taxman

In this British political cartoon, Americans are depicted as barbarians who would tar and feather a customs official, or tax collector, and pour hot tea down his throat.

A Liberty Tree as a gallows

B Stamp Act posted upside down

C Protesters in Boston

D Customs official tarred and feathered

Colonial Resistance Grows

To raise money to pay for expenses in America, the British Parliament passed the Townshend Acts in 1767. The first of these acts suspended New York's assembly until New Yorkers agreed to house British troops. The other acts placed duties, or import taxes, on various goods.

The colonists felt that the Townshend Acts were a serious threat to their rights and freedoms. To protest these acts, colonists announced another boycott of British goods. The driving force behind this protest was Samuel Adams, a leader of the Boston Sons of Liberty. The Sons of Liberty was a secret society that opposed British policies.

On March 5, 1770, a fight broke out between youths and British soldiers in Boston. The soldiers began firing, killing five civilians. Called the Boston Massacre, this incident became a major source for anti-British propaganda.

Parliament repealed the Townshend Acts but, in 1773, passed the Tea Act. The Tea Act gave the British East India Company control over the American tea trade. This enraged colonial shippers and merchants. In Boston, the Sons of Liberty organized the Boston Tea Party. On December 16, 1773, a group of men disguised as Native Americans boarded three British tea ships. They destroyed 342 chests of tea.

Reading **History**
A. Recognizing Propaganda How did the use of the word *massacre* show an anti-British view?

The Road to Lexington and Concord

The Boston Tea Party aroused fury in Britain. In 1774, Parliament passed a series of laws to punish the Massachusetts colony and to warn other colonies not to rebel. These laws were so harsh that the colonists called them the Intolerable Acts. Among other things, these acts closed the port of Boston until colonists paid for the destroyed tea.

In 1774, delegates from all the colonies except Georgia met in Philadelphia. At this meeting, called the First Continental Congress, delegates voted to ban all trade with Britain until the Intolerable Acts were repealed. They also called on each colony to begin training troops. In response, Parliament increased restrictions on colonial trade and sent more troops. On April 18, 1775, British general Thomas Gage ordered his troops to arrest Sam Adams and John Hancock in Lexington. The troops were also to destroy colonial ammunition supplies in Concord.

Paul Revere spread the news about British troop movements. On April 19, some 700 British troops reached Lexington, where they found about 70 colonists waiting. After a skirmish, eight colonists lay dead. The British marched to Concord, Massachusetts, where a battle broke out. As the British retreated, nearly 4,000 colonists lined the road from Concord to Lexington, Massachusetts, and peppered the redcoats with musket fire. These confrontations were the first battles of the Revolutionary War.

Declaring Independence

After the fighting at Lexington and Concord, Ethan Allen and his band of backwoodsmen captured Britain's Fort Ticonderoga in New York and its large supply of artillery—cannon and large guns. On May 10, 1775, the Second Continental Congress began meeting in Philadelphia. They agreed to form the Continental Army with **George Washington** as its commander.

In June 1775, British soldiers attacked militiamen holding down Bunker Hill and Breed's Hill near Boston. The redcoats won the battle, but more than 1,000 were killed or wounded. By 1776, the Continental Army had surrounded British forces in Boston. General Howe, in charge of British forces, decided to withdraw his troops.

On June 7, a resolution that declared the colonies "free and independent states" was introduced to the Continental Congress. Congress debated the resolution and appointed a committee to draft the **Declaration of Independence.** The committee included Benjamin Franklin, John Adams, Roger Sherman, Robert Livingston, and **Thomas Jefferson.** The group chose Jefferson to write the Declaration. On July 4, 1776, Congress adopted the Declaration of Independence. It stated that people have unalienable rights, or rights that government cannot take away.

The Early Years of the War

*Reading*History
B. Making Inferences
Why do you think the colonists disagreed about independence?

Historians estimate that roughly 20 to 30 percent of Americans were **Loyalists,** supporters of Britain. And roughly 40 to 45 percent were **Patriots,** supporters of the Revolution. The rest of the white population remained neutral. Some Iroquois nations fought with the British and others with the Americans. African Americans also fought on both sides.

Because not everyone supported the war, raising an army was difficult. Men began to enlist, but most of

AMERICA'S HISTORY MAKERS

THOMAS JEFFERSON
1743–1826

Jefferson was just 33 when chosen to write the Declaration of Independence. He was already a brilliant thinker and writer and a highly respected political leader. Jefferson came from a wealthy Virginia family. As a child, he was interested in everything, and he became an inventor, scientist, and architect, among other things. In 1769, he began his political career in the House of Burgesses.

Jefferson felt that writing the Declaration was a major achievement of his life. He had that fact carved on his tombstone.

Why do you think Jefferson felt the Declaration was one of his greatest achievements?

them didn't serve long. At the start of the war, Congress asked men to enlist for only one year. Congress's inability to deliver supplies to the army was also frustrating.

In late 1776, the British and American armies fought for New York State. The British forced Washington and his troops to retreat through New Jersey. The American army was in terrible condition when it crossed the Delaware River into Pennsylvania in December. However, later that month, Washington's troops launched surprise attacks against British allies at Trenton and Princeton, New Jersey. The Americans won both battles. The following year, the Continental Army defeated the British army at the Battles of Saratoga in upstate New York. This victory was the turning point in the Revolution.

*Reading*History
C. Analyzing Causes Why would the lack of agreement about the war make it hard to raise an army?

The War Expands

In 1778, France signed two treaties of alliance with the United States. As part of its new alliance, France sent badly needed funds, supplies, and troops to America. Several military officers also came to Washington's aid, including men from France, Poland, and the German states. A French nobleman named the Marquis de Lafayette was given the command of an army division. He also persuaded the French king to send a 6,000-man army to America.

In the winter of 1777–1778, Washington and his army camped at Valley Forge in southeast Pennsylvania. Roughly a quarter of the soldiers there died from malnutrition, exposure to the cold, or disease. Despite the hardships, Washington and his soldiers showed amazing endurance.

Throughout the war, Britain controlled the Atlantic trade routes. There was no way the Americans could defeat the powerful British navy. But American privateers attacked British merchant ships. A privateer is a privately owned ship with permission to attack enemy ships. During the war, privateers captured hundreds of British ships. Also, Commander John Paul Jones and his crew achieved a major naval victory against the British in 1779.

War in the South, 1778–1781

American forces and allies
British forces
American victory
British victory

0   100 Miles
0   200 Kilometers

N

New York
Washington and Rochambeau
Valley Forge
Ft. Pitt
MD.
Lafayette
VA.
British fleet, 1781
French fleet
Cornwallis
Yorktown
40°N
N.C.
35°N
Morgan
Greene
Cowpens
Kings Mt.
Camden
Cornwallis
Marion
S.C.
Wilmington
1780
British fleet 1778
GA.
Charles Town
Savannah
ATLANTIC OCEAN

GEOGRAPHY SKILLBUILDER Interpreting Maps
1. **Place** *What ports did the British use to invade the South?*
2. **Movement** *Who traveled from Wilmington to Yorktown, and who traveled from New York?*

The victorious American forces accept the British surrender at Yorktown. George Washington is to the left of the American flag.

The Path to Victory

The British believed that most Southerners were loyalists, so they decided to move the war to the South in 1778. The British took control of most of Georgia and Charles Town (now Charleston), South Carolina. However, Francis Marion and his band of followers weakened the British with surprise raids and hit-and-run attacks.

In July 1781, British general Cornwallis set up his base at Yorktown, Virginia, on a peninsula in Chesapeake Bay. The following month, the French fleet blocked the bay. These ships prevented the British from receiving supplies or escaping. Washington moved his army from the north and trapped Cornwallis. American and French troops bombarded Yorktown with cannon fire. With no way out, Cornwallis surrendered on October 19, 1781. Although some fighting continued, Yorktown was the last major battle of the war. In November 1783, the last British troops left New York City. As the winners, the Americans won favorable terms in the **Treaty of Paris of 1783,** which ended the Revolutionary War. The United States had won its independence.

Reading **History**

D. Forming and Supporting Opinions Was setting up base at Yorktown a sound military move by Cornwallis? Why or why not?

Section ❸ Assessment

1. Terms & Names

Explain the significance of:
- George Washington
- Declaration of Independence
- Thomas Jefferson
- Loyalists
- Patriots
- Treaty of Paris of 1783

2. Taking Notes

Use a diagram like the one below to show events that led to the Revolutionary War.

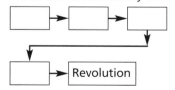

3. Main Ideas

a. How did colonists react to the Stamp Act?

b. How were Americans divided over the issue of separating from Great Britain?

c. How did European officers aid America in the Revolutionary War?

4. Critical Thinking

Drawing Conclusions Why did it take colonists so long to declare their independence?

THINK ABOUT
- the colonists' British traditions
- the risk of revolution
- divided loyalties of Americans

ACTIVITY OPTIONS

TECHNOLOGY

MUSIC

Imagine that Congress has asked you to commemorate the Battle of Yorktown. Design a **Web page** or write a **song** celebrating the U.S. victory.

The Declaration of Independence

Setting the Stage On July 4, 1776, the Second Continental Congress adopted what became one of America's most cherished documents. Written by Thomas Jefferson, the Declaration of Independence voiced the reasons for separating from Britain and provided the principles of government upon which the United States would be built. **See Primary Source Explorer**

[Preamble]

When in the Course of human events, it becomes necessary for one people to dissolve the political bands which have connected them with another, and to assume among the powers of the earth, the separate and equal station to which the Laws of Nature and of Nature's God entitle them, a decent respect to the opinions of mankind requires that they should declare the causes which impel them to the separation.

[The Right of the People to Control Their Government]

We hold these truths to be self-evident, that all men are created equal, that they are **endowed**[1] by their Creator with certain **unalienable**[2] Rights, that among these are Life, Liberty and the pursuit of Happiness; that, to secure these rights, Governments are instituted among Men, deriving their just powers from the consent of the governed; that whenever any Form of Government becomes destructive of these ends, it is the Right of the People to alter or to abolish it, and to institute new Government, laying its foundation on such principles and organizing its powers in such form, as to them shall seem most likely to effect their Safety and Happiness. Prudence, indeed, will dictate that Governments long established should not be changed for light and transient causes; and accordingly all experience hath shewn that mankind are more disposed to suffer, while evils are sufferable, than to right themselves by abolishing the forms to which they are accustomed. But when a long train of abuses and **usurpations**,[3] pursuing invariably the same Object, evinces a design to reduce them under absolute **Despotism**,[4] it is their right, it is their duty, to throw off such Government, and to provide new Guards for their future security.

Such has been the patient sufferance of these Colonies; and such is now the necessity which constrains them to alter their former Systems of Government. The history of the present King of Great Britain is a history of repeated injuries and usurpations, all having in direct object the establishment of an absolute Tyranny over these States. To prove this, let facts be submitted to a **candid**[5] world.

A CLOSER LOOK

RIGHTS OF THE PEOPLE

The ideas in this passage reflect the views of John Locke. Locke was an English philosopher who believed that the natural rights of individuals came from God, but that a government's power comes from the consent of the governed. This belief is the foundation of modern democracy.

1. In what way can American voters bring about changes in their government?

---

1. **endowed:** provided.
2. **unalienable:** unable to be taken away.
3. **usurpations:** unjust seizures of power.
4. **Despotism:** rule by a tyrant with absolute power.
5. **candid:** fair, impartial.

[Tyrannical Acts of the British King]

He has refused his Assent to Laws, the most wholesome and necessary for the public good.

He has forbidden his Governors to pass Laws of immediate and pressing importance, unless suspended in their operation till his assent should be obtained; and, when so suspended, he has utterly neglected to attend to them.

He has refused to pass other Laws for the accommodation of large districts of people, unless those people would **relinquish**[6] the right of Representation in the Legislature, a right inestimable to them, and formidable to tyrants only.

He has called together legislative bodies at places unusual, uncomfortable, and distant from the depository of their public Records, for the sole purpose of fatiguing them into compliance with his measures.

He has dissolved Representative Houses repeatedly, for opposing with manly firmness his invasions on the rights of the people.

He has refused for a long time, after such dissolutions, to cause others to be elected; whereby the Legislative powers, incapable of Annihilation, have returned to the people at large for their exercise; the State remaining in the mean time exposed to all the dangers of invasions from without, and **convulsions**[7] within.

He has endeavoured to prevent the population of these States; for that purpose obstructing the Laws for **Naturalization**[8] of Foreigners; refusing to pass others to encourage their migration hither, and raising the conditions of new Appropriations of Lands.

He has obstructed the Administration of Justice, by refusing his Assent to Laws for establishing Judiciary powers.

He has made Judges dependent on his Will alone, for the **tenure**[9] of their offices, and the amount and payment of their salaries.

He has erected a multitude of New Offices, and sent hither swarms of Officers to harass our people and **eat out their substance**.[10]

He has kept among us, in times of peace, Standing Armies, without the Consent of our legislatures.

He has affected to render the Military independent of and superior to the Civil power. He has combined with others to subject us to a jurisdiction foreign to our constitution and unacknowledged by our laws; giving his Assent to their Acts of pretended Legislation:

For **quartering**[11] large bodies of armed troops among us;

For protecting them, by a mock Trial, from punishment for any Murders which they should commit on the Inhabitants of these States;

For cutting off our Trade with all parts of the world;

A CLOSER LOOK

GRIEVANCES AGAINST BRITAIN

The list contains 27 offenses by the British king and others against the colonies. It helps explain why it became necessary to seek independence.

2. Which offense do you think was the worst? Why?

A CLOSER LOOK

LOSS OF REPRESENTATIVE GOVERNMENT

One of the Intolerable Acts of 1774 stripped the Massachusetts Legislature of many powers and gave them to the colony's British governor.

3. Why was this action so "intolerable"?

A CLOSER LOOK

QUARTERING TROOPS WITHOUT CONSENT

The Quartering Act of 1765 required colonists to provide housing and supplies for British troops in America.

4. Why did colonists object to this act?

---

6. **relinquish:** give up.

7. **convulsions:** violent disturbances.

8. **Naturalization:** process of becoming a citizen.

9. **tenure:** term.

10. **eat out their substance:** drain their resources.

11. **quartering:** housing or giving lodging to.

A CLOSER LOOK

TAXATION WITHOUT REPRESENTATION

The colonists believed in the long-standing British tradition that Parliament could tax only those citizens it represented—and the colonists claimed to have no representation in Parliament.

5. How do persons today give consent to taxation?

For imposing Taxes on us without our Consent;

For depriving us, in many cases, of the benefits of Trial by Jury;

For transporting us beyond Seas to be tried for pretended offenses;

For abolishing the free System of English Laws in a neighboring Province, establishing therein an **Arbitrary**[12] government, and enlarging its Boundaries so as to render it at once an example and fit instrument for introducing the same absolute rule into these Colonies;

For taking away our Charters, abolishing our most valuable laws, and altering fundamentally the Forms of our Governments;

For suspending our own Legislatures, and declaring themselves invested with power to legislate for us in all cases whatsoever.

He has **abdicated**[13] Government here, by declaring us out of his Protection and waging War against us.

He has plundered our seas, ravaged our Coasts, burnt our towns, and destroyed the lives of our people.

He is at this time transporting large Armies of **foreign Mercenaries**[14] to compleat the works of death, desolation, and tyranny, already begun with circumstances of Cruelty & **perfidy**[15] scarcely paralleled in the most barbarous ages, and totally unworthy the Head of a civilized nation.

He has constrained our fellow Citizens, taken Captive on the high Seas, to bear Arms against their Country, to become the executioners of their friends and Brethren, or to fall themselves by their Hands.

He has excited **domestic insurrections**[16] amongst us, and has endeavoured to bring on the inhabitants of our frontiers the merciless Indian Savages, whose known rule of warfare is an undistinguished destruction of all ages, sexes and conditions.

[Efforts of the Colonies to Avoid Separation]

In every stage of these Oppressions We have **Petitioned for Redress**[17] in the most humble terms; Our repeated Petitions have been answered only by repeated injury. A Prince, whose character is thus marked by every act which may define a Tyrant, is unfit to be the ruler of a free people.

Nor have We been wanting in attentions to our British brethren. We have warned them from time to time of attempts by their legislature to extend an unwarrantable jurisdiction over us. We have reminded them of the circumstances of our emigration and settlement here. We have appealed to their native justice and **magnanimity,**[18] and we have conjured them by the ties of our common kindred, to disavow these usurpations, which would inevitably interrupt our connections and correspondence. They too have been deaf to

A CLOSER LOOK

PETITIONING THE KING

The colonists sent many petitions to King George III. In the Olive Branch Petition of 1775, the colonists expressed their desire to achieve "a happy and permanent reconciliation." The king rejected the petition.

6. Why did the colonists at first attempt to solve the dispute and remain loyal?

12. **Arbitrary:** not limited by law.
13. **abdicated:** given up.
14. **foreign Mercenaries:** professional soldiers hired to serve in a foreign army.
15. **perfidy:** dishonesty, disloyalty.
16. **domestic insurrections:** rebellions at home.
17. **Petitioned for Redress:** asked for the correction of wrongs.
18. **magnanimity:** generosity, forgiveness.

the voice of justice and of **consanguinity**.[19] We must, therefore, **acquiesce**[20] in the necessity, which denounces our Separation, and hold them, as we hold the rest of mankind, Enemies in War, in Peace Friends.

[The Colonies Are Declared Free and Independent]

We, therefore, the Representatives of the United States of America, in General Congress, Assembled, appealing to the Supreme Judge of the world for the **rectitude**[21] of our intentions, do, in the name, and by the Authority of the good People of these Colonies solemnly publish and declare, That these United Colonies are, and of Right ought to be, Free and Independent States; that they are Absolved from all Allegiance to the British Crown, and that all political connection between them and the State of Great Britain is, and ought to be, totally dissolved; and that as Free and Independent States, they have full Power to levy War, conclude Peace, contract Alliances, establish Commerce, and do all other Acts and Things which Independent States may of right do.

And for the support of this Declaration, with a firm reliance on the protection of divine Providence, we mutually pledge to each other our Lives, our Fortunes, and our sacred Honor. [Signed by]

John Hancock *President, from Massachusetts*

[Georgia] Button Gwinnett; Lyman Hall; George Walton

[Rhode Island] Stephen Hopkins; William Ellery

[Connecticut] Roger Sherman; Samuel Huntington; William Williams; Oliver Wolcott

[North Carolina] William Hooper; Joseph Hewes; John Penn

[South Carolina] Edward Rutledge; Thomas Heyward, Jr.; Thomas Lynch, Jr.; Arthur Middleton

[Maryland] Samuel Chase; William Paca; Thomas Stone; Charles Carroll

[Virginia] George Wythe; Richard Henry Lee; Thomas Jefferson;

Benjamin Harrison; Thomas Nelson, Jr.; Francis Lightfoot Lee; Carter Braxton

[Pennsylvania] Robert Morris; Benjamin Rush; Benjamin Franklin; John Morton; George Clymer; James Smith; George Taylor; James Wilson; George Ross

[Delaware] Caesar Rodney; George Read; Thomas McKean

[New York] William Floyd; Philip Livingston; Francis Lewis; Lewis Morris

[New Jersey] Richard Stockton; John Witherspoon; Francis Hopkinson; John Hart; Abraham Clark

[New Hampshire] Josiah Bartlett; William Whipple; Matthew Thornton

[Massachusetts] Samuel Adams; John Adams; Robert Treat Paine; Elbridge Gerry

19. **consanguinity:** relationship by a common ancestor; close connection.

20. **acquiesce:** accept without protest.

21. **rectitude:** moral uprightness.

A CLOSER LOOK

POWERS OF AN INDEPENDENT GOVERNMENT

The colonists identified the ability to wage war and agree to peace; to make alliances with other nations; and to set up an economic system as powers of a free and independent government.

7. What other powers are held by an independent government?

A CLOSER LOOK

DECLARATION SIGNERS

The Declaration was signed by 56 representatives from the 13 original states.

8. Which signers do you recognize? Write one line about each of those signers.

Interactive Primary Source Assessment

1. Main Ideas

a. What is the purpose of the Declaration of Independence as stated in the Preamble?

b. What are the five main parts of the Declaration?

c. What are three rights that all people have?

2. Critical Thinking

Drawing Conclusions Why did the colonies feel that they had to declare their independence?

THINK ABOUT

• colonial grievances against Britain

• Britain's response to these grievances

Chapter 1 ASSESSMENT

VISUAL SUMMARY

Colonization to Revolution

From 30,000 B.C. to 12,000 B.C, people migrate to the Americas from Asia.

By A.D. 1500, people in Europe, Africa, and the Americas develop diverse cultures and civilizations.

Beginning in 1492, the voyages of Columbus bring the people of all four continents into contact.

From the 1500s through the 1700s, European nations compete for colonies.

In the 1600s and 1700s, the British establish colonies in North America.

The British win the French and Indian War (1754–1763) and claim control of North America east of the Mississippi River.

The British begin to tighten control over their colonies. The colonists resist these efforts.

In 1776, the colonists declare their independence from Britain.

In 1781, the colonists win the last major battle of the Revolutionary War. In 1783, the war ends.

46 CHAPTER 1

TERMS & NAMES

Briefly explain the significance of each of the following.
1. Christopher Columbus
2. Columbian Exchange
3. slavery
4. Jamestown
5. Mayflower Compact
6. triangular trade
7. George Washington
8. Declaration of Independence
9. Loyalist
10. Patriot

REVIEW QUESTIONS

Three Worlds Meet (pages 27–31)
1. What are two theories about migration to the Americas?
2. What were three Native American civilizations located in what is now Mexico?
3. What were three reasons for the European voyages of exploration in the 1400s and 1500s?

The English Colonies (pages 32–36)
4. What sorts of crops were particularly well suited to the soil and climate in the Southern Colonies?
5. How were farms in the Middle Colonies different from those in New England?
6. What did England gain as a result of the French and Indian War?

The American Revolution (pages 37–41)
7. Why did Britain tax the colonies?
8. What was the core idea of the Declaration of Independence?
9. What were conditions like at Valley Forge?
10. How did America's ally France contribute to the victory at Yorktown?

CRITICAL THINKING

1. USING YOUR NOTES

Event/Idea	Notes
Exploration	
Establishing Colonies	
Slavery in the Americas	
Colonial Conflict with Britain	
Revolutionary War	

Using your completed chart, answer the questions below.
a. How did European exploration affect Native Americans?
b. How did the establishment of colonies in the Americas lead to slavery?
c. What event or idea in the chart contributed most to the Revolutionary War?

2. APPLYING CITIZENSHIP SKILLS
What were some of the common ideals that link the Mayflower Compact and the establishment of the House of Burgesses?

3. THEME: DEMOCRATIC IDEALS
What democratic ideals did Americans inherit from England?

4. CONTRASTING
How did colonial government differ from present-day government in the United States?

5. DRAWING CONCLUSIONS
What factors and events led the colonies to seek independence?

Interact with History
How would the choice that you made at the beginning of the chapter have varied according to the year that you arrived and the region in which you lived? Would you still make the same choice?

HISTORY SKILLS

1. INTERPRETING MAPS: HUMAN–ENVIRONMENT INTERACTION

Study the map. Answer the questions.

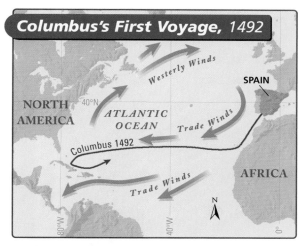

Columbus's First Voyage, 1492

Basic Map Elements

a. What is the name of the winds blowing west across the Atlantic? Blowing east?

b. In what direction did Columbus sail on his first journey from Europe?

Interpreting the Map

a. How did the winds affect Columbus's journey?

b. If Columbus's route had been farther north, would his voyage have taken more or less time? Explain.

Interpreting Primary Sources

Read the passage below, which deals with the difficulties faced by colonists during the Revolutionary War.

> These are the times that try men's souls. The summer soldier and the sunshine patriot will, in this crisis, shrink from the service of their country; but he that stands it now, deserves the love and thanks of man and woman. Tyranny, like hell, is not easily conquered; yet we have this consolation with us, that the harder the conflict, the more glorious the triumph. What we obtain too cheap, we esteem too lightly: it is dearness only that gives everything its value.
>
> **Thomas Paine,** from *The American Crisis*

a. In your own words, explain who "the summer soldier and the sunshine patriot" are.

b. What does Paine promise will be the reward of a hard conflict?

ALTERNATIVE ASSESSMENT

1. INTERDISCIPLINARY ACTIVITY: LITERATURE

Retelling a Folk Tale Many North American Indian tales give insight into the relationship between Native Americans and their environment. Select a tale from a collection of Native American literature and retell the tale for the class.

2. COOPERATIVE LEARNING ACTIVITY

Performing a Talk Show In a small group, prepare to hold a talk show in which the guests discuss which side to take in the Revolutionary War. One member of your group should be the talk-show host. The others should play the roles of various Americans. Each person should explain the reasons for his or her position. Perform the talk show before the class. Students might choose from the following roles:

a. the wife of an American soldier

b. an enslaved African American

c. an Iroquois chief

d. a Quaker minister

e. an employee of the British government

3. 💿 PRIMARY SOURCE EXPLORER

Planning a Government As with any group of people living in a community, some sort of government was needed in Plymouth. The Pilgrims devised the Mayflower Compact. Using the CD-ROM, library, and Internet, find out more about the Mayflower Compact.

Create your own plan for a government, using the following suggestions:

- Draw up a plan for a government that will apply to your class.
- Adapt ideas from the Mayflower Compact that you think will work for the class.
- Decide what rules are needed in your government. Decide who will hold office, how they will be appointed or selected, and how long they will serve.
- Decide whether there should be limits on majority rule in your government.

4. HISTORY PORTFOLIO

Review your section and chapter assessment activities. Select the one that you think is your best work. Then use comments made by your teacher or classmates to improve your work, and add it to your portfolio.

Additional Test Practice, pp. S1–S33

TEST PRACTICE
CLASSZONE.COM

REVIEW CHAPTER

2

Confederation to Constitution

1776–1791

Section 1 **Creating the Constitution**
Section 2 **Ratifying the Constitution**

Delegates to the Constitutional
Convention in 1787 gathered
in Philadelphia. They held their
meetings in the Pennsylvania
State House, now known as
Independence Hall.

Delegates kept the windows closed during meetings so that the proceedings would be secret.

Some of the most respected men in the nation served as delegates, including Alexander Hamilton and Benjamin Franklin.

The delegates chose George Washington, hero of the Revolutionary War, to be president of the convention.

The year is 1787, and your young country needs to reform its government. Now everyone is wondering what the new government will be like. You have been called to a convention to decide how the new government should be organized.

What Do You Think?

• What will be your main goal in creating a new government?

• How will you get the people at the convention to agree on important issues?

How do you form a government?

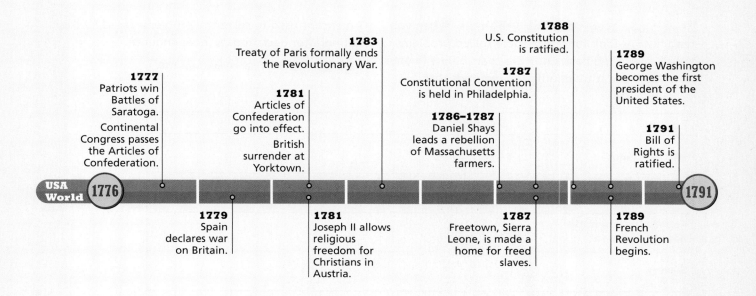

1777
Patriots win Battles of Saratoga.
Continental Congress passes the Articles of Confederation.

1781
Articles of Confederation go into effect.
British surrender at Yorktown.

1783
Treaty of Paris formally ends the Revolutionary War.

1786–1787
Daniel Shays leads a rebellion of Massachusetts farmers.

1787
Constitutional Convention is held in Philadelphia.

1788
U.S. Constitution is ratified.

1789
George Washington becomes the first president of the United States.

1791
Bill of Rights is ratified.

USA World 1776 — 1791

1779
Spain declares war on Britain.

1781
Joseph II allows religious freedom for Christians in Austria.

1787
Freetown, Sierra Leone, is made a home for freed slaves.

1789
French Revolution begins.

BEFORE YOU READ

Previewing the Theme

Democratic Ideals Between 1776 and 1791, the United States strug-gled to set up a national government. The Articles of Confederation established the first federal government. Chapter 2 explains how the weaknesses of the Articles led Americans to write a new constitution for the United States.

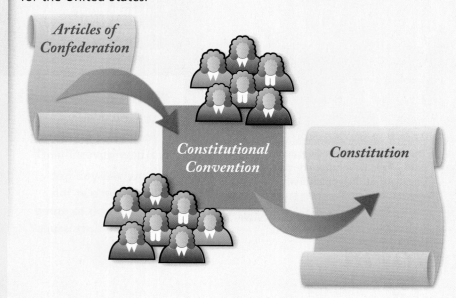

Articles of Confederation

Constitutional Convention

Constitution

What Do You Know?

What do you think of when people talk about the U.S. gov-ernment? Why do nations have governments? What does the U.S. government do?

THINK ABOUT

• what you've learned about the U.S. government from the news or your teachers
• what the purpose of a govern-ment is
• how the government affects your everyday life

What Do You Want to Know?

What questions do you have about the creation of the U.S. Constitution? Write those questions in your notebook before you read the chapter.

READ AND TAKE NOTES

Reading Strategy: Solving Problems When you read history, look for how people solved problems they faced in the past. Copy the chart below in your notebook. Use it to identify the methods that

Americans used to solve the problems faced by the nation after declaring its independence.

 See Skillbuilder Handbook, page R18.

Problems	Solutions
Western lands	
Economic crises	
Representation in the new government	
Slavery	

① Creating the Constitution

TERMS & NAMES
Articles of
Confederation
Constitutional
Convention
Virginia Plan
New Jersey Plan
Great Compromise
Three-Fifths
Compromise

MAIN IDEA	WHY IT MATTERS NOW
The states sent delegates to a convention to solve the weaknesses of the Articles of Confederation.	The Constitutional Convention formed the plan of government that the United States still has today.

ONE AMERICAN'S STORY

In the mid-1780s, Massachusetts faced serious economic problems, as did other states. People had little money, but the state continued to demand high taxes. Many people, such as Revolutionary War veteran Daniel Shays, fell deeply into debt. People who could not repay their debts would have their property sold at an auction. If the auction did not raise enough money to settle the debts, officials could put the debtor in jail.

Farmers asked the Massachusetts legislature to provide debt relief. But the legislators refused—and the farmers rebelled. Daniel Shays was one of the leaders of the rebellion. In January 1787, Shays and his men marched on a federal arsenal, a place to store weapons. Nine hundred soldiers from the state militia defended the arsenal. The militia quickly defeated Shays's men. But Shays's Rebellion, as the uprising came to be known, won the sympathy of many people. America's leaders realized that an armed uprising of common farmers spelled danger for the nation.

A stone marker rests on the spot of Shays's Rebellion.

Some leaders hoped that strengthening the national government could solve the nation's ills. In this section, you will read how Americans held a convention to change the Articles of Confederation.

The Articles of Confederation

During the Revolutionary War, Americans realized that they needed to unite to win the war against Britain. In 1776, the Continental Congress began to develop a plan for a national government. The Congress eventually arrived at a final plan, called the **Articles of Confederation.**

Under the Articles, the national government had few powers because many Americans feared that a strong government would threaten liberty. A Confederation Congress ran the national government. Each state had one vote in the Congress. The national government had the power to wage war, make peace, and sign treaties. But the Articles left most important powers to the states. Those powers included the authority to

U.S. Government, 1776–1787

Successes of the Confederation Congress

- Governed the nation during the Revolutionary War
- Negotiated the Treaty of Paris at the end of the war
- Passed the Land Ordinance of 1785
- Passed the Northwest Ordinance (1787)

- Lacked power to enforce laws
- Lacked power to levy taxes
- Lacked power to regulate trade among the states
- Required all 13 states to approve changes in the Articles

Weaknesses of the Articles of Confederation

SKILLBUILDER Interpreting Charts

1. *What do you think was the greatest success of the Confederation Congress?*
2. *What do you think was the greatest weakness of the Articles of Confederation?*

set taxes and enforce national laws. The Articles also proposed to leave the states in control of the lands west of the Appalachians.

The Continental Congress passed the Articles of Confederation in November 1777. It then sent the Articles to the states for ratification, or approval. By July 1778, eight states had ratified the Articles. But some of the small states that did not have Western land claims refused to sign. They argued that states that owned Western lands had an advantage because they could sell the land to pay off debts left from the Revolution. States without lands would have difficulty paying off the high war debts. Eventually, all the states gave up their claims to Western lands. The small states then ratified the Articles.

One task the Confederation Congress faced was to decide how to handle the Western lands it now controlled. Congress passed important laws on how to divide and govern these lands. The Land Ordinance of 1785 outlined how the land would be divided. (See Geography in History on pages 56–57.) And the Northwest Ordinance (1787) described how the land was to be governed.

Aside from its handling of land issues, however, the Confederation Congress had few successes. By the end of the Revolutionary War, the United States faced serious problems, such as those that led to Shays's Rebellion. Many states faced deep debts. They set high taxes to repay them, hurting poor people. In addition, Congress did not have the power to levy taxes to pay its own debts. Many people began to call for change.

Reading **History**

A. Finding Main Ideas Why did the states without Western land claims want the other states to give up their claims?

The Constitutional Convention

In 1786, a series of events began that would lead to a new form of government for the United States. In September, delegates from five states met in Annapolis, Maryland, to discuss ways to promote trade among their states. At the time, most states placed high taxes on goods from other states. The delegates to the Annapolis Convention believed that creating national trade laws would help the economies of all states.

Reading History

B. Making Inferences Why didn't the Articles of Confederation give the national government the power to regulate trade among states?

Making such changes required amending the Articles of Confederation, because the national government had been granted no power to regulate trade among the states. The Annapolis delegates, led by Alexander Hamilton of New York, called for the states to send representatives to Philadelphia the following May to discuss such changes.

At first, many Americans doubted that the national government needed strengthening. But news of Shays's Rebellion in late 1786 and early 1787 quickly changed people's minds. Many citizens began to see the need for a government that could maintain order. Even so, they did not want a government so strong that it could not be controlled. James Madison later wrote about this problem.

A VOICE FROM THE PAST

If men were angels, no government would be necessary. If angels were to govern men, neither external nor internal controls on government would be necessary. In framing a government which is to be administered by men over men, the great difficulty lies in this: you must first enable the government to control the governed; and in the next place oblige it [the government] to control itself.

James Madison, *The Federalist* "Number 51"

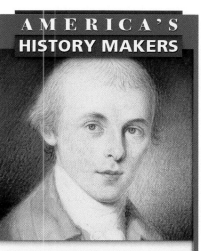

AMERICA'S HISTORY MAKERS

JAMES MADISON
1751–1836

James Madison was a short, soft-spoken man, but he may have made the greatest contribution of any of the Founders at the Constitutional Convention. He took thorough notes of the convention's proceedings. His notes are the most detailed picture we have of the debates and drama of the convention.

But Madison did not just observe the convention. He was perhaps the most important participant. One of the other delegates called him "the best informed Man of any point in debate." Madison was so important that he earned the title "Father of the Constitution."

How did Madison contribute to the Constitutional Convention?

This was the challenge that faced delegates to the **Constitutional Convention,** as the Philadelphia meeting became known. Among the delegates who would face this challenge were some of America's most famous men, including George Washington, Benjamin Franklin, and James Madison. In late May 1787, the convention officially began.

The Virginia Plan

After establishing rules and electing a president, the delegates began the work of designing a new national government. On May 29, George Washington, who presided over the convention, recognized Edmund Randolph of Virginia as the first speaker. Randolph offered a plan for the new government that became known as the **Virginia Plan.** Madison, Randolph, and the other Virginia delegates had drawn up the plan while they waited for the convention to open.

Reading History

C. Summarizing What was the Virginia Plan?

The Virginia Plan proposed a government with three branches. The first branch was the legislature, which made the laws. The second branch was the executive, which enforced the laws. The third branch was the judiciary, which interpreted the laws.

This plan also proposed a legislature with two houses. In both houses, the number of representatives from each state would be based on the state's population or its wealth. The legislature would have the power to levy taxes and regulate commerce.

The Virginia Plan sparked weeks of debate. Larger states supported the plan because it would give them greater representation in the legislature. Smaller states opposed the plan because they worried that the larger states would end up ruling the others.

The Great Compromise

In response to the Virginia Plan, New Jersey delegate William Paterson presented an alternative. The New Jersey Plan called for a legislature with only one house. In it, each state would have one vote. In providing equal representation to each state, the **New Jersey Plan** was similar to the Articles of Confederation.

The New Jersey Plan gave the legislature the power to regulate trade and to raise money by taxing foreign goods. But it did not offer the broad powers proposed by the Virginia Plan. The delegates voted on these two plans. The Virginia Plan won and became the framework for drafting the Constitution.

For weeks, the delegates argued over representation in the legislature. Emotions ran high as the delegates struggled for a solution. In desperation, the delegates selected a committee to work out a compromise in early July. The committee offered the **Great Compromise**.

To satisfy the smaller states, each state would have an equal number of votes in the Senate. To satisfy the larger states, the committee set representation in the House of Representatives according to state populations. The convention passed the proposal on July 16.

Background
Roger Sherman of Connecticut is widely credited with proposing the Great Compromise.

Slavery and the Constitution

Because representation in the House of Representatives would be based on the population of each state, the delegates had to decide who would be counted in that population. The Southern states had many more

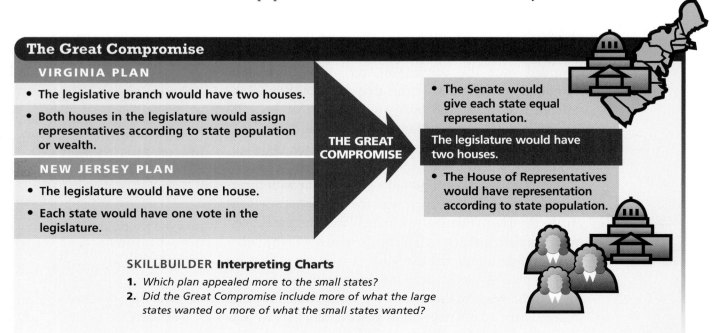

The Great Compromise

VIRGINIA PLAN
- The legislative branch would have two houses.
- Both houses in the legislature would assign representatives according to state population or wealth.

NEW JERSEY PLAN
- The legislature would have one house.
- Each state would have one vote in the legislature.

THE GREAT COMPROMISE

- The Senate would give each state equal representation.
- The legislature would have two houses.
- The House of Representatives would have representation according to state population.

SKILLBUILDER Interpreting Charts
1. *Which plan appealed more to the small states?*
2. *Did the Great Compromise include more of what the large states wanted or more of what the small states wanted?*

slaves than the Northern states. Southerners wanted the slaves to be counted as part of the general population for representation but not for taxation. Northerners argued that slaves were not citizens and should not be counted for representation but should be counted for taxation.

Reading **History**
D. Forming and Supporting Opinions Did the delegates do the right thing in agreeing to the Three-Fifths Compromise? Explain.

On this issue, the delegates reached another compromise, known as the **Three-Fifths Compromise.** Under this compromise, three-fifths of the slave population would be counted when setting direct taxes on the states. This three-fifths ratio would also be used to determine representation in the legislature.

The delegates had another heated debate about the slave trade. Slavery had already been outlawed in several states. All of the Northern states and several of the Southern states had banned the importation of slaves. Many Northerners wanted to see this ban extended to the rest of the nation. But Southern slaveholders strongly disagreed. The delegates from South Carolina and Georgia stated that they would never accept any plan "unless their right to import slaves be untouched." Again, the delegates settled on a compromise. They agreed that Congress could not ban the slave trade until 1808.

The Constitutional Convention continued to meet into September. On Saturday, September 15, 1787, the delegates voted their support for the Constitution in its final form. On Sunday, it was written out on four sheets of thick parchment. On Monday, all but three delegates signed the Constitution. It was sent, with a letter signed by George Washington, to the Confederation Congress, which sent it to the states for ratification. In the next section, you will read about the debate over ratification.

Now and then

PRESERVING THE CONSTITUTION

The National Archives is responsible for preserving the 200-year-old sheets of parchment on which the original Constitution was first written.

The Archives stores the document in an airtight glass case enclosed in a 55-ton vault of steel and concrete. Every few years, scientists examine the pages with the latest technology. For the last examination in 1995, they used fiber-optic light sources and computer-guided electronic cameras designed for space exploration.

Section 1 Assessment

1. Terms & Names

Explain the significance of:
- Articles of Confederation
- Constitutional Convention
- Virginia Plan
- New Jersey Plan
- Great Compromise
- Three-Fifths Compromise

2. Taking Notes

Use a diagram like the one below to list some of the challenges Americans faced in shaping a new government.

Which challenge do you think was the toughest? Why?

3. Main Ideas

a. What were the strengths and weaknesses of the Articles of Confederation?

b. What is the significance of the date 1787?

c. How did the Constitutional Convention reach a compromise on the issue of slavery?

4. Critical Thinking

Analyzing Points of View How did the delegates at the convention differ on the issue of representation in the new government?

THINK ABOUT
- the large states and the small states
- the Virginia Plan
- the New Jersey Plan
- the Great Compromise

ACTIVITY OPTIONS

TECHNOLOGY

ART

Think about the Three-Fifths Compromise. Make an **audio recording** of a speech or draw a **political cartoon** that expresses your views on the issue.

The Northwest Territory

The Northwest Territory was officially known as "the Territory Northwest of the River Ohio." In the mid-1780s, Congress decided to sell the land in the territory to settlers. The sale of land solved two problems. First, it provided cash for the government. Second, it increased American control over the land.

The Land Ordinance of 1785 outlined how the land in the Northwest Territory would be divided. Congress split the land into grids with clearly defined boundaries. It created townships that could be divided into sections, as shown on the map below. Each township was six miles by six miles. This was an improvement over earlier methods of setting boundaries. Previously, people had used rocks, trees, or other landmarks to set boundaries. There had been constant fights over disputed claims.

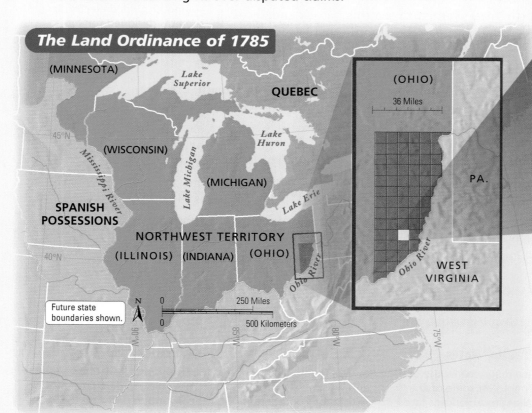

The Land Ordinance of 1785

(MINNESOTA)

Lake Superior

QUEBEC

45°N

(WISCONSIN)

Lake Huron

(MICHIGAN)

Lake Michigan

SPANISH POSSESSIONS

Lake Erie

NORTHWEST TERRITORY

(ILLINOIS) (INDIANA) (OHIO)

40°N

Mississippi River

Ohio River

(OHIO)

36 Miles

PA.

WEST VIRGINIA

Future state boundaries shown.

N

0   250 Miles

0   500 Kilometers

90°W   85°W   80°W   75°W

TOWNSHIP, 1785

36	30	24	18	12	6
35	29	23	17	11	5
34	28	22	16	10	4
33	27	21	15	9	3
32	26	20	14	8	2
31	25	19	13	7	1

Each township contained 36 sections. Each section was one square mile.

ARTIFACT FILE

The Theodolite The theodolite is a surveying tool. It consists of a telescope that can be moved from side to side and up and down. A theodolite measures angles and determines alignment. These functions are necessary for land surveyors to establish accurate boundaries for land claims.

Township Map Congress reserved several plots (outlined on map) for special purposes. A few were set aside for later sale to raise money for the government. One plot was reserved to support a local school.

1. The first things settlers needed were food and shelter. Cutting trees provided fields for crops and wood for log cabins. The first crop most farmers planted was corn. Even if the land was not fully cleared of trees, farmers planted corn between the stumps.

2. A shortage of labor meant that a farmer working alone was doing well if he cleared several acres a year. As a result, few farms were completely fenced in, and forest covered most of the property. Hogs were allowed to find food in the woods. Farmers collected apples from trees and used sap to make syrup.

3. Over time, families planted fruits and vegetables. Cattle raising also became more common. Beef cattle supplied families with meat. Dairy cattle provided milk. Families could sell extra fruits, vegetables, and dairy products, such as butter and cheese.

On-Line Field Trip

The Ohio Historical Society is located in Columbus, Ohio. It maintains a Web site called Ohio History Central that includes information on the Ohio portion of the Northwest Territory.

For more about the Northwest Territory . . .

RESEARCH LINKS
CLASSZONE.COM

CONNECT TO GEOGRAPHY

1. **Region** What was the land in the Northwest Territory like before Americans settled there?

2. **Human-Environment Interaction** How did American settlers affect the landscape in the territory?

G See Geography Handbook, pages 4–5.

CONNECT TO HISTORY

3. **Making Inferences** Why did so many people buy land in the new territory?

② Ratifying the Constitution

TERMS & NAMES
federalism
Federalists
Antifederalists
The Federalist papers
George Mason
Bill of Rights

MAIN IDEA	WHY IT MATTERS NOW
Americans across the nation debated whether the Constitution would produce the best government.	American liberties today are protected by the U.S. Constitution, including the Bill of Rights.

ONE AMERICAN'S STORY

For a week in early January 1788, a church in Hartford, Connecticut, was filled to capacity. Inside, 168 delegates were meeting to decide whether their state should ratify the U.S. Constitution. Samuel Huntington, Connecticut's governor, addressed the assembly.

A VOICE FROM THE PAST

This is a new event in the history of mankind. Heretofore, most governments have been formed by tyrants and imposed on mankind by force. Never before did a people, in time of peace and tranquillity, meet together by their representatives and, with calm deliberation, frame for themselves a system of government.

Samuel Huntington, quoted in *Original Meanings*

The governor supported the new Constitution and wanted to see it ratified. Not everyone agreed with him. In this section, you will learn about the debates that led to the ratification of the Constitution.

Samuel Huntington

Federalists and Antifederalists

By the time the convention in Connecticut opened, Americans had already been debating the new Constitution for months. The document had been printed in newspapers and handed out in pamphlets across the United States. The framers of the Constitution knew that the document would cause controversy. They immediately began to campaign for ratification, or approval, of the Constitution.

The framers suspected that people might be afraid the Constitution would take too much power away from the states. To address this fear, the framers explained that the Constitution was based on federalism. **Federalism** is a system of government in which power is shared between the central (or federal) government and the states. Linking themselves to the idea of federalism, the people who supported the Constitution took the name **Federalists.**

People who opposed the Constitution were called **Antifederalists.** They thought the Constitution took too much power away from the states and did not guarantee rights for the people. Some were afraid that a strong president might be declared king. Others thought the Senate might turn into a powerful aristocracy. In either case, the liberties won at great cost during the Revolution might be lost.

Antifederalists published their views about the Constitution in newspapers and pamphlets. They used logical arguments to convince people to oppose the Constitution. But they also tried to stir people's emotions by charging that it would destroy American liberties. As one Antifederalist wrote, "After so recent a triumph over British despots [oppressive rulers], . . . it is truly astonishing that a set of men among ourselves should have had the effrontery [nerve] to attempt the destruction of our liberties."

The Federalist Papers

The Federalists did not sit still while the Antifederalists attacked the Constitution. They wrote essays to answer the Antifederalists' attacks. The best known of the Federalist essays are ***The Federalist* papers.** These essays first appeared as letters in New York newspapers. They were later published together in a book called *The Federalist.*

Three well-known politicians wrote *The Federalist* papers—James Madison, Alexander Hamilton, and John Jay, the secretary of foreign affairs for the Confederation Congress. Like the Antifederalists, the Federalists appealed to reason and emotion. In *The Federalist* papers, Hamilton described why people should support ratification.

A VOICE FROM THE PAST

Yes, my countrymen, . . . I am clearly of opinion it is in your interest to adopt it [the Constitution]. I am convinced that this is the safest course for your liberty, your dignity, and your happiness.

Alexander Hamilton, *The Federalist* "Number 1"

Federalists and Antifederalists

FEDERALISTS	ANTIFEDERALISTS
• Supported removing some powers from the states and giving more powers to the national government	• Wanted important political powers to remain with the states
• Favored dividing powers among different branches of government	• Wanted the legislative branch to have more power than the executive
• Proposed a single person to lead the executive branch	• Feared that a strong executive might become a king or tyrant
	• Believed a bill of rights needed to be added to the Constitution to protect people's rights

SKILLBUILDER Interpreting Charts
1. *Which group wanted a stronger central government?*
2. *If you had been alive in 1787, would you have been a Federalist or an Antifederalist?*

John Jay

George Mason

HISTORY through ART

Supporters of the Constitution turned out in parades like this one in New York in 1788. The "Ship of State" float has Alexander Hamilton's name on it to celebrate his role in creating the Constitution.

What does the picture indicate about the importance of the Constitution in people's lives?

The Federalists had an important advantage over the Antifederalists. Most of the newspapers supported the Constitution, giving the Federalists more publicity than the Antifederalists. Even so, there was strong opposition to ratification in Massachusetts, North Carolina, Rhode Island, New York, and Virginia. If some of these states failed to ratify the Constitution, the United States might not survive.

The Battle for Ratification

The first four state conventions to ratify the Constitution were held in December 1787. It was a good month for the Federalists. Delaware, New Jersey, and Pennsylvania voted for ratification. In January 1788, Georgia and Connecticut ratified the Constitution. Massachusetts joined these states in early February.

By late June, nine states had voted to ratify the Constitution. That meant that the document was now officially ratified. But New York and Virginia had not yet cast their votes. There were many powerful Antifederalists in both of those states. Without Virginia, the new government would lack the support of the largest state. Without New York, the nation would be separated into two parts geographically.

Virginia's convention opened the first week in June. The patriot Patrick Henry fought against ratification. **George Mason,** perhaps the most influential Virginian aside from Washington, also was opposed to it. Mason had been a delegate to the Constitutional Convention in Philadelphia, but he had refused to sign the final document. Both Henry and Mason would not consider voting for the Constitution until a bill of rights was added. A bill of rights is a set of rules that defines people's rights.

James Madison was also at Virginia's convention. He suggested that Virginia follow Massachusetts's lead and ratify the Constitution, and he recommended the addition of a bill of rights. With the addition of a bill of rights likely, Virginia ratified the Constitution at the end of June.

*Reading*History
B. Drawing Conclusions How did the lack of a bill of rights endanger the Constitution?

The news of Virginia's vote arrived while the New York convention was in debate. The Antifederalists had outnumbered the Federalists when the convention had begun. But with the news of Virginia's ratification, New Yorkers decided to join the Union. New York also called for a bill of rights.

It was another year before North Carolina ratified the Constitution. In 1790, Rhode Island became the last state to ratify it. By then, the new Congress had already written a bill of rights and submitted it to the states for approval.

The Bill of Rights

Background
The seven states that asked for a bill of rights were Massachusetts, South Carolina, New Hampshire, Virginia, New York, North Carolina, and Rhode Island.

At the same time that seven of the states ratified the Constitution, they asked that it be amended to include a bill of rights. Supporters of a bill of rights hoped that it would set forth the rights of all Americans. They believed it was needed to protect people against the power of the national government.

Madison, who was elected to the new Congress in the winter of 1789, took up the cause. He proposed a set of changes to the Constitution. Congress edited Madison's list and proposed placing the amendments at the end of the Constitution in a separate section.

The amendments went to the states for ratification. As with the Constitution, three-quarters of the states had to ratify the amendments for them to take effect. With Virginia's vote in 1791, ten of the amendments were ratified and became law. These ten amendments to the U.S. Constitution became known as the **Bill of Rights**. (See the Constitution Handbook, pages 88–90.)

The passage of the Bill of Rights was one of the first acts of the new government. In the next chapter, you will read about other issues that faced the new government.

America's HERITAGE

RELIGIOUS FREEDOM
Freedom of religion was an important part of the First Amendment. Jefferson and Madison believed that government enforcement of religious laws was the source of much social conflict. They supported freedom of religion as a way to prevent such conflict.

Even before Madison wrote the Bill of Rights, he worked to ensure religious liberty in Virginia. In 1786, he helped pass the Virginia Statute for Religious Freedom, originally written by Jefferson in 1777.

Section 2 Assessment

1. Terms & Names
Explain the significance of:
- federalism
- Federalists
- Antifederalists
- *The Federalist* papers
- George Mason
- Bill of Rights

2. Taking Notes
Use a diagram like the one below to compare and contrast the Federalists and the Antifederalists.

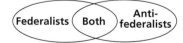

Which group do you think made the stronger argument about ratification? Why?

3. Main Ideas
a. What were Patrick Henry's and George Mason's views on ratification?

b. How did the Federalists and the Antifederalists try to convince people to take their sides in the debate over the Constitution?

c. What was the significance of the Bill of Rights?

4. Critical Thinking
Recognizing Propaganda
Reread the quotation by Hamilton on page 59. Is it an example of propaganda? Why or why not?

THINK ABOUT
- Hamilton's use of the word *countrymen*
- Hamilton's reference to liberty, dignity, and happiness

ACTIVITY OPTIONS

SPEECH
LANGUAGE ARTS

Review the major arguments for and against ratification of the Constitution. Hold a **press conference** or write a **news report** on the ratification debate.

VISUAL SUMMARY

Confederation to Constitution

Articles of Confederation

★

1777
Continental Congress passes the Articles of Confederation.

★

1777–1781
States debate ratification of the Articles of Confederation.

★

1781
Articles of Confederation go into effect.

★

1786
Annapolis Convention is held.

★

1786–1787
Shays's Rebellion occurs.

★

1787
Constitutional Convention is held in Philadelphia.

★

1788
U.S. Constitution is ratified.

★

1789
Government created by the new Constitution takes power.

★

1791
Bill of Rights is added to the Constitution.

Constitution

Bill of Rights

TERMS & NAMES

Briefly explain the significance of each of the following.

1. Articles of Confederation
2. Constitutional Convention
3. Virginia Plan
4. New Jersey Plan
5. Great Compromise
6. Three-Fifths Compromise
7. Federalists
8. *The Federalist* papers
9. George Mason
10. Bill of Rights

REVIEW QUESTIONS

Creating the Constitution (pages 51–57)

1. What were the problems with the Articles of Confederation?
2. How did Shays's Rebellion affect people's views on the Articles of Confederation?
3. What were the two main plans for the Constitution, and how did they differ?
4. Why was James Madison called the "Father of the Constitution?
5. What compromises did the delegates make during the convention?

Ratifying the Constitution (pages 58–61)

6. What is federalism?
7. What were two reasons why some people opposed the Constitution?
8. How did the supporters and opponents of the Constitution get their messages across?
9. Why were Virginia and New York important in the battle for ratification of the Constitution?
10. Why did some states think that it was necessary to add a bill of rights to the Constitution?

CRITICAL THINKING

1. USING YOUR NOTES

Problems	Solutions
Western lands	
Economic crises	
Representation in the new government	
Slavery	

Using your completed chart, answer the questions below.

a. What were the major problems facing the nation during the Confederation Era?

b. How well did the nation solve these problems? Explain.

2. ANALYZING LEADERSHIP

Think about the leaders discussed in this chapter. Based on their actions, which leader do you think made the greatest contribution to the Constitutional Convention? Why?

3. THEME: DEMOCRATIC IDEALS

How do the Articles of Confederation and the Constitution each carry out democratic ideals?

4. APPLYING CITIZENSHIP SKILLS

Do you think the delegates were right to make the compromises they did in the Constitution on the issues of representation and slavery? What might have happened if they had not compromised?

5. RECOGNIZING EFFECTS

How might U.S. history be different if Virginia had refused to ratify the Constitution? If New York had refused? If both had refused?

Interact *with* History

How did your ideas about how you would form a government change after reading this chapter?

HISTORY SKILLS

1. INTERPRETING MAPS: Region

Study the map and then answer the questions.

Ratification in Middle States, 1790

- Federalist majority
- Antifederalist majority
- Evenly divided
- Sparsely populated

NEW YORK

PENNSYLVANIA

New York

Philadelphia

NEW JERSEY

ATLANTIC OCEAN

DELAWARE

N

0 100 Miles

0 200 Kilometers

Source: *American Heritage Pictorial Atlas of United States History*

Basic Map Elements

a. Which states are identified on the map?

b. In which states did the Federalists have statewide majorities?

Interpreting the Map

c. Why do you think the two cities on the map were strong Federalist supporters?

2. INTERPRETING PRIMARY SOURCES

The following law was put into effect in Virginia in 1786. Read the law and answer the questions.

> *Be it enacted by the General Assembly,* That no man shall be compelled to frequent or support any religious worship, place, or ministry, whatsoever . . . but that all men shall be free to profess, and by argument maintain, their opinion in matters of religion, and that the same shall in no way diminish, enlarge, or affect their civil capacities.
>
> *The Statute of Virginia for Religious Freedom, 1786*

a. How would you summarize this law?

b. Which right in the Bill of Rights was based on this law?

c. Based on what you know about colonial history, how had American society changed between the early 1600s and the late 1700s?

ALTERNATIVE ASSESSMENT

1. INTERDISCIPLINARY ACTIVITY: Government

Making a Chart Do research to learn how the U.S. Constitution has been used as a model by other nations. Make a chart to summarize the information you find about one specific nation. Include the country, the date the country's constitution was ratified, and two ways in which that nation's constitution is similar to and different from the U.S. Constitution.

2. COOPERATIVE LEARNING ACTIVITY

Staging a Debate Stage a debate between a Federalist and an Antifederalist. Work in small groups to read some of the different arguments each side used. Look for discussions of one or more of the issues listed below. Pick one of the issues and stage a debate, using the strongest arguments from each side. Let the class determine who won the debate and why.

a. the representation of people in Congress

b. the strength of the president and Senate

c. the need for a bill of rights

3. ◉ PRIMARY SOURCE EXPLORER

Creating a Museum Exhibit The creation of the U.S. Constitution was one of the most important events in the nation's history. There is a great amount of information about the Constitution. Using the Primary Source Explorer CD-ROM and your local library, collect information on different topics relating to the Constitution.

Create a museum exhibit about the Constitution, using the suggestions below.

- Include information on the historical background of the Constitutional Convention, such as Shays's Rebellion and Enlightenment ideas about government.
- Find biographies about the delegates to the convention, including portraits.
- Collect important primary sources, such as Madison's notes and *The Federalist* papers.
- Include photographs or facsimiles of the documents.
- Draw a diagram that shows a layout for the exhibit.

4. HISTORY PORTFOLIO

Review your section and chapter assessment activities. Select one that you think shows your best work. Then use comments made by your teacher or classmates to improve your work and add it to your portfolio.

Additional Test Practice, pp. S1–S33

TEST PRACTICE
CLASSZONE.COM

The Living Constitution

The Framers of the Constitution created a flexible plan for governing the United States far into the future. They also described ways to allow changes in the Constitution. For over 200 years, the Constitution has guided the American people. It remains a "living document." The Constitution still thrives, in part, because it echoes the principles the delegates valued. Each generation of Americans renews the meaning of the Constitution's timeless ideas. These two pages show you some ways in which the Constitution has shaped events in American history. **See Primary Source Explorer** ◎

"In framing a system which we wish to last for ages, we should not lose sight of the changes which ages will produce."

—JAMES MADISON, CONSTITUTIONAL CONVENTION

1787

Delegates in Philadelphia sign the Constitution.

1965

Civil rights leaders protest to end the violation of their constitutional rights. Dr. Martin Luther King, Jr., Coretta Scott King, and others march from Selma toward Montgomery, Alabama, to gain voting rights.

1971

The 26th Amendment to the Constitution gives young people "18 years of age or older" the right to vote.

PCT. 423

1981

A Supreme Court decision rules that Congress can exclude women from the draft. Still, many women who have joined the armed forces have served in combat.

HOW TO READ THE CONSTITUTION

The complete text of the Constitution of the United States begins on page 70. The main column has the actual text. Some of the spellings and punctuation have been updated for easier reading. Headings and subheadings have been added to the Constitution to help you find specific topics. Those parts of the Constitution that are no longer in use have been crossed out. "A Closer Look" notes and charts will help you understand issues related to the Constitution.

The New York Times

National Edition

Midwest: Mostly sunny, breezy and seasonable in the Great Lakes area and Ohio Valley. Becoming very warm after a cold start in the western Plains. Weather map is on page A8.

"All the News That's Fit to Print"

ONE DOLLAR

SATURDAY, FEBRUARY 13, 1999

VOL. CXLVIII ... No. 51,432   Copyright © 1999 The New York Times

CLINTON ACQUITTED DECISIVELY: NO MAJORITY FOR EITHER CHARGE

CENSURE IS BARRED

President Says He Is Sorry And Seeks Reconciliation

By JAMES BENNET and JOHN M. BRODER

But Rebuke From Both Sides of Aisle Dilutes President's Victory

By ALISON MITCHELL

Two hours after the Senate voted yesterday, President Clinton spoke in the Rose Garden of the White House.

The Fallout Of the Trial

Effects on the Office Are Far From Certain

'Senators, How Say You?'

1999

The Senate tries President Bill Clinton for the impeachment charges brought against him by the House of Representatives. As required by the Constitution, the Senate needs a two-thirds majority vote to convict him. This rule saves his presidency.

Seven Principles of the Constitution

The Framers of the Constitution constructed a new system of government. Seven principles supported their efforts. To picture how these principles work, imagine seven building blocks. Together they form the foundation of the United States Constitution. In the pages that follow, you will find the definitions and main ideas of the principles shown in the graphic below.

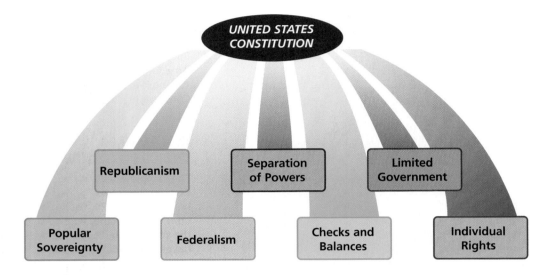

UNITED STATES CONSTITUTION

Republicanism

Separation of Powers

Limited Government

Popular Sovereignty

Federalism

Checks and Balances

Individual Rights

1 Popular Sovereignty
Who Gives the Government Its Power?

"We the people of the United States . . . establish this Constitution for the United States of America." These words from the Preamble, or introduction, to the Constitution clearly spell out the source of the government's power. The Constitution rests on the idea of **popular sovereignty**—a government in which the people rule. As the nation changed and grew, popular sovereignty took on new meaning. A broader range of Americans shared in the power to govern themselves.

In 1987, Americans gathered in Washington, D.C., to celebrate the 200th anniversary of the Constitution. The banner proudly displays that the power to govern belongs to the people.

In a republican government, voting citizens make their voices heard at the polls. The power of the ballot prompts candidates to listen to people's concerns.

② Republicanism
How Are People's Views Represented in Government?

The Framers of the Constitution wanted the people to have a voice in government. Yet the Framers also feared that public opinion might stand in the way of sound decision making. To solve this problem, they looked to republicanism as a model of government.

Republicanism is based on this belief: The people exercise their power by voting for their political representatives. According to the Framers, these lawmakers played the key role in making a republican government work. Article 4, Section 4, of the Constitution also calls for every state to have a "republican form of government."

③ Federalism
How Is Power Shared?

The Framers wanted the states and the nation to become partners in governing. To build cooperation, the Framers turned to federalism. **Federalism** is a system of government in which power is divided between a central government and smaller political units, such as states. Before the Civil War, federalism in the United States was closely related to dual sovereignty, the idea that the federal government and the states each had exclusive power over their own spheres.

The Framers used federalism to structure the Constitution. The Constitution assigns certain powers to the national government. These are *delegated powers*. Powers kept by the states are *reserved powers*. Powers shared or exercised by national and state governments are known as *concurrent powers*.

Federalism

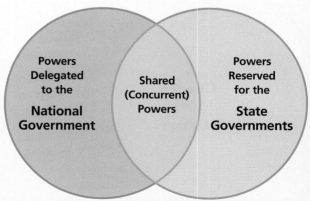

Powers Delegated to the **National Government**

Shared (Concurrent) Powers

Powers Reserved for the **State Governments**

The overlapping spheres of power bind the American people together.

4 Separation of Powers
How Is Power Divided?

The Framers were concerned that too much power might fall into the hands of a single group. To avoid this problem, they built the idea of **separation of powers** into the Constitution. This principle means the division of basic government roles into branches. No one branch is given all the power. Articles 1, 2, and 3 of the Constitution detail how powers are split among the three branches.

Separation of Powers

```
            UNITED STATES
            CONSTITUTION
        ↓        ↓        ↓
```

Article 1	Article 2	Article 3
Legislative Branch	**Executive Branch**	**Judicial Branch**
Congress makes the laws.	President enforces the laws.	Supreme Court interprets the law.

5 Checks and Balances
How Is Power Evenly Distributed?

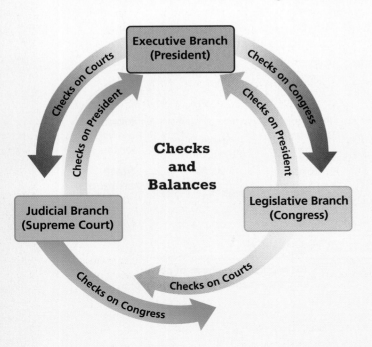

Baron de Montesquieu, an 18th-century French thinker, wrote, "Power should be a check to power." His comment refers to the principle of **checks and balances**. Each branch of government can exercise checks, or controls, over the other branches. Though the branches of government are separate, they rely on one another to perform the work of government.

The Framers included a system of checks and balances in the Constitution to help make sure that the branches work together fairly. For example, only Congress can pass laws. Yet the president can check this power by refusing to sign a law into action. In turn, the Supreme Court can declare that a law, passed by Congress and signed by the president, violates the Constitution.

6 Limited Government
How Is Abuse of Power Prevented?

The Framers restricted the power of government. Article 1, Section 9, of the Constitution lists the powers denied to the Congress. Article 1, Section 10, forbids the states to take certain actions.

The principle of **limited government** is also closely related to the "rule of law": In the American government everyone, citizens and powerful leaders alike, must obey the law. Individuals or groups cannot twist or bypass the law to serve their own interests.

'I AM THE LAW!'

In this political cartoon, President Richard Nixon shakes his fist as he defies the "rule of law." Faced with charges of violating the Constitution, Nixon resigned as president in 1974.

Students exercise their right to protest. They urge the community to protect the environment.

7 Individual Rights
How Are Personal Freedoms Protected?

The first ten amendments to the Constitution shield people from an overly powerful government. These amendments are called the Bill of Rights. The Bill of Rights guarantees certain **individual rights,** or personal liberties and privileges. For example, government cannot control what people write or say. People also have the right to meet peacefully and to ask the government to correct a problem. Later amendments to the Constitution also advanced the cause of individual rights.

Assessment: Principles of the Constitution

1. Main Ideas

a. What are the seven principles of government?

b. How does the Constitution reflect the principle of separation of powers?

c. Why did the Framers include a system of checks and balances in the Constitution?

2. Critical Thinking

Forming Opinions How do the rights and responsibilities of U.S. citizenship reflect American national identity?

THINK ABOUT

• what it means to be an American

• the rights and responsibilities of U.S. citizens

The Constitution of the United States

See Primary Source Explorer

" In 1787, I was not included in that 'We the people.' . . . But through the process of amendment, interpretation, and court decision, I have finally been included in 'We the people.'"

—BARBARA JORDAN, 1974
The first African-American congresswoman from the South (Texas)

Preamble. *Purpose of the Constitution*

We the people of the United States, in order to form a more perfect Union, establish justice, insure domestic tranquility, provide for the common defense, promote the general welfare, and secure the blessings of liberty to ourselves and our posterity, do ordain and establish this Constitution for the United States of America.

A CLOSER LOOK Goals of the Preamble

PREAMBLE	EXPLANATION	EXAMPLES
"Form a more perfect Union"	Create a nation in which states work together	• U.S. Postal System • U.S. coins, paper money
"Establish justice"	Make laws and set up courts that are fair	• Court system • Jury system
"Insure domestic tranquility"	Keep peace within the country	• National Guard • Federal marshals
"Provide for the common defense"	Safeguard the country against attack	• Army • Navy
"Promote the general welfare"	Contribute to the happiness and well-being of all the people	• Birth certificate • Marriage license
"Secure the blessings of liberty to ourselves and our posterity"	Make sure future citizens remain free	• Commission on Civil Rights • National Council on Disability

SKILLBUILDER Interpreting Charts

1. *Which goal of the Preamble do you think is most important? Why?*
2. *How does the Preamble reflect the principle of popular sovereignty?*

Article 1. *The Legislature*

> **MAIN IDEA** The main role of Congress, the legislative branch, is to make laws. Congress is made up of two houses—the Senate and the House of Representatives. Candidates for each house must meet certain requirements. Congress performs specific duties, also called delegated powers.
>
> **WHY IT MATTERS NOW** Representatives in Congress still voice the views and concerns of the people.

Section 1. Congress All legislative powers herein granted shall be vested in a Congress of the United States, which shall consist of a Senate and House of Representatives.

Section 2. The House of Representatives

1. Elections The House of Representatives shall be composed of members chosen every second year by the people of the several states, and the **electors** in each state shall have the qualifications requisite for electors of the most numerous branch of the state legislature.

2. Qualifications No person shall be a Representative who shall not have attained to the age of twenty-five years, and been seven years a citizen of the United States, and who shall not, when elected, be an inhabitant of that state in which he shall be chosen.

3. Number of Representatives Representatives and direct taxes shall be apportioned among the several states which may be included within this Union, according to their respective numbers, which shall be determined by adding to the whole number of free persons, including those bound to service for a term of years, and excluding Indians not taxed, three-fifths of all other Persons. The actual **enumeration** shall be made within three years after the first meeting of the Congress of the United States, and within every subsequent term of ten years, in such manner as they shall by law direct. The number of Representatives shall not exceed one for every thirty thousand, but each state shall have at least one Representative; and until such enumeration shall be made, the state of New Hampshire shall be entitled to choose three, Massachusetts eight, Rhode Island and Providence Plantations one, Connecticut five, New York six, New Jersey four, Pennsylvania eight, Delaware one, Maryland six, Virginia ten, North Carolina five, South Carolina five, and Georgia three.

4. Vacancies When vacancies happen in the representation from any state, the executive authority thereof shall issue writs of election to fill such vacancies.

5. Officers and Impeachment The House of Representatives shall choose their Speaker and other officers; and shall have the sole power of **impeachment**.

VOCABULARY

electors voters

enumeration an official count, such as a census

impeachment the process of accusing a public official of wrongdoing

---

A CLOSER LOOK

ELECTIONS

Representatives are elected every two years. There are no limits on the number of terms a person can serve.

1. What do you think are the advantages of holding frequent elections of representatives?

A CLOSER LOOK

REPRESENTATION

Some delegates, such as Gouverneur Morris, thought that representation should be based on wealth as well as population. Others, such as James Wilson, thought representation should be based on population only. Ultimately, the delegates voted against including wealth as a basis for apportioning representatives.

2. How do you think the United States would be different today if representation were based on wealth?

Section 3. The Senate

1. Numbers The Senate of the United States shall be composed of two Senators from each state, ~~chosen by the legislature thereof~~, for six years; and each Senator shall have one vote.

2. Classifying Terms Immediately after they shall be assembled in consequence of the first election, they shall be divided as equally as may be into three classes. The seats of the Senators of the first class shall be vacated at the expiration of the second year, of the second class at the expiration of the fourth year, and of the third class at the expiration of the sixth year, so that one-third may be chosen every second year; ~~and if vacancies happen by resignation, or otherwise, during the recess of the legislature of any state, the executive thereof may make temporary appointments until the next meeting of the legislature, which shall then fill such vacancies.~~

3. Qualifications No person shall be a Senator who shall not have attained to the age of thirty years, and been nine years a citizen of the United States, and who shall not, when elected, be an inhabitant of that state for which he shall be chosen.

A CLOSER LOOK Federal Office Terms and Requirements

POSITION	TERM	MINIMUM AGE	RESIDENCY	CITIZENSHIP
Representative	2 years	25	state in which elected	7 years
Senator	6 years	30	state in which elected	9 years
President	4 years	35	14 years in the U.S.	natural-born
Supreme Court Justice	unlimited	none	none	none

SKILLBUILDER Interpreting Charts
Why do you think the term and qualifications for a senator are more demanding than for a representative?

4. Role of Vice-President The Vice-President of the United States shall be President of the Senate, but shall have no vote, unless they be equally divided.

5. Officers The Senate shall choose their other officers, and also a President **pro tempore**, in the absence of the Vice-President, or when he shall exercise the office of President of the United States.

6. Impeachment Trials The Senate shall have the sole power to try all impeachments. When sitting for that purpose, they shall be on oath or affirmation. When the President of the United States is tried, the Chief Justice shall preside: and no person shall be convicted without the concurrence of two-thirds of the members present.

7. Punishment for Impeachment Judgment in cases of impeachment shall not extend further than to removal from office, and disqualification to hold and enjoy any office of honor, trust or profit under the United States; but the party convicted shall nevertheless be liable and subject to **indictment**, trial, judgment and punishment, according to law.

A CLOSER LOOK

IMPEACHMENT

The House brings charges against the president. The Senate acts as the jury. The Chief Justice of the Supreme Court presides over the hearings.

3. How many presidents have been impeached?

Section 4. Congressional Elections

1. Regulations The times, places and manner of holding elections for Senators and Representatives shall be prescribed in each state by the legislature thereof; but the Congress may at any time by law make or alter such regulations, except as to the places of choosing Senators.

2. Sessions The Congress shall assemble at least once in every year, ~~and such meeting shall be on the first Monday in December, unless they shall by law appoint a different day.~~

Section 5. Rules and Procedures

1. Quorum Each house shall be the judge of the elections, returns and qualifications of its own members, and a majority of each shall constitute a **quorum** to do business; but a smaller number may adjourn from day to day, and may be authorized to compel the attendance of absent members, in such manner, and under such penalties as each house may provide.

2. Rules and Conduct Each house may determine the rules of its proceedings, punish its members for disorderly behavior, and, with the concurrence of two-thirds, expel a member.

3. Congressional Records Each house shall keep a journal of its proceedings, and from time to time publish the same, excepting such parts as may in their judgment require secrecy; and the yeas and nays of the members of either house on any question shall, at the desire of one-fifth of those present, be entered on the journal.

4. Adjournment Neither house, during the session of Congress, shall, without the consent of the other, adjourn for more than three days, nor to any other place than that in which the two houses shall be sitting.

Section 6. Payment and Privileges

1. Salary The Senators and Representatives shall receive a compensation for their services, to be ascertained by law, and paid out of the treasury of the United States. They shall in all cases, except treason, felony and breach of the peace, be privileged from arrest during their attendance at the session of their respective houses, and in going to and returning from the same; and for any speech or debate in either house, they shall not be questioned in any other place.

2. Restrictions No Senator or Representative shall, during the time for which he was elected, be appointed to any civil office under the authority of the United States, which shall have been created, or the emoluments whereof shall have been increased during such time; and no person holding any office under the United States, shall be a member of either house during his continuance in office.

A CLOSER LOOK

SENATE RULES

Senate rules allow for debate on the floor. Using a tactic called filibustering, senators give long speeches to block the passage of a bill. Senator Strom Thurmond holds the filibustering record—24 hours, 18 minutes.

4. Why might a senator choose filibustering as a tactic to block a bill?

A CLOSER LOOK

SALARIES

Senators and representatives are paid $136,700 a year. The Speaker of the House is paid $175,400— the same as the vice-president.

5. How do the salaries of members of Congress compare to those of adults you know?

revenue income a government collects to cover expenses

naturalization a way to give full citizenship to a person of foreign birth

tribunals courts

felonies serious crimes

appropriation public funds set aside for a specific purpose

Section 7. How a Bill Becomes a Law

1. Tax Bills All bills for raising <u>revenue</u> shall originate in the House of Representatives; but the Senate may propose or concur with amendments as on other Bills.

2. Lawmaking Process Every bill which shall have passed the House of Representatives and the Senate, shall, before it become a law, be presented to the President of the United States; if he approves he shall sign it, but if not he shall return it, with his objections to that house in which it shall have originated, who shall enter the objections at large on their journal, and proceed to reconsider it. If after such reconsideration two-thirds of that house shall agree to pass the bill, it shall be sent, together with the objections, to the other house, by which it shall likewise be reconsidered, and if approved by two-thirds of that house, it shall become a law. But in all such cases the votes of both houses shall be determined by yeas and nays, and the names of the persons voting for and against the bill shall be entered on the journal of each house respectively. If any bill shall not be returned by the President within ten days (Sundays excepted) after it shall have been presented to him, the same shall be a law, in like manner as if he had signed it, unless the Congress by their adjournment prevent its return, in which case it shall not be a law.

3. Role of the President Every order, resolution, or vote to which the concurrence of the Senate and House of Representatives may be necessary (except on a question of adjournment) shall be presented to the President of the United States; and before the same shall take effect, shall be approved by him, or being disapproved by him, shall be repassed by two-thirds of the Senate and House of Representatives, according to the rules and limitations prescribed in the case of a bill.

A CLOSER LOOK   How a Bill Becomes a Law

Introduction

The House introduces a bill and refers it to a committee.

The Senate introduces a bill and refers it to a committee.

Committee Action

The House committee may approve, rewrite, or kill the bill.

The Senate committee may approve, rewrite, or kill the bill.

Floor Action

The House debates and votes on its version of the bill.

The Senate debates and votes on its version of the bill.

House and Senate committee members work out the differences between the two versions.

Section 8. Powers Granted to Congress

1. Taxation The Congress shall have power to lay and collect taxes, duties, imposts and excises, to pay the debts and provide for the common defense and general welfare of the United States; but all duties, imposts and excises shall be uniform throughout the United States;

2. Credit To borrow money on the credit of the United States;

3. Commerce To regulate commerce with foreign nations, and among the several states, and with the Indian tribes;

4. Naturalization, Bankruptcy To establish a uniform rule of **naturalization,** and uniform laws on the subject of bankruptcies throughout the United States;

5. Money To coin money, regulate the value thereof, and of foreign coin, and fix the standard of weights and measures;

6. Counterfeiting To provide for the punishment of counterfeiting the securities and current coin of the United States;

7. Post Office To establish post offices and post roads;

8. Patents, Copyrights To promote the progress of science and useful arts, by securing for limited times to authors and inventors the exclusive right to their respective writings and discoveries;

9. Federal Courts To constitute **tribunals** inferior to the Supreme Court;

10. International Law To define and punish piracies and **felonies** committed on the high seas, and offenses against the law of nations;

11. War To declare war, grant letters of marque and reprisal, and make rules concerning captures on land and water;

12. Army To raise and support armies, but no **appropriation** of money to that use shall be for a longer term than two years;

13. Navy To provide and maintain a navy;

Final Approval   ### Enactment

President signs the bill.

OR

President vetoes the bill.

Bill Becomes Law.

5 Both houses of Congress pass the revised bill.

6

7 Two-thirds majority vote of Congress is needed to approve a vetoed bill.

8 LAW

SKILLBUILDER Interpreting Charts

1. How can a president block a bill?

2. What examples of checks and balances are shown in the chart?

14. Regulation of Armed Forces To make rules for the government and regulation of the land and naval forces;

15. Militia To provide for calling forth the **militia** to execute the laws of the Union, suppress insurrections and repel invasions;

16. Regulations for Militia To provide for organizing, arming, and disciplining the militia, and for governing such part of them as may be employed in the service of the United States, reserving to the states respectively the appointment of the officers, and the authority of training the militia according to the discipline prescribed by Congress;

17. District of Columbia To exercise exclusive legislation in all cases whatsoever, over such district (not exceeding ten miles square) as may, by cession of particular states, and the acceptance of Congress, become the seat of the government of the United States, and to exercise like authority over all places purchased by the consent of the legislature of the state in which the same shall be, for the erection of forts, magazines, arsenals, dockyards, and other needful buildings;—and

18. Elastic Clause To make all laws which shall be necessary and proper for carrying into execution the foregoing powers, and all other powers vested by this Constitution in the government of the United States, or in any department or officer thereof.

A CLOSER LOOK **The Elastic Clause**

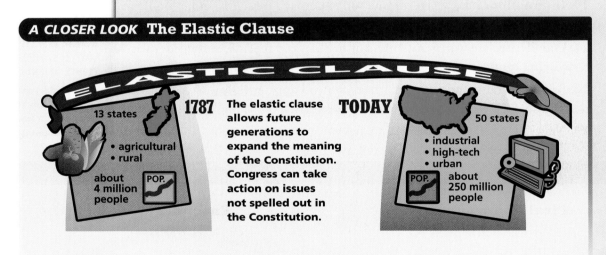

1787 The elastic clause allows future generations to expand the meaning of the Constitution. Congress can take action on issues not spelled out in the Constitution.

13 states
• agricultural
• rural
about 4 million people
POP.

TODAY

50 states
• industrial
• high-tech
• urban
POP. about 250 million people

A CLOSER LOOK

HABEAS CORPUS

A writ of habeas corpus is a legal order. It protects people from being held in prison or jail without formal charges of a crime. In 1992, the Supreme Court recognized that "habeas corpus is the [basic] instrument for safeguarding individual freedom."

8. How does habeas corpus help ensure fairness and justice?

Section 9. Powers Denied Congress

1. **Slave Trade** The migration or importation of such persons as any of the states now existing shall think proper to admit, shall not be prohibited by the Congress prior to the year one thousand eight hundred and eight, but a tax or duty may be imposed on such importation, not exceeding ten dollars for each person.

2. Habeas Corpus The privilege of the writ of habeas corpus shall not be suspended, unless when in cases of rebellion or invasion the public safety may require it.

3. Illegal Punishment No <u>bill of attainder</u> or <u>ex post facto law</u> shall be passed.

4. Direct Taxes No capitation, ~~or other direct,~~ tax shall be laid, ~~unless in proportion to the census or enumeration herein before directed to be taken.~~

5. Export Taxes No tax or duty shall be laid on articles exported from any state.

6. No Favorites No preference shall be given by any regulation of commerce or revenue to the ports of one state over those of another: nor shall vessels bound to, or from, one state be obliged to enter, clear, or pay duties in another.

7. Public Money No money shall be drawn from the treasury, but in consequence of appropriations made by law; and a regular statement and account of the receipts and expenditures of all public money shall be published from time to time.

8. Titles of Nobility No title of nobility shall be granted by the United States: and no person holding any office of profit or trust under them shall, without the consent of the Congress, accept of any present, emolument, office, or title, of any kind whatever, from any king, prince, or foreign state.

Section 10. Powers Denied the States

1. Restrictions No state shall enter into any treaty, alliance, or confederation; grant letters of marque and reprisal; coin money; emit bills of credit; make anything but gold and silver coin a **tender** in payment of debts; pass any bill of attainder, ex post facto law, or law impairing the obligation of contracts, or grant any title of nobility.

2. Import and Export Taxes No state shall, without the consent of the Congress, lay any imposts or duties on imports or exports, except what may be absolutely necessary for executing its inspection laws; and the net produce of all duties and imposts, laid by any state on imports or exports, shall be for the use of the treasury of the United States; and all such laws shall be subject to the revision and control of the Congress.

3. Peacetime and War Restraints No state shall, without the consent of Congress, lay any duty of tonnage, keep troops or ships of war in time of peace, enter into any agreement or compact with another state, or with a foreign power, or engage in war, unless actually invaded, or in such imminent danger as will not admit of delay.

A CLOSER LOOK

DIRECT TAX

In 1913, the 16th Amendment allowed Congress to collect an income tax—a direct tax on the amount of money a person earns. Americans today pay much more in taxes than their ancestors would have imagined.

9. Why do you think the issue of taxes is so important to people?

A CLOSER LOOK

TITLES OF NOBILITY

The Framers disapproved of titles of nobility. The list of grievances in the Declaration of Independence included numerous examples of King George III's abuses of power. Symbols of these abuses included English titles of nobility, such as "king," "queen," and "duke." The Framers said clearly that there would be no such titles in the new republic.

10. How do TV news reporters address members of Congress and the president?

Article 1 Assessment

1. Main Ideas

a. What is the main job of the legislative branch?

b. What role does the vice-president of the United States play in the Senate?

c. Why are there more members in the House of Representatives than the Senate?

d. What is one of the powers denied to Congress?

2. Critical Thinking

Drawing Conclusions How does Article 1 show that the Constitution is a clearly defined yet flexible document?

THINK ABOUT
• the powers of Congress
• the "elastic clause"

Article 2. *The Executive*

> **MAIN IDEA** The president and vice-president are the leaders of the executive branch. Their main role is to enforce the laws. The president commands the military and makes foreign treaties with the Senate's approval.
>
> **WHY IT MATTERS NOW** As the United States has become a world power, the authority of the president has also expanded.

Section 1. The Presidency

1. Terms of Office The executive power shall be vested in a President of the United States of America. He shall hold his office during the term of four years, and, together with the Vice-President, chosen for the same term, be elected, as follows:

2. Electoral College Each state shall appoint, in such manner as the Legislature thereof may direct, a number of electors, equal to the whole number of Senators and Representatives to which the State may be entitled in the Congress; but no Senator or Representative, or person holding an office of trust or profit under the United States, shall be appointed an elector.

A CLOSER LOOK Electoral College (based on 2000 Census)

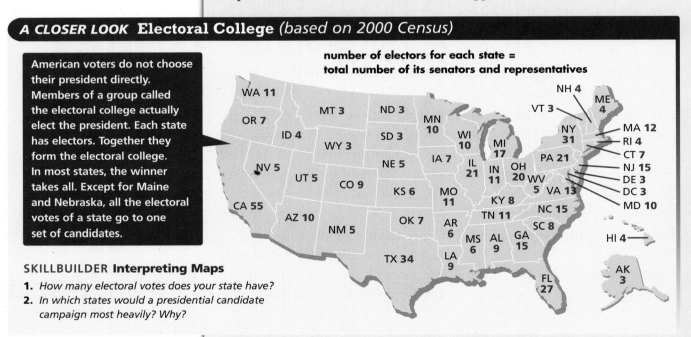

American voters do not choose their president directly. Members of a group called the electoral college actually elect the president. Each state has electors. Together they form the electoral college. In most states, the winner takes all. Except for Maine and Nebraska, all the electoral votes of a state go to one set of candidates.

number of electors for each state = total number of its senators and representatives

WA 11, OR 7, MT 3, ND 3, MN 10, NH 4, VT 3, ME 4, NY 31, MA 12, RI 4, CT 7, ID 4, WY 3, SD 3, WI 10, MI 17, NJ 15, DE 3, DC 3, NV 5, UT 5, NE 5, IA 7, IL 21, IN 11, OH 20, PA 21, WV 5, VA 13, MD 10, CA 55, CO 9, KS 6, MO 11, KY 8, NC 15, AZ 10, NM 5, OK 7, AR 6, TN 11, SC 8, HI 4, MS 6, AL 9, GA 15, TX 34, LA 9, FL 27, AK 3

SKILLBUILDER Interpreting Maps

1. *How many electoral votes does your state have?*
2. *In which states would a presidential candidate campaign most heavily? Why?*

~~**3. Former Method of Electing President** The electors shall meet in their respective states, and vote by ballot for two persons, of whom one at least shall not be an inhabitant of the same state with themselves. And they shall make a list of all the persons voted for, and of the number of votes for each; which list they shall sign and certify, and transmit sealed to the seat of the government of the United States, directed to the President of the Senate. The President of the Senate shall, in the presence of the Senate and House of Representatives, open all the certificates, and the votes shall then be counted. The person having the greatest number of votes shall be the~~

President, if such number be a majority of the whole number of electors appointed; and if there be more than one who have such majority, and have an equal number of votes, then the House of Representatives shall immediately choose by ballot one of them for President; and if no person have a majority, then from the five highest on the list the said House shall in like manner choose the President. But in choosing the President, the votes shall be taken by States, the representation from each state having one vote; a quorum for this purpose shall consist of a member or members from two-thirds of the states, and a majority of all the states shall be necessary to a choice. In every case, after the choice of the President, the person having the greatest number of votes of the electors shall be the Vice-President. But if there should remain two or more who have equal votes, the Senate shall choose from them by ballot the Vice-President.

A CLOSER LOOK

Vice-President Lyndon Johnson, next in line of succession, takes the oath of office after the assassination of President John F. Kennedy in 1963. Johnson, like every U.S. president, promises to uphold the Constitution. The 25th Amendment sets up clearer procedures for presidential succession.

4. Election Day The Congress may determine the time of choosing the electors, and the day on which they shall give their votes, which day shall be the same throughout the United States.

5. Qualifications No person except a **natural-born citizen,** or a citizen of the United States at the time of the adoption of this Constitution, shall be eligible to the office of President; neither shall any person be eligible to that office who shall not have attained to the age of thirty-five years, and been fourteen years a resident within the United States.

6. Succession In case of the removal of the President from office, or of his death, resignation, or inability to discharge the powers and duties of the said office, the same shall devolve on the Vice-President, and the Congress may by law provide for the case of removal, death, resignation or inability, both of the President and Vice-President, declaring what officer shall then act as President, and such officer shall act accordingly, until the disability be removed, or a President shall be elected.

7. Salary The President shall, at stated times, receive for his services, a compensation, which shall neither be increased nor diminished during the period for which he shall have been elected, and he shall not receive within that period any other emolument from the United States, or any of them.

8. Oath of Office Before he enter on the execution of his office, he shall take the following oath or **affirmation:**—"I do solemnly swear (or affirm) that I will faithfully execute the office of President of the United States, and will to the best of my ability, preserve, protect and defend the Constitution of the United States."

A CLOSER LOOK

PRESIDENT'S SALARY

The president's yearly salary is $400,000. The president also gets special allowances, such as funds for travel expenses. Here are some other benefits:
- living in a mansion, the White House
- vacationing at Camp David, an estate in Maryland
- using *Air Force One*, a personal jet plane

11. Why do you think the president needs to have a plane and a vacation spot?

Commander in Chief

As a military leader, President Abraham Lincoln meets with his generals during the Civil War.

Chief Executive

Like a business executive, the president solves problems and makes key decisions. President John F. Kennedy is shown in the oval office in 1962.

Chief Diplomat and Chief of State

As a foreign policy maker, President Richard M. Nixon visits the People's Republic of China in 1972.

Legislative Leader

President Lyndon Johnson signs the Civil Rights Act of 1964. All modern presidents have legislative programs they want Congress to pass.

Head of a Political Party

President Ronald Reagan rallies support at the 1984 Republican Convention. By this time, Reagan had put together a strong bloc of voters who supported the Republican Party's policies. During his presidency (1981–1989), Reagan helped build new unity among party members.

Section 2. Powers of the President

1. Military Powers The President shall be commander in chief of the Army and Navy of the United States, and of the militia of the several states, when called into the actual service of the United States; he may require the opinion, in writing, of the principal officer in each of the executive departments, upon any subject relating to the duties of their respective offices, and he shall have power to grant **reprieves** and pardons for offenses against the United States, except in cases of impeachment.

2. Treaties, Appointments He shall have power, by and with the advice and consent of the Senate, to make treaties, provided two-thirds of the Senators present concur; and he shall nominate, and by and with the advice and consent of the Senate, shall appoint ambassadors, other public ministers and consuls, judges of the Supreme Court, and all other officers of the United States, whose appointments are not herein otherwise provided for, and which shall be established by law; but the Congress may by law vest the appointment of such inferior officers, as they think proper, in the President alone, in the courts of law, or in the heads of departments.

3. Vacancies The President shall have power to fill up all vacancies that may happen during the recess of the Senate, by granting commissions which shall expire at the end of their next session.

Section 3. Presidential Duties

He shall from time to time give to the Congress information of the State of the Union, and recommend to their consideration such measures as he shall judge necessary and expedient; he may, on extraordinary occasions, **convene** both houses, or either of them, and in case of disagreement between them, with respect to the time of adjournment, he may adjourn them to such time as he shall think proper; he shall receive ambassadors and other public ministers; he shall take care that the laws be faithfully executed, and shall commission all the officers of the United States.

Section 4. Impeachment

The President, Vice-President and all civil officers of the United States shall be removed from office on impeachment for, and conviction of, treason, bribery, or other high crimes and **misdemeanors**.

A CLOSER LOOK

SUPREME COURT APPOINTMENTS

Recent presidents have used their power of appointment to add minorities and women to the Supreme Court. In 1967, President Lyndon Johnson appointed the first African-American justice, Thurgood Marshall. In 1981, President Ronald Reagan appointed the first woman, Sandra Day O'Connor.

12. What do you think influences a president's choice for a Supreme Court justice?

A CLOSER LOOK

STATE OF THE UNION

Major TV networks broadcast the State of the Union address to the whole nation. In this yearly message, the president urges Congress to achieve certain lawmaking goals. The president's speech also must gain the attention of TV viewers.

13. Why is the president's power to persuade an important political skill?

Article 2 Assessment

1. Main Ideas

a. What is the chief purpose of the executive branch?

b. What are the requirements for becoming president?

c. How does the Constitution limit the president's power to make appointments and treaties?

2. Critical Thinking

Analyzing Issues Why do you think the Constitution states that the president must seek approval from the Senate for most political appointments and treaties?

THINK ABOUT
• the abuse of power
• the will of the voters

A CLOSER LOOK

ORGANIZING FEDERAL COURTS

The Judiciary Act of 1789, passed by the First Congress, included establishing a Supreme Court with a chief justice and five associate justices and other lower federal courts.

14. How many Supreme Court justices are there today?

A CLOSER LOOK

JUDICIAL POWER

Judicial power gives the Supreme Court and other federal courts the authority to hear certain kinds of cases. These courts have the power to rule in cases involving the Constitution, national laws, treaties, and states' conflicts.

15. What federal cases have you seen reported on TV?

Article 3. *The Judiciary*

> **MAIN IDEA** The judicial branch interprets the laws. This branch includes the Supreme Court, the highest court in the nation, and other federal courts.
>
> **WHY IT MATTERS NOW** Supreme Court rulings can shape government policies on hotly debated issues.

Section 1. Federal Courts and Judges

The judicial power of the United States shall be vested in one Supreme Court, and in such **inferior courts** as the Congress may from time to time ordain and establish. The judges, both of the Supreme and inferior courts, shall hold their offices during good behavior, and shall, at stated times, receive for their services a compensation, which shall not be diminished during their continuance in office.

Section 2. The Courts' Authority

1. General Authority The judicial power shall extend to all cases, in law and equity, arising under this Constitution, the laws of the United States, and treaties made, or which shall be made, under their authority;—to all cases affecting ambassadors, other public ministers and consuls;—to all cases of admiralty and maritime jurisdiction;—to controversies to which the United States shall be a party;—to controversies between two or more states;— between a state and citizens of another state;—between citizens of different states;—between citizens of the same state claiming lands under grants of different states, and between a state, or the citizens thereof, and foreign states, citizens or subjects.

A CLOSER LOOK Judicial Review

Judicial review allows the Supreme Court and other federal courts to play a key role in lawmaking. The judges examine a law or government activity. They then decide whether it violates the Constitution. The Supreme Court established this important right in the case of *Marbury* v. *Madison* (1803). (See Chapter 3.)

2. Supreme Court In all cases affecting ambassadors, other public ministers and consuls, and those in which a state shall be party, the Supreme Court shall have original jurisdiction. In all the other cases before mentioned, the Supreme Court shall have **appellate** jurisdiction, both as to law and fact, with such exceptions, and under such regulations, as the Congress shall make.

A CLOSER LOOK Checks and Balances

CHECKS ON COURTS
- Appoints federal judges
- Can grant reprieves and pardons for federal crimes

Executive Branch (President)

CHECKS ON CONGRESS
- Can veto acts of Congress
- Can call special sessions of Congress
- Can suggest laws and send messages to Congress

CHECKS ON PRESIDENT
- Can declare executive acts unconstitutional
- Judges, appointed for life, are free from executive control

Judicial Branch (Supreme Court)

CHECKS ON CONGRESS
- Judicial review—Can declare acts of Congress unconstitutional

CHECKS ON PRESIDENT
- Can impeach and remove the president
- Can override veto
- Controls spending of money
- Senate can refuse to confirm presidential appointments and to ratify treaties

Legislative Branch (Congress)

CHECKS ON COURT
- Can impeach and remove federal judges
- Establishes lower federal courts
- Can refuse to confirm judicial appointments

SKILLBUILDER Interpreting Charts
1. *Why is judicial review an important action of the Supreme Court?*
2. *Which check do you think is most powerful? Why?*

3. Trial by Jury The trial of all crimes, except in cases of impeachment, shall be by jury; and such trial shall be held in the state where the said crimes shall have been committed; but when not committed within any state, the trial shall be at such place or places as the Congress may by law have directed.

Section 3. Treason

1. Definition Treason against the United States shall consist only in levying war against them, or in adhering to their enemies, giving them aid and comfort. No person shall be convicted of treason unless on the testimony of two witnesses to the same overt act, or on confession in open court.

2. Punishment The Congress shall have power to declare the punishment of treason, but no attainder of treason shall work corruption of blood, or forfeiture except during the life of the person attained.

Article 3 Assessment

1. Main Ideas
a. What is the main purpose of the judicial branch?

b. What is judicial review?

c. What are two kinds of cases that can begin in the Supreme Court?

2. Critical Thinking
Drawing Conclusions Why might the Supreme Court feel less political pressure than Congress in making judgments about the Constitution?

THINK ABOUT
- the appointment of Supreme Court justices
- Congress members' obligation to voters

A CLOSER LOOK Federalism

Americans live under both national and state governments.

NATIONAL POWERS
- Maintain military
- Declare war
- Establish postal system
- Set standards for weights and measures
- Protect copyrights and patents

SHARED POWERS
- Collect taxes
- Establish courts
- Regulate interstate commerce
- Regulate banks
- Borrow money
- Provide for the general welfare
- Punish criminals

STATE POWERS
- Establish local governments
- Set up schools
- Regulate state commerce
- Make regulations for marriage
- Establish and regulate corporations

SKILLBUILDER Interpreting Charts
What do you think is the purpose of dividing the powers between national and state governments?

Article 4. *Relations Among States*

MAIN IDEA States must honor one another's laws, records, and court rulings.

WHY IT MATTERS NOW Article 4 promotes cooperation, equality, and fair treatment of citizens from all the states.

Section 1. State Acts and Records Full faith and credit shall be given in each state to the public acts, records, and judicial proceedings of every other state. And the Congress may by general laws prescribe the manner in which such acts, records and proceedings shall be proved, and the effect thereof.

Section 2. Rights of Citizens

1. Citizenship The citizens of each state shall be entitled to all privileges and **immunities** of citizens in the several states.

2. Extradition A person charged in any state with treason, felony, or other crime, who shall flee from justice, and be found in another state, shall on demand of the executive authority of the state from which he fled, be delivered up, to be removed to the state having jurisdiction of the crime.

3. Fugitive Slaves ~~No person held to service or labor in one state, under the laws thereof, escaping into another, shall, in consequence of any law or regulation therein, be discharged from such service or labor, but shall be delivered up on claim of the party to whom such service or labor may be due.~~

A CLOSER LOOK

EXTRADITION

Persons charged with serious crimes cannot escape punishment by fleeing to another state. They must be returned to the first state and stand trial there.

16. Why do you think the Framers included the power of extradition?

Section 3. New States

1. Admission New states may be admitted by the Congress into this Union; but no new state shall be formed or erected within the jurisdiction of any other state; nor any state be formed by the junction of two or more states, or parts of states, without the consent of the legislatures of the states concerned as well as of the Congress.

2. Congressional Authority The Congress shall have power to dispose of and make all needful rules and regulations respecting the territory or other property belonging to the United States; and nothing in this Constitution shall be so construed as to prejudice any claims of the United States, or of any particular state.

Section 4. Guarantees to the States

The United States shall guarantee to every state in this Union a republican form of government, and shall protect each of them against invasion; and on application of the legislature, or of the executive (when the legislature cannot be convened) against domestic violence.

A CLOSER LOOK

ADMISSION TO STATEHOOD

In 1998, Puerto Ricans voted against their island becoming the 51st state. A lawyer in Puerto Rico summed up a main reason: "Puerto Ricans want to have ties to the U. S., but they want to protect their language and culture." Also, as a U.S. commonwealth, Puerto Rico makes its own laws and handles its own finances.

17. Do you think Puerto Rico should become a state? Why or why not?

Article 5. *Amending the Constitution*

> **MAIN IDEA** The Constitution can be amended, or formally changed.
> **WHY IT MATTERS NOW** The amendment process allows the Constitution to adapt to modern times.

The Congress, whenever two-thirds of both houses shall deem it necessary, shall propose amendments to this Constitution, or, on the application of the legislatures of two-thirds of the several states, shall call a convention for proposing amendments, which, in either case, shall be valid to all intents and purposes, as part of this Constitution, when ratified by the legislatures of three-fourths of the several states, or by conventions in three-fourths thereof, as the one or the other mode of ratification may be proposed by the Congress; provided that no amendment which may be made prior to the year one thousand eight hundred and eight shall in any manner affect the first and fourth clauses in the ninth section of the first article; and that no state, without its consent, shall be deprived of its equal **suffrage** in the Senate.

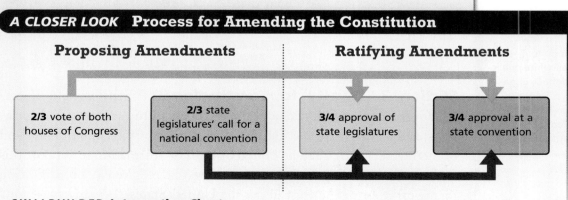

A CLOSER LOOK Process for Amending the Constitution

Proposing Amendments   **Ratifying Amendments**

| **2/3** vote of both houses of Congress | **2/3** state legislatures' call for a national convention | **3/4** approval of state legislatures | **3/4** approval at a state convention |

SKILLBUILDER Interpreting Charts
Why do you think more votes are needed to ratify an amendment than to propose one?

PAYING DEBTS

The U.S. government agreed to pay all debts held under the Articles of Confederation. For example, the United States still owed money from the costs of the Revolutionary War.

18. What problems might arise in a country that has a huge national debt?

Article 6. *Supremacy of the National Government*

> **MAIN IDEA** The Constitution, national laws, and treaties are the supreme, or highest, law of the land. All government officials must promise to support the Constitution.
>
> **WHY IT MATTERS NOW** The authority of federal laws over state laws helps keep the nation unified.

Section 1. Valid Debts All debts contracted and engagements entered into, before the adoption of this Constitution, shall be as valid against the United States under this Constitution, as under the Confederation.

Section 2. Supreme Law This Constitution, and the laws of the United States which shall be made in pursuance thereof; and all treaties made, or which shall be made, under the authority of the United States, shall be the supreme law of the land; and the judges in every state shall be bound thereby, anything in the constitution or laws of any state to the contrary notwithstanding.

In 1957, the "supreme law of the land" was put to a test. The governor of Arkansas defied a Supreme Court order. The Court ruled that African-American students could go to all-white public schools. President Dwight D. Eisenhower then sent federal troops to protect the first African-American students to enroll in Central High School in Little Rock, Arkansas.

Section 3. Loyalty to Constitution The Senators and Representatives before mentioned, and the members of the several state legislatures, and all executive and judicial officers, both of the United States and of the several states, shall be bound by oath or affirmation to support this Constitution; but no religious test shall ever be required as a qualification to any office or public trust under the United States.

REDEUNT SATURNIA REGNA.

On the erection of the Eleventh PILLAR of the great National DOME, we beg leave most sincerely to felicitate " OUR DEAR COUNTRY "

Rise it will.

The foundation good—it may yet be SAVED.

The FEDERAL EDIFICE.

A CLOSER LOOK

This political cartoon shows that New York was the 11th state to ratify the Constitution. Each of the 13 states is represented by a pillar.

Article 7. *Ratification*

MAIN IDEA Nine of the 13 states had to ratify, or approve, the Constitution before it could go into effect.

WHY IT MATTERS NOW The approval of the Constitution launched a new plan of government still followed today.

The **ratification** of the conventions of nine states shall be sufficient for the establishment of this Constitution between the states so ratifying the same. Done in convention by the **unanimous consent** of the states present, the seventeenth day of September in the year of our Lord one thousand seven hundred and eighty-seven and of the independence of the United States of America the twelfth. In witness whereof we have hereunto subscribed our names.

George Washington—President and deputy from Virginia

New Hampshire: *John Langdon, Nicholas Gilman*

Massachusetts: *Nathaniel Gorham, Rufus King*

Connecticut: *William Samuel Johnson, Roger Sherman*

New York: *Alexander Hamilton*

New Jersey: *William Livingston, David Brearley, William Paterson, Jonathan Dayton*

Pennsylvania: *Benjamin Franklin, Thomas Mifflin, Robert Morris, George Clymer, Thomas FitzSimons, Jared Ingersoll, James Wilson, Gouverneur Morris*

Delaware: *George Read, Gunning Bedford, Jr., John Dickinson, Richard Bassett, Jacob Broom*

Maryland: *James McHenry, Dan of St. Thomas Jenifer, Daniel Carroll*

Virginia: *John Blair, James Madison, Jr.*

North Carolina: *William Blount, Richard Dobbs Spaight, Hugh Williamson*

South Carolina: *John Rutledge, Charles Cotesworth Pinckney, Charles Pinckney, Pierce Butler*

Georgia: *William Few, Abraham Baldwin*

A CLOSER LOOK

THE SIGNERS

The 39 men who signed the Constitution were wealthy and well-educated. About half of them were trained in law. Others were doctors, merchants, bankers, and slaveholding planters. Missing from the list of signatures are the names of African Americans, Native Americans, and women. These groups reflected the varied population of the United States in the 1780s.

19. How do you think the absence of these groups affected the decisions made in creating the Constitution?

Articles 4–7 Assessment

1. Main Ideas

a. What rights does Article 4 guarantee to citizens if they go to other states in the nation?

b. What are two ways of proposing an amendment to the Constitution?

c. What makes up "the supreme law of the land"?

2. Critical Thinking

Forming and Supporting Opinions Should the Framers of the Constitution have allowed the people to vote directly for ratification of the Constitution? Why or why not?

THINK ABOUT

- the idea that the government belongs to the people
- the general public's ability to make sound political decisions

The Bill of Rights and Amendments 11–27

In 1787, Thomas Jefferson sent James Madison a letter about the Constitution. Jefferson wrote, "I will now add what I do not like . . . [there is no] bill of rights." He explained his reasons: "A bill of rights is what the people are entitled to against every government on earth . . . and what no just government should refuse." Jefferson's disapproval is not surprising. In writing the Declaration of Independence, he spelled out basic individual rights that cannot be taken way. These are "life, liberty, and the pursuit of happiness." The Declaration states that governments are formed to protect these rights.

Several states approved the Constitution only if a list of guaranteed freedoms was added. While serving in the nation's first Congress, James Madison helped draft the Bill of Rights. In 1791, these first ten amendments became part of the Constitution.

AMENDMENTS 1–10. *The Bill of Rights*

MAIN IDEA The Bill of Rights protects citizens from government interference.

WHY IT MATTERS NOW Issues related to the Bill of Rights are still being applied, tested, and interpreted.

AMENDMENT 1. Religious and Political Freedom (1791)

Congress shall make no law respecting an establishment of religion, or prohibiting the free exercise thereof; or **abridging** the freedom of speech, or of the press; or the right of the people peaceably to assemble, and to petition the Government for a redress of grievances.

A CLOSER LOOK The Five Freedoms

Freedom of Religion
Right to worship

Freedom of Speech
Right to state ideas

Freedom of the Press
Right to publish ideas

WE SAY NO!

Freedom of Assembly
Right to meet peacefully in groups

Freedom to Petition
Right to protest the government

PETITION

SKILLBUILDER Interpreting Charts
1. *Why is freedom of speech and the press important in a democratic society?*
2. *What impact has religious freedom had on the American way of life?*

AMENDMENT 2. Right to Bear Arms (1791)

A well-regulated militia, being necessary to the security of a free state, the right of the people to keep and bear arms, shall not be infringed.

AMENDMENT 3. Quartering Troops (1791)

No soldier shall, in time of peace be **quartered** in any house, without the consent of the owner, nor in time of war, but in a manner to be prescribed by law.

AMENDMENT 4. Search and Seizure (1791)

The right of the people to be secure in their persons, houses, papers, and effects, against unreasonable searches and seizures, shall not be violated, and no warrants shall issue, but upon probable cause, supported by oath or affirmation, and particularly describing the place to be searched, and the persons or things to be seized.

AMENDMENT 5. Rights of Accused Persons (1791)

No person shall be held to answer for a capital, or otherwise infamous crime, unless on a presentment or indictment of a Grand Jury, except in cases arising in the land or naval forces, or in the militia, when in actual service in time of war or public danger; nor shall any person be subject for the same offense to be twice put in jeopardy of life or limb; nor shall be compelled in any criminal case to be a witness against himself, nor be deprived of life, liberty, or property, without **due process of law**; nor shall private property be taken for public use, without just compensation.

AMENDMENT 6. Right to a Speedy, Public Trial (1791)

In all criminal prosecutions, the accused shall enjoy the right to a speedy and public trial, by an impartial jury of the State and district wherein the crime shall have been committed, which district shall have been previously ascertained by law, and to be informed of the nature and cause of the accusation; to be confronted with the witnesses against him; to have **compulsory process** for obtaining witnesses in his favor, and to have the assistance of **counsel** for his defense.

A CLOSER LOOK

SEARCHES

Metal detectors at airports search passengers. Airline workers search all carry-on luggage. Do these actions violate the 4th Amendment? The courts say no. They have cited many situations that allow for searches without a warrant, or written order. A person's right to privacy is balanced against the government's need to prevent crime.

20. What does the right to privacy mean to you at home and at school?

A CLOSER LOOK

In 1966, the Supreme Court made a decision based on the 5th and 6th Amendments. The warnings outlined in this ruling are often called "Miranda rights." Miranda rights protect suspects from giving forced confessions. Police must read these rights to a suspect they are questioning. For example:

• "You have the right to remain silent."

• "Anything that you say can and will be used against you in a court of law."

• "You have the right to an attorney."

A CLOSER LOOK

Protesters such as the young woman at left claim that the death penalty violates the 8th Amendment, which protects people against "cruel and unusual punishment." Supporters (above) believe that the death penalty is a justly deserved punishment.

A CLOSER LOOK

STATES' POWERS

The 10th Amendment gives the states reserved powers. Any powers not clearly given to the national government by the U.S. Constitution or denied to the states in Article I, Section 10, belong to the states. State constitutions sometimes assume authority in unexpected areas. For example, California's constitution sets rules for governing the use of fishing nets.

21. What are some common areas in which states have authority?

AMENDMENT 7. Trial by Jury in Civil Cases (1791) In suits at **common law,** where the value in controversy shall exceed twenty dollars, the right of trial by jury shall be preserved, and no fact tried by a jury, shall be otherwise reexamined in any court of the United States, than according to the rules of the common law.

AMENDMENT 8. Limits of Fines and Punishments (1791) Excessive **bail** shall not be required, nor excessive fines imposed, nor cruel and unusual punishments inflicted.

AMENDMENT 9. Rights of People (1791) The enumeration in the Constitution of certain rights shall not be construed to deny or disparage others retained by the people.

AMENDMENT 10. Powers of States and People (1791) The powers not delegated to the United States by the Constitution, nor prohibited by it to the States, are reserved to the States respectively, or to the people.

Bill of Rights Assessment

1. Main Ideas

a. Which amendment protects your privacy?

b. Which amendments guarantee fair legal treatment?

c. Which amendment prevents the federal government from taking powers away from the states and the people?

2. Critical Thinking

Forming and Supporting Opinions The 4th, 5th, 6th, 7th, and 8th Amendments protect innocent people accused of crimes. Do you think these five amendments also favor the rights of actual criminals? Explain.

THINK ABOUT

- criminals who go free if valuable evidence is found after their trials
- criminals released on bail

Amendments 11–27

> **MAIN IDEA** The Constitution has adapted to social changes and historical trends.
> **WHY IT MATTERS NOW** Amendments 11–27 show that the Constitution is a living document.

AMENDMENT 11. Lawsuits Against States (1798)

Passed by Congress March 4, 1794. Ratified February 7, 1795. Proclaimed 1798.
Note: Article 3, Section 2, of the Constitution was modified by Amendment 11.

The Judicial power of the United States shall not be construed to extend to any suit in law or **equity,** commenced or prosecuted against one of the United States by citizens of another state, or by citizens or subjects of any foreign state.

AMENDMENT 12. Election of Executives (1804)

Passed by Congress December 9, 1803. Ratified June 15, 1804.
Note: Part of Article 2, Section 1, of the Constitution was replaced by the 12th Amendment.

The electors shall meet in their respective states and vote by ballot for President and Vice-President, one of whom, at least, shall not be an inhabitant of the same state with themselves; they shall name in their ballots the person voted for as President, and in distinct ballots the person voted for as Vice-President, and they shall make distinct lists of all persons voted for as President, and of all persons voted for as Vice-President, and of the number of votes for each, which lists they shall sign and certify, and transmit sealed to the seat of the government of the United States, directed to the President of the Senate;—the President of the Senate shall, in the presence of the Senate and House of Representatives, open all the certificates and the votes shall then be counted;—the person having the greatest number of votes for President, shall be the President, if such number be a majority of the whole number of electors appointed; and if no person have such majority, then from the persons having the highest numbers not exceeding three on the list of those voted for as President, the House of Representatives shall choose immediately, by ballot, the President. But in choosing the President, the votes shall be taken by states, the representation from each state having one vote; a quorum for this purpose shall consist of a member or members from two-thirds of the states, and a majority of all the states shall be necessary to a choice. And if the House of Representatives shall not choose a President whenever the right of choice shall devolve upon them, ~~before the fourth day of March next following,~~ then the Vice-President shall act as President, as in the case of the death or other constitutional disability of the President. The person having the greatest number of votes as Vice-President, shall be the Vice-President, if such number be a majority of the whole number of Electors appointed, and if no person have a majority, then from the two highest numbers on the list, the Senate shall choose the Vice-President; a quorum for the purpose shall consist of two-thirds of the whole number of Senators, and a majority of the whole number shall be necessary to a choice. But no person constitutionally ineligible to the office of President shall be eligible to that of Vice-President of the United States.

A CLOSER LOOK

SEPARATE BALLOTS

The presidential election of 1800 ended in a tie between Thomas Jefferson and Aaron Burr. At this time, the candidate with the most votes became president. The runner-up became vice-president. The 12th Amendment calls for separate ballots for the president and vice-president. The vice-president is specifically elected to the office, rather than being the presidential candidate with the second-most votes.

22. Why do you think it's important for a presidential election to result in a clear-cut winner?

AMENDMENT 13. Slavery Abolished (1865)

Passed by Congress January 31, 1865. Ratified December 6, 1865.

Note: A portion of Article 4, Section 2, of the Constitution was superseded by the 13th Amendment.

Section 1. Neither slavery nor involuntary **servitude,** except as a punishment for crime whereof the party shall have been duly convicted, shall exist within the United States, or any place subject to their jurisdiction.

Section 2. Congress shall have power to enforce this article by appropriate legislation.

AMENDMENT 14. Civil Rights (1868)

Passed by Congress June 13, 1866. Ratified July 9, 1868.

Note: Article 1, Section 2, of the Constitution was modified by Section 2 of the 14th Amendment.

Section 1. All persons born or **naturalized** in the United States, and subject to the jurisdiction thereof, are citizens of the United States and of the state wherein they reside. No state shall make or enforce any law which shall abridge the privileges or immunities of citizens of the United States; nor shall any state deprive any person of life, liberty, or property, without due process of law; nor deny to any person within its jurisdiction the equal protection of the laws.

Section 2. Representatives shall be apportioned among the several states according to their respective numbers, counting the whole number of persons in each state, excluding Indians not taxed. But when the right to vote at any election for the choice of electors for President and Vice-President of the United States, Representatives in Congress, the executive and judicial officers of a state, or the members of the legislature thereof, is denied to any of the male inhabitants of such state, being twenty-one years of age, and citizens of the United States, or in any way abridged, except for participation in rebellion, or other crime, the basis of representation therein shall be reduced in the proportion which the number of such male citizens shall bear to the whole number of male citizens twenty-one years of age in such state.

A CLOSER LOOK

The 14th Amendment laid the groundwork for many civil rights laws, such as the Americans with Disabilities Act (1990). This act gave people with mental or physical disabilities "equal protection of the laws." For example, public places had to be designed for wheelchair use. Wider doors and ramps allow disabled people to go in and out of buildings.

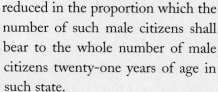

Section 3. No person shall be a Senator or Representative in Congress, or elector of President and Vice-President, or hold any office, civil or military, under the United States, or under any state, who, having previously taken an oath, as a member of Congress, or as an officer of the United States, or as a member of any state legislature, or as an executive or judicial officer of any state, to support the Constitution of the United States, shall have engaged in **insurrection** or rebellion against the same, or given aid or comfort to the enemies thereof. But Congress may, by a vote of two-thirds of each house, remove such disability.

Section 4. The validity of the public debt of the United States, authorized by law, including debts incurred for payment of pensions and **bounties** for services in suppressing insurrection or rebellion, shall not be questioned. But neither the United States nor any state shall assume or pay any debt or obligation incurred in aid of insurrection or rebellion against the United States, or any claim for the loss or emancipation of any slave; but all such debts, obligations and claims shall be held illegal and void.

Section 5. The Congress shall have power to enforce, by appropriate legislation, the provisions of this article.

AMENDMENT 15. Right to Vote (1870)
Passed by Congress February 26, 1869. Ratified February 3, 1870.

Section 1. The right of citizens of the United States to vote shall not be denied or abridged by the United States or by any state on account of race, color, or previous condition of servitude.

Section 2. The Congress shall have power to enforce this article by appropriate legislation.

A CLOSER LOOK Reconstruction Amendments

The 13th, 14th, and 15th Amendments are often called the Reconstruction Amendments. They were passed after the Civil War during the government's attempt to rebuild the Union and to grant rights to recently freed African Americans.

Amendment 13

1865
• Ended slavery in the United States

Amendment 14

1868
• Defined national and state citizenship
• Protected citizens' rights
• Promised "equal protection of the laws"

Amendment 15

1870
• Designed to protect African Americans' voting rights

SKILLBUILDER Interpreting Charts
What problems did these amendments try to solve?

A CLOSER LOOK

VOTING RIGHTS

The Voting Rights Act of 1965 extended the 15th Amendment. To qualify as voters, African Americans were no longer required to take tests proving that they could read and write. Also, federal examiners could help register voters. As a result, the number of African-American voters rose sharply.

23. What effect do you think the Voting Rights Act had on candidates running for office?

INCOME TAX

People below the poverty level, as defined by the federal government, do not have to pay income tax. In 1997, the poverty level for a family of four was $16,400 per year. About 13.3 percent of all Americans were considered poor in 1997.

24. Why do you think people below the poverty level do not pay any income tax?

AMENDMENT 16. Income Tax (1913)

Passed by Congress July 12, 1909. Ratified February 3, 1913.

Note: Article 1, Section 9, of the Constitution was modified by the 16th Amendment.

The Congress shall have power to lay and collect taxes on incomes, from whatever source derived, without apportionment among the several states, and without regard to any census or enumeration.

AMENDMENT 17. Direct Election of Senators (1913)

Passed by Congress May 13, 1912. Ratified April 8, 1913.

Note: Article 1, Section 3, of the Constitution was modified by the 17th Amendment.

Section 1. The Senate of the United States shall be composed of two Senators from each state, elected by the people thereof, for six years; and each Senator shall have one vote. The electors in each state shall have the qualifications requisite for electors of the most numerous branch of the state legislatures.

Section 2. When vacancies happen in the representation of any state in the Senate, the executive authority of such state shall issue writs of election to fill such vacancies: Provided, that the legislature of any state may empower the executive thereof to make temporary appointments until the people fill the vacancies by election as the legislature may direct.

Section 3. This amendment shall not be so construed as to affect the election or term of any Senator chosen before it becomes valid as part of the Constitution.

AMENDMENT 18. Prohibition (1919)

Passed by Congress December 18, 1917. Ratified January 16, 1919. Repealed by the 21st Amendment.

Section 1. After one year from the ratification of this article the manufacture, sale, or transportation of intoxicating liquors within, the importation thereof into, or the exportation thereof from the United States and all territory subject to the jurisdiction thereof for beverage purposes is hereby prohibited.

Section 2. The Congress and the several states shall have concurrent power to enforce this article by appropriate legislation.

Section 3. This article shall be inoperative unless it shall have been ratified as an amendment to the Constitution by the legislatures of the several states, as provided in the Constitution, within seven years from the date of the submission hereof to the states by the Congress.

Under Prohibition, people broke the law if they made, sold, or shipped alcoholic beverages. Powerful crime gangs turned selling illegal liquor into a big business. This photo shows federal agents getting ready to smash containers of illegal whiskey. The 21st Amendment ended Prohibition.

AMENDMENT 19. Woman Suffrage (1920)

Passed by Congress June 4, 1919. Ratified August 18, 1920.

Section 1. The right of citizens of the United States to vote shall not be denied or abridged by the United States or by any state on account of sex.

Section 2. Congress shall have power to enforce this article by appropriate legislation.

AMENDMENT 20. "Lame Duck" Sessions (1933)

Passed by Congress March 2, 1932. Ratified January 23, 1933.

Note: Article 1, Section 4, of the Constitution was modified by Section 2 of this amendment. In addition, a portion of the 12th Amendment was superseded by Section 3.

Section 1. The terms of the President and Vice-President shall end at noon on the 20th day of January, and the terms of Senators and Representatives at noon on the 3rd day of January, of the years in which such terms would have ended if this article had not been ratified; and the terms of their successors shall then begin.

Section 2. The Congress shall assemble at least once in every year, and such meeting shall begin at noon on the 3rd day of January, unless they shall by law appoint a different day.

Section 3. If, at the time fixed for the beginning of the term of the President, the President elect shall have died, the Vice-President elect shall become President. If a President shall not have been chosen before the time fixed for the beginning of his term, or if the President elect shall have failed to qualify, then the Vice-President elect shall act as President until a President shall have qualified; and the Congress may by law provide for the case wherein neither a President elect nor a Vice-President elect shall have

VOCABULARY

inoperative no longer in force
primary an election in which registered members of a political party nominate candidates for office

qualified, declaring who shall then act as President, or the manner in which one who is to act shall be selected, and such person shall act accordingly until a President or Vice-President shall have qualified.

Section 4. The Congress may by law provide for the case of the death of any of the persons from whom the House of Representatives may choose a President whenever the right of choice shall have devolved upon them, and for the case of the death of any of the persons from whom the Senate may choose a Vice-President whenever the right of choice shall have devolved upon them.

Section 5. Sections 1 and 2 shall take effect on the 15th day of October following the ratification of this article.

Section 6. This article shall be **inoperative** unless it shall have been ratified as an amendment to the Constitution by the legislatures of three-fourths of the several states within seven years from the date of its submission.

AMENDMENT 21. Repeal of Prohibition (1933)
Passed by Congress February 20, 1933. Ratified December 5, 1933.

Section 1. The eighteenth article of amendment to the Constitution of the United States is hereby repealed.

Section 2. The transportation or importation into any state, territory, or possession of the United States for delivery or use therein of intoxicating liquors, in violation of the laws thereof, is hereby prohibited.

Section 3. This article shall be inoperative unless it shall have been ratified as an amendment to the Constitution by conventions in the several states, as provided in the Constitution, within seven years from the date of the submission hereof to the states by the Congress.

AMENDMENT 22. Limit on Presidential Terms (1951)
Passed by Congress March 21, 1947. Ratified February 27, 1951.

Section 1. No person shall be elected to the office of the President more than twice, and no person who has held the office of President, or acted as President, for more than two years of a term to which some other person was elected President shall be elected to the office of the President more than once. But this article shall not apply to any person holding the office of President when this article was proposed by the Congress, and shall not prevent any person who may be holding the office of President, or acting as President, during the term within which this article becomes operative from holding the office of President or acting as President during the remainder of such term.

Section 2. This article shall be inoperative unless it shall have been ratified as an amendment to the Constitution by the legislatures of three-fourths of the several states within seven years from the date of its submission to the states by the Congress.

A CLOSER LOOK

George Washington set the tradition of limiting the presidency to two terms. Franklin Roosevelt broke this custom when he was elected president four terms in a row—1932, 1936, 1940, and 1944. His record-long presidency led to the 22nd Amendment. A two-term limit, written into the Constitution, checks the president's power.

AMENDMENT 23. Voting in District of Columbia (1961)

Passed by Congress June 17, 1960. Ratified March 29, 1961.

Section 1. The district constituting the seat of government of the United States shall appoint in such manner as Congress may direct: a number of electors of President and Vice-President equal to the whole number of Senators and Representatives in Congress to which the district would be entitled if it were a state, but in no event more than the least populous state; they shall be in addition to those appointed by the states, but they shall be considered, for the purposes of the election of President and Vice-President, to be electors appointed by a state; and they shall meet in the district and perform such duties as provided by the twelfth article of amendment.

Section 2. The Congress shall have power to enforce this article by appropriate legislation.

AMENDMENT 24. Abolition of Poll Taxes (1964)

Passed by Congress August 27, 1962. Ratified January 23, 1964.

Section 1. The right of citizens of the United States to vote in any **primary** or other election for President or Vice-President, for electors for President or Vice-President, or for Senator or Representative in Congress, shall not be denied or abridged by the United States or any state by reason of failure to pay any poll tax or other tax.

Section 2. The Congress shall have power to enforce this article by appropriate legislation.

AMENDMENT 25. Presidential Disability, Succession (1967)

Passed by Congress July 6, 1965. Ratified February 10, 1967.

Note: Article 2, Section 1, of the Constitution was affected by the 25th Amendment.

Section 1. In case of the removal of the President from office or of his death or resignation, the Vice-President shall become President.

Section 2. Whenever there is a vacancy in the office of the Vice-President, the President shall nominate a Vice-President who shall take office upon confirmation by a majority vote of both houses of Congress.

Section 3. Whenever the President transmits to the President pro tempore of the Senate and the Speaker of the House of Representatives his written declaration that he is unable to discharge the powers and duties of his office, and until he transmits to them a written declaration to the contrary, such powers and duties shall be discharged by the Vice-President as Acting President.

A CLOSER LOOK

POLL TAX

The poll tax was aimed at preventing African Americans from exercising their rights. Many could not afford to pay this fee required for voting.

26. How do you think the 24th Amendment affected elections?

A CLOSER LOOK

PRESIDENTIAL DISABILITY

President John F. Kennedy's death in 1963 signaled the need for the 25th Amendment. The Constitution did not explain what to do in the case of a disabled president. James Reston, a writer for *The New York Times*, summed up the problem: Suppose Kennedy was "strong enough to survive [the bullet wounds], but too weak to govern." The 25th Amendment provides for an orderly transfer of power.

27. What do you think can happen in a country where the rules for succession are not clear?

A CLOSER LOOK

SUCCESSION

Who takes over if a president dies in office or is unable to serve? The top five in the line of succession follow:

- vice-president
- speaker of the house
- president pro tempore of the Senate
- secretary of state
- secretary of the treasury

28. Why should voters know the views of the vice-president?

Section 4. Whenever the Vice-President and a majority of either the principal officers of the executive departments or of such other body as Congress may by law provide, transmit to the President pro tempore of the Senate and the Speaker of the House of Representatives their written declaration that the President is unable to discharge the powers and duties of his office, the Vice-President shall immediately assume the powers and duties of the office as Acting President. Thereafter, when the President transmits to the President pro tempore of the Senate and the Speaker of the House of Representatives his written declaration that no inability exists, he shall resume the powers and duties of his office unless the Vice-President and a majority of either the principal officers of the executive department[s] or of such other body as Congress may by law provide, transmit within four days to the President pro tempore of the Senate and the Speaker of the House of Representatives their written declaration that the President is unable to discharge the powers and duties of his office. Thereupon Congress shall decide the issue, assembling within forty-eight hours for that purpose if not in session. If the Congress, within twenty-one days after receipt of the latter written declaration, or, if Congress is not in session, within twenty-one days after Congress is required to assemble, determines by two thirds vote of both houses that the President is unable to discharge the powers and duties of his office, the Vice-President shall continue to discharge the same as Acting President; otherwise, the President shall resume the powers and duties of his office.

A CLOSER LOOK Amendments Time Line *1791–1992*

Use the key below to help you categorize the amendments.

- ■ **Voting Rights**
- ■ **Social Changes**
- ■ **Overturned Supreme Court Decisions**
- ■ **Election Procedures and Conditions of Office**

**Amendment 15
1870**
Stops national and state governments from denying the vote based on race.

**Bill of Rights
Amendments 1–10
1791**

**Amendment 13
1865**
Bans slavery.

1790

**Amendment 11
1798**
Protects state from lawsuits filed by citizens of other states or countries.

**Amendment 12
1804**
Requires separate electoral ballots for president and vice-president.

**Amendment 14
1868**
Defines American citizenship and citizens' rights.

AMENDMENT 26. 18-year-old Vote (1971)

Passed by Congress March 23, 1971. Ratified July 1, 1971.

Note: Amendment 14, Section 2, of the Constitution was modified by Section 1 of the 26th Amendment.

Section 1. The right of citizens of the United States, who are eighteen years of age or older, to vote shall not be denied or abridged by the United States or by any state on account of age.

Section 2. The Congress shall have power to enforce this article by appropriate legislation.

AMENDMENT 27. Congressional Pay (1992)

Passed by Congress September 25, 1789. Ratified May 7, 1992.

No law, varying the compensation for the services of the Senators and Representatives, shall take effect, until an election of Representatives shall have intervened.

A CLOSER LOOK

Members of the recording industry founded Rock the Vote. They urge young people to vote in elections.

Amendments 11–27 Assessment

1. Main Ideas

a. Which amendments affected the office of president?

b. Which pair of amendments shows the failure of laws to solve a social problem?

c. Which amendments corrected unfair treatment toward African Americans and women?

2. Critical Thinking

Summarizing What is the purpose of amending the Constitution?

THINK ABOUT

• the purpose of the Constitution
• problems and issues that Americans have faced throughout U.S. history

---

Amendment 23
1961
Gives citizens of Washington, D.C., right to vote in presidential elections.

Amendment 19
1920
Extends the vote to women.

Amendment 24
1964
Bans poll taxes.

Amendment 18
1919
Prohibits making, selling, and shipping alcoholic beverages.

Amendment 21
1933
Repeals Amendment 18.

Amendment 26
1971
Gives 18-year-olds right to vote in federal and state elections.

2000

Amendment 16
1913
Allows Congress to tax incomes.

Amendment 20
1933
Changes date for starting new Congress and inaugurating new president.

Amendment 25
1967
Sets procedures for presidential succession.

Amendment 27
1992
Limits ability of Congress to increase its pay.

Amendment 17
1913
Establishes direct election of U.S. senators.

Amendment 22
1951
Limits terms president can serve to two.

VISUAL SUMMARY

The Constitution of the United States

Preamble

WE THE PEOPLE

Article 1   Article 2   Article 3

The Branches of Government

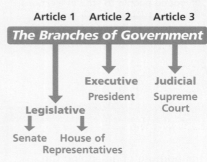

Executive
President

Judicial
Supreme Court

Legislative

Senate   House of Representatives

Article 4   Article 6

The Federal System

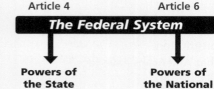

Powers of the State

Powers of the National Government

"Supreme law of the land"

Article 5

Amending the Constitution

Making Changes

Bill of Rights

Amendments 1–10

Personal Freedoms   Personal Security   Rights of the Accused

Amendments 11–27

The living Constitution changes with the times.

VOCABULARY

Briefly explain the significance of each of the following.

1. electors
2. impeachment
3. naturalization
4. felonies
5. bill of attainder
6. ex post facto law
7. suffrage
8. due process of law
9. servitude
10. primary

SEVEN PRINCIPLES OF THE CONSTITUTION

Make a chart like the one shown. Then fill it in with a definition of each principle and an example from the Constitution.

Principle	Definition	Example
1. popular sovereignty		
2. republicanism		
3. federalism		
4. separation of powers		
5. checks and balances		
6. limited government		
7. individual rights		

REVIEW QUESTIONS

Article 1 (pages 71–77)

1. What are the requirements for becoming a member of the House of Representatives and the Senate?
2. What are two military powers granted to Congress?

Article 2 (pages 78–81)

3. How does the electoral college choose the president?
4. What are three powers of the president?

Article 3 (pages 82–83)

5. What are the two most important powers of the federal courts?

Articles 4–7 (pages 84–87)

6. How can the Constitution be changed?
7. If a state law and a federal law conflict, which law must be obeyed? Why?
8. How was the Constitution ratified?

Bill of Rights and Amendments 11–27 (pages 88–99)

9. What five freedoms are guaranteed in the First Amendment?
10. Which amendments extend voting rights to a broader range of Americans?

CRITICAL THINKING

1. DRAWING CONCLUSIONS

In a two-column chart, summarize the processes for changing the Constitution. Then use your completed chart to answer the questions below.

Proposing Amendments	Ratifying Amendments
1.	1.
2.	2.

a. What role can citizens play in proposing amendments?

b. What do you think are the main reasons for changing the Constitution?

2. MAKING INFERENCES

Explain how the "elastic clause" in Article 1 gives Congress the authority to take action on other issues unknown to the Framers of the Constitution.

3. ANALYZING LEADERSHIP

Think about the president's roles described in the Constitution. What qualities does a president need to succeed as a leader in so many different areas?

4. RECOGNIZING EFFECTS

How would you describe the impact of the 14th, 15th, and 16th Amendments on life in the United States?

5. APPLYING CITIZENSHIP

Suppose you and your family go on a road trip across several states. According to Article 4 of the Constitution, what citizens' rights do you have in the states you are visiting?

HISTORY SKILLS

INTERPRETING PRIMARY SOURCES

In 1937, President Franklin D. Roosevelt gave a speech over the radio. He used interesting comparisons to explain how the government works.

> I described the American form of government as a three-horse team provided by the Constitution to the American people so that their field might be plowed. The three horses are, of course, the three branches of government—the Congress, the Executive, and the Courts. . . . It is the American people themselves who are in the driver's seat. It is the American people themselves who want the furrow plowed.
>
> **Franklin D. Roosevelt,** Radio Address

• How does Roosevelt describe the separation of powers?

• How does Roosevelt explain popular sovereignty?

ALTERNATIVE ASSESSMENT

1. INTERDISCIPLINARY ACTIVITY: Government

Creating a Database Review the grievances against King George III listed in the Declaration of Independence. Then create a database that shows how specific sections of the U.S. Constitution addressed those grievances. Write a brief summary stating how well the Constitution addressed the grievances.

2. COOPERATIVE LEARNING ACTIVITY

Drafting a Constitution Imagine you are asked to write a constitution for a newly formed country. Working with a group, use the outline below to organize and write your constitution.

  I. Purpose of the Constitution (Preamble)

  II. Making Laws (Legislative Branch)

  III. Carrying Out the Laws (Executive Branch)

  IV. Making Laws Fair (Judicial Branch)

  V. Choosing Leaders

  VI. Citizens' Rights (Bill of Rights)

3. PRIMARY SOURCE EXPLORER

Making a Learning Center Creating the U.S. Constitution was one of the most important events in the nation's history. Use the CD-ROM and the library to collect information on different topics related to the Constitution.

Create a learning center featuring the suggestions below.

• Find biographies and portraits of the Framers.

• Collect important primary sources such as James Madison's notes and *The Federalist* papers.

• Gather recent pictures and news articles about the Congress, the president, the Supreme Court, and the Bill of Rights.

4. HISTORY PORTFOLIO

Review your draft of the constitution you wrote for the assessment activity. Choose one of these options below.

 Option 1 Use comments made by your teacher or classmates to improve your work.

 Option 2 Illustrate your constitution. Add your work to your history portfolio.

Additional Test Practice, pp. S1–S33

The Role of the Citizen

Citizens of the United States enjoy many basic rights and freedoms. Freedom of speech and religion are examples. These rights are guaranteed by the Constitution, the Bill of Rights, and other amendments to the Constitution. Along with these rights, however, come responsibilities. Obeying rules and laws, voting, and serving on juries are some examples.

Active citizenship is not limited to adults. Younger citizens can help their communities become better places. The following pages will help you to learn about your rights and responsibilities. Knowing them will help you to become an active and involved citizen of your community, state, and nation.

In this book you will find examples of active citizenship by young people like yourself. **Look for the Citizenship Today features.**

Citizen ▶ KNOW YOUR RIGHTS ▶ BE RESPONSIBLE ▶ STAY INFORMED ▶ MAKE GOOD DECISIONS ▶ PARTICIPATE IN YOUR COMMUNITY ▶ **Model Citizen**

President John F. Kennedy urged all Americans to become active citizens and work to improve their communities.

The weather was sunny but cold on January 20, 1961—the day that John F. Kennedy became the 35th president of the United States. In his first speech as president, he urged all Americans to serve their country. Since then, Kennedy's words have inspired millions of Americans to become more active citizens.

> *"Ask not what your country can do for you—ask what you can do for your country!"*
>
> —JOHN F. KENNEDY

What Is a Citizen?

A citizen is a legal member of a nation and pledges loyalty to that nation. A citizen has certain guaranteed rights, protections, and responsibilities. A citizen is a member of a community and wants to make it a good place to live.

Today in the United States there are a number of ways to become a citizen. The most familiar are citizenship by birth and citizenship by naturalization. All citizens have the right to equal protection under the law.

CITIZENSHIP BY BIRTH A child born in the United States is a citizen by birth. Children born to U.S. citizens traveling or living outside the country, such as military personnel, are citizens. Even children born in the United States to parents who are not citizens of the United States are considered U.S. citizens. These children have dual citizenship. This means they are citizens of two countries—both the United States and the country of their parents' citizenship. At the age of 18, the child may choose one of the countries for permanent citizenship.

CITIZENSHIP BY NATURALIZATION A person who is not a citizen of the United States may become one through a process called naturalization. The steps in this process are shown below. To become a naturalized citizen, a person must meet certain requirements.

- Be at least 18 years old. Children under the age of 18 automatically become naturalized citizens when their parents do.
- Enter the United States legally.
- Live in the United States for at least five years immediately prior to application.
- Read, write, and speak English.
- Show knowledge of American history and government.

Steps in the Naturalization Process

1. **File an application.**
2. **Take an examination.**
3. **File a legal petition for naturalization.**
4. **Appear at a court hearing.**
5. **Take an oath of allegiance.**

Hundreds of people become new citizens at a single ceremony in San Antonio, Texas.

What Are Your Rights?

Citizens of the United States are guaranteed rights by the U.S. Constitution, state constitutions, and state and federal laws. All citizens have three kinds of rights: basic freedoms, protection from unfair government actions, and equal treatment under the law.

Citizens' basic rights and freedoms are sometimes called **civil rights**. Some of these rights are personal, and others are political.

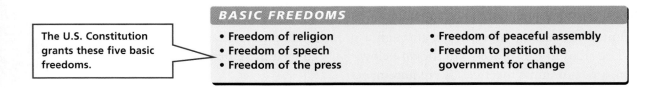

The U.S. Constitution grants these five basic freedoms.

BASIC FREEDOMS
- Freedom of religion
- Freedom of speech
- Freedom of the press
- Freedom of peaceful assembly
- Freedom to petition the government for change

The second category of rights is intended to protect citizens from unfair government actions.

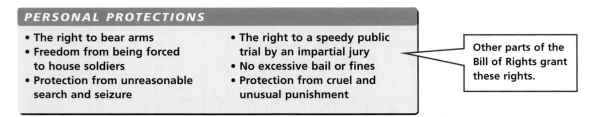

PERSONAL PROTECTIONS
- The right to bear arms
- Freedom from being forced to house soldiers
- Protection from unreasonable search and seizure
- The right to a speedy public trial by an impartial jury
- No excessive bail or fines
- Protection from cruel and unusual punishment

Other parts of the Bill of Rights grant these rights.

The third category is the right to equal treatment under the law. The government cannot treat one individual or group differently from another.

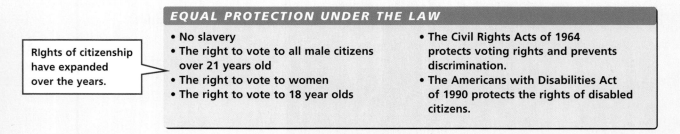

Rights of citizenship have expanded over the years.

EQUAL PROTECTION UNDER THE LAW
- No slavery
- The right to vote to all male citizens over 21 years old
- The right to vote to women
- The right to vote to 18 year olds
- The Civil Rights Acts of 1964 protects voting rights and prevents discrimination.
- The Americans with Disabilities Act of 1990 protects the rights of disabled citizens.

LIMITS TO RIGHTS The rights guaranteed to citizens have sensible limits. For example, the right to free speech does not allow a person to falsely shout, "Fire!" at a crowded concert. The government may place limits on certain rights to protect national security or to provide equal opportunities for all citizens. And rights come with responsibilities.

What Are Your Responsibilities?

For American democracy to work, citizens must carry out important responsibilities. There are two kinds of responsibilities—personal and civic. Personal responsibilities include taking care of yourself, helping your family, knowing right from wrong, and behaving in a respectful way.

Civic responsibilities are those that involve your government and community. They include obeying rules and laws, serving on juries, paying taxes, and defending your country when called upon. One of the most important responsibilities is voting. When you turn 18, you will have that right.

As a young person, you can be a good citizen in a number of ways. You might work with other people in your community to make it a fair and just place to live. Working for a political party or writing to your elected officials about issues that concern you are some other examples.

The chart below shows how responsibilities change with a citizen's age. Notice that all citizens share the responsibility to obey the laws of their communities.

Responsibilities of a Citizen

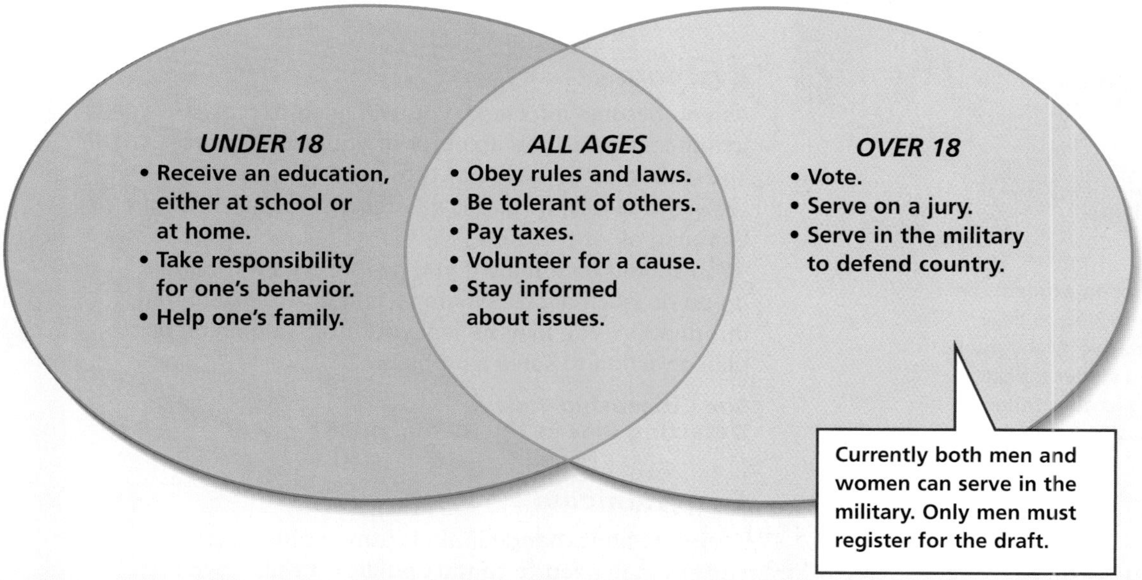

UNDER 18
- Receive an education, either at school or at home.
- Take responsibility for one's behavior.
- Help one's family.

ALL AGES
- Obey rules and laws.
- Be tolerant of others.
- Pay taxes.
- Volunteer for a cause.
- Stay informed about issues.

OVER 18
- Vote.
- Serve on a jury.
- Serve in the military to defend country.

Currently both men and women can serve in the military. Only men must register for the draft.

CITIZENSHIP ACTIVITIES

1. Interview a recently naturalized citizen. Ask about the test he or she took to become a U.S. citizen. Write a report of your findings.

2. Using newspapers or magazines, find examples of citizens using their unalienable rights or practicing responsible citizenship. Cut out five articles to illustrate the points. Mount them and write a one-sentence explanation of each article.

Building Citizenship Skills

Good citizenship skills include **staying informed, solving problems** or **making decisions,** and **taking action.** Every citizen can find ways to build citizenship skills. By showing respect for the law and for the rights of others in your daily life, you promote democracy. You can also work to change conditions in your community to make sure all citizens experience freedom and justice.

How Do You Stay Informed?

Americans can sometimes feel that they have access to too much information. It may seem overwhelming. Even so, you should stay informed on issues that affect your life. Staying informed gives you the information you need to make wise decisions and helps you find ways to solve problems.

These Texas middle school students are staying informed by talking to their Texas state representative. Many public officials enjoy having students visit and ask them questions about their jobs, and about issues students think are important.

Watch, Listen, and Read

The first step in practicing good citizenship is to know how to find information that you need.

Sources of information include broadcast and print media and the Internet. Public officials and civic organizations are also good sources for additional information. Remember as you are reading to evaluate your sources.

Evaluate

As you become informed, you will need to make judgments about the accuracy of your news sources. You must also be aware of those sources' points of view and biases. (A bias is a judgment formed without knowing all of the facts.)

You should determine if you need more information. If you do, then decide where to find it. After gathering information, you may be ready to form an opinion or a plan of action to solve a problem.

See Citizenship Today: Detecting Bias in the Media, p. 262

Communicate

To bring about change in their communities, active citizens may need to contact public officials. In today's world, making contact is easy.

You can reach most public officials by telephone, voice mail, fax, or letter. Many public officials also have Internet pages or e-mail that encourages input from the public.

See Citizenship Today: Writing to Government Officials, p. 374

How Do You Make Wise Decisions?

Civic life involves making important decisions. As a voter, whom should you vote for? As a juror, should you find the defendant guilty or not guilty? As an informed citizen, should you support or oppose a proposed government action? Unlike decisions about which video to rent, civic decisions cannot be made by a process as easy as tossing a coin. Instead, you should use a problem-solving approach like the one shown in the chart below. Decision making won't always proceed directly from step to step. Sometimes it's necessary to backtrack a little. For example, you may get to the "Analyze the Information" step and realize that you don't have enough information to analyze. Then you can go back a step and gather more information.

Problem-Solving and Decision-Making Process

Problem-solving and decision-making involves many steps. This diagram shows you how to take those steps. Notice that you may have to repeat some steps depending on the information you gather.

EVALUATE THE SOLUTION
Review the results of putting your solution into action. Did the solution work? Do you need to adjust the solution in some way?

IMPLEMENT THE SOLUTION
Take action or plan to take action on a chosen solution.

CHOOSE A SOLUTION
Choose the solution you believe will best solve the problem and help you reach your goal.

CONSIDER OPTIONS
Think of as many ways as possible to solve the problem. Don't be afraid to include ideas that others might think are unacceptable.

ANALYZE THE INFORMATION
Look at the information and determine what it reveals about solving the problem.

GATHER INFORMATION
Get to know the basics of the problem. Find out as much as possible about the issues.

IDENTIFY THE PROBLEM
Decide what the main issues are and what your goal is.

Students working on an environmental project are gathering and analyzing information to help them make decisions.

How Do You Participate in Your Community?

Across the country many young people have come up with ways to make their communities better places to live. Thirteen-year-old Aubyn Burnside of Hickory, North Carolina, is just one example. Aubyn felt sorry for foster children she saw moving their belongings in plastic trash bags. She founded Suitcases for Kids. This program provides used luggage for foster children who are moving from one home to another. Her program has been adopted by other young people in several states. Below are some ways in which you can participate in your community.

See Citizenship Today: Community Service, p. 210

Students participate in a rally to promote safety in their school.

Find a Cause

How can you become involved in your community? First, select a community problem or issue that interests you. Some ideas from other young people include starting a support group for children with cancer, publishing a neighborhood newspaper with children's stories and art, and putting on performances to entertain people in shelters and hospitals.

Develop Solutions

Once you have found a cause on which you want to work, develop a plan for solving the problem. Use the decision-making or problem-solving skills you have learned to find ways to approach the problem. You may want to involve other people in your activities.

Follow Through

Solving problems takes time. You'll need to be patient in developing a plan. You can show leadership in working with your group by following through on meetings you set up and plans you make. When you finally solve the problem, you will feel proud of your accomplishments.

CITIZENSHIP ACTIVITIES

1. Use the telephone directory to make a list of names, addresses, and phone numbers of public officials or organizations that could provide information about solving problems in your community.

2. Copy the steps in the problem-solving and decision-making diagram and show how you followed them to solve a problem or make a decision. Be sure to clearly state the problem and the final decision.

Practicing Citizenship Skills

You have learned that good citizenship involves three skills: staying informed, solving problems, and taking action. Below are some activities to help you improve your citizenship skills. By practicing these skills you can work to make a difference in your own life and in the lives of those in your community.

CITIZENSHIP ACTIVITIES

Stay Informed

CREATE A PAMPHLET OR RECRUITING COMMERCIAL

Ask your school counselors or write to your state department of education to get information on state-run colleges, universities, or technical schools. Use this information to create a brochure or recruiting commercial showing these schools and the different programs and degrees they offer.

KEEP IN MIND

What's there for me? It may help you think about what areas students are interested in and may want to pursue in later life.

Where is it? You may want to have a map showing where the schools are located in your state.

How can I afford it? Students might want to know if financial aid is available to attend the schools you have featured.

Make Wise Decisions

CREATE A GAME BOARD OR SKIT

Study the decision-making diagram on page 107. With a small group, develop a skit that explains the steps in problem solving. Present your skit to younger students in your school. As an alternative, create a game board that would help younger students understand the steps in making a decision.

KEEP IN MIND

What do children this age understand? Be sure to create a skit or game at an age-appropriate level.

What kinds of decisions do younger students make? Think about the kinds of decisions that the viewers of your skit or players of the game might make.

How can I make it interesting? Use visual aids to help students understand the steps in decision making.

Take Action

CREATE A BULLETIN BOARD FOR YOUR CLASS

Do some research on the Internet or consult the yellow pages under "Social Services" to find the names of organizations that have volunteer opportunities for young people. Call or write for more information. Then create a bulletin board for your class showing groups that would like volunteer help.

KEEP IN MIND

What kinds of jobs are they? You may want to list the types of skills or jobs volunteer groups are looking for.

How old do I have to be? Some groups may be looking for younger volunteers; others may need older persons.

How do I get there? How easy is it to get to the volunteer group's location?

REVIEW CHAPTER

3

The Growth of a Young Nation

1789–1853

The Erie Canal, which opened in 1825, increased western trade and migration.

rotary printing press

steamboat

steam locomotive

telegraph

This Currier and Ives print, *Progress of the Century,* shows some inventions of the 1800s.

You have seen many changes in American life from 1789 to 1850. Some of these are the result of new inventions, including the railroad and the telegraph. Some of your neighbors are leaving their farms to run machines in new factories. You sense the country is changing rapidly.

What Do You Think?

• What would it mean to be able to grow more grain and cotton?

• What would it mean to communicate and travel more quickly?

• How might it feel to do factory work instead of farm work?

How will new inventions change your country?

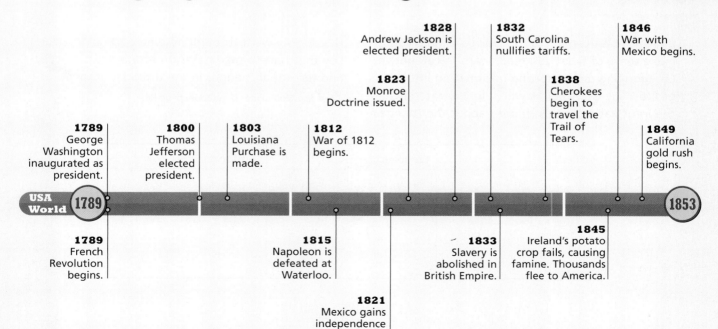

1828
Andrew Jackson is elected president.

1832
South Carolina nullifies tariffs.

1846
War with Mexico begins.

1823
Monroe Doctrine issued.

1838
Cherokees begin to travel the Trail of Tears.

1789
George Washington inaugurated as president.

1800
Thomas Jefferson elected president.

1803
Louisiana Purchase is made.

1812
War of 1812 begins.

1849
California gold rush begins.

USA
World 1789

1853

1789
French Revolution begins.

1815
Napoleon is defeated at Waterloo.

1833
Slavery is abolished in British Empire.

1845
Ireland's potato crop fails, causing famine. Thousands flee to America.

1821
Mexico gains independence from Spain.

BEFORE YOU READ

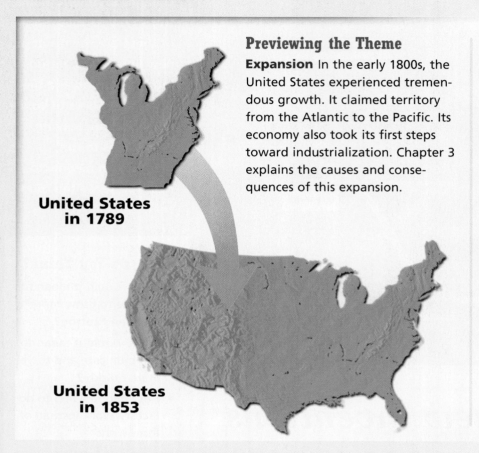

United States in 1789

United States in 1853

Previewing the Theme

Expansion In the early 1800s, the United States experienced tremendous growth. It claimed territory from the Atlantic to the Pacific. Its economy also took its first steps toward industrialization. Chapter 3 explains the causes and consequences of this expansion.

What Do You Know?

What do you think of when you hear the term *expansion*? Is expansion always a good thing?

THINK ABOUT

• what you know about inventions of the early 1800s
• how the United States extended its territory to the Pacific Ocean

What Do You Want to Know?

What questions do you have about westward expansion and early U.S. industry? Record these questions in your notebook before you read the chapter.

READ AND TAKE NOTES

Reading Strategy: Categorizing To help you make sense of what you read, learn to categorize. Categorizing means sorting information into groups. The chart below will help you categorize the information in this chapter about the changes U.S. society went through between 1789 and 1853. Use the chart to take notes on economic, political, and territorial changes in the United States.

 See Skillbuilder Handbook, page R6.

Political	Economic	Territorial

① **The Early Republic**

TERMS & NAMES
tariff
Marbury v. Madison
Louisiana Purchase
Tecumseh
Monroe Doctrine

MAIN IDEA

The United States faced great challenges in its early years.

WHY IT MATTERS NOW

Early policies and actions helped set a course for the nation.

ONE AMERICAN'S STORY

Charles Thomson had known George Washington for many years. Thomson had served as secretary of the Continental Congress when delegates from the colonies first met in Philadelphia in 1774.

Now, 15 years later, on April 14, 1789, he had come to Mount Vernon, Washington's home, with a letter announcing Washington's election as the nation's first president. Before giving Washington the letter, Thomson made a short speech.

Charles Thomson delivers the letter to Washington announcing his election as president.

A VOICE FROM THE PAST

I have now Sir to inform you that . . . your patriotism and your readiness to sacrifice . . . private enjoyments to preserve the liberty and promote the happiness of your Country [convinced the Congress that you would accept] this important Office to which you are called not only by the unanimous votes of the Electors but by the voice of America.

Charles Thomson, quoted in Washington's Papers, Library of Congress

As you will read in this section, Washington accepted the honor and the burden of his new office. He guided the nation through its early years.

The Washington Presidency

As the nation's first president, Washington faced many difficult tasks. One of the most challenging problems was managing the economy. The country had to repay war debts of more than $52 million. To win the respect of both foreign countries and its own citizens, the new nation had to show that it could manage its budget.

The job of creating an economic plan fell to Alexander Hamilton, the new secretary of the treasury. Hamilton believed in a strong central government that supported business and industry. Hamilton's plan called for the federal government to pay off all war debts. It also called for **tariffs**—taxes on imported goods—to raise money and encourage the growth of

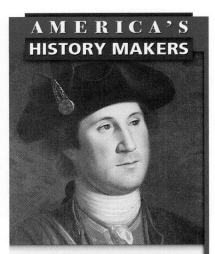

GEORGE WASHINGTON
1732–1799

At the age of 16, George Washington worked as a surveyor, setting land boundaries in the wilderness. He learned to handle hardship by hunting for food and sleeping outdoors.

In the French and Indian War, Washington had many brushes with death. Yet he wrote, "I heard the bullets whistle, and, believe me, there is something charming in the sound."

That war made him the most famous American officer. People loved him for his courage. As commander of the Continental Army, Washington's popularity helped unite Americans.

How did Washington's military record prepare him to lead the nation?

American industry. In addition, it called for the creation of a national bank that could make loans and issue currency. Hamilton's plan helped stabilize the U.S. economy and increase the power of the federal government.

In 1794, a challenge to federal taxes arose on the frontier. A group of Pennsylvania farmers refused to pay a tax on whiskey. The farmers beat up a tax collector and threatened other attacks. Washington sent troops to put down this Whiskey Rebellion, as the event was known. In doing so, he demonstrated the power and authority of the government.

Reading **History**

A. Making Inferences Why might Washington have felt it was crucial to put down the Whiskey Rebellion?

Relations with Native Americans and Other Nations

Another challenge facing the new government was how to control the Northwest Territory, the land between the Ohio River and Canada. Britain had given up its claim on this region after the American Revolution but still kept troops there. In addition, Native American groups hoped to set up an independent nation in the territory with British support.

As white American settlers moved into the Ohio Valley, they clashed with Native Americans. Washington sent in federal troops and eventually won control of the territory. Native Americans then signed a treaty surrendering much of present-day Ohio and Indiana to the U.S. government.

Events in Europe also occupied the government's attention. In 1789, a revolution in France toppled the monarchy and led to war between France and Britain.

The United States decided not to take sides in the conflict. Britain made that choice difficult by seizing U.S. ships traveling from the French West Indies. When the United States protested, Britain agreed to pay for damages to U.S. ships. Britain also agreed to withdraw its forces from the Ohio Valley.

In 1795, the United States signed a treaty with Spain. At the time, Spain controlled Florida, New Orleans, and much of North America west of the Mississippi River. The treaty gave Americans the right to travel freely on the Mississippi River. It also set clear boundaries between Spanish Florida and the United States.

After eight years in office, Washington decided to step down. In 1796, two newly formed political parties fought for the presidency: the Federalists, led by John Adams, and the Democratic-Republicans, led by Thomas Jefferson. The two parties represented different interests. The Federalists wanted a strong national government and tended to support Britain. The Democratic-Republicans wanted a limited national government and tended to support France.

The First Political Parties

FEDERALISTS	DEMOCRATIC-REPUBLICANS
Strong national government	Limited national government
Fear of mob rule	Fear of rule by one person or a powerful few
Loose construction (interpretation) of the Constitution	Strict construction (interpretation) of the Constitution
Favored national bank	Opposed national bank
Economy based on manufacturing and shipping	Economy based on farming
Supporters: lawyers, merchants, manufacturers, clergy	Supporters: farmers, tradespeople

SKILLBUILDER Interpreting Charts

1. *Which economic interests were served by the Federalists?*
2. *Which party favored a ruling elite? Which put more trust in the common people?*

*Reading*History
B. Drawing Conclusions Why did political parties develop?

Adams won the election, but Jefferson got enough votes to become vice-president. The Adams presidency was troubled by the threat of war with France and by political disputes between the two parties. Although Adams managed to avoid war, the political feuding left bitter feelings.

The Jefferson Presidency

The presidential election of 1800 produced another tough political battle. This time Jefferson defeated Adams, shifting power from the Federalists to the Democratic-Republicans.

Jefferson wanted the United States to remain a nation of small, independent farmers. Such a nation, he believed, would uphold the strong morals and democratic values he associated with country living. Jefferson believed in a modest role for the federal government and sought to end many Federalist programs. He cut the number of federal employees and reduced the size of the military.

Jefferson had less impact on the courts, however. Before leaving office, Adams had appointed many Federalist judges. One of these, John Marshall, was the Chief Justice of the Supreme Court. In a key ruling, *Marbury* **v.** *Madison* (1803), the Court established the principle of judicial review, which gives the Supreme Court final say in interpreting the Constitution. This ruling gave the Court more power than Jefferson would have liked.

In one case, however, Jefferson himself increased federal power. In 1803, France offered to sell the Louisiana Territory—a vast area stretching from the Mississippi River to the Rocky Mountains—to the United States. Although the Constitution did not specifically give the president such power, Jefferson approved the **Louisiana Purchase** for $15 million. This purchase doubled the size of the United States. Soon after, Jefferson sent Meriwether Lewis and William Clark to explore the new land.

While the United States was expanding, it also faced troubles abroad. The ongoing conflict between France and England continued to affect U.S. shipping. Both Britain and France tried to disrupt U.S. trade with their enemy.

Britain also continued to encourage Native American unrest in the Northwest Territory. James Madison, who won the presidential election of 1808, faced strong pressure to defend U.S. interests against foreign powers.

The War of 1812

As tensions increased with Britain, some Americans began to call for war. One of the key issues was the impressment, or kidnapping, of U.S. sailors by the British navy. Another was British support for **Tecumseh,** a Shawnee chief who was attempting to unite Native Americans against U.S. settlers.

When Tecumseh's warriors were forced to flee in 1811, they were welcomed in British Canada. Some American leaders called for Britain's removal from Canada, while others urged retaliation against British aggression at sea. Congress declared war on Britain on June 18, 1812.

The War of 1812 had two main phases. In the first phase, Britain focused on its war against France and devoted little energy to the North American conflict. The U.S. Navy won several key victories, including a hard-fought battle on Lake Erie.

The second phase began after Britain defeated France in 1814 and turned its full attention to the American campaign. British troops sacked Washington, D.C., burning the Capitol and the president's mansion. Then they laid siege to Fort McHenry at Baltimore. During that battle, Francis Scott Key, an American prisoner on a British ship, was inspired to write the "Star-Spangled Banner," which became the national anthem in 1931.

At Lake Champlain, the Americans fought back, preventing a British invasion from Canada. In the last battle of the war, Andrew Jackson's troops scored a dramatic victory over the British at New Orleans. This battle actually took place after a peace treaty had been signed in Europe but before the news could reach the city.

The War of 1812 had no clear winner. No land changed hands, and trade disputes were left unresolved. Even so, the war did have important effects. The actions of heroic military leaders like Andrew Jackson fueled American patriotism. The war also broke the strength of Native American resistance to U.S. expansion.

*Reading*History
C. Analyzing Causes How could the Battle of New Orleans have taken place after a peace treaty was signed?

The Effects of the War

WAR

| Increased American patriotism | Weakened Native American resistance | U.S. manufacturing grew |

SKILLBUILDER Interpreting Charts
Which effect do you think resulted from the war's interruption of U.S. trade?

In addition, the disruption of trade caused by the war encouraged the growth of U.S. manufacturing. Above all, the United States showed that it could defend itself against the mightiest military power of the time. Many Americans now believed that the country would survive and prosper.

The Monroe Doctrine

After the war, a strong feeling of national unity swept the United States. In 1816, Democratic-Republican James Monroe was elected president. He faced little opposition from the Federalist Party. In 1820, Monroe was reelected.

One of Monroe's goals was to protect the country from any interference from foreign powers. The main threat seemed to come from European monarchies that hoped to regain control of Latin American territories that had recently won their independence. Monroe feared that European meddling in Latin America might threaten the United States.

Background
Latin America refers to the Spanish- and Portuguese-speaking nations of the Western Hemisphere south of the United States.

In December 1823, the president issued a statement that became known as the **Monroe Doctrine.** Monroe said that the Americas were closed to further colonization. He also warned that any European efforts to reestablish colonies would be considered "dangerous to our peace and safety." Over time, the Monroe Doctrine became an important part of U.S. foreign policy. It was used to justify many U.S. actions in the Western Hemisphere.

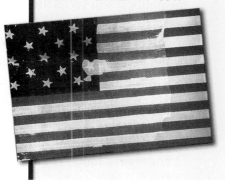

America's HERITAGE

THE STAR-SPANGLED BANNER

The "Star-Spangled Banner," inspired by the flag that flew over Fort McHenry (see below), continues to move Americans. On hearing this national anthem, patriotic listeners stand, take off their hats, and put their hands over their hearts. These actions pay respect to the American flag and the song that celebrates it.

Francis Scott Key's song enjoyed widespread popularity for more than 100 years before an act of Congress made it the national anthem in 1931.

 Section 1 Assessment

1. Terms & Names

Explain the significance of:
- tariff
- *Marbury* v. *Madison*
- Louisiana Purchase
- Tecumseh
- Monroe Doctrine

2. Taking Notes

Use a chart like the one below to show causes and effects of the War of 1812.

Causes		Effects
	→	

3. Main Ideas

a. What were the elements of Alexander Hamilton's economic plan?

b. Why was the Northwest Territory an area of conflict?

c. What was Thomas Jefferson's vision for the United States?

4. Critical Thinking

Analyzing Points of View Why did Tecumseh think it was important for Native Americans to unite?

THINK ABOUT
- what he observed about white settlement
- what Native Americans would lose if they did not act together

ACTIVITY OPTIONS

LANGUAGE ARTS
ART

Imagine that you are a member of the Lewis and Clark expedition. Write a **letter** or illustrate a **journal entry** about one of the places you see on your journey.

② Jackson and Reform

TERMS & NAMES
Jacksonian
 democracy
Indian Removal Act
Trail of Tears
nullification
cotton gin
Frederick Douglass
abolition
Seneca Falls
 Convention

MAIN IDEA	WHY IT MATTERS NOW
Democracy expanded and reform movements changed American society in the early 1800s.	Many reforms of the period still influence democratic institutions in the United States today.

ONE AMERICAN'S STORY

Margaret Bayard Smith was 22 years old when she married and moved to Washington, D.C., in 1800. For the next 40 years, she and her husband, a government official, were central figures in the political and social life of Washington. They entertained presidents from Thomas Jefferson to Andrew Jackson.

Smith wrote about life in Washington. In 1824, she described how John Quincy Adams reacted to his election as president.

A VOICE FROM THE PAST

When the news of his election was communicated to Mr. Adams by the Committee . . . the sweat rolled down his face—he shook from head to foot and was so agitated that he could scarcely stand or speak.

Margaret Bayard Smith, *The First Forty Years of Washington Society*

Adams had reason to be shaken by his election. It had been hotly contested, and he knew that he would face much opposition as he tried to govern. In this section, you will learn how Adams defeated Andrew Jackson in 1824, only to lose to him four years later.

Margaret Bayard Smith wrote about life in the nation's capital in the first half of the 19th century.

Jackson Takes Office

In the election of 1824, Jackson won more votes than any other candidate. He did not, however, get a majority of electoral votes. According to the Constitution, the House of Representatives had to choose the president, and it chose John Quincy Adams.

Charging that the presidency had been stolen from him, Jackson waged a tough campaign for the 1828 election. He claimed that Adams represented wealthy Easterners, while he stood for the common man. He pledged to extend power to more of the people. This idea became known as **Jacksonian democracy**. After winning a resounding victory, Jackson set out to reform government to reflect his ideas of democracy. As a first step, he appointed many of his supporters to official positions.

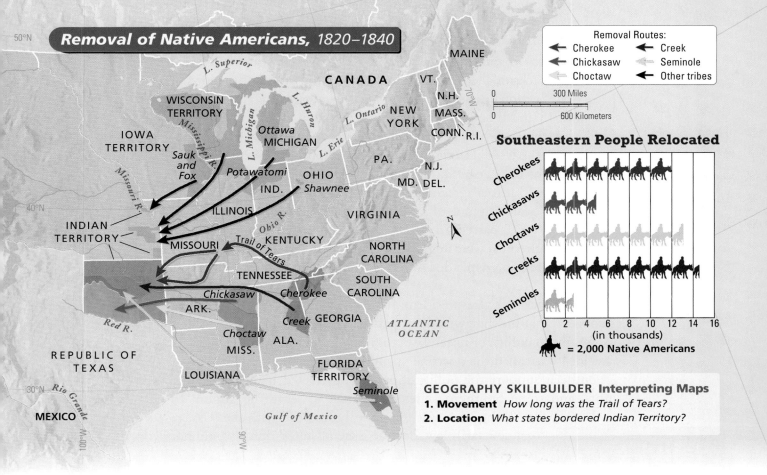

Removal of Native Americans, 1820–1840

Removal Routes:
- ← Cherokee ← Creek
- ← Chickasaw ← Seminole
- ← Choctaw ← Other tribes

Southeastern People Relocated

= 2,000 Native Americans

GEOGRAPHY SKILLBUILDER Interpreting Maps
1. **Movement** *How long was the Trail of Tears?*
2. **Location** *What states bordered Indian Territory?*

Jackson's Native American Policy

One of the most important issues Jackson faced as president was the place of Native Americans in the United States. Many Native Americans still lived east of the Mississippi River, particularly in the Southeast. White settlers wanted their land, and tensions grew. The discovery of gold on Cherokee lands in Georgia fueled demands by many white Americans to move Native Americans westward.

Jackson favored government controls over Native Americans. He regarded them as conquered subjects with limited rights. In 1830, he signed the **Indian Removal Act,** which called for the government to negotiate treaties that would require Native Americans to move west.

Most Southeast tribes signed the treaties and relocated to Indian Territory, an area covering modern-day Oklahoma and parts of Kansas and Nebraska. But many Cherokees refused to move. They were rounded up and forcibly marched west in the winter of 1838–1839. This harsh journey, in which one-fourth of the marchers died, became known as the **Trail of Tears.**

Some Native Americans fought back. Seminoles battled U.S. troops in Florida for years, while tribes in the Ohio Valley rose up in the Black Hawk War. Eventually, though, the government subdued Native American resistance east of the Mississippi River.

Reading **History**

A. Forming and Supporting Opinions Did the government have a right to relocate Native Americans? Why or why not?

The Nullification Crisis

In addition to growing tensions between Native Americans and white Americans, Jackson also faced tensions among the different sections of the nation. Sectional tensions had previously emerged over the issue of slavery. In 1819, Missouri had applied for statehood as a slave state. This application threatened to overturn the balance between slave states and free states in the Union. In the Missouri Compromise of 1820, Congress maintained the balance by admitting Missouri as a slave state and Maine as a free state. But this agreement did not end sectional conflict.

By the time Jackson took office in 1829, another sectional dispute was brewing. A tariff passed in 1828 raised the cost of manufactured imports. Southerners were angry about this tariff because the South, an agricultural region, depended on imported products more than the North did.

In 1830, Jackson's vice-president, John C. Calhoun of South Carolina, announced that his state would not pay the tariff. He claimed that states had a right to nullify, or reject, laws they believed were unconstitutional. This idea was called the doctrine of **nullification.**

Southern support for nullification prompted a debate over states' rights, and some Southern states threatened to leave the Union. In 1833, the issue was temporarily resolved with the passage of a new tariff law. But the issue of states' rights would not go away.

*Reading*History

B. Analyzing Causes Why was the South more dependent on imports than the North?

daily *life*

SPIRITUALS
Singing spirituals offered comfort for pain, bound people together at religious meetings, and eased the boredom of daily tasks. This verse came from a spiritual sung by slaves in Missouri.

Dear Lord, dear lord, when slavery'll cease
Then we poor souls will have our peace;—
There's a better day a coming,
Will you go along with me?
There's a better day a coming,
Go sound the jubilee!

The Expansion of Slavery

Tariffs, however, were not at the heart of sectional tensions. Slavery was. The Southern economy depended on slave labor. In 1793, the invention of the **cotton gin**—a machine that cleaned cotton—stimulated a boom in cotton production. Before long, cotton plantations and slavery were expanding westward.

Most cotton was grown on large plantations that had many slaves. But even whites who were small farmers with no slaves still supported slavery. They hoped that they, too, would someday become plantation owners and slaveholders themselves.

Enslaved African Americans made up about one-third of the South's population in 1840. Some worked as domestic servants or factory hands. Most, however, performed back-breaking labor in the fields.

To survive the brutal conditions of plantation life, African Americans relied on the strength of their emerging culture. This culture featured strong religious convictions and music. Family bonds were also very important, but the slave system often separated

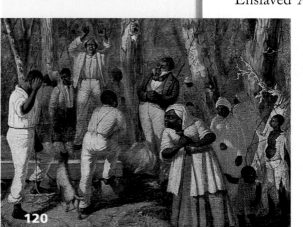

families, including children from their parents. **Frederick Douglass** recalled his experience of slavery.

> *A VOICE FROM THE PAST*
>
> I do not recollect of [remember] ever seeing my mother by the light of day. She was with me in the night. She would lie down with me, and get me to sleep, but long before I waked she was gone.
>
> **Frederick Douglass,** *Narrative of the Life of Frederick Douglass*

*Reading*History

C. Recognizing Effects What effects did slavery have on enslaved people?

Douglass later resisted slavery by running away to the North. Other enslaved people resisted slavery with violence. Over the years, numerous slave rebellions erupted across the South. Fearful whites responded by placing even harsher controls on the slave population.

Reform Movements

The evils of slavery gave rise to the movement to end slavery, called **abolition.** It began in the late 1700s. By 1804, most Northern states had abolished slavery. Abolitionists then began to push for a law ending slavery in the South.

Free blacks, such as Frederick Douglass and Sojourner Truth, were prominent abolitionists. Both Douglass and Truth were former slaves. Douglass published an antislavery paper, the *North Star,* and was a powerful speaker. Truth was also a powerful speaker who drew huge crowds to hear her. Perhaps the most famous abolitionist was William Lloyd Garrison, a white Northerner. He published an abolitionist newspaper, *The Liberator.*

Reformers' Hall of Fame

William Lloyd Garrison

Even after being threatened with hanging, Garrison continued to publish his antislavery newspaper, *The Liberator.*

Sojourner Truth and Harriet Tubman

Truth spoke out for both abolition and women's rights. Tubman risked her life leading people to freedom on the Underground Railroad.

Lucretia Mott and Susan B. Anthony

An abolitionist, Mott also helped lead the movement for women's rights. Anthony fought for women's suffrage into the 20th century.

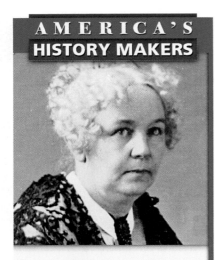

ELIZABETH CADY STANTON
1815–1902

Elizabeth Cady Stanton's first memory was the birth of a sister when she was four. So many people said, "What a pity it is she's a girl!" that Stanton felt sorry for the new baby. She later wrote, "I did not understand at that time that girls were considered an inferior order of beings."

When Stanton was 11, her only brother died. Her father said, "Oh, my daughter, I wish you were a boy!" That sealed Stanton's determination to prove that girls were just as important as boys.

How did Stanton's childhood experiences motivate her to help other people besides herself?

Other abolitionists helped slaves escape to freedom. They developed the Underground Railroad—a series of escape routes from the South to the North. Runaway slaves traveled by night and hid by day. The people who led them to freedom were called conductors. One of the most famous conductors was an escaped slave named Harriet Tubman. Tubman made 19 dangerous journeys to free enslaved persons.

Abolition helped give rise to the struggle for women's rights. In 1840, two abolitionists—Lucretia Mott and Elizabeth Cady Stanton—traveled to an antislavery conference in London. When they arrived, they were told that women would not be allowed to speak at the convention. This experience convinced them to fight for women's rights.

In the 1800s, women enjoyed few legal or political rights. They could not vote, sit on juries, or hold public office. In 1848, Mott and Stanton organized a women's rights convention in Seneca Falls, New York. The **Seneca Falls Convention** published a declaration calling for equality and basic rights for women.

Other women also joined the struggle. Susan B. Anthony was a skilled organizer who built the women's movement into a national organization. Her efforts helped produce laws that gave married women the right to own property.

The early 1800s also saw reform efforts in other areas. Reformers fought for workers' rights and a public education system. They also worked to improve conditions for the needy. These reform movements laid the foundation for many traits of modern American society.

Reading **History**

D. Forming and Supporting Opinions Why do you think women were denied equal rights? Are they still?

Section 2 Assessment

1. Terms & Names

Explain the significance of:
• Jacksonian democracy
• Indian Removal Act
• Trail of Tears
• nullification
• cotton gin
• Frederick Douglass
• abolition
• Seneca Falls Convention

2. Taking Notes

On a time line like the one below, record significant events covered in this section.

1804   1848

3. Main Ideas

a. What was Andrew Jackson's policy toward Native Americans?

b. Why did slavery expand in the South?

c. What did abolitionists do to fight slavery?

4. Critical Thinking

Drawing Conclusions Why did the idea of nullification provoke a crisis?

THINK ABOUT
• what Southern states were demanding
• what those demands meant for the Union

ACTIVITY OPTIONS

TECHNOLOGY

DRAMA

With a partner, act out a meeting between two of the people discussed in this section. **Videotape** their conversation or **perform** it for the class.

(3) Manifest Destiny

TERMS & NAMES

Industrial
 Revolution

manifest destiny

War with Mexico

Treaty of
 Guadalupe
 Hidalgo

California gold
 rush

MAIN IDEA	WHY IT MATTERS NOW
The United States experienced great economic and geographic expansion by 1853.	Size and economic strength have helped make the United States a world power.

ONE AMERICAN'S STORY

In 1789, the Englishman Samuel Slater sailed to the United States under a false name. It was illegal for textile workers like him to leave the country. Britain wanted no other nation to copy its new machines for making thread and cloth. But Slater was going to bring the secret to America. When he got to New York, he wrote a letter to Rhode Island investor Moses Brown.

A VOICE FROM THE PAST

A few days ago I was informed that you wanted a manager of *cotton spinning* . . . in which business I flatter myself that I can give the greatest satisfaction, in making machinery, making good yarn, either for stockings or twist, as any that is made in England.

Samuel Slater, quoted in *Samuel Slater: Father of American Manufactures*

Samuel Slater's mill was located in Pawtucket, Rhode Island.

   With Brown's backing, Slater built the first successful water-powered textile mill in America. In this section, you will learn about the economic growth and development of the United States in the early 1800s.

Economic Growth

The growth of textile mills was part of the **Industrial Revolution**. During this period of change—from the late 1700s to the late 1800s—factory machines replaced hand tools, and large-scale manufacturing replaced farming as the main form of work for many people. Factories brought many workers and machines together under one roof. Towns like Waltham and Lowell, Massachusetts, attracted workers to jobs in clothing factories. Often, these mills employed young women, who made higher wages than they could on farms.

   New inventions and methods of production had a tremendous impact on the American economy and society. For example, the development of interchangeable parts—parts that are exactly alike—allowed for more efficient manufacturing. The steamboat and the telegraph improved transportation and communication. Other inventions—like the cotton gin and the mechanical reaper—increased farm production.

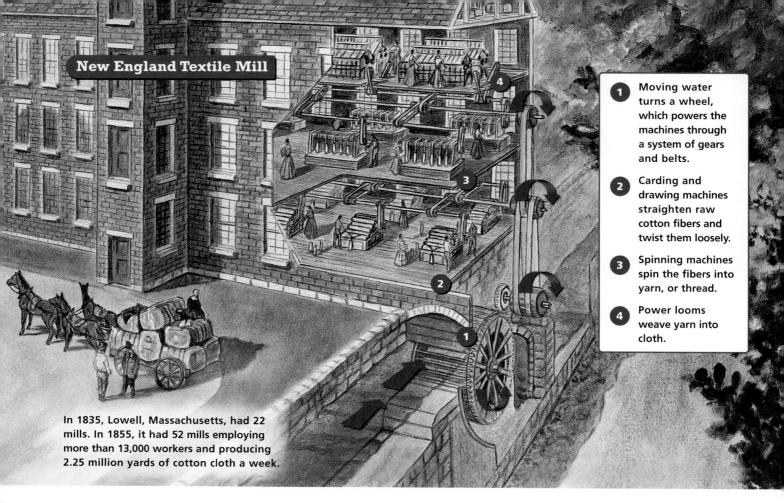

New England Textile Mill

1. Moving water turns a wheel, which powers the machines through a system of gears and belts.

2. Carding and drawing machines straighten raw cotton fibers and twist them loosely.

3. Spinning machines spin the fibers into yarn, or thread.

4. Power looms weave yarn into cloth.

In 1835, Lowell, Massachusetts, had 22 mills. In 1855, it had 52 mills employing more than 13,000 workers and producing 2.25 million yards of cotton cloth a week.

Improvements in production and transportation meant that rural farm regions could provide food for urban industrial areas, and receive factory goods in return. New roads, canals, and railroads were built to link the different parts of the country. Completion of the Erie Canal, in 1825, connected the Great Lakes with the Atlantic Ocean and helped make New York City the country's leading commercial center. Railroads, first used in the 1830s, were also expanding rapidly by 1850.

Reading **History**
A. Drawing Conclusions How do you think Americans felt about the economic changes taking place in the early 1800s?

Trails West

Another important change taking place in American life was the quickening pace of movement to the West. Following the Louisiana Purchase in 1803, the American West extended far west of the Mississippi River. Many Americans believed that the nation would extend its territory from the Atlantic Ocean to the Pacific. This belief is called **manifest destiny**. To many people, the West offered a chance to make money or start a new life.

At first only a few white Americans traveled west of the Mississippi. Some of these people were called mountain men. They trapped small animals and sold the furs to eastern businessmen. On their journeys, the mountain men blazed trails for others to follow. Soon, settlers were moving west to farm. They were joined by manufacturers and merchants, who hoped to earn money by making and selling items that farmers needed.

ReadingHistory

B. Finding Main Ideas What were the Santa Fe Trail and Oregon Trail?

One of the first major routes west was the Santa Fe Trail, which stretched from Missouri to Santa Fe, New Mexico. Traders made large profits bringing American goods to New Mexican settlers.

Another important westward route was the Oregon Trail, which ran from Independence, Missouri, to the Oregon Territory. The first travelers on this route were missionaries, who sent back glowing reports about Oregon. These stories tempted people to make the journey. In 1843, nearly 1,000 people traveled to Oregon. The next year, twice as many went.

The War with Mexico

In the 1820s, Texas was a Mexican territory. Mexico encouraged U.S. settlers to move there. The American settlers were required to obey Mexican law. Over time, tensions grew between the Americans and the Mexican government. Some settlers began to talk of independence.

To maintain control, Mexico's president, General Antonio López de Santa Anna, sent troops to Texas. Fighting soon broke out. At the Battle of the Alamo, a small band of rebels was crushed by a much larger Mexican force. The Texans fought back, though. At the Battle of San Jacinto, they defeated the Mexican army and forced Santa Anna to surrender. In 1836, Texas became an independent republic.

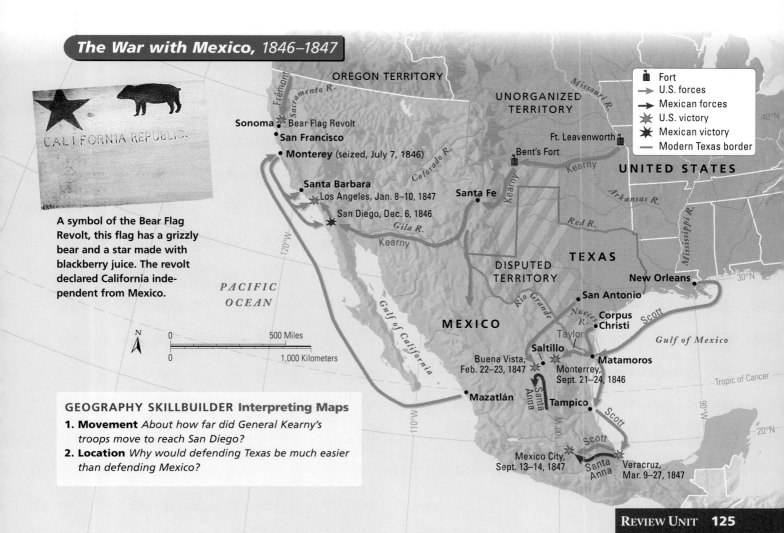

The War with Mexico, 1846–1847

A symbol of the Bear Flag Revolt, this flag has a grizzly bear and a star made with blackberry juice. The revolt declared California independent from Mexico.

GEOGRAPHY SKILLBUILDER Interpreting Maps

1. **Movement** About how far did General Kearny's troops move to reach San Diego?
2. **Location** Why would defending Texas be much easier than defending Mexico?

Many Southerners wanted to bring Texas into the Union as a slave state. Northerners objected because it would give the slave states more power in Congress. But the pressures for expansion grew, and Congress admitted Texas as a slave state in 1845.

Mexico was furious at the annexation of Texas. It still claimed Texas and said it would fight to defend its claim. In 1846, fighting broke out between Mexico and the United States. The **War with Mexico** would result in great territorial gain for the United States.

Despite protests from some Americans—who charged that the United States had provoked Mexico—the U.S. Army moved quickly to win the war. One U.S. force entered northern Mexico and defeated Santa Anna's army. Another U.S. force headed west and captured New Mexico. Meanwhile, Americans in California rebelled against Mexican rule. U.S. troops joined the rebels and took California. Then, U.S. forces landed at Veracruz and marched to Mexico City. Despite fierce resistance, the U.S. Army captured Mexico City in 1847.

In 1848, the war officially ended with the **Treaty of Guadalupe Hidalgo.** In this treaty, Mexico recognized Texas as part of the United States and set the border at the Rio Grande. Mexico also gave up a vast region that included the present-day states of California, Nevada, Utah, most of Arizona, and parts of New Mexico, Colorado, and Wyoming.

Growth of the United States, *1783–1853*

Ceded to Great Britain, 1818

Ceded by Great Britain, 1818

Ceded by Great Britain, Webster-Ashburton Treaty, 1842

CANADA

OREGON TERRITORY
From Great Britain, 1846

LOUISIANA PURCHASE
Bought from France, 1803

From Great Britain by Treaty of Paris, 1783

Original 13 Colonies

MEXICAN CESSION
From Mexico by Treaty of Guadalupe Hidalgo, 1848

PACIFIC OCEAN

ATLANTIC OCEAN

GADSDEN PURCHASE
Bought from Mexico, 1853

TEXAS ANNEXATION
Annexed Independent Republic, 1845

Ceded by Spain, 1818

1810 Annexed by United States

1813

FLORIDA CESSION
From Spain, 1819

Modern U.S. boundaries shown.

Gulf of Mexico

GEOGRAPHY SKILLBUILDER Interpreting Maps

1. Region *How many states or parts of states were created by all the lands added after 1844?*

2. Region *Which addition to the United States after 1783 added the greatest area of land?*

0   300 Miles
0   600 Kilometers

This transfer of territory is called the Mexican Cession. The loss was a bitter defeat for Mexico. In return, the United States paid Mexico $15 million. In 1853, the United States paid Mexico another $10 million for a strip of land just west of Texas. This purchase, called the Gadsden Purchase, gave the continental United States its modern borders.

The California Gold Rush

The war was barely over when astounding news came from California. Gold had been discovered in the Sacramento Valley. Soon, miners found more gold in the Sierra Nevada Mountains.

Almost overnight, the **California gold rush** had begun. By 1849, thousands of gold-seekers rushed to California. About two-thirds of the forty-niners, as the miners were known, were white American men. But Native Americans and African Americans also arrived. So did immigrants from overseas, including many from China. A few of these miners made fortunes, but most struggled to survive.

By 1852, the gold rush was over. Although short, its impact was far-reaching. While it lasted, about 250,000 people flooded into California. This huge migration caused economic growth that changed California permanently. The port city of San Francisco grew rapidly to become a center of banking, manufacturing, shipping, and trade.

One major effect of the gold rush was that California had enough people to apply for statehood. Skipping the territorial stage, California applied to Congress for admission to the Union and was admitted as a free state in 1850. On a national level, California's statehood created turmoil. Before 1850, there were an equal number of slave states and free states. Now the balance had tipped to the free states. Southerners feared that Northerners might use their majority to abolish slavery. In the next chapter, you will read how tensions over slavery led to the Civil War.

Reading **History**

C. Identifying Problems What do you think some negative effects of the gold rush were?

Section 3 Assessment

1. Terms & Names

Explain the significance of:
- Industrial Revolution
- manifest destiny
- War with Mexico
- Treaty of Guadalupe Hidalgo
- California gold rush

2. Taking Notes

Use a cluster diagram like the one shown below to review details about the War with Mexico.

3. Main Ideas

a. Why did Americans travel west in the early 1800s?

b. How did Texas gain independence from Mexico?

c. What were some effects of the California gold rush?

4. Critical Thinking

Evaluating Information How did the Industrial Revolution promote economic growth?

THINK ABOUT
- new inventions and factories
- transportation and communication

ACTIVITY OPTIONS

MATH

GEOGRAPHY

In an almanac, find the current population of the states formed from the Mexican Cession. Create a **graph** or a **map** to display the information.

The Growth of a Young Nation

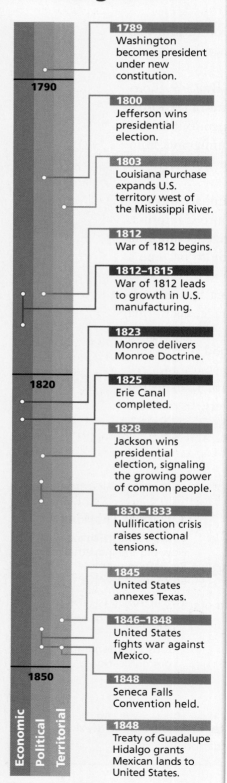

1789
Washington becomes president under new constitution.

1790

1800
Jefferson wins presidential election.

1803
Louisiana Purchase expands U.S. territory west of the Mississippi River.

1812
War of 1812 begins.

1812–1815
War of 1812 leads to growth in U.S. manufacturing.

1823
Monroe delivers Monroe Doctrine.

1820

1825
Erie Canal completed.

1828
Jackson wins presidential election, signaling the growing power of common people.

1830–1833
Nullification crisis raises sectional tensions.

1845
United States annexes Texas.

1846–1848
United States fights war against Mexico.

1850

1848
Seneca Falls Convention held.

1848
Treaty of Guadalupe Hidalgo grants Mexican lands to United States.

Economic Political Territorial

TERMS & NAMES

Briefly explain the significance of each of the following.

1. *Marbury v. Madison*
2. Louisiana Purchase
3. Monroe Doctrine
4. Trail of Tears
5. Frederick Douglass
6. abolition
7. Industrial Revolution
8. manifest destiny
9. Treaty of Guadalupe Hidalgo
10. California gold rush

REVIEW QUESTIONS

The Early Republic (pages 113–117)

1. What were two major problems that arose on the Western frontier during the early years of the American republic?
2. Why did the United States have trouble remaining neutral in European conflicts?
3. How did the War of 1812 boost American confidence?

Jackson and Reform (pages 118–122)

4. What caused the nullification crisis?
5. How did slavery expand in the early 1800s?
6. What were four key reform movements of the early 1800s?

Manifest Destiny (pages 123–127)

7. How did the U.S. economy change in the early 1800s?
8. What caused westward migration?
9. What were the results of the War with Mexico?
10. How did California gain statehood?

CRITICAL THINKING

1. USING YOUR NOTES

Political	Economic	Territorial

Using your completed chart, answer the questions below.

a. What political changes occurred with Andrew Jackson's rise to the presidency?

b. How did the War of 1812 affect the U.S. economy?

c. How did the War with Mexico affect U.S. territorial claims?

2. FORMING AND SUPPORTING OPINIONS

What was the most crucial issue facing the United States during the early years of the republic? Why?

3. MAKING GENERALIZATIONS

What were two differences that divided North and South in the early 1800s? How were the issues linked?

4. ANALYZING LEADERSHIP

Which leader or public figure discussed in this chapter had the greatest influence on U.S. history? Explain your answer.

5. THEME: EXPANSION

How did the idea of manifest destiny help bring about the expansion of the United States?

Interact *with* History

Did you predict the ways that new inventions would change the country? What surprised you?

HISTORY SKILLS

1. INTERPRETING MAPS: Movement
Study the map. Answer the questions.

Settlement of Texas

- Amarillo
- Dallas
- El Paso
- Austin
- Houston
- San Antonio

T E X A S

Gulf of Mexico

35°N
30°N
25°N
105°W
100°W
95°W

N

Legend:
- Before 1800
- Between 1800 and 1850
- Between 1850 and 1870
- Between 1870 and 1890
- After 1890

Basic Map Elements
a. What is the subject of the map?
b. What years are covered by the map?
c. What do the colors indicate?

Interpreting the Map
d. Which area of Texas was settled first?
e. In what general direction was Texas settled?

2. INTERPRETING PRIMARY SOURCES
This photograph was taken of a man who planned to go to California to find gold. Study the photo carefully. Answer the questions.

a. What does the photo reveal about the man's expectations of danger?

b. What does the photo suggest about how successful he hopes to be?

ALTERNATIVE ASSESSMENT

1. INTERDISCIPLINARY ACTIVITY: SCIENCE
Creating a Diagram Do research to learn how gold is deposited into veins in the earth and how erosion later exposes the gold. Draw diagrams showing the processes of gold vein formation and erosion. Share your diagram with the class.

2. COOPERATIVE LEARNING ACTIVITY
Planning an Exhibit As a class, plan a museum exhibit to show what slavery was like on cotton plantations. Break into small groups to research different topics—for example, what enslaved people wore, what their houses were like, what rules they lived under, and what stories they told. Bring back your research and decide how you can best share what you learned with an audience. Part of your exhibit might be a model of a plantation or dramatic readings from slave narratives.

3. PRIMARY SOURCE EXPLORER
Planning Foreign Policy The Monroe Doctrine was President Monroe's outline for U.S. foreign policy early in the 19th century. Using the Primary Source Explorer CD-ROM, library, and Internet, find out more about the Monroe Doctrine.

Imagine that you are president of the United States. Come up with four main principles of foreign policy that this country should follow in the 21st century.

- With classmates, talk about broad principles from the Monroe Doctrine, such as keeping out of European conflicts or protecting free republics.

- Decide whether you agree or disagree with these principles. Think of current U.S. policies that follow or reject them.

- As president, decide how you will communicate U.S. foreign policy for the 21st century to the public. If you make a televised speech, what facts and visual aids would be most persuasive?

4. HISTORY PORTFOLIO
Review your section and chapter assessment activities. Select one that you think is your best work. Then use comments made by your teacher or classmates to improve your work and add it to your portfolio.

Additional Test Practice, pp. S1–S33

TEST PRACTICE
CLASSZONE.COM

The Union in Peril 1850–1877

In this vivid engraving, South Carolina shore guns fire on Fort Sumter in Charleston's harbor.

Interact *with* History

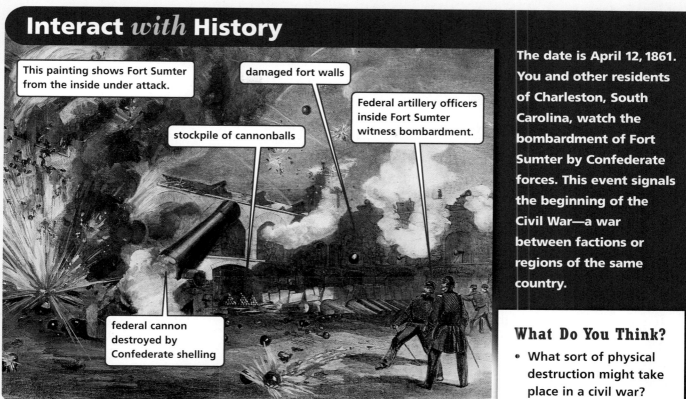

This painting shows Fort Sumter from the inside under attack.

damaged fort walls

Federal artillery officers inside Fort Sumter witness bombardment.

stockpile of cannonballs

federal cannon destroyed by Confederate shelling

The date is April 12, 1861. You and other residents of Charleston, South Carolina, watch the bombardment of Fort Sumter by Confederate forces. This event signals the beginning of the Civil War—a war between factions or regions of the same country.

What Do You Think?

- What sort of physical destruction might take place in a civil war?
- What social, political, and economic trouble might be likely to occur in a civil war?
- What might happen when a civil war breaks out?

How might a civil war be worse than other wars?

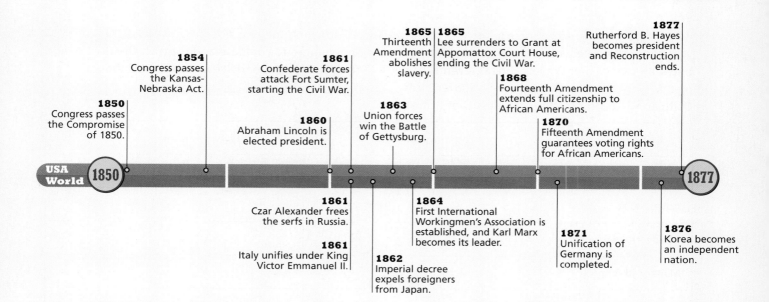

1850 Congress passes the Compromise of 1850.

1854 Congress passes the Kansas-Nebraska Act.

1860 Abraham Lincoln is elected president.

1861 Confederate forces attack Fort Sumter, starting the Civil War.

1863 Union forces win the Battle of Gettysburg.

1865 Thirteenth Amendment abolishes slavery.

1865 Lee surrenders to Grant at Appomattox Court House, ending the Civil War.

1868 Fourteenth Amendment extends full citizenship to African Americans.

1870 Fifteenth Amendment guarantees voting rights for African Americans.

1877 Rutherford B. Hayes becomes president and Reconstruction ends.

USA World

1850

1877

1861 Czar Alexander frees the serfs in Russia.

1861 Italy unifies under King Victor Emmanuel II.

1862 Imperial decree expels foreigners from Japan.

1864 First International Workingmen's Association is established, and Karl Marx becomes its leader.

1871 Unification of Germany is completed.

1876 Korea becomes an independent nation.

BEFORE YOU READ

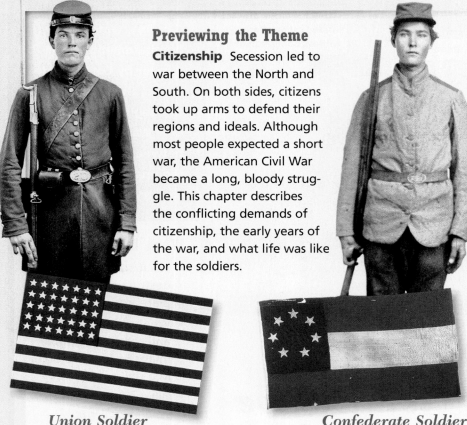

Previewing the Theme

Citizenship Secession led to war between the North and South. On both sides, citizens took up arms to defend their regions and ideals. Although most people expected a short war, the American Civil War became a long, bloody struggle. This chapter describes the conflicting demands of citizenship, the early years of the war, and what life was like for the soldiers.

Union Soldier

Confederate Soldier

What Do You Know?

What do you think of when you hear the phrase *civil war*? What would it be like to fight in a war of brother against brother? Where and how did the Civil War begin?

THINK ABOUT

- what a civil war is
- what you've learned about the Civil War from movies, television, and books
- reasons that countries threaten to break apart in today's world

What Do You Want to Know?

What details do you need to help you understand the outbreak of the Civil War? Make a list of those details in your notebook before you read the chapter.

READ AND TAKE NOTES

Reading Strategy: Comparing and Contrasting
When you compare, you look for similarities between two or more objects, ideas, events, or people. When you contrast, you look for differences. Comparing and contrasting can be a useful strategy for studying the two sides in a war. Use the chart shown here to compare and contrast the North and the South in the early years of the Civil War.

S See Skillbuilder Handbook, page R11.

	North	South
Reasons for fighting		
Advantages		
Disadvantages		
Military strategy		
Battle victories		

① The Nation Breaking Apart

TERMS & NAMES
Compromise of 1850
Dred Scott v. *Sandford*
Abraham Lincoln
secede
Confederate States of America
Jefferson Davis

MAIN IDEA	WHY IT MATTERS NOW
Disagreements over slavery led the Southern states to secede from the Union.	The sectional crisis caused by slavery led to the Civil War.

ONE EUROPEAN'S STORY

Alexis de Tocqueville [TOHK•vihl] was a young French government official from a wealthy family. In 1831, he set out to study American prisons and politics. At one point, Tocqueville traveled by steamship down the Ohio River. The river was the border between Ohio, a free state, and Kentucky, a slave state. Tocqueville noted what he saw on both sides of the river.

Alexis de Tocqueville

A VOICE FROM THE PAST

The State of Ohio is separated from Kentucky just by one river; on either side of it the soil is equally fertile, and the situation equally favourable, and yet everything is different. Here [on the Ohio side] a population devoured by feverish activity, trying every means to make its fortune. . . . There [on the Kentucky side] are people who make others work for them and show little compassion, a people without energy, mettle or the spirit of enterprise. . . . These differences cannot be attributed to any other cause but slavery. It degrades the black population and enervates [saps the energy of] the white.

Alexis de Tocqueville, *Journey to America*

Tocqueville's comment was aimed not at the southern people as individuals but at the system of slavery itself. In this section, you'll read about the differences between the North and the South. You'll learn how slavery led to political tensions that threatened to tear the nation apart.

Sectional Tensions

The economies of the North and the South developed differently in the early 1800s. While the North began to develop more industry and commerce, the Southern economy relied on plantation farming. In the South, a few wealthy planters made great profits from the labor of their slaves, especially by exporting cotton.

The issue of slavery caused tension between the North and the South. Some Northerners opposed slavery because they thought it was unjust. Others viewed it as a threat to workers who might lose jobs to slave labor. But slaveholders were determined to defend slavery.

The expansion of slavery into the territories taken after the War with Mexico brought the North and the South into conflict. Many Northerners opposed the spread of slavery into the territories. White Southerners viewed slaves as property and said the Constitution gave them the right to take their property anywhere. They also believed that if slavery were banned in the territories, it would destroy the balance of power in Congress between the North and the South.

*Reading*History

A. Making Generalizations How did white Southerners defend slavery?

The Compromise of 1850

In 1850, California applied to join the Union as a free state. California could not gain statehood, however, without the approval of Congress, and Congress was divided. To resolve the division, Senator Henry Clay of Kentucky made a proposal to appeal to both regions.

1. To please the North, California would be admitted as a free state, and the slave trade would be abolished in Washington, D.C.
2. To please the South, Congress would not pass laws regarding slavery for the rest of the territories gained from the War with Mexico. Congress also would pass a stronger law to help slaveholders recapture runaway slaves.

Congress passed these proposals, which together became known as the **Compromise of 1850.** This compromise was designed to save the Union, but it actually deepened the division between the North and the South.

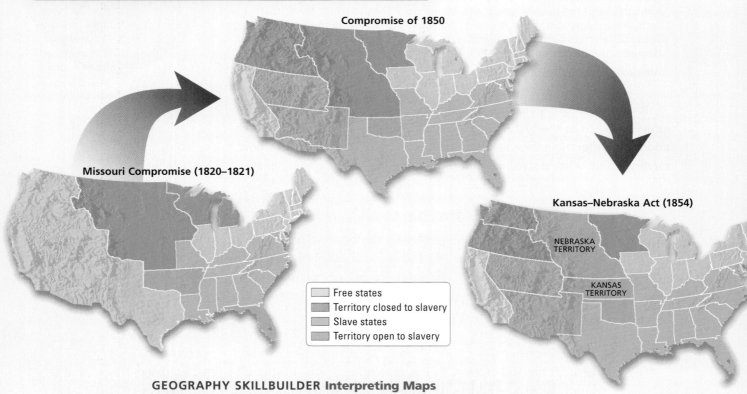

Free and Slave States and Territories, *1820–1854*

Compromise of 1850

Missouri Compromise (1820–1821)

Kansas–Nebraska Act (1854)

NEBRASKA TERRITORY

KANSAS TERRITORY

- Free states
- Territory closed to slavery
- Slave states
- Territory open to slavery

GEOGRAPHY SKILLBUILDER Interpreting Maps

1. **Region** *What new free states and slave states entered the Union between 1820 and 1854?*
2. **Region** *How did the Kansas–Nebraska Act change the amount of territory open to slavery?*

The Crisis Deepens

The part of the Compromise of 1850 that dealt with runaway slaves was called the Fugitive Slave Act. It required citizens to help recapture runaway slaves. Northerners faced an unpleasant choice. They could obey the law and support slavery or oppose slavery and break the law.

Background
The Nebraska Territory was part of the Louisiana Purchase. It lay north of the 36° 30′ line, so the Missouri Compromise banned slavery there.

Meanwhile, the issue of slavery in the territories brought bloodshed to the West. In 1854, Congress passed a law to organize territorial governments for the Nebraska Territory. The bill divided the area into two territories—Nebraska and Kansas. The law, called the Kansas-Nebraska Act, allowed people to vote for slavery in territories even though the Missouri Compromise had banned it.

Proslavery and antislavery settlers rushed into the Kansas Territory to vote for the territorial legislature. The two sides clashed, and eventually civil war broke out in Kansas. It continued for three years.

The Kansas-Nebraska Act of 1854 also caused political parties to realign. In the South, supporters of slavery flocked to the Democratic Party. In the North, slavery opponents formed a new, antislavery party called the Republican Party.

The *Dred Scott* Case

The Supreme Court decision in the case of Dred Scott, a slave from Missouri, worsened sectional tensions. Scott's owner took him to live in territories where slavery was illegal. Then they returned to Missouri. After his owner's death, Scott sued for his freedom. He argued that he was a free man because he had lived in territories where slavery was illegal. His case, ***Dred Scott* v. *Sandford***, reached the Supreme Court in 1856.

Dred Scott (below left) first sued for his freedom in 1846. The Supreme Court, led by Chief Justice Roger B. Taney (below right), did not rule on the case until 1857.

In 1857, the Court ruled against Scott. Chief Justice Roger B. Taney stated that Scott was not a U.S. citizen and so could not sue in federal courts. In addition, Taney ruled that Congress could not ban slavery in the territories. To do so would violate the slaveholders' property.

Reading **History**
B. Making Inferences How do you think Republicans would respond to Taney's opinion in the *Dred Scott* case?

After the *Dred Scott* decision, Republicans charged that the Democrats wanted to legalize slavery throughout the United States. They used this charge to attack Stephen A. Douglas, sponsor of the Kansas-Nebraska Act. In 1858, Illinois Republicans nominated **Abraham Lincoln** to challenge Douglas for his U.S. Senate seat. The two men held formal debates across Illinois. Lincoln argued against the expansion of slavery. Douglas argued for popular sovereignty, the rights of people in the territories to decide issues for themselves. Lincoln countered by bringing up the *Dred Scott* decision. Douglas won reelection. Lincoln, despite his loss, became a national figure and strengthened his standing in the Republican Party.

The Election of 1860

By 1860, the issue of slavery had raised sectional tensions to the boiling point. At Harpers Ferry, Virginia, on October 16, 1859, an extreme abolitionist named John Brown and his followers captured a federal arsenal, killing four people. The group planned to arm local slaves so that they could fight for their freedom. Brown was captured, tried, and hanged. On the day of his hanging, abolitionists tolled bells and fired guns in salute. Southerners were enraged by Brown's actions and horrified by Northern reactions.

A POLITICAL RACE

The presidential election of 1860 reflected the split in the nation. Four candidates with differing views on slavery ran. Many Southerners warned that if the Republican candidate Abraham Lincoln won, the Southern states would **secede,** or withdraw, from the Union. Lincoln opposed the expansion of slavery into the territories, but he said he would not abolish slavery. White Southerners did not believe him.

After Lincoln won the election, seven Southern states seceded and formed the **Confederate States of America**. They named **Jefferson Davis** to be their president. In the next section, you will read how secession led to war.

This cartoon of the long-legged Abe Lincoln shows him to be the fittest candidate in the 1860 presidential election.

Reading **History**

C. Making Inferences Why were popular sovereignty and the opinion in the *Dred Scott* case inconsistent?

Background
The first seven states to secede were South Carolina, Mississippi, Florida, Alabama, Georgia, Louisiana, and Texas.

Section 1 Assessment

1. Terms & Names
Explain the significance of:
- Compromise of 1850
- *Dred Scott* v. *Sandford*
- Abraham Lincoln
- secede
- Confederate States of America
- Jefferson Davis

2. Taking Notes
Use a chart like the one below to compare Northern and Southern views of the issues listed.

Northern View	Issue	Southern View
	Fugitive Slave Act	
	Kansas–Nebraska Act	
	Harpers Ferry raid	

3. Main Ideas
a. How did the issue of slavery divide the North and the South?

b. What was the cause of violence in the Kansas territory?

c. Why did the Southern states secede?

4. Critical Thinking
Solving Problems What would you have done to resolve the differences between the North and the South?

THINK ABOUT
- differences in the economy of the two sections
- their differing views on slavery

ACTIVITY OPTIONS

MATH
GEOGRAPHY

Do research to find election returns from the 1860 presidential election. Make **graphs** or draw a **map** to illustrate the results.

② The Civil War

TERMS & NAMES
Fort Sumter
Robert E. Lee
Ulysses S. Grant
Emancipation Proclamation
Battle of Gettysburg
Appomattox Court House
Thirteenth Amendment

MAIN IDEA	WHY IT MATTERS NOW
The Civil War was destructive but preserved the Union and abolished slavery in the United States.	The Civil War brought changes that helped shape modern American life.

ONE AMERICAN'S STORY

Two months before the Civil War broke out, 22-year-old Emma Holmes of Charleston began keeping a detailed diary. From a rooftop, she witnessed the event that started the war. She wrote about South Carolina's attack on Fort Sumter, a federal fort in Charleston's harbor, in her diary.

This photograph of Emma Holmes was taken in 1900.

A VOICE FROM THE PAST

[A]t half past four this morning, the heavy booming of cannons woke the city from its slumbers. . . . Every body seems relieved that what has been so long dreaded has come at last and so confident of victory that they seem not to think of the danger of their friends. . . . I had a splendid view of the harbor with the naked eye. We could distinctly see flames amidst the smoke. All the barracks were on fire. . . . With the telescope I saw the shots as they struck the fort and [saw] the masonry crumbling.

Emma Holmes, *The Diary of Emma Holmes 1861–1866*

Many Southerners expected a short war that they would easily win. Northerners expected the same. In this section, you'll read about the course and consequences of the war.

War Erupts

The Southern states took over most of the federal forts inside their borders when they seceded from the Union. President Lincoln had to decide what to do about the forts that remained under federal control. One was **Fort Sumter** in the harbor of Charleston, South Carolina. The fort was running out of supplies. If Lincoln supplied the fort, he risked war. If he did not, he would be giving in to the rebels. Lincoln informed South Carolina that he was resupplying Fort Sumter. Confederate leaders decided to take over the fort before the supply ships arrived.

On April 12, 1861, the Confederates opened fire on the fort. The attack continued for 34 hours, until the fort surrendered. The Confederate attack on Fort Sumter was the beginning of the Civil War.

Lincoln asked the Union states to provide 75,000 militiamen for 90 days to put down the uprising in the South. In the upper South, some

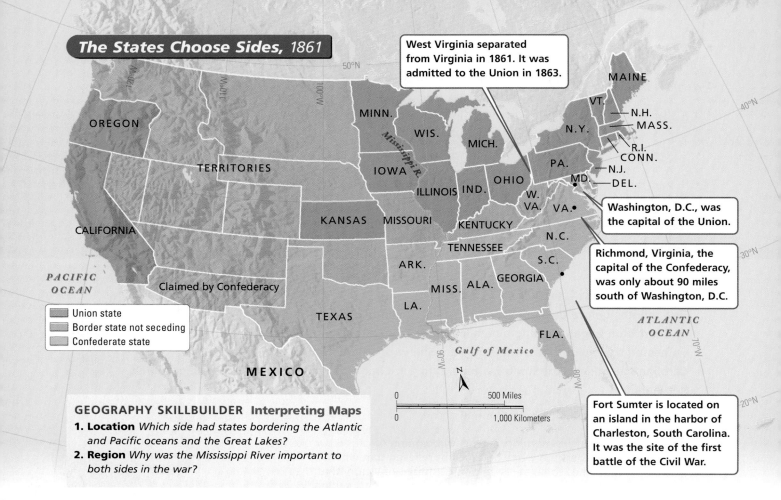

The States Choose Sides, 1861

West Virginia separated from Virginia in 1861. It was admitted to the Union in 1863.

Washington, D.C., was the capital of the Union.

Richmond, Virginia, the capital of the Confederacy, was only about 90 miles south of Washington, D.C.

Fort Sumter is located on an island in the harbor of Charleston, South Carolina. It was the site of the first battle of the Civil War.

Claimed by Confederacy

- Union state
- Border state not seceding
- Confederate state

GEOGRAPHY SKILLBUILDER Interpreting Maps
1. **Location** *Which side had states bordering the Atlantic and Pacific oceans and the Great Lakes?*
2. **Region** *Why was the Mississippi River important to both sides in the war?*

state leaders refused to supply troops to subdue neighboring Southern states. In the following weeks, Virginia, North Carolina, Tennessee, and Arkansas joined the Confederacy.

Attention focused on the border states of Delaware, Maryland, Kentucky, and Missouri. These slave states bordered free states. Because of their location and resources, the border states could tip the scales toward one side. All stayed in the Union. In addition, a group of western counties in Virginia formed the state of West Virginia in 1863 and supported the Union. In the end, 24 states remained in the Union and 11 joined the Confederacy.

The Union had huge advantages at the start of the war. It had more people, factories, railroads, ships, and shipyards than the South. The Union also had President Lincoln, who was a remarkable leader. He convinced Northerners that democracy depended on preserving the Union.

The main advantage of the Confederacy was its talented military leaders, such as **Robert E. Lee,** whom Lincoln had tried recruit to head the Union army. Lee became the commanding general of the Army of Northern Virginia. The South also benefited from fighting on its own territory. There it knew the land and received help from local people.

The North suffered early losses despite its advantages. In the summer of 1861, Lincoln ordered an invasion of Virginia in order to take the Confederate capital of Richmond. But the Confederates defeated Union

Reading **History**
A. Supporting Opinions At the beginning of the Civil War, which side would you have predicted to win? Why?

Background
The state militias were armies of ordinary citizens rather than professional soldiers.

forces in the First Battle of Bull Run north of Manassas, Virginia. This victory thrilled the South and shocked the North. The North realized it had underestimated its opponent. Lincoln sent the 90-day militias home and called for a real army of 500,000 volunteers for three years.

Life in the Army

Volunteers largely made up both armies. In all, about 2 million soldiers served the Union, and less than 1 million served the Confederacy. The majority were between 18 and 30 years of age. Neither the North nor the South accepted African Americans into their armies at the beginning of the war. Later, the North took African Americans into its ranks.

Civil War soldiers faced many hardships. Conditions were often wet, muddy, or cold, and soldiers had inadequate clothing and lived in crude shelters. They sometimes marched over frozen ground in bare feet. After battles, needy soldiers took clothing from the dead.

Many army camps were unsanitary. Soldiers often went weeks without bathing or washing their clothes. Their bodies, clothing, and bedding became infested with lice and fleas. The lack of hygiene—conditions and practices that promote health—resulted in widespread sickness. Most soldiers had chronic diarrhea or other disorders. These disorders were caused by contaminated water or food or by germ-carrying insects. In addition, doctors often failed to wash their hands or their instruments when attending patients.

Reading**History**
B. Making Inferences What changes could have helped lower the spread of disease among soldiers?

No End in Sight

In the first two years of the war, neither side gained a decisive victory. In November of 1861, Lincoln made George McClellan general in chief of the entire Union army. But Lincoln grew frustrated with McClellan because he kept training his troops instead of attacking.

While McClellan stalled, **Ulysses S. Grant** won victories for the Union in the West. Early in 1862, General Grant captured two Confederate river forts in Tennessee, opening up a river highway into the heart of the South. On April 6, 1862, Grant won another victory at the Battle of Shiloh, in Tennessee. But the victory came at a staggering cost. Union casualties at Shiloh numbered over 13,000, about one-fourth of those who had fought. Congressmen criticized Grant for the high casualties and urged Lincoln to replace him. But Lincoln replied, "I can't spare this man—he fights."

In the East, the story was different. In the summer of 1862, Lee forced McClellan's troops to withdraw from Virginia. Lee then decided to

Vocabulary
casualties: number of people killed or injured

STRANGE _but_ True

DEADLIER THAN BULLETS

"Look at our company—21 have died of disease, 18 have become so unhealthy as to be discharged, and only four have been killed in battle." So a Louisiana officer explained the high death rate in the Civil War.

More than twice as many men died of disease as died of battle wounds. Intestinal disorders, including typhoid fever, diarrhea, and dysentery, killed the most. Pneumonia, tuberculosis, and malaria killed many others. Bad water and food, poor diet, exposure to cold and rain, unsanitary conditions, and disease-carrying insects all contributed to the high rate of disease.

invade the North. By chance, McClellan got hold of Lee's battle plans. On September 17, 1862, at Antietam Creek in Maryland, McClellan's army met Lee's. The resulting Battle of Antietam caused the bloodiest day in American history. About 25,000 men died or were wounded. Lee lost nearly one-third of his fighting force and withdrew to Virginia. But McClellan did not pursue him and so missed a chance to finish off Lee's army. Lincoln was so angry he fired McClellan.

*Reading*History
C. Contrasting
How did Grant differ from McClellan as a military leader?

The Emancipation Proclamation

After Lee's forces were stopped at Antietam, Lincoln decided to emancipate, or free, the slaves in the Confederacy. Abolitionists had been urging Lincoln to do so since the beginning of the war. Lincoln, however, did not believe he had the power under the Constitution to abolish slavery where it already existed. Nor did he want to anger the four slave states that remained in the Union. He also knew that most Northern Democrats opposed emancipation.

Lincoln did not want the issue of slavery to divide the nation further than it already had. Although he disliked slavery, Lincoln's first priority was to preserve the Union. But if freeing the slaves would help weaken the Confederacy, then Lincoln would do it.

On January 1, 1863, Lincoln issued the **Emancipation Proclamation,** which freed all slaves in Confederate territory. The proclamation had a tremendous impact on the public, but it freed very few slaves on that day. Most of the slaves lived in areas far from the Union troops that could enforce emancipation. Nevertheless, the Emancipation Proclamation was an important symbolic measure. For the North, the Civil War was no longer just to preserve the Union. It had become a war of liberation.

Many African Americans had escaped to Union lines before 1863. Now they had legal freedom and were encouraged even more to join their liberators. These runaways deprived the Confederacy of labor and provided the Union with soldiers. The Emancipation Proclamation also declared that African-American men willing to fight "will be received into the armed service of the United States." By war's end, about 180,000 African-American soldiers had served in the Union army.

*Reading*History
D. Drawing Conclusions
Why did Lincoln choose to limit his proclamation mostly to rebellious states?

War Affects Society

As the Civil War entered its third year, the constant demand for men and resources began to take its toll. Economic hardship was especially severe in the South, where most of the battles were fought. Food shortages were common. Inflation—an increase in prices and decrease in

AMERICA'S HISTORY MAKERS

ABRAHAM LINCOLN
1809–1865

Today, Abraham Lincoln is considered one of the great men of all time. Yet early in his presidency, he was widely criticized and ridiculed. Critics labeled him ignorant, incompetent, and socially crude. As Lincoln grew into his job, however, he gained the respect and affection of many Northerners.

Even as a youth, Lincoln had displayed a gift for public speaking. During the Civil War, through his speeches and writings, Lincoln inspired fellow Americans to "dare to do our duty as we understand it."

Why would the ability to inspire people be important in a wartime leader?

the value of money—made life hard for working people. Over the course of the war, prices rose 9,000 percent in the South. This increase made goods 90 times more expensive than in 1861. Riots broke out. Mobs broke into shops and stole food, clothing, and other goods.

Inflation was much lower in the North. Overall, war production boosted Northern industry and fueled the economy. This gave the North an even larger economic advantage over the South.

In 1863, Confederate soldiers began to leave the army in increasing numbers. By the end of the year, the Confederate army had lost nearly 40 percent of its men. Some were on leave, but many deserted. Both the Union and the Confederacy instituted a draft, which required men to serve in the army.

With so many men away at war, women had to run farms and take over jobs in offices and factories. Thousands of women also served on the front lines as volunteer workers and nurses.

The North Wins

In 1863, the tide of the war turned in favor of the North with two important victories. One was the **Battle of Gettysburg,** in which Union troops led by General George Meade fought for three days against Confederate troops led by Lee. From July 1 to July 3, about 90,000 Union troops clashed with 75,000 Confederates near Gettysburg, Pennsylvania.

On July 3, some 13,000 rebel troops under General George Pickett charged up a ridge into heavy Union fire. They were torn to pieces, and the Union army won the battle. Lee lost over one-third of his army at the battle and retreated to Virginia.

The day after Pickett's Charge, Grant's Union forces forced the Confederates at Vicksburg, Mississippi, to surrender after a long siege. This victory gave the Union complete control of the Mississippi River.

In March 1864, Lincoln named Grant commander of all the Union armies. Grant then developed a plan to defeat the Confederacy. He would pursue Lee's army in Virginia, while Union forces under General William Tecumseh Sherman pushed through the Deep South to Atlanta and the Atlantic Coast.

Sherman waged total war, or war against everything that supported the enemy. His troops tore up rail lines, destroyed crops, and burned towns. Sherman took Atlanta in September 1864, and then Savannah, Georgia, in December.

In the East, Grant fought savage battles against Lee's forces. In June 1864, Grant's armies settled in for a long siege of Richmond. After ten

Reading **History**
E. Analyzing Causes Why were economic problems particularly bad in the South?

Vocabulary
siege: the surrounding of a city, town, or fortress by an army trying to capture it

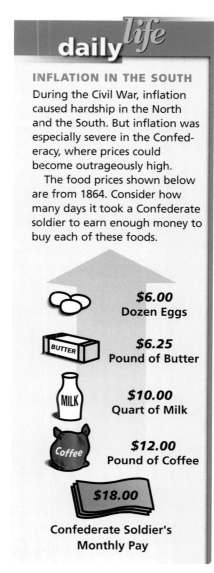

daily *life*

INFLATION IN THE SOUTH
During the Civil War, inflation caused hardship in the North and the South. But inflation was especially severe in the Confederacy, where prices could become outrageously high.

The food prices shown below are from 1864. Consider how many days it took a Confederate soldier to earn enough money to buy each of these foods.

$6.00
Dozen Eggs

$6.25
Pound of Butter

$10.00
Quart of Milk

$12.00
Pound of Coffee

$18.00

Confederate Soldier's Monthly Pay

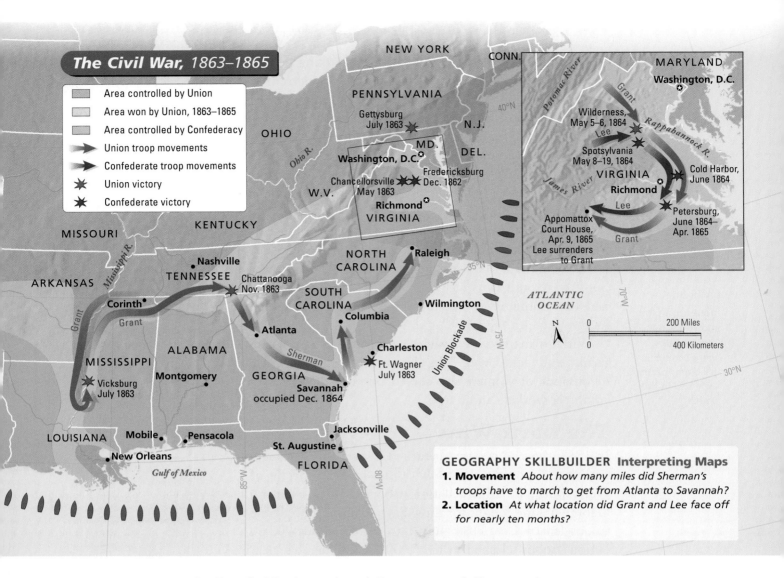

The Civil War, 1863–1865

Legend:
- Area controlled by Union
- Area won by Union, 1863–1865
- Area controlled by Confederacy
- Union troop movements
- Confederate troop movements
- Union victory
- Confederate victory

NEW YORK
CONN.
MARYLAND
Washington, D.C.

PENNSYLVANIA

Gettysburg
July 1863

N.J.

OHIO

Obio R.

MD.

DEL.

Washington, D.C.

Chancellorsville
May 1863

Fredericksburg
Dec. 1862

W.V.

Richmond

VIRGINIA

KENTUCKY

MISSOURI

NORTH
CAROLINA

Raleigh

Nashville

TENNESSEE

Chattanooga
Nov. 1863

ARKANSAS

Corinth

Grant

SOUTH
CAROLINA

Wilmington

Grant

Columbia

ATLANTIC
OCEAN

Atlanta

ALABAMA

Sherman

Charleston

Ft. Wagner
July 1863

MISSISSIPPI

Montgomery

GEORGIA

Vicksburg
July 1863

Savannah
occupied Dec. 1864

Union Blockade

LOUISIANA

Mobile

Pensacola

Jacksonville

New Orleans

St. Augustine

FLORIDA

Gulf of Mexico

Virginia inset:
Potomac River
MARYLAND
Washington, D.C.
Grant
Wilderness,
May 5–6, 1864
Lee
Rappahannock R.
Spotsylvania
May 8–19, 1864
VIRGINIA
Cold Harbor,
June 1864
James River
Richmond
Lee
Petersburg,
June 1864–
Apr. 1865
Appomattox
Court House,
Apr. 9, 1865
Lee surrenders
to Grant
Grant

0   200 Miles
0   400 Kilometers

GEOGRAPHY SKILLBUILDER Interpreting Maps
1. **Movement** *About how many miles did Sherman's troops have to march to get from Atlanta to Savannah?*
2. **Location** *At what location did Grant and Lee face off for nearly ten months?*

months, Lee fled Richmond, and Grant pursued. Knowing his situation was hopeless, Lee sent a message to Grant that he was ready to surrender. On April 9, 1865, Lee and Grant met in the small Virginia town of **Appomattox Court House** to arrange the surrender. After four long years, the Civil War had ended.

The Legacy of the War

The Civil War left bitter feelings between the North and the South, in part because its costs were so great. The Civil War was the deadliest war in U.S. history. About 620,000 soldiers died—360,000 for the Union and 260,000 for the Confederacy. Another 275,000 Union soldiers and 260,000 Confederate soldiers were wounded. The war also had great economic costs. Together, the North and the South spent more than five times what the government had spent in the previous eight decades. Years later, the federal government was still paying interest on war loans.

For the South, the war brought economic disaster. Farms, plantations, factories, and thousands of miles of railroad track were destroyed. Before the war, the South accounted for 30 percent of the nation's wealth. After, it accounted for only 12 percent. In the North, on the other hand, industry had grown rapidly. These economic differences would last for decades.

To deal with the demands of war, the national government grew larger and more powerful. It instituted an income tax, issued paper currency, and established a new federal banking system. It also funded railroads, gave western land to settlers, and provided for state colleges. This growth of federal power continued long after the war.

One of the greatest effects of the war was the end of slavery. The Emancipation Proclamation applied primarily to slaves in the Confederacy. In 1864, Lincoln had approved of a constitutional amendment to end slavery entirely, but it failed to pass Congress. In January 1865, Lincoln urged Congress to try again. The measure, known as the **Thirteenth Amendment,** passed. By year's end, 27 states had ratified the amendment. From then on, slavery was banned in the United States.

Lincoln did not live to see the end of slavery, however. Five days after Lee's surrender at Appomattox, Lincoln was shot by John Wilkes Booth, a Confederate supporter. Lincoln died the next day—on April 15, 1865. He was the first U.S. president to be assassinated.

The loss of Lincoln's experience and political skills was a terrible tragedy for a people facing the challenges of rebuilding their nation. You will read more about these challenges in the next section.

Vocabulary
income tax: tax on earnings

Reading**History**
F. Making Inferences Why was an amendment needed to free enslaved persons even after the Emancipation Proclamation?

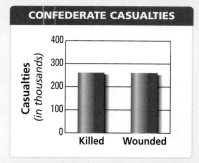

CONNECTIONS TO MATH
Costs of the Civil War

CONFEDERATE CASUALTIES

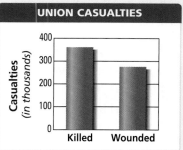

UNION CASUALTIES

Source: _World Book; Historical Statistics of the United States; The United States Civil War Center_

SKILLBUILDER

Interpreting Graphs
1. _About how many Confederate soldiers were killed in the Civil War?_
2. _Approximately how many soldiers were wounded in the war?_

Section 2 Assessment

1. Terms & Names

Explain the significance of:
• Fort Sumter
• Robert E. Lee
• Ulysses S. Grant
• Emancipation Proclamation
• Battle of Gettysburg
• Appomattox Court House
• Thirteenth Amendment

2. Taking Notes

Use a time line like the one below to record key events from Section 2.

1861   1865

Which events mark the turning point of the war?

3. Main Ideas

a. What was life in the army like for Civil War soldiers?

b. Why was the immediate impact of the Emancipation Proclamation limited?

c. What were some of the human and economic costs of the Civil War?

4. Critical Thinking

Comparing How was the South's situation in the Civil War similar to the situation of the Patriots in the Revolutionary War?

THINK ABOUT
• their reasons for fighting
• their opponents' strengths

ACTIVITY OPTIONS

GEOGRAPHY
LANGUAGE ARTS

Research the Siege of Vicksburg. Make a **topographic map** of the area or write an **article** describing the soldiers' hardships during the siege.

TERMS & NAMES
Reconstruction
Andrew Johnson
Fourteenth
 Amendment
Fifteenth
 Amendment
Ku Klux Klan

③ Reconstruction

MAIN IDEA

During Reconstruction, the country struggled over how to rebuild the South and create racial equality.

WHY IT MATTERS NOW

Reconstruction was an important step in the African-American struggle for civil rights.

ONE AMERICAN'S STORY

After the Civil War ended in 1865, Pennsylvania congressman Thaddeus Stevens became a leader of the Radical Republicans. This group of congressmen favored using federal power to reshape the South and promote full citizenship for African Americans.

A VOICE FROM THE PAST

The whole fabric of southern society must be changed. . . . If the South is ever to be made a safe Republic let her lands be cultivated by the toil of the owners, or the free labor of intelligent citizens.

Thaddeus Stevens, quoted in *The Era of Reconstruction* by Kenneth Stampp

In this section, you will read about the gains and setbacks in rebuilding the South and gaining equality for African Americans.

Thaddeus Stevens addresses Congress.

Reconstruction Begins

The process the federal government used to readmit Confederate states to the Union is known as **Reconstruction.** It lasted from 1865 to 1877. After Lincoln's assassination, Vice-President **Andrew Johnson** became president. Johnson called for a moderate program for bringing the South back into the Union. He offered to pardon most white Southerners in return for a pledge of loyalty to the United States. He also required the new state governments to ratify the Thirteenth Amendment prohibiting slavery. But the Southern states set up governments that limited the freedom of former slaves. Some states even refused to ratify the Thirteenth Amendment.

New Civil Rights Laws

Some Republicans in Congress wanted to take a forceful approach toward Reconstruction. These people were called Radical Republicans. Urged on by the Radicals, Congress passed the Civil Rights Act of 1866.

His First Vote, an 1868 oil painting by Thomas Waterman Wood, shows a new African-American voter.

How do you think the man felt about voting?

Vocabulary
civil rights: those rights granted to all citizens

It declared that all persons born in the United States (except Native Americans) were citizens and entitled to equal rights.

Republicans also wanted equality to be protected by the Constitution itself. To achieve this goal, Congress proposed a new constitutional amendment in 1866. This proposed amendment stated that all people born in the United States were citizens and had the same rights. Johnson refused to support the amendment. Only one former Confederate state approved it.

Outraged Republicans then passed the Reconstruction Acts of 1867, which began a period known as Radical Reconstruction. From this point on, Congress controlled Reconstruction. It divided the South into five military districts and took away the right of Confederate leaders to vote. Before Southern states could reenter the Union, they had to approve new state constitutions giving the vote to all adult men. They also had to ratify the amendment to extend citizenship to African Americans. When they did so in 1868, it became the **Fourteenth Amendment**.

*Reading*History
A. Contrasting
How did Radical Reconstruction differ from Andrew Johnson's plan?

In 1867, Southern voters chose delegates to draft new state constitutions. About three-fourths of the delegates were Republicans. About half of these were poor white farmers. They were called scalawags (scoundrels) for going along with Radical Reconstruction. Another one-fourth of the Republican delegates were known as carpetbaggers— white Northerners who had come to the South after the war. Many Southerners accused them, often unfairly, of seeking only to get rich or gain political power. African Americans made up the rest of the Republican delegates. Most were ministers, teachers, or skilled workers.

Background
Carpetbaggers were said to have headed south carrying only a cheap suitcase, known as a carpetbag.

By 1870, voters in all the Southern states had approved the new constitutions written by these delegates. The states then were let back into the Union and allowed to send representatives to Congress.

Johnson and Grant

President Johnson fought against many of the Radical Republican reform efforts. The conflict between Johnson and Congress came to a showdown. In 1867, Congress passed the Tenure of Office Act, which prohibited the president from firing government officials without Senate approval. In February 1868, Johnson fired his secretary of war without getting Senate approval. The House of Representatives voted to impeach him, or formally accuse him of improper conduct. The case moved to the Senate for a trial, where Johnson was acquitted by one vote.

*Reading*History

B. Drawing Conclusions Why did Congress decide to impeach President Johnson?

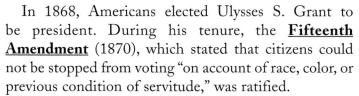

Now and then

AFRICAN AMERICANS IN CONGRESS

Between 1870 and 1877, 16 African Americans served in Congress. Seven are shown in the picture below. Two were senators: Hiram R. Revels and Blanche K. Bruce, both of whom were from Mississippi.

In 1999, there were 38 African Americans in Congress. The longest-serving member was John Conyers, a representative from Michigan elected in 1964. Only two African-American senators were elected in the 20th century. Massachusetts senator Edward W. Brooke served from 1967 to 1979. Illinois senator Carol Moseley-Braun served from 1993 to 1999.

In 1868, Americans elected Ulysses S. Grant to be president. During his tenure, the **Fifteenth Amendment** (1870), which stated that citizens could not be stopped from voting "on account of race, color, or previous condition of servitude," was ratified.

Grant won a second term, but his support declined because of political scandals involving officials in his administration. In addition, a five-year economic depression began in 1873. During the depression, many white Americans lost interest in Reconstruction.

Daily Life During Reconstruction

Reconstruction spelled a new beginning for recently freed African Americans. To assist former slaves, Lincoln had established the Freedmen's Bureau. This federal agency set up schools and hospitals for African Americans and distributed clothes, food, and fuel. Children and adults flocked to freedmen's schools to learn to read and write. The Freedmen's Bureau also helped reunite many family members who had been separated during slavery.

With freedom, African Americans no longer had to work for an owner's benefit. However, without their own land to support themselves, many African Americans returned to work on plantations as wage earners. They earned very low wages, and many owners cheated workers out of wages. Some African Americans decided to turn to sharecropping. In this system, a worker rents land to farm and gives the landowner a share of the crop.

Landowners forced sharecroppers to grow cash crops, such as cotton, instead of food. As a result, farmers had to buy food from the local store, which was usually owned by the landlord. Most farmers did not have money and so bought on credit. Many got caught in a cycle of debt that kept them poor.

Besides poverty, African Americans in the South continued to face racial violence. Many white Southerners did not want African Americans to achieve equality. In 1866, such feelings spurred the rise of the **Ku Klux Klan.** This secret group aimed to keep former slaves powerless. Klansmen burned houses and beat and killed people. As gun-toting Klansmen kept Republicans from voting, the Democrats increased their power.

The End of Reconstruction

Supreme Court decisions also prevented African Americans from exercising their rights. For example, the Court ruled in 1876 that the federal

Reconstruction: Civil Rights Amendments and Laws

Civil Rights Act of 1866	• Granted citizenship and equal rights to all persons born in the United States (except Native Americans)
Fourteenth Amendment (1868)	• Granted citizenship and equal protection of the laws to all persons born in the United States (except Native Americans)
Fifteenth Amendment (1870)	• Protected the voting rights of African Americans
Civil Rights Act of 1875	• Outlawed racial segregation in public services • Ensured the right of African Americans to serve as jurors

SKILLBUILDER Interpreting Charts

1. *Which amendment and law are most similar?*
2. *Which amendment specifically protects voting rights?*

government could not punish individuals, such as Klansmen, who violated the civil rights of African Americans.

The final blow to Reconstruction came with the 1876 presidential election. The race between Democratic candidate Samuel J. Tilden and Republican candidate Rutherford B. Hayes was so close that both parties claimed victory. Leaders of the two parties then agreed to a deal that made Hayes president. In exchange, the South won several promises, including a pledge to remove federal troops from the South. After the election, Reconstruction governments in the South collapsed, and the Democrats returned to power. The new Southern state governments quickly gutted the Reconstruction civil rights laws.

Reconstruction had mixed results. African Americans did not achieve equality. Most still lived in poverty and faced violence and prejudice. However, the nation did reunite. Black schools and churches endured. And civil rights protections that became part of the Constitution supported the civil rights struggles of the 20th century.

 *Reading***History**

B. Summarizing What events weakened support for Reconstruction?

Section 3 Assessment

1. Terms & Names

Explain the significance of:
• Reconstruction
• Andrew Johnson
• Fourteenth Amendment
• Fifteenth Amendment
• Ku Klux Klan

2. Taking Notes

Review the section and find five significant events to place on a time line as shown.

1865 ——————— 1877

In your opinion, which event was most important and why?

3. Main Ideas

a. What role did the Radical Republicans play in Reconstruction?

b. What impact did the Reconstruction Acts of 1867 have on the South?

c. How did the lives of African Americans improve during Reconstruction?

4. Critical Thinking

Analyzing Causes Despite greater civil rights, why did African Americans still face difficulty in improving their lives?

THINK ABOUT
• ownership of farm land
• the Ku Klux Klan's rise
• Supreme Court rulings

ACTIVITY OPTIONS

 **LANGUAGE ARTS**

CIVICS

Research Ku Klux Klan activities barring African Americans from voting. Then write a protest **letter to the editor** or propose a **law** to protect voting rights.

TERMS & NAMES

Briefly explain the significance of each of the following.

1. Compromise of 1850
2. Abraham Lincoln
3. Confederate States of America
4. Robert E. Lee
5. Ulysses S. Grant
6. Battle of Gettysburg
7. Thirteenth Amendment
8. Reconstruction
9. Fourteenth Amendment
10. Ku Klux Klan

REVIEW QUESTIONS

The Nation Breaking Apart (pages 133–136)

1. What was the source of sectional tensions in the 1850s?
2. What did Chief Justice Taney argue in his opinion in the *Dred Scott* case?
3. What happened as a result of the presidential election of 1860?

The Civil War (pages 137–143)

4. What advantages did the Union have at the start of the Civil War?
5. Why did Lincoln issue the Emancipation Proclamation?
6. What happened at the Battle of Gettysburg?
7. How did the war affect the Southern economy?

Reconstruction (pages 144–147)

8. What was the purpose of the Fourteenth Amendment?
9. Why did Congress impeach Andrew Johnson?
10. What led to the end of Reconstruction?

CRITICAL THINKING

1. USING YOUR NOTES

	North	South
Reasons for fighting		
Advantages		
Disadvantages		
Military strategy		
Battle victories		

Using your completed chart, answer the questions.

a. Which side seemed more likely to win the war? Why?
b. Which side followed more closely its original strategy in the first two years of the war?

2. ANALYZING LEADERSHIP

Think about the leaders discussed in this chapter. Choose one. What character traits helped make him an effective leader?

3. APPLYING CITIZENSHIP SKILLS

Which individuals or groups of people demonstrated good or poor citizenship during the war? Explain your choices.

4. THEME: CITIZENSHIP

How could people on both sides of the Civil War believe that they were being good citizens by fighting?

5. MAKING DECISIONS

In your opinion, was Lincoln correct in deciding to go to war to save the Union? Explain your answer.

Interact *with* History

How did the consequences and effects of civil war that you predicted before you read the chapter compare with the actual conditions you read about?

VISUAL SUMMARY

The Union in Peril

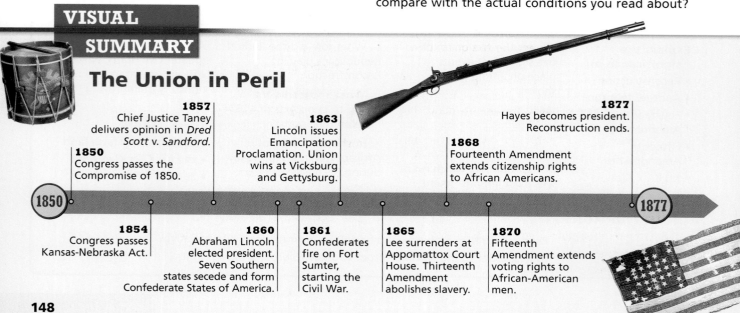

1850 Congress passes the Compromise of 1850.

1854 Congress passes Kansas-Nebraska Act.

1857 Chief Justice Taney delivers opinion in *Dred Scott v. Sandford.*

1860 Abraham Lincoln elected president. Seven Southern states secede and form Confederate States of America.

1861 Confederates fire on Fort Sumter, starting the Civil War.

1863 Lincoln issues Emancipation Proclamation. Union wins at Vicksburg and Gettysburg.

1865 Lee surrenders at Appomattox Court House. Thirteenth Amendment abolishes slavery.

1868 Fourteenth Amendment extends citizenship rights to African Americans.

1870 Fifteenth Amendment extends voting rights to African-American men.

1877 Hayes becomes president. Reconstruction ends.

1850 — 1877

HISTORY SKILLS

1. INTERPRETING MAPS: Movement
Study the map and answer the questions.

Anaconda Plan, 1861

Richmond
New Orleans
Gulf of Mexico
Mississippi R.
Naval Blockade
ATLANTIC OCEAN

→ Union army movements
■ Union
■ Border states
■ Confederacy

Basic Map Elements
a. What is the subject of the map?
b. What do the colors of the states indicate?

Interpreting the Map
c. What does the arrow in the East indicate?
d. What two bodies of water did the blockade cover?

2. INTERPRETING PRIMARY SOURCES
The following quotation comes from a letter that Robert E. Lee wrote to his sister after Virginia had seceded from the Union and he had resigned from the U.S. Army. Read the quotation and then answer the questions.

> With all my devotion to the Union and the feeling of loyalty and duty of an American citizen, I have not been able to make up my mind to raise my hand against my relatives, my children, my home. I have, therefore, resigned my commission in the Army, and, save in defense of my native state, with the sincere hope that my poor services may never be needed, I hope I may never be called on to draw my sword.
>
> **Robert E. Lee**, quoted in *The Annals of America*

a. What inner conflict does Lee express?
b. What obligation or loyalty does Lee consider greater than his duty to his country?

ALTERNATIVE ASSESSMENT

1. INTERDISCIPLINARY ACTIVITY: Literature
Reading Letters Using the library or the Internet, find firsthand accounts of the Civil War and read some letters written by soldiers. Choose one letter to read aloud to the class. Then, pretend you are the person receiving the letter, and describe your reaction to it.

2. COOPERATIVE LEARNING ACTIVITY
Developing a Peace Proposal The Civil War broke out because the two sides could not reach a compromise. Work in a small group to develop a compromise that would have resolved the conflict between the North and the South. Have one person in the group take the position of an antislavery Northerner, another a proslavery Southerner, and the third a mediator between the two. Present your proposal to the class for their comments.

3. TECHNOLOGY ACTIVITY
Making a Class Presentation Life in the army training camps during the Civil War was hard. Information about life in the camps comes from primary sources. Using the library and the Internet, find diaries, letters, photographs, and news articles about daily life.

For more about Civil War army camps . . .

INTERNET ACTIVITY
CLASSZONE.COM

Plan an electronic presentation on army life for your class. Use the list of suggested topics below to begin brainstorming.

- Drawings, maps, and photos that show the design of a typical camp
- Items used for cooking, lodging, sanitation, military drilling, and recreation
- Drills and maneuvers soldiers learned
- Personal belongings of the Yankees and rebels
- Firsthand accounts of camp life from letters and diaries
- Changes in camp life as the war dragged on

4. HISTORY PORTFOLIO
Review the questions that you wrote for What Do You Want to Know? on page 132. Then write a short report in which you explain the answers to your questions. Be sure to use standard grammar, spelling, sentence structure, and punctuation in your report. If any questions were not answered, do research to answer them. Add your report to your portfolio.

Additional Test Practice, pp. S1–S33

TEST PRACTICE
CLASSZONE.COM

America Transformed

"Give me your tired, your poor,
Your huddled masses, yearning
to breathe free…"

—Emma Lazarus

European immigrants such as those
shown in this photograph (taken
around 1900) streamed into Ellis
Island at the turn of the century.

CHAPTER 5

Growth in the West 1860–1900

Life in the West was hard and dangerous, as this Charles M. Russell painting of cowhands shows.

farmland

sod house built into side of hill

horse and wagon

A Nebraska "sodbuster" family takes time away from their chores to pose in front of their sod house.

It is 1865, and the Civil War has just ended. You are drawn to the West by stories of gold, silver, fertile soil, and free land, and by tales of adventure and new opportunities. Yet you know there would be hardships and unknown dangers. Your life would never be the same.

What Do You Think?

- What might be some of the ways to make a living in the West?
- What do you think your daily life would be like in the West?
- What would be the biggest difference in your life?

How might your life change in the West?

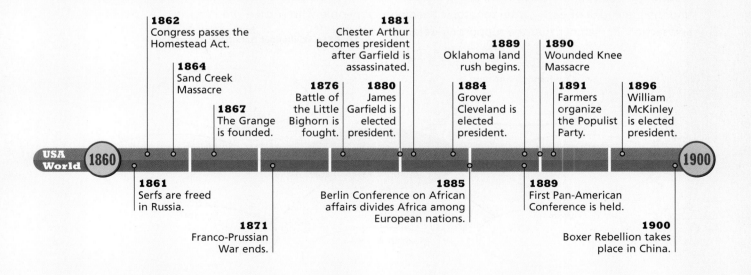

1862 Congress passes the Homestead Act.

1864 Sand Creek Massacre

1867 The Grange is founded.

1876 Battle of the Little Bighorn is fought.

1880 James Garfield is elected president.

1881 Chester Arthur becomes president after Garfield is assassinated.

1884 Grover Cleveland is elected president.

1889 Oklahoma land rush begins.

1890 Wounded Knee Massacre

1891 Farmers organize the Populist Party.

1896 William McKinley is elected president.

USA
World

1860

1861 Serfs are freed in Russia.

1871 Franco-Prussian War ends.

1885 Berlin Conference on African affairs divides Africa among European nations.

1889 First Pan-American Conference is held.

1900 Boxer Rebellion takes place in China.

1900

BEFORE YOU READ

Preview the Theme

Diversity and Unity As Chapter 5 explains, hundreds of thousands of men, women, and children packed up their belongings and went to the West after the Civil War. Most were looking for new opportunities and land of their own; some were seeking freedom or adventure. Their arrival led to conflict with the Native Americans, who were the first occupants of the area.

The West

What Do You Know?

What do you think about when you hear terms like *cowboy* and *Wild West*? What do you already know about the people, places, and events in the West in the last half of the 19th century?

THINK ABOUT
- what you have learned about the West from books, movies, and television
- what happens when different cultures clash

What Do You Want to Know?

What details do you need to help you understand the settling of the West? Make a list of those details in your notebook before you read the chapter.

READ AND TAKE NOTES

Reading Strategy: Finding Main Ideas To make it easier for you to understand what you read, learn to find the main idea of each paragraph, topic heading, and section. Remember that the supporting details help to explain the main ideas. On the chart below, write down the main ideas about the many diverse people who settled the West.

 See Skillbuilder Handbook, page R5.

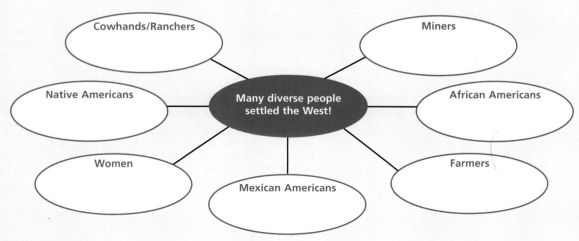

Cowhands/Ranchers

Miners

Native Americans

Many diverse people settled the West!

African Americans

Women

Farmers

Mexican Americans

TERMS & NAMES
frontier
Great Plains
boomtown
long drive
vaquero
vigilante

MAIN IDEA	WHY IT MATTERS NOW
Miners, ranchers, and cowhands settled in the West seeking economic opportunities.	The mining and cattle industries that developed then still contribute to American economic growth.

ONE AMERICAN'S STORY

Nat Love was born a slave in Tennessee in 1854. After the Civil War, he was one of thousands of African Americans who left the South and went west. In 1869, Love headed for Dodge City, Kansas. He was 15 and now free.

Love's horse taming skills landed him a job as a cowhand. For 20 years, he took part in the cattle drives that brought Texas cattle to Kansas stockyards. He became well known for his expert horsemanship and his rodeo riding and roping. In his 1907 autobiography, Love offered a lively but exaggerated account of his life. He told how he braved hailstorms, fought wild animals, and held off human attackers.

A VOICE FROM THE PAST

I carry the marks of fourteen bullet wounds on different parts of my body, most any one of which would be sufficient to kill an ordinary man. . . . Horses were shot from under me, men killed around me, but always I escaped with a trifling wound at the worst.

Nat Love, *The Life and Adventures of Nat Love*

Nat Love was an African-American cowhand who became a rodeo star.

As you will read in this section, few cowhands led lives as exciting as that described by Nat Love, but they all helped to open a new chapter in the history of the American West.

Geography and Population of the West

In the mid-1800s, towns such as St. Joseph and Independence, Missouri, were jumping-off places for settlers going west. They were the last cities and towns before the frontier. The **frontier** was the unsettled or sparsely settled area of the country occupied largely by Native Americans.

Many white settlers thought of the **Great Plains**—the area from the Missouri River to the Rocky Mountains—as empty. (See map on page 156.) Few had been attracted to its rolling plains, dry plateaus, and deserts. However, west of the Rockies, on the Pacific Coast, settlers had followed miners streaming into California after the 1849 gold rush. By 1850, California had gained statehood. Oregon followed in 1859.

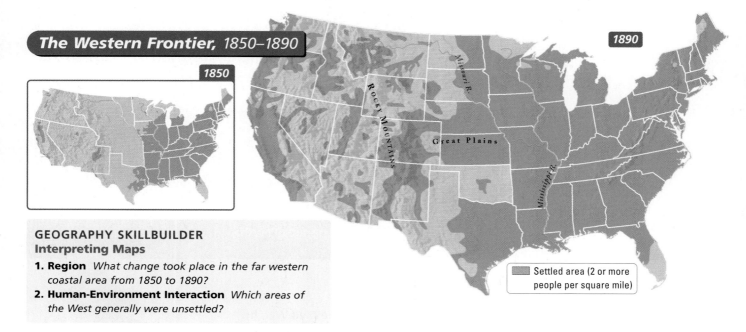

The Western Frontier, 1850–1890

1850

1890

Settled area (2 or more people per square mile)

GEOGRAPHY SKILLBUILDER
Interpreting Maps

1. **Region** *What change took place in the far western coastal area from 1850 to 1890?*
2. **Human-Environment Interaction** *Which areas of the West generally were unsettled?*

The Great Plains had few trees, but its grasslands were home to about 300,000 Native Americans in the mid-1800s. Most followed the buffalo herds that rumbled across the open plains. Despite the presence of these peoples, the United States claimed ownership of the area.

Railroads played a key role in settling the western United States. Trains carried the natural resources of the West—minerals, timber, crops, and cattle—to eastern markets. In turn, trains brought miners, ranchers, and farmers west to develop these resources further. As the railroads opened new areas to white settlement, they also helped to bring an end to the way of life of the West's first settlers—the Native Americans.

Reading **History**

A. Making Inferences Why were railroads so important to the West?

Mining in the West

In 1859, gold and silver strikes drew fortune seekers to Colorado and Nevada. As many as 100,000 miners raced to the Rocky Mountains in Colorado after gold was discovered near Pikes Peak. Also in 1859, prospectors hit "pay dirt" at the Comstock Lode in western Nevada. (A lode is a deposit of a valuable mineral buried in layers of rock.) From 1859 to 1880, the Comstock mine produced some $300 million in silver and gold.

Vocabulary
strike: valuable discovery of a precious mineral

Nearby Virginia City, Nevada, became a **boomtown,** a town that has a sudden burst of economic or population growth. Population jumped from 3,000 in the 1860s to over 20,000 in the 1870s. The writer Samuel Clemens, better known as Mark Twain, captured the excitement of life there.

> **A VOICE FROM THE PAST**
>
> The sidewalks swarmed with people. . . . Money was as plenty as dust; [everyone] considered himself wealthy. . . . There were . . . fire companies, brass bands, banks, hotels, theaters . . . gambling palaces . . . street-fights, murders, . . . riots, . . . and a half dozen jails . . . in full operation.
>
> **Mark Twain,** *Roughing It*

Other major strikes took place in the Black Hills of South Dakota in 1874 and at Cripple Creek, Colorado, in 1891. In 1896, gold was discovered in

Canada's Yukon Territory. News of the strike set off a fresh epidemic of gold fever. Prospectors rushed to the Yukon's Klondike region.

The chance to strike it rich drew Americans from both East and West coasts. Gold fever also attracted miners from other parts of the world, including Europe, South America, Mexico, and China. Unfortunately, few prospectors became rich. Most left, disappointed and broke.

Early miners used panning and sluicing to wash sand and gravel from a stream to separate out any bits of precious metal, as you read in Chapter 3. Large mining companies moved in after surface mines no longer yielded gold or silver. Only they could buy the costly, heavy equipment needed to take the precious metals from underground. Water cannons blasted away hillsides to expose gold deposits. In other places, workers sank shafts thousands of feet into the ground to create underground mines. These new methods recovered more precious metals, but in the process stripped hillsides of vegetation and left rivers polluted.

Paid workers in company mines replaced independent prospectors. The work was hard and dangerous. Dust caused lung problems, and deadly cave-ins could trap miners hundreds of feet below the surface.

By the 1890s, the mining boom was over. Many mines closed because the costs had become too high, and the quality of the ore had dropped. Jobless workers moved elsewhere. Once-thriving communities became ghost towns. Still, the mining boom had lasting effects. Nevada, Colorado, and South Dakota all grew so rapidly that they soon gained statehood.

The Rise of the Cattle Industry

The cattle trade had existed in the Southwest since the Spanish arrived there in the 1500s. But cattle herds remained small until the Civil War. There were few buyers for Western beef because there was no efficient way to get the beef to markets in the more heavily populated cities of the East. The ranchers mostly sold their cattle locally.

The extension of railroad lines from Chicago and St. Louis into Kansas by the 1860s brought changes. An Illinois livestock dealer named Joseph McCoy realized that railroads could bring cattle from Texas ranches to meat-hungry Eastern cities. Cowhands had only to drive cattle herds north from Texas to his stockyards in Abilene, Kansas. From there, the beef could be shipped to Chicago and points east by rail car.

Reading **History**
B. Recognizing Effects Why did large mining companies replace individual prospectors?

Miners brought ore, like the gold nugget shown, from underground mines that dotted the hillsides.

McCoy's plan turned cattle ranching into a very profitable business. Cattle fed on the open range for a year or two and cost the rancher nothing. Ranchers then hired cowhands to round up the cattle and take them to Abilene. There they were sold for as much as ten times their original price. The success of the Abilene stockyards spurred the growth of other Kansas cow towns, including Wichita and Dodge City. The cattle drives to cow towns along the railways were called the **long drives**.

Over time, cowhands followed specific trails across the plains. The first was the Chisholm Trail, which stretched from San Antonio, Texas, to Abilene, Kansas. It was named for Jesse Chisholm, a trader who marked the northern part of the route. From 1867 to 1884, about four million cattle were driven to market on this trail. As cattle raising became more profitable, ranching spread north across the plains from Texas to Montana.

Reading **History**

C. Reading a Map
Use the map on page 179 to locate the Chisholm Trail.

Vaqueros and Cowhands

The first cowhands, or <u>*vaqueros,*</u> as they were known in Spanish, came from Mexico with the Spaniards in the 1500s. They settled in the Southwest. The *vaqueros* helped Spanish, and later Mexican, ranchers manage their herds. From the *vaquero*, the American cowhand learned to rope and ride. Cowhands also adapted the saddle, spurs, lariat (which they used to rope a calf or steer), and chaps of the *vaqueros*.

About one in three cowhands in the West was either Mexican or African-American. Many Mexican cowhands were descendants of the *vaqueros*. Some African-American cowhands were former slaves. They came west at the end of Reconstruction because the enactment of Black Codes in the South put restrictions on their freedom. Also among the cowhands were a large number of former Confederate and Union soldiers.

Background
Chaps, from the Spanish word *chaperejos*, were seatless leather pants worn over trousers to protect legs from scrub brush, snakes, and cactus.

The "Wild West"

At first, the rapidly growing cow towns had no local governments. There were no law officers to handle the fights that broke out as cowhands drank and gambled after a long drive. A more serious threat to law and order came from "con men." These swindlers saw new towns as places to get rich quick by cheating others.

Vocabulary
con man: a person who cheats victims by first gaining their confidence

daily *life*

LIFE OF A COWHAND: THE ROUNDUP

During some parts of the year, the cowhand's life was downright dull. While cattle grazed on the open range, cowhands sat around the ranch, repairing their gear and doing odd jobs. The pace quickened at roundup time in the spring and fall.

For several weeks, 150 to 250 cowhands from nearby ranches rode hundreds of miles locating cattle. Cowhands from each ranch collected their cattle, removed sick or weak animals, and branded new calves. Then the cowhands were ready for the long drive. A roundup by *vaqueros* is shown in this painting by James Walker.

Some Union and Confederate veterans were led to crime by hard feelings left over from the Civil War. Outlaws like John Wesley Hardin, "Billy the Kid," and Jesse and Frank James made crime a way of life. Some women became outlaws, too. Belle Starr, better known as the Bandit Queen, was a legendary horse thief.

For protection, citizens formed vigilante groups. **Vigilantes** were people who took the law into their own hands. They caught suspected criminals and punished them without a trial. Vigilante justice often consisted of hanging suspects from the nearest tree or shooting them on the spot. As towns became more settled, citizens elected a local sheriff or asked the federal government for a marshal. These law officers would arrest lawbreakers and hold them in jail until the time of trial.

Bandit Queen Belle Starr sits atop a horse she just might have stolen.

End of the Long Drives

For about 20 years, the cattle industry boomed. As the railroads extended farther west and south into Texas, the long drives grew shorter. The future looked bright. But by 1886, several developments had brought the cattle boom to an end. First, the price of beef dropped sharply as the supply increased in the early 1880s. It fell from more than $30 a head to $7. Then came the newly invented barbed wire. As more settlers moved to the Great Plains to farm or raise sheep, they fenced in their lands with barbed wire. The open range disappeared, and cattle could no longer pass freely over the trails. Finally, in the harsh winter of 1886–1887, thousands of cattle on the northern Plains froze to death. Many ranchers were put out of business.

Meanwhile, as the mining and cattle industries were developing, the Native Americans of the Great Plains were being pushed off their land, as you will read in the next section.

Reading **History**
D. Analyzing Causes What caused the decline of cattle ranching on the open range?

Section ❶ Assessment

1. Terms & Names

Explain the significance of:
- frontier
- Great Plains
- boomtown
- long drive
- *vaquero*
- vigilante

2. Taking Notes

Use a diagram to review the rise and fall of the cattle industry.

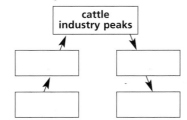

```
        cattle
   industry peaks
      ↗        ↘
  ┌──────┐  ┌──────┐
  └──────┘  └──────┘
     ↗          ↘
  ┌──────┐  ┌──────┐
  └──────┘  └──────┘
```

3. Main Ideas

a. What economic opportunities drew large numbers of people to the West beginning in the 1860s?

b. How did the transcontinental railroad spur Western settlement?

c. What did cowhands learn from the *vaqueros*?

4. Critical Thinking

Evaluating Could cattle ranchers have stopped the decline of the cattle industry that occurred in the late 1880s?

THINK ABOUT
- economic causes
- impact of weather
- changing settlement patterns

ACTIVITY OPTIONS

LANGUAGE ARTS

MUSIC

Do research on a legendary figure of the West such as Wyatt Earp, "Calamity Jane," or Nat Love. Then write a **biographical sketch** or **song** about the person.

TERMS & NAMES
reservation
Sand Creek
  Massacre
Sitting Bull
George A. Custer
Battle of the Little
  Bighorn
Wounded Knee
  Massacre
Dawes Act

MAIN IDEA	WHY IT MATTERS NOW
The Native Americans of the Great Plains fought to maintain their way of life as settlers poured onto their lands.	The taking of their lands led to social and economic problems for Native Americans that continue to this day.

ONE AMERICAN'S STORY

Buffalo Bird Woman was a Hidatsa who lived almost 100 years. She was born in 1840. As a child, she and her family made their home along the Missouri River. Later the federal government forced her family onto a reservation. A **reservation** is land set aside for Native American tribes.

The federal government attempted to "Americanize" Native American children, including Buffalo Bird Woman, by sending them away to boarding schools. But Buffalo Bird Woman struggled to hold on to Hidatsa customs. She spoke only her native language and wore traditional dress. As an old woman, she looked back on her early years.

A VOICE FROM THE PAST

Sometimes at evening I sit, looking out on the . . . Missouri [river]. . . . In the shadows I seem . . . to see our Indian village, with smoke curling upward from the earth lodges; and in the river's roar I hear the yells of the warriors, the laughter of . . . children as of old. It is but an old woman's dream. . . . Our Indian life, I know, is gone forever.

Buffalo Bird Woman, quoted in *Native American Testimony,* edited by Peter Nabokov

Buffalo Bird Woman's life spanned the years when Native Americans waged their final fight to keep lands guaranteed to them by treaties. As white settlers claimed Native American hunting grounds, Plains peoples fought a losing battle to save not only their land but their way of life.

Buffalo Bird Woman saw the Native American way of life change forever during her almost 100 years of life.

Native American Life on the Plains

Before the arrival of Europeans in the 1500s, most Plains tribes lived in villages along rivers and streams. The women tended crops of beans, corn, and squash. The men hunted deer and elk and in the summer stalked the vast buffalo herds that inhabited the Plains.

In the early 1540s, the Spanish brought the first horses to the Great Plains. The arrival of horses changed the way of life of the Plains people. They quickly became expert riders. By the late 1700s, most Plains tribes kept their own herds of horses. Mounted on horseback, hunters traveled far from their villages seeking buffalo.

The buffalo was central to the life of Plains tribes. Its meat became the chief food in their diet, while its skins served as portable shelters called tepees. Plains women turned buffalo hides into clothing, shoes, and blankets and used buffalo chips (dried manure) as cooking fuel. Bones and horns became tools and bowls. Over time, many Plains tribes developed a nomadic way of life tied to buffalo hunting.

Vocabulary
nomadic: wandering from place to place

A Clash of Cultures

When the federal government first forced Native American tribes of the Southeast to move west of the Mississippi in the 1830s, it settled them in Indian Territory. This territory was a huge area that included almost all of the land between the Missouri River and Oregon Territory. Most treaties made by the government with Native Americans promised that this land would remain theirs "as long as Grass grows or water runs."

Reading **History**

A. Analyzing Causes What was the major source of conflict between white settlers and Native Americans?

Unfortunately, these treaty promises would be broken. Government policy was based on the belief that white settlers were not interested in the Plains. The land was considered too dry for farming. However, as wagon trains bound for Oregon and California crossed the Great Plains in the 1850s, some pioneers saw possibilities for farming and ranching on its grasslands. Soon white settlers moved onto the prairies.

These settlers pressured the federal government for more land. They also wanted protection from Native Americans in the area. In 1851, the government responded by calling the Sioux, Cheyenne, Arapaho, and

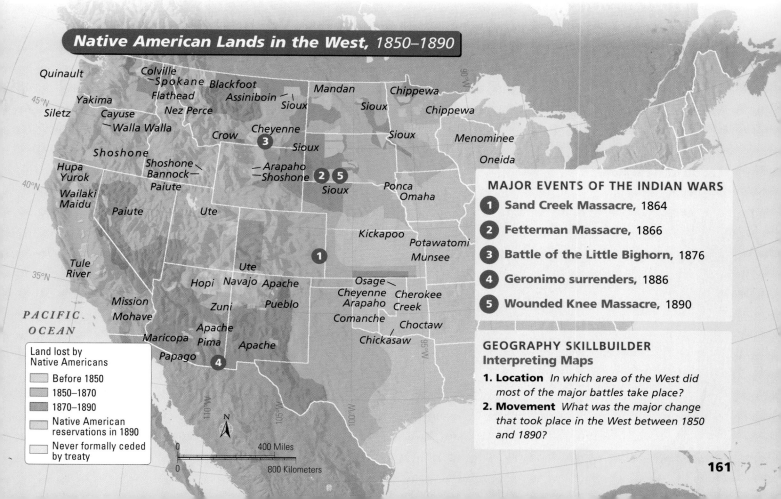

Native American Lands in the West, 1850–1890

MAJOR EVENTS OF THE INDIAN WARS

1. **Sand Creek Massacre,** 1864
2. **Fetterman Massacre,** 1866
3. **Battle of the Little Bighorn,** 1876
4. **Geronimo surrenders,** 1886
5. **Wounded Knee Massacre,** 1890

GEOGRAPHY SKILLBUILDER
Interpreting Maps

1. **Location** In which area of the West did most of the major battles take place?
2. **Movement** What was the major change that took place in the West between 1850 and 1890?

Land lost by Native Americans
- Before 1850
- 1850–1870
- 1870–1890
- Native American reservations in 1890
- Never formally ceded by treaty

other Plains tribes together near Fort Laramie in present-day Wyoming. Government officials tried to buy back some Native American land and also set boundaries for tribal lands. Many Plains tribes signed the First Treaty of Fort Laramie (1851)—they saw no other choice.

But some Cheyennes and Sioux resisted. They preferred conflict with settlers and soldiers to the restrictions of reservation life. In southeastern Colorado, bands of Cheyenne warriors attacked miners and soldiers. In response, about 1,200 Colorado militia led by Colonel John Chivington opened fire on a peaceful Cheyenne village along Sand Creek in 1864. More than 150 Cheyenne men, women, and children were killed in what came to be known as the **Sand Creek Massacre.**

*Reading*History

B. Reading a Map
Locate the site of the Sand Creek Massacre on the map on page 161.

The Plains tribes reacted to such attacks by raiding white settlements. One of the fiercest battles took place in Montana. There the government had begun to build a road called the Bozeman Trail across Sioux hunting grounds. To stop construction, the Sioux attacked construction workers. In 1866, Captain W. J. Fetterman and 80 troopers stumbled into a deadly ambush set by the Sioux. All the soldiers were killed in what was called the Fetterman Massacre.

Such incidents finally forced the government to try to find a way to end the fighting. In 1868, U.S. officials signed the Second Treaty of Fort Laramie with the Sioux, Northern Cheyenne, and Arapaho. The treaty gave these tribes a large reservation in the Black Hills of South Dakota.

HISTORY through ART

Artist Edgar S. Paxson researched the Battle of the Little Bighorn for 20 years to try to accurately re-create the last moments of the fighting. Custer is at the center clutching at a bullet wound in his chest.

What do you think this painting shows about the fighting at the Little Bighorn?

Battle of the Little Bighorn

The Second Treaty of Fort Laramie did not end the trouble between the Sioux and white settlers, though. In 1874, white prospectors discovered gold in the Black Hills. Paying no attention to the Fort Laramie treaty, thousands of miners rushed onto Sioux land. Tribal leaders angrily rejected a government offer to buy back the land. Many Sioux warriors fled the reservation during the

winter of 1875–1876. They united under the leadership of two Sioux chiefs—**Sitting Bull** and Crazy Horse—to push back the intruders.

The Seventh Cavalry set out to return the Sioux to the reservations. It was commanded by Lieutenant Colonel **George A. Custer,** a hero of the Civil War and of other campaigns against Plains tribes. On June 25, his forces met several thousand Sioux and Cheyennes near the Little Bighorn River in Montana in the **Battle of the Little Bighorn.** In less than two hours, Custer and his men—211 in all—were wiped out.

News of Custer's defeat shocked the nation. The government responded by stepping up military action. As a result, Little Bighorn was the last major Native American victory. In 1877, Crazy Horse surrendered and Sitting Bull and his followers fled to Canada. In 1881, Sitting Bull's starving band surrendered to U.S. troops and were returned to the reservation.

*Reading*History
C. Recognizing Effects What were the results of the Battle of the Little Bighorn?

Resistance in the Northwest and Southwest

Background
Nez Perce means "pierced nose" in French. French-Canadian trappers gave this name to these Native American people because some of them wore jewelry in their noses.

The Nez Perce (nehz PURS) was a Northwest tribe that lived in eastern Oregon and Idaho. Until the 1860s, the Nez Perce lived peacefully on land guaranteed to them by an 1855 treaty. However, as white settlement increased, the government forced them to sell most of their land and move to a narrow strip of territory in Idaho. Most reluctantly agreed, but a group of Nez Perce led by Chief Joseph refused.

In 1877, Chief Joseph and his followers fled north to seek refuge in Canada. For four months, the Nez Perce traveled across 1,000 miles of rugged terrain with army troops in pursuit. About 40 miles from the Canadian border, the army caught up with them. Greatly outnumbered, the Nez Perce surrendered. Chief Joseph spoke for his people when he said, "I will fight no more, forever."

In the Southwest, both the Navajos and Apaches fought against being removed to reservations. U.S. troops ended Navajo resistance in Arizona in 1863 by burning Navajo homes and crops. Most Navajos surrendered. Nearly 8,000 took what they called the "Long Walk," a brutal journey of 300 miles to a reservation in eastern New Mexico. Hundreds died on the way. Their new home was a parched strip of land near the Pecos River. After four years, the government allowed the Navajos to return to Arizona, where many live today.

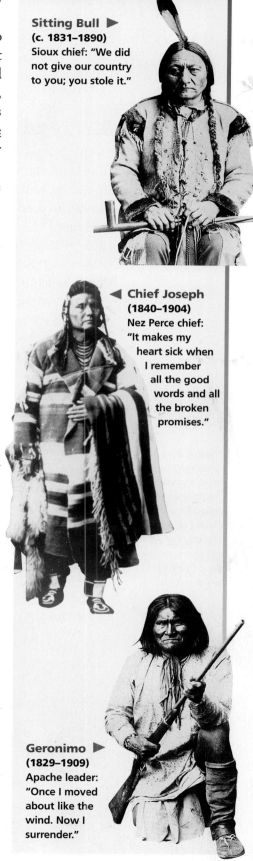

Native American Leaders

**Sitting Bull ▶
(c. 1831–1890)**
Sioux chief: "We did not give our country to you; you stole it."

**◀ Chief Joseph
(1840–1904)**
Nez Perce chief: "It makes my heart sick when I remember all the good words and all the broken promises."

**Geronimo ▶
(1829–1909)**
Apache leader: "Once I moved about like the wind. Now I surrender."

> ## "Once I moved about like the wind. Now I surrender."
> Geronimo

In the early 1870s, the government forced many Apaches to settle on a barren reservation in eastern Arizona. But a group led by Geronimo refused to remain. Escaping the reservation, these Apaches survived by raiding settlers' homes. Geronimo was captured many times but always managed to escape. In 1886, however, he finally surrendered and was sent to prison.

A Way of Life Ends

As the Native Americans of the Plains battled to remain free, the buffalo herds that they depended upon for survival dwindled. At one time, 30 million buffalo roamed the Plains. However, hired hunters killed the animals to feed crews building railroads. Others shot buffalo as a sport or to supply Eastern factories with leather for robes, shoes, and belts. From 1872 to 1882, hunters killed more than one million buffalo each year.

Background
In 1889, fewer than 100 buffalo remained.

By the 1880s, most Plains tribes had been forced onto reservations. With their hunting grounds fast disappearing, some turned in despair to a Paiute prophet named Wovoka. He preached a vision of a new age in which whites would be removed and Native Americans would once again freely hunt the buffalo. To prepare for this time, Wovoka urged Native Americans to perform the chants and movements of the Ghost Dance. Wovoka's hopeful vision quickly spread among the Plains peoples.

Many of Wovoka's followers, especially among the Sioux, fled their reservations and gathered at the Pine Ridge Reservation in South Dakota. White settlers and government officials began to fear that they were preparing for war. The army was sent to track down the Ghost Dancers. They rounded them up, and a temporary camp was made along Wounded Knee Creek in South Dakota, on December 28, 1890. The next day, as the Sioux were giving up their weapons, someone fired a shot. The troopers responded to the gunfire, killing about 300 men, women, and children. The **Wounded Knee Massacre**, as it was called, ended armed resistance in the West.

These Native American students in Oklahoma Territory in 1901 posed for a class picture at the school where they were sent to learn the culture of white people.

Reading **History**
D. Drawing Conclusions What was the most important factor in the defeat of the Native Americans?

The Dawes Act Fails

Some white Americans had been calling for better treatment of Native Americans for years. In 1881, Helen Hunt Jackson published *A Century of Dishonor*, which listed the failures of the federal government's policies toward Native Americans. About the same time, Sarah Winnemucca, a Paiute reformer, lectured in the East about the injustices of reservation life.

*Reading*History

E. Analyzing Points of View
Why did reformers support assimilation?

Many well-meaning reformers felt that assimilation was the only way for Native Americans to survive. Assimilation meant adopting the culture of the people around them. Reformers wanted to make Native Americans like whites—to "Americanize" them.

The **Dawes Act,** passed in 1887, was intended to encourage Native Americans to give up their traditional ways and become farmers. The act divided reservations into individual plots of land for each family. The government sold leftover land to white settlers. The government also sent many Native American children to special boarding schools where they were taught white culture. In "One American's Story," you read about the effort to Americanize Buffalo Bird Woman. But these attempts to Americanize the children still did not make them part of white society.

In the end, the Dawes Act did little to benefit Native Americans. Not all of them wanted to be farmers. Those who did lacked the tools, training, and money to be successful. Over time, many sold their land for a fraction of its real value to white land promoters or settlers.

The situation of Native Americans at the end of the 1800s was tragic. Their lands had been taken and their culture treated with contempt. Not until decades later would the federal government recognize the importance of their way of life. In the next section, you will read about some of the people who settled on Native American lands.

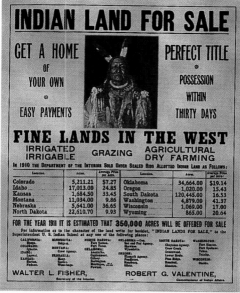

This poster advertised the sale of Native American lands to white settlers.

Section 2 Assessment

1. Terms & Names

Explain the significance of:
- reservation
- Sand Creek Massacre
- Sitting Bull
- George A. Custer
- Battle of the Little Bighorn
- Wounded Knee Massacre
- Dawes Act

2. Taking Notes

Use a chart to compare the life of Plains people before and after the arrival of white settlers.

	Before	After
Meeting survival needs		
Customs		
Land use		

3. Main Ideas

a. How did federal government policy toward Native Americans change as white settlers moved to the West?

b. How did the destruction of the buffalo affect Plains peoples?

c. Why was Wounded Knee a turning point in relations between Native Americans and the government?

4. Critical Thinking

Recognizing Effects How were the effects of the Dawes Act different from what was intended?

THINK ABOUT
- goals of the act
- impact on the land use, culture, and independence of the Plains peoples

ACTIVITY OPTIONS

TECHNOLOGY

SPEECH

Research the life of a Native American leader discussed in this section. Create that person's **Web page** or give a **speech** from this person's perspective.

3 Life in the West

TERMS & NAMES
homestead
Mexicano
William "Buffalo Bill" Cody
buffalo soldier

MAIN IDEA	WHY IT MATTERS NOW
Diverse groups of people helped to shape both the reality and the myth of the West.	The myth of the West continues to be a part of our culture.

ONE AMERICAN'S STORY

Abigail Scott was born in Illinois in 1834. She was told that her mother remarked at the time, "Poor baby! She'll be a woman some day! . . . A woman's lot is so hard!" At 17, Abigail moved to Oregon by wagon train with her family. Her mother died on the journey. In Oregon, Abigail taught school until she married a farmer named Benjamin Duniway in 1853. When he was disabled in an accident, Abigail assumed the support of her family. She wrote about a day on a pioneer farm with its endless chores.

A VOICE FROM THE PAST

[W]ashing, scrubbing, churning . . . preparing . . . meals in our lean-to kitchen . . . [having] to bake and clean and stew and fry; to be in short, a general pioneer drudge, with never a penny of my own, was not pleasant business.

Abigail Scott Duniway, in her autobiography, *Path Breaking*

Later, Duniway grew committed to the cause of women's rights. In 1871, she started a weekly pro-suffrage newspaper. Two years later, she founded the Oregon Equal Suffrage Association.

Oregon honored Duniway for her part in the suffrage struggle by registering her as the state's first woman voter. As you will read in this section, women like Duniway helped to shape the West.

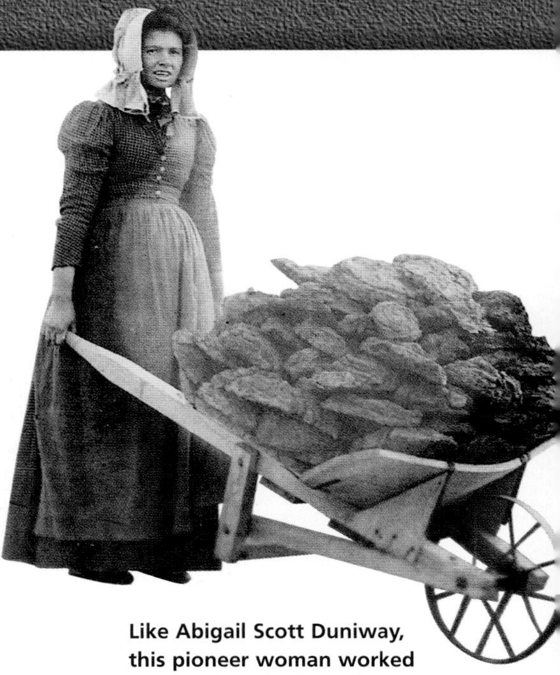

Like Abigail Scott Duniway, this pioneer woman worked long and hard. She is shown here with buffalo chips she has collected on the treeless prairie to use as fuel.

Women in the West

Women often were not given recognition for their efforts to turn scattered Western farms and ranches into settled communities. In their letters and diaries, many women recorded the harshness of pioneer life. Others talked about the loneliness. While men went to town for supplies or did farm chores with other men, women rarely saw their neighbors. Mari Sandoz lived in Nebraska on a **homestead,** a piece of land and the house on it. She wrote that women "had only the wind and the cold and the problems of clothing [and] shelter." Living miles from others, women were their family's doctors—setting broken bones and delivering babies—as well as cooks.

Despite its challenges, Western life provided opportunities for women. Most who worked held traditional jobs. They were teachers or servants or gave their families financial support by taking in sewing or laundry. However, a few became sheriffs, gamblers, and even outlaws. In mining camps and cow towns, some even ran dance halls and boarding houses.

Western lawmakers recognized the contributions women made to Western settlement by giving them more legal rights than women had in the East. In most territories, women could own property and control their own money. In 1869, Wyoming Territory led the nation in giving women the vote. Esther Morris, who headed the suffrage fight there, convinced lawmakers women would bring law and order to the territory.

When Wyoming sought statehood in 1890, many in Congress demanded that the state repeal its woman suffrage law. But Wyoming lawmakers stood firm. They told Washington, "We may stay out of the Union for 100 years, but we will come in with our women." Congress backed down. By 1900, women had also won the right to vote in Colorado, Utah, and Idaho.

*Reading*History
A. Making Inferences Why were women in the West the first to win the right to vote?

The Rise of Western Cities

Cities seemed to grow overnight in the West. Gold and silver strikes made instant cities of places like Denver in Colorado Territory and brought new life to sleepy towns like San Francisco in California. These cities prospered, while much of the area around them remained barely settled. San Francisco grew from a small town to a city of about 25,000 in just one year after the 1849 gold rush.

Miners who flocked to the "Pikes Peak" gold rush of 1859 stopped first in Denver to buy supplies. Not even a town in 1857, Denver was the capital of Colorado Territory by 1867. A decade later, it became the state capital when Colorado was admitted into the Union. The decision by Denver citizens to build a railroad to link their city with the transcontinental railroad sent population soaring. In 1870, it had about 4,800 residents. In 1890, it had nearly 107,000.

The railroads also brought rapid growth to other towns in the West. Omaha, Nebraska, flourished as a meat-processing center for cattle ranches in the area. Portland, Oregon, became a regional

Population of Western Cities		
CITY	1860	1890
Denver	2,603*	106,713
Omaha	1,883	140,452
Portland	2,874	46,385
San Francisco	56,802	298,997

SKILLBUILDER Interpreting Charts
Which city had the largest increase in numbers of people, 1860–1890?

*1861 Territorial Census
Sources: *Population Abstract of the United States; Colorado Republic*

San Francisco, 1847

San Francisco, 1850

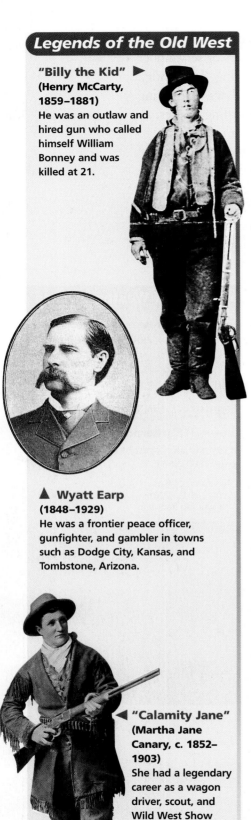

"Billy the Kid" ▶
(Henry McCarty, 1859–1881)
He was an outlaw and hired gun who called himself William Bonney and was killed at 21.

▲ **Wyatt Earp**
(1848–1929)
He was a frontier peace officer, gunfighter, and gambler in towns such as Dodge City, Kansas, and Tombstone, Arizona.

◀ **"Calamity Jane"**
(Martha Jane Canary, c. 1852–1903)
She had a legendary career as a wagon driver, scout, and Wild West Show performer.

market for fish, grain, and lumber. While these cities were growing on the Great Plains and Pacific coast, the Southwest was also developing.

Mexicanos in the Southwest

The Southwest included what are now New Mexico, Texas, Arizona, and California. For centuries, it had been home to people of Spanish descent whose ancestors had come from Mexico. These Spanish-speaking southwesterners called themselves **Mexicanos.**

In the 1840s, the annexation of Texas and Mexico's defeat in the Mexican War brought much of the Southwest under the control of the United States. Soon after, English-speaking white settlers—called Anglos by the Mexicanos—began arriving. These pioneers were attracted to the Southwest by opportunities in ranching, farming, and mining. Their numbers grew in the 1880s and 1890s, as railroads connected the region with the rest of the country.

As American settlers crowded into the Southwest, the Mexicanos lost economic and political power. Many also lost land. They claimed their land through grants from Spain and Mexico. But American courts did not usually recognize these grants. One Mexicano remarked that "the North Americans . . . consider us unworthy to form with them one nation and one society." Only in New Mexico Territory did Hispanic society survive despite Anglo-American settlement.

The Myth of the Old West

America's love affair with the West began just as the cowboy way of life was vanishing in the late 1800s. To most Americans, the West had become a larger-than-life place where brave men and women tested themselves against hazards of all kinds and won. Easterners eagerly bought "dime novels" filled with tales of daring adventures. Sometimes the hero was a real person like Wyatt Earp or "Calamity Jane." But the plots were fiction or exaggerated accounts of real-life incidents.

Also adding to the myth were more serious works of fiction, like Owen Wister's bestselling novel about Wyoming cowhands, *The Virginian* (1902). Such works showed little of the drabness of daily life in the West. White settlers—miners, ranchers, farmers, cowhands, and law officers—played heroic roles not only in novels but also in plays and, later, in movies.

Reading **History**
B. Summarizing
Who were the Mexicanos?

Native Americans generally appeared as villains. African Americans were not even mentioned.

William "Buffalo Bill" Cody, a buffalo hunter turned showman, brought the West to the rest of the world through his Wild West show. Cody recognized people's fascination with the West. His show, with its reenactments of frontier life, played before enthusiastic audiences across the country and in Europe.

The Real West

Background
From 1866 to 1898, some 12,500 African Americans served in the West in the 9th and 10th Cavalry and the 24th and 25th Infantry regiments.

The myth of the Old West overlooked the contributions of many peoples. The first cowhands, as you read earlier, were the Mexican *vaqueros*. Native Americans and African Americans played a role in cattle ranching, too. Many African Americans also served in the U.S. Army in the West, where Native Americans nicknamed them **"buffalo soldiers."** And the railroads would not have been built without the labor of Chinese immigrants.

Western legends often highlighted the attacks by Native Americans on soldiers or settlers. But the misunderstandings and broken treaties that led to the conflicts were usually overlooked.

Reading **History**
C. Comparing
How does the real West compare to the myth of the West?

Historians also say that the image of the self-reliant Westerner who tames the wild frontier ignores the important role played by the government in Western settlement. Settlers needed the help of the army to remove Native Americans. The government also aided in the building of the railroads and gave the free land that drew homesteaders to the West. You will read about these homesteaders and the problems that they faced in the next section.

Now and **then**

THE WEST IN POPULAR CULTURE

The distorted picture of life in the West that had been part of popular culture for decades eventually changed. Starting in the late 1970s, the view became more realistic, especially in motion pictures.

For example, the hardships of the cattle drives were shown in *Lonesome Dove* (1989). The sufferings of Native Americans were portrayed in *Dances With Wolves* (1990). The role of women in the West was dramatized in *Sarah, Plain and Tall* (1991). And the contributions of African Americans were noted in *Buffalo Soldiers* (1997), pictured below.

Section 3 Assessment

1. Terms & Names

Explain the significance of:
• homestead
• Mexicano
• William "Buffalo Bill" Cody
• buffalo soldier

2. Taking Notes

Use a chart to compare Wild West myths with the realities of Western life.

Myth	Real life

What do you think is the most well-known myth about the West?

3. Main Ideas

a. How were women's contributions to the West recognized by Western lawmakers?

b. Which factors led to the growth of such Western cities as Denver, Omaha, and San Francisco?

c. How did the arrival of Anglo-Americans change life for Spanish-speaking residents of the Southwest?

4. Critical Thinking

Making Inferences What changed the attitudes of Western lawmakers about giving women voting rights?

THINK ABOUT
• new roles for women
• need for stability in Western communities
• part played by women in settlement

ACTIVITY OPTIONS

MATH

SPEECH

Pick a Western city mentioned in this section. Create a **database** of information about the city or give a **short speech** describing its growth.

Stage a Wild West Show!

You are the manager of Buffalo Bill's Wild West, the biggest and most famous of the 50 outdoor circuses and shows performing in the United States in the 1880s. Your job is to keep the show running smoothly. You oversee publicity and keep performers and livestock housed, fed, and supplied with the gear they need. You also manage finances.

COOPERATIVE LEARNING On this page are three challenges you face as the manager of Buffalo Bill's Wild West show. Working with a small group, decide how to deal with each challenge. Choose an option, assign a task to each group member, and do the activity. You will find useful information in the Data File.

MATH CHALLENGE

"over $280,000"

What a season you had from May to September of 1886! The show took in more than $280,000. But you had big expenses, too. You want to compare income and expenses so you can make changes to increase profits. Use the Data File for more statistics. Then present your summary using one of these options:

- Make a line graph comparing income and expenses.
- Make a pie chart showing how you spent the income— that is, what your expenses were. Include one sector for profit (the difference between total income and total expenses). Label each sector with the percentage.

LANGUAGE ARTS CHALLENGE

"the thunder of hoofs"

Over the last three days, attendance at the show has slacked off. To meet expenses and generate a profit, you need to fill 15,000 seats. You decide to stir up interest using the local newspaper. Use the Data File for information. Then promote the show.

- Write an article dramatizing the Wild West show.
- Write a script to be used by the master of ceremonies.

BUFFALO BILL'S WILD WEST
AND CONGRESS OF ROUGH RIDERS OF THE WORLD.

ART CHALLENGE

"History . . . in Living Legends"

You need more posters right away because splashy posters are your best advertising. They dazzle people with thrilling Western scenes. They also give show times and admission fees. Use the Data File for help. Then present your ideas using one of these options:

- Design a 2' x 3' poster showing the excitement of the Wild West show.
- Sketch two small action posters, each showing one event, for shop windows.

ACTIVITY WRAP-UP

Present to the class Meet as a group to review your methods of promoting and charting the success of your Wild West show. Evaluate which of your solutions is the best for each challenge. Once you have chosen one solution for each, make a class presentation. Each group member should take part.

📁 **DATA FILE**

WILD WEST SHOW

- 3-hour show; admission, 50¢

Major Show Acts

- "Star-Spangled Banner" Overture
- Grand Review of Buffalo Bill Cody and cast on horseback
- Annie Oakley shoots card targets, apple off her poodle's head
- Reenactments of covered wagons crossing the prairie; a Native American buffalo hunt; outlaws attacking a mail coach; a battle between army and Native Americans
- Sharpshooting by Buffalo Bill

Show Crew and Gear

- crew of 700—including Buffalo Bill, Annie Oakley, Sitting Bull, cowhands, Native Americans, 36-piece band, cooks, blacksmiths, teams to set up grandstand and tents
- animals—including 500 horses, 10 mules, 5 steers, 18 buffalo
- gear—including covered wagons and tepees, guns and ammunition, living and dressing room tents, dining tents, booths selling popcorn, souvenirs, and canvas scenery backdrops, 26-car train for transport

INCOME AND EXPENSES

May 9–September 25, 1886

Total income: $287,000 (from attendance)

Total expenses: $285,000

Owners', managers', key performers' salaries: $55,000

Rents: $58,000

Advertising: $17,000

Printing: $4,000

Groceries/ammunition: $7,000

Miscellaneous expenses: $144,000 (other wages, livestock feed, electricity, medical, security, etc.)

For more about the Old West . . .

 **RESEARCH LINKS**
CLASSZONE.COM

④ Farming and Populism

TERMS & NAMES
Homestead Act
Exoduster
sodbuster
Grange
cooperative
Populist Party
gold standard
William Jennings
Bryan

MAIN IDEA	WHY IT MATTERS NOW
A wave of farmers moved to the Plains in the 1800s and faced many economic problems.	Farmers are facing similar economic problems today.

ONE AMERICAN'S STORY

From 1865 to 1900, about 800,000 Swedes left their homeland in northern Europe. Sweden's population was soaring, and good farmland was becoming scarce. Most Swedes were farmers. They were drawn to the United States by the promise of more and better land.

For Olaf Olsson, the acres of free land offered to settlers by the U.S. government was an unbelievable opportunity. Shortly after he arrived in 1869, Olsson wrote home to tell friends and family what awaited them in America.

A VOICE FROM THE PAST

We do not dig gold with pocket knives, we do not expect to become . . . rich in a few days or in a few years, but what we aim at is to own our own homes. . . . The advantage which America offers is not to make everyone rich at once, without toil or trouble, but . . . that the poor . . . [can] secure a large piece of good land almost without cost, that they can work up little by little.

Olaf Olsson, quoted in *The Swedish Americans,* by Allyson McGill

As you will read in this section, many Americans as well as immigrants from all parts of Europe shared Olsson's optimism. They uprooted their families to start a new life on the Plains.

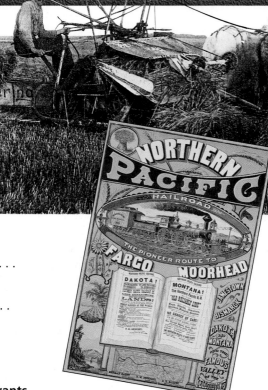

Railroad posters advertise lands in the West.

U.S. Government Encourages Settlement

For years, people had been calling on the federal government to sell Western land at low prices. Before the Civil War, Southern states fought such a policy. They feared that a big westward migration would result in more nonslave states. Once the South left the Union, however, the way was clear for a new land policy. To interest both American and immigrant families like the Olssons in going west, the federal government passed the **Homestead Act** in 1862. This law offered 160 acres of land free to anyone who agreed to live on and improve the land for five years.

After Reconstruction ended in 1877, African Americans in the South faced harsh new forms of discrimination. (See Chapter 4.) By 1879, leaders like Benjamin "Pap" Singleton of Tennessee had convinced thousands to migrate to new homes in Kansas. They compared themselves to the biblical Hebrews led out of slavery in Egypt and called themselves **Exodusters.** One of them, John Solomon Lewis, remarked, "When I landed on the soil of Kansas, I looked on the ground and I says this is free ground." In all, some 50,000 African Americans settled in Kansas, Missouri, Indiana, and Illinois.

Thousands of European immigrants also sought a new start in the West. Swedes, like Olaf Olsson, joined Germans, Norwegians, Ukrainians, and Russians on the Great Plains. They often first learned about the West from land agents for American railroad companies. These salesmen traveled throughout Europe with pamphlets proclaiming "Land for the Landless! Homes for the Homeless."

*Reading*History

A. Analyzing Causes How did the railroads help to settle the West?

From 1850 to 1870, the government gave millions of acres of public land to the railroads to promote railroad expansion. The railroads resold much of the land to settlers. This not only made the railroad companies rich, but it also supplied new customers for railroad services. The railroads' sales pitch worked. In the 1860s, so many Swedes and Norwegians settled in Minnesota that a local editor wrote, "It seems as if the Scandinavian Kingdoms were being emptied into this state."

Life on the Farming Frontier

Once pioneers reached their new homes on the plains, they faced many challenges never mentioned by the land agents. The plains were nearly treeless. So farmers were forced to build their first homes from blocks of sod. Sod is the top layer of prairie soil that is thickly matted with grass roots.

For fuel, the **sodbusters,** as the farmers were called, burned corn cobs or "cow chips" (dried manure). In many places, sodbusters had to dig wells more than 280 feet deep to reach the only water. Blizzards, prairie fires, hailstorms, tornadoes, grasshoppers, and drought added to the misery of life on the plains. Many settlers, such as Katherine Kirk of South Dakota, wondered whether they had the courage "to stick it out."

Connections TO SCIENCE

SOD HOUSES

To build their dwellings, Plains farmers, or sodbusters, like the Nebraska family pictured here, cut the tough buffalo grass of the prairie into two-or three-foot strips. Then they laid chunks of sod into two rows as walls. The walls were often 36 inches thick.

Prairie grass was thick. Its roots grew outward under the soil, often connecting with one another. This held the sod together. The roots also provided a layer of insulation. So sod houses, or soddies, stayed warm in the winter and cool in the summer. But their roofs leaked rain and dirt, and the walls housed mice, snakes, and insects.

New inventions helped farmers to meet some of these challenges. A steel plow invented by John Deere in 1838 and improved upon by James Oliver in 1868 sliced through the tough sod. Windmills adapted to the plains pumped water from deep wells to the surface. Barbed wire allowed farmers to fence in land and livestock. Reapers made the harvesting of crops much easier, and threshers helped farmers to separate grain or seed from straw. These inventions also made farm work more efficient. From 1860 to 1890, farmers doubled their production of wheat.

The Problems of Farmers

As farmers became more efficient, they grew more and more food. The result was that farmers in the West and South watched with alarm as prices for farm crops began to drop lower and lower in the 1870s.

Economics *in* History

Supply and Demand

Farmers in the West were having economic problems in the 1880s. The supply of food was increasing rapidly, but consumer demand was growing slowly. To attract more consumers, farmers had to drop the prices of their products.

The farmers were experiencing the **law of supply and demand**. The amount of economic goods available for sale is the **supply**. The willingness and ability of consumers to spend money for goods and services is **demand**. The price of goods is set by the supply of that good and the demand for that good.

At a lower price, businesses produce less of a good because they will make less money. As the price rises, they produce more. Consumer demand works in the opposite way. Consumers want to buy more of the good when the price is lower—after all, it costs them less. They buy less when the price is higher. The actual price of a good results from a compromise—how much consumers are willing to pay and how little businesses are willing to take for the good.

CONNECT TO HISTORY

1. **Recognizing Effects** Suppose farmers found a new market for their wheat—the people in another country, for instance. What effect would that have on price? Why?

   See Skillbuilder Handbook, page R11.

CONNECT TO TODAY

2. **Comparing** How does the price of blue jeans show the law of supply and demand?

For more about supply and demand . . .

RESEARCH LINKS
CLASSZONE.COM

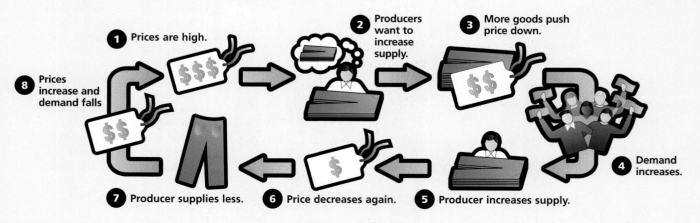

1 Prices are high.
2 Producers want to increase supply.
3 More goods push price down.
4 Demand increases.
5 Producer increases supply.
6 Price decreases again.
7 Producer supplies less.
8 Prices increase and demand falls

(See "Economics in History" on page 174.) Wheat that sold for $1.45 a bushel after the Civil War was 49 cents 30 years later. One reason for lower prices was overproduction. Farmers were growing more food because additional farmland had been opened up and farming methods and machines had improved.

Receiving less money for their crops was bad enough. But at the same time farmers had to spend more to run a farm. New farm machinery and railroad rates were especially costly. Railroads charged the farmers high fees to carry their crops to market. The railroads also usually owned the grain elevators where crops were stored until shipment. Farmers had no choice but to pay the high costs of storage that railroads charged.

"The Grange Awakening the Sleepers" (1873) shows a farmer trying to warn the country about the menace of the railroads.

Farmers were angry. They began to work together to seek solutions to their problems. In 1867, farmers had formed the **Grange,** officially known as the Patrons of Husbandry. The group's main purpose at first had been to meet the social needs of farm families who lived great distances from one another. However, as economic conditions got worse, Grange members took action. They formed **cooperatives.** These are organizations owned and run by their members. The cooperatives bought grain elevators and sold crops directly to merchants. This allowed farmers to keep more of their profits.

Farmers also began to demand action from the government to change their circumstances. For example, Grangers asked states to regulate railroad freight rates and storage charges. Illinois, Minnesota, Wisconsin, and Iowa did so. In 1877, the Supreme Court backed the farmers in their fight against the railroads. In *Munn* v. *Illinois,* the Court ruled that states and the federal government could regulate the railroads because they were businesses that served the public interest.

The Rise of Populism

In 1890, several farm groups joined together to try to gain political power. They formed the **Populist Party,** or People's Party. The Populists wanted the government to adopt a free silver policy, that is, the unlimited coining of silver. Since silver was plentiful, more money would be put in circulation. They believed that increasing the money supply would cause inflation. Inflation, in turn, would result in rising prices. Higher prices for crops would help farmers pay back the money that they had borrowed to improve their farms.

Opponents of free silver wanted to keep the gold standard. Under the **gold standard,** the government backs every dollar with a certain amount

Reading **History**

B. Summarizing What steps did farmers take to seek solutions to their problems?

WILLIAM JENNINGS BRYAN
1860–1925
William Jennings Bryan was known as the "silver-tongued orator from Nebraska." His powerful voice and his strong belief in the "common people" won him two terms in Congress and a presidential nomination at age 36. He made and lost two more bids for president in 1900 and 1908.

Although he never again held elective office, Bryan remained influential in the Democratic Party. Many reforms that he fought for, such as an eight-hour workday and woman suffrage, later became law.

How do you think Bryan was able to influence reform without being elected president?

of gold. Since the gold supply is limited, fewer dollars are in circulation. Inflation is less likely. This protects the value of money by keeping prices down.

In 1892, the Populist Party platform called for free silver to expand the money supply, government ownership of railroads, shorter working hours, and other political reforms. The Populist presidential candidate, James B. Weaver, lost to Grover Cleveland. But he won more than a million votes—a good showing for a third-party candidate.

The Election of 1896

By the next presidential campaign, money issues mattered much more to voters. The nation had suffered through a serious depression, the Panic of 1893. The Republican candidate, William McKinley, favored the gold standard. He warned that "free silver" would mean higher prices for food and other goods.

The Populists joined the Democratic Party in supporting **William Jennings Bryan** of Nebraska. Bryan urged the Democratic convention to support free silver in his stirring "Cross of Gold" speech.

A VOICE FROM THE PAST

Burn down your cities and leave our farms, and your cities will spring up again as if by magic; but destroy our farms and the grass will grow in the street of every city in the country. . . . [We] . . . answer . . . their demand for a gold standard by saying . . . : You shall not press down upon the brow of labor this crown of thorns. You shall not crucify mankind upon a cross of gold.

William Jennings Bryan, Democratic Convention speech, July 8, 1896

Reading **History**

C. Analyzing Points of View
What point was William Jennings Bryan making about the importance of farms?

Farmers in the South and the West voted overwhelmingly for Bryan. But McKinley, who was backed by industrialists, bankers, and other business leaders, won the East and the election by about half a million votes. This election was the beginning of the end for the Populist Party.

The Closing of the Frontier

By the late 1880s, fenced-in fields had replaced open plains. The last remaining open land was in Indian Territory. The Oklahoma land rush of 1889 symbolized the closing of the frontier. At the blast of the starting gun on April 22, thousands of white settlers rushed to claim two million acres of land that had once belonged to Native Americans. In May 1890, this part of Indian Territory officially became Oklahoma Territory. In 1890, 17 million people lived between the Mississippi and the Pacific. That year the Census Bureau declared that the country no longer had a continuous frontier line—the frontier no longer existed.

To many, the frontier was what had made America unique. In 1893, historian Frederick Jackson Turner wrote an influential essay on the frontier. Turner said that the frontier was a promise to all Americans, no matter how poor, that they could advance as far as their abilities allowed. To Turner the frontier meant opportunity, and its closing marked the end of an era.

Thousands of settlers rushed into Oklahoma Territory in 1889 to claim the last open land on the frontier.

Reading **History**

D. Using Secondary Sources What did Frederick Jackson Turner believe about the frontier?

A VOICE FROM THE PAST

Up to our own day American history has been in a large degree the history of the colonization of the Great West. The existence of an area of free land, its continuous recession, and the advance of American settlement westward, explain American development.

Frederick Jackson Turner, "The Significance of the American Frontier"

Today many historians question Turner's view. They think he gave too much importance to the frontier in the nation's development and in shaping a special American character. These historians point out that the United States remains a land of opportunity long after the frontier's closing.

In the next chapter, you will learn how an industrial society developed in the East during the same period that the West was settled.

Section 4 Assessment

1. Terms & Names
Explain the significance of:
• Homestead Act
• Exoduster
• sodbuster
• Grange
• cooperative
• Populist Party
• gold standard
• William Jennings Bryan

2. Taking Notes
Review the chapter and find five key events to place on a time line as shown.

```
1860   event   event   1890

  event   event   event
```

What do you think was the most important event?

3. Main Ideas
a. How did the federal government encourage and support settlement of the Plains?

b. Which groups of people moved onto the Plains in the late 1800s? Why did they come?

c. Which problems in the 1890s led farmers to take political action?

4. Critical Thinking
Drawing Conclusions
Why did the Grange favor government regulation of the railroads?

THINK ABOUT
• powers of monopolies
• importance of railroads to farmers
• railroad freight and storage rates

ACTIVITY OPTIONS

TECHNOLOGY

SPEECH

Pick one invention that helped farmers on the Plains. Plan an **electronic presentation** on the invention or deliver a **sales pitch** to potential buyers.

Growth of the West

The West

Miners

Miners were attracted to the West by gold and silver strikes. Mining contributed to the population growth of many Western territories.

Cowhands & Ranchers

Ranchers and cowhands established a thriving cattle industry. New settlement, barbed wire, and bad weather ended the cattle boom.

Native Americans

Government policies, wars, and the destruction of the buffalo led to the defeat of the Plains peoples and to their placement on reservations.

Homesteaders

Hundreds of thousands of homesteaders settled on the Plains. Their life was hard, but they used new technologies to increase their output.

TERMS & NAMES

Briefly explain the significance of each of the following.

1. frontier
2. long drive
3. reservation
4. Battle of the Little Bighorn
5. Dawes Act
6. homestead
7. Mexicano
8. Homestead Act
9. sodbuster
10. Populist Party

REVIEW QUESTIONS

Miners, Ranchers, and Cowhands (pages 155–159)

1. What role did miners play in the settlement of the West?
2. What made cattle ranching so profitable in the late 1800s?
3. What ended the boom in the cattle business?

Native Americans Fight to Survive (pages 160–165)

4. What caused conflict between Native Americans and white settlers on the Great Plains?
5. How did Native Americans resist white settlement?

Life in the West (pages 166–171)

6. What rights did women in the West gain before women in Eastern states?
7. How has the myth of the "Wild West" been revised?

Farming and Populism (pages 172–177)

8. How did the federal government encourage people to settle on the Great Plains?
9. What were the goals of the Grange?
10. What marked the closing of the frontier?

CRITICAL THINKING

1. USING YOUR NOTES

Using your completed chart, answer the questions below.

a. What were the main reasons that drew people to the West?
b. Which groups do you think benefited from being in the West and which groups did not? Explain.

2. APPLYING CITIZENSHIP SKILLS

What are the dangers of vigilante justice?

3. THEME: DIVERSITY AND UNITY

Why might the contributions of women and Native Americans, African Americans, and other ethnic groups have been overlooked in early books and films on the West?

4. ANALYZING LEADERSHIP

Why did the Nez Perce Chief Joseph decide to surrender? What other choices might he have made?

5. CONTRASTING

How did ranchers and sodbusters differ over land use? Why did these differences lead to conflict?

6. FORMING AND SUPPORTING OPINIONS

What do you think would be the most difficult challenge in starting a new life on the Great Plains? Give reasons for your answer.

Interact with History

Now that you have read the chapter, would you still make the same statements about how your life would change in the West? Explain.

HISTORY SKILLS

1. INTERPRETING MAPS: Movement

Study the map. Answer the questions.

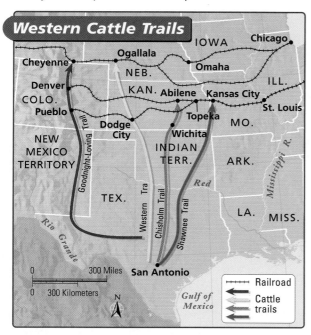

Western Cattle Trails

Basic Map Elements

a. What is the subject of the map?

b. What do the arrows indicate?

Interpreting the Map

c. What is the longest cattle trail?

d. How many miles did it cover?

2. INTERPRETING PRIMARY SOURCES

This quotation by Charles Goodnight, a Texas rancher and founder of the Goodnight-Loving Trail (see above map), appeared in *The West* by Geoffrey Ward.

> All in all, my years on the trail were the happiest I ever lived. There were many hardships and dangers, of course, that called on all a man had of endurance and bravery; but when all went well there was no other life so pleasant. Most of the time we were solitary adventurers in a great land as fresh and new as a spring morning, and we were free and full of the zest of darers.

a. What does Goodnight think about life on a cattle trail?

b. How does Goodnight describe the West?

ALTERNATIVE ASSESSMENT

1. INTERDISCIPLINARY ACTIVITIES: Art

Analyzing Visual Images of the West Look through magazines and books to find images that portray the West today. Create a display of pictures with captions that explains whether each picture portrays the real or legendary Wild West.

2. COOPERATIVE LEARNING ACTIVITY

Performing Dramatic Readings Drawing on the many journals, diaries, and other primary sources left by sodbusters, create a Voices of the Plains play. Working in small groups, have students research such topics as "the journey west," "first impressions," "dugouts and soddies," "farming the plains," and "women's work and worries." Within groups, members can create presentations using these suggestions.

- Choose and research a topic.
- Select quotations related to the topic.
- Pick writers to compose lines to introduce and make transitions between quotations, and choose readers to perform readings.

3. TECHNOLOGY ACTIVITY

Designing a "Legends of the West" Web Site The "Wild West" of the late 1800s was a land of myth and legend. It was peopled by a cast of memorable characters whose exploits, real and imagined, have been portrayed in books, motion pictures, and television. Use the library or search the Internet for information on the "Wild West."

For more about the West . . .

INTERNET ACTIVITY
CLASSZONE.COM

Design a "Wild West" Web site following the suggestions below.
- Select the legendary personalities to be featured.
- Include words and images that capture the flavor of the West.
- Choose musical selections to add background.
- Find Web sites that would be good links for visitors to your page.

4. PORTFOLIO ACTIVITY

Review the list of details that you wanted to know about the West on page 154. Then write a short report in which you explain the details you have learned. Be sure to use standard grammar, spelling, sentence structure, and punctuation in your report. Add this report to your portfolio.

Additional Test Practice, pp. S1–S33

TEST PRACTICE
CLASSZONE.COM

CHAPTER

6

An Industrial Society 1860–1914

Section 1 **The Growth of Industry**
Section 2 **Railroads Transform the Nation**
Section 3 **The Rise of Big Business**
Section 4 **Workers Organize**

These laborers are working in a foundry, a place where metal is cast.

This image shows policemen and soldiers attacking workers who are on strike.

Most of the workers have only bricks, stones, or sticks for weapons.

There were no laws protecting children from dangerous work or long hours.

The year is 1894. You work in a factory that is unheated and badly lit. The machine that you operate is dangerous. The economy is doing poorly, so the factory has cut your wages. Some of your coworkers have gone out on strike. They want better pay and working conditions.

Would you join the strike? Why or why not?

What Do You Think?

- What are some risks you would be taking if you join the strike?
- What might you gain if you take part in the strike?
- What other methods might you use to persuade your employer to meet your demands?

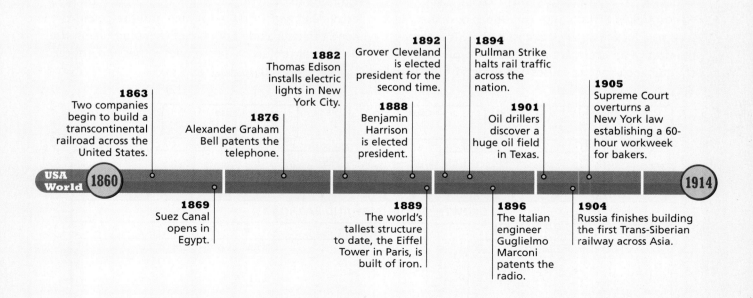

1863
Two companies begin to build a transcontinental railroad across the United States.

1876
Alexander Graham Bell patents the telephone.

1882
Thomas Edison installs electric lights in New York City.

1888
Benjamin Harrison is elected president.

1892
Grover Cleveland is elected president for the second time.

1894
Pullman Strike halts rail traffic across the nation.

1901
Oil drillers discover a huge oil field in Texas.

1905
Supreme Court overturns a New York law establishing a 60-hour workweek for bakers.

USA
World   1860 ——————————————————————————————— 1914

1869
Suez Canal opens in Egypt.

1889
The world's tallest structure to date, the Eiffel Tower in Paris, is built of iron.

1896
The Italian engineer Guglielmo Marconi patents the radio.

1904
Russia finishes building the first Trans-Siberian railway across Asia.

BEFORE YOU READ

Business leader John D. Rockefeller is shown as a wealthy king. Notice which industries are the "jewels in his crown."

Previewing the Theme

Economics in History As Chapter 6 explains, natural resources and new inventions caused industry to boom in the late 1800s. Some businesses grew very large and made great profits by wiping out competitors and paying low wages. Workers banded together to demand higher pay and better working conditions.

What Do You Know?

Do you know of any businesses that started back in the 1800s? How do businesses grow?

THINK ABOUT

• businesses that you see in your community
• businesses that are advertised on television, in magazines or newspapers, or on the Internet

What Do You Want to Know?

What facts and details would help you understand how a nation of small businesses became a nation of giant corporations? In your notebook, list the facts and details you hope to learn from this chapter.

READ AND TAKE NOTES

Reading Strategy: Analyzing Causes and Recognizing Effects The conditions or actions that lead to a historical event are its causes. The consequences of an event are its effects. As you read the chapter, look for the causes and effects of industrial and railroad growth. Causes include geographical factors and actions by individuals and the government. Effects include both benefits and problems. Use the diagram below to record both causes and effects.

S **See Skillbuilder Handbook, page R11.**

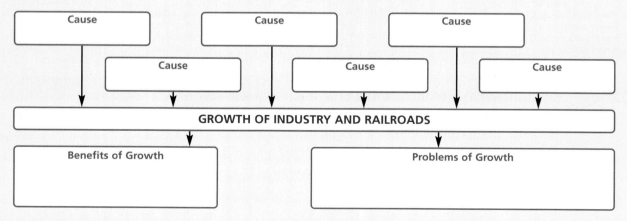

Cause	Cause	Cause
Cause	Cause	Cause

GROWTH OF INDUSTRY AND RAILROADS

Benefits of Growth	Problems of Growth

petroleum
patent
business cycle
Bessemer steel
  process
generator
Thomas Edison
Alexander Graham
  Bell
Centennial Exhibition

MAIN IDEA	WHY IT MATTERS NOW
The growth of industry during the years 1860 to 1914 transformed life in America.	Modern businesses rely on many of the inventions and products developed during that time.

ONE AMERICAN'S STORY

In the 1850s, most Americans lit their homes with oil lamps. They could have used kerosene, an oil made from coal, but it was expensive. Then, in 1855, a chemist reported that kerosene could be made more cheaply from an oily liquid called **petroleum**.

However, people didn't know how to obtain petroleum from underground. They just gathered it slowly when it seeped to the surface. In 1857, Edwin Drake visited a site in Pennsylvania where petroleum oozed to the surface.

A VOICE FROM THE PAST

Within ten minutes after my arrival . . . I had made up my mind that [petroleum] could be obtained in large quantities by Boreing as for Salt Water.

Edwin Drake, quoted in *The Americans: The Democratic Experience*

Drake began drilling in 1859. He struck oil in August. This event launched the oil industry—one of many new industries that developed in the late 1800s, as this section explains.

The wooden structure is Drake's first oil well.

The Industrial Revolution Continues

Throughout the 1800s, factory production expanded in the United States. By the Civil War, factory production had spread beyond New England textiles to other regions and industries. Several factors encouraged this growth.

1. **Plentiful natural resources.** America had immense forests and large supplies of water. It also had vast mineral wealth, including coal, iron, copper, silver, and gold. Industry used these resources to manufacture a variety of goods.
2. **Growing population.** From 1860 to 1900, the U.S. population grew from 31.5 million to 76 million. This led to a growing need for goods. The demand for goods spurred the growth of industry.

3. **Improved transportation.** In the early 1800s, steamboats, canals, and railroads made it possible to ship items long distances more quickly. Railroad building boomed after the Civil War. As shipping raw materials and finished goods to markets became even easier, industry grew.

4. **High immigration.** Between 1860 and 1900, about 14 million people immigrated to the United States. Many of them knew specialized trades, such as metalworking. Such knowledge was valuable to industries. In addition, unskilled immigrants supplied the labor that growing industry needed.

5. **New inventions.** New machines and improved processes helped industry produce goods more efficiently. Inventors applied for patents for the machines or processes they invented. A **patent** is a government document giving an inventor the exclusive right to make and sell his or her invention for a specific number of years.

6. **Investment capital.** When the economy was thriving, many businesses made large profits. Hoping to share in those profits, banks and wealthy people lent businesses money. The businesses used this capital to build factories and buy equipment.

7. **Government assistance.** State and federal governments used tariffs, land grants, and subsidies to help businesses grow.

The Business Cycle

American industry did not grow at a steady pace; it experienced ups and downs. This pattern of good and bad times is called the **business cycle**. During good times, called booms, people buy more, and some invest in business. As a result, industries and businesses grow. During bad times, called busts, spending and investing decrease. Industries lay off workers and make fewer goods. Businesses may shrink—or even close. Such a period of low economic activity is a depression.

America experienced depressions in 1837 and 1857. Both were eventually followed by periods of strong economic growth. In the late 1800s, there were two harsh depressions, also called panics. The depression of 1873 lasted five years. At its height, three million people were out of work. During the depression that began in 1893, thousands of businesses failed, including more than 300 railroads.

The Business Cycle

Peak
(high point)

Contraction
(decrease)

Expansion
(growth)

Expansion

Peak

Trough
(low point)

Change in volume of what businesses produce

Passage of time

SKILLBUILDER Interpreting Charts
1. *How does the amount of goods produced at the peak compare to the amount at the trough?*
2. *Are all peaks equally prosperous? Explain.*

Even with these economic highs and lows, industries in the United States grew tremendously between 1860 and 1900. Overall, the amount of manufactured goods increased six times during these years.

Steel: The Backbone of Industry

The steel industry contributed to America's industrial growth. Before the mid-1800s, steel was very expensive to manufacture because the steel-making process used huge amounts of coal. In the 1850s, William Kelly in the United States and Henry Bessemer in England independently developed a new process for making steel. It used less than one-seventh of the coal that the older process used. This new manufacturing technique was called the **Bessemer steel process**.

Because the Bessemer process cut the cost of steel, the nation's steel output increased 500 times between 1867 and 1900. Industry began to make many products out of steel instead of iron. These products included plows, barbed wire, nails, and beams for buildings. But the main use of steel throughout the late 1800s was for rails for the expanding railroads. (See Section 2.)

Edison and Electricity

Another industry that grew during the late 1800s was the electric-power industry. By the 1870s, inventors had designed efficient generators. A **generator** is a machine that produces electric current. As a result, people grew eager to tap the power of electricity.

The inventor who found the most ways to use electricity was **Thomas Edison.** In 1876, he opened a laboratory in Menlo Park, New Jersey. He employed many assistants, whom he organized into teams to do research. Edison's laboratory invented so many things that Edison received more than 1,000 U.S. patents, more than any other individual inventor.

Edison would start with an idea for a possible invention. Then he would work hard to make that idea a reality—even if problems arose.

A VOICE FROM THE PAST

It has been just so in all my inventions. The first step is an intuition—and comes with a burst, *then* difficulties arise. . . . "Bugs"—as such little faults and difficulties are called—show themselves and months of anxious watching, study and labor are requisite [needed] before commercial success—or failure—is certainly reached.

Thomas Edison, quoted in *Edison* by Matthew Josephson

Edison's most famous invention was practical electric lighting. Other inventors had already created electric lights, but they were too bright and

*Reading*History

B. Drawing Conclusions Which industries benefited from the steel products mentioned here?

*Reading*History

C. Finding Main Ideas According to Edison, is inventing easy?

Connections TO SCIENCE

IRON VS. STEEL

Why is the comic book hero Superman also called the man of steel? People often use the word *steel* as a synonym for strength.

Steel is an iron alloy—a blend of iron and other materials such as carbon. But steel is stronger and more durable than iron. That is why steel replaced iron in many industries in the late 1800s. A giant ladle (bucket) used to pour melted steel is pictured below.

Stainless steel, invented in the early 1900s, has an additional benefit: it doesn't rust. Stainless steel is used in tools, machines, and many household items, such as pots, pans, and utensils.

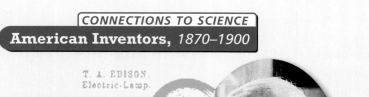

T. A. EDISON.
Electric-Lamp.

Thomas A. Edison

Imagine life without being able to burn lights 24 hours a day. Or without movies and recorded music. Edison invented not only the light bulb but also the phonograph and a moving-picture viewer.

A. G. BELL.
TELEGRAPHY.
No. 174,465. Patented March 7, 1876.

Alexander Graham Bell

As a teacher of the deaf, Bell experimented to learn how vowel sounds are produced. This led to his interest in the electrical transmission of speech.

flickery for home use. Edison figured out how to make a safe, steady light bulb. He also invented a system to deliver electricity to buildings.

By 1882, he had installed electric lighting in a half-mile-square area of New York City. Electric lighting quickly replaced gaslights. By the late 1880s, Edison's factory produced about a million light bulbs a year.

Bell and the Telephone

Electricity played a role in communications devices invented during the 1800s. In 1835, Samuel Morse developed the telegraph. It allowed people to use electrical impulses to send messages over long distances.

The next step in communications was the telephone, invented by **Alexander Graham Bell.** He was a Scottish immigrant who taught deaf students in Boston. At night, Bell and his assistant, Thomas Watson, tried to invent a device to transmit human speech using electricity.

After years of experiments, Bell succeeded. One day in March 1876, he was adjusting the transmitter in the laboratory in his apartment. Watson was in another room with the receiver. The two doors between the rooms were shut. According to Watson's memoirs, Bell accidentally spilled acid on himself and said, "Mr. Watson, come here. I want you." Watson rushed down the hall. He burst into the laboratory, exclaiming that he had heard and understood Bell's words through the receiver.

Bell showed his telephone at the **Centennial Exhibition** in June 1876. That was an exhibition in Philadelphia to celebrate America's 100th birthday. There, several of the world's leading scientists and the emperor of Brazil saw his demonstration. Afterward, they declared, "Here is the greatest marvel ever achieved in electrical science."

Reading **History**
D. Analyzing Points of View
Why do you think the scientists said this about the telephone?

Inventions Change Industry

The telephone industry grew rapidly. By 1880, more than 50,000 telephones had been sold. The invention of the switchboard allowed more and more people to connect into a telephone network. Women commonly worked in the new job of switchboard operator.

The typewriter also opened jobs for women. Christopher Latham Sholes helped invent the first practical typewriter in 1867. He also

J. E. MATZELIGER.
LASTING MACHINE.

Patented Mar. 20, 1883.

Jan Matzeliger

An immigrant from Dutch Guiana, Matzeliger worked in a shoe factory. To reduce the time needed to fasten shoe leather to the sole by hand, he invented a machine to do the job. It increased production by 1,400 percent!

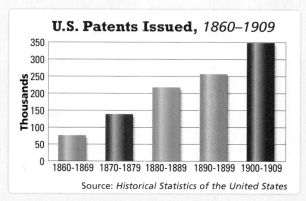

U.S. Patents Issued, *1860–1909*

Source: *Historical Statistics of the United States*

SKILLBUILDER Interpreting Graphs

1. *How many more patents were issued from 1900 to 1909 than from 1860 to 1869?*
2. *Was this a time of increasing or decreasing inventiveness?*

improved the machine and sold his rights to it to a manufacturer who began to make typewriters in the 1870s.

The sewing machine also changed American life. Elias Howe first patented it in 1846. In the next few years, the sewing machine received many design improvements. Isaac Singer patented a sewing machine in 1851 and continued to improve it. It became a bestseller and led to a new industry. In factories, people produced ready-made clothes. Instead of being fitted to each buyer, clothes came in standard sizes and popular styles. Increasingly, people bought clothes instead of making their own.

Other inventors helped industry advance. African-American inventor Granville T. Woods patented devices to improve telephone and telegraph systems. Margaret Knight invented machines for the packaging and shoemaking industries and also improved motors and engines.

Of all the up-and-coming industries of the middle 1800s, one would have a larger impact on American life than any other. That was the railroad industry. You will read about railroads in Section 2.

Section 1 Assessment

1. Terms & Names

Explain the significance of:
• petroleum
• patent
• business cycle
• Bessemer steel process
• generator
• Thomas Edison
• Alexander Graham Bell
• Centennial Exhibition

2. Taking Notes

Use a cluster diagram like the one below to list some of the inventions of the late 1800s.

Inventions

How has one of these inventions recently been improved?

3. Main Ideas

a. What factors contributed to industrial growth in the United States?

b. What is the business cycle?

c. What caused the steel-making industry to boom and why?

4. Critical Thinking

Recognizing Effects How did the inventions of the late 1800s make it easier to do business?

THINK ABOUT

• electric generators and light bulbs
• the telephone
• the typewriter

ACTIVITY OPTIONS

SCIENCE
TECHNOLOGY

Choose an invention and learn more about it. Create a **display** explaining how it works or design a **Web page** linking to sites with more information.

2 Railroads Transform the Nation

transcontinental
railroad
standard time

MAIN IDEA	WHY IT MATTERS NOW
The railroads tied the nation together, speeded industrial growth, and changed U.S. life.	The railroad first made possible our modern system of shipping goods across the country.

ONE AMERICAN'S STORY

Ah Goong was one of thousands of Chinese workers on the Western railroads in the late 1800s. Building a railroad across steep mountains was dangerous. In some places, the workers had to blast rock from a cliff wall to build bridges and tunnels. The lightest Chinese climbed into wicker baskets at the top of the cliff. Others lowered the baskets hundreds of feet to the blasting site. Years later, Ah Goong's granddaughter described her grandfather's job.

A VOICE FROM THE PAST

Swinging near the cliff, Ah Goong . . . dug holes, then inserted gunpowder and fuses. He worked neither too fast nor too slow, keeping even with the others. The basketmen signaled one another to light the fuses. He struck match after match and dropped the burnt matches over the sides. At last his fuse caught; he waved, and the men above pulled hand over hand hauling him up, pulleys creaking.

Maxine Hong Kingston, *China Men*

Chinese immigrants—like the one at the lower left—helped build several railroads in the West.

Irishmen and Americans also worked on the railroads. This section discusses the building of the railroads and how they changed America.

Deciding to Span the Continent

Americans had talked about building a **transcontinental railroad**—one that spanned the entire continent—for years. Such a railroad would encourage people to settle the West and develop its economy. In 1862, Congress passed a bill that called for two companies to build a transcontinental railroad across the center of the United States.

The Central Pacific, led by Leland Stanford, was to start in Sacramento, California, and build east. The Union Pacific was to start in Omaha, Nebraska, and build west. To build the railroad, these two companies had to raise large sums of money. The government lent them millions of dollars. It also gave them 20 square miles of public land for every mile of track they laid. The railroad companies could then sell the land to raise money.

With the guarantees of loans and land, the railroads attracted many investors. The Central Pacific began to lay its first track in 1863. The

Union Pacific laid its first rail in July 1865 (after the Civil War had ended).

Building the Railroad

The Central Pacific faced a labor shortage because most men preferred to try to strike it rich as miners. Desperate for workers, the Central Pacific's managers overcame the widespread prejudice against the Chinese and hired several dozen of them. The Chinese were small and weighed, on average, no more than 110 pounds. But they were efficient, fearless, and hard working.

They also followed their own customs, which led to an unexpected benefit for the railroad company. The Chinese drank tea instead of unboiled water, so they were sick less often than other workers. Pleased with the Chinese workers, the company brought more men over from China. At the peak of construction, more than 10,000 Chinese worked on the Central Pacific.

The Union Pacific hired workers from a variety of backgrounds. After the Civil War ended in 1865, former soldiers from both North and South flocked to work on the railroad. Freed slaves came, too. But one of the largest groups of Union Pacific workers was immigrants, many from Ireland.

Both railroads occasionally hired Native Americans. Washos, Shoshones, and Paiutes all assisted the race of the rails across the deserts of Nevada and Utah.

Railroads Tie the Nation Together

Only short, undergrown trees dotted the vast open space. To the south shimmered the Great Salt Lake. In the east rose the bluish shapes of the Rocky Mountains. Across that space, from opposite directions, the workers of the Central Pacific and the Union Pacific toiled. By May 10, 1869, Central Pacific workers had laid 690 miles of track. Union Pacific workers had laid 1,086 miles. Only one span of track separated the two lines at their meeting point at Promontory, Utah.

Hundreds of railroad workers, managers, spectators, and journalists gathered on that cool, windy day to see the transcontinental railroad completed. Millions of Americans waited to hear the news by telegraph. A band played as a Chinese crew and an Irish crew laid the last rails. The last spike, a golden one, was set in place. First, the president of the Central Pacific raised a hammer to drive in the spike. After he swung the hammer down, the crowd roared with laughter. He had missed. The vice-president of the Union Pacific took a turn and also missed. But the telegraph operator couldn't see and had already sent the message: "done." People across the nation celebrated.

Background
Boiling water kills germs.

*Reading*History
A. Drawing Conclusions Why did the Union Pacific have a larger supply of workers?

*Reading*History
B. Reading a Map Using the map on page 190, find the Union Pacific and Central Pacific Railroads. Notice how they connect Omaha to Sacramento.

daily *life*

RAILROAD CAMPS
Union Pacific workers often worked 12-hour days. Graders had the job of leveling the roadbed. After a day of hard labor, they slept in small dirt shanties like the one below.

Track layers lived together in groups of 100 to 135, in railroad cars with three layers of bunk beds. The cars were parked at the end of the just-finished track. Workers ate in a dining car with their plates nailed to the table. They gobbled a quick meal of beef, beans, and bread. As soon as one group of 125 workers was done, the next group filed in.

This golden spike united the Central Pacific and Union Pacific Railroads.

The Union Pacific-Central Pacific line was the first transcontinental railroad. By 1895, four more U.S. lines had been built across the continent. Between 1869 and 1890, the amount of money railroads earned carrying freight grew from $300 million to $734 million per year.

Background
Canada had also built a transcontinental railroad, so there were six altogether.

Railroad Time

The railroads changed America in a surprising way: they altered time. Before the railroads, each community determined its own time, based on calculations about the sun's travels. This system was called "solar time." Solar time caused problems for people who scheduled trains crossing several time zones and for travelers.

A VOICE FROM THE PAST

I have been annoyed and perplexed by the changes in the time schedules of connecting railroads. My watch could give me no information as to the arrival and departure of trains, nor of the time for meals.

John Rodgers, quoted in *Passage to Union*

To solve this problem, the railroad companies set up **standard time.** It was a system that divided the United States into four time zones. Although the plan went into effect on November 18, 1883, Congress did not adopt standard time until 1918. By then, most Americans saw its benefit because following schedules had become part of daily life.

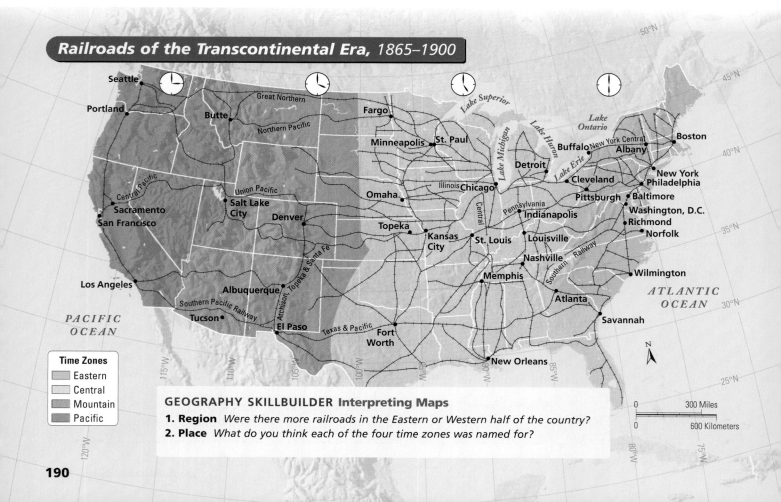

Railroads of the Transcontinental Era, *1865–1900*

Time Zones
- Eastern
- Central
- Mountain
- Pacific

GEOGRAPHY SKILLBUILDER Interpreting Maps
1. **Region** *Were there more railroads in the Eastern or Western half of the country?*
2. **Place** *What do you think each of the four time zones was named for?*

0   300 Miles
0   600 Kilometers

Economic and Social Changes

The railroads changed people's lives in many other important ways. They helped create modern America.

1. **Linked the economies of the West and East.** From the West, the railroads carried eastward raw materials such as lumber, livestock, and grain. Materials like these were processed in Midwestern cities such as Chicago and Cleveland. (See Geography in History on pages 196–197.) From Eastern cities, in turn, came manufactured goods, which were sold to Westerners.

2. **Helped people settle the West.** Railroads were lifelines for settlers. Trains brought them lumber, farm equipment, food, and other necessities and hauled their crops to market.

3. **Weakened the Native American hold on the West.** As Chapter 5 explained, the railroads carried hunters who killed off the herds of buffalo. They also brought settlers and miners who laid claim to Native American land.

4. **Gave people more control of the environment.** Before railroads, people lived mainly where there were waterways, such as rivers. Roads were primitive. Railroads made possible cities such as Denver, Colorado, which had no usable waterways.

Reading **History**

C. Evaluating
Which of these four changes do you think were positive, and which were negative?

Just as railroads changed life for many Americans in the late 1800s, so did big business. You will read about big business in Section 3.

Connections TO
ART & MUSIC

RAILROAD HEROES

Several American songs celebrate railroad heroes. One tells of Casey Jones, an engineer who saved lives. He slammed on the brakes as his train rounded a bend and plowed into a stalled freight train. He died but slowed the train enough to save his passengers.

Another song tells of a mythical worker named John Henry, shown below. This ballad celebrates an African American's strength in a track-laying race against a steam-driven machine.

Section 2 Assessment

1. Terms & Names

Explain the significance of:
- transcontinental railroad
- standard time

2. Taking Notes

Using a chart like the one below, record which groups of people helped build the transcontinental railroad.

Central Pacific	Union Pacific

Which group worked on both railroads?

3. Main Ideas

a. Why did the federal government want a transcontinental railroad built?

b. How did the government encourage the building of the railroad?

c. Why was standard time created?

4. Critical Thinking

Recognizing Effects
Which of the trends started by railroads are still part of the modern business world?

THINK ABOUT
- railroads' effect on time
- the way they linked the economy
- the way they changed where people settled

ACTIVITY OPTIONS

ART

TECHNOLOGY

You have been asked to honor those who built the transcontinental railroad. Design a **memorial** or create the opening screen of a **multimedia presentation**.

TERMS & NAMES
robber baron
corporation
John D. Rockefeller
Andrew Carnegie
monopoly
trust
philanthropist
Gilded Age

3 The Rise of Big Business

MAIN IDEA	WHY IT MATTERS NOW
Business leaders guided industrial expansion and created new ways of doing business.	These leaders developed the modern corporation, which dominates business today.

ONE AMERICAN'S STORY

In 1853, when Jay Gould was 17, he visited New York. Big-city wealth impressed Gould. After returning to his small hometown, he told a friend, "Crosby, I'm going to be rich. I've seen enough to realize what can be accomplished by means of riches, and I tell you I'm going to be rich."

"What's your plan?" his friend asked.

"I have no immediate plan," Gould replied. "I only see the goal. Plans must be formed along the way."

Gould achieved his goal. By the time he died in 1892, he was worth $77 million. He made a lot of his money using methods that are illegal today—such as bribing officials and selling fake stock. Most of his deals involved railroads, including the Union Pacific.

Jay Gould was a robber baron. A **robber baron** was a business leader who became wealthy through dishonest methods. This section discusses other business leaders and their companies.

Jay Gould used methods such as trickery and false reports to "bowl over" his competition.

The Growth of Corporations

Until the late 1800s, most businesses were owned directly by one person or by a few partners. Then advances in technology made many business owners want to buy new equipment. One way to raise money to do so was to turn their businesses into corporations. A **corporation** is a business owned by investors who buy part of the company through shares of stock. A corporation has advantages over a privately owned business:

1. By selling stock, a corporation can raise large amounts of money.
2. A corporation has a special legal status and continues to exist after its founders die. Banks are more likely to lend a corporation money.
3. A corporation limits the risks to its investors, who do not have to pay off the corporation's debts.

In the late 1800s, few laws regulated corporations. This led to the growth of a few giant corporations that dominated American industry. The oil and steel industries are examples of this process.

The Oil and Steel Industries

As Section 1 explained, the oil and steel industries began to grow in the late 1800s. Two men dominated these industries. **John D. Rockefeller** led the oil industry, and **Andrew Carnegie** controlled the steel industry.

John D. Rockefeller built his first refinery in 1863. He decided that the best way to make money was to put his competitors out of business. A company that wipes out its competitors and controls an industry is a **monopoly.** Rockefeller bought other refineries. He made secret deals with railroads to carry his oil at a lower rate than his competitors' oil. He also built and purchased his own pipelines to carry oil.

Rockefeller's most famous move to end competition was to develop the trust in 1882. A **trust** is a legal body created to hold stock in many companies, often in the same industry. Rockefeller persuaded other oil companies to join his Standard Oil Trust. By 1880, the trust controlled 95 percent of all oil refining in the United States—and was able to set a high price for oil. The public had to pay that price because they couldn't buy oil from anyone else. As head of Standard Oil, Rockefeller earned millions of dollars. He also gained a reputation as a ruthless robber baron.

Businessmen in other industries began to follow Rockefeller's example. Trusts were formed in the sugar, cottonseed oil, and lead-mining industries. Many people felt that these monopolies were unfair and hurt the economy. But the government was slow to regulate them.

Rockefeller tried to control all the companies in his industry. By contrast, Andrew Carnegie tried to beat his competition in the steel industry

Vocabulary
refinery: a plant that purifies oil

Reading **History**
A. Analyzing Points of View
Why do you think people thought monopolies were unfair?

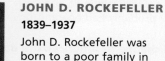

AMERICA'S HISTORY MAKERS

JOHN D. ROCKEFELLER
1839–1937
John D. Rockefeller was born to a poor family in upstate New York. From his mother, he learned the habit of frugality—he avoided unnecessary spending. "Willful waste makes woeful want" was a saying that Rockefeller's mother passed down to him.

By 1897, he had made millions and millions of dollars. Instead of keeping all that vast fortune for himself and his family, he spent the rest of his life donating money to several worthy causes.

ANDREW CARNEGIE
1835–1919
When Andrew Carnegie was 12, he and his family moved from Scotland to Pennsylvania. Carnegie's first job was in a cotton mill.

Later he worked in a telegraph office. There he was noticed by a railroad superintendent, who hired Carnegie as his assistant. Carnegie learned not only about running a big business but also about investing money. Eventually, he quit to start his own business.

Despite his fortune, Carnegie once wrote that none of his earnings gave him as much happiness as his first week's pay.

Compare the characters of Rockefeller and Carnegie. What do you think made each of them successful?

by making the best and cheapest product. To do so, he sought to control all the processes related to the manufacture of steel. He bought the mines that supplied his iron ore, and the ships and railroads that carried that ore to his mills. Carnegie's company dominated the U.S. steel industry from 1889 to 1901, when he sold it to J.P. Morgan, the nation's most prominent banker.

Rockefeller and Carnegie were multimillionaires. They also were both **philanthropists,** people who give large sums of money to charities. Rockefeller donated money to the University of Chicago and Rockefeller University in New York. Carnegie also gave money to universities, and he built hundreds of public libraries. During his life, Rockefeller gave away more than $500 million. Carnegie gave away more than $350 million.

*Reading*History

B. Contrasting
How did the methods that Carnegie and Rockefeller used to eliminate competition differ?

The Gilded Age

The rags-to-riches stories of people such as Rockefeller and Carnegie inspired many Americans to believe that they too could grow rich. Stories like theirs also inspired writer Horatio Alger. He wrote popular stories about poor boys who worked hard and became quite successful.

Inspiring as these stories were, they hid an important truth. Most people who made millions of dollars had not been raised in poverty. Many belonged to the upper classes and had attended college. Most began their careers with the advantage of money or family connections.

For the rich, the late 1800s was a time of fabulous wealth. Writers Mark Twain and Charles Warner named the era the **Gilded Age.** To

HISTORY *through* ART

Artist Eastman Johnson painted this portrait of Alfredrick Smith Hatch's family, one of the wealthiest families in America, in 1870–1871. It shows the family in their New York mansion. Notice the expensive furnishings.

Photographer Jessie Tarbox Beals shot this photograph of a poor family in a tenement in 1910. A tenement is an apartment house that is usually rundown and overcrowded. This family probably had only this tiny space.

How do these two images reflect continuity and change in American life during the Gilded Age?

Vocabulary
gold leaf: gold that has been pounded into thin sheets

gild is to coat an object with gold leaf. Gilded decorations were popular during the era. But the name has a deeper meaning. Just as gold leaf can disguise an object of lesser value, so did the wealth of a few people mask society's problems, including corrupt politics and widespread poverty.

The South Remains Agricultural

One region that knew great poverty was the South. The Civil War had left the South in ruins. Industry did grow in some Southern areas, such as Birmingham, Alabama. Founded in 1871, Birmingham developed as an iron- and steel-producing town. In addition, cotton mills opened from southern Virginia to Alabama. Compared with the Northern economy, however, the Southern economy grew very slowly after the war.

Most of the South remained agricultural. As you have read, many Southern landowners rented their land to sharecroppers who paid a large portion of their crops as rent. Often sharecroppers had to buy their seed and tools on credit. The price of cotton, the South's main crop, was very low. Sharecroppers made little money from selling cotton and had difficulty paying what they owed. And because most sharecroppers had little education, merchants cheated them, increasing their debt.

Reading **History**
C. Making Inferences What is Fortune implying about the storekeeper?

A VOICE FROM THE PAST

My father once kept an account . . . of the things he "took up" at the store as well as the storekeeper. When the accounts were footed [added] up at the end of the year the thing became serious. The storekeeper had $150 more against my father than appeared on the latter's book. . . . It is by this means that [sharecroppers] are swindled and kept forever in debt.

T. Thomas Fortune, testimony to a Senate committee, 1883

At the same time that sharecroppers struggled to break free of debt, workers in the industrial North also faced injustices. In the next section, you will learn how labor unions tried to fight back.

Section **3** **Assessment**

1. Terms & Names

Explain the significance of:
• robber baron
• corporation
• John D. Rockefeller
• Andrew Carnegie
• monopoly
• trust
• philanthropist
• Gilded Age

2. Taking Notes

Use a Venn diagram like the one shown to compare and contrast Rockefeller and Carnegie.

Rockefeller (Both) Carnegie

Whose business methods do you agree with more?

3. Main Ideas

a. Why did the number of corporations grow in the late 1800s?

b. Who is an example of a robber baron? Why?

c. Why was the South so much less industrial than the North?

4. Critical Thinking

Forming and Supporting Opinions Do you think that wealthy people have a duty to become philanthropists? Explain your opinion.

THINK ABOUT
• Carnegie and Rockefeller
• how most wealthy people gain their money
• the differences between the rich and the poor

ACTIVITY OPTIONS

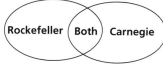

MATH

SPEECH

In your local or school library, look up the business cycle. Create a **graph** of the cycle for the last century or prepare an **oral report** to Congress on the trends.

Industry in the Midwest

The Midwest is the region around the Great Lakes and the Upper Mississippi Valley. The region saw explosive growth during the 1800s. The first wave came after 1825, when the Erie Canal linked the East with the Great Lakes region. The second wave, caused by investments in products related to the Civil War (1861–1865), saw a boom in mining, farming, forestry, and meat-packing. By 1890, 29 percent of the country's manufacturing employment was in the Midwest, and the next big wave of growth was just beginning. New industries included steel and steel products, such as train rails and skyscraper beams.

Transportation and resources spurred the region's growth. Coal, oil, iron ore, limestone, and lumber were abundant, and the land was fertile. Trains, rivers, and lakes connected the Midwest to markets in the East and South and brought in raw materials from the West. The map on page 197 shows the resources of the lower Great Lakes and how transportation by rail and water joined regions.

The industries of the Midwest used raw materials that came both from their own region and from other regions of the country. For example, the cattle in this photograph of the Chicago stockyards came by rail from the ranches of the West. In contrast, the logs being floated down the river came from the pine forests of Michigan and Wisconsin.

ARTIFACT FILE

A Quick Dinner Midwestern meat-packing companies advertised canned meats as a way to save time feeding a hungry family.

Affordable Housing People began to build with wooden siding over a frame of wooden two-by-fours. These homes were cheap and quick to construct.

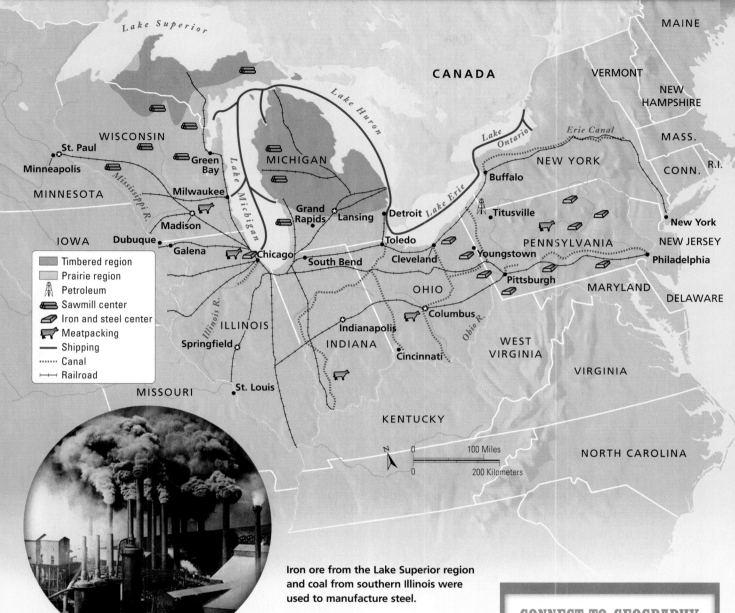

Map Legend

- Timbered region
- Prairie region
- ⛏ Petroleum
- Sawmill center
- Iron and steel center
- 🐄 Meatpacking
- —— Shipping
- ······ Canal
- ⊢——⊣ Railroad

Iron ore from the Lake Superior region and coal from southern Illinois were used to manufacture steel.

On-Line Field Trip

The Chicago Historical Society

in Chicago, Illinois, contains photographs, documents, and artifacts such as this Western Electric typewriter, made in 1900. Typewriters enabled office workers to produce neat, clean documents quickly.

For more about the Midwest . . .

RESEARCH LINKS
CLASSZONE.COM

CONNECT TO GEOGRAPHY

1. **Region** What advantages did the Midwest have that helped it become highly industrialized?
2. **Human-Environment Interaction** How did the development of railroads add to the region's advantages?

    G See Geography Handbook, pages 4–5.

CONNECT TO HISTORY

3. **Analyzing Causes** Chicago was a big meatpacking center. Why do you think that industry chose to locate there?

4 Workers Organize

sweatshop
Knights of Labor
socialism
Haymarket affair
Pullman Strike
Eugene V. Debs
Samuel Gompers
American Federation
of Labor (AFL)

MAIN IDEA	WHY IT MATTERS NOW
To increase their ability to bargain with management, workers formed labor unions.	Many of the modern benefits that workers take for granted were won by early unions.

Mother Jones won the love of working people by fighting for their rights.

ONE AMERICAN'S STORY

In 1867, Mary Harris Jones lost her husband and four children during a yellow fever epidemic in Memphis. For the rest of her life, she dressed in black as a sign of mourning. Moving from Memphis to Chicago, Jones started a dressmaking business. But the great Chicago fire of 1871 destroyed everything she owned. Instead of giving up in despair, Jones found a cause to fight for.

A VOICE FROM THE PAST

From the time of the Chicago fire I became more and more engrossed [interested] in the labor struggle and I decided to take an active part in the efforts of the working people to better the conditions under which they worked and lived.

Mary Harris Jones, *Autobiography of Mother Jones*

Jones became an effective labor leader who organized meetings, gave speeches, and helped strikers. Workers loved her so much that they called her Mother Jones. In this section, you will learn why workers went on strike in the late 1800s and the results of those strikes.

Workers Face Hardships

Business owners of the late 1800s wanted to keep their profits high, so they ran their factories as cheaply as possible. Some cut costs by requiring workers to buy their own tools or to bring coal to heat the factories. Others refused to buy safety equipment. For example, railroads would not buy air brakes or automatic train-car couplers. Because of this, 30,000 railroad workers were injured and 2,000 killed every year.

If a factory became too crowded, the owner rarely built a larger one. Instead, the owner sent part of the work to be done by smaller businesses that critics called sweatshops. **Sweatshops** were places where workers labored long hours under poor conditions for low wages. Often both children and adults worked there.

Factory and sweatshop workers did the same jobs, such as sewing collars or making buttonholes, all day long. They grew bored and did not experience the satisfaction that came from making an entire product themselves. Further, both factory and sweatshop owners kept wages low. In the 1880s, the average weekly wage was less than $10. This barely paid a family's expenses. If a worker missed work due to illness or had any unexpected bills, the family went into debt. Workers began to feel that only other working people could understand their troubles.

> **A VOICE FROM THE PAST**
>
> They know what it is to bring up a family on ninety cents a day, to live on beans and corn meal week in and week out, to run in debt at the stores until you cannot get trusted [credit] any longer, to see the wife breaking down . . . , and the children growing sharp and fierce like wolves day after day because they don't get enough to eat.
>
> **A railroad worker**, quoted in the *Philadelphia Inquirer*, July 23, 1877

Child labor was common in the late 1800s, and as this boy's bare feet demonstrate, safety practices were rare.

So discontented workers joined together to try to improve their lives. They formed labor unions—groups of workers that negotiated with business owners to obtain better wages and working conditions.

Early Unions

As you read in Chapter 3, the first labor unions began in the mid-1800s but were unable to win many improvements for workers. After the Civil War, some unions started to form national organizations. One of these was the **Knights of Labor.** This was a loose federation of workers from all different trades. Unlike many labor organizations, the Knights allowed women and, after 1878, African-American workers to join their union. They inspired many people to support their cause.

Then, beginning in 1873, the United States fell into a serious economic depression. Over the next four years, millions of workers took pay cuts, and about one-fifth lost their jobs. In July 1877, the Baltimore and Ohio (B & O) Railroad declared a wage cut of 10 percent. The day the pay cut was to go into effect, B & O workers in Martinsburg, West Virginia, refused to run the trains. No labor union had called the strike. The workers themselves had stopped working on their own.

"[Working people] know what it is to bring up a family on ninety cents a day."
A railroad worker, 1877

This work stoppage was the Railroad Strike of 1877. As the news spread, workers in many cities and in other industries joined in. This threw the country into turmoil. In several cities, state militias battled angry mobs. President Rutherford B. Hayes called out federal troops. Before the two-week strike ended, dozens of people were killed.

The strike did not prevent the railroad pay cut, but it showed how angry American workers had become. In 1884–1885, railroaders again went out on strike. This time they went on strike against the Union

Pacific and two other railroads. The strikers, who were members of the Knights of Labor, gained nationwide attention when they won their strike. Hundreds of thousands of new workers joined the union.

Union Setbacks

The growth of labor unions scared many business leaders. They blamed the labor movement on socialists and anarchists. Socialists believe in **socialism.** In that economic system, all members of a society are equal owners of all businesses—they share the work and the profits. Anarchists are far more extreme. They want to abolish all governments.

Business and government leaders feared that unions might spread such ideas, so they tried to break union power. In Chicago in 1886, the McCormick Harvester Company locked out striking union members and hired strikebreakers to replace them. On May 3, union members, strikebreakers, and police clashed. One union member was killed.

The next day, union leaders called a protest meeting at Haymarket Square. Held on a rainy evening, the rally was small. As police moved in to end the meeting, an unknown person threw a bomb. It killed 7 police and wounded about 60. The police then opened fire on the crowd, killing several people and wounding about a hundred. This conflict was called the **Haymarket affair.**

Afterward, the Chicago police arrested hundreds of union leaders, socialists, and anarchists. Opposition to unions increased. The membership in the Knights of Labor dropped rapidly—even though that wasn't the union that had called the meeting at Haymarket Square.

Reading **History**
B. Recognizing Effects Did the action of the bomber make it seem more or less likely that anarchists were behind union activity? Explain.

The Homestead and Pullman Strikes

Labor conflicts grew more bitter. In 1892, Andrew Carnegie reduced wages at his steel mills in Homestead, Pennsylvania, but the union refused to accept the cut. The company responded by locking out union workers from the mills and announcing that it would hire nonunion labor. The company also hired 300 armed guards. In response, the locked-out workers gathered weapons. The guards arrived on July 6, and a battle broke out that left ten people dead. The Pennsylvania state militia began to escort the nonunion workers to the mills. After four months, the strike collapsed, breaking the union.

Workers lost another dispute in 1894. In that depression year, many railroad companies went bankrupt. To stay in business, the Pullman Palace Car Company, which made railroad cars,

Reading **History**
C. Analyzing Causes Why was it so difficult for early unions to win against big business?

One night during the Pullman Strike, some 600 freight cars were burned.

200

cut workers' pay 25 percent. But Pullman did not lower the rent it charged workers to live in company housing. After their rent was deducted from the lower pay, many Pullman workers took home almost nothing.

The Pullman workers began the **Pullman Strike,** a strike which spread throughout the rail industry in 1894. When the Pullman Company refused to negotiate, American Railway Union president **Eugene V. Debs** called on all U.S. railroad workers to refuse to handle Pullman cars. Rail traffic in much of the country came to a halt. President Grover Cleveland called out federal troops, which ended the strike. Debs was put in jail.

Gompers Founds the AFL

Not all companies treated workers as harshly as Carnegie and Pullman did. For instance, in the 1880s, the soap company Procter & Gamble began to give its employees an extra half day off a week. It also began a profit-sharing plan, in which a company gives part of its profits to workers.

However, workers at most companies received low wages and few benefits. So in spite of the opposition to unions, the labor movement did not die. In 1886, labor leader **Samuel Gompers** helped found a new national organization of unions called the **American Federation of Labor (AFL).** Gompers served as AFL president for 37 years.

The AFL focused on improving working conditions. By using strikes, boycotts, and negotiation, the AFL won shorter working hours and better pay for workers. By 1904, it had about 1.7 million members.

In the next few decades, labor unions helped change the way all Americans worked. At the same time, city growth and immigration transformed America. You will read about that in Chapter 7.

*Reading*History

D. Identifying Problems What problems did the AFL try to solve?

Section **4** Assessment

1. Terms & Names

Explain the significance of:
- sweatshop
- Knights of Labor
- socialism
- Haymarket affair
- Pullman Strike
- Eugene V. Debs
- Samuel Gompers
- American Federation of Labor (AFL)

2. Taking Notes

Review this section and find five key events to place on a time line like the one below.

1870   event   event   1910

event   event   event

What individuals played significant roles in these events?

3. Main Ideas

a. What hardships did workers face in the late 1800s?

b. What happened to unions after the protest at Haymarket Square?

c. How did Carnegie's company break the union at the Homestead mills?

4. Critical Thinking

Drawing Conclusions In your opinion, was the government more supportive of unions or business in the late 1800s? Explain.

THINK ABOUT
- the Railroad Strike of 1877
- the Homestead Strike
- the Pullman Strike

ACTIVITY OPTIONS

LANGUAGE ARTS

ART

Decide whether unions should be encouraged. Write an **editorial** or create a **public message poster** expressing your opinion.

An Industrial Society **201**

VISUAL SUMMARY

An Industrial Society

Long-Term Causes
- plentiful natural resources
- building of canals and railroads in early 1800s

Immediate Causes
- continued building of railroads in late 1800s
- growing population and high immigration
- new inventions and industrial processes
- investment capital and development of corporations

GROWTH of INDUSTRY

Immediate Effects
- increased amount of manufactured goods
- growth of large corporations, monopolies, and trusts
- poor conditions for workers in factories and sweatshops
- labor unions and strikes

Long-Term Effects
- economies of East and West linked together
- labor movement wins permanent changes, such as reduced working hours

TERMS & NAMES

Briefly explain the significance of each of the following.

1. patent
2. business cycle
3. transcontinental railroad
4. standard time
5. corporation
6. John D. Rockefeller
7. Andrew Carnegie
8. Haymarket affair
9. Pullman Strike
10. American Federation of Labor (AFL)

REVIEW QUESTIONS

The Growth of Industry (pages 183–187)

1. How do inventors protect their rights to what they invent?
2. What did Thomas Edison and Alexander Graham Bell invent?

Railroads Transform the Nation (pages 188–191)

3. What geographic feature made building the Central Pacific difficult?
4. What took place when workers connected the Central Pacific and the Union Pacific?

The Rise of Big Business (pages 192–197)

5. What is a monopoly?
6. What are trusts, and why did some people think they were bad for the country?
7. Why did writers Mark Twain and Charles Warner name the late 1800s the Gilded Age?

Workers Organize (pages 198–201)

8. What ideas did business leaders fear that unions would spread?
9. How did the Pullman Strike begin and end?
10. Which unions were led by Eugene V. Debs and Samuel Gompers?

CRITICAL THINKING

1. USING YOUR NOTES

Using your completed chart, answer the questions below.

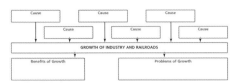

a. How did the growth of railroads act as a cause of industrial growth?
b. Who do you think benefited most from the growth of industry? Explain.

2. THEME: ECONOMICS IN HISTORY

Who is someone from this chapter that might view the United States as a land of economic opportunity? Explain your answer.

3. ANALYZING LEADERSHIP

What characteristics of a good leader did Mother Jones possess?

4. APPLYING CITIZENSHIP SKILLS

Were John D. Rockefeller and Andrew Carnegie good citizens? Support your answer with details from this chapter.

5. COMPARING

How were the problems of sharecroppers, described on page 195, similar to those of Pullman workers, described on pages 200–201?

6. DRAWING CONCLUSIONS

Why do you think unions were more successful at attracting members in the late 1800s than in the early 1800s?

Interact with History

Now that you have read the chapter, would you change your mind about joining the strike? Explain.

HISTORY SKILLS

1. INTERPRETING GRAPHS

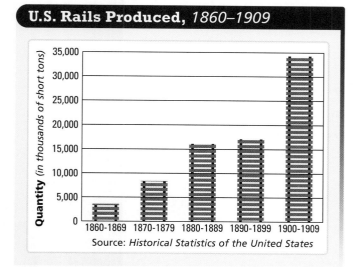

U.S. Rails Produced, *1860–1909*

Source: *Historical Statistics of the United States*

Basic Graph Elements

a. What period of time does this graph cover?

b. What was the general trend in rail production?

Interpreting the Graph

c. Which decade saw the biggest change in rail production?

d. What does this graph indicate about what was happening in the railroad industry?

2. INTERPRETING PRIMARY SOURCES

This memoir was written by James Davis, who was secretary of labor during the 1920s. In 1886, when he was 12, he worked in a mill making wrought iron.

> In this mill there is a constant din by day and night. Patches of white heat glare from the opened furnace doors like the teeth of some great, dark dingy devil grinning across the smoky vapors of the Pit. Half-naked, soot-smeared fellows fight the furnace hearths with hooks, rabbles, and paddles. Their scowling faces are lit with fire like sailors manning their guns in a night fight when a blazing fire ship is bearing down upon them. The sweat runs down their backs and arms and glistens in the changing lights. Brilliant blues and rays of green and bronze come from the coruscating [sparkling] metal, molten yet crystallizing into white-hot frost within the furnace puddle.
>
> **James Davis,** *The Iron Puddler*

a. What were working conditions like in the mill where Davis worked?

b. Do you think Davis liked his work? Use details from the passage to support your answer.

ALTERNATIVE ASSESSMENT

1. INTERDISCIPLINARY ACTIVITY: Science

Diagramming a Process Do research to find out how iron is converted to steel in the Bessemer process. Make a diagram that shows the process. Use terms from science to describe what happens to different elements during the heating process. Share your diagram with the class.

2. COOPERATIVE LEARNING ACTIVITY

Performing a Monologue Working in a small group, research the life of a business or labor leader from this chapter. Write and perform a monologue in which the leader discusses his or her life. After the presentation, ask the class to discuss what they learned from your monologue. Assign group members one or more of the following tasks:

a. researching the person's life

b. writing the monologue

c. editing the monologue

d. finding costumes and props

e. creating sound effects (if necessary)

f. directing the rehearsals

g. acting out the monologue

3. TECHNOLOGY ACTIVITY

Writing a Report Using the Internet, reference materials, and other printed material, write a report that describes how scientific ideas influenced technological developments during different periods in U.S. history. Consider the following topics:

- how Enlightenment ideas affected 17th-century science
- how scientific ideas affected industrialization in the 19th century

For more about industrialization in the United States . . .

INTERNET ACTIVITY
CLASSZONE.COM

4. HISTORY PORTFOLIO

Option 1 Review your section and chapter assessment activities. Select one that you think is your best work. Then use comments made by your teacher or classmates to improve your work and add it to your portfolio.

Option 2 Review the scientific and technological developments discussed in this chapter. Create a chart that lists the ways these developments affected daily life in the United States. Add your chart to your portfolio.

Additional Test Practice, pp. S1–S33

TEST PRACTICE
CLASSZONE.COM

CHAPTER
7

Changes in American Life

1880–1914

Crowds of people walk, work,
and shop on Mulberry Street in
New York's Lower East Side.

Ellis Island in New York Harbor was the port of entry for most European immigrants. It opened in 1892.

Many immigrants looked for friends who had already come to America.

Most immigrants came to America with just a few dollars and a small number of treasured personal possessions.

It is 1900, and you have decided to leave your native country. After a long and difficult voyage, you arrive in the United States. Now you need to find a new home and a job. You have to create a new life in a strange land.

What Do You Think?
- What caused you to leave your native country?
- What problems did you face on your voyage?
- What do you hope to find in the United States?

How will you make a home in your new country?

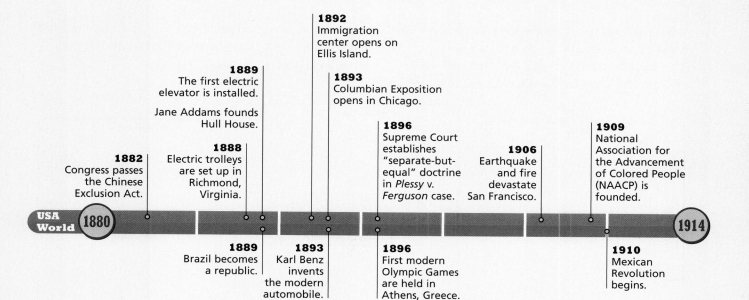

1892
Immigration center opens on Ellis Island.

1889
The first electric elevator is installed.

Jane Addams founds Hull House.

1893
Columbian Exposition opens in Chicago.

1888
Electric trolleys are set up in Richmond, Virginia.

1896
Supreme Court establishes "separate-but-equal" doctrine in *Plessy* v. *Ferguson* case.

1906
Earthquake and fire devastate San Francisco.

1909
National Association for the Advancement of Colored People (NAACP) is founded.

1882
Congress passes the Chinese Exclusion Act.

USA World 1880

1889
Brazil becomes a republic.

1893
Karl Benz invents the modern automobile.

1896
First modern Olympic Games are held in Athens, Greece.

1910
Mexican Revolution begins.

1914

BEFORE YOU READ

Previewing the Theme

Diversity and Unity Chapter 7 discusses how American society went through deep changes at the end of the 19th century. The economy became more industrial. Millions of immigrants came to the United States. Cities grew rapidly. These changes caused tensions in the nation. Immigrants and racial minorities faced discrimination.

Asia

Europe

Latin America

What Do You Know?

What do you think about when you hear the term *immigration*? Why do people move to different countries? What kinds of challenges might immigrants face in their new country?

THINK ABOUT

• what you know about immigration from your own experience or the experience of your family
• what would make you want to move away from your home

What Do You Want to Know?

What questions do you have about American life around 1900? Write them in your notebook before you read the chapter.

READ AND TAKE NOTES

Reading Strategy: Categorizing To help you make sense of what you read, learn to categorize. Categorizing means sorting information into groups. The chart below will help you take notes and categorize the changes in American life that occurred during the late 19th and early 20th centuries.

S **See Skillbuilder Handbook, page R6.**

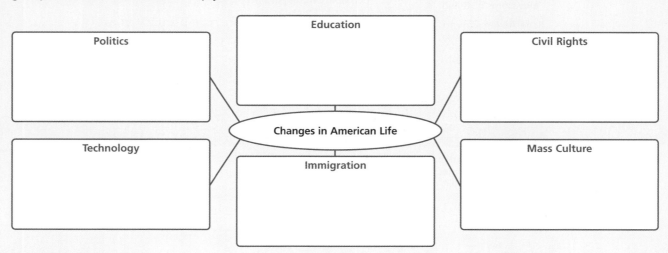

Politics

Education

Civil Rights

Changes in American Life

Technology

Immigration

Mass Culture

① Cities Grow and Change

TERMS & NAMES
urbanization
tenement
slum
social gospel
Jane Addams
Hull House
political machine
Tammany Hall

MAIN IDEA

Industrialization and immigration caused American cities to grow rapidly.

WHY IT MATTERS NOW

Modern American city life first emerged during this period.

ONE AMERICAN'S STORY

Carl Jensen came to the United States from Denmark in 1906. Like most of the millions of immigrants who came to America around the turn of the century, he immediately began to look for work. He described the crush of people, including himself, who were searching for jobs in New York.

A VOICE FROM THE PAST

Along thirty miles of water front I wandered in search of work . . . waiting through rain and sleet and snow with gangs of longshoremen [dockworkers] to reach the boss before he finished picking the men he wanted. . . . Strong men crushed each other to the ground in their passion for work.

Carl Jensen, quoted in *A Sunday Between Wars*

Jensen eventually found work in New York's garment, or clothing, district. At the turn of the century, the promise of work drew millions of people like Carl Jensen from around the world to American cities. In this section, you will read about the rapid growth of American cities.

Shipyards in growing cities provided jobs for many Americans.

Industrialization Expands Cities

The Industrial Revolution, which had been changing how people worked, also changed *where* people worked. Since colonial days, most Americans had lived and worked in rural areas. But in the late 1800s, that began to change as more and more people moved to cities to find jobs.

Industries were drawn to cities because cities offered good transportation and plentiful workers. Increasing numbers of factory jobs appeared in America's cities, followed by more workers to fill those jobs. The growth of cities that resulted from these changes is called **urbanization.**

Many of the people who moved to American cities were immigrants like Carl Jensen. People also migrated from America's farms to the cities. Once there, even workers with few skills could usually find steady work.

Building a Skyscraper

Modern cities depend on skyscrapers to increase the space for people to live and work. Steel, electricity, and elevators make skyscrapers possible.

1 STEEL FRAMES Steel beams can carry much more weight than brick or stone walls. The strength of the steel allows architects to design extremely tall buildings.

2 WINDOWS In skyscrapers, the outer walls do not support the weight of the building; the steel beams do. As a result, many skyscrapers have outer walls made of glass to allow sunlight inside.

3 ELEVATOR Tall buildings would be useless if people could not reach all of the floors. Elevators powered by electricity make such tall buildings practical.

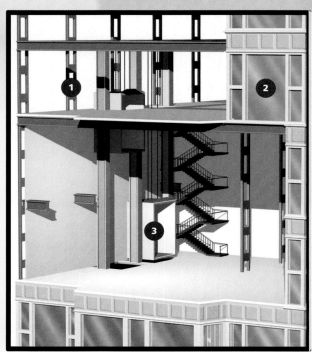

Technology Changes City Life

New technologies helped cities absorb the millions of people who flocked there. For example, new technologies made possible the construction of skyscrapers, buildings that looked tall enough to scrape the sky. Skyscrapers helped cities grow and made modern city life possible.

The elevator was a key invention for constructing tall buildings that could hold greater numbers of people. Before the 1860s, buildings rarely rose higher than four stories because it was hard for people to climb to the top. In 1889, the Otis Elevator Company installed the first electric elevator. Now buildings could be more than a few stories tall because people no longer had to walk up to the higher floors. As a result, buildings could hold more people.

The use of steel also helped to increase the height of buildings. In 1885, the Home Insurance Building in Chicago boasted an iron and steel skeleton that could hold the immense weight of the skyscraper's floors and walls. The building climbed to ten stories. Skyscrapers changed city skylines forever.

*Reading*History
A. Recognizing Effects How did industry and technology help cities grow?

The Streetcar City

As electricity helped change the way people traveled inside buildings, it also changed how people traveled around cities. Before industrialization, people walked or used horse-drawn vehicles to travel over land. But by 1900, electric streetcars in American cities were carrying more than 5 billion passengers a year. Streetcars and trains changed the walking city into the streetcar city.

Background
Streetcars are also called trolleys.

In 1888, Richmond, Virginia, became the first American city to have a transportation system powered by electricity. Other cities soon installed their own electric streetcars. The streetcars could quickly carry people to work and play all over the city. Some cities, such as Chicago, moved their electric streetcars above the street level, creating elevated, or "el," lines. Other cities, like New York, placed their city rail lines in underground tunnels, making subways.

The streetcar city spread outward from the city's center in ways the walking city never could. The ability to live farther away from work helped new suburbs to develop around cities. Some people in the suburbs wanted to become part of the city they bordered. That way they also could be served by the city's transportation system. Largely due to public transportation, cities expanded. For example, in 1889, Chicago annexed several suburbs and more than doubled its population as well as its area.

Vocabulary
annex: to add

Urban Disasters and Slums

The concentration of people in cities increased the danger of disasters because people and buildings were packed closely together. For example, in 1906, a powerful earthquake rocked San Francisco. The tremors caused large fires to tear through the city. The central business district was destroyed. About 700 people died, and nearly $400 million in property was damaged. But natural disasters were not the only source of danger for the people of the cities. Poverty and disease also threatened their lives.

As people flocked to cities, overcrowding became a serious problem. It was especially serious for families who could not afford to buy a house. Such families usually lived in rented apartments or tenements. A **tenement** is an apartment house that is usually run-down and overcrowded.

Old buildings, landlord neglect, poor design, and little government control led to dangerous conditions in many tenements. Poor families who could not afford to rent a place of their own often needed to move in with other families. This resulted in severely overcrowded tenements. Inadequate garbage pick-up also caused problems. Tenants sometimes dumped their garbage into the narrow air shafts between tenements. There was little fresh air, and the smell was awful.

Many tenements had no running water. Residents had to collect water

*Reading*History
B. Summarizing
What was it like to live in a turn-of-the-century tenement?

HISTORY *through*ART

This photograph by Lewis Hine shows a family of Italian immigrants in their cramped, decaying tenement in New York City in 1912. Often photographers, such as Hine, had their subjects pose for their pictures to create the strongest effect.

What effect do you think Hine wanted this photograph to have?

from a faucet on the street. The water could be heated for bathing. But it was often unsafe for drinking. Sewage flowed in open gutters and threatened to spread disease among tenement dwellers.

A neighborhood with such overcrowded, dangerous housing was called a **slum**. The most famous example was New York City's Lower East Side. But every city had slums. After visiting Chicago's slums, the British writer Rudyard Kipling wrote in disgust, "Having seen it [Chicago], I urgently desire never to see it again."

Reformers Attack Urban Problems

Many Americans were also disgusted by poverty and slums. Some people fought to reform, or create changes, that would solve these problems. They were known as urban reformers.

The social gospel movement provided one basis for these beliefs. The **social gospel** movement aimed to improve the lives of the poor. Led by Protestant ministers, the ideas of the movement were based on Christian values. The most important concerns of the social gospel movement were labor reforms, such as abolishing child labor. Some reformers inspired by the movement opened settlement houses. They helped the poor and immigrants improve their lives. Settlement houses offered services such as daycare, education, and health care to needy people in slum neighborhoods.

*Reading*History
C. Making Inferences How did Christian values support the social gospel movement?

CITIZENSHIP TODAY

Community Service

Since the United States began, citizens have shared concerns about their communities. Many citizens, such as Jane Addams in 1889, have identified problems and proposed solutions to them.

In 1993, sixth-grader David Levitt asked his principal if the leftover food from the school cafeteria could be sent to a program to feed needy people. David was told that many restrictions prevented giving away the food.

Determined to get food to people who needed it, David talked to the school board, the state health department, and private companies to convince them to back his program. Today, more than 500,000 pounds of food from schools has been given to hungry people in the Seminole, Florida, area.

David Levitt carries supplies for his food pantry program.

How Do You Participate in Your Community?

1. In a small group, think about problems within your community. Make a list of those problems.

2. Choose one problem to work on.

3. Gather information about the problem. Keep a log of your sources to use again.

4. After you gather information, brainstorm solutions to the problem. Create a plan to carry out one solution.

5. Present the problem and your plan to the class.

See the Citizenship Handbook, page 108.

For more about community service . . .

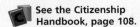
RESEARCH LINKS
CLASSZONE.COM

Many settlement house founders were educated middle-class women. **Jane Addams** founded Chicago's **Hull House** in 1889 with Ellen Gates Starr. Hull House soon became a model for other settlement houses, including New York's Henry Street Settlement House, which Lillian D. Wald established in 1889.

Political Machines Run Cities

Political machines were another type of organization that addressed the problems of the city. A **political machine** is an organization that influences enough votes to control a local government.

Political machines gained support by trading favors for votes. For example, machine bosses gave jobs or food to supporters. In return, supporters worked and voted for the machine. Political machines also did many illegal things. They broke rules to win elections. They accepted bribes to affect government actions.

The most famous political machine was **Tammany Hall** in New York City. It was led by William Marcy Tweed. Along with his greedy friends, "Boss" Tweed stole enormous amounts of money from the city.

Reading **History**
D. Comparing and Contrasting How were settlement houses and political machines similar? How were they different?

Despite such corruption, political machines did a number of good things for cities. They built parks, sewers, schools, roads, and orphanages in many cities. In addition, machine politicians often helped immigrants get settled in the United States by helping them find jobs or homes. Many immigrants gratefully supported the political machine after this kind of help. In the next section, you will learn more about immigration.

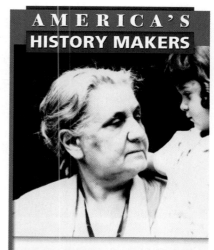

AMERICA'S HISTORY MAKERS

JANE ADDAMS
1860–1935

Jane Addams founded Hull House as an "effort to aid in the solution of the social and industrial problems which are [caused] by the modern conditions of life in a great city."

In addition to Hull House, Addams was active in many other areas. She fought for the passage of laws to protect women workers and outlaw child labor. She also worked to improve housing and public health. In 1931, she was awarded a share of the Nobel Peace Prize for her efforts.

Why did Jane Addams found Hull House?

Section 1 Assessment

1. Terms & Names

Explain the significance of:
- urbanization
- tenement
- slum
- social gospel
- Jane Addams
- Hull House
- political machine
- Tammany Hall

2. Taking Notes

Use a chart like the one below to show the causes and effects of urban growth.

Cause	Effect
Steel	
Elevators	
Streetcars	
Immigration	

3. Main Ideas

a. Why did immigrants and farmers settle in big cities at the end of the 19th century?

b. What are two inventions that made modern city life possible?

c. What urban problems did reformers try to solve?

4. Critical Thinking

Evaluating What were some of the advantages and disadvantages of machine politics?

THINK ABOUT
- the problems faced by immigrants and cities
- Tammany Hall and "Boss" Tweed

ACTIVITY OPTIONS

LANGUAGE ARTS

ART

It is 1900, and you have just moved to an American city. Write a **letter** to friends back home or draw a **picture** that describes your new home.

② The New Immigrants

TERMS & NAMES
new immigrants
Ellis Island
Angel Island
melting pot
assimilation
Chinese Exclusion
  Act

MAIN IDEA	WHY IT MATTERS NOW
Millions of immigrants—mostly from southern and eastern Europe—moved to the United States.	The new immigrants had an important role in shaping American culture in the 20th century.

ONE AMERICAN'S STORY

In 1907, 10-year-old Edward Corsi left Italy to come to America. After two weeks at sea, he caught his first sight of the Statue of Liberty. He described the reaction of the people on the ship.

A VOICE FROM THE PAST

This symbol of America . . . inspired awe in the hopeful immigrants. Many older persons among us, burdened with a thousand memories of what they were leaving behind, had been openly weeping. . . . Now somehow steadied, I suppose, by the concreteness of the symbol of America's freedom, they dried their tears.

Edward Corsi, *In the Shadow of Liberty*

The Statue of Liberty and Ellis Island were two of the first things many immigrants saw of the United States.

Every day, thousands of immigrants like Corsi streamed through Ellis Island, the nation's immigration station. In this section, you will learn about the immigrants who came to the United States around 1900 and how they affected the nation.

The New Immigrants

Until the 1890s, most immigrants to the United States had come from northern and western Europe. But after 1900, fewer northern Europeans immigrated, and more southern and eastern Europeans did. This later group of immigrants came to be known as the **new immigrants**. Southern Italy sent large numbers of immigrants. Many Jews from eastern Europe and Slavic peoples, such as Poles and Russians, also immigrated.

Ellis Island was the first stop for most immigrants from Europe. There, they were processed before they could enter the United States. First, they had to pass a physical examination. Those with serious health problems or diseases were sent home. Next, they were asked a series of questions: Name? Occupation? How much money do you have?

Louis Adamic came to America from Slovenia, in southeastern Europe, in 1913. Adamic described the night he spent on Ellis Island. He and many other immigrants slept on bunk beds in a huge hall. Lacking a warm blanket, the young man "shivered, sleepless, all night, listening to snores" and dreams "in perhaps a dozen different languages."

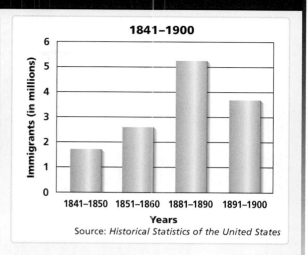

CONNECTIONS TO MATH

U.S. Immigration, *1841–1900*

1841–1860

0.7%
1%
2%
3.3%

93%

1881–1900

0.5%
1.5%
6%
31%

61%

■ Northern and western Europe   ■ Southern and eastern Europe   ■ Americas   ■ Asia   ■ All others

1841–1900

Immigrants (in millions)

6 — 5 — 4 — 3 — 2 — 1 — 0

1841–1850   1851–1860   1881–1890   1891–1900

Years

Source: *Historical Statistics of the United States*

SKILLBUILDER Interpreting Graphs

1. *About how many immigrants came to the United States from 1841 to 1860?*
2. *About how many southern and eastern European immigrants came to the United States from 1881 to 1900?*

While European immigrants passed through Ellis Island on the East Coast, Asians landed at **Angel Island** in San Francisco Bay. In Angel Island's filthy buildings, most Chinese immigrants were held for several weeks. One unhappy prisoner carved in the wall, "For what reason must I sit in jail? It is only because my country is weak and my family poor."

Many Mexican immigrants entered the United States through Texas. Jesús [heh•SOOS] Garza recalled how simple his journey was. "I paid my $8, passed my examination, then changed my Mexican coins for American money and went to San Antonio, Texas."

Settling in America

Immigrants settled where they could find jobs. Many found work in American factories. The immigrants contributed to the growth of cities such as New York, Boston, Philadelphia, Pittsburgh, and Chicago. About half of the new immigrants settled in four industrial states: Massachusetts, New York, Pennsylvania, and Illinois.

Once in America, newer immigrants looked for people from the same village in the old country to help them find jobs and housing. People with similar ethnic backgrounds often moved to the same neighborhoods. As a result, ethnic neighborhoods with names like "Little Italy" and "Chinatown" became common in American cities.

The immigrants living in these communities pooled money to build places of worship for their neighborhoods. They published newspapers in their native languages. They commonly supported political machines, often led by politicians who had also come from their country of origin. Such politicians could speak the native language and help new arrivals feel comfortable. Most importantly, politicians could help immigrants find jobs.

Reading **History**
A. Identifying Problems How did immigrants show creativity in solving problems?

"I paid my $8, passed my examination, . . . and went to San Antonio."

Jesús Garza

Changes in American Life   **213**

Labor unions helped immigrants fit into American life. The various languages on the signs at this rally show the ethnic diversity in the labor movement.

Immigrants Take Tough Jobs

Immigrants took whatever jobs they could get. Many immigrants worked in Northern factories. As you read in Chapter 6, most factories offered low wages, long hours, and unsafe conditions. Many European immigrants who had settled in the East found jobs in sweatshops for about $10 a week. One observer of textile sweatshops noted, "The faces, hands, and arms to the elbows of everyone in the room are black with the color of the cloth on which they are working."

While European immigrants settled mostly in the East and Midwest, Asian immigrants settled mostly in the West. Many Chinese immigrants worked on the railroad. Others settled in Western cities where they set up businesses such as restaurants and stores. Large numbers of Japanese immigrants first came to Hawaii in 1885 to work on sugar plantations. Others settled on the mainland, where they fished, farmed, and worked in mines.

Immigrants from Mexico came to the Southwest. Mexican immigration increased after 1910 when revolution in that country forced people to flee. Growers and ranchers in California and Texas used the cheap labor Mexican immigrants offered. Owners of copper mines in Arizona hired Mexicans as well.

Reading **History**
B. Making Inferences What did all the immigrants seem to have in common?

Becoming Americans

Some Americans have described the United States as a **melting pot**, or a place where cultures blend. The new immigrants blended into American society as earlier immigrants had. This process of blending into society is called **assimilation**. Most new immigrants were eager to assimilate. To do so, they studied English and how to be American citizens.

Many workers began to assimilate at work. Employers and labor unions both tried to "Americanize" immigrant workers by offering classes in citizenship and English. A Lithuanian worker explained that his labor union helped him learn to "read and speak and enjoy life like an American." He then became an interpreter for the union to help other Lithuanians become Americans.

At the same time the immigrants were learning about America, they were also *changing* America. Immigrants did not give up their cultures right away. Bits and pieces of immigrant languages, foods, and music worked their way into the rest of American culture.

Despite their efforts to assimilate, immigrants faced prejudice from native-born Americans. Many Protestants feared the arrival of Catholics and Jews. Other native-born Americans thought immigrants would not fit into democratic society because they would be controlled by political machines. Such prejudices led some native-born Americans to push for restrictions to reduce the numbers of new immigrants coming to America.

Restrictions on Immigration

Many native-born Americans also feared they would have to compete with immigrants for jobs. Immigrants were desperate for jobs and would often take work for lower wages in worse conditions than other Americans. Some Americans worried that there would not be enough jobs for everyone. These fears led to an upsurge in nativist opposition to immigration. In 1882, Congress began to pass laws to restrict immigration. They placed taxes on new immigrants

Background
The Chinese Exclusion Act was renewed in 1892. In 1902, the ban was made permanent. It was not repealed until 1943.

and banned specific groups, such as beggars and people with diseases. Nonwhites faced deeper prejudice than European immigrants, and Asians faced some of the worst. In 1882, Congress passed the **Chinese Exclusion Act**. It banned Chinese immigration for ten years.

The Chinese Exclusion Act was not the only example of prejudice in America around 1900. As you will read in the next section, racial discrimination was common throughout the United States.

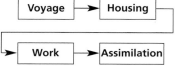

Now and then

LATE 20TH-CENTURY IMMIGRATION

Historians refer to the people who came to the United States around 1900 as the "new immigrants." But an even newer wave of immigrants has been coming to the United States since the 1980s.

From 1981 to 1996, nearly 13.5 million people immigrated to the United States. About 6.5 million came from other nations in the Western Hemisphere. In the same period, 4.8 million people came from Asia.

Section 2 Assessment

1. Terms & Names

Explain the significance of:
- new immigrants
- Ellis Island
- Angel Island
- melting pot
- assimilation
- Chinese Exclusion Act

2. Taking Notes

Use a chart to take notes on immigrant experiences in the United States.

Voyage → Housing

Work → Assimilation

Which part of the immigrant experience was the most difficult?

3. Main Ideas

a. How were the new immigrants different from earlier immigrants?

b. How did immigrants support one another?

c. Why did nonwhite immigrants have a harder time assimilating than European immigrants did?

4. Critical Thinking

Making Generalizations
How well does the idea of the melting pot reflect U.S. immigration around 1900?

THINK ABOUT
- assimilation
- immigrant languages and cultures
- ethnic neighborhoods

ACTIVITY OPTIONS

MATH
GEOGRAPHY

Research immigration to your city or state. Create a **spreadsheet** of this information or draw a **map** showing immigration routes.

from
Dragonwings
by Laurence Yep

In 1903, eight-year-old Moon Shadow makes the long journey from China to join his father in San Francisco. After living for a time in Chinatown, the two move into a white neighborhood where Moon Shadow's father takes a job as a handyman working for Miss Whitlaw, who runs a boarding house for elderly people. Moon Shadow makes friends with Miss Whitlaw's niece Robin. In April of 1906, their world is turned upside down. As Moon Shadow goes outside to fetch water from the pump, an earthquake hits San Francisco, endangering rich and poor, young and old, American and immigrant alike.

The morning was filled with that soft, gentle twilight of spring, when everything is filled with soft, dreamy colors and shapes; so when the earthquake hit, I did not believe it at first. It seemed like a nightmare where everything you take to be the rock-hard, solid basis for reality becomes unreal.

Wood and stone and brick and the very earth became fluidlike. The pail beneath the pump jumped and rattled like a spider dancing on a hot stove. The ground deliberately seemed to slide right out from under me. I landed on my back hard enough to drive the wind from my lungs. The whole world had become unglued. Our stable and Miss Whitlaw's house and the tenements to either side heaved and bobbed up and down, riding the ground like ships on a heavy sea. Down the alley mouth, I could see the cobblestone street **undulate**[1] and twist like a red-backed snake.

From inside our stable, I could hear the cups and plates begin to rattle on their shelves, and the equipment on Father's work table clattered and rumbled **ominously**.[2]

Suddenly the door banged open and Father stumbled out with his clothes all in a bundle. "It's an earthquake, I think," he shouted. He had washed his hair the night before and had not had time to twist it into a **queue**,[3] so it hung down his back long and black.

He looked around in the back yard. It was such a wide, open space that we were fairly safe there. Certainly more safe than in the frame doorway of our stable. He got into his pants and shirt and then his socks and boots.

"Do you think one of the mean dragons is doing all this?" I asked him.

"Maybe. Maybe not." Father had sat down to stuff his feet into his boots. "Time to wonder about that later. Now you wait here."

He started to get to his feet when the second tremor shook and he fell forward flat on his face. I heard the city bells ringing. They were rung by no human hand—the earthquake had just shaken them in their steeples. The second tremor was worse than the first. From all over came an immense wall of noise: of metal tearing, of bricks crashing, of wood breaking free from wood nails, and all. Everywhere, what man had built came undone. I was looking at a tenement house to our right and it just seemed to shudder and then collapse. One moment there were solid wooden walls and the next moment it had fallen with the cracking of wood and the tinkling of glass and the screams of people inside.

---

1. **undulate:** to move like a wave.
2. **ominously:** threateningly.
3. **queue:** a long braid of hair hanging down the back.

Mercifully, for a moment, it was lost to view in the cloud of dust that rose up. The debris surged against Miss Whitlaw's fence and toppled it over with a creak and a groan and a crash. I saw an arm sticking up from the mound of rubble and the hand was twisted at an impossible angle from the wrist. Coughing, Father pulled at my arm. "Stay here now," he ordered and started for Miss Whitlaw's.

I turned. Her house was still standing, but the tenement house to the left had partially collapsed; the wall on our side and part of the front and back had just fallen down, revealing the apartments within: the laundry hanging from lines, the old brass beds, and a few lucky if astonished people just looking out dazedly on what had once been walls. I could see Jack sitting up in bed with his two brothers. His mother and father were standing by the bed holding on to Maisie. Their whole family crowded into a tiny two-room apartment. Then they were gone, disappearing in a cloud of dust and debris as the walls and floor collapsed. Father held me as I cried.

Miss Whitlaw came out onto her porch in her nightdress and a shawl. She pulled the shawl tighter about her shoulders. *"Are you all right?"*

"Yes," Father said, patting me on the back.

"Aren't we, Moon Shadow?"

"Yes." I wiped my eyes on my sleeves.

"Is everyone okay inside?" Father asked Miss Whitlaw.

She nodded. We joined her on the porch and walked with her into her house. Robin was sitting on the stairs that led up to the second floor. She huddled up, looking no longer like the noisy, **boisterous**[4] girl I knew. The front door was open before her. She must have gone outside to look. *"Just about the whole street's gone."*

From up the stairs we could hear the **querulous**[5] old voices of the boarders demanding to know what had happened. Miss Whitlaw shouted up the stairs, "Everything's all right."

"Are you sure?" Father asked quietly.

Miss Whitlaw laughed. *"From top to bottom. Papa always built well. He said he wanted a house that could hold a herd of thundering elephants—that was what he always called Mama's folks. He never liked them much."*

"It's gone," Robin repeated. *"Just about the whole street's gone."*

"Oh, really now." Miss Whitlaw walked past Robin. We followed her out the front door to the front porch. Robin was right.

---

4. **boisterous:** loud, noisy.

5. **querulous:** complaining.

San Franciscans watch the destruction caused by the 1906 earthquake and the resulting fire.

CONNECT TO HISTORY

1. **Finding Main Ideas** How does the earthquake affect the neighborhood that Moon Shadow lives in?

    See Skillbuilder Handbook, page R5.

CONNECT TO TODAY

2. **Researching** What happened in San Francisco after the quake? Did it affect the immigrants differently than others?

For more about the San Francisco earthquake . . .

Segregation and Discrimination

TERMS & NAMES
racial
  discrimination
Jim Crow
segregation
Plessy v. *Ferguson*
**Booker T.
  Washington**
W. E. B. Du Bois
NAACP
Ida B. Wells

MAIN IDEA	WHY IT MATTERS NOW
Racial discrimination ran through American society in the late 19th and early 20th centuries.	Modern American society continues to face the problems caused by racism and discrimination.

ONE AMERICAN'S STORY

African-American sisters Bessie and Sadie Delany grew up in Raleigh, North Carolina, in the early 20th century. Almost 100 years later, they still remembered their first taste of <u>racial discrimination</u>, different treatment on the basis of race.

A VOICE FROM THE PAST

We were about five and seven years old at the time. Mama and Papa used to take us to Pullen Park in Raleigh for picnics, and that particular day, the trolley driver told us to go to the back. We children objected loudly, because we always liked to sit in the front, where the breeze would blow your hair. That had been part of the fun for us. But Mama and Papa just gently told us to hush and took us to the back without making a fuss.

Sarah L. Delany and A. Elizabeth Delany, *Having Our Say*

Bessie (left) and Sadie Delany

Millions of Americans were familiar with the racial discrimination described by the Delanys. As you will read in this section, it was common throughout the United States.

Racism Causes Discrimination

As you read in earlier chapters, racist attitudes had been developing in America since the introduction of slavery. The low social rank held by slaves led many whites to believe that whites were superior to blacks. Most whites held similar attitudes toward Asians, Native Americans, and Latin Americans. Even most scientists of the day believed that whites were superior to nonwhites. However, no scientists believe this today.

Such attitudes led whites to discriminate against nonwhites across the country. The most obvious example of racial discrimination was in the South. Southern blacks had their first taste of political power during Reconstruction. (See Chapter 4.) But when Reconstruction ended in 1877, Southern states began to restrict African Americans' rights.

Segregation Expands in the South

One way for whites to weaken African-American political power was to restrict their voting rights. For example, Southern states passed laws that set up literacy, or reading, tests and poll taxes to prevent African Americans from voting. White officials made sure that blacks failed literacy tests by giving unfair exams. For example, white officials sometimes gave blacks tests written in Latin. Poll taxes kept many blacks from voting because they didn't have enough cash to pay the tax.

*Reading*History

A. Recognizing Effects What was the purpose behind literacy tests, poll taxes, and grandfather clauses?

Such laws threatened to prevent poor whites from voting, too. To keep them from losing the vote, several Southern states added grandfather clauses to their constitutions. Grandfather clauses stated that a man could vote if he or an ancestor, such as a grandfather, had been eligible to vote before 1867. Before that date, most African Americans, free or enslaved, did not have the right to vote. Whites could use the grandfather clause to protect their voting rights. Blacks could not.

In addition to voting restrictions, African Americans faced Jim Crow laws. **Jim Crow** laws were meant to enforce **segregation,** or separation, of white and black people in public places. As a result, separate schools, trolley seats, and restrooms were common throughout the South.

Plessy v. Ferguson

African Americans resisted segregation, but they had little power to stop it. In 1892, Homer Plessy, an African American, sued a railroad company, arguing that segregated seating violated his Fourteenth Amendment right to "equal protection of the laws."

In 1896, the case of *Plessy v. Ferguson* reached the Supreme Court. The Court ruled against Plessy. It argued that "separate but equal" facilities did not violate the Fourteenth Amendment. This decision allowed Southern states to maintain segregated institutions.

*Reading*History

B. Identifying Problems Why was a policy of "separate but equal" unfair?

But the separate facilities were not equal. White-controlled governments and companies allowed the facilities for African Americans to decay. African Americans would have to organize to fight for equality.

Segregation forced African Americans to use separate entrances from whites and to attend separate, usually inferior, schools like the one shown below.

African Americans Organize

<u>Booker T. Washington</u> was an early leader in the effort to achieve equality. He had been born into slavery. But after the Civil War, he became a teacher. In 1881, he founded the Tuskegee Institute in Alabama to help African Americans learn trades and gain economic strength. Washington hired talented teachers and scholars, such as George Washington Carver.

To gain white support for Tuskegee, Washington did not openly challenge segregation. As he said in an 1895 speech in Atlanta, in "purely social matters" whites and blacks "can be as separate as the fingers, yet one as the hand in all things essential to mutual progress."

However, some blacks disagreed with Washington's views. <u>W. E. B. Du Bois</u> (doo•BOYS) encouraged African Americans to reject segregation.

AMERICA'S HISTORY MAKERS

W. E. B. DU BOIS
1868–1963

W. E. B. Du Bois grew up in a middle-class home. He went to college and earned his doctorate at Harvard. Du Bois became one of the most distinguished scholars of the 20th century.

Du Bois fought against segregation. He believed that the best way to end it would be to have educated African Americans lead the fight. He referred to this group of educated African Americans as the "Talented Tenth"—the most educated 10 percent of African Americans.

Why do you think Du Bois believed the Talented Tenth should lead the fight against segregation?

A VOICE FROM THE PAST

Is it possible . . . that nine millions of men can make effective progress in economic lines if they are deprived of political rights? . . . If history and reason give any distinct answer to these questions, it is an emphatic *No.*

W. E. B. Du Bois, *The Souls of Black Folk*

Reading **History**

C. Making Inferences In what way did Washington and Du Bois disagree about how to achieve African-American progress?

In 1909, Du Bois and other reformers founded the National Association for the Advancement of Colored People, or the **NAACP**. The NAACP played a major role in ending segregation in the 20th century.

Violence in the South and North

Besides discrimination, African Americans in the South also faced violence. The Ku Klux Klan, which first appeared during Reconstruction, used violence to keep blacks from challenging segregation. More than 2,500 African Americans were lynched between 1885 and 1900.

<u>Ida B. Wells,</u> an African-American journalist from Memphis, led the fight against lynching. After three of her friends were lynched in 1892, she mounted an anti-lynching campaign in her newspaper. When whites called for Wells herself to be lynched, she moved to Chicago. But she continued her work against lynching. (See Interactive Primary Sources, page 222.)

Like Wells, many blacks moved north to escape discrimination. Public facilities there were not segregated by law. But Northern whites still discriminated against blacks. Blacks could not get housing in white neighborhoods and usually were denied good jobs. Anti-black feelings among whites sometimes led to violence. In 1908, whites in Springfield, Illinois, attacked blacks who had moved there. The whites lynched two blacks within a half mile of Abraham Lincoln's home.

Racism in the West

Chinese immigrants who came to the West in the 1800s also faced severe discrimination. Chinese laborers received lower wages than whites for the same work. Sometimes, Chinese workers faced violence. In 1885, white workers in Rock Springs, Wyoming, refused to work in the same mine as Chinese workers. The whites stormed through the Chinese part of town, shooting Chinese people and burning buildings. During the attack, 28 Chinese people were killed and 15 were wounded.

At the same time, Mexicans and African Americans who came to the American Southwest were forced into peonage (PEE•uh•nihj). In this system of labor, people are forced to work until they have paid off debts. Congress outlawed peonage in 1867, but some workers were still forced to work to repay debts. In 1911, the U.S. Supreme Court declared such labor to be the same as peonage. As a result, the Court struck down such forms of labor as a violation of the Thirteenth Amendment.

Background
The Thirteenth Amendment banned "involuntary servitude"—another term for slavery.

Despite the problems caused by racism, many Americans had new opportunities to enjoy their lives at the turn of the century. In the next section, you will learn about changes in people's daily lives.

The Workingmen's Party of California produced this anti-Chinese poster during the 1880s.

Section 3 Assessment

1. Terms & Names

Explain the significance of:
- racial discrimination
- Jim Crow
- segregation
- *Plessy* v. *Ferguson*
- Booker T. Washington
- W. E. B. Du Bois
- NAACP
- Ida B. Wells

2. Taking Notes

Use a chart to identify people and events related to racial discrimination at the turn of the century.

People	
Events	

Which person do you think did the most to end racial discrimination?

3. Main Ideas

a. What were Jim Crow laws?

b. How did discrimination against African Americans in the North differ from discrimination in the South?

c. What did Chinese immigrants and Mexican immigrants have in common?

4. Critical Thinking

Solving Problems What could have been done to end racial discrimination against nonwhites in the United States at the turn of the century?

THINK ABOUT
- attitudes of whites about nonwhites
- the efforts of nonwhites to find jobs and security
- competition for jobs

ACTIVITY OPTIONS

LANGUAGE ARTS
TECHNOLOGY

Research a civil rights leader from the turn of the century. Write a short **biography** of that person or design a **Web site** devoted to the work of that person.

from *Crusade for Justice* (1892)

Setting the Stage Ida B. Wells was the editor of the *Free Speech and Headlight,* a small Baptist newspaper in Memphis, Tennessee. She used the paper to attack the evils of Jim Crow, especially lynching. In her auto-biography, *Crusade for Justice,* she described the events that led to the lynching of three of her friends. **See Primary Source Explorer**

A CLOSER LOOK

ECONOMIC COMPETITION

Moss, McDowell, and Stewart were African Americans who opened a grocery store near a white-owned store in a black neighborhood.

1. Why might the opening of the black-owned grocery store lead to problems?

A CLOSER LOOK

LYNCHINGS

There was a sharp increase in the number of lynchings in the United States in the 1890s. From 1891 to 1900, more than 1,100 African Americans were lynched.

2. Why do you think the number of lynchings increased in this period?

A CLOSER LOOK

THE GREAT MIGRATION

Between 1890 and 1920, hundreds of thousands of African Americans left the South to escape racism. This movement is called the Great Migration.

3. Why does Wells's newspaper advise African Americans to move away in the wake of the lynching?

While I was thus carrying on the work of my newspaper . . . there came the lynching in Memphis which changed the whole course of my life. . . .

Thomas Moss, Calvin McDowell, and Henry Stewart owned and operated a grocery store. . . . There was already a grocery owned and operated by a white man who **hitherto**[1] had had a **monopoly**[2] on the trade of this thickly populated colored suburb. Thomas's grocery changed all that, and he and his **associates**[3] were made to feel that they were not welcome by the white grocer. . . .

About ten o'clock that [one Saturday] night, . . . shots rang out in the back room of the store. The men stationed there had seen several white men steal-ing through the rear door and fired on them without a moment's pause. Three of these men were wounded, and others fled and gave the alarm.

Sunday morning's paper came out with **lurid**[4] headlines telling how officers of the law had been wounded while in the **discharge**[5] of their duties. . . . The same newspaper told of the arrest and jailing of the **proprietor**[6] of the store and many of the colored people. . . .

On Tuesday following, . . . a body of picked [white] men was admitted to the jail. . . . This mob took out of their cells Thomas Moss, Calvin McDowell, and Henry Stewart. . . . They were loaded on a switch engine of the railroad which ran back of the jail, carried a mile north of the city limits, and horribly shot to death.

Although stunned by the events of that hectic week, the *Free Speech* [Wells's newspaper] felt that it must carry on. Its [lead article] for that week said:

The city of Memphis has demonstrated that neither character nor standing **avails**[7] the Negro if he dares to protect himself against the white man or become his rival. There is nothing we can do about the lynching now, as we are out-numbered and without arms. The white mob could help itself to ammunition without pay, but the order was rigidly enforced against the selling of guns to Negroes. There is therefore only one thing left that we can do; save our money and leave a town which will neither protect our lives and property, nor give us a fair trial in the courts, but takes us out and murders us in cold blood when accused by white persons.

1. **hitherto:** until this time.
2. **monopoly:** exclusive control by one person or group.
3. **associates:** friends or partners.
4. **lurid:** causing shock or horror.
5. **discharge:** performance of duty.
6. **proprietor:** owner.
7. **avails:** helps.

Like Country Pretty Much

Setting the Stage Kee Low was a Chinese immigrant. He had come to the United States in 1876. He was interviewed in 1924 as part of a project by scholars to create a "Survey of Race Relations." This is an excerpt from that interview. In it, Kee Low tells his story. Despite the racism, he still "like country pretty much." **See Primary Source Explorer** ◎

I arrived in San Francisco in 1876, 49 years ago. Come to San Francisco when country one hundred years old. People treat Chinese rotten then. Don't blame people much at that time. Chinese and European not educated as much then as today. More civilized today. People drive Chinese out of country. . . .

I was living on the waterfront, and they told me to get out one day. Sunday morning, they come together and drive Chinese out. . . . They want to get us out to San Francisco, to go on steamer, and we stayed on the **wharf**[1] all night, and they bring us little black coffee and little bread in morning. We pretty hungry. The last day, some of the citizens, Judge Greene, Judge Hanford, United States Attorney, nice fellow want to help us. . . . Judge Greene told the Chinese that those who wanted to stay and make good citizens could stay, and those who wanted to go could go. One half wanted to go, and one half wanted to stay. . . .

There were so many around the streets that they had to have somebody to protect these people. Some of the **hobos**[2] tried to make them go back to the wharf, but volunteers tried to keep these fellows away. They **commenced**[3] shooting and kill one of them. So Chinese people get excited when gun begin to sound, so they throw shoes, blankets and everything and run. I was uptown myself. I didn't intend to go. I ran outside to see what happened because I was so excited. . . . Call up one or two friends of mine and tell them get killed, and we better get out of the way. We run out in woods. Build fire. Pretty cold. I told friends, we got to protect ourselves. We got to get out of here.

1. **wharf:** landing place for ships. 2. **hobos:** homeless people. 3. **commenced:** began.

A CLOSER LOOK

RACIST ATTITUDES

Some people believe that racism is caused by ignorance.

4. Why does Kee Low believe that discrimination against the Chinese was worse in the 1870s than in the 1920s?

A CLOSER LOOK

REASONS TO STAY

Despite the violence that they faced for having Asian ancestry, half of the Chinese with Kee Low wanted to stay in the United States.

5. Why do you think Asian-Americans stayed in the United States despite discrimination?

Interactive Primary Sources Assessment

1. Main Ideas

a. What do the accounts of Wells and Low have in common?

b. How did the officers of the law behave differently in the report by Low than in the one by Wells?

c. What conclusions do Wells and Low come to about how someone should respond to discrimination?

2. Critical Thinking

Forming and Supporting Opinions Do you think Wells and Low were right to flee racism? Why?

THINK ABOUT
• the causes of racism
• the threat of violence to Wells and Low

4 Society and Mass Culture

TERMS & NAMES
mass culture
Joseph Pulitzer
William Randolph
  Hearst
department store
mail-order catalog
leisure
vaudeville
ragtime

MAIN IDEA	WHY IT MATTERS NOW
Industrialization and new technologies created a mass culture in the United States.	Modern American mass culture had its beginnings during this period.

ONE AMERICAN'S STORY

Mary Ellen Chase dreaded her first day of teaching at a new school. Many of the boys were larger than she and were known to be troublemakers. But she would do her best to control the class.

A VOICE FROM THE PAST

I stormed up and down. . . . This pathetic pretense of courage, aided by the mad flourishing of my razor strop, brought forth . . . the expression of respectful fear on the faces of the young giants.

Mary Ellen Chase, quoted in *The Good Old Days—They Were Terrible!*

Discipline was a key goal of education in the 1800s. Education also helped create a common culture for the millions of Americans who went to school. In this section, you will learn how education helped create an American **mass culture**— a common culture experienced by large numbers of people.

Students work on their lessons in this New York City classroom in 1906.

Education and Publishing Grow

Immigration caused enormous growth in American schools. To teach citizenship and English to immigrants, new city and state laws required children to attend school. Between 1880 and 1920, the number of children attending school more than doubled. To serve the growing number of students, the number of public high schools increased from 2,526 in 1890 to 14,326 in 1920.

The growth of education increased American literacy. Reading became more popular. Americans read large numbers of novels. Dime novels were especially popular. They sold for ten cents each and told exciting tales of romance and adventure, often set in the West or on the high seas.

Americans also read more newspapers. Tough competition pushed newspaper publishers to try all sorts of gimmicks to outsell their rivals. For example, **Joseph Pulitzer,** owner of the *New York World*, and

William Randolph Hearst, owner of the *New York Morning Journal,* were fierce competitors. They filled the pages of their papers with spectacular stories. They also added special features, such as comics and sports.

Modern Advertising and New Products

Newspapers had a wide influence on American life, including the rise of modern advertising. Advertisers used images of celebrities in newspapers and magazines to tempt people to buy products. They advertised everything from cereal to jewelry to soap. Some ads played on people's fears. For example, advertisers might scare a young woman concerned about her appearance into buying a particular brand of face cream. Advertising was effective in turning brand names into household words.

Advertisements also helped people learn about new products. At the turn of the century, new inventions, such as the electric washing machine, promised to help people do their household chores more easily. Because women did most of these chores as well as most of the shopping, manufacturers marketed these new devices to women.

One of the places people could buy these—and many other—goods was in department stores. **Department stores** sold everything from clothing to furniture to hardware. The Chicago businessman Marshall Field discovered as a sales clerk that he could increase his sales by paying close attention to each woman customer. Field opened his own department store in downtown Chicago with the motto, "Give the lady what she wants."

People who did not live near a department store could order goods through the mail. Companies like Montgomery Ward and Sears Roebuck sent catalogs to customers. These **mail-order catalogs** included pictures and descriptions of merchandise. People could place their orders by mail, and the company would deliver the product. Richard Sears claimed that he sold 10,000 items a minute.

In 1896, the post office made it easier for people to receive goods through the mail by establishing a new delivery system. Rural free delivery brought packages directly to homes in rural areas. Now people in these areas could get the same goods as people in the cities.

STRANGE *but* True

BICYCLES TO AIRPLANES

At the turn of the century, two bicycle mechanics invented a machine that would help advertisers and businessmen reach new customers. In 1892, Orville and Wilbur Wright opened a bicycle shop in Ohio. They used the profits to fund experiments in aeronautics, the construction of aircraft.

In 1903, the Wright brothers took a gasoline-powered airplane that they had designed to a sandy hill outside Kitty Hawk, North Carolina. On December 17 of that year, Orville made the first successful flight of a powered aircraft in history. By 1918, the U.S. Postal Service began airmail service that made it faster and easier for people to get goods.

Urban Parks and World's Fairs

Advertising and shopping were not the only daily activities changing at this time. **Leisure,** or free time, activities also changed. In cities, new parks provided people with entertainment. The increasing number of people working in factories and offices liked going to parks to get some sunshine and fresh air. Parks helped bring grass and trees back into city landscapes.

▼ **Coney Island**
Visitors to New York's Coney Island cool off in the Steeple-chase Pool.

▼ **World's Fair**
Visitors to the 1893 world's fair in Chicago saw exotic sights, such as elephants.

▼ **Football**
Excited fans watch the 1881 Harvard–Yale football game at the Polo Grounds in New York.

Central Park in New York City is the nation's best-known urban park. Opened in 1876, Central Park looked like the country. Trees and shrubs dotted its gently rolling landscape. Winding walkways let city dwellers imagine they were strolling in the woods. People could also ride bicycles and play sports in the park.

In addition to urban parks, amusement parks provided a place people could go for fun. The most famous amusement park was Coney Island in New York City. Completed in 1904, Coney Island had shops, food vendors, and exciting rides like roller coasters. One immigrant woman said Coney Island "is just like what I see when I dream of heaven!"

World's fairs provided another wildly popular form of entertainment for Americans. Between 1876 and 1916, several U.S. cities, including Philadelphia, Chicago, St. Louis, and San Francisco, hosted world's fairs. The fairs were designed to show off American technology. The 1876 fair in Philadelphia displayed Alexander Graham Bell's newly invented telephone. Millions of people attended these fairs. Nearly 10 million attended the Philadelphia fair alone. Visitors were drawn to foods, shows, and amusements. The historian Thomas Schlereth described the giant wheel built by George Ferris at the 1893 Chicago fair.

Reading **History**
B. Comparing and Contrasting What did urban parks and world's fairs have in common?

A VOICE FROM THE PAST

Chicago's answer to Paris's 1889 Eiffel Tower, Ferris's 264-foot bicycle wheel in the sky dominated the landscape. With thirty-six cars, each larger than a Pullman coach and capable of holding 60 people, the wheel, when fully loaded, rotated 2,160 people in the air.

Thomas Schlereth, *Victorian America*

Spectator Sports

During this time, spectator sports also became popular entertainment. Baseball, football, boxing, and many other sports drew thousands of people to fields and gyms around the country.

Baseball was the most popular sport. Summer games drew crowds of enthusiastic fans. By the 1890s, baseball had standardized rules and a published schedule of games. Racial discrimination kept African-American baseball players out of baseball's American and National Leagues. In order to compete, African Americans formed their own teams in the Negro American League and the Negro National League. (See Geography in History, pages 320–321.)

Going to the Show

In addition to sports, other forms of live entertainment attracted large audiences. **Vaudeville,** for example, featured a mixture of song, dance, and comedy. A show would have a series of acts leading up to an exciting end, which advertisers billed as the "wow finish."

New types of music also began to be heard. **Ragtime,** a blend of African-American songs and European musical forms, was an important new musical form. African-American composer Scott Joplin heard ragtime while he traveled through black communities from New Orleans to Chicago. Joplin's "Maple Leaf Rag," published in 1899, became a hit in the first decade of the 20th century.

Early in the 20th century, movies began to compete with live entertainment. The first movies were silent and were added as the final feature of a vaudeville show. Soon storefront theaters appeared that showed only movies. After 1905, these movie theaters were called nickelodeons because they charged just a nickel for admission.

Reading **History**

C. Making Inferences How do you think movies contributed to mass culture?

Movies, music, sports, and advertising contributed to shaping modern American mass culture. People across the nation experienced many of these things. In the next chapter, you will learn about different nationwide changes—the reform movements of the Progressive era.

America's HERITAGE

RAGTIME

Tired of slow waltz music, young people eagerly embraced ragtime at the turn of the century. The name probably came from a description of the rhythm of black dance music as "ragged time." Ragtime's exciting beat inspired the names of such songs as "Irresistible Fox Trot Rag," "That Fascinating Rag," and "That Nifty Rag."

Ragtime had an enormous influence on American music. Throughout the 20th century, American musical styles such as jazz, blues, rock-and-roll, rap, and rhythm-and-blues built on the style of ragtime.

Scott Joplin

Section 4 Assessment

1. Terms & Names

Explain the significance of:
- mass culture
- Joseph Pulitzer
- William Randolph Hearst
- department store
- mail-order catalog
- leisure
- vaudeville
- ragtime

2. Taking Notes

Use a diagram like the one below to note the changes that created a mass culture at the turn of the century.

3. Main Ideas

a. What did dime novels and newspapers have in common?

b. How did new technologies change the way people bought goods?

c. What did visitors see at world's fairs?

4. Critical Thinking

Making Inferences Why did mass culture emerge during this period?

THINK ABOUT
- the impact of newspapers
- advertising and catalogs
- the development of leisure time

ACTIVITY OPTIONS

ART

LANGUAGE ARTS

Research a world's fair from the turn of the century. Then make a **poster** or write a **newspaper advertisement** that will attract people to the fair.

TERMS & NAMES

Briefly explain the significance of each of the following.

1. urbanization
2. Jane Addams
3. political machine
4. Ellis Island
5. assimilation
6. Jim Crow
7. *Plessy* v. *Ferguson*
8. W. E. B. Du Bois
9. Joseph Pulitzer
10. leisure

REVIEW QUESTIONS

Cities Grow and Change (pages 207–211)

1. How did public transportation change city life?
2. What dangers did urban overcrowding pose to tenement dwellers?
3. How did big-city political machines keep their power?

The New Immigrants (pages 212–217)

4. Where did most American immigrants come from around 1900?
5. How did immigrants enter the United States?
6. Why have some people described the United States as a melting pot?

Segregation and Discrimination (pages 218–223)

7. Why was *Plessy* v. *Ferguson* an important Supreme Court decision?
8. What did African-American leaders do to fight discrimination?

Society and Mass Culture (pages 224–227)

9. What is mass culture?
10. How did city parks improve city life?

CRITICAL THINKING

1. USING YOUR NOTES

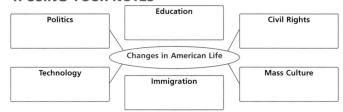

Using your completed chart, answer the questions below:

a. What changes did increased immigration cause?
b. How did the growing popularity of spectator sports and movies help bring about mass culture?
c. Which changes helped immigrants assimilate into American life?

2. ANALYZING LEADERSHIP

Think about the actions of Booker T. Washington and W. E. B. Du Bois. What approach did each take against discrimination? Whose approach do you think was the most likely to be effective?

3. THEME: DIVERSITY AND UNITY

How do you think the emergence of mass culture around 1900 affected immigrants and nonwhites?

4. APPLYING CITIZENSHIP SKILLS

What kinds of things prevented African Americans and immigrants from having full citizenship? How did they attempt to participate in American politics?

Interact *with* History

Have your ideas about how you'll make a home in the United States changed after reading the chapter? Explain.

VISUAL SUMMARY

Changes in American Life

Cities Grow and Change
Industrialization caused American cities to grow.

The New Immigrants
Large numbers of immigrants, especially from southern and eastern Europe, came to the United States.

American Life Around 1900

Segregation and Discrimination
Racial and ethnic minorities faced discrimination across the country.

Society and Mass Culture
New leisure activities and mass culture emerged at this time.

HISTORY SKILLS

1. INTERPRETING GRAPHS

Study the graph and answer the questions.

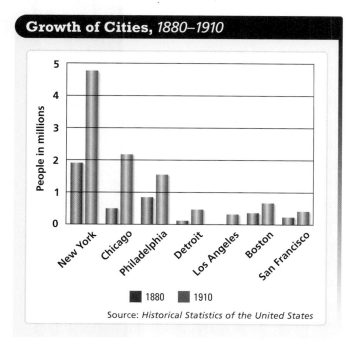

Growth of Cities, *1880–1910*

People in millions — New York, Chicago, Philadelphia, Detroit, Los Angeles, Boston, San Francisco

■ 1880 ■ 1910

Source: *Historical Statistics of the United States*

Basic Graph Elements

a. What cities are shown on the graph?

b. What were the three largest U.S. cities in 1910?

Interpreting the Graph

c. Which city's population increased by the greatest amount between 1880 and 1910?

d. Which city's population increased by the greatest percentage between 1880 and 1910?

2. INTERPRETING PRIMARY SOURCES

Advertisements urged Americans to buy all sorts of goods, such as bicycles. Study the ad carefully. Answer the questions.

a. How does the picture portray the activity of cycling?

b. How do you think this advertisement might convince people to buy bicycles?

ALTERNATIVE ASSESSMENT

1. INTERDISCIPLINARY ACTIVITY: Math

Making a Graph Do research to determine the number of immigrants who came from various countries between 1880 and 1914. Find out where immigrants come from today. Make a graph that displays your findings. Explain your graph to the class.

2. COOPERATIVE LEARNING ACTIVITY

Designing a Park Cities across the United States built parks at the turn of the century. They wanted to provide city dwellers with places to enjoy grass, trees, and fresh air as well as all sorts of leisure activities. What kinds of things would you want to be able to do in a park?

Working in small groups, research city parks built in the late 1800s. Design a park that could please as many urban residents as possible. Make sure to take into account the following.

a. sports fields

b. areas for rest and relaxation

c. places for nature and wildlife

d. buildings for food and restrooms

3. ◉ PRIMARY SOURCE EXPLORER

Creating a Museum Exhibit Racial discrimination has been a sad feature of American history. There is a large amount of information about racism and the ways that racial and ethnic minorities have tried to overcome it. Using the CD-ROM or your local library, collect information on discrimination and civil rights.

Create a museum exhibit about discrimination and civil rights in your hometown using the ideas below.

• Include information on groups that faced discrimination.

• Find biographies about any important civil rights leaders in your town.

• Collect primary sources, such as newspaper articles or autobiographies, that discuss important events.

• Draw a diagram that shows a floor plan for your exhibit.

4. HISTORY PORTFOLIO

Review your section and chapter assessment activities. Select one that you think was your best work. Then use comments made by your teacher or classmates to improve your work, and add it to your portfolio.

Additional Test Practice, pp. S1–S33

TEST PRACTICE
CLASSZONE.COM

Create an Exhibit

In 1904 the Louisiana Purchase Exposition, better known as the St. Louis World's Fair, opened to great fanfare. The event celebrated the 100th anniversary of the U.S. purchase of the Louisiana Territory from France in 1803. Taking five years to plan and opening a year late, the fair focused on education and American technology. The automobile was among the most notable attractions at the fair. People from 63 countries and 43 states gathered in St. Louis.

People stroll down The Great Pike at the St. Louis World's Fair.

ACTIVITY Create an exhibit that reflects some aspect of technology at the end of the 19th century. Then make a classroom fair. Write an article about it and give a speech describing your favorite exhibit.

TOOLBOX

Each group will need:

bifold (type of poster board that folds open)	scissors
	pencils
poster board	glue
drawing paper	cardboard
markers	

STEP BY STEP

1 **Form groups.** Each group should consist of three or four students. During the workshop, each group will be expected to:

- research technology and inventions just prior to 1904
- design and create an exhibit for a classroom fair
- write a news report about the fair
- give a speech in praise of a favorite exhibit at the fair

2 **Research the fair.** Using this chapter, books on the St. Louis fair, or the Internet, find out what kinds of exhibits were displayed. Also research the technology and inventions of the time. Some themes of the fair's massive exhibit halls are listed below. Pick one theme on which to focus. Then brainstorm ideas for your exhibit and choose the best one.

World's Fair Themes	
transportation	education
technology	the arts

The New York-to-St. Louis Automobile Parade arrives at the St. Louis World's Fair.

HELP DESK

For related information, see pages 225–226 in Chapter 7.

Researching Your Project

• *The Song of the Molimo* by Jane Cutler

For more about world's fairs . . .

RESEARCH LINKS
CLASSZONE.COM

Did You Know?

One vender at the fair had difficulty selling tea in the hot St. Louis summer. As a result, he began putting ice cubes in the tea, and sales of his "iced tea" soared.

Though there has been some controversy over who invented the ice-cream cone, the St. Louis World's Fair was the place it became popular. One story states that a vendor at the fair rolled a waffle into a cone-shaped holder when another vendor ran out of dishes. However, Italo Marchiony of New York City claimed to have been selling ice-cream cones since 1896.

3 **Design your exhibit.** Think about what your group wants to create. Using drawing paper, sketch a design of the exhibit in pencil. Next to your sketch, list all the items you'll need for the exhibit. Assign each person in your group certain items to bring for the next class period.

4 **Lay out your display.** Use the images and text you found to visually organize the three-panel display. Vary the size of the images, type-size of the text, and include color to make your layout clear and interesting. Remember to create a title.

5 **Create a mini St. Louis fair.** Along with the other groups, arrange the exhibits around the classroom. Walk around the room and look at the other groups' exhibits. Discuss with other groups how you created your exhibit.

REFLECT & ASSESS

• How did your group come up with its idea?

• How does your design fit into the theme of the St. Louis fair?

• What criteria did you use when judging the exhibits?

WRITE AND SPEAK

Write a newspaper article. Cover the fair as a journalist from another city. Write an article about the classroom fair, describing the atmosphere as well as the exhibits. Then give a speech in praise of the outstanding exhibit of the fair.

Modern America Emerges

"Woman must not depend upon
the protection of man, but must
be taught to protect herself."
—Susan B. Anthony

Suffragists marched in Washington, D.C., in
1914 in support of a constitutional amendment giving women the right to vote.

The Progressive Era 1890–1920

CHAPTER 8

Section 1 **Roosevelt and Progressivism**
Section 2 **Taft and Wilson as Progressives**
Section 3 **Women Win New Rights**

Homelessness—Children sleep in the street.

Poor sanitation—Dead horse rots in city street while children play in the gutter.

Poverty—Family earns money by making artificial flowers in its tenement.

Progressive Era

SOCIAL PROBLEMS

Child labor—Children work in a Pennsylvania coal mine.

Interact *with* History

Theodore Roosevelt gives a speech. He faces difficult social problems, such as those shown to the left.

It is 1901, and Theodore Roosevelt has suddenly become president. You and all Americans are counting on him to help end child labor, poverty, business abuses, and political corruption. You're anxious to see what actions the new president will take to solve these problems.

What Do You Think?

• What different problems do the photographs show?

• What qualities would a leader need to tackle such problems?

• What might be the cause of these different problems?

How would you solve one of these problems?

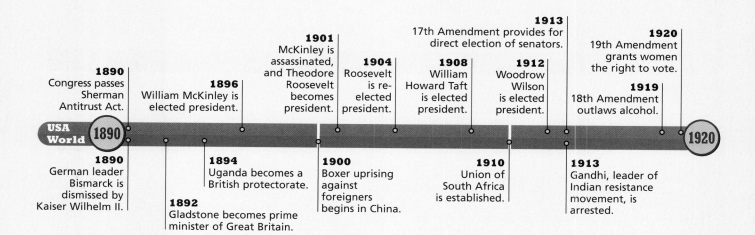

1890
Congress passes Sherman Antitrust Act.

1896
William McKinley is elected president.

1901
McKinley is assassinated, and Theodore Roosevelt becomes president.

1904
Roosevelt is re-elected president.

1908
William Howard Taft is elected president.

1913
17th Amendment provides for direct election of senators.

1912
Woodrow Wilson is elected president.

1920
19th Amendment grants women the right to vote.

1919
18th Amendment outlaws alcohol.

USA **1890** — World — **1920**

1890
German leader Bismarck is dismissed by Kaiser Wilhelm II.

1892
Gladstone becomes prime minister of Great Britain.

1894
Uganda becomes a British protectorate.

1900
Boxer uprising against foreigners begins in China.

1910
Union of South Africa is established.

1913
Gandhi, leader of Indian resistance movement, is arrested.

BEFORE YOU READ

Previewing the Theme

Impact of the Individual The problems caused by the growth of industries and cities sparked a variety of reform movements. This chapter shows that individual reformers and reform groups shared a strong desire to solve problems in American society.

A social worker pays a visit to a poor family.

What Do You Know?

What do you know about life in American cities in the early 1900s? What problems plagued the cities? How have people living in cities overcome obstacles?

THINK ABOUT
- what you've learned in previous chapters
- what you know about urban problems today

What Do You Want to Know?

What questions do you have about the reform movements of the early 1900s? Record your questions in your notebook before you read the chapter.

READ AND TAKE NOTES

Reading Strategy: Identifying and Solving Problems This chapter focuses on the problems that Americans faced at the turn of the century and how they worked to solve those problems. A graphic organizer can help you keep track of problems and solutions. Major problems faced by the nation at the turn of the century are listed in the first column of the chart below. As you read, record solutions for these problems in the second column of the chart.

S See Skillbuilder Handbook, page R18.

PROBLEM	SOLUTION
Political: patronage; limited suffrage and democracy	
Social: poverty; alcohol abuse	
Economic: power of big corporations; unemployment	
Environmental: impure food and water; diminishing natural resources	

TERMS & NAMES
progressivism
muckrakers
direct primary
initiative
referendum
recall
Sherman Antitrust Act
Theodore Roosevelt

1 Roosevelt and Progressivism

MAIN IDEA

Reformers tried to solve the problems of the cities. They gained a champion in Theodore Roosevelt.

WHY IT MATTERS NOW

Many of the reforms of the Progressive Era have had an effect on life in America today.

Nellie Bly

ONE AMERICAN'S STORY

Newspaper journalist Nellie Bly worked for *The New York World*. In 1887, Bly wanted to investigate the Women's Lunatic Asylum in New York City. An asylum is a place where people with mental illness can get help. She faked mental illness and fooled doctors so that she could become a patient there. After spending ten days in the asylum, Bly wrote a newspaper article about what she had witnessed. She described being forced to take ice cold baths.

A VOICE FROM THE PAST

My teeth chattered and my limbs were goose-fleshed and blue with cold. Suddenly I got, one after the other, three buckets of water over my head—ice-cold water, too—into my eyes, my ears, my nose and my mouth.

Nellie Bly, quoted in *Nellie Bly: Daredevil, Reporter, Feminist*

She reported that nurses choked and beat patients. Shortly after Bly's stories appeared, conditions at the asylum improved.

Bly also wrote about poor conditions in slums, factories, prisons, and nursing homes. Like other reformers, she wanted to correct the wrongs in American society. All of these reformers made up the Progressive movement around the turn of the century.

The Rise of Progressivism

As you saw in Chapter 7, the rapid growth of cities and industries in the United States at the turn of the century brought many problems. Among them were poverty, the spread of slums, and poor conditions in factories. A depression in the 1890s made problems worse. In addition, corrupt political machines had won control of many city and state governments. Big corporations had gained power over the economy and government.

To attack these problems, individuals organized a number of reform movements. These reformers believed in the basic goodness of people. They also believed in democracy. The reformers were mostly native born and middle-class. They could be found in either political party. Their reform movements came to be grouped under the label **progressivism**.

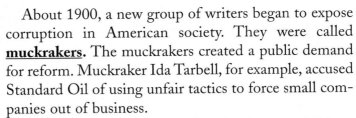

In the late 1800s, John D. Rockefeller made a fortune as he gained control of most of the nation's oil refineries, oil fields, and pipelines. In 1906, the government filed an antitrust suit against Rockefeller's Standard Oil. This resulted in its breakup in 1911. The cartoon below shows Standard Oil as an octopus.

In the 1990s, Bill Gates became the richest man in the world as he built Seattle-based Microsoft into a computer software giant. In 1998, the government filed an antitrust suit against Microsoft. It charged the company with using illegal tactics to gain a monopoly with its computer operating system and Web browser.

About 1900, a new group of writers began to expose corruption in American society. They were called **muckrakers**. The muckrakers created a public demand for reform. Muckraker Ida Tarbell, for example, accused Standard Oil of using unfair tactics to force small companies out of business.

The progressive reformers shared at least one of three basic goals: first, to reform government and expand democracy; second, to promote social welfare; third, to create economic reform.

Reforming Government and Expanding Democracy

In the 1870s and 1880s, elected officials often handed out government jobs and contracts. In return, they won political support. This practice was called patronage. It became a hot political issue during the presidencies of Rutherford B. Hayes, James Garfield, and Chester Arthur. Finally, Congress passed the Pendleton Civil Service Act in 1883. This law required people to take civil service exams for certain government jobs. It also prevented elected officials from firing civil service workers for political reasons.

In the 1890s and early 1900s, progressive leaders in a number of states sought to expand democracy. They wanted to give voters more control over their government. In 1903, under progressive governor Robert M. La Follette, Wisconsin became the first state to establish a direct primary. In a **direct primary**, voters, rather than party conventions, choose candidates to run for public office.

Reading **History**
A. Finding Main Ideas What was the main goal behind the progressive reforms of government?

In Oregon, newspaper editor William S. U'Ren promoted three reforms besides the direct primary.

1. **Initiative**—This reform allowed voters to propose a law directly.
2. **Referendum**—In this reform, a proposed law was submitted to the vote of the people.
3. **Recall**—This reform allowed people to vote an official out of office.

In the years that followed, many other states adopted one or more of these progressive reforms.

Promoting Social Welfare

This goal addressed such problems as poverty, unemployment, and poor working conditions. You read about the social gospel and settlement house movements in Chapter 7. Leaders in these movements promoted many social-welfare reforms. For example, Jane Addams provided social services to the poor at Hull House. She also worked to help the unemployed. Florence Kelley, also from Hull House, pushed for minimum wage laws and limits on women's working hours.

Another group of reformers who wanted to improve social welfare were the prohibitionists. They worked to prevent alcohol from ruining people's lives. The prohibitionists built on the temperance movement of the 1800s.

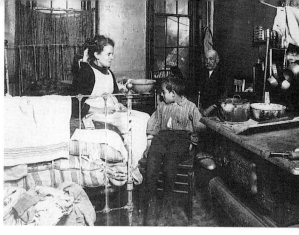

This photograph shows an immigrant family in a crowded tenement at the turn of the century.

Creating Economic Reform

The third progressive goal was to create economic reform. This meant limiting the power of big business and regulating its activities. By the late 1800s, business leaders in some major industries had formed trusts. These were combinations of businesses. The business firms in a trust worked together to cut prices and squeeze out competitors. Then the trust would raise prices and make larger profits.

*Reading*History

B. Summarizing How did progressives pursue their three basic goals?

The **Sherman Antitrust Act** of 1890 made it illegal for corporations to gain control of industries by forming trusts. However, the government did not enforce the law at first. Enforcement required a strong president.

Roosevelt and the Square Deal

Theodore Roosevelt—the first progressive president—provided this strength and leadership. He came to the presidency by accident, however. In 1898, Roosevelt won fame fighting in the Spanish-American War in Cuba. He returned from Cuba a war hero and was elected governor of New York. In 1900, Roosevelt ran on the Republican ticket as President McKinley's vice president.

Then an assassin shot McKinley, just six months after his inauguration. Roosevelt became president when McKinley died on September 14, 1901. At age 42, Roosevelt was the youngest person ever to become president. He brought his boundless energy to the office. The president often joined his six children in playing in the White House. Americans admired Roosevelt's zest for living. He gained the public's support for reform.

"I believe in a square deal."
Theodore Roosevelt

Roosevelt began his reforms with an effort to break up the corporate trusts. He thought industries should be regulated for the public interest.

A VOICE FROM THE PAST

When I say I believe in a square deal I do not mean, and nobody who speaks the truth can mean, that he believes it possible to give every man the best hand. If the cards do not come to any man, or if they do come, and he has not got the power to play them, that is his affair. All I mean is that there shall not be any crookedness in the dealing.

Theodore Roosevelt, speech on April 5, 1905

Roosevelt saw government as an umpire. Its purpose was to ensure fairness, or a "square deal," for workers, consumers, and big business.

To root out "crookedness," Roosevelt used the Sherman Antitrust Act. Since its passage in 1890, many corporations had ignored the law, which was intended to regulate the trusts. No one had enforced it—no one, that is, until Roosevelt became president in 1901.

At the end of 1901, the nation's railroads were run by a handful of companies. The power of railroads continued to grow. It was not surprising, therefore, that one of Roosevelt's first targets was the railroads. He used the Sherman Antitrust Act to bust up a railroad trust.

Roosevelt was not against big business as such. However, he opposed any trust he thought worked against the national interest. In addition to the railroad trust, Roosevelt broke up the Standard Oil Company and a tobacco trust. In all, the government filed suit against 44 corporations during Roosevelt's presidency.

*Reading*History
C. Making Inferences How do you think big business leaders regarded President Roosevelt? Why?

Roosevelt Leads Progressive Reforms

As president, Roosevelt had a great deal of power to push progressive ideas. To make such ideas into law, however, he needed help. Roosevelt got it as voters began pressuring their senators and representatives. As a result, Congress passed laws that helped change American society.

Roosevelt acted to regulate the meat-packing industry after reading Upton Sinclair's *The Jungle*. The novel describes a packing plant in which dead rats end up in the sausage. Sinclair focused attention on the poor sanitary conditions under which the meat-packers worked. "I aimed at the public's heart, and by accident I hit it in the stomach," he noted.

Roosevelt launched an investigation of the meat-packing industry. In 1906, he signed the Meat Inspection Act. This act created a government meat inspection program. Roosevelt also signed the Pure Food and Drug Act. This law banned the sale of impure foods and medicines.

While Roosevelt tried to win a square deal for most Americans, he did not push for civil rights for African Americans. He believed that discrimination was morally wrong. However, he did not take the political risk of leading a fight for civil rights.

Shown at the left is the cover of Upton Sinclair's novel, *The Jungle*. The photograph shows immigrant workers stuffing sausages in a Chicago meat-packing house.

Conservation

Roosevelt was a strong crusader for conservation—controlling how America's natural resources were used. As an outdoorsman and hunter, he had observed the gradual loss of natural resources. He camped with naturalist John Muir for four days in Yosemite, California. Because he loved the Yosemite Valley so much, he set out to preserve Yosemite and other areas for people's "children and their children's children."

Roosevelt preserved more than 200 million acres of public lands. He established the nation's first wildlife refuge at Pelican Island, Florida. He doubled the number of national parks in the United States. At one point, Congress refused to establish any more national parks. Roosevelt used the Antiquities Act to create national monuments instead. In this way, he preserved the Grand Canyon and the Petrified Forest in Arizona. Roosevelt spoke of the glories of the Grand Canyon while visiting the site in 1903.

Reading **History**

D. Finding Main Ideas Why did President Roosevelt bypass Congress?

A VOICE FROM THE PAST

Leave it as it is. You cannot improve on it. The ages have been at work on it, and man can only mar it.

Theodore Roosevelt, quoted in *Yellowstone*

Both the Grand Canyon and the Petrified Forest have since become national parks. America's next president, William Howard Taft, was not as interested in conservation. However, he did continue Roosevelt's progressive reforms, as you will read in the next section.

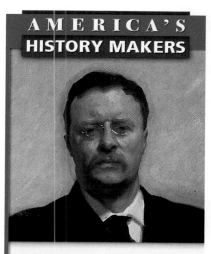

AMERICA'S HISTORY MAKERS

THEODORE ROOSEVELT
1858–1919

From his youth on, Theodore Roosevelt lived what he called the "strenuous life." He rode horses, hiked, boxed, wrestled, and played tennis. In winter, he swam in the icy Potomac River. He hunted rhinoceros in Africa, harpooned devilfish in Florida, and boated down the Amazon.

Americans loved reading of his exploits and affectionately referred to him as "Teddy" or "T.R." Once, on a hunting trip, he refused to shoot a bear cub. News of the event resulted in a new toy—the teddy bear.

How did Roosevelt's active style of living carry over into his presidency?

Section 1 Assessment

1. Terms & Names

Explain the significance of:
- progressivism
- muckrakers
- direct primary
- initiative
- referendum
- recall
- Sherman Antitrust Act
- Theodore Roosevelt

2. Taking Notes

Use a chart to list examples of progressive reforms.

Goals	Reforms
To expand democracy	
To protect social welfare	
To create economic reform	

Which reform was most important? Explain.

3. Main Ideas

a. What kinds of problems did progressives attempt to solve?

b. What did President Roosevelt mean by a "square deal," and how did he try to achieve it?

c. What were Roosevelt's achievements in the field of conservation?

4. Critical Thinking

Recognizing Effects In what ways do the reforms that President Roosevelt promoted affect your life today?

THINK ABOUT
- the quality of the food you eat
- natural resources that have been preserved

ACTIVITY OPTIONS

ART

GEOGRAPHY

Do research on one of the natural areas that President Roosevelt preserved. Create a **travel brochure** or an illustrated **map** of the area.

The National Parks Movement

As the United States expanded westward, two things became evident. First, this was a land of astonishing beauty. Second, this unspoiled beauty would not last if it wasn't protected.

President Theodore Roosevelt may have given the conservation movement its most significant boost. An outdoorsman, naturalist, and visionary, he established the U.S. Forest Service and set aside more than 200 million acres of public lands as national parks, forests, monuments, and wildlife refuges.

Creating parks was just the first step in protecting these lands. Problems arose that had not been foreseen. These problems included a lack of funds and growing numbers of tourists and researchers. In 1916, the National Park Service was established with the goal of saving the parks for future generations.

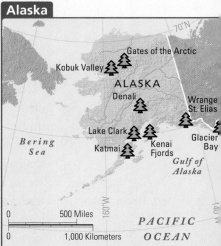
Alaska

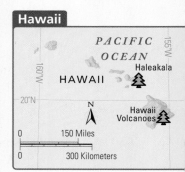
Hawaii

In 1903, Teddy Roosevelt (left) joined conservationist John Muir (right) for a camping trip. Their trip took them from the "big trees" of the Sequoia forest to the wonders of the Yosemite Valley. This photo of Roosevelt and Muir was taken at Glacier Point in Yosemite. Both men wanted to protect the magnificent beauty of America's most spectacular regions.

ARTIFACT FILE

Sequoia National Park is a land of giants. In a forest where many trees are more than 250 feet high, it is difficult to get a sense of scale when looking at the biggest of these giants. The General Sherman Tree, shown here, is the largest tree by volume in the world. A number of trees in Sequoia National Park are named for Civil War generals.

GENERAL SHERMAN

Everglades National Park in Florida is part of the approximately 1,500,000-acre Everglades region. This wetland habitat is home to birds, especially waders such as herons, egrets, and ibis, and is famous for its alligators.

The National Parks Today

Olympic
North Cascades
Mount Rainier
Glacier
Crater Lake
Redwood
Yellowstone
Grand Teton
Theodore Roosevelt
Voyageurs
Isle Royale
Acadia
Lassen Volcanic
Wind Cave
Badlands
Yosemite
Great Basin
Capitol Reef
Rocky Mountain
Shenandoah
Kings Canyon
Zion
Arches
Black Canyon of the Gunnison
Canyonlands
Sequoia
Bryce Canyon
Death Valley
Grand Canyon
Mesa Verde
Mammoth Cave
Great Smoky Mountains
Channel Islands
Joshua Tree
Petrified Forest
Hot Springs
Saguaro
Carlsbad Caverns
Guadalupe Mountains
Big Bend
Everglades
Biscayne
Dry Tortugas

PACIFIC OCEAN

ATLANTIC OCEAN

Gulf of Mexico

50°N
40°N
30°N
110°W

N

0   500 Miles
0   1000 Kilometers

National parks are identified on the map above. The National Park System includes many areas, all of which are under the management of the National Park Service (NPS).

On-Line Field Trip

Yellowstone National Park was designated the world's first national park in 1872. Covering about 2,200,000 acres, Yellowstone is still the largest national park in the United States. There are many geysers in Yellowstone, including Old Faithful (at right).

For more about national parks . . .

CONNECT TO GEOGRAPHY

1. **Region** What might be two reasons the national parks are concentrated where they are?
2. **Human-Environment Interaction** What effects might visits from many tourists have on a national park?

   G See Geography Handbook, page 17.

CONNECT TO HISTORY

3. **Analyzing Causes** What general mood of the era made the late 1800s a likely time for successfully starting a national park?

Taft and Wilson as Progressives

TERMS & NAMES
William Howard
   Taft
Sixteenth
   Amendment
Seventeenth
   Amendment
Clayton Antitrust
   Act
Federal Reserve Act

MAIN IDEA	WHY IT MATTERS NOW
Progressive reforms continued under William Howard Taft and Woodrow Wilson.	Constitutional amendments passed during this time affect Americans today.

ONE AMERICAN'S STORY

During the Progressive Era, many Americans became disturbed by the problems caused by capitalism. Some even turned to socialism. This is a system in which business and industry are totally controlled by the state. Labor leader Eugene V. Debs became a socialist while serving time in prison for his role in a labor strike. In 1894, as head of the American Railway Union, Debs supported a strike by the workers who made railroad cars. When the federal government broke up the strike, Debs defied the courts. He was sent to prison for six months.

In the 1908 presidential election, Debs ran as the Socialist Party candidate. In his campaign, he urged American workers to consider what competition was like in a capitalist system.

The forceful speeches of Eugene V. Debs attracted large audiences.

A VOICE FROM THE PAST

Competition was natural enough at one time, but do you think you are competing today? . . . Against whom? Against Rockefeller? About as I would if I had a wheelbarrow and competed with the Santa Fe [railroad] from here to Kansas City.

Eugene V. Debs, quoted in *The Annals of America*

Debs made a decent showing in the election, winning more than 420,000 votes. However, the Republican candidate Taft did better and was elected.

Taft and Progressivism

In the 1908 election, Debs ran against Republican **William Howard Taft** and Democrat William Jennings Bryan. Neither Debs nor Bryan stood much of a chance against Taft. He was Roosevelt's handpicked successor. Roosevelt's popularity swayed many people to vote for Taft, who promised to follow Roosevelt's progressive policies.

Taft continued Roosevelt's attack on trusts. During his four years in office, Taft pursued almost twice as many antitrust suits as Roosevelt had in nearly eight years in office. But Taft received less credit for his progressivism because he became allied with conservative Republicans rather than Roosevelt's progressive Republicans. Nevertheless, Taft did move forward with progressive reforms. His reforms addressed the progressive goals of democracy, social welfare, and economic reform. Two of the major progressive achievements under President Taft were constitutional amendments.

Two Progressive Amendments

The **Sixteenth Amendment** was passed in 1909 and ratified in 1913. It gave Congress the power to create income taxes. The Constitution previously did not allow direct taxes on an individual's income. This amendment was intended to provide a means of spreading the cost of running the government among more people. The income tax soon became the main source of federal revenue.

Economics *in* History

Types of Taxes

The Sixteenth Amendment, ratified in 1913, made it constitutional for the federal government to have an income tax. Congress quickly passed an income tax law the same year. The income tax provides revenue to the federal government by taxing profits and earnings. In a graduated income tax, larger incomes are taxed at higher rates than smaller incomes. The income tax is only one of several taxes that governments use to raise money.

CONNECT TO HISTORY

1. **Making Inferences** How might a corporate income tax fit the goals of the Progressive Era?

   See Skillbuilder Handbook, page R12.

CONNECT TO TODAY

2. **Drawing Conclusions** Some states that have a sales tax do not charge that tax on the purchase of goods like food or clothing. Why do you think they make an exception for these purchases?

For more about taxes . . .

RESEARCH LINKS
CLASSZONE.COM

INCOME TAXES

1. **Individual:** You pay a percentage of what you earn at work or from investments. Under the payroll deduction plan, income taxes are deducted (taken out) from your wages or salary before you get your paycheck.
2. **Corporate:** Corporations pay a percentage of their profits in income tax.

PROPERTY TAXES

People pay taxes on property they own, such as land or a house. Property taxes are often used to support public services such as schools.

TYPES OF TAXES

SALES TAXES

Sales tax is imposed on the retail price of merchandise and collected by the retailer. For example, when you buy a pair of jeans, you pay sales tax, which will be listed on your receipt.

ESTATE TAXES

This tax is charged against the value of the property of a person who has died. It is also called the "death tax" because it is collected from the dead person's estate before the estate is passed on to the heirs.

FROM PRESIDENT TO CHIEF JUSTICE

William Howard Taft was the only man in American history to serve first as president and then as chief justice of the U.S. Supreme Court. He had always wanted to be a Supreme Court justice. Even his mother said, "I do not want my son to be President. His is a judicial mind and he loves the law."

Taft was unhappy as president. When he left office, he said: "I'm glad to be going. This is the lonesomest place in the world." Eight years later, in 1921, President Warren G. Harding appointed Taft to the Supreme Court. Taft is shown here in his judicial robes.

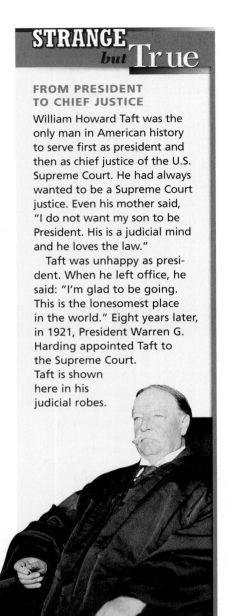

The **Seventeenth Amendment** was ratified in 1913. It provided for the direct election of U.S. senators by voters in each state. Formerly, state legislatures had chosen U.S. senators. Under this system, many senators obtained their positions through corrupt bargains. Because of this, the Senate was called the "Millionaires' Club." The Seventeenth Amendment gave people a more direct voice in the government.

*Reading*History
A. Drawing Conclusions Why are the Sixteenth and Seventeenth amendments considered progressive?

The Election of 1912

Taft achieved a number of progressive reforms. However, a deep split developed between him and progressive leaders in the Republican Party. Still, with the support of conservative Republicans, Taft won the party's nomination as its presidential candidate in 1912.

However, many progressive Republicans supported Theodore Roosevelt. He had entered the race and formed the Progressive Party, also known as the Bull Moose Party.

The Democrats chose Governor Woodrow Wilson of New Jersey as their presidential candidate. Eugene Debs again entered the race as the Socialist candidate. With the Republicans deeply divided, Wilson won the election.

The Wilson Presidency

As president, Wilson established a progressive record. Wilson believed that "bigness" itself was dangerous. He wanted the government to use its powers to break up monopolies—groups that sought complete control over an industry. He also wanted the government to help workers in their struggles against business owners.

At Wilson's urging, Congress passed the **Clayton Antitrust Act** of 1914. The new law laid down rules forbidding business practices that lessened competition. A business, for example, could no longer buy the stock of a competitor. The Clayton Act gave the government more power to regulate trusts. In addition, the Clayton Act was also prolabor:

1. It said labor unions and farm organizations could merge and expand.
2. It limited the ability of the courts to force workers to end strikes.
3. It legalized such labor tactics as strikes, picketing, and boycotts.

During Wilson's two terms, reforms to the nation's financial system occurred. In 1913, the **Federal Reserve Act** was passed. This improved the nation's monetary and banking system. The law created the modern banking system, which resembles a pyramid. At the top is the Federal Reserve Board, which is appointed by the president. Next are 12 Federal Reserve Banks for different regions of the country. These are "bankers'

Vocabulary
boycott: an attempt to pressure a business by refusing to buy a product or use a service

banks." They serve the bottom level—the member banks.

The Federal Reserve Act created a more flexible currency system by allowing banks to control the money supply. To raise money, for example, the Federal Reserve Board, or "Fed," lowers the interest rate that it charges member banks. These banks then borrow more from the Fed and thus have more money to lend to people and businesses.

*Reading*History
B. Summarizing
What were some of Wilson's achievements as a progressive president?

Wilson did no more to advance civil rights for African Americans than Roosevelt did. In fact, Wilson approved the segregation, or separation, of African-American and white employees in the federal government. Throughout the Progressive Era, presidents Roosevelt, Taft, and Wilson did not actively promote civil rights for African Americans.

President Wilson throws out a baseball at the opening game of the 1916 season.

The Eighteenth Amendment

Another amendment passed during the Progressive Era was the Eighteenth Amendment. This is also called the Prohibition Amendment. During Wilson's administration, supporters of prohibition gained strength. Reformers thought an alcohol ban would reduce poverty. They argued that liquor added to unemployment and violence. Business leaders saw that alcohol made workers less efficient. Finally, in 1917, Congress passed a constitutional amendment. The Eighteenth Amendment prohibited the manufacture and sale of alcoholic beverages. The states ratified the amendment in 1919.

In the next section, you will read about the most important amendment of the era—the Nineteenth Amendment, which gave women the vote.

Section 2 Assessment

1. Terms & Names

Explain the significance of:
- William Howard Taft
- Sixteenth Amendment
- Seventeenth Amendment
- Clayton Antitrust Act
- Federal Reserve Act

2. Taking Notes

Complete the chart to review some of the major reforms of both the Taft and Wilson administrations.

Law	Description
Sixteenth Amendment	
Clayton Antitrust Act	
Federal Reserve Act	

3. Main Ideas

a. What caused the Republican Party to split in 1912?

b. What were the major progressive accomplishments of Wilson's presidency?

c. What did the Federal Reserve Act do?

4. Critical Thinking

Making Inferences Why did progressive presidents do little to advance civil rights for African Americans?

THINK ABOUT
- the goals of progressivism
- the groups of people that progressivism aimed to help

ACTIVITY OPTIONS

LANGUAGE ARTS
TECHNOLOGY

Research one of the people mentioned in this section. Then write the **script** for the first 10 minutes of his documentary or design his **Web page**.

Women Win New Rights

MAIN IDEA	WHY IT MATTERS NOW
Women became leaders in social reform movements and won the right to vote during the Progressive Era.	Today, American women enjoy the right to vote because of women reformers in the Progressive Era.

ONE AMERICAN'S STORY

After graduating from nursing school in 1891, Lillian Wald briefly studied medicine. Then a friend asked her to teach a home nursing class at a school for immigrants in New York City. One day a child asked Wald to help her sick mother, who was absent from the class. Following the child home, Wald was shocked by what she saw.

> *A VOICE FROM THE PAST*
>
> Over broken asphalt, over dirty mattresses and heaps of refuse we went. The tall houses reeked with rubbish. . . . There were two rooms and a family of seven not only lived here but shared their quarters with boarders.
>
> **Lillian Wald,** quoted in *Always a Sister*

The experience gave Wald a new mission. Inspired to help such poor immigrants, she founded the Nurses' Settlement. This was later called the Henry Street Settlement. It was the first visiting nurse program in the country not run by a religious group. The program mainly helped poor women and children.

In this section, you will read about others like Wald who worked to make life better for all women.

(Above left) Lillian Wald. (Above) A visiting nurse takes a shortcut between two tenements.

New Roles for Women

The social reform movements of the Progressive Era were led by educated, middle-class women. At the turn of the century, women like Wald were looking for new roles outside the home. The growth of industry had changed many urban, middle-class homes. These homes now had indoor running water and electric power for lamps and vacuum cleaners.

In addition, factories produced the products that women once made in the home, such as soap, clothing, and canned goods. Such technological advances reduced some of the unpleasant work of homemaking. At the same time, families were becoming smaller as women had fewer children.

As a result, the homemaker's role began to change. High schools, colleges, and women's clubs offered courses in home economics and domestic science. In these courses, women were encouraged to apply the latest methods to running their homes.

Other women responded to changes in the home by taking jobs in factories, offices, and stores. Women worked as telephone operators, store clerks, and typists. Those who gained a college education could pursue a profession. The choices were limited to such fields as teaching and nursing. Women who could afford to were expected to quit their jobs when they married. In 1890, approximately 30 percent of women between the ages of 20 and 24 worked outside the home. However, only about 15 percent between the ages of 25 and 44 did so.

*Reading*History
A. Finding Main Ideas How and why did women's roles begin to change around the turn of the century?

Women Progressives

The social reform movements that many middle-class, college-educated women took part in were focused on helping people. These included the settlement house and prohibition movements. A settlement house is a community center providing assistance to residents—particularly immigrants—in a slum neighborhood.

Jane Addams was a good example of the progressive female leader. After graduating from college, Addams sought a meaningful way to participate in society. She was financially independent. A visit to a settlement house in a London slum inspired her to start a similar program in Chicago. She was helped by her friend Ellen Starr.

With donations from wealthy Chicagoans, Addams and Starr rented an old mansion. Hull House was located in a poor, immigrant neighborhood. Within just a few years, they organized a full program of services, classes, and clubs. These were run by a group of young women residents and over 90 volunteers. Hull House served as an information bureau for new immigrants. It also helped the unemployed find jobs. It offered a kindergarten, a day nursery, after-school youth clubs, nutrition classes, and a concert program. Workers also pressured politicians for improved city services for the neighborhood.

Connections TO LITERATURE

WOMEN OUTSIDE THE HOME
Charlotte Perkins Gilman (shown below) was an influential writer on women's rights. She wanted to free women from housework to pursue careers. In *Women and Economics* (1898), Gilman argued that a wife's dependency on her husband limited her personal development.

In *Concerning Children* (1900) and *The Home* (1903), she proposed that families live in large apartments. These would have centralized nurseries and a staff devoted to cooking, cleaning, and child-care. This support would free women to work outside the home.

A VOICE FROM THE PAST

One function of the settlement to its neighborhood somewhat resembled that of the big brother whose mere presence in the playground protected the little ones from bullies.

Jane Addams, quoted in *Women and the American Experience*

The young women residents of Hull House received no salary and had to pay for their room and board. This meant that they had to be financially independent. For some, Hull House provided training for other public service. Florence Kelley, for example, worked at Hull House from 1891 to 1898. She later became secretary of the National Consumers' League. This group promoted better working conditions in factories and stores.

Another prominent but controversial progressive leader was Carry Nation. She campaigned for prohibition. Nation had once been married to an alcoholic. Tall and strong, she adopted dramatic methods in her opposition to alcoholic beverages. In the 1890s, she smashed saloons with a hatchet. This caused law enforcement officials to arrest her for disturbing the peace. Although some people criticized Nation, her efforts helped bring about passage of the Eighteenth Amendment in 1919.

Suffrage for Women

Many women progressives were active in the struggle for woman suffrage, or the right to vote. American women fought longer for the right to vote than they did for any other reform. Some leaders in the fight died before realizing their goal.

In 1890, two separate woman suffrage groups merged to form the National American Woman Suffrage Association (NAWSA). Elizabeth Cady Stanton served as its first president. Two years later, in 1892, **Susan B. Anthony** became president. She held the position until 1900. Expressing their frustration over the difficulty of gaining suffrage, Elizabeth Cady Stanton and Susan B. Anthony wrote, "Words can not describe the indignation, the humiliation a proud woman feels for her sex in disfranchisement [being deprived of the right to vote]."

NAWSA at first focused on state campaigns to win the right to vote, since earlier efforts at passing a federal amendment had failed. But by 1896, only four states allowed women to vote. These were Wyoming, Utah, Idaho, and Colorado. Between 1896 and 1910, women did not gain the right to vote in a single state. Then, between 1910 and 1914, seven more Western states approved full suffrage for women.

Background
Because she helped organize the woman suffrage movement, Susan B. Anthony became the first woman to be pictured on a U.S. coin.

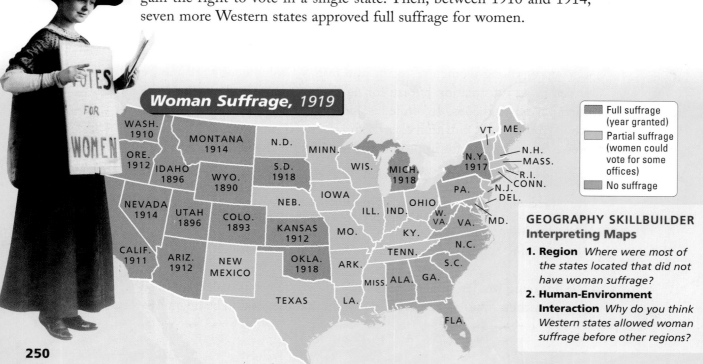

Woman Suffrage, 1919

WASH. 1910
MONTANA 1914
N.D.
MINN.
VT. ME.
N.H.
N.Y. 1917
MASS.
R.I.
CONN.
ORE. 1912
IDAHO 1896
WYO. 1890
S.D. 1918
WIS.
MICH. 1918
PA.
N.J.
DEL.
NEVADA 1914
UTAH 1896
COLO. 1893
NEB.
IOWA
ILL. IND.
OHIO
W. VA.
VA. MD.
CALIF. 1911
ARIZ. 1912
NEW MEXICO
KANSAS 1912
MO.
KY.
N.C.
OKLA. 1918
ARK.
TENN.
S.C.
GA.
MISS. ALA.
TEXAS
LA.
FLA.

Full suffrage (year granted)
Partial suffrage (women could vote for some offices)
No suffrage

GEOGRAPHY SKILLBUILDER
Interpreting Maps

1. **Region** *Where were most of the states located that did not have woman suffrage?*

2. **Human-Environment Interaction** *Why do you think Western states allowed woman suffrage before other regions?*

The Progressive Amendments, 1909–1920

Number	Description	Passed by Congress	Ratified by States
16th	Federal income tax	1909	1913
17th	Senators elected by people rather than state legislatures	1912	1913
18th	Manufacture, sale, or transport of alcohol prohibited	1917	1919
19th	Woman suffrage	1919	1920

SKILLBUILDER Interpreting Charts

1. *For which amendment was there the longest gap between passage by Congress and ratification by states?*
2. *What do the dates 1909 and 1920 represent in this chart?*

The Nineteenth Amendment

The Western successes turned the tide in favor of woman suffrage. The United States' entry into World War I in 1917 made the final difference. During the war, membership in NAWSA reached 2 million. **Carrie Chapman Catt,** president of NAWSA, argued that the nation could no longer deny the right to vote to women, who were supporting the war effort by selling war bonds and organizing benefits. President Wilson urged the Senate to pass a women's suffrage amendment. He called passage "vital to the winning of the war."

In 1918, the House passed the **Nineteenth Amendment,** which gave women full voting rights. The Senate approved the amendment in 1919. In 1920, the states ratified it. In the final state campaigns, women staged marches, parades, and rallies around the country. Charlotte Woodard had attended the first women's rights convention in 1848 at Seneca Falls as a teenager. In 1920, the 91-year-old Woodard voted in a presidential election for the first time.

Reading **History**

B. Recognizing Effects What factors helped women gain the right to vote?

Section ❸ Assessment

1. Terms & Names

Explain the significance of:
- Susan B. Anthony
- Carrie Chapman Catt
- Nineteenth Amendment

2. Taking Notes

Use a chart to record the achievements of some women leaders of the era.

Progressive Achievements	
Lillian Wald	
Jane Addams	
Florence Kelley	

Which achievement seems greatest and why?

3. Main Ideas

a. How did women's roles expand near the turn of the century?

b. What was the background of many women who became leaders in social reform movements?

c. How did World War I influence the passage of the Nineteenth Amendment?

4. Critical Thinking

Comparing and Contrasting In what ways was the struggle for woman suffrage similar to and different from African Americans' struggle for equal rights?

THINK ABOUT
- the restrictions that both groups faced
- how long they struggled for basic rights

ACTIVITY OPTIONS

LANGUAGE ARTS
TECHNOLOGY

Research one of the women reformers discussed in this chapter. Then write the **script** for the first 10 minutes of her documentary or design her **Web page.**

TERMS & NAMES

Briefly explain the significance of each of the following.

1. progressivism
2. muckrakers
3. referendum
4. Theodore Roosevelt
5. William Howard Taft
6. Sixteenth Amendment
7. Seventeenth Amendment
8. Susan B. Anthony
9. Carrie Chapman Catt
10. Nineteenth Amendment

REVIEW QUESTIONS

Roosevelt and Progressivism (pages 237–243)

1. What problems did progressivism address?
2. How did progressive reformers expand democracy in the states?
3. What was Roosevelt's "square deal"?
4. What were Roosevelt's achievements in the area of conservation?

Taft and Wilson as Progressives (pages 244–247)

5. In what area did Taft achieve a more impressive progressive record than Roosevelt?
6. What progressive goals did the Sixteenth and Seventeenth amendments address?
7. How did Wilson's position on big business differ from Roosevelt's?

Women Win New Rights (pages 248–251)

8. How did women's lives change around 1900?
9. What was the background of many women progressives?
10. What helped further the passage of the Nineteenth Amendment in 1918?

CRITICAL THINKING

1. USING YOUR NOTES

PROBLEM	SOLUTION
Political: patronage; limited suffrage and democracy	
Social: poverty; alcohol abuse	
Economic: power of big corporations; unemployment	
Environmental: impure food and water; diminishing natural resources	

Use your completed chart from the beginning of this chapter to answer these questions.

a. Which solution to a problem do you think was most effective? Why?

`b. Which solution was least effective and why?

c. To which problem on the chart might you offer a different solution, and what is your solution?

2. ANALYZING LEADERSHIP

Based on their domestic record, which president— Roosevelt, Taft, or Wilson—was most effective? Why?

3. APPLYING CITIZENSHIP SKILLS

Why might women at the turn of the century consider the right to vote important enough to devote their lives to fighting for it?

4. THEME: IMPACT OF THE INDIVIDUAL

In what ways did individuals affect the political, social, and economic life of the country during the Progressive Era?

Interact *with* History

How did your solution to one of the social problems of the Progressive Era compare to the solutions proposed by reformers?

VISUAL SUMMARY

The Progressive Era

Corruption plagues the government.

Congress passes the Pendleton Civil Service Act (1883).

Theodore Roosevelt becomes president.

Roosevelt breaks up trusts, establishes "square deal," and advocates national parks.

Abuses in industry, politics, business, and labor are widespread.

Congress passes the Pure Food and Drug Act (1906), progressive amendments, Federal Reserve Act (1913), and the Clayton Antitrust Act (1914).

Women lack social justice and equality.

Vote for WOMEN

Women work to establish settlement houses, fight for woman suffrage, and gain 19th Amendment (1920).

HISTORY SKILLS

1. INTERPRETING GRAPHS

Study the graph below. Then answer the questions that follow.

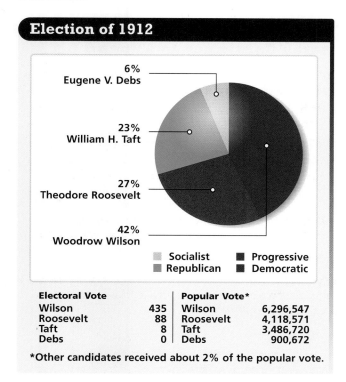

Election of 1912

6%
Eugene V. Debs

23%
William H. Taft

27%
Theodore Roosevelt

42%
Woodrow Wilson

■ Socialist ■ Progressive
■ Republican ■ Democratic

Electoral Vote		Popular Vote*	
Wilson	435	Wilson	6,296,547
Roosevelt	88	Roosevelt	4,118,571
Taft	8	Taft	3,486,720
Debs	0	Debs	900,672

*Other candidates received about 2% of the popular vote.

a. What percentage of the popular vote did Eugene V. Debs win?

b. How many electoral votes did Woodrow Wilson win?

c. Who won the second greatest total of popular votes?

2. INTERPRETING PRIMARY SOURCES

Following is an excerpt from Woodrow Wilson's first inaugural address, delivered on March 4, 1913. Read the excerpt and then answer the questions that follow.

> There can be no equality of opportunity . . . if men and women and children be not shielded in their lives . . . from the consequences of great industrial and social processes which they cannot alter, control, or singly cope with. . . . Sanitary laws, pure-food laws, and laws determining conditions of labor which individuals are powerless to determine for themselves are intimate parts of the very business of justice and legal efficiency.
>
> **Woodrow Wilson,** First Inaugural Address, March 4, 1913

a. What is Wilson promoting in this passage?

b. What values are reflected in this passage?

ALTERNATIVE ASSESSMENT

1. INTERDISCIPLINARY ACTIVITY: Geography

Creating a Map Investigate women's suffrage in other parts of the world. Create a world map on which you show the date that women gained the right to vote in selected countries throughout the world. What conclusions can you draw from your map?

2. COOPERATIVE LEARNING ACTIVITY

Performing a Play Working in a small group, research the problems that African Americans faced in the United States during the Progressive Era, and investigate President Wilson's attitudes toward civil rights. Imagine a small group of African-American leaders visiting President Wilson to confront him about his record. Write a script for the meeting, and assign roles to each group member. Then practice and stage a performance for the class.

3. TECHNOLOGY ACTIVITY

Making an Electronic Presentation America's national parks offer a variety of educational and recreational experiences. Information about the parks is available from many different sources. Using the library and the Internet, find information about national parks that interest you. Which park or parks would you most like to visit? If you were designing a national park, which features would you most like to include?

For more about national parks . . .

INTERNET ACTIVITY
CLASSZONE.COM

Create a class presentation about the national parks using presentation software and the suggestions below.

- A map of a national park, showing the location of various features and attractions.

- Lodging for a national park that you would like to use. Incorporate features from hotels and lodgings in national parks that you have researched.

- Your description of the most important features of a national park that you would like to visit.

- A database of facts about the national parks.

4. HISTORY PORTFOLIO

Review this chapter and make a list of the major characteristics of the Progressive era. Then create a time line and place the Progressive era in chronological sequence with other significant eras in U.S. history. Add your time line to your portfolio.

Additional Test Practice, pp. S1–S33

TEST PRACTICE
CLASSZONE.COM

CHAPTER 9

Becoming a World Power
1880–1917

Section 1 **The United States Continues to Expand**
Section 2 **The Spanish-American War**
Section 3 **U.S. Involvement Overseas**

The United States "Great White Fleet" symbolized the nation's presence as a global power at the beginning of the 20th century.

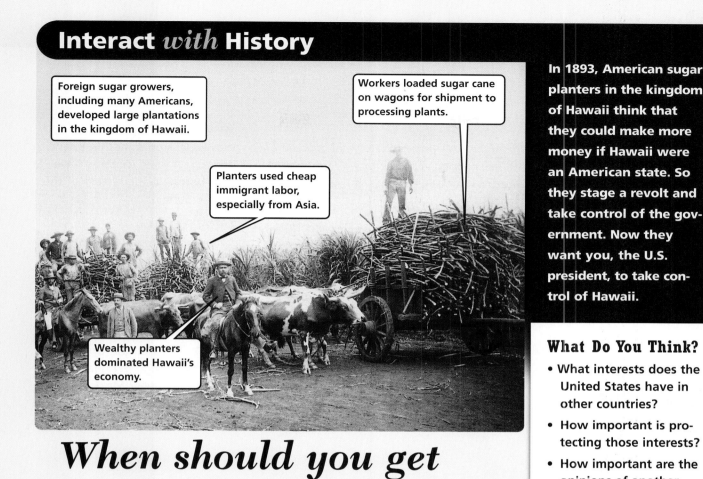

Foreign sugar growers, including many Americans, developed large plantations in the kingdom of Hawaii.

Workers loaded sugar cane on wagons for shipment to processing plants.

Planters used cheap immigrant labor, especially from Asia.

Wealthy planters dominated Hawaii's economy.

In 1893, American sugar planters in the kingdom of Hawaii think that they could make more money if Hawaii were an American state. So they stage a revolt and take control of the government. Now they want you, the U.S. president, to take control of Hawaii.

When should you get involved in the affairs of another country?

What Do You Think?
- What interests does the United States have in other countries?
- How important is protecting those interests?
- How important are the opinions of another country's citizens?

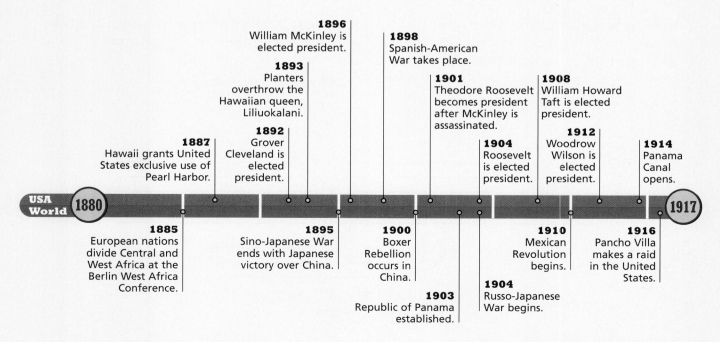

1896 William McKinley is elected president.

1898 Spanish-American War takes place.

1893 Planters overthrow the Hawaiian queen, Liliuokalani.

1901 Theodore Roosevelt becomes president after McKinley is assassinated.

1908 William Howard Taft is elected president.

1892 Grover Cleveland is elected president.

1887 Hawaii grants United States exclusive use of Pearl Harbor.

1904 Roosevelt is elected president.

1912 Woodrow Wilson is elected president.

1914 Panama Canal opens.

USA World 1880 — 1917

1885 European nations divide Central and West Africa at the Berlin West Africa Conference.

1895 Sino-Japanese War ends with Japanese victory over China.

1900 Boxer Rebellion occurs in China.

1910 Mexican Revolution begins.

1916 Pancho Villa makes a raid in the United States.

1903 Republic of Panama established.

1904 Russo-Japanese War begins.

BEFORE YOU READ

Previewing the Theme

Expansion By the end of the 1800s, the United States had become a world power. The nation used its economic and military strength to expand its influence in both Latin America—the part of the Americas south of the United States—and Asia. Some Americans worried that U.S. expansion overseas might weaken the nation's democratic principles. These are the issues and events explored in Chapter 9.

The American eagle spreads its wings over Asia and Latin America in this political cartoon from 1904.

What Do You Know?

Was expansion something new, or was it a force that you have seen before in the history of the United States?

THINK ABOUT
• the idea of Manifest Destiny
• the Louisiana Purchase
• the War with Mexico

What Do You Want to Know?

What do you think might have caused the United States to expand overseas at the end of the 1800s? Make a list of the possible reasons before you read the chapter.

READ AND TAKE NOTES

Reading Strategy: Finding Main Ideas An important skill for reading history is the ability to find main ideas. Identifying main ideas helps you to organize and understand the variety of details and examples that support those ideas. Use a chart like the one below to write main ideas about U.S. expansion overseas.

 See Skillbuilder Handbook, page R5.

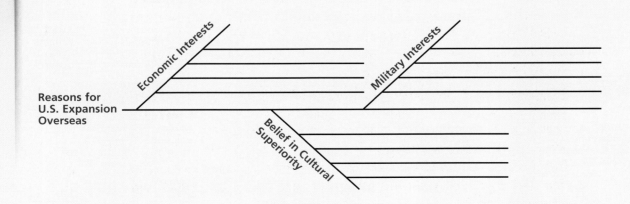

① The United States Continues to Expand

MAIN IDEA	WHY IT MATTERS NOW
The United States expanded its interest in world affairs and acquired new territories.	During this period, the United States acquired Alaska and Hawaii as territories.

ONE AMERICAN'S STORY

Alfred T. Mahan joined the U.S. Navy in the 1850s and served for nearly 40 years. In the 1890s, Mahan made use of his decades of experience to write several books on the historical importance of sea power. In one passage, he discussed the economic importance of trading stations and colonies.

A VOICE FROM THE PAST

The trading-station . . . [was] the same as the . . . colony. In both cases the mother-country had won a foothold in a foreign land, seeking a new outlet for what it had to sell, a new sphere for its shipping, more employment for its people, and more comfort and wealth for itself.

A. T. Mahan, *The Influence of Sea Power upon History, 1660–1805*

Naval historian Alfred Thayer Mahan at the turn of the century

Mahan encouraged government officials to build up American naval forces so that the United States could compete with other powerful nations. In this section you will learn how the United States began to extend its influence beyond the national boundaries.

Reasons for U.S. Expansion

Americans had always sought to expand the size of their nation. Throughout the 19th century, they extended their control toward the Pacific Coast. By the 1880s, however, many leaders became convinced that the United States should join the imperialist powers of Europe and establish colonies overseas. **Imperialism**—the policy by which stronger nations extend their economic, political, or military control over weaker territories—was a trend around the world.

European nations had been establishing colonies for centuries. In the late 19th century, Africa became a major area of European expansion. By the early 20th century, only two countries in Africa—Ethiopia and Liberia—remained independent.

Imperialist countries also competed for territory in Asia, especially in China. There, European nations had to compete with Japan, which had also become a world power by the end of the 1800s.

Becoming a World Power **257**

Most Americans gradually came to approve of the idea of expansion overseas. Three factors helped to fuel the development of American imperialism.

1. **Economic Interests.** Economic leaders argued that expansion would increase U.S. financial prosperity. Industry had greatly expanded after the Civil War. Many industrialists saw new colonies as a potential source of cheap raw materials. Agriculture had also expanded. Farmers pointed out that colonies would mean new markets for their products.

2. **Military Interests.** In his books, Alfred T. Mahan had argued that economic interests went hand-in-hand with military interests. Foreign policy experts agreed. They urged U.S. leaders to follow the European example and establish a military presence overseas.

3. **Belief in Cultural Superiority.** Many Americans believed that their government, religion, and even race were superior to those of other societies. Some people hoped to spread democratic ideas overseas. Others saw a chance to advance Christianity. Racist ideas about the inferiority of the nonwhite populations in many foreign countries were also used to justify American imperialism.

Each of these developments—economic interests, military interests, and a belief in cultural superiority—led the United States to a larger role on the world stage.

Reading **History**
A. Making Inferences Why might economic and military interests go hand in hand?

Alaska, 1867 & Hawaii, 1898

RUSSIA
Arctic Circle

Alaska, 1867

United States and its possessions

60°N

PACIFIC OCEAN

Hawaiian Islands, 1898
Kauai
Oahu
Molokai
Pearl Harbor
Maui

40°N

Hawaii

NORTH AMERICA

UNITED STATES

Tropic of Cancer

20°N

N

0   2,000 Miles
0   4,000 Kilometers

GEOGRAPHY SKILLBUILDER
Interpreting Maps

1. **Location** *What country lies to the west of Alaska?*
2. **Location** *On which Hawaiian island is Pearl Harbor?*

Seward and Alaska

A strong backer of expansion was **William Seward,** Secretary of State under presidents Abraham Lincoln and Andrew Johnson. Seward made his biggest move in 1867, when he arranged the purchase of Alaska from Russia.

Not everyone was pleased by Seward's move, though. At the time, the $7.2-million deal was widely criticized. Newspapers called Alaska a "Polar Bear Garden" and "Seward's Icebox." Even so, the purchase of the resource-rich territory turned out to be a great bargain for the United States.

Throughout his career, Seward continued to pursue new territory. Before he retired in 1869, he considered acquiring the Hawaiian Islands, a group of volcanic and coral islands in the central Pacific Ocean. That would not happen, however, for almost 30 more years.

Background
In the late 1800s, large gold fields were discovered in Alaska. The territory was also rich in fur-bearing animals, timber, copper, coal, and oil.

The Annexation of Hawaii

Reading History
B. Reading a Map
Locate the Hawaiian Islands on the map on page 258.

In the early 1800s, Christian missionaries from the United States had moved to the Kingdom of Hawaii to convert the local population. Some of the missionaries' descendants started sugar plantations. By the late 1800s, wealthy planters dominated Hawaii's economy.

In 1891, **Queen Liliuokalani** (lee•LEE•oo•oh•kah•LAH•nee) became the leader of Hawaii. Believing that planters had too much influence, she wanted to limit their power. Around the same time, U.S. trade laws changed to favor sugar grown exclusively in American states.

American planters in Hawaii were upset by these threats to their political and economic interests. In January 1893, they staged a revolt. With the help of U.S. Marines, they overthrew the queen and set up their own government. They then asked to be annexed by the United States.

Vocabulary
annex: to add

U.S. leaders already understood the value of the islands. In 1887, they had pressured Hawaii to allow a U.S. naval base at Pearl Harbor, the kingdom's best port. The base became an important refueling station for American merchant and military ships bound for Asia.

Thus, when President Benjamin Harrison received the planters' request in 1893, he gave his approval and sent a treaty to the Senate. But before the Senate could act, Grover Cleveland became president. He did not approve of the planters' actions and withdrew the treaty. Hawaii would not be annexed until 1898, during the Spanish-American War. In the next section, you will read about the events that led to that war.

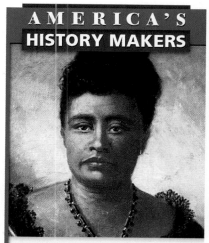

AMERICA'S HISTORY MAKERS

QUEEN LILIUOKALANI
1838–1917

As a young princess, Liliuokalani received a Western education and toured the world. Although she learned about many cultures, she remained committed to Hawaii. An excellent musician, she wrote the famous Hawaiian song "Aloha Oe [Farewell to Thee]."

She was the first queen of Hawaii and proved to be a good leader. She resisted the foreign takeover of Hawaii and inspired a revolt against the planters. Only in 1895, when the safety of her supporters was threatened, did she agree to give up her throne.

How did Queen Liliuokalani protect her followers after planters seized power?

Section ① Assessment

1. Terms & Names

Explain the significance of:
- imperialism
- William Seward
- Queen Liliuokalani

2. Taking Notes

Use a chart like the one shown to record causes of U.S. expansion overseas in the late 1800s.

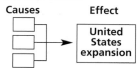

Causes → Effect: United States expansion

Which was the most important cause?

3. Main Ideas

a. Where was the focus of U.S. expansion before the late 1800s?

b. How did William Seward contribute to U.S. expansion?

c. Why did the American planters' request for the annexation of Hawaii fail in the early 1890s?

4. Critical Thinking

Making Inferences What benefits were American planters looking for when they staged a revolt in 1893?

THINK ABOUT
- the new policies of Queen Liliuokalani
- changes in U.S. trade laws

ACTIVITY OPTIONS

TECHNOLOGY
ART

Read more about Hawaii's Queen Liliuokalani. Outline a **video presentation** on the overthrow of the queen or plan a **mural** that depicts the event.

The Spanish-American War

TERMS & NAMES
yellow journalism
U.S.S. *Maine*
Spanish-American War
Rough Riders
Platt Amendment
Anti-Imperialist League
Luis Muñoz Rivera

MAIN IDEA	WHY IT MATTERS NOW
Independence movements in Spanish colonies led to the Spanish-American War in 1898.	U.S. involvement in Latin America and Asia expanded greatly after the Spanish-American War.

ONE AMERICAN'S STORY

José Martí was forced to leave Cuba in the 1870s, when he was still a teenager. In those years, the Caribbean island was a Spanish colony, and he had spoken out for independence. Martí later described the terrible conditions that existed under Spanish rule.

A VOICE FROM THE PAST

Cuba's children . . . suffer in indescribable bitterness as they see their fertile nation enchained and also their human dignity stifled . . . all for the necessities and vices of the [Spanish] monarchy.

José Martí, quoted in *José Martí, Mentor of the Cuban Nation*

José Martí dedicated his life to the Cuban struggle for independence from Spain.

After being forced out of Cuba, Martí spent much of his life in the United States. In 1892, he was elected to lead the Cuban Revolutionary Party. At the Party's headquarters in New York City, Martí began to plan a revolt against Spain that began in 1895.

Martí's lifelong struggle for Cuban independence made him a symbol of liberty throughout Latin America. In this section, you will read how U.S. disapproval of Spain's treatment of Cubans led to the Spanish-American War.

Rebellion Against Spain

The Spanish empire was crumbling at the end of the 19th century. Spain had once controlled most of the Americas, including land that became part of the United States. By the 1890s, however, it owned only a few colonies. Among them were the Philippine Islands in the Pacific and the Caribbean islands of Cuba and Puerto Rico. (See the maps on page 263.) Many of the inhabitants of these colonies had begun to demand independence.

Cubans had revolted against Spain several times in the second half of the nineteenth century. Each time, Spanish soldiers defeated the rebels. In 1895, an ongoing economic depression had increased Cubans' anger over Spanish rule, and they rebelled again. José Martí, who had helped to organize the rebellion from New York, returned to Cuba. He was killed in a skirmish with Spanish troops shortly after, but the revolt continued.

Spain sent General Valeriano "the Butcher" Weyler to crush the rebels. Weyler's methods were harsh. He forced many Cubans from their homes and placed them in camps guarded by Spanish troops. Thousands died of starvation and disease in the camps.

The revolt in Cuba caused alarm in the United States. Business leaders were concerned because the fighting disrupted U.S. trade with Cuba. Most Americans, however, became outraged when the press began to describe the brutality of Spanish officials. Two New York City newspapers, in particular, stirred up people's emotions.

*Reading*History
A. Forming Opinions How can newspapers affect public opinion?

The *World,* owned by Joseph Pulitzer, and the *New York Journal,* owned by William Randolph Hearst, were battling for customers. Both owners were able to attract readers by printing stories that described—and often exaggerated—news about Spanish cruelty. This sensational style of writing was known as **yellow journalism**. It was named after "The Yellow Kid," a popular comic strip that ran in the two New York papers.

The United States Goes to War

William McKinley, the U.S. president in 1898, did not want war. "I have been through [the Civil War]," he told a friend. "I have seen the dead piled up, and I do not want to see another."

Even so, public opinion—stirred up by sensational newspaper reports—forced McKinley to take action. He demanded that Spain halt its harsh treatment of Cubans. Spain did bring General Weyler home, but conditions remained severe.

In January 1898, McKinley sent the **U.S.S. *Maine*** to Cuba. Riots had broken out in the capital, Havana, and the battleship was dispatched to protect U.S. citizens. Then, the following month, the *Maine* exploded and sank in Havana's harbor, killing 260 sailors.

No one knows what caused the explosion. Most historians today believe that it was an accident. For example, a spark might have set off an explosion in the ship's coal bunker. Even so, Americans blamed Spain.

The explosion of the *Maine* and accounts of the event by yellow journalists led many Americans to favor war against Spain.

Detecting Bias in the Media

Modern journalists try to report the news without bias—that is, without letting their personal opinions or those of their employer influence what they write. Unbiased reporting is one of the responsibilities of a free press. It allows citizens to weigh the facts and come to their own understanding of issues and events.

As you have read, journalists and their employers do not always avoid bias. In fact, in the 1890s, journalists were not concerned with bias. Before the United States declared war on Spain in 1898, 'yellow journalists' exaggerated stories to help sell newspapers. These stories helped turn U.S. public opinion in favor of war against Spain. They used words and images to reflect their bias that the United States should declare war on Spain—and sell more papers along the way.

William Randolph Hearst ran this headline in his *New York Journal* before authorities had a chance to determine the cause of the *Maine's* explosion.

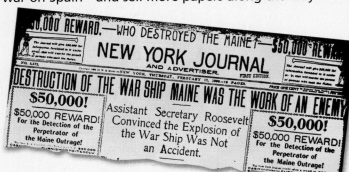

Can You Find Bias in the Media?

1. With a small group, collect news stories from different sources that cover the same issue or event.

2. Record any differences in the way a specific issue or event is covered by the oral, written, or visual sources you have selected.

3. Review the differences and decide whether any of the authors of the sources showed bias in their coverage.

4. Write a report that describes any bias you might detect. Explain why the biased source might have reported the story the way it did.

   See Citizenship Handbook, page 106.

For more about the news media . . .

RESEARCH LINKS
CLASSZONE.COM

"Remember the Maine!" became a call to arms. On April 20, 1898, President McKinley signed a congressional resolution that called for Cuba's independence and demanded a withdrawal of Spanish forces. He gave Spain three days to respond. Spain refused, and the **Spanish-American War** began.

The War in the Philippines

The United States went to war to fight for Cuban freedom. But the first major battle of the Spanish-American War took place in a Spanish colony on the other side of the world—the Philippine Islands. Many Filipinos, as the inhabitants of the islands were called, had also revolted against Spanish rule in the 1890s.

Before the war began, the Filipino independence movement had attracted the attention of Theodore Roosevelt. At that time, Roosevelt was assistant secretary of the navy. He put a fleet of American ships in Hong Kong on alert. Their leader, Commodore George Dewey, prepared his forces and made contact with the head of the Filipino rebel forces, Emilio Aguinaldo (eh•MEE•lyoh AH•gee•NAHL•doh).

When the war began, Dewey set out for Manila, the Philippine capital, where part of the Spanish fleet was located. The battle in Manila Bay began early on the morning of May 1, 1898. By a little past noon,

Reading **History**
B. Making Inferences Why did Theodore Roosevelt put the U.S. fleet in Hong Kong on alert?

Dewey's forces had destroyed the Spanish fleet. About 380 Spanish sailors were dead or wounded. No Americans died. U.S. troops, aided by Filipino rebels, took control of Manila in August.

Dewey became an instant hero in the United States. Thousands of babies born at the time of the victory in Manila Bay were named for him, and a chewing gum called "Dewey's Chewies" became popular.

The War in the Caribbean

When the Spanish-American War began, the U.S. Army had only 28,000 men. Within four months, over 200,000 more joined up. Among the new recruits was Theodore Roosevelt, who had resigned from the Navy Department to volunteer.

Roosevelt helped to organize the First United States Volunteer Cavalry. This unit was nicknamed the **Rough Riders**. Its recruits included cowboys, miners, college students, New York policemen, athletes, and Native Americans.

In June, the Rough Riders and about 16,000 other soldiers—nearly a quarter of them African American—gathered in Tampa, Florida. They then set out for Santiago, a Spanish stronghold in southern Cuba. When the Rough Riders arrived, their dark-blue wool uniforms were too hot for the Cuban climate. Also, many of the soldiers came down with tropical diseases. Even so, they fought their way toward Santiago.

In order to gain control of Santiago's port, American troops had to capture San Juan Hill. They attacked the Spanish on July 1.

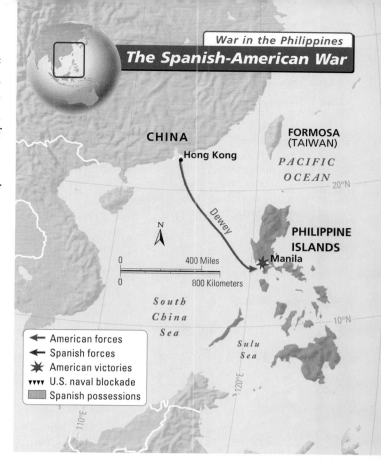

War in the Philippines
The Spanish-American War

CHINA
Hong Kong
FORMOSA (TAIWAN)
PACIFIC OCEAN
20°N
PHILIPPINE ISLANDS
Manila
South China Sea
Sulu Sea
10°N
120°E
110°E

← American forces
← Spanish forces
✶ American victories
▼▼▼ U.S. naval blockade
▨ Spanish possessions

0 — 400 Miles
0 — 800 Kilometers

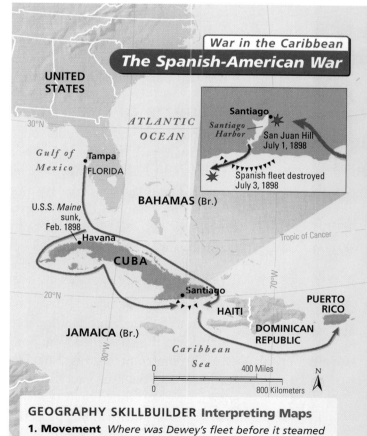

War in the Caribbean
The Spanish-American War

UNITED STATES
ATLANTIC OCEAN
30°N
Gulf of Mexico
Tampa
FLORIDA
U.S.S. *Maine* sunk, Feb. 1898
Havana
CUBA
20°N
Santiago
JAMAICA (Br.)
BAHAMAS (Br.)
Tropic of Cancer
70°W
HAITI
DOMINICAN REPUBLIC
PUERTO RICO
80°W
Caribbean Sea
90°W

Santiago
Santiago Harbor
San Juan Hill July 1, 1898
Spanish fleet destroyed July 3, 1898

0 — 400 Miles
0 — 800 Kilometers

GEOGRAPHY SKILLBUILDER Interpreting Maps
1. **Movement** *Where was Dewey's fleet before it steamed toward the Philippines?*
2. **Location** *About how far is Havana from the tip of southern Florida?*

HISTORY through ART

On July 1, 1898, U.S. troops, including the Rough Riders, attacked San Juan Hill outside of Santiago, Cuba. This painting shows Theodore Roosevelt leading a cavalry charge up the hill—even though the regiment's horses had been left behind in Florida.

Why did the artist show the Rough Riders on horses when they made their charge on foot?

African-American soldiers from the Tenth Cavalry began to drive the Spanish back. Roosevelt and the Rough Riders joined them as they rushed forward and captured the hill.

Two days later, American ships destroyed Spain's fleet as it tried to escape Santiago Harbor. On July 17, the city surrendered. A week later, U.S. forces took Puerto Rico. Finally, on August 12, 1898, Spain signed a truce. To U.S. Secretary of State John Hay, it had been "a splendid little war." For Spain, four centuries of glory had come to an end.

Results of the War

Although the war had been fought over Cuba, U.S. leaders demanded that Spain give up other colonies after the war—including Puerto Rico, the island of Guam, and the Philippines. Spain had no choice but to agree. The final peace treaty was signed in Paris in December 1898.

One of the most difficult questions for U.S. leaders after the war was what to do with the Philippines. Filipinos had fought alongside Americans during the war and believed that Spain's defeat would bring them independence. But President McKinley eventually decided that the Philippines should become an American colony.

Filipinos were bitterly disappointed. Led by Emilio Aguinaldo, they began to fight against their new colonial rulers. American troops sent to put down the resistance were not able to restore order until 1902.

The United States was also reluctant to grant Cuba complete independence. First, Cuba had to add the **Platt Amendment** to its constitution. This gave the United States the right to intervene in Cuban affairs anytime there was a threat to "life, property, and individual liberty." Cuba also had to allow a U.S. naval base at Guantánamo Bay.

Puerto Rico became an American territory. The United States set up a government and appointed the top officials. Puerto Ricans had little to

Reading **History**

C. Making Inferences Why did the United States demand that Spain give up territories in addition to Cuba?

say in their own affairs. Only in 1917 would the United States agree to make Puerto Rico a self-governing territory and grant U.S. citizenship to all Puerto Ricans.

The Anti-Imperialist League

U.S. treatment of Spain's former colonies after the Spanish-American War disappointed many people in the United States.

Several well-known Americans, including businessman Andrew Carnegie, reformer Jane Addams, and writer Mark Twain, joined with others to form the **Anti-Imperialist League.** Members of the League believed that Americans should not deny other people the right to govern themselves.

*Reading*History
D. Finding Main Ideas Why did the Anti-Imperialist League oppose U.S. efforts to collect colonies?

A VOICE FROM THE PAST

We hold that the policy known as imperialism is hostile to liberty. . . . We regret that it has become necessary in the land of Washington and Lincoln to reaffirm that all men, of whatever race or color, are entitled to life, liberty, and the pursuit of happiness.

From the *Platform of the American Anti-Imperialist League*

The voice of the Anti-Imperialist League was lost, however, in the roar of popular approval of the Spanish-American War.

Many Americans hoped that their nation would surpass the glory of the old Spanish empire. In the next section, you will read more about how the United States continued its involvement overseas.

AMERICA'S HISTORY MAKERS

LUIS MUÑOZ RIVERA
1859–1916

Luis Muñoz Rivera devoted his life to obtaining self-government for Puerto Rico—first from Spain and then from the United States.

After Spain granted Puerto Rico self-rule in 1897, Muñoz Rivera joined the government. He resigned and renewed his struggle when Puerto Rico became a U.S. territory.

Muñoz Rivera died just before the United States granted Puerto Ricans U.S. citizenship and a large measure of self-government.

In what ways did Muñoz Rivera use his leadership skills to help his country?

Section 2 Assessment

1. Terms & Names
Explain the significance of:
• yellow journalism
• U.S.S. *Maine*
• Spanish-American War
• Rough Riders
• Platt Amendment
• Anti-Imperialist League
• Luis Muñoz Rivera

2. Taking Notes
Use a time line to record the major events of the Spanish-American War.

Spanish-American War, 1898

About how long did the Spanish-American War last?

3. Main Ideas
a. What led to the Cuban rebellion against Spain in 1895?

b. What was the first major military event of the Spanish-American War?

c. What happened in the Philippines after the war?

4. Critical Thinking
Forming Opinions Did the United States betray its democratic principles when it made the Philippines a colony?

THINK ABOUT
• the public's response to yellow journalists and U.S. military victories
• the work of the Anti-Imperialist League

ACTIVITY OPTIONS

LANGUAGE ARTS
MATH

Research the Spanish-American War. Write a **television news script** covering a major battle or create a **database** of wartime casualties.

U.S. Involvement Overseas

TERMS & NAMES
sphere of influence
Open Door Policy
Boxer Rebellion
Panama Canal
Roosevelt Corollary

MAIN IDEA

In the early 1900s, the United States expanded its involvement in Asia and Latin America.

WHY IT MATTERS NOW

The United States still trades extensively with Asian and Latin American countries.

ONE AMERICAN'S STORY

In 1852, President Millard Fillmore sent Commodore Matthew Perry on a mission to open Japan to U.S. trade. For over two centuries, Japan's rulers had kept the country closed to most foreigners. Perry wanted to break Japan's traditional policy with a demonstration of American power.

A VOICE FROM THE PAST

[I was determined] to adopt an entirely contrary plan of proceedings from that of all others who had . . . visited Japan on the same errand [to open up trade]: to demand as a right and not to [ask] as a favor those acts of courtesy which are due from one civilized nation to another.

Commodore Matthew Perry, *Personal Journal*

A Japanese artist portrayed Commodore Matthew Perry's meeting with Japanese officials in 1853.

   Perry arrived in Japan in July 1853 but was not able to win a trade agreement. He departed but returned the next year with more warships. Under the threat of force, the Japanese gave in. In March 1854, Japan signed a treaty giving American ships access to its ports. In this section, you will read more about U.S. involvement in Asia, as well as in Latin America.

A Power in the Pacific

Throughout the 1800s, the United States continued to expand its involvement in Asia. Toward the end of the century, the United States acquired a chain of islands—including Hawaii and Guam—that stretched across the Pacific Ocean to Asia.

   During the Spanish-American War, Americans fought in the Philippine Islands, a Spanish colony in eastern Asia. After the war, the United States annexed the islands and put down the Filipino independence movement.

   Some Americans objected to the annexation of the Philippines. However, supporters of imperialism, such as Indiana senator Albert Beveridge, applauded U.S. actions. Beveridge boasted, "The Philippines are ours forever. And just beyond the Philippines are China's [unlimited] markets. We will not retreat from either. . . . The power that rules the Pacific is the power that rules the world."

Many Americans looked forward to the profits promised by Asian markets and resources. Others saw a chance to extend U.S. democracy and culture in the region. The Philippines would provide a base for these activities.

"The power that rules the Pacific . . . rules the world."

Albert Beveridge

The United States in China

As Senator Beveridge noted, control of the Philippines gave Americans greater access to China. However, by the time the United States acquired the islands, other imperialist nations, including Japan, were already deeply involved in China.

When Commodore Perry opened Japan to U.S. trade in the 1850s, he also opened the nation to Western ideas. After Perry's voyages, Japan began to modernize and soon emerged as a world power. In the 1890s, Japan demonstrated its strength in a successful war against China.

After the war, both Japan and the major European powers expanded their **spheres of influence** in China. These were areas where foreign nations claimed special rights and economic privileges. By the late 1890s, France, Germany, Britain, Japan, and Russia had established prosperous settlements along the coast of China. They also claimed exclusive rights to railroad construction and mining development in the nation's interior.

The competition for spheres of influence worried U.S. leaders who wanted access to China's markets and resources. In 1899, Secretary of State John Hay asked nations involved in the region to follow an **Open Door Policy**. This meant that no single country should have a monopoly on trade with China. Eventually, most of the nations accepted Hay's proposal.

Many Chinese people were not pleased by the presence of foreigners. One group, called the "Boxers," was angered by the privileges given to foreigners and the disrespect they showed toward Chinese traditions. In 1900, Chinese resentment toward foreigners' attitude of cultural superiority led to a violent uprising known as the **Boxer Rebellion**. Many foreigners were killed before the uprising was put down by an international force.

*Reading*History
A. Analyzing Causes Why did John Hay propose the Open Door Policy?

Imperialism in Asia, *1900*

MANCHURIA
MONGOLIA
Beijing (Peking)
JAPAN
KOREA
CHINA
Shanghai
PACIFIC OCEAN
Macao (Portuguese)
Hong Kong (Br.)
FORMOSA (TAIWAN)
PHILIPPINE ISLANDS (U.S.)

0   1,000 Miles
0   2,000 Kilometers

Russian sphere
German sphere
British sphere
French sphere
Japanese sphere

GEOGRAPHY SKILLBUILDER Interpreting Maps
1. **Place** *What country controlled the port of Macao?*
2. **Region** *What country had the largest sphere of influence in the coastal region of China?*

The Panama Canal

As American interests in the Pacific expanded, easy access to the region became vital. For that reason, U.S. leaders proposed a canal to connect the Atlantic and Pacific oceans. A canal would mean that U.S. ships would not have to travel around South America. The Spanish-American War, fought in both oceans, also made clear the need for such a shortcut.

The South American nation of Colombia controlled the best spot for the canal—the Isthmus of Panama. But Colombia was unwilling to give up this land. Ignoring Colombia's right to control its territory, President Roosevelt sent the U.S. Navy to support a revolution on the isthmus. Out of this revolution, the new nation of Panama was created in 1903.

The new Panamanian leaders granted the U.S. government rights to a ten-mile-wide strip of land called the Canal Zone. In return, the United States paid Panama $10 million and an annual fee of $250,000. There, the United States would build the **Panama Canal,** the shortcut that would connect the Atlantic and Pacific oceans.

Some people in Latin America and the United States opposed Roosevelt's actions. They believed that he had interfered in Colombia's affairs in order to cheat it out of land. In 1921, the United States finally paid Colombia $25 million for the loss of Panama.

Vocabulary
isthmus: a narrow strip of land connecting two larger masses of land

Reading **History**
B. Summarizing What political difficulty faced U.S. leaders who wanted to build the Panama Canal?

Building the Canal

Building the canal was extremely difficult. The land was swampy and full of mosquitoes that carried the organism that causes malaria. In spite of the difficulties, the project moved forward. When Roosevelt visited Panama in 1906, he wrote a letter describing the work.

A VOICE FROM THE PAST

Steam shovels are hard at it; scooping huge masses of rock and gravel and dirt previously loosened by the drillers and dynamite blasters, loading it on trains which take it away. . . . They are eating steadily into the mountain cutting it down and down. . . . It is an epic feat.

Theodore Roosevelt, from a letter sent to his son

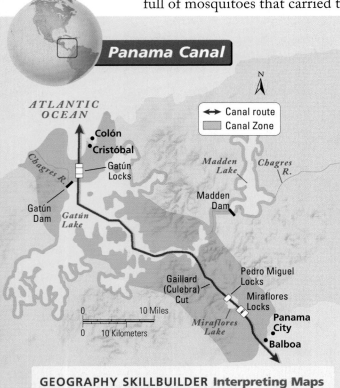

Panama Canal

N

ATLANTIC OCEAN

Colón
Cristóbal
Gatún Locks
Madden Lake
Chagres R.
Chagres R.
Madden Dam
Gatún Dam
Gatún Lake
Gaillard (Culebra) Cut
Pedro Miguel Locks
Miraflores Locks
Miraflores Lake
Panama City
Balboa

← → Canal route
▨ Canal Zone

0   10 Miles
0   10 Kilometers

GEOGRAPHY SKILLBUILDER Interpreting Maps
1. **Location** *Which locks are closest to Panama City?*
2. **Movement** *In which direction do ships move through the canal from the Atlantic Ocean to the Pacific Ocean?*

More than 45,000 workers, including many black West Indians, labored for years on the canal. They did not finish the work until 1914. The canal cost $352 million, the most expensive project up to that time. It was expensive in human terms, too. More than 5,000 workers died from diseases or accidents.

Background
In 1977, the United States signed a treaty that transferred ownership of the canal to Panama on December 31, 1999.

How the Panama Canal Works

Engineers faced a problem in building the Panama Canal. Because of the region's different landscape elevations, no waterway would remain level. They solved this dilemma by building three sets of *locks*—water-filled chambers that raise or lower ships to match a canal's different water levels.

1 The lock gates open on one end to allow the ship to enter.

2 The gates close, and water is pumped in or out depending on whether the ship is moving up or down.

3 Once the water in the chamber and the canal ahead is level, the second gate opens and the ship moves on.

The locks, whose steel gates rise six stories high, can hold as much as 26 million gallons of water—enough to supply a major U.S. city for one day.

Gatún Locks   Culebra Cut   Pedro Miguel Locks
Gatún Lake   Miraflores Lake   Miraflores Locks
Atlantic Ocean   Pacific Ocean

← 51 miles →

This cross-section shows the different elevations and locks that a ship moves through on the 8–9 hour trip through the canal. Before the canal was built, a trip around South America could take two months.

CONNECT TO HISTORY

1. **Drawing Conclusions** Why did the United States want a shorter route between the Atlantic and Pacific oceans?

CONNECT TO TODAY

2. **Researching** What is the economic and political status of the Panama Canal today?

For more about the Panama Canal . . .

RESEARCH LINKS
CLASSZONE.COM

269

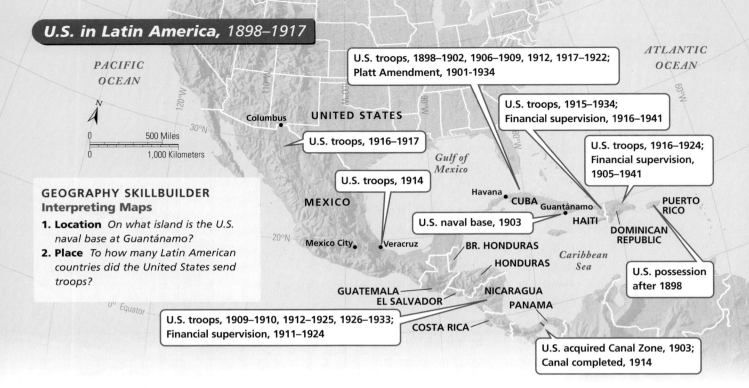

U.S. in Latin America, 1898–1917

PACIFIC OCEAN

ATLANTIC OCEAN

U.S. troops, 1898–1902, 1906–1909, 1912, 1917–1922; Platt Amendment, 1901-1934

U.S. troops, 1915–1934; Financial supervision, 1916–1941

U.S. troops, 1916–1924; Financial supervision, 1905–1941

U.S. troops, 1916–1917

U.S. troops, 1914

Gulf of Mexico

Havana

CUBA

Guantánamo

HAITI

PUERTO RICO

UNITED STATES

Columbus

MEXICO

U.S. naval base, 1903

DOMINICAN REPUBLIC

Mexico City

Veracruz

BR. HONDURAS

Caribbean Sea

U.S. possession after 1898

HONDURAS

GUATEMALA

EL SALVADOR

NICARAGUA

PANAMA

U.S. troops, 1909–1910, 1912–1925, 1926–1933; Financial supervision, 1911–1924

COSTA RICA

U.S. acquired Canal Zone, 1903; Canal completed, 1914

Equator

GEOGRAPHY SKILLBUILDER
Interpreting Maps
1. **Location** On what island is the U.S. naval base at Guantánamo?
2. **Place** To how many Latin American countries did the United States send troops?

U.S. Involvement in Latin America

The Panama Canal was only one sign of U.S. involvement in Latin America. As the U.S. economy continued to grow, so did Americans' interest in the resources of their southern neighbors.

Businesses in the United States found that they could cheaply buy food and raw materials—for example, bananas, coffee, and copper— from Latin America. They shipped these goods to the United States and sold them for higher prices. U.S. companies also bought large amounts of land in the region for farming and mining.

As economic interests drew the United States deeper into Latin American affairs, U.S. leaders became concerned about political stability in the region. They were especially worried that instability might tempt European nations to intervene in the region.

Reading **History**
C. Making Inferences Why was the United States interested in the political stability of Latin America?

Policing the Hemisphere

During his presidency, Theodore Roosevelt made it clear that the United States would remain the dominant power in the Western Hemisphere. He summed up his foreign policy toward the region with an African saying: "Speak softly, but carry a big stick." Roosevelt, however, rarely spoke softly. He made sure that everyone knew the United States would use military force if its interests were threatened.

Roosevelt reminded European powers of the Monroe Doctrine—the policy that prevented other nations from intervening in Latin America. In 1904, he added the **Roosevelt Corollary**. Now, the doctrine would not only prevent European intervention in Latin America; it also authorized the United States to act as a "policeman" in the region. That is, U.S. leaders would now intervene in Latin America's domestic affairs

Vocabulary
corollary: a statement that follows logically from an earlier statement

when they believed that such action was necessary to maintain stability.

In 1905, the United States used the Roosevelt Corollary to take control of the Dominican Republic's finances after the country failed to pay its foreign debts. A year later, when a revolt threatened Cuba's government, the policy was used to send troops there.

Later presidents expanded on Roosevelt's "big stick diplomacy." William Howard Taft urged American businesses to invest in Latin America, promising military action if anything threatened these investments. He kept his word. In 1912, Taft sent marines to Nicaragua to restore order.

Background
Taft's policy was known as "dollar diplomacy."

President Taft's successor, Woodrow Wilson, also intervened in Latin America. When a revolution in Mexico began to threaten U.S. interests, Wilson took action. In 1914, he sent a fleet to Veracruz after U.S. sailors were arrested. Two years later, he sent troops into Mexico after a Mexican revolutionary named Pancho Villa (PAHN•choh VEE•yah) raided New Mexico and killed 19 Americans in the town of Columbus.

Americans rarely questioned U.S. actions in Latin America. They saw their nation as a good police officer, maintaining peace and preventing disorder. But many Latin Americans saw the United States as an imperial power that cared only about its own interests. This mistrust continues to trouble U.S. relations with its neighbors. In the next chapter, you will read about U.S. involvement in another part of the world—Europe.

Now *and* then

GLOBO COP?

In the early 1900s, the United States used its "police powers" in the Western Hemisphere. Today, U.S. forces participate in police actions all over the globe. This fact has led some journalists to call the United States the "Globo Cop."

In the 1990s, U.S. forces helped lead international police actions in Somalia (see photo below), Yugoslavia, and other areas in crisis. The United States also led the Gulf War forces that liberated Kuwait after it was seized by Iraq.

The United States continues to patrol its own hemisphere, too. In 1989, U.S. troops invaded Panama to overthrow dictator Manuel Noriega.

Section 3 Assessment

1. Terms & Names

Explain the significance of:
• sphere of influence
• Open Door Policy
• Boxer Rebellion
• Panama Canal
• Roosevelt Corollary

2. Taking Notes

Use a chart like the one below to record details about U.S. involvement in Asia and Latin America.

Asia	Latin America

How was U.S. involvement in Asia different from that in Latin America?

3. Main Ideas

a. Why was the United States interested in the Philippines?

b. Why was the nation of Panama created in 1903?

c. How did the Roosevelt Corollary change U.S. foreign policy?

4. Critical Thinking

Drawing Conclusions
Why did the United States become so heavily involved in Asia and Latin America?

THINK ABOUT
• U.S. economic growth
• American military interests

ACTIVITY OPTIONS

SCIENCE

MATH

Research the Panama Canal. Build a simple **model** of the canal or create a **graph** that shows how many ships use the canal each year.

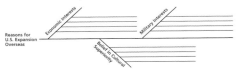

Becoming a World Power

The United States Continues to Expand

In the late 1800s, the United States began to expand overseas.
- Alaska was purchased from Russia.
- Planters took over Hawaii's government.

The Spanish-American War

Events in Cuba, a Spanish colony in the Caribbean, led to the Spanish-American War.
- U.S. forces won victories in the Caribbean and in Asia.
- Spain gave up its colonies in Cuba, Puerto Rico, the Philippines, and Guam.

U.S. Involvement Overseas

In both Asia and Latin America, the United States began to play a larger role.
- U.S. leaders insisted on an Open Door Policy in China.
- The United States built the Panama Canal.

TERMS & NAMES

Briefly explain the significance of each of the following.

1. imperialism
2. Queen Liliuokalani
3. yellow journalism
4. Spanish-American War
5. Rough Riders
6. Anti-Imperialist League
7. Open Door Policy
8. Boxer Rebellion
9. Panama Canal
10. Roosevelt Corollary

REVIEW QUESTIONS

The United States Continues to Expand (pages 257–259)

1. Why did Americans become interested in overseas expansion in the late 1800s?
2. How did the public react when William Seward negotiated the purchase of Alaska in 1867?
3. Why did the United States take an interest in Hawaii?
4. Why might President Cleveland have wanted to restore Liliuokalani to the Hawaiian throne?

The Spanish-American War (pages 260–265)

5. How did the Spanish-American War begin?
6. What were the most important battles of the war?
7. What territories did the United States take control of as a result of its victory over the Spanish?

U.S. Involvement Overseas (pages 266–271)

8. Why did U.S. leaders want access to China's markets after the Spanish-American War?
9. Why was there an interest in building a canal across Latin America?
10. How were the Latin American policies of Roosevelt, Taft, and Wilson similar?

CRITICAL THINKING

1. USING YOUR NOTES

Using your completed chart, answer the questions below.

a. How did U.S. economic interests in Latin America influence the foreign policy of the United States?
b. In what ways was the Boxer Rebellion a reaction to the attitude of foreigners in China?

2. ANALYZING LEADERSHIP

What qualities made Theodore Roosevelt an effective leader?

3. THEME: EXPANSION

How did U.S. expansion at the end of the 19th century compare with expansion that occurred earlier? Discuss both similarities and differences.

4. APPLYING CITIZENSHIP SKILLS

How might the activities of the Anti-Imperialist League have helped to remind citizens of their democratic responsibilities?

5. FORMING OPINIONS

The "yellow journalism" of major newspapers influenced U.S. foreign policy at the turn of the century. How does modern media, such as television, shape public opinion today?

Interact *with* History

How has your study of U.S. involvement overseas at the turn of the century influenced your opinion about getting involved in the affairs of another country?

HISTORY SKILLS

1. INTERPRETING GRAPHS

Study the graph and then answer the questions.

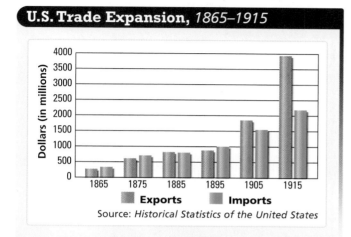

U.S. Trade Expansion, 1865–1915

Source: *Historical Statistics of the United States*

Basic Graph Elements

a. What does this graph represent?

Interpreting the Graph

b. What were the values of U.S. exports in 1865 and 1915?

c. What were the values of U.S. imports in 1865 and 1915?

2. INTERPRETING PRIMARY SOURCES

W. A. Rogers's political cartoon from 1904 shows Theodore Roosevelt tugging the U.S. Navy around the Caribbean.

a. What do you think this cartoon is about?

b. Why did the cartoonist portray Roosevelt with a big stick?

ALTERNATIVE ASSESSMENT

1. INTERDISCIPLINARY ACTIVITY: Geography

Making a Map During the 19th century, the United States acquired several islands in the Pacific Ocean. Do more research on U.S. possessions in the Pacific and make a map that shows the islands' locations.

2. COOPERATIVE LEARNING ACTIVITY

Creating a News Story Imagine that you are a journalist in the late 1800s. The publisher of the *New York Journal,* William Randolph Hearst, has asked you to put together a team of reporters and artists. With your team, plan and write an illustrated news story for the *Journal* that features an important event from the Spanish-American War. Be sure to use standard grammar, spelling, sentence structure, and punctuation in your news story.

3. TECHNOLOGY ACTIVITY

Creating a Multimedia Presentation When the United States annexed the Philippines after the Spanish-American War, Filipinos rose in rebellion. Use the Internet, books, and other resources for a multimedia presentation on the Philippine-American war that resulted from the rebellion.

For more about U.S. imperialism . . .

INTERNET ACTIVITY
CLASSZONE.COM

Using presentation software, consider including the following content:

- descriptions or images of battles
- the views of Filipino and American soldiers, including African-American troops
- public opinion in the two countries
- statistics of casualties suffered by both sides during the conflict

4. HISTORY PORTFOLIO

Option 1 Review your section and chapter assessment activities. Select one that you think is your best work. Then use comments made by your teacher or classmates to improve your work and add it to your portfolio.

Option 2 Review the questions that you wrote for What Do You Want to Know? on page 256. Then write a short report in which you explain the answers to your questions. If any questions were not answered, do research to answer them. Add your answers to your portfolio.

Additional Test Practice, pp. S1–S33

TEST PRACTICE
CLASSZONE.COM

CHAPTER
10

World War I
1914–1920

This photograph shows a battlefield view of trench warfare during World War I.

274

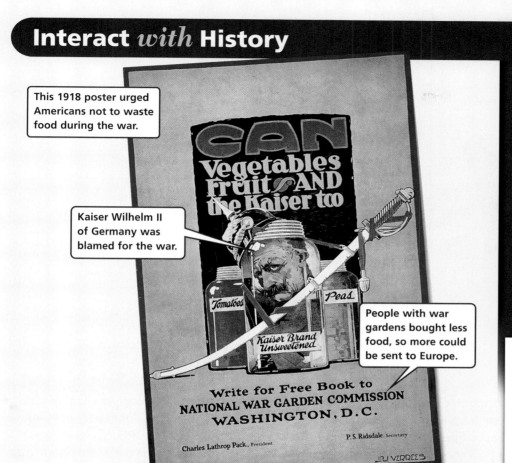

This 1918 poster urged Americans not to waste food during the war.

CAN Vegetables Fruit AND the Kaiser too

Kaiser Wilhelm II of Germany was blamed for the war.

Tomatoes

Peas

Kaiser Brand Unsweetened

People with war gardens bought less food, so more could be sent to Europe.

Write for Free Book to
NATIONAL WAR GARDEN COMMISSION
WASHINGTON, D.C.

Charles Lathrop Pack, President

P.S. Ridsdale, Secretary

The year is 1917, and the United States has been drawn into World War I. Each citizen is called upon to help the war effort. Some will join the American armed forces and go to fight in Europe. Others will work in factories at home, producing weapons and supplies. Even children will do their part.

What Do You Think?

- How can Americans at home help win the war?
- What might U.S. soldiers experience in Europe?
- How might being at war affect the country?

How will you support the war effort?

November 7, 1916
Woodrow Wilson is reelected president.

April 2, 1917
Wilson asks Congress to declare war on Germany.

November 2, 1920
Warren G. Harding is elected president.

August 15, 1914
U.S.-built Panama Canal officially opens.

May 7, 1915
Many Americans die as German U-boat sinks *Lusitania*.

January 8, 1918
President Wilson proposes League of Nations.

USA World 1914 ——————————————————————— 1920

June 28, 1914
Austria-Hungary's Archduke Franz Ferdinand is assassinated, starting World War I.

February–December, 1915
Allies and Central Powers clash at Gallipoli in the Ottoman Empire.

July–November, 1916
French, British, and Germans suffer huge losses at the Battle of the Somme.

June 28, 1919
The Allies and Germany sign the Treaty of Versailles.

March 3, 1918
Russia withdraws from the war.

November 11, 1918
The Allies defeat the Central Powers, ending World War I.

BEFORE YOU READ

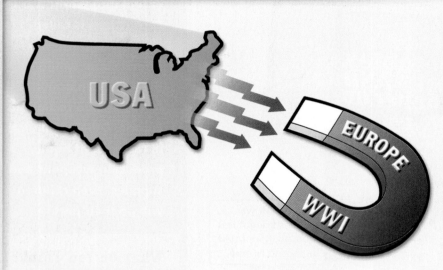

Previewing the Theme

America in the World Although the United States was reluctant to join World War I, American involvement helped the Allies win the war. The war also brought about permanent changes in American society. Chapter 10 explains how the United States became involved in the war, how it mobilized for war, and how it tried to establish a lasting peace.

What Do You Know?

What do you think of when you hear the phrase "world war"? How many countries might have participated in the war? Where did most of the fighting take place?

THINK ABOUT

• what you've learned about World War I from movies or television

• reasons that millions of people might choose to risk their lives in a global conflict

What Do You Want to Know?

What details do you need to help you understand what is involved in waging a world war? Make a list of these details in your notebook before you read the chapter.

READ AND TAKE NOTES

Reading Strategy: Recognizing Effects To help you make sense of what you read, learn to analyze the effects of important historical events. The chart below will help you analyze some of the effects of World War I, both on the world and on the United States. In each box, fill in a different effect. Add more boxes if you need to.

 See Skillbuilder Handbook, page R11.

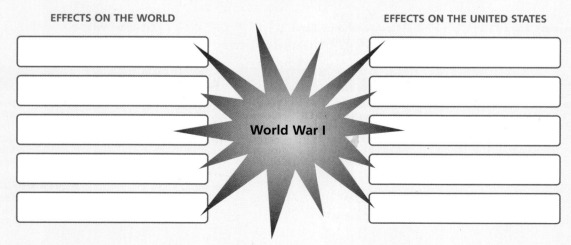

EFFECTS ON THE WORLD

EFFECTS ON THE UNITED STATES

World War I

① War Breaks Out in Europe

TERMS & NAMES
militarism
Central Powers
Allies
trench warfare
U-boat
Woodrow Wilson
neutrality
Zimmermann
  telegram

MAIN IDEA	WHY IT MATTERS NOW
After World War I broke out, the United States eventually joined the Allied side.	This was the first time that the United States was involved in a European conflict.

ONE AMERICAN'S STORY

While the United States was forming its own empire, European nations were competing to expand their empires. Rivalry poisoned relationships among these nations. In the spring of 1914, tensions were running high in Europe. President Woodrow Wilson sent Colonel Edward M. House, his trusted advisor, to study the situation.

House gave the president a troubling report. He compared Europe to an open keg of gunpowder. "It only requires a spark," he said, "to set the whole thing off." Soon the spark ignited. On June 28, 1914, a young Serbian man shot and killed Archduke Franz Ferdinand. The archduke was the heir to the throne of Austria-Hungary. One month later, Austria declared war on Serbia. One by one, the nations of Europe chose sides and the Great War, later called World War I, began.

Archduke Franz Ferdinand and his wife are murdered at Sarajevo on June 28, 1914.

Causes of World War I

A single action, the assassination of the archduke, started World War I. But the conflict had many underlying causes.

1. **Imperialism.** Britain, France, Germany, and Italy competed for colonies in Africa and Asia. Because it had fewer colonies than Britain and France, Germany felt it deserved more colonies to provide it with resources and buy its goods.

2. **Nationalism.** Europeans were very nationalistic, meaning that they had strong feelings of pride, loyalty, and protectiveness toward their own countries. They wanted to prove their nations were the best. They placed their countries' interests above all other concerns. In addition, some ethnic groups hoped to form their own separate nations and were willing to fight for such a cause.

3. **Militarism.** The belief that a nation needs a large military force is **militarism**. In the decades before the war, the major powers built up their armies and navies.

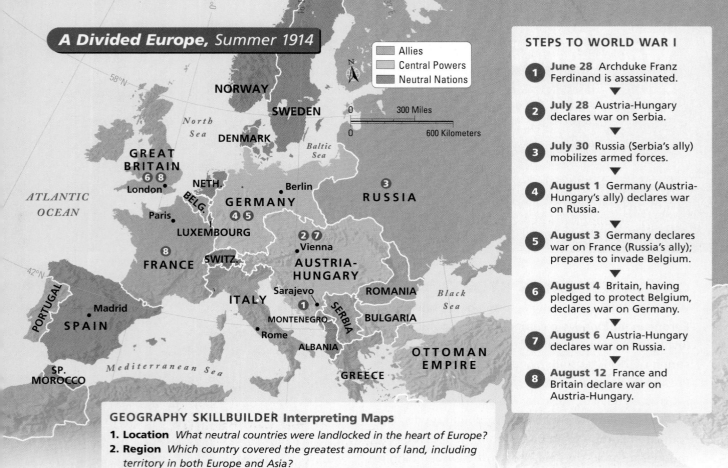

A Divided Europe, Summer 1914

Legend:
- Allies
- Central Powers
- Neutral Nations

NORWAY
SWEDEN
DENMARK
GREAT BRITAIN
London ⑥ ⑧
NETH.
BELG.
Berlin
GERMANY ④⑤
Paris
LUXEMBOURG
RUSSIA ③
FRANCE ⑧
SWITZ.
Vienna ②⑦
AUSTRIA-HUNGARY
ROMANIA
Sarajevo ①
ITALY
MONTENEGRO
Rome
SERBIA
BULGARIA
ALBANIA
OTTOMAN EMPIRE
GREECE
PORTUGAL
Madrid
SPAIN
SP. MOROCCO

North Sea
Baltic Sea
ATLANTIC OCEAN
Black Sea
Mediterranean Sea

0 — 300 Miles
0 — 600 Kilometers

STEPS TO WORLD WAR I

1. **June 28** Archduke Franz Ferdinand is assassinated.
2. **July 28** Austria-Hungary declares war on Serbia.
3. **July 30** Russia (Serbia's ally) mobilizes armed forces.
4. **August 1** Germany (Austria-Hungary's ally) declares war on Russia.
5. **August 3** Germany declares war on France (Russia's ally); prepares to invade Belgium.
6. **August 4** Britain, having pledged to protect Belgium, declares war on Germany.
7. **August 6** Austria-Hungary declares war on Russia.
8. **August 12** France and Britain declare war on Austria-Hungary.

GEOGRAPHY SKILLBUILDER Interpreting Maps
1. **Location** What neutral countries were landlocked in the heart of Europe?
2. **Region** Which country covered the greatest amount of land, including territory in both Europe and Asia?

4. **Alliances** In 1914, a tangled network of competing alliances bound European nations together. An attack on one nation forced all its allies to come to its aid. Any small conflict could become a larger war.

European nations had divided into two opposing alliances. The **Central Powers** were made up of Austria-Hungary, Germany, the Ottoman Empire, and Bulgaria. They faced the Allied Powers, or **Allies,** consisting of Serbia, Russia, France, Great Britain, Italy, and seven other countries.

Stalemate in the Trenches

When the war began in August, most people on both sides assumed it would be over within a few months. With France as its goal, the German army invaded Belgium on August 4, 1914. Despite stiff resistance, the Germans fought their way west into France. They reached the Marne River about 40 miles from Paris. There the French, supported by the British, rallied and prepared to fight back. The First Battle of the Marne, in September 1914, stopped the German advance.

Instead of one side quickly defeating the other, the two sides stayed stuck in the mud for more than three years. The soldiers were fighting a new kind of battle, **trench warfare.** Troops huddled at the bottom of rat-infested trenches. They fired artillery and machine guns at each other. Lines of trenches stretched across France from the English Channel to the border with Switzerland. (See pages 282–283 for an

Background
The Ottoman Empire included modern-day Turkey and Syria.

Reading **History**
A. Reading a Map On the map on page 286, find the site of the first Battle of the Marne.

Vocabulary
trench: a long, deep ditch dug for protection

illustration of the trenches.) For more than three years, the battle lines remained almost unchanged. Neither side could win a clear victory.

In the trenches, soldiers faced the constant threat of sniper fire. Artillery shelling turned the area between the two opposing armies into a "no man's land" too dangerous to occupy. When soldiers left their trenches to attack enemy lines, they rushed into a hail of bullets and clouds of poison gas.

*Reading*History
B. Reading a Map
Find the site of the Battle of the Somme on the map on page 286.

When battles did take place, they cost many thousands of lives, often without gaining an inch for either side. The Battle of the Somme (SAHM), between July and November 1916, resulted in more than 1.2 million casualties. British dead or wounded numbered over 400,000. German losses totaled over 600,000, and French nearly 200,000. Despite this, the Allies gained only about seven miles.

A War of New Technology

New technology raised the death toll. The tank, a British invention, smashed through barbed wire, crossed trenches, and cleared paths through no man's land. Soldiers also had machine guns that fired 600 bullets a minute. Poison gas, used by both sides, burned and blinded soldiers.

World War I was the first major conflict in which airplanes were used in combat. By 1917, fighter planes fought each other far above the clouds. Manfred von Richthofen, known as the Red Baron, was Germany's top ace. An ace was an aviator who had downed five or more enemy aircraft. Von Richthofen shot down over 80 enemy planes.

Background
U-boat was short for "undersea boat."

At sea, the Germans used submarines, which they called **U-boats,** to block trade. They were equipped with both guns and torpedoes. German U-boats sank over 11 million tons of Allied shipping.

New Technology of War

First used effectively during World War I, these new weapons caused high casualties.

Airplane

Poison Gas

Machine Gun

Tank

279

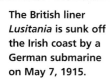

The British liner *Lusitania* is sunk off the Irish coast by a German submarine on May 7, 1915.

America's Path to War

When the war started in 1914, President **Woodrow Wilson** announced a policy of **neutrality,** refusing to take sides in the war. A popular song, "I Didn't Raise My Boy to Be a Soldier," expressed the antiwar sentiment of many Americans.

Over time, however, German attacks shifted public opinion to the Allied cause. In the fall of 1914, Britain set up a naval blockade of German ports, seizing all goods bound for Germany. In response, German submarines sank all Allied merchant ships they found off the British coast. In May 1915, a German U-boat torpedoed the British passenger ship *Lusitania,* killing 1,198 people, including 128 Americans. The sinking turned many Americans against Germany.

But President Wilson kept the United States neutral. He demanded that the German government halt unrestricted submarine warfare, and it agreed. In the election of 1916, the Democratic Party's campaign slogan, "He kept us out of war," appealed to voters. Wilson won reelection.

Desperate to defeat Britain, Germany resumed unrestricted submarine warfare at the end of January 1917. Its military leaders knew this action would bring the United States into the war. However, they hoped to win the war before the Americans arrived.

The next month, another blow to German-American relations came from the **Zimmermann telegram.** The telegram was discovered by the British, who passed it on to the Americans. In it, Arthur Zimmermann, the German foreign minister, told the German ambassador in Mexico to propose that Mexico join the Germans. In exchange, Germany would help Mexico get back its "lost" territories of Texas, New Mexico, and Arizona. Americans were furious.

Reading **History**

C. Making Inferences Why did the sinking of the *Lusitania* turn Americans against Germany?

In March, German submarines sank three American ships. President Wilson asked for a declaration of war.

> ## *"The world must be made safe for democracy."*
> Woodrow Wilson

A VOICE FROM THE PAST

The world must be made safe for democracy. . . . We desire no conquest. . . . We are but one of the champions of the rights of mankind. We shall be satisfied when those rights have been made . . . secure.

Woodrow Wilson, message to Congress, April 2, 1917

Six senators and 50 representatives, including the first woman in Congress, Jeannette Rankin of Montana, voted against going to war. But the majority shared the president's commitment to join the Allies.

Revolution in Russia

Events in Russia made U.S. entry into the war more urgent for the Allies. By early 1915, the huge Russian army had been outfought by a smaller German army led by better-trained officers. In August 1915, Czar Nicholas II insisted on taking control of the troops himself. His poor leadership was blamed for more deaths. By 1917, food shortages led to riots, and soaring inflation led to strikes by angry workers in Russia.

In March 1917, Czar Nicholas II was forced to step down. A temporary government continued the unpopular war until November. In that month the Bolsheviks, a communist group led by Vladimir Ilich Lenin, took power. Communism is a political system in which the government owns key parts of the economy, and there is no private property.

Reading **History**
D. Analyzing Causes What led Russia to pull out of the war?

Because the war had devastated Russia, Lenin at once began peace talks with Germany. In March 1918, Russia withdrew from the war by signing the Treaty of Brest-Litovsk. German troops could now turn from Russia to the Western front. The Allies urged American troops to come quickly, as you will read in the next section.

Section 1 Assessment

1. Terms & Names

Explain the significance of:
- militarism
- Central Powers
- Allies
- trench warfare
- U-boat
- Woodrow Wilson
- neutrality
- Zimmermann telegram

2. Taking Notes

Write at least four events that brought the United States into World War I.

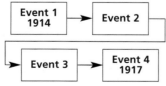

Which of these events was most important? Why?

3. Main Ideas

a. What were the long-term causes of World War I?

b. Why were Americans divided over the issue of remaining neutral?

c. Why was Russia's withdrawal from the war in 1917 a blow to Allies?

4. Critical Thinking

Analyzing Causes How did imperialism, nationalism, and militarism work to reinforce each other?

THINK ABOUT
- the goals of each
- how nationalism might encourage military buildup
- how nationalism contributed to the race for colonies

ACTIVITY OPTIONS

SCIENCE

ART

Research one of the new weapons of World War I. Explain how it works using a **model,** or draw an illustrated **diagram** of a defense against the weapon.

Survive Trench Warfare

You are a platoon leader assigned to a section of the front in central France. You have 60 men under your command. Day and night, through constant rain, earthen trenches full of sticky mud serve as your only protection. Sometimes, you think, the cold, rain, mud, rats, and fatigue are tougher to endure than a German bombardment.

COOPERATIVE LEARNING On this page are two challenges you face as a soldier during World War I. Working with a small group, decide how to deal with each challenge. Choose an option, assign a task to each group member, and do the activity. You will find useful information in the Data File. Be prepared to present your solutions to the class.

PHYSICAL EDUCATION CHALLENGE

"They must have 20 or 30 pounds of mud on them."

Until now, no one thought the trenches would be a permanent part of this war. So you, like the other soldiers along the front, weren't trained to cope with heavy, thick mud, 70-pound backpacks, and the other demands of living and fighting in these conditions. You learned on the job. Now you've been ordered to contribute ideas for a training program that will prepare recruits for the trenches. Look at the Data File for help. Then present your ideas using one of these options:

• Design an exercise regimen to strengthen troops for the trenches.

• Write a booklet of survival tips based on your platoon's experiences.

THE TRENCHES

- Trenches covered about 450 miles between the North Sea and the Swiss border.
- In France, ten-foot-deep trenches were dug into the ground and topped with sandbag parapets.
- Inside was a fire step, a ledge two or three feet up from bottom of the trench, used by sentries or troops firing.
- The sides were held up by sandbags and timber.

A SOLDIER'S GEAR

60–75 pounds of gear, including blankets, waterproof ground-sheet, extra boots and occasion-ally waterproof gum boots, quilted coat, shovel for digging trenches, helmet, wire clippers, pail for rations, 2 quarts of water, 4 days' food, 200 cartridges, 6 hand grenades, gas mask, 3 pairs of socks, soap, toothbrush, bottle of whale oil, towel, rifle, bayonet

TRENCH FOOD

beef stew, corned beef, bread, hard biscuits, pork and beans, tins of jam, butter, sugar, tea

PROBLEMS

- **trench foot:** condition caused by feet staying wet 24 hours a day; feet swell, turn numb and blue; if not treated, gangrene sets in and feet must be amputated; helped by rubbing whale oil on feet, changing to dry socks three times daily
- **mud:** mud traps the wounded until some drown, clogs rifles and gear, weighs men down, causes trench walls to fall in
- **rats:** huge rats, as big as rabbits, infest the trenches

For more about trench warfare . . .

RESEARCH LINKS
CLASSZONE.COM

HEALTH CHALLENGE

"Your feet swell to two or three times . . . normal size."

You're worried about your men getting trench foot. You've heard horror stories about men whose feet swelled so much they couldn't pull off their boots. Some of these men developed gangrene and had their feet amputated. The key to preventing trench foot is staying dry. What will you do? Use the Data File for help. Then present your solution using one of these options:

- Come up with a way to keep the men's feet dry.
- Role-play a conversation with veteran soldiers about preventing trench foot.

ACTIVITY WRAP-UP

Present to the Class As a group, review your methods of surviving the trenches. Pick the most creative solution for each challenge, and present these solutions to the class.

② America Joins the Fight

TERMS & NAMES
John J. Pershing
American Expeditionary Force
convoy system
Second Battle of the Marne
Alvin York
armistice

MAIN IDEA

U.S. forces helped the Allies win World War I.

WHY IT MATTERS NOW

For the first time, the United States asserted itself as a world power.

ONE AMERICAN'S STORY

Eddie Rickenbacker was America's most famous flying ace. He was one of the first Americans to get a look at the trenches from the cockpit of an airplane. The date was March 6, 1918. It was, recalled Rickenbacker, the first flyover of the battlefield by a "made-in-America Squadron." What Rickenbacker saw shocked him.

A VOICE FROM THE PAST

[T]here appeared to be nothing below but these old battered ditches . . . and billions of shell holes. . . . [N]ot a tree, a fence . . . nothing but . . . ruin and desolation. The whole scene was appalling.

Eddie Rickenbacker, *Fighting the Flying Circus*

An American gun crew advances against German positions in 1918. The ruin that Rickenbacker described is apparent.

Rickenbacker went on to distinguished service as a wartime aviator. As you will read in this section, he and other U.S. soldiers helped the Allies win the war.

Raising an Army and a Navy

The U.S. Army was not ready for war. American fighting forces consisted of fewer than 200,000 soldiers, many of them recent recruits. To meet its need for troops, the government began a draft. This system of choosing people for forced military service was first used during the Civil War. In May 1917, Congress passed the Selective Service Act. This act required all males between the ages of 21 and 30 to sign up for military service. By the end of 1918, nearly 3 million men had been drafted.

About 2 million American soldiers went to France. They served under General **John J. Pershing** as the **American Expeditionary Force,** or AEF. British commanders asked the U.S. government to have AEF troops join existing French and British combat units. Wilson refused. He believed that having "distinct and separate" American combat units would guarantee the United States a major role in the peace talks at war's end. Most U.S. troops fought separately, but some fought under Allied command.

*Reading*History
A. Finding Main Ideas How did women serve in the U.S. armed forces?

Close to 50,000 American women also served in World War I. Some volunteered for overseas duty with the American Red Cross. However, for the first time in American history, women also served in the military. The Navy, desperate for clerical workers, took about 12,000 female volunteers. The Marine Corps accepted 305 female recruits, known as Marinettes. Over 1,000 women went overseas for the Army. Nurses made up the largest group of females in the armed forces. However, women also acted as interpreters, operated switchboards, entertained troops, and drove ambulances for the AEF.

Around 400,000 African Americans served in the armed forces. More than half of them served in France. As they had at home, African-American troops overseas faced discrimination. However, it came from white American soldiers rather than from their European allies. At first, the Army refused to take black draftees. However, responding to pressure from African-American groups, the military eventually created two African-American combat divisions.

American Ships Make a Difference

In the first years of the war, German U-boat attacks on supply ships were a serious threat to the Allied war effort. American Rear Admiral William S. Sims convinced the Allies to adopt a system of protection. In a **convoy system,** a heavy guard of destroyers escorted merchant ships across the Atlantic in groups. Begun in May 1917, this strategy quickly reduced the loss rate.

Another American tactic gave the Allies added protection from the U-boat menace. Beginning in June 1918, the Allies laid a barrier of 70,000 mines in the North Sea. The 180-mile-long minefield made U-boat access to the North Atlantic almost impossible. Admiral Sims called the North Sea minefield "one of the wonders of the war."

Vocabulary
mines: hidden explosive devices

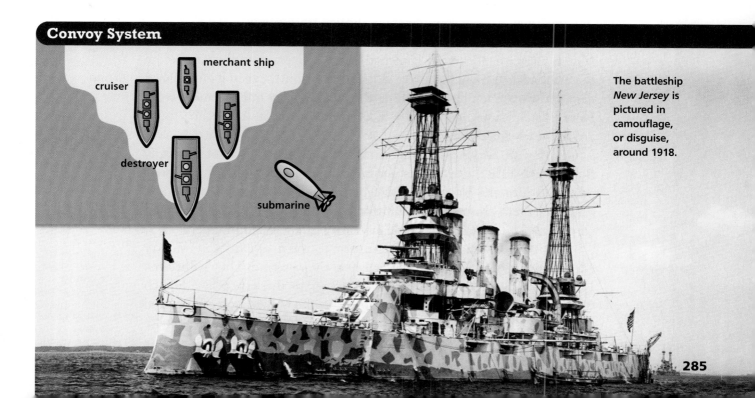

Convoy System

cruiser
merchant ship
destroyer
submarine

The battleship *New Jersey* is pictured in camouflage, or disguise, around 1918.

The Western Front, 1914–1918

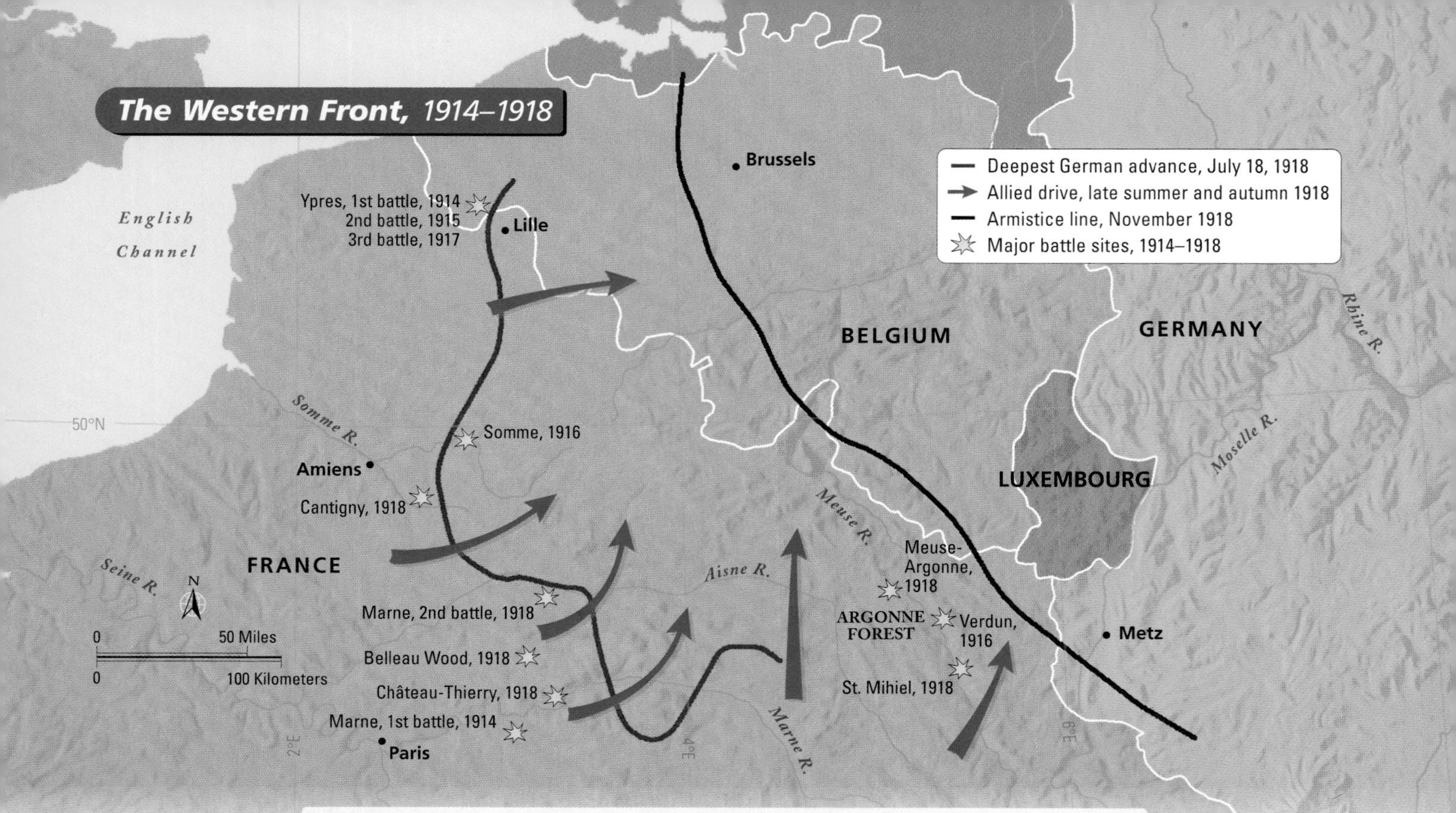

Deepest German advance, July 18, 1918
Allied drive, late summer and autumn 1918
Armistice line, November 1918
Major battle sites, 1914–1918
English Channel
Brussels
Ypres, 1st battle, 1914
2nd battle, 1915
3rd battle, 1917
Lille
BELGIUM
GERMANY
Rhine R.
50°N
Somme R.
Somme, 1916
Amiens
Cantigny, 1918
LUXEMBOURG
Moselle R.
Meuse R.
Seine R.
FRANCE
Aisne R.
Meuse-Argonne, 1918
N
Marne, 2nd battle, 1918
ARGONNE FOREST
Verdun, 1916
Metz
0
50 Miles
0
100 Kilometers
Belleau Wood, 1918
St. Mihiel, 1918
Château-Thierry, 1918
Marne, 1st battle, 1914
Paris
2°E
4°E
6°E
Marne R.

GEOGRAPHY SKILLBUILDER Interpreting Maps

1. Location *What three battles occurred closest to the Armistice line?*

2. Movement *In what two directions did the Allied drives move?*

American Troops Enter the War

By the time the first American troops arrived in France in June 1917, the Allies had been at war for almost three years. The small force of 14,000 Yanks boosted the morale of the battle-weary Allies. However, almost a year would pass before the bulk of the American troops landed in Europe.

Background
American soldiers were also called *doughboys.* This term was used even during the Civil War.

After their Russian opponents withdrew from the war, the Germans and the other Central Powers prepared to finish the fight in France. In March 1918, the Germans launched an offensive to end the war before the Americans arrived in force. Within two months, they had smashed through the French lines, reaching the Marne River only 50 miles from Paris. Just in time, in May 1918, one million fresh American troops arrived ready for action.

On May 28, American soldiers attacked the French town of Cantigny (kahn•tee•NYEE), which was occupied by the Germans. The soldiers advanced into the town, blasting enemy soldiers out of trenches and dragging them from cellars. Within two hours, the Yanks had taken control of Cantigny. The American victory lifted Allied morale.

When the Germans moved against the town of Château-Thierry (shah•toh•tyeh•REE), the Americans held their ground. They helped the French stop the German advance. Encouraged by these successes, French General Ferdinand Foch, commander of the Allied forces, ordered General Pershing's American forces to retake Belleau (beh•LOH) Wood.

This was a forest near the Marne River well defended by German troops. American soldiers succeeded, but at a fearful cost. One unit lost 380 of its 400 men. However, the Americans had proved themselves in combat.

Pushing the Germans Back

The **Second Battle of the Marne** in the summer of 1918 was the turning point of the war. It began with a German drive against the French line. During three days of heavy fighting, about 85,000 Americans helped the Allies halt the German advance. The Allies then took the initiative. They cut the enemy off from its supply lines and forced the Germans back.

For the rest of the war, the Allies advanced steadily. By early September, the Germans had lost all the territory they had gained since the spring. September 26, 1918, marked the beginning of the final Meuse-Argonne (myooz•ahr•GAHN) offensive. Around 1.2 million U.S. soldiers took part in a massive drive to push back the German line between the Argonne Forest and the Meuse River. The war's final battle left 26,000 Americans dead. But by November, the Germans were retreating.

Reading **History**
B. Recognizing Effects What was the effect of the Meuse-Argonne offensive?

The Meuse-Argonne offensive made a hero of American soldier **Alvin York.** At first, Tennessee-born Sergeant York seemed an unlikely candidate for military fame. Because of his religious beliefs, he tried unsuccessfully to avoid the draft. He refused to bear arms on religious grounds. An army captain convinced him to change his mind. In October 1918, in the Argonne Forest, York attacked German machine gunners, killing 25 of them. Other German soldiers surrendered, and York returned to the American lines with 132 captives.

Reading **History**
C. Evaluating What was heroic about Sergeant York?

Another American hero was pilot Eddie Rickenbacker. He won fame as the U.S. "ace of aces" for shooting down a total of 26 enemy planes. Just before the Meuse-Argonne offensive, he attacked seven German planes, sending two of them crashing to the ground. This action won him the Medal of Honor.

Four African-American combat units also received recognition for their battlefield valor. Fighting under French commanders, the 369th, 371st, and 372nd regiments (and part of the 370th) were awarded France's highest honor, the Croix de Guerre. The 369th spent more continuous time on the front lines than any other American unit. Although under intense fire for 191 days, it never lost a foot of ground.

Connections TO LITERATURE

LITERATURE OF WORLD WAR I

Several notable American writers served in World War I. They included Ernest Hemingway, the poet E. E. Cummings, and John Dos Passos. Hemingway drove an ambulance for the Italian army. He put this experience into his war novel *A Farewell to Arms.* Cummings wrote of his time in France in *The Enormous Room.*

Dos Passos, who also worked as an ambulance driver, once explained what attracted him to the battlefront: "What was war like, we wanted to see with our own eyes. I wanted to see the show."

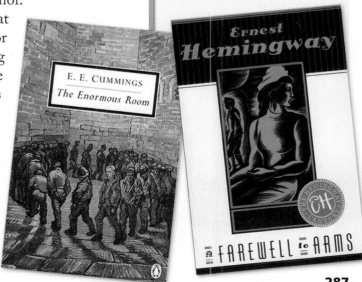

Americans were proud of the contribution their troops made to the war effort. They helped shift the balance in favor of the Allies.

Germany Stops Fighting

After the defeat of the Meuse-Argonne, General Erich Ludendorff advised the German government to seek peace. In early November, Germany's navy mutinied and its allies dropped out. On November 9, the Kaiser stepped down. Two days later Germany agreed to an **armistice**, an end to fighting. On November 11, 1918, at 11:00 A.M.—the 11th hour of the 11th day of the 11th month—all fighting ceased.

About 8.5 million soldiers died in the war, and about 21 million were wounded. Before he was killed in battle, one British soldier summed up the war's tragic costs.

Background
For many years after the war, Americans celebrated Armistice Day as a national holiday.

A VOICE FROM THE PAST

The sufferings of the men at the Front, of the wounded whose flesh and bodies are torn in a way you cannot conceive; the sorrow of those at home. . . . What a cruel and mad diversion of human activity!

William John Mason, quoted in *The Lost Generation of 1914*

Millions of civilians in Europe, Asia, and Africa also died in the war—from starvation and disease. In the next section, you will learn how the war affected U.S. civilians.

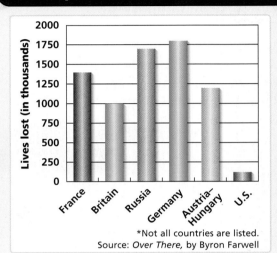

CONNECTIONS TO MATH

Military Deaths in World War I*

Lives lost (in thousands)

France, Britain, Russia, Germany, Austria-Hungary, U.S.

*Not all countries are listed.
Source: *Over There,* by Byron Farwell

SKILLBUILDER
Interpreting Graphs

1. *Which two nations on the chart suffered the most deaths?*
2. *U.S. deaths were about what percentage of combined French and British deaths?*

Section 2 Assessment

1. Terms & Names

Explain the significance of:
- John J. Pershing
- American Expeditionary Force
- convoy system
- Second Battle of the Marne
- Alvin York
- armistice

2. Taking Notes

Create a web to show how American groups or individuals helped fight the war.

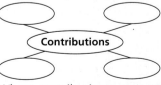

Contributions

Whose contribution was most surprising?

3. Main Ideas

a. Why did Wilson want U.S. forces to fight as a separate American combat unit?

b. What were two ways the U.S. Navy countered the U-boat threat?

c. Why was the Meuse-Argonne offensive a turning point in the war?

4. Critical Thinking

Recognizing Effects How important was America's entry into the war to the Allied cause?

THINK ABOUT
- the morale of Allied troops
- troop strength
- performance in battle

ACTIVITY OPTIONS

MUSIC

LANGUAGE ARTS

Make an **audiotape** of music or sounds that suggest the stages of the war, or write a **letter** in the voice of a soldier in the war.

3 Life on the Home Front

MAIN IDEA	WHY IT MATTERS NOW
The war required sacrifice for Americans at home and changed life in other ways.	Some wartime changes were permanent, such as black migration to Northern cities.

ONE AMERICAN'S STORY

On the home front, the war opened up new jobs for women. Most of the women who took these jobs were already in the work force. Carrie Fearing worked for the Railroad Administration. When the war ended, female workers were laid off. Fearing wrote to the railroad director, hoping to keep her job.

A VOICE FROM THE PAST

We never took a soldier's place, a soldier would not do the work we did . . . such as sweeping, picking up waste and paper and hauling steel shavings. . . . We . . . were liked and respected by all who knew us. . . . We like our job very much and I hope you will . . . place us back at the shop.

Carrie Fearing, quoted in *Women, War, and Work*

In May 1918, these women worked in the Union Pacific Railroad freight yard in Cheyenne, Wyoming.

Like Fearing, most women who helped the country get ready for war were pleased to have wartime jobs. They were proud of the part they had played in getting the country ready for war.

Mobilizing for War

To prepare for war, the government needed money. World War I cost the United States $35.5 billion. Americans helped pay almost two-thirds of that amount by buying government war bonds. **War bonds** were low-interest loans by civilians to the government, meant to be repaid in a number of years. To sell the bonds, officials held Liberty Loan drives. Posters urged citizens to "Come Across or the Kaiser Will." Hollywood actors like Charlie Chaplin toured the country selling bonds to starstruck audiences.

Schoolchildren rolled bandages and collected tin cans, paper, toothpaste tubes, and apricot pits. The pits were burned and made into charcoal for gas mask filters. Some Boy Scout troops even sold war bonds. So that more food could be sent to soldiers, people planted "victory gardens" in backyards and vacant lots. Women's groups came together in homes and churches to knit socks and sweaters and sew hospital gowns.

To persuade women to buy war bonds, this poster appealed to their love of family.

Patriotic citizens also saved food by observing wheatless Mondays and Wednesdays, when they ate no bread, and meatless Tuesdays. To save gas, they stopped their Sunday pleasure drives. The government limited civilian use of steel and other metals. Women donated their corsets with metal stays to scrap drives. Manufacturers stopped making tin toys for children and removed metal from caskets.

The war brought more government control of the economy. To produce needed war supplies, in 1917 President Wilson set up the War Industries Board. The board had great power. It managed the buying and distributing of war materials. It also set production goals and ordered construction of new factories. With the president's approval, the board also set prices. Another government agency, the National War Labor Board, settled conflicts between workers and factory owners.

To rally citizen support, Wilson created the Committee on Public Information. The committee's writers, artists, photographers, and film-makers produced **propaganda,** opinions expressed for the purpose of influencing the actions of others. The committee sold the war through posters, pamphlets, and movies. One popular pamphlet, "How the War Came to America," came out in Polish, German, Swedish, Bohemian, and Spanish. In movie houses, audiences watched such patriotic films as *Under Four Flags* and *Pershing's Crusaders.*

Intolerance and Suspicion

Patriotic propaganda did much to win support for the war. But its anti-German, anti-foreign focus also fueled prejudice. Suddenly people distrusted anything German. A number of towns with German names changed their names. Berlin, Maryland, became Brunswick. People called sauerkraut "liberty cabbage," and hamburger became "Salisbury steak." Owners of German shepherds took to calling their pets "police dogs."

On June 15, 1917, Congress passed the **Espionage Act.** The **Sedition Act** followed in May 1918. These laws set heavy fines and long prison terms for such antiwar activities as encouraging draft resisters. The laws made it illegal to criticize the war. U.S. courts tried more than 1,500 pacifists, socialists, and other war critics. Hundreds went to jail. Socialist Party leader Eugene Debs gave a speech arguing that the war was fought by poor workingmen for the profit of wealthy business owners. For this talk, a judge sentenced him to ten years in prison.

The government ignored complaints that the rights of Americans were being trampled. In the 1919 decision in *Schenck* v. *United States,* the Supreme Court upheld the Espionage Act. Schenck, convicted of

*Reading*History

A. Finding Main Ideas What were civilians asked to do for the war effort?

*Reading*History

B. Recognizing Effects How did war propaganda fuel prejudice?

distributing pamphlets against the draft, had argued that the Espionage Act violated his right to free speech. Justice **Oliver Wendell Holmes, Jr.,** wrote the court's opinion.

A VOICE FROM THE PAST

The most stringent [strict] protection of free speech would not protect a man in falsely shouting fire in a theater and causing a panic. . . . The question in every case is whether the words used . . . are of such a nature as to create a clear and present danger that they will bring about . . . evils that Congress has a right to prevent.

Oliver Wendell Holmes, Jr., *Schenck v. United States,* 1919

*Reading*History

C. Analyzing Points of View Why did Justice Holmes believe that free speech could be limited?

Justice Holmes argued that free speech, guaranteed by the First Amendment, could be limited, especially in wartime.

New Jobs and the Great Migration

As soldiers went off to battle, the United States faced a labor shortage. Northern factories gearing up for war were suddenly willing to hire workers they had once rejected. Throughout the South, African Americans heeded the call. Between 1910 and 1920, about 500,000 African Americans moved north to such cities as New York, Chicago, Detroit, Cleveland, and St. Louis. This movement became known as the **Great Migration**. African Americans left to escape the bigotry, poverty, and racial violence of the South. They hoped for a better life in the North.

HISTORY *through*ART

The Migration of the Negro, Panel No. 1 (1940–41), by Jacob Lawrence, shows three of the most common destinations for African Americans leaving the South.

How does Lawrence's painting reflect continuity and change in American life?

New jobs were opening up in the American Southwest. These jobs were fueled by the growth of railroads and irrigated farming. A revolution was under way in Mexico, and the chaos led many Mexicans to flee across the border after 1910. Many immigrants settled in Texas, Arizona, Colorado, and California. Most became farm workers. During the war years, some went to Northern cities to take better-paying factory jobs.

The wartime labor shortage also meant new job choices for women. Women replaced male workers in steel mills, ammunition factories, and assembly lines. Women served as streetcar conductors and elevator operators. The war created few permanent openings for women, but their presence in these jobs gave the public a wider view of their abilities. Women's contributions during the war helped them win the vote.

Reading **History**
D. Recognizing Effects What groups gained new jobs as a result of the war?

Now and then

THE FLU EPIDEMIC

In 1918, flu victims often came down with pneumonia and died within a week. Today, bacterial infections such as pneumonia resulting from the flu can be controlled with antibiotics.

The 1998 discovery of the frozen remains of a 1918 flu victim in an Alaskan cemetery may one day lead to a better understanding of the virus. Scientists have found a genetic link between the 1918 flu virus and swine flu, a virus first found in pigs. The Alaskan find may help scientists develop vaccines to protect against future flu outbreaks.

The Flu Epidemic of 1918

Another result of the war was a deadly flu epidemic that swept the globe in 1918. It killed more than 20 million people on six continents by the time it disappeared in 1919. It had no known cure. Spread around the world by soldiers, the virus took some 500,000 American lives. People tried desperately to protect themselves. Everywhere, schools and other public places shut down to limit the flu's spread.

In the army, more than a quarter of the soldiers caught the disease. In some AEF units, one-third of the troops died. Germans fell victim in even larger numbers than the Allies. World War I brought death and disease to millions. It would also have longer-term effects, as you will read in Section 4.

Section 3 Assessment

1. Terms & Names

Explain the significance of:
- war bonds
- propaganda
- Espionage Act
- Sedition Act
- Oliver Wendell Holmes
- Great Migration

2. Taking Notes

Make a chart like the one below to show reasons for wartime shifts in population.

	Shift	Reason(s)
African Americans		
Mexicans		

How similar were the two groups' reasons for moving?

3. Main Ideas

a. What were three ways American families could contribute to the war effort?

b. What was the purpose of the Espionage and Sedition Acts? What groups were most affected by them?

c. What kinds of new job opportunities did the war create for women and minorities?

4. Critical Thinking

Making Inferences What were the positive and the negative consequences of American wartime propaganda?

THINK ABOUT
- contributions to war effort
- effect on opponents of war and on German-Americans

ACTIVITY OPTIONS

SPEECH

MATH

Deliver a **radio broadcast** on the importance of conserving food, or make a **calculation** of the amount of food your class wastes monthly.

The Legacy of World War I

TERMS & NAMES
League of Nations
Fourteen Points
Treaty of Versailles
reparations
Red Scare
Palmer raids

MAIN IDEA

After the war, Americans were divided over foreign policy and domestic issues.

WHY IT MATTERS NOW

The war affected the role the United States played in the world during the rest of the century.

ONE AMERICAN'S STORY

Massachusetts Senator Henry Cabot Lodge had favored U.S. entry into the war. However, he opposed President Wilson's idea that the United States join an international organization. The **League of Nations** was such an organization set up to settle conflicts through negotiation. Lodge warned against joining an alliance that would require the United States to guarantee the freedom of other nations.

A VOICE FROM THE PAST

If we guarantee any country . . . its independence . . . we must [keep] at any cost . . . our word. . . . I wish [the American people] carefully to consider . . . whether they are willing to have the youth of America ordered to war by other nations.

Henry Cabot Lodge, speech to the Senate, February 28, 1919

Speeches like Lodge's helped turn the public against the League and gave President Wilson the most crushing defeat of his political career. In this section, you will learn how the United States and Europe adjusted to the end of the war.

Senator Henry Cabot Lodge (1850–1924) opposed U.S. entry into the League of Nations.

Wilson's Fourteen Points

In January 1918, President Wilson spoke to Congress about his goals for peace. This was ten months before the end of the war. His statement became known as the **Fourteen Points** (see page 297). The speech called for smaller military forces, an end to secret treaties, freedom of the seas, and free trade. It also called for changes in national boundaries. Most of these changes gave independence to peoples formerly ruled by Austria-Hungary or the Ottoman Empire.

For Wilson, the fourteenth point mattered most. He called for an association of nations to peacefully settle disputes. This association was to become the League of Nations, which Republicans like Lodge opposed. Wilson firmly believed that acceptance of his Fourteen Points by the warring parties would bring about what he called a "peace without victory."

Treaty of Versailles

Wilson led the U.S. delegation to the peace conference in France. Though many Europeans considered him a hero, conference leaders did not. The leaders of Britain, France, and Italy did not share Wilson's vision of "peace without victory." They wanted Germany to pay heavily for its part in the war.

The **Treaty of Versailles** (vuhr•SY) forced Germany to accept full blame for the war. Germany was stripped of its colonies and most of its armed forces. It was also burdened with $33 billion in **reparations**—money that a defeated nation pays for the destruction caused by a war. The treaty divided up the empires of Austria-Hungary and the Ottomans. It created Yugoslavia and Czechoslovakia and recognized Poland's independence.

Wilson managed to include the League of Nations in the treaty. He firmly believed the League would help to keep the peace. He returned home to seek Senate approval for the treaty. But the Republican-run Senate was dead set against it. Senator Henry Cabot Lodge kept delaying a vote on the treaty.

After weeks of delay, Wilson decided to make his case to the public. In September of 1919, he began a cross-country speaking trip to build support for the League. In about 21 days, he traveled almost 10,000 miles and gave over 30 speeches.

*Reading*History

A. Recognizing Effects How were the Central Powers punished by the Treaty of Versailles?

A VOICE FROM THE PAST

In the covenant [agreement] of the League of Nations, the moral forces of the world are mobilized . . . . They consent . . . to submit every matter of difference between them to the judgment of mankind, and just so certainly as they do that, . . . war will be pushed out of the foreground of terror in which it has kept the world.

Woodrow Wilson, speech in Pueblo, Colorado, on September 25, 1919

Shortly after giving this speech, Wilson collapsed from strain. Later, he suffered a stroke from which he never fully recovered.

Negotiations to get the treaty through Congress continued, but Americans were not eager for more foreign commitments. Lodge and his supporters offered to accept the treaty if major changes were made in the League. Wilson refused to compromise. As a result, the United States did not ratify the treaty. The League of Nations was formed without the United States.

The war and the Treaty of Versailles failed to make Europe "safe for democracy." In the next decades, Germany's resentment of the treaty grew. The treaty planted the seeds of World War II, an even more deadly conflict to come.

*Reading*History

B. Analyzing Causes Why didn't the United States ratify the Treaty of Versailles?

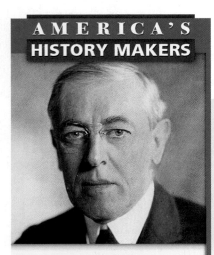

AMERICA'S HISTORY MAKERS

WOODROW WILSON

1856–1924

A gifted speaker, Woodrow Wilson had a strong sense of duty, and he inspired great loyalty. Yet he could be a harsh judge of others, stiff and unbending in his relations with people. Sculptor Jo Davidson remarked that "He invoked fear and respect . . . but not affection." Though not America's best-loved president, he still commands respect. When historians list the nation's best presidents, Wilson often ranks in the top ten.

How might Wilson's character have worked against approval of the Treaty of Versailles?

Postwar Europe, 1919

☐ New nations

0 — 400 Miles
0 — 800 Kilometers

NORWAY FINLAND
SWEDEN ESTONIA SOVIET
          RUSSIA
North   LATVIA
Sea DENMARK LITHUANIA
IRELAND   Baltic Sea
GREAT
BRITAIN NETH.
          GERMANY
BELGIUM   POLAND
LUX.   CZECHOSLOVAKIA
FRANCE SWITZ. AUSTRIA
          HUNGARY
          YUGOSLAVIA ROMANIA
PORTUGAL   Black Sea
SPAIN   ITALY   BULGARIA
      Mediterranean Sea ALBANIA GREECE

ATLANTIC
OCEAN

GEOGRAPHY SKILLBUILDER Interpreting Maps
1. **Region** *What new nations were created after the war?*
2. **Region** *In what part of Europe were most of the new nations located?*

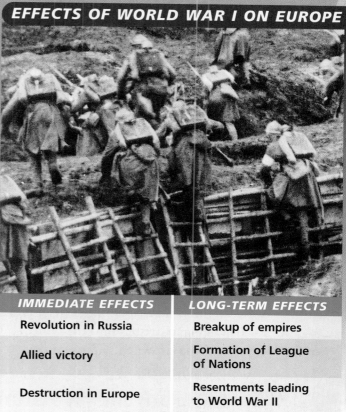

EFFECTS OF WORLD WAR I ON EUROPE

IMMEDIATE EFFECTS	LONG-TERM EFFECTS
Revolution in Russia	Breakup of empires
Allied victory	Formation of League of Nations
Destruction in Europe	Resentments leading to World War II

Strikes and the Red Scare

Background
In 1919, police, steelworkers, and coal miners also went on strike.

The Treaty of Versailles was not the only issue that divided Americans after the war. Shortly after the war ended, the United States experienced a number of labor strikes. For example, in Seattle, Washington, in February 1919, more than 55,000 workers took part in a peaceful general strike. The shutdown paralyzed the city.

Some Americans saw efforts to organize labor unions as the work of radicals, people who favor extreme measures to bring about change. The strikes sparked fears of a communist revolution like the one that toppled the Russian czar. In 1919–1920, this fear created a wave of panic called the **Red Scare** (communists were called *reds*). Public fear was heightened by the discovery of mail bombs sent to government officials. Many believed the bombs were the work of anarchists. Anarchists are radicals who do not believe in any form of government.

Reading **History**
C. **Recognizing Effects** What resulted from the Red Scare?

In January 1920, Attorney General A. Mitchell Palmer took action. He ordered federal agents and local police to raid the homes and headquarters of suspected radicals. His agents arrested at least 6,000 people in the **Palmer raids.** Without search warrants, agents burst into homes and offices and dragged citizens off to jail.

The Red Scare was not only antiradical but also antiforeign. During the Red Scare, two Italian-born anarchists, Nicola Sacco and Bartolomeo Vanzetti, were arrested for killing two men in an armed robbery in

Massachusetts. They claimed they were innocent, but both were found guilty and executed. Their trial attracted worldwide attention.

Racial Tensions Increase

Americans also saw a rise in racial tensions after the war. Between 1910 and 1920, the Great Migration brought a half million African Americans to Northern cities. In the cities where African Americans had settled in large numbers, whites and blacks competed for factory jobs and housing.

On July 2, 1917, tensions erupted into a race riot in East St. Louis, Illinois. The trouble began when blacks were brought in to take the jobs of white union members who had gone on strike. A shooting incident touched off a full-scale riot.

Two years later, African-American soldiers returning from the war found their social plight unchanged. They had fought to make the world "safe for democracy." At home, though, they were still second-class citizens.

Simmering resentments over housing, job competition, and segregation exploded during the summer of 1919. In 25 cities around the country, race riots flared. In Chicago, a black man swimming in Lake Michigan drifted into the white section of a beach. Whites stoned him until he drowned. Thirteen days of rioting followed. Before it ended, 38 people were dead.

Reading **History**

D. Analyzing Causes How did the war contribute to racial tensions?

Longing for "Normalcy"

By the time campaigning began for the 1920 election, Americans felt drained. Labor strikes, race riots, the Red Scare, and the fight over the Treaty of Versailles and the League of Nations had worn them out. Voters were ready for a break. Republican candidate Warren G. Harding of Ohio offered them one. His promise to "return to normalcy" appealed to voters. Harding won a landslide victory. In the next chapter, you will learn about American life after his election.

Section **4** *Assessment*

1. Terms & Names

Explain the significance of:
- League of Nations
- Fourteen Points
- Treaty of Versailles
- reparations
- Red Scare
- Palmer raids

2. Taking Notes

Create a diagram to examine the war's effects on Europe and America.

Effects of World War I	
Europe	United States

Which effects were positive and which were negative?

3. Main Ideas

a. Why did Germany resent the Treaty of Versailles?

b. Why did Lodge and other Republicans oppose joining the League of Nations?

c. What caused the Red Scare? Who was most affected by it?

4. Critical Thinking

Analyzing Points of View
Why was Wilson unable to get other powers to accept his goals for the peace conference?

THINK ABOUT
- conflicting goals
- practicality of Wilson's aims
- attitudes of other nations toward U.S. contributions during the war

ACTIVITY OPTIONS
LANGUAGE ARTS
ART

Imagine that you work for a newspaper. Write an **editorial** about the Palmer raids, or draw a political **cartoon** about the raids.

The Fourteen Points

Setting the Stage Nine months after the United States entered World War I, President Wilson delivered to Congress a statement of war aims. This statement became known as the "Fourteen Points." In the speech, President Wilson set forth 14 proposals for reducing the risk of war in the future. Numbers have been inserted to help identify the main points, as well as those omitted. **See Primary Source Explorer**

All the peoples of the world are in effect partners . . . , and for our own part we see very clearly that unless justice be done to others it will not be done to us. The program of the world's peace, therefore, is our program; and that program, . . . as we see it, is this:

[1] Open **covenants**¹ of peace, openly arrived at, after which there shall be no private international understandings of any kind but diplomacy shall proceed always frankly and in the public view.

[2] Absolute freedom of navigation upon the seas . . . in peace and in war. . . .

[3] The removal, so far as possible, of all economic barriers and the establishment of an equality of trade conditions among all the nations. . . .

[4] Adequate guarantees given and taken that national **armaments**² will be reduced. . . .

[5] A free, open-minded, and absolutely impartial adjustment of all colonial claims, based upon . . . the principle that . . . the interests of the populations concerned must have equal weight with the . . . claims of the government whose title is to be determined.

[6–13: These eight points deal with specific boundary changes.]

[14] A general association of nations must be formed under specific covenants for the purpose of affording mutual guarantees of political independence and territorial **integrity**³ to great and small states alike.

—*Woodrow Wilson*

A CLOSER LOOK

THE VALUE OF OPENNESS

The first of Wilson's points attempts to solve one of the problems that caused the outbreak of World War I—agreements between nations arrived at in secret.

1. How might agreements arrived at in public prevent another world war?

A CLOSER LOOK

BALANCING CLAIMS

Wilson frequently appeals to fairness, balance, and impartiality in settling competing claims.

2. What might be unusual about a leader such as Wilson calling for an impartial adjustment of colonial claims?

A CLOSER LOOK

LEAGUE OF NATIONS

Wilson proposes that nations join a formal organization to protect one another.

3. Why did Wilson believe that such an organization would benefit the world?

---

1. **covenants:** binding agreements.
2. **armaments:** weapons and supplies of war.
3. **integrity:** the condition of being whole or undivided; completeness.

Interactive Primary Source Assessment

1. Main Ideas

a. Why should diplomacy avoid private dealings and proceed in public view?

b. How might equality of trade be important to keeping the peace?

c. What must nations join together to guarantee?

2. Critical Thinking

Evaluating The first five points address issues that Wilson believed had caused the war. How successful do you think Wilson's ideas have been in the rest of the 20th century?

THINK ABOUT
• other conflicts since World War I
• peacekeeping efforts around the world

TERMS & NAMES

Briefly explain the significance of each of the following.

1. militarism
2. Allies
3. trench warfare
4. Zimmermann telegram
5. American Expeditionary Force
6. convoy system
7. propaganda
8. Great Migration
9. Treaty of Versailles
10. Red Scare

REVIEW QUESTIONS

War Breaks Out in Europe (pages 277–283)

1. What were the sources of tension between the European powers that led to war?
2. Why did the United States at first remain neutral in the war between the Allies and the Central Powers?
3. What brought the United States into the war on the Allied side?

America Joins the Fight (pages 284–288)

4. How did the Allies fight the German U-boat threat?
5. How did U.S. entry into the war affect the Allies?
6. What led Germany to agree to an armistice?

Life on the Home Front (pages 289–292)

7. How did U.S. civilians aid the war effort?
8. How did Congress contribute to increased prejudice and intolerance on the home front?

The Legacy of World War I (pages 293–297)

9. How did Wilson's goals for the peace conference differ from those of his European allies?
10. Why did the Senate reject the Treaty of Versailles?

CRITICAL THINKING

1. USING YOUR NOTES

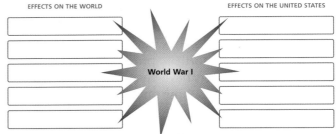

EFFECTS ON THE WORLD

EFFECTS ON THE UNITED STATES

World War I

Using your chart, answer the questions below.

a. Were the effects of the war greater in Europe or the United States?
b. What political effects did the war have on the United States?
c. How did the war affect African-American civilians?

2. APPLYING CITIZENSHIP SKILLS

Are limitations on freedom of speech justified by war? Explain your opinion.

3. THEME: AMERICA IN THE WORLD

How did Wilson's view of the role the United States should play in world affairs compare with Theodore Roosevelt's view of America's role?

4. ANALYZING LEADERSHIP

Do you think Wilson's refusal to compromise to get the Treaty of Versailles through Congress was a good decision? Why?

Interact *with* History

How accurately did you predict the ways in which American citizens might support the war effort?

VISUAL SUMMARY

World War I

War Breaks Out in Europe

When the Allies and the Central Powers went to war in Europe, the United States reluctantly joined the Allies.

America Joins the Fight

Millions of U.S. soldiers and civilian volunteers went abroad and helped the Allies win the war.

Life on the Home Front

The war required Americans to sacrifice many things, even political freedoms. The war also brought new jobs.

The Legacy of World War I

The war broke up European empires and left lasting social changes in the United States.

HISTORY SKILLS

1. INTERPRETING MAPS: Movement

Study the map. Answer the questions.

Great Migration, 1910–1920

Northeast
201,000

Midwest
233,000

West Coast
16,000

← Movement of African Americans
201,000 Number of migrants

Source: *Historical Statistics of the United States*

Basic Map Elements

a. What is the subject of the map?

b. What do the arrows indicate?

Interpreting the Map

c. In what general directions did migration take place?

d. Of these directions, in which direction did the fewest African Americans move?

2. INTERPRETING PRIMARY SOURCES

This famous World War I poster shows Uncle Sam, a national symbol. Study the poster and answer the questions.

a. How does Uncle Sam's clothing show that he stands for the United States?

b. What was the purpose of this propaganda poster?

I WANT YOU
FOR U.S. ARMY
NEAREST RECRUITING STATION

ALTERNATIVE ASSESSMENT

1. INTERDISCIPLINARY ACTIVITY: Music

Analyzing Music of the War Years During World War I, songs such as "Johnny I Hardly Knew You" protested the war, while "Over There" and "Pack Up Your Troubles" cheered the troops. Analyze the lyrics of a wartime song, examining its attitude toward the war.

2. COOPERATIVE LEARNING ACTIVITY

Negotiating a Treaty Working in seven groups, do research on the Paris peace conference that created the Treaty of Versailles. Have each group represent one of these nations: Germany, France, Britain, the United States, Italy, Japan, Poland. Hold a mock conference in which delegates present their goals and debate resolutions to be included in the treaty. Compare your treaty with the actual historical results.

- Identify the national interests of your country for the postwar settlement.

- Make a list of goals and issues you want discussed at the conference.

- Choose a chief spokesperson for your group.

3. PRIMARY SOURCE EXPLORER

Planning Peace Shortly after America's entry into World War I, President Wilson was planning for peace. He wanted to reduce the risk of war in the future. For this purpose, he came up with his Fourteen Points. Using the CD-ROM, the library, and the Internet, find out more about the Fourteen Points.

Create your own plan for peace using the suggestions below.

- Draw up a plan for peace that might apply to your classroom or community.

- Adapt ideas from the Fourteen Points that you think will work for your classroom or community.

- Decide how peace can be enforced in the classroom and in wider communities.

- Discuss whether working to establish peace might involve setting restrictions on personal liberty.

4. HISTORY PORTFOLIO

Review your section and chapter assessment activities. Select one that you think is your best work. Then use comments made by your teacher or classmates to improve your work and add it to your portfolio.

Additional Test Practice, pp. S1–S33

TEST PRACTICE
CLASSZONE.COM

Campaign for Liberty Bonds

To rally Americans to support World War I, the government set up the Committee on Public Information (CPI). This agency called on creative individuals to join "the world's greatest adventure in advertising." Speakers gave patriotic speeches in theaters, hotels, and restaurants. Artists designed posters persuading Americans to buy Liberty Bonds. These loans to the government helped fund the war effort. Liberty Bonds were actually sold through four Liberty Loan drives in 1917 and 1918.

ACTIVITY Create a poster to help the government raise money for World War I. In addition, write and present a patriotic speech that wins public support of the war.

TOOLBOX

Each group will need:

poster board	drawing paper
colored markers	glue
pencils	scissors

WOMEN! HELP AMERICA'S SONS WIN THE WAR

BUY U.S. GOVERNMENT BONDS 2ND LIBERTY LOAN OF 1917

STEP BY STEP

1 **Form an imaginary ad agency.** Meet with three or four other students to discuss your latest contract: The CPI has hired your agency to create a poster as part of a nationwide campaign to sell Liberty Bonds and promote World War I. Your group will:

- do research on Liberty Bonds
- design and create a poster advertising Liberty Bonds
- write and deliver a "pep talk" persuading people to buy Liberty Bonds

2 **Research Liberty Bonds.** Look on the Internet, in this chapter, or in books about World War I to find out more about Liberty Bonds and to see actual posters. As you look over the posters, think about the feelings the posters bring out. What images and words seem most powerful or persuasive?

Posters such as this one appealed to patriotism and love of family to sell Liberty Bonds.

3 **Choose a theme for your poster.** Persuading people to buy Liberty Bonds means that you need to show that winning World War I is important. One way is to appeal to people's emotions. For example, the poster can appeal to their sense of fear, pride, or love of family.

4 **Sketch out your idea.** Write out a slogan and choose images based on the theme of your poster. Make sure your words and pictures communicate the same feeling and message. Draw an outline of the images and the letters. Then cut both the letters and images out. Be sure that they're large enough to be seen from several yards away.

5 **Create the poster.** Decide where the art and writing will appear. Experiment with the arrangement of the art and the writing. Move them around. Do not overwhelm your viewers with too many images or too many words. Use vivid, patriotic colors for your poster.

6 **Create a bulletin board display.** Pin or tape your poster on the wall, along with the posters of the other groups. As you examine the other posters, compare and contrast your poster with the others.

WRITE AND SPEAK

Write a patriotic speech. As a group, write a two-minute "pep talk" persuading people to buy Liberty Bonds and to support the soldiers fighting overseas. Include reasons why the war is worth fighting. Each group member should be prepared to deliver the speech, using the poster you made as a visual aid.

HELP DESK

For related information, see pages 289–290 in Chapter 10.

Researching Your Project
- *World War I* by Gail Stewart
- *Causes and Consequences of World War I* by Stewart Ross

For more about World War I . . .

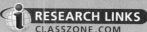

RESEARCH LINKS
CLASSZONE.COM

Did You Know?
The CPI used about 75,000 lecturers. They gave around 755,190 speeches to about 300 million people in 5,000 towns.

Even children were moved by advertising slogans to help fund the war: "Lick a stamp and lick the kaiser." Children filled books with war stamps, each worth 25 cents. These stamps were then converted into government bonds.

Even President Wilson helped to raise money for the war effort. He sold wool from sheep raised on the White House lawn.

REFLECT & ASSESS
- What aspects of your poster do you think will inspire people to buy Liberty Bonds?
- How well does your speech inspire patriotic feeling about the war?
- Which do you think is a more powerful means of persuasion—your poster or your speech?

Depression, War, and Recovery

This panel of a WPA mural shows
California workers picking oranges,
tilling the soil, and collecting flowers
during the 1920s and 1930s.

"The test of our progress . . . is whether we provide enough for those who have too little."

—Franklin Delano Roosevelt

CHAPTER 11

The Roaring Twenties 1919–1929

Section 1 **The Business of America**

Section 2 **Changes in Society**

Section 3 **The Jazz Age and the Harlem Renaissance**

The carefree spirit of the Roaring Twenties is captured on this magazine cover from 1926.

Interact *with* History

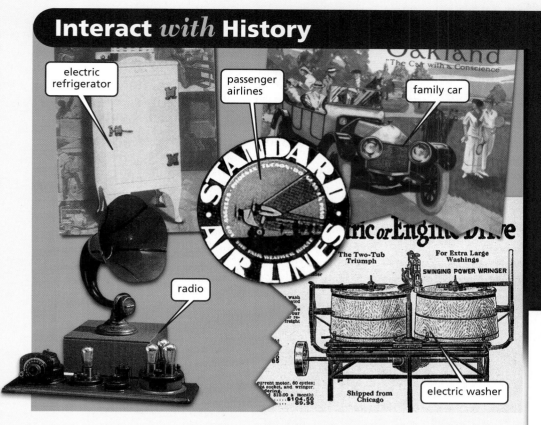

electric refrigerator

passenger airlines

family car

radio

The Two-Tub Triumph

For Extra Large Washings

SWINGING POWER WRINGER

Shipped from Chicago

electric washer

World War I is over, and a new decade has begun. There is peace in the world and prosperity at home. It is a time of exciting social, cultural, economic, and technological change. You see new products and new ideas coming into your life.

Which changes in culture or technology will affect your life the most?

What Do You Think?
- How will these new ideas and products change your life?
- Will these changes make life better and easier? How?
- Which class of people will be affected most by these changes?

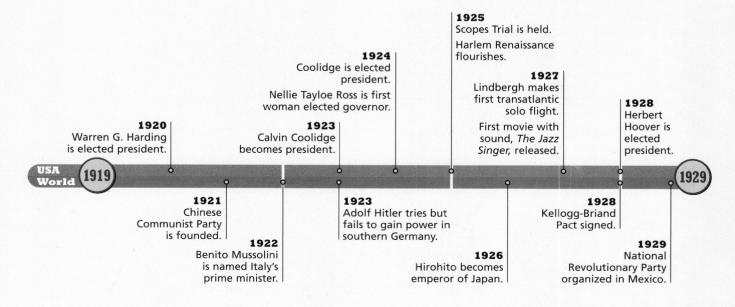

1925
Scopes Trial is held.
Harlem Renaissance flourishes.

1924
Coolidge is elected president.
Nellie Tayloe Ross is first woman elected governor.

1927
Lindbergh makes first transatlantic solo flight.
First movie with sound, *The Jazz Singer,* released.

1928
Herbert Hoover is elected president.

1920
Warren G. Harding is elected president.

1923
Calvin Coolidge becomes president.

USA
World
1919

1929

1921
Chinese Communist Party is founded.

1923
Adolf Hitler tries but fails to gain power in southern Germany.

1928
Kellogg-Briand Pact signed.

1922
Benito Mussolini is named Italy's prime minister.

1926
Hirohito becomes emperor of Japan.

1929
National Revolutionary Party organized in Mexico.

BEFORE YOU READ

Previewing the Theme

Science and Technology As Chapter 11 explains, the 1920s were a time of peace and economic prosperity for many Americans. Consumer buying, the growth of the automobile industry, and the development of new technologies helped business to expand and changed the way people lived. The Roaring Twenties also brought new ideas, new attitudes, and new forms of entertainment.

More cars meant traffic jams—like this one in St. Louis in 1920.

What Do You Know?

What do you already know about the Roaring Twenties? What were the issues and who were the personalities that made this decade "roar"?

THINK ABOUT
- how the 1920s have been portrayed in movies, television, and historical fiction
- what happens to a country when rapid changes take place

What Do You Want to Know?

What additional information do you want about the issues and personalities of the 1920s? Record questions you may have in your notebook before you read the chapter.

READ AND TAKE NOTES

Reading Strategy: Finding Main Ideas To understand what you read, learn to find the main idea of each paragraph, topic heading, and section. Remember that the supporting details help to explain the main idea. On the chart below, write down the main idea in this chapter for each category of American life.

 See Skillbuilder Handbook, page R5.

Categories	Main Ideas
Government	
Business	
Agriculture	
Technology	
Society	
Popular Culture	

The Business of America

TERMS & NAMES
Warren G. Harding
Teapot Dome Scandal
Calvin Coolidge
laissez faire
isolationist
Kellogg-Briand Pact
assembly line
installment buying

MAIN IDEA	WHY IT MATTERS NOW
The government supported business and kept a hands-off policy in other matters.	How involved the government should be in the economy remains an issue today.

ONE AMERICAN'S STORY

Warren G. Harding was a pleasant man of whom it was said he "looked like a president." He was happiest relaxing or playing cards with his closest friends. But urged on by his wealthy and ambitious wife, Florence Kling Harding, he rose from small-town newspaper publisher, to U.S. senator from Ohio, to Republican presidential candidate.

The advice from Republican Party leaders in 1920 was "Keep Warren at home. Don't let him make any speeches." So Harding spent most of the 1920 election race campaigning from his front porch in Marion, Ohio. But Harding was what the voters wanted. He promised them prosperity at home and peace abroad, and they elected him president. Mrs. Harding supposedly said, "Well, Warren Harding, I have got you the Presidency; what are you going to do with it?"

In this section, you will read about Presidents Warren G. Harding and Calvin Coolidge, the booming economy of the Roaring Twenties, and the new technologies that helped businesses to grow.

Warren G. Harding and his wife, Florence Kling Harding, at their home in Marion, Ohio.

Harding and the "Return to Normalcy"

After some 20 years of reform and war, Americans were ready for the "normalcy" promised by Harding in the election and at his inauguration.

A VOICE FROM THE PAST

Our supreme task is the resumption of our onward, normal way. Reconstruction, readjustment, restoration all these must follow. I would like to hasten them.

Warren G. Harding, Inaugural Address, March 4, 1921

As president, Harding wanted to lift the burden of taxes and regulations from the shoulders of Americans. To do this, he proposed lower taxes and "less government in business and more business in government." He also sought higher tariffs on foreign goods to help American companies.

Harding chose a pro-business cabinet. The secretary of the treasury was Andrew W. Mellon, one of the wealthiest men in the United States.

The New York Times. EXTRA

PRESIDENT HARDING DIES SUDDENLY; STROKE OF APOPLEXY AT 7:30 P. M.; CALVIN COOLIDGE IS PRESIDENT

Mellon persuaded Congress to lower taxes and balance the budget. Herbert Hoover, an engineer who organized aid to Europe in World War I, was secretary of commerce. He worked to cut federal government waste.

While some of Harding's cabinet choices, like Mellon and Hoover, were excellent, a number were unqualified, and even corrupt. These men had been Harding's friends back in Ohio and were known as the "Ohio Gang." They used their government positions to make money illegally. Their actions helped to wreck the Harding presidency. The worst scandal involved Secretary of the Interior Albert Fall. It was called the **Teapot Dome Scandal.** Fall took bribes and made illegal deals with oil executives to drill on oil-rich government land in Teapot Dome, Wyoming.

Rumors of corruption in the Harding administration began to be heard in 1923. Harding, who was politically and personally honest, was alarmed. He had once said, "I knew that this job would be too much for me." Tired and depressed, Harding went on a speaking tour in the summer of 1923. It was then that he learned the full extent of the corruption. He died suddenly while on the trip, on August 2, 1923. The American people mourned his death, but they were shocked when the scandals became public.

Reading **History**

A. Drawing Conclusions How did members of the Ohio Gang take advantage of their friendship with Harding?

Coolidge Takes Over

Vice-President **Calvin Coolidge** became president when Harding died. He moved quickly to try to clean up the scandals. His efforts limited the political damage to the Republican Party, and Coolidge was elected president in his own right in 1924. He defeated Democrat John W. Davis and Robert M. La Follette, the Progressive Party nominee.

Coolidge and those who voted for him felt that prosperity would be the reward of those who worked hard. As a friend of business, Coolidge agreed with the economic theory of **laissez faire.** It stated that business, if left unregulated by the government, would act in a way that would benefit the nation. In 1925, Coolidge stated his belief that "the chief business of the American people is business." He said that Americans were concerned with "prospering in the world." Under the Coolidge administration, business prospered and so did many Americans.

Vocabulary
laissez faire: to allow to do (French)

Coolidge also believed that it was not the government's job to help people with social and economic problems. Farmers were one group that Coolidge refused to help. Because new machinery had been introduced, farmers were producing more food than the nation needed. So food prices were dropping.

"The chief business of the American people is business."

Calvin Coolidge

Congress passed a bill that required the government to buy the extra food. This would have raised prices. But Coolidge vetoed the bill.

Like Harding, Coolidge was an **isolationist**. Both believed that the United States should stay out of other nations' affairs except in matters of self-defense. Both supported efforts to avoid war.

Coolidge's major peace effort was the **Kellogg-Briand Pact** of 1928. This pact, or treaty, was signed by 15 nations who pledged not to make war against one another except in self-defense. Most Americans supported the treaty. They hoped that if war were outlawed, it would disappear. Then they could concentrate on their own lives.

Technology Changes American Life

The economy was booming in the 1920s. Both Harding and Coolidge kept government regulation to a minimum, and business flourished. Part of the "roar" in the Roaring Twenties was the growth in the nation's wealth. The average annual income per person rose more than 35 percent during the period—from $522 to $716. This increase in income gave Americans more money to buy goods and to spend on leisure activities.

Automobiles had the greatest impact on life during the 1920s. Henry Ford, who built his first successful automobile in 1896, was determined to make a car that most people could afford. At the Ford Motor Company in Detroit, his dream came true with a car called the Model T. In 1920, Ford produced more than a million automobiles, at a rate of one per minute. Each car cost the consumer $335.

Reading **History**

B. Recognizing Effects What effect did the assembly line have on the price of cars?

To speed up production and lower costs and prices, Ford used an **assembly line.** In an assembly line, the product moves along a conveyor belt across the factory. Workers at various stations add parts as the belt moves past them. By the mid-1920s, a Model T came off a Ford assembly line every ten seconds.

1923 Model T Ford

How an Automobile Assembly Line Works

3 Roof and sides are attached and secured at various stations.

4 Assembled auto body is joined to a chassis (frame) that has been put together on another conveyer.

1 The auto body is placed on the conveyor belt.

2 Workers add parts at each station as it moves past them—here the seats are attached.

OIL HEAT
FOR
small homes

$50

DOWN—*balance on liberal terms*

WILLIAMS
DISTO·MATIC
HEATING

Credit allowed consumers to buy the latest products—$50 down and small monthly payments bought this new oil heater.

Other advances in technology improved life. New machines turned out products faster and cheaper. Once-costly items were now available to many consumers. Some consumers used credit and paid for their purchases through **installment buying.** This allowed repaying the amount borrowed in small monthly payments. National advertising also got its start at this time, as a way of helping to promote new products.

Cheap fuel powered the new prosperity. Petroleum and electricity became widely available. These power sources made possible new inventions and advances in technology that made life easier, such as electric vacuum cleaners, washers, sewing machines, toasters, and fans. However, it was mostly only the white middle class that could afford these new products.

Reading **History**
C. Summarizing
How did advances in technology change the lives of Americans?

The Air Age Begins

The 1920s also marked the beginning of the air age. After World War I, many former military pilots bought old war planes and worked as crop-dusters, stunt fliers, and flight instructors. In 1918, the Post Office Department began air mail service. Airplanes had found new uses.

Transatlantic flights by Charles A. Lindbergh in 1927 and Amelia Earhart in 1928 and 1932 helped to promote the idea of commercial air transportation. Pan American Airways, founded in 1927, became the nation's first passenger airline. By the end of the decade, its operations were drawing distant cities closer together both in North and South America.

In the next section, you will read about more changes in life in the United States and the conflicts these changes caused.

Section **1** *Assessment*

1. Terms & Names
Explain the significance of:
- Warren G. Harding
- Teapot Dome Scandal
- Calvin Coolidge
- laissez faire
- isolationist
- Kellogg-Briand Pact
- assembly line
- installment buying

2. Taking Notes
Use a chart like the one below to review details about the people in this section.

People	Details
Warren G. Harding	
Calvin Coolidge	
Henry Ford	

3. Main Ideas
a. What were Harding's and Coolidge's policies toward business?

b. How did corruption affect the Harding administration?

c. How did new technology help business to grow during the 1920s?

4. Critical Thinking
Drawing Conclusions
Which developments in the 1920s added to prosperity?

THINK ABOUT
- government's role in the economy
- advances made in technology

ACTIVITY OPTIONS

TECHNOLOGY

ART

Research an aspect of the American automobile industry. Either draw a **diagram** of how a car works or design an **advertisement** for an automobile.

TERMS & NAMES
flapper
Prohibition
Al Capone
NAACP
Marcus Garvey
fundamentalism
Ku Klux Klan

② Changes in Society

MAIN IDEA	WHY IT MATTERS NOW
Changes in society in the 1920s brought new attitudes and lifestyles but also caused divisions and conflict.	Many of the social issues of the 1920s continue to challenge American society today.

ONE AMERICAN'S STORY

Poet Edna St. Vincent Millay was one of many young people who rebelled against traditional values in the 1920s. She had left her home in Maine to study poetry at Vassar College in New York. She graduated in 1917 as World War I neared its end. Then she moved to the Greenwich Village section of New York City. There Millay lived among artists and writers whose ideas were different from those traditionally held by society. She wrote poems about love and the carefree lifestyle of the 1920s.

A VOICE FROM THE PAST

My candle burns at both ends;
It will not last the night;
But ah, my foes, and oh, my friends—
It gives a lovely light!

Edna St. Vincent Millay, "First Fig," from *A Few Figs from Thistles*

Edna St. Vincent Millay became a bestselling poet and a symbol of her time.

Millay was a symbol of the 1920s woman. In this section, you will read about the changing roles of young people and women, problems facing African Americans, and conflicts that came to divide society.

Youth in the Roaring Twenties

The 1920s were called the Roaring Twenties. According to author F. Scott Fitzgerald, "The uncertainties of 1919 were over. America was going on the greatest, gaudiest spree in history." During the decade, youth and its culture were celebrated. For the first time, young people as a group rebelled against the values of the past and the authority of their elders. The under-25 generation wanted fun and freedom. Many of them experimented with new fashions, attitudes, and ways of behavior.

Young people stayed in school longer, and more went to college. School became a place for socializing as well as learning. Young people expressed their new freedom in daring new clothes, lively songs and dances, and silly fads. Men wore extra-wide floppy pants and sported hair slicked down close to the head. Women wore a shorter hairstyle called a *bob* to match the shorter dresses of the period.

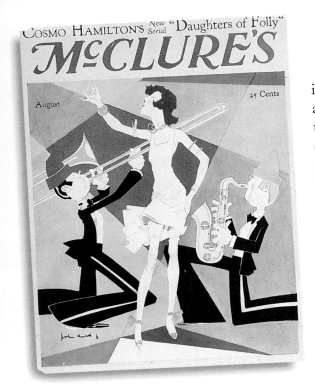

COSMO HAMILTON'S *New Serial* "Daughters of Folly"

McCLURE'S

August — 25 Cents

The flapper appeared on many magazine covers during the 1920s.

The Charleston was a favorite dance. It involved wild, flailing movements of the arms and legs. Dance marathons became the rage. In these contests, couples would dance nonstop for days. Songs also captured the high spirits of the decade. Among the most popular tunes were "Runnin' Wild" and "Ain't We Got Fun." Many young people imitated the behavior of favorite stars from Hollywood movies. Other fads included crossword puzzles, mah-jongg, and flagpole sitting (sitting on a platform on top of a flagpole for days).

The spirited behavior of young women during the decade was just one way women's lives changed.

Background
Mah-jongg was a game from China played with small painted tiles.

New Roles for Women

The symbol of the 1920s American woman was the **flapper**. The flapper was the creation of John Held, Jr., a magazine illustrator. Flappers often wore bobbed hair, makeup, and dresses that fell to just below the knee. They were always eager to try something new, whether it was a new fashion, behavior, dance, or fad.

During the 1920s, women took more active roles in their life than ever before. They had more personal freedom. They drove cars, played sports, went to college, and took jobs. Margaret Sanger, a reformer who focused on women's health issues, described these women.

A VOICE FROM THE PAST

Today women are on the whole much more individual. They possess as strong likes and dislikes as men. They live more and more on the plane of social equality with men . . . [and] there is more enjoyable companionship and real friendship between men and women.

Margaret Sanger, quoted in *A More Perfect Union*

The prosperity of the 1920s opened new job opportunities for women in business offices, retail stores, factories, and various professions. College graduates most often became teachers and nurses, but also librarians, social workers, and bankers. Women with less education worked in factories or in offices as typists and secretaries or in stores as clerks and cashiers. Attitudes toward marriage also changed. Men and women came to view marriage as more of an equal partnership. Women still had the responsibility of housework and child rearing. But labor-saving appliances and timesaving convenience foods made life easier.

The 19th Amendment ensured women the right to vote. Some women even ran for political office. In 1924, two were elected governor—Nellie Tayloe Ross in Wyoming and Miriam "Ma" Ferguson in Texas. In 1923, an equal rights amendment was introduced in Congress. It would be almost 50 years, however, before such an amendment would pass Congress.

*Reading*History
A. Recognizing Effects What were some of the effects of women's greater opportunities?

Prohibition and Lawlessness

Another change in American society came on January 16, 1920. That was the date when the 18th Amendment went into effect. The amendment was commonly called **Prohibition,** the ban on the manufacture and sale of alcohol. Many people saw Prohibition as a victory of small-town, Protestant Americans over city dwellers. Supporters felt that Prohibition would promote morality and good health. To enforce the ban, Congress had passed the Volstead Act in 1919.

Background
Bootlegger came from the old smugglers' practice of carrying liquor in the legs of boots.

Saloons were forced to close their doors. But many Americans did not consider drinking harmful or sinful. They resented government interference. People who wanted alcohol found endless ways to get it. For instance, illegal nightclubs known as speakeasies sold liquor. People called bootleggers made their living by transporting and selling liquor illegally. Others simply brewed their own homemade liquor.

One unfortunate result of Prohibition was the growth of organized crime. In nearly every major city, criminal gangs battled for control of bootlegging operations. The most ruthless crime boss of the era was **Al Capone** in Chicago. With a private army of 700 criminals, he violently seized control of the city's 10,000 speakeasies. By the late 1920s, most Americans had come to see Prohibition as a failure. It was repealed by the 21st Amendment in 1933. Prohibition ended, but organized crime did not end with it.

Marcus Garvey led a Back-to-Africa movement in the 1920s.

Changes for African Americans

Reading **History**
B. Reading a Map
Locate cities with significant African-American populations on the map on page 321.

The 1920s also brought major changes to the lives of many African Americans. To find better jobs, African Americans had begun moving north in the early 1900s. As you read in Chapter 10, this movement was called the Great Migration. The jobs that they held in industries during World War I raised their expectations for a better life.

In the North, African Americans gained some economic and political power. But they still faced discrimination in jobs and housing. Rising tensions between African Americans and whites in Northern cities led to over 25 race riots in 1919 alone. The movement of an additional 1.5 million African Americans to these cities during the 1920s increased tensions even more.

The National Association for the Advancement of Colored People **(NAACP)** tried to protect the constitutional rights of African Americans. The NAACP worked to make people aware of crimes against African Americans. But it was unable to get Congress to pass legislation to help African Americans fight against discrimination.

Reading **History**
C. Analyzing Points of View
What action did Marcus Garvey believe would improve the lives of African Americans?

Daily threats and discrimination made some African Americans lose faith in America. **Marcus Garvey,** the founder of the Universal Negro Improvement Association, called for a return to Africa and the formation of a separate nation there. He said, "If Europe is for the Europeans, then Africa shall be for the black peoples of the world." Few African Americans migrated to Africa. But Garvey set an example for future black political movements.

More than 40,000 Ku Klux Klan members march in Washington, D.C., in 1925, to show their growing political power.

A Divided Society

Some groups felt threatened by the changes in society in the 1920s. Conflicts developed over ideas and values. Divisions between groups resulted—between African Americans and whites, the native-born and immigrants, and the urban and rural communities. Science and religion also were in conflict.

In religion, a movement called **fundamentalism** gained both recognition and political power. Fundamentalists believed in a literal, or word-for-word, interpretation of the Bible. They did not want the theory of evolution taught in public schools because it opposed their belief in the biblical story of creation. Evolution is the scientific theory that living things developed over millions of years from earlier and simpler forms of life.

Fundamentalists succeeded in banning the teaching of evolution in Tennessee and 12 other states. In 1925, in Dayton, Tennessee, biology teacher John Scopes broke this law. He took this action to test whether the law could be enforced. Scopes's trial attracted national attention. The jury found Scopes guilty, but the Tennessee Supreme Court reversed the decision. Controversy over the teaching of evolution continues today.

Another reaction to changes in society was the rebirth of the **Ku Klux Klan**. The Klan called for a "racially and morally pure" America. It became strong in several states, including some outside the South. By 1924, the Klan claimed as many as five million members. It tried to influence national, state, and local politics by using violence against African Americans and other groups. Its power began to decrease by the end of the decade because of personal and financial scandals in the organization.

In this section, you read about divisions in society. In the next, you will learn how mass media and popular culture brought Americans together.

*Reading*History

D. Analyzing Causes What action taken by fundamentalists caused John Scopes to break the law in Tennessee?

Section 2 Assessment

1. Terms & Names

Explain the significance of:
- flapper
- Prohibition
- Al Capone
- NAACP
- Marcus Garvey
- fundamentalism
- Ku Klux Klan

2. Taking Notes

Use a cluster diagram to review the fads of the Roaring Twenties.

the Roaring Twenties

Which fads of the 1920s had lasting influence?

3. Main Ideas

a. How did the Roaring Twenties change the lives of young people?

b. What factors were responsible for the changes in women's lives?

c. What were the conflicts that divided society?

4. Critical Thinking

Recognizing Effects How was American society transformed in the 1920s?

THINK ABOUT
- roles of young people and women
- migration of African Americans
- conflicts between groups

ACTIVITY OPTIONS

ART

MUSIC

Draw a **poster** with an image that represents the Roaring Twenties or write a **song** capturing the spirit of the times.

The Jazz Age and the Harlem Renaissance

TERMS & NAMES
jazz
mass media
popular culture
Harlem Renaissance
Lost Generation
expatriate

MAIN IDEA	WHY IT MATTERS NOW
Popular culture was influenced by the mass media, sports, and the contributions of African Americans.	Much of today's popular culture had its origins in this period.

ONE AMERICAN'S STORY

The decade known as the Roaring Twenties was also called the Jazz Age, because the lively, loose beat of **jazz** captured the carefree spirit of the times. Jazz was developed by African-American musicians in New Orleans. That city was the home of Louis Armstrong, who became one of the world's great jazz musicians.

As a child, Armstrong often listened to jazz played at funeral processions and dance halls. He was raised by a poor, single mother and started working at age seven. His job was collecting junk in a horse-drawn wagon. While in the wagon, Armstrong often played a small tin horn.

A VOICE FROM THE PAST

I had a little tin horn, the kind the people celebrate with. I would blow this long tin horn without the top on it. Just hold my fingers close together. Blow it as a call for old rags, bones, bottles or anything that people had to sell. . . . The kids loved the sounds of my tin horn!

Louis Armstrong, quoted in *Louis Armstrong* by Sandford Brown

Louis Armstrong brought New Orleans jazz to the North in the 1920s.

Later, Armstrong learned to play the trumpet. With other jazz musicians, he spread this new music to other parts of the country—from Chicago to New York's Harlem—and then to Europe.

In this section, you will read more about the spread of popular culture, the Harlem Renaissance, and the artists of the Lost Generation.

More Leisure Time for Americans

Laborsaving appliances and shorter working hours gave Americans more leisure time. Higher wages also gave them money to spend on leisure activities. People wanted more fun, and they were willing to spend money to have it. Americans paid 25 cents or more to see a movie—an increase of at least 5 times the price in the previous decade. By the end of the 1920s, there were more than 100 million weekly moviegoers.

In addition to attending movies, some Americans went to museums and public libraries. Others bought books and magazines. Sales rose by

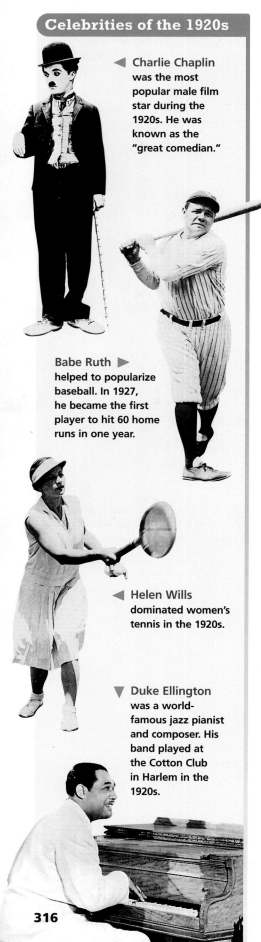

◄ **Charlie Chaplin** was the most popular male film star during the 1920s. He was known as the "great comedian."

Babe Ruth ▶ helped to popularize baseball. In 1927, he became the first player to hit 60 home runs in one year.

◄ **Helen Wills** dominated women's tennis in the 1920s.

▼ **Duke Ellington** was a world-famous jazz pianist and composer. His band played at the Cotton Club in Harlem in the 1920s.

50 percent. Americans also spent time listening to the radio, talking on the telephone, playing games, and driving their cars. In 1929, Americans spent about $4 billion on entertainment—a 100 percent jump in a decade.

But not all Americans were able to take part equally in leisure-time activities or in the consumer culture of the 1920s. Some, like African Americans and Hispanic Americans, had their time and choices limited by factors such as income and race.

Mass Media and Popular Culture

New types of **mass media**—communications that reach a large audience—began to take hold in the 1920s. Radio and movies provided entertainment and spread the latest ideas about fashions and lifestyles.

The first commercial radio broadcast took place in Pittsburgh at station KDKA in 1920. Other radio stations soon emerged. The number of households with radios jumped from about 60,000 in 1922 to 10 million in 1929. Radio stations broadcast news, sports, music, comedy, and commercials. Not only were Americans better informed than before, but listening to the same radio programs united the nation.

Of all the powerful new influences of the 1920s, none shaped the ideas and dreams of Americans more than motion pictures. The moviemaking industry was centered in Hollywood, California.

Movies gave people an escape into worlds of glamour and excitement they could never enter. Audiences flocked to movie theaters to see their favorite actors and actresses. These included Charlie Chaplin, Mary Pickford, Douglas Fairbanks, Clara Bow, and Rudolph Valentino. Movies also spread American popular culture to Europe. **Popular culture** included songs, dances, fashions, and even slang expressions like *scram* (leave in a hurry) and *ritzy* (elegant).

Moviemakers like Samuel Goldwyn, the Warner brothers, and Louis B. Mayer made fortunes overnight. For most of the 1920s, films were silent. In 1927, *The Jazz Singer* introduced sound. Another *talkie* caused a sensation in 1928—Walt Disney's cartoon *Steamboat Willie*, featuring Mickey Mouse. Within a few years, all movies were talkies.

Reading **History**

A. Recognizing Effects What was the main effect that laborsaving devices and reduced working hours had on Americans' lives?

A Search for Heroes

Another leisure activity was watching sporting events and listening to them on the radio. Sporting events of all types—baseball, football, hockey, boxing, golf, and tennis—enjoyed rising attendance. Boxing became very popular. Fans who could not attend the fights listened to matches on the radio or saw them on newsreels shown at movie theaters. The Jack Dempsey–Gene Tunney boxing match of 1926 drew 120,000 fans.

In the 1920s, professional baseball gained many new fans because games were broadcast on radio. As a result, fans flocked to major league ballparks. In New York City, fans went to Yankee Stadium, which opened in 1923, to watch the "Bronx Bombers"—the nickname for the New York Yankees. Even college football and basketball attracted huge crowds.

Sports figures captured the imagination of the American public. They became heroes because they restored Americans' belief in the power of the individual to improve his or her life. Babe Ruth of the Yankees was baseball's top home-run hitter. Someone once asked Ruth why his $80,000 salary was higher than the president's. Ruth supposedly replied, "Well, I had a better year."

Baseball players weren't the only sports heroes. Golfers idolized Bobby Jones. People cheered Helen Wills and Bill Tilden on the tennis courts. In 1926, New York City threw a huge homecoming parade for Gertrude Ederle, the first woman to swim the English Channel. Americans also made national heroes of two daring young fliers—Charles A. Lindbergh and Amelia Earhart.

*Reading*History

B. Summarizing What were some of the changes that came about in popular entertainment in the 1920s?

AMERICA'S HISTORY MAKERS

CHARLES A. LINDBERGH
1902–1974

Charles A. Lindbergh took flying lessons in 1922 and bought his first airplane in 1923. Four years later, in May 1927, he became the first person to fly nonstop alone across the Atlantic Ocean.

Lindbergh had heard about an offer of $25,000 to anyone who could fly nonstop from New York to Paris. Piloting his single engine monoplane, the *Spirit of St. Louis,* without radio or parachute, Lindbergh flew some 3,600 miles in 33½ hours. "Lucky Lindy" became an instant hero.

AMELIA EARHART
1897–1937

Amelia Earhart was often called "Lady Lindy" because of both her physical resemblance to Charles Lindbergh and her similar accomplishments as a pilot.

Earhart took flying lessons in 1921 and bought her first plane in 1922. Noted for her courage and independence, she flew where no women had gone before. She was the first woman to cross the Atlantic in a plane (as a passenger) in 1928 and the first to fly solo across the Atlantic in 1932. She disappeared on a round-the-world flight in 1937. What happened remains a mystery to this day.

Why do you think Lindbergh and Earhart became American heroes?

Artists of the Harlem Renaissance celebrated the cultural traditions and the life experiences of African Americans. This painting by Lois Mailou Jones is entitled *The Ascent of Ethiopia.*

How does the artist show the link between African and American cultures?

The Harlem Renaissance

Wartime military service and work in war industries had given African Americans a new sense of freedom. They migrated to many cities across the country, but it was New York City that turned into the unofficial capital of black America. In the 1920s, Harlem, a neighborhood on New York's West Side, was the world's largest black urban community.

The migrants from the South brought with them new ideas and a new kind of music called jazz. Soon Harlem produced a burst of African-American cultural activity known as the **Harlem Renaissance,** which began in the 1920s and lasted into the 1930s. It was called a renaissance because it symbolized a rebirth of hope for African Americans.

Vocabulary
renaissance: rebirth (French)

Harlem became home to writers, musicians, singers, painters, sculptors, and scholars. There they were able to exchange ideas and develop their creativity. Among Harlem's residents were poets Langston Hughes, James Weldon Johnson, and Countee Cullen and novelists Claude McKay and Zora Neale Hurston. Hughes was perhaps Harlem's most famous writer. He wrote about the difficult conditions under which African Americans lived.

Jazz became widely popular in the 1920s. It was a form of music that combined African rhythms, blues, and ragtime to produce a unique sound. Jazz spread from its birthplace in New Orleans to other parts of the country and made its way into the nightclubs of Harlem. These nightclubs featured popular jazz musicians such as Louis Armstrong and Duke Ellington, and singers such as the jazz and blues great, Bessie Smith. Harlem's most famous nightclub was the Cotton Club. It made stars of many African-American performers, but only white customers were allowed in the club.

Reading History

C. Recognizing Effects What changes to popular culture resulted from the migration of African Americans to the North?

The Lost Generation

For some artists and writers, the decade after the war was not a time of celebration but a time of deep despair. They had seen the ideas of the Progressives end in a senseless war. They were filled with resentment and they saw little hope for the future. They were called the **Lost Generation.**

Reading History
D. Analyzing Causes Why did many American writers become expatriates and live in Paris?

For many of them, only one place offered freedom and tolerance. That was Paris. The French capital became a gathering place for American **expatriates,** people who choose to live in a country other than their own. Among the American expatriates living in Paris was the young novelist Ernest Hemingway. As an ambulance driver in Europe during World War I, he had seen the war's worst. His early novels, *The Sun Also Rises* and *A Farewell to Arms*, reflected the mood of despair that followed the war.

Novelists F. Scott Fitzgerald and Sinclair Lewis were two other members of the Lost Generation. Fitzgerald and his wife, Zelda, lived the whirlwind life of the Jazz Age—fast cars, nightclubs, wild parties, and trips to Paris. His masterpiece, *The Great Gatsby*, is a tragic story of wealthy New Yorkers whose lives spin out of control. The novel is a portrait of the dark side of the Roaring Twenties.

Lewis wrote *Babbitt,* a novel that satirized, or made fun of, the American middle class and its concern for material possessions.

F. Scott Fitzgerald is pictured here in France with his wife, Zelda. He published his masterpiece, *The Great Gatsby*, while living there.

A VOICE FROM THE PAST

It's the fellow with four to ten thousand a year . . . and an automobile and a nice little family in a bungalow . . . that makes the wheels of progress go round! . . . That's the type of fellow that's ruling America today; in fact, it's the ideal type to which the entire world must tend, if there's to be a decent, well-balanced . . . future for this little old planet!

Sinclair Lewis, *Babbitt*

The social values and materialistic lifestyles criticized by Lewis soon came to an end. As you will read in the next chapter, the soaring economy that brought prosperity in the 1920s came to a crashing halt. It was followed by a worldwide economic depression in the 1930s.

Section 3 Assessment

1. Terms & Names
Explain the significance of:
- jazz
- mass media
- popular culture
- Harlem Renaissance
- Lost Generation
- expatriate

2. Taking Notes
Use the chart to review facts about mass media.

Radio	Movies

How did mass media change the lives of Americans?

3. Main Ideas
a. Which two factors gave Americans more leisure time?

b. What effect did radio have on sports?

c. Why was Harlem called the unofficial capital of black America?

4. Critical Thinking
Evaluating What contributions to popular culture occurred in the 1920s?

THINK ABOUT
- the impact of World War I
- the power of mass media
- new social values

ACTIVITY OPTIONS

ART

TECHNOLOGY

Find an image and important facts about a noted person in this section. Draw a **trading card** or plan that person's **home page** for the Internet.

African-American Baseball Leagues

More than a million African Americans left the South from 1917 to 1929. They were lured to large cities by the offer of higher wages and the increased demand for labor. It was during this period of growing urbanization that the Negro baseball leagues were formed. The map on the next page shows cities with notable teams in the 1920s and 1930s. Each city had an African-American population large enough and wealthy enough to support a team.

Most teams were owned by African Americans. To raise money for expenses, teams needed to play as many games as possible. Thus, they traveled constantly. Stopping in big cities and small towns, they played other African-American teams or white amateur and professional teams. Eventually, teams of African-American all-stars played exhibitions against professional white all-stars.

In 1920, Andrew "Rube" Foster persuaded owners of seven other teams to join him in forming the first Negro baseball league—the Negro National League. Foster (pictured in suit at right) was a former player and then owner of the Chicago American Giants. The Negro American League got started in 1937. After major league baseball was integrated by Jackie Robinson in 1947, the Negro leagues began to decline.

ARTIFACT FILE

Memorabilia

The baseball jersey and shoes pictured here are part of the uniform worn by a player from one of the traveling teams of the period.

Pittsburgh Crawfords

The Pittsburgh Crawfords, shown here with the team's bus, was one of the best teams in the Negro leagues in the 1930s. The success of traveling teams helped to boost revenues of African-American-owned hotels and restaurants in every city that they played.

Cities with Notable African-American Baseball Teams, 1920s–1930s

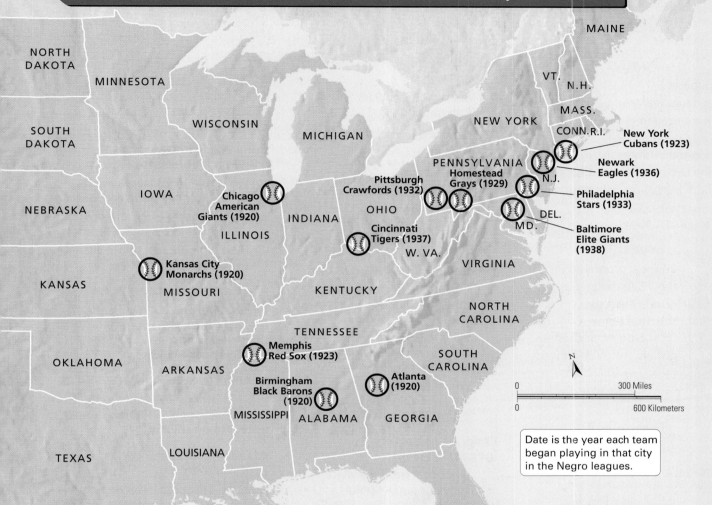

MAINE

NORTH DAKOTA

MINNESOTA

SOUTH DAKOTA

WISCONSIN

MICHIGAN

VT.

N.H.

MASS.

NEW YORK

CONN. R.I.

New York Cubans (1923)

PENNSYLVANIA

Newark Eagles (1936)

N.J.

IOWA

Chicago American Giants (1920)

INDIANA

Pittsburgh Crawfords (1932)

Homestead Grays (1929)

Philadelphia Stars (1933)

NEBRASKA

ILLINOIS

OHIO

Cincinnati Tigers (1937)

DEL.

MD.

Baltimore Elite Giants (1938)

Kansas City Monarchs (1920)

W. VA.

VIRGINIA

KANSAS

MISSOURI

KENTUCKY

NORTH CAROLINA

TENNESSEE

OKLAHOMA

ARKANSAS

Memphis Red Sox (1923)

SOUTH CAROLINA

Birmingham Black Barons (1920)

Atlanta (1920)

MISSISSIPPI

ALABAMA

GEORGIA

TEXAS

LOUISIANA

N

0   300 Miles

0   600 Kilometers

Date is the year each team began playing in that city in the Negro leagues.

FLORIDA

On-Line Field Trip

National Baseball Hall of Fame and Museum

The Negro leagues have been widely honored. This poster is from the National Baseball Hall of Fame and Museum in Cooperstown, New York. In Kansas City, Missouri, the Negro Leagues Baseball Museum also keeps the memory of these teams alive.

For more about the Negro leagues . . .

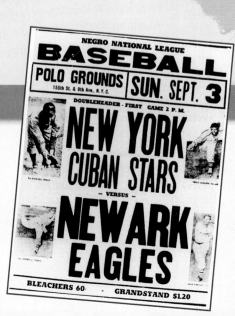

CONNECT TO GEOGRAPHY

1. **Location** Which cities had notable teams in the 1920s and 1930s?

2. **Region** Why do you think that African-American teams were located mainly in cities in the East?

See Geography Handbook, pp. 4–5.

CONNECT TO HISTORY

3. **Evaluating** How did the migration of African Americans from the South to Northern cities lead to the rise of Negro baseball leagues?

VISUAL SUMMARY

The Roaring Twenties

Politics

Republican presidents Warren G. Harding and Calvin Coolidge supported business in the United States and isolationism in foreign relations.

Economics

Business prospered in the 1920s, helped by government support and the development of new technologies. But some groups, notably farmers, faced hardships.

Technology

Technological developments, such as the assembly line, and cheap, available sources of power, such as electricity and petroleum, powered the new prosperity.

Society and Culture

Changes in society brought new attitudes and lifestyles, especially for young people and women. Movies, radio, jazz, and sports became popular forms of entertainment.

TERMS & NAMES

Briefly explain the significance of each of the following.
1. Warren G. Harding
2. Calvin Coolidge
3. isolationist
4. Kellogg-Briand Pact
5. NAACP
6. Marcus Garvey
7. fundamentalism
8. mass media
9. Harlem Renaissance
10. Lost Generation

REVIEW QUESTIONS

The Business of America (pages 307–310)
1. How was the foreign policy of Harding and Coolidge isolationist?
2. What was the economic theory of laissez faire?
3. Which factors contributed to the nation's growing wealth during the 1920s?

Changes in Society (pages 311–314)
4. What changes took place in the behavior and values of young people during the 1920s?
5. What was the image of the *flapper?*
6. How did the 19th Amendment change women's lives?
7. What were some of the divisions in society in the 1920s?

The Jazz Age and the Harlem Renaissance (pages 315–321)
8. What were three examples of American popular culture?
9. Which factors contributed to the popularity of sports?
10. Why are the 1920s also called the Jazz Age?

CRITICAL THINKING

1. USING YOUR NOTES

Categories	Main Ideas
Government	
Business	
Agriculture	
Technology	
Society	
Popular Culture	

Using your completed chart, answer the questions below.
a. What role did government choose to play in the economy?
b. How did technology affect life during the 1920s?
c. How did popular culture change the habits of society?

2. ANALYZING LEADERSHIP
Think about the political leaders discussed in this chapter. Which of their characteristics made them good or poor leaders?

3. APPLYING CITIZENSHIP SKILLS
In what other ways could people have protested Prohibition besides disregarding the law?

4. THEME: SCIENCE AND TECHNOLOGY
How did advances in technology contribute to the prosperity of the United States during the 1920s?

5. DRAWING CONCLUSIONS
Explain how the African-American migration to the North and the spread of jazz contributed to the cultural diversity of the United States.

Interact *with* History

In your opinion, which changes in American life discussed in this chapter would have affected you the most?

HISTORY SKILLS

1. INTERPRETING GRAPHS

Study the graph and then answer the questions.

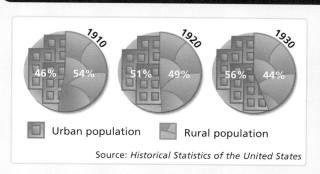

Urbanization of America, *1910–1930*

1910: 46% 54%
1920: 51% 49%
1930: 56% 44%

☐ Urban population ☐ Rural population

Source: *Historical Statistics of the United States*

a. What was the total percentage increase in the urban population from 1910 to 1930?

b. During which 10-year period did the United States become more urban than rural?

2. INTERPRETING PRIMARY SOURCES

Read the poem below, which was written by Langston Hughes, an African American. Then answer the questions that follow.

> I, too, sing America.
>
> I am the darker brother.
> They send me to eat in the kitchen
> When company comes,
> But I laugh,
> And eat well,
> And grow strong.
>
> Tomorrow,
> I'll be at the table
> When company comes.
> Nobody'll dare
> Say to me,
> "Eat in the kitchen,"
> Then.
>
> Besides,
> They'll see how beautiful I am
> And be ashamed—
>
> I, too, am America.

Langston Hughes, "I, Too"

a. What is the subject of the poem?

b. What change does Hughes see taking place?

ALTERNATIVE ASSESSMENT

1. INTERDISCIPLINARY ACTIVITY: Language Arts

Writing a Report Do research to learn how cars are made on an assembly line today. Describe the procedure for manufacturing a car from start to finish. Include the method of production, materials used, and the time it takes to make a car. Share your report with the class.

2. COOPERATIVE LEARNING ACTIVITY

Writing or Drawing an Advertisement National advertising became an important way to promote new products to the public during the 1920s. Working in a small group, write a radio ad or draw a magazine ad for a product that made life easier during the 1920s, such as a car, refrigerator, toaster, vacuum cleaner, sewing machine, fan, or washer. Make sure your advertisement covers the following ideas:

a. Do research on the product. Describe the product in the 1920s.

b. How will the product improve life for Americans?

c. How much does the product cost?

3. TECHNOLOGY ACTIVITY

Planning a Web Page on the Roaring Twenties The 1920s were years of great creativity. American popular culture was being spread throughout the nation and abroad by radio and movies. Use the library or search the Internet for information about the music, fashions, fads, and celebrities of the period.

For more about the Roaring Twenties . . .

INTERNET ACTIVITY
CLASSZONE.COM

Create a Roaring Twenties Web page by following the suggestions below.

• Select appropriate images of personalities, fashions, and fads.

• Include biographical information and quotations.

• Choose music that captures the spirit of the era.

• Decide which Web sites would be good links for visitors to your page.

4. PORTFOLIO ACTIVITY

Review your section and chapter assessment activities. Select one that you think was your best work. Use comments made by your teacher or classmates to improve your work, and then add it to your portfolio.

Additional Test Practice, pp. S1–S33

TEST PRACTICE
CLASSZONE.COM

CHAPTER 12

The Great Depression and New Deal 1929–1940

Section 1 **Hoover and the Crash**
Section 2 **Roosevelt and the New Deal**
Section 3 **Life During the Depression**
Section 4 **The Effects of the New Deal**

Homeless people used scrap materials to build shacks in a New York City alley during the Great Depression.

Interact *with* History

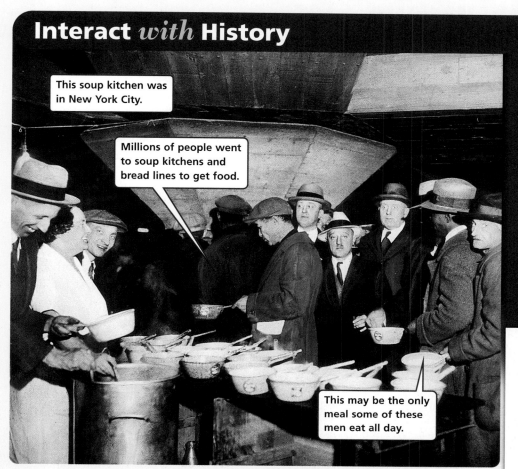

This soup kitchen was in New York City.

Millions of people went to soup kitchens and bread lines to get food.

This may be the only meal some of these men eat all day.

It's 1932. The economy is bad, and millions of people are out of work. Some are starving.

Two men are running for president. One says the government should give money to the poor. The other says this will make people stop looking for jobs. He wants charity groups to help people in need.

What Do You Think?

- Is the government responsible for everyone's well-being?
- What responsibility do individuals have to help others?
- What is the best way to help people out of poverty?

Who do you think should help the poor?

1929
U.S. stock market crashes. Great Depression begins.

1931
President Hoover declares that the country will work itself out of the Depression.

1932
Americans turn against Hoover. Franklin Delano Roosevelt is elected president.

1933
Roosevelt initiates government programs to help the economy.

1935
Congress passes the Social Security Act.

1936
Roosevelt is reelected.

1937
Roosevelt tries but fails to add justices to the Supreme Court.

1939
John Steinbeck publishes *The Grapes of Wrath* about migrant workers.

USA World **1929**

1940

1931
Affected by the Depression, Japan invades Manchuria, partially to expand its economy.

1933
Adolf Hitler becomes dictator of Germany.

1936
Léon Blum, Socialist premier of France, introduces reforms such as the 40-hour workweek.

1939
Germany invades Poland, starting World War II.

BEFORE YOU READ

Previewing the Theme

Economics in History Chapter 12 explains how the prosperity of the 1920s ended suddenly. The years of unemployment and hard times that followed are known as the Great Depression. To improve economic conditions, President Roosevelt and Congress enacted programs that permanently changed the U.S. government.

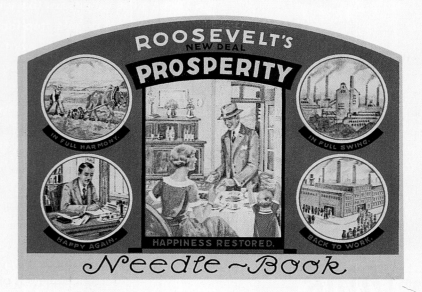

What Do You Know?

What do people do to get by when they are unable to find work? Where can they turn for help besides the government?

THINK ABOUT

- stories you may have heard about the Great Depression
- movies and books about people with economic struggles

What Do You Want to Know?

What questions do you have about how the Great Depression affected Americans? What facts and details would you like to learn about government actions during that period? In your notebook, list the things you hope to learn from this chapter.

READ AND TAKE NOTES

Reading Strategy: Evaluating To evaluate is to make a judgment about something. As you read this chapter, look for details about how the following people responded to the Great Depression: President Herbert Hoover, President Franklin Delano Roosevelt, and ordinary citizens (civilians). Record those details in a chart like the one below. Then evaluate how effective those responses were at making the situation better.

 See Skillbuilder Handbook, page R19.

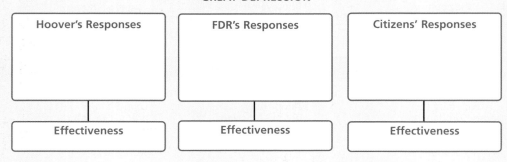

GREAT DEPRESSION

Hoover's Responses	FDR's Responses	Citizens' Responses
Effectiveness	Effectiveness	Effectiveness

TERMS & NAMES
Herbert Hoover
speculation
buying on margin
Black Tuesday
Crash of 1929
Great Depression
public works
  projects
Bonus Army

MAIN IDEA	WHY IT MATTERS NOW
After the stock market crash of 1929, the U.S. economy sank into the worst depression in its history.	Today the government regulates banking and the stock exchange to prevent such severe depressions.

ONE AMERICAN'S STORY

Not everyone prospered in the 1920s. For example, many farmers suffered poverty because farm prices stayed low. Republican senator George Norris from Nebraska joined a group of lawmakers called the farm bloc, who sought to pass new laws to aid farmers. Norris also criticized bankers for not caring about farmers' problems.

Instead of holding to pure Republican ideas, Norris said he "would rather be right than regular."

A VOICE FROM THE PAST

When the great leaders of banking and industry can see no further than the artificial prosperity that comes to Big Business while those who toil on farms are getting no return for their labor, then indeed we have a right to question the wisdom of our financial leaders.

George Norris, "The Farmers' Situation, a National Danger"

Norris also urged the building of government-owned power plants in rural areas. He was unusual because most Republicans believed that government should not interfere in the economy. Section 1 explains how Republican policies came under attack when the economy failed.

Problems in the Economy

Secretary of Commerce **Herbert Hoover** became the Republican candidate for president in 1928. In a speech, he stated, "We shall soon . . . be in sight of the day when poverty will be banished from this nation." But the overall prosperity of the 1920s hid the fact that some industries were in trouble. These included agriculture, railroads, textile mills, and mines.

The growing wealth of the richest Americans also hid the struggle of the majority. By 1929, 71 percent of American families earned less than $2,500 per year, the minimum needed to live decently. Some people had no jobs. African Americans in particular had high jobless rates.

During the 1920s, industries had improved efficiency and begun to produce more goods. But the income of middle-class and poor people didn't rise enough for them to purchase the extra goods. Products piled up in warehouses, causing a problem. Unless businesses sold their products, they couldn't pay for materials, salaries, equipment, or shipping.

Economic Problems, *1920–1929*

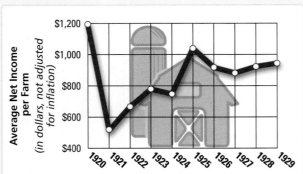

Average Net Income per Farm Notice the big drop in average farm income between 1920 and 1921. Although farm income generally rose during the decade, it did not reach the 1920 level.

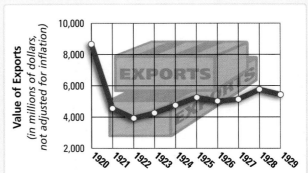

Value of Exports Notice the drop between 1920 and 1921. For the next eight years, exports remained generally the same. U.S. businesses barely increased the amount they sold overseas.

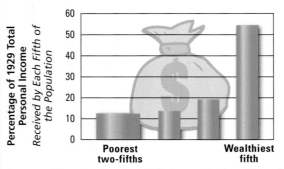

Income Distribution In 1929, the wealthiest fifth of the population had more income than the other four-fifths combined. Poor and middle-class people could not afford to buy many consumer goods. This hurt business.

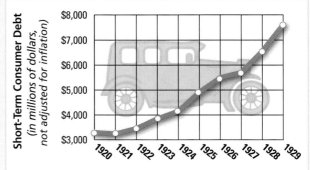

Short-Term Consumer Debt If people do not earn enough to buy what they want, they may take out loans or buy on credit. Short-term consumer debt skyrocketed from 1920 to 1929.

Sources: *Historical Statistics of the United States; A Study of Saving in the United States*

SKILLBUILDER Interpreting Graphs

1. *Which of these problems affected individuals, and which affected businesses?*

2. *By how much did short-term consumer debt rise from 1920 to 1929?*

Some consumers bought goods anyway—on credit. But when their debt grew higher than they could repay, they stopped buying new items. Unsold goods piled up even more.

Yet stock market prices kept climbing. Americans who could afford it rushed to buy stocks. Increasingly, investors bought on **speculation,** buying and selling stocks in the hope of making a quick profit.

Investors also began **buying on margin**—they paid a small part of a stock's price as a down payment and borrowed the rest. When they sold the stock, they repaid the loan and kept the profit. The system worked as long as prices rose. But if prices fell, borrowers couldn't repay their loans because they had to sell the stock for less than they paid for it.

Despite these problems, people believed Hoover when he predicted growing prosperity. In 1928, he won the presidency by a landslide.

Vocabulary
credit: an agreement to pay over time, instead of all at once

The Crash and the Great Depression

On September 3, 1929, the value of stocks on the New York Stock Exchange reached a high point. Then prices drifted downward. On October 23, prices dropped sharply. The next morning, people tried to sell thousands of shares before their value dropped further. Many of those who had bought on margin were forced to sell stocks to pay off their loans.

This heavy selling drove prices even lower. Because more people wanted to sell stocks than to buy them, prices had to go down to attract purchasers. But the quickly falling prices scared off buyers. Meanwhile, sellers hurried to unload their shares at the best price they could get.

On October 24, a record 12.9 million shares were traded. But the worst was yet to come. On October 29, **Black Tuesday,** investors sold 16.4 million shares of stocks at prices much lower than they had been selling for a month earlier. The plunge in stock market prices, called the **Crash of 1929,** was the first event of a terrible economic depression.

After the stock market crash, banks began to demand that people pay back the money they had borrowed to buy stocks. When people could not repay these loans, banks ran short of money. This frightening news

sent people running to the banks to withdraw their savings. But banks typically do not keep enough cash on hand to pay all of their depositors at once. Unable to pay their depositors, many banks simply closed. By March 1933, about 9,000 banks had gone out of business.

Businesses felt the impact next. Many already had warehouses filled with more goods than they could sell. Because the economy's problems scared people, they stopped buying new goods. As a result, businesses sold less and less. Tens of thousands of businesses went bankrupt.

To survive, many businesses fired workers. Unemployment grew to 25 percent by 1933. As more people lost jobs, they bought fewer products—and companies laid off even more workers. Unable to pay their bills, thousands of people lost their homes, and millions went hungry.

The United States had experienced economic depressions before. But no depression caused as much suffering or lasted as long as this one— from 1929 to World War II. Therefore, it is called the **Great Depression**.

The Great Depression also affected millions of people around the world. For example, many European countries had borrowed money from U.S. banks to rebuild after World War I. When the American economy failed, so did Europe's. Hard times spread around the globe.

Hoover Acts Conservatively

Americans looked to the president to end the hard times. Along with most Republicans, Hoover feared that government interference might hurt the economy even more. Even so, he did try to fight the Depression, but his actions often backfired. For example, he tried to balance the

Economics *in* History

Recession and Depression

Many people hoped the economy would fix itself because they believed depressions were a natural part of the business cycle (shown below). Economies go through ups and downs. The period when an economy is at its worst is a trough. There are two kinds of troughs—recessions and depressions. A depression is more severe.

CONNECT TO HISTORY
1. **Evaluating** Why were the hard times of the 1930s a depression, not a recession?

S See Skillbuilder Handbook, page R19.

CONNECT TO TODAY
2. **Making Inferences** How would today's world be affected differently by a depression in the United States than by one in Holland? Explain.

For more about economics . . .

RESEARCH LINKS
CLASSZONE.COM

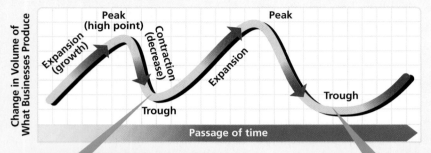

Change in Volume of What Businesses Produce

Peak (high point) · Expansion (growth) · Contraction (decrease) · Trough · Expansion · Peak · Expansion · Trough

Passage of time

Recession
- The production of a nation's goods and services goes down each month for six months.
- Business owners produce less and invest less in new equipment and facilities. They also lay off workers.
- Consumers buy fewer goods.

Depression
- The production of goods and services drops lower than in a recession.
- The period of no economic growth is longer than in a recession. Unemployment is higher.
- The slowdown may spread to other countries; international trade declines dramatically.

WHY CAN'T YO GIVE MY DAD A JOB?

federal budget by cutting government spending and raising taxes. This pulled money out of the economy, which made the slump worse.

Some of Hoover's actions made him very unpopular. For example, he believed that federal relief—aid to the poor—would make people too dependent on government. So he would not support giving relief. In his view, one answer to the hard times was a quality he called "rugged individualism." In 1931, Hoover said, "We cannot legislate ourselves out of a world economic depression. We can and will work ourselves out."

Hoover also stressed the value of volunteer efforts. He encouraged churches and private charities such as the Salvation Army and the Red Cross to help needy Americans. In 1932, private giving did reach a record level—but it still wasn't enough to help everyone in need.

As unemployment, hunger, and homelessness grew, people became bitter toward the president. They blamed him for their suffering. They called empty pockets turned inside out "Hoover flags." And they called villages of wretched huts that housed homeless people "Hoovervilles."

Finally, Hoover softened his stand against government relief. States received some federal money to give to the needy. And in 1932, Hoover set up an agency to lend money to states, cities, and towns. This money would be used for **public works projects**—government-funded projects to build public resources such as roads and dams. These projects would create jobs. But Hoover's actions proved to be too little and too late.

*Reading*History

B. Solving Problems What were Hoover's solutions to the problems caused by the Depression, and did they succeed?

Hoover Loses to Roosevelt

In the summer of 1932, a dramatic event made Hoover even more unpopular. Congress had promised World War I veterans a bonus for wartime service. The bonuses were not due to be paid until the 1940s. But many of the ex-soldiers were jobless and wanted early payment. Some decided to march to Washington, D.C., to ask Congress to pass such a law. Through May and June, the **Bonus Army** of 12,000 to 15,000 veterans poured into Washington and set up camps around the city. Some of them were accompanied by their families.

U.S. troops used tanks and grenades to force the Bonus Army from their camps.

The Senate, backed by Hoover, voted down a bill that called for a bonus payment. Most veterans gave up and returned home, but a few thousand remained to protest.

At the end of July, General Douglas MacArthur decided on his own to drive the Bonus Army from Washington. MacArthur's troops threw tear gas and prodded the veterans and their children with bayonets. One veteran was shot to death. The American public reacted angrily.

Reading History
C. Making Inferences Why do you think Evalyn McLean became so angry?

A VOICE FROM THE PAST

I saw in a news reel the tanks, the cavalry, and the gas-bomb throwers running those wretched Americans out of our capital. I was so raging mad I could have torn the theater down.

Evalyn Walsh McLean, *Father Struck It Rich*

Because of the attack, Americans turned against Hoover more than ever. In the 1932 presidential election, Democratic candidate Franklin Delano Roosevelt carried all but six states. Section 2 explains how Roosevelt tried to end the Depression with new federal programs.

Section 1 Assessment

1. Terms & Names

Explain the significance of:
- Herbert Hoover
- speculation
- buying on margin
- Black Tuesday
- Crash of 1929
- Great Depression
- public works projects
- Bonus Army

2. Taking Notes

Use a diagram like the one below to show the sequence of events that led from the stock market crash to massive unemployment.

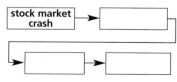

3. Main Ideas

a. What weaknesses existed in the economy during the 1920s?

b. What is buying on margin, and how was it a problem?

c. Why did Hoover become unpopular with many Americans?

4. Critical Thinking

Contrasting How did Hoover's view of the federal government and that of most Americans differ?

THINK ABOUT
- Hoover's attitude about federal relief
- why Americans blamed Hoover for their suffering
- what Americans might have expected from Hoover

ACTIVITY OPTIONS

MATH

SPEECH

Research the changes in stock market value from September through October 1929. Create a **graph** or give a series of **radio news bulletins** about the changes.

TERMS & NAMES

Franklin Delano
  Roosevelt

fireside chat

New Deal

Hundred Days

Social Security Act

Second New Deal

deficit spending

MAIN IDEA	WHY IT MATTERS NOW
After becoming president, Franklin D. Roosevelt took many actions to fight the Great Depression.	Roosevelt increased government's role in helping needy Americans and regulating the financial industry.

ONE AMERICAN'S STORY

Dynamite Garland's father had worked for the railroad. But when the Depression struck, Dynamite's father lost his job, and her family had to move into a garage that a landlord let them have rent-free.

A VOICE FROM THE PAST

We had a coal stove, and we had to each take turns, the three of us kids, to warm our legs. It was awfully cold when you opened those garage doors. . . . In the morning, we'd get out and get some snow and put it on the stove and melt it and wash around our faces. Never the neck or anything. Put on our two pairs of socks on each hand and two pairs of socks on our feet, and long underwear and lace it up with Goodwill shoes. Off we'd walk, three, four miles to school.

Dynamite Garland, quoted in *Hard Times*

Children such as Dynamite Garland and the girls in this photograph suffered greatly from hunger and poverty during the Depression.

Starting in 1933, **Franklin Delano Roosevelt**, the new Democratic president, created a number of programs to help the economy and people like Dynamite. This section describes those programs.

Roosevelt Takes Charge

Millions of people lacked food and shelter. Yet the country had to endure a frustrating four-month wait from the November election to Roosevelt's inauguration. The Twentieth Amendment, which moved the inauguration date to January, was not ratified until 1933. President Roosevelt, nicknamed FDR, was finally inaugurated on March 4, 1933.

Roosevelt differed from Hoover in two important ways. First, he gave Americans hope, beginning with his inaugural address: "Let me assert my firm belief that the only thing we have to fear is fear itself." Second, he was willing to try new ideas and change the way government worked. Though he had no fixed plan to end the Depression, he set up a "brain trust" of advisers, including college professors and economists.

Roosevelt took three immediate steps that boosted public confidence. First, he declared a "bank holiday"—a temporary shutdown of all banks.

Reading History

A. Drawing
Conclusions Did
Roosevelt's first
fireside chat
affect the public
the way he
wanted? Explain.

Second, he promised that only the banks that were in good shape would be allowed to reopen.

Third, the day before the banks reopened, FDR gave the first of many **fireside chats.** In these radio talks, he explained his policies in a warm, friendly style. He said it was safer to "keep your money in a reopened bank than under the mattress." The next day, people deposited more money into the banks than they withdrew.

The Hundred Days

During the campaign, FDR had pledged a "new deal" for Americans. This snappy phrase, the **New Deal,** came to stand for FDR's programs to fight the Depression.

In the session of Congress lasting from March 9 to mid-June 1933, Roosevelt sent Congress a pile of new bills. Many of them passed with little debate in this famous session of Congress, called the **Hundred Days.**

The laws passed during the Hundred Days had three major goals, known as the "three Rs."

1. **relief** for the hungry and jobless
2. **recovery** for agriculture and industry
3. **reforms** to change the way the economy worked

FDR wanted not only to ease suffering but also to try to prevent such a severe depression from happening again. The major programs passed during the Hundred Days included relief, recovery, and reform plans that related to jobs, banking, wages, and agriculture. The chart on page 335 lists several major programs and explains what those programs accomplished.

Responses to the New Deal

Some conservatives thought the New Deal went too far. They opposed the growth of the federal government and questioned how it would pay for all the new programs. They also feared that the New Deal was moving the country toward socialism.

Vocabulary
socialism: an eco-
nomic system in
which businesses
are owned by the
government, not
individuals

Yet, other critics charged that the New Deal didn't go far enough. Louisiana senator Huey Long declared, "Unless we provide for redistribution of wealth in this country, the country is doomed." But Long's motives were far from noble. For years, he had ruled his state like a dictator. Attacking FDR was a way to increase his own power.

Father Charles Coughlin, a priest with a popular radio program, also argued for changing the economy to help the poor. He eventually began to blame Jews for the nation's problems. In the 1940s, the Catholic Church stopped his broadcasts. Another critic, Francis Townshend, proposed giving $200 a month to every American over age 60. He said a sales tax would pay for the pension, but economists disputed his figures.

AMERICA'S HISTORY MAKERS

FRANKLIN DELANO ROOSEVELT

1882–1945

A distant cousin of Theodore Roosevelt, Franklin D. Roosevelt became a New York state senator when he was 29. Later, he served as assistant secretary of the Navy.

At the age of 39, FDR caught polio. For the rest of his life, he walked with braces or rode in a wheelchair. Despite this, he continued in politics and was elected governor of New York in 1928.

The public rarely saw photos revealing FDR's disability. Even so, many Americans sensed that he was a man who understood trouble. This quality helped him as a leader during the Depression.

How would an understanding of trouble help Roosevelt to lead?

The Tennessee Valley Authority

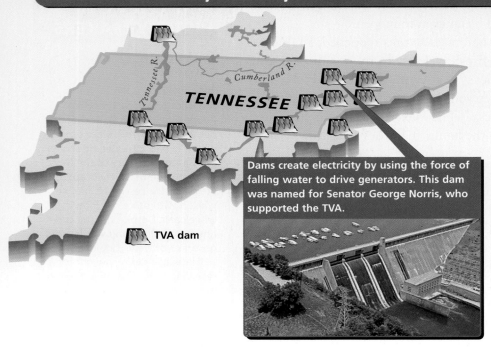

Dams create electricity by using the force of falling water to drive generators. This dam was named for Senator George Norris, who supported the TVA.

TVA dam

FACTS ABOUT THE TVA

- The TVA supplies power to an area of about 80,000 square miles, shown in dark and light green to the left. The region uses more than 100 billion kilowatt-hours of electricity. This is 65 times as much as in 1933.

- There are more than 40 TVA dams.

- Users of TVA power pay about a third less for their electricity than other Americans.

- The TVA dams also help control flooding on the Tennessee River.

In the 1934 congressional elections, voters had a chance to react to these criticisms. The party in power usually loses seats in a nonpresidential election. But, indicating their support for Roosevelt, voters in this election sent even more Democrats to Congress.

The Second New Deal

Although he rejected Townshend's plan, FDR did want to help the elderly. Bank failures and the stock market crash had stolen the savings of many old people. Some had lost their homes or had to beg for food.

In August 1935, Congress passed one of the most important bills of the century. Under the **Social Security Act,** workers and employers made payments into a special fund, from which they would draw a pension after they retired. The act also gave help to laid-off workers, disabled workers, and needy families with dependent children.

Background
Townshend's plan had been very popular with the public. FDR knew his own popularity would increase if he proposed a pension.

A VOICE FROM THE PAST

We have tried to frame a law which will give some measure of protection to the average citizen and to his family against the loss of a job and against poverty-ridden old age.

Franklin D. Roosevelt, quoted in *Promises to Keep*

Social Security was part of a set of programs passed in 1935. These became known as the **Second New Deal.** Other programs of the Second New Deal are listed in the chart on the next page.

In 1936, the Democrats nominated Roosevelt for a second term. Business leaders opposed his reelection because they feared higher taxes. They also thought he was increasing government power at their expense. But a widespread alliance of working-class Americans supported FDR.

Major Programs of the New Deal

	PROGRAMS	ACCOMPLISHMENTS
Hundred Days, 1933	**FERA** (Federal Emergency Relief Administration)	Provided federal money for relief projects to the roughly 13 million unemployed
	PWA (Public Works Administration)	Created jobs by having people build highways, bridges, and other public works
	AAA (Agricultural Adjustment Administration)	Regulated farm production and promoted soil conservation
	TVA (Tennessee Valley Authority)	Planned development of the Tennessee Valley region
	CCC (Civilian Conservation Corps)	Hired young men to plant trees, build dams, and work on other conservation projects
	FDIC (Federal Deposit Insurance Corporation)	Protected the money of depositors in insured banks
	NRA (National Recovery Administration)	Regulated industry and raised wages and prices
Second New Deal, 1935	**WPA** (Works Progress Administration)	Established large-scale national works programs to create jobs
	REA (Rural Electrification Administration)	Brought electricity to rural areas
	NYA (National Youth Administration)	Set up job programs for young people and helped them continue their education
	Wagner Act	Protected labor's right to form unions and set up a board to hear labor disputes
	Social Security Act	Provided workers with unemployment insurance and retirement benefits

SKILLBUILDER Interpreting Charts

1. *How did the PWA and the CCC help both those who were hired and the nation as a whole?*
2. *How did the Second New Deal help both young and old workers?*

*Reading*History
B. Analyzing Causes Why did many African Americans switch to the Democratic Party?

They included African Americans, who until then had remained loyal to the Republican Party—the party of Lincoln, who had issued the Emancipation Proclamation during the Civil War. However, FDR's programs to help the poor convinced many African Americans to vote Democrat. On Election Day, FDR won every state except Maine and Vermont.

Roosevelt Fights the Supreme Court

From the high point of his 1936 victory, Roosevelt's presidency took a downward turn. Most of the nine justices of the Supreme Court didn't support FDR's programs. Using the power of judicial review (see Chapter 3), in 1935 the Court struck down laws that it believed gave the federal government too much power. These actions threatened to destroy the New Deal.

In 1937, FDR asked Congress to pass a bill allowing him to add up to six justices to the Supreme Court. He planned to appoint justices who shared his ideas about government. This would give him the majority he

"THERE'S NOTHING
THE MATTER WITH YOU—
YOUR NURSE IS NOT
GIVING YOU PROPER
TREATMENT!"

"Dr. Roosevelt" reassures the Constitution that the New Deal won't harm it. Instead, FDR blames "Nurse Supreme Court" for any problems.

needed to save his programs from being overturned. Both Republicans and Democrats harshly criticized FDR's Court-packing bill. They said it interfered with the system of checks and balances that were set up by the U.S. Constitution. Congress agreed and voted it down.

In the end, Roosevelt did achieve his goal of a more sympathetic Court. Within the next two and a half years, retirements and deaths allowed Roosevelt to name five liberal justices to the bench. But the president may have lost more than he won. His clumsy attempt to pack the Court with allies damaged his image and gave ammunition to his critics.

*Reading*History

C. Recognizing Effects What was the outcome of Roosevelt's attempt to pack the Court?

The New Deal Slows Down

Opposition to Roosevelt grew after the Court-packing attempt. Then in late 1937, the economy worsened again. The amount of goods produced by industry fell, and unemployment rose. Many Americans blamed Roosevelt for the downturn.

Critics also attacked Roosevelt's use of **deficit spending,** or using borrowed money to fund government programs. Roosevelt himself had doubts about it. Even though some economists said that huge amounts of deficit spending were needed to boost the economy, FDR hesitated to take that course. He proposed few new programs in his second term. Meanwhile, as Section 3 explains, Americans continued to suffer from harsh economic conditions.

Section **2** Assessment

1. Terms & Names

Explain the significance of:
- Franklin Delano Roosevelt
- fireside chat
- New Deal
- Hundred Days
- Social Security Act
- Second New Deal
- deficit spending

2. Taking Notes

Use a chart like the one below to list FDR's major programs and whether you think each program's goal was relief, recovery, or reform (or a combination of these).

Program	Goal

Which programs created jobs?

3. Main Ideas

a. How did Roosevelt give Americans hope?

b. What happened during the period known as the Hundred Days?

c. What were the consequences of FDR's attempt to increase the size of the Supreme Court?

4. Critical Thinking

Analyzing Points of View
What were some of the different reasons that people criticized FDR?

THINK ABOUT
- the conservatives
- Huey Long, Father Coughlin, and Francis Townshend
- those who opposed the Court-packing bill

ACTIVITY OPTIONS

ART

TECHNOLOGY

Choose one aspect of the New Deal that you have an opinion about. Create a **political cartoon** or design a **Web page** expressing your opinion.

③ Life During the Depression

TERMS & NAMES
Dust Bowl
Eleanor Roosevelt
Congress of
  Industrial
  Organizations (CIO)
sit-down strike

MAIN IDEA	WHY IT MATTERS NOW
During the Depression, most Americans knew great hardship.	Because of this, a generation was scarred by suffering in ways that later generations were not.

ONE AMERICAN'S STORY

Born to former slaves, Mary McLeod Bethune refused to accept the racial stereotype that all she could be was a servant. She gained an education and went on to found Bethune-Cookman College. In 1936, FDR named her director of the Division of Negro Affairs at the National Youth Administration. Bethune ran training programs for 600,000 African-American young people. She also supervised her college from afar. Because of her health, her doctor told her to stop working so hard.

A VOICE FROM THE PAST

I promise to reform, but in an hour the promise is forgotten. For I am my mother's daughter, and the drums of Africa still beat in my heart. They will not let me rest while there is a single Negro boy or girl without a chance to prove his worth.

Mary McLeod Bethune, "Faith That Moved a Dump Heap"

A friend of Mrs. Roosevelt, Mary McLeod Bethune became the first African-American woman to head a federal agency.

Section 3 discusses the difficulty of living during the Depression— and the efforts of people like Bethune to make the hard times easier.

The Dust Bowl Destroys Lives

In the early 1930s, a drought hit the Great Plains and lasted for several years. Even before then, the overgrazing of livestock and the overplowing of fields had damaged the land by destroying the natural grasses whose roots anchored the soil. A journalist wrote, "You could hear the fields crack and dry, and the only movement in the down-driving heat was the dead withering of the dry blighted leaves on the twigs."

Winds picked up dirt from the dry, exposed fields. During dust storms, noon turned into night as walls of dust filled the air and hid the sun. Dust damaged farms across a 150,000-square-mile region called the **Dust Bowl,** which covered parts of Kansas, Oklahoma, Texas, Colorado, and New Mexico. Dust storms ripped through the plains for years until rain and improved farming methods finally brought relief.

With their crops buried under layers of dirt, ruined farmers loaded their belongings onto trucks and set off with their families to find work.

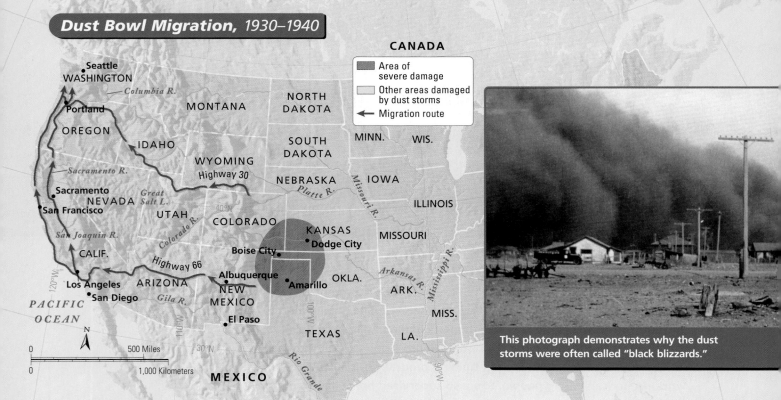

Dust Bowl Migration, 1930–1940

CANADA

- ▨ Area of severe damage
- ▢ Other areas damaged by dust storms
- ← Migration route

Seattle
WASHINGTON
Columbia R.
Portland
OREGON
MONTANA
NORTH DAKOTA
MINN.
WIS.
IDAHO
SOUTH DAKOTA
Sacramento R.
WYOMING
Highway 30
NEBRASKA
IOWA
Sacramento
NEVADA
Great Salt L.
Platte R.
Missouri R.
ILLINOIS
San Francisco
UTAH
40°N
San Joaquin R.
Colorado R.
COLORADO
KANSAS
Dodge City
MISSOURI
CALIF.
Highway 66
Boise City
Arkansas R.
Mississippi R.
Los Angeles
ARIZONA
Albuquerque
NEW MEXICO
Amarillo
OKLA.
ARK.
San Diego
Gila R.
100°W
MISS.
PACIFIC OCEAN
El Paso
120°W
N
TEXAS
LA.
0   500 Miles
30°N
0   1,000 Kilometers
Rio Grande
MEXICO
90°W

This photograph demonstrates why the dust storms were often called "black blizzards."

GEOGRAPHY SKILLBUILDER Interpreting Maps

1. **Place** Which states suffered the most damage from the dust storms?
2. **Movement** What were the main highways that people took to leave the Dust Bowl, and where did they lead?

Many drove west on Route 66, the main highway to California. They had heard that California's farms needed workers.

But as the newcomers poured in, California farm towns quickly became overcrowded. Families lived in tiny shacks. By 1940, about 2.5 million people fleeing the Dust Bowl had made their way to California and other Pacific coast states. Because many had come from Oklahoma, they were sometimes called "Okies."

Living Through Hard Times

Not just in the Dust Bowl, but all over the country, families suffered. Even after the recovery measures of the New Deal, unemployment remained high. In 1936, for example, 9 million people had no jobs.

Without work, families couldn't afford to buy food. Bread lines offering food to the hungry appeared across the country. In January 1931, New York's 82 bread lines served an average of 85,000 small meals a day: bread and soup or bread and stew. Men, women, and children waited in these lines for their daily food. Some fainted from hunger while they waited.

Many people also lost their homes. Thousands of homeless people sought shelter under bridges and overpasses. One woman remembered "people living in old, rusted out car bodies. . . . There were people living in shacks made of orange crates. One family with a whole lot of kids were living in a piano box."

Reading **History**

A. Reading a Map Look at the map above. Notice the three states that most Dust Bowl migrants went to.

Children had to grow up fast during the Depression. To add to their family's income, boys worked after school or even dropped out of school. Often girls had to stay home to look after younger children. Sometimes teenagers who failed to find jobs ran away from home to avoid burdening their families. By late 1932, perhaps a quarter million teens roamed the country. They sneaked onto freight trains, begged for food, and lived in squatter camps along the railroad tracks.

*Reading*History
B. Summarizing
What were the various hardships suffered by families during the Depression?

Family life suffered as many unemployed men felt a loss of status. They sometimes became irritable and quarreled with their families. Working women came under pressure to give up their jobs to jobless men. In fact, some New Deal projects would hire a woman only if her husband had a job. Even so, poverty forced many women to work as servants or at other low-paying jobs that men didn't want.

Artists Portray the Struggle

Many books of the period described the hard times. *Let Us Now Praise Famous Men* (1941) by James Agee and Walker Evans reported on the harsh lives of tenant farmers. John Steinbeck's novel *The Grapes of Wrath* (1939) told of Okies who had been evicted from their farms.

Vocabulary
evicted: forced to leave property

A VOICE FROM THE PAST

Carloads, caravans, homeless and hungry; twenty thousand and fifty thousand and a hundred thousand and two hundred thousand. They streamed over the mountains, hungry and restless—restless as ants, scurrying to find work to do—to lift, to push, to pull, to pick, to cut—anything, any burden to bear, for food. The kids are hungry. We got no place to live. Like ants scurrying for work, for food, and most of all for land.

John Steinbeck, *The Grapes of Wrath*

The African-American writer Richard Wright was one of many writers who were hired by the Works Progress Administration. Freed from his economic worries, he also wrote creatively in his spare time and produced the novel *Native Son* (1940). It depicts one African American's anger about society's racism.

daily *life*

HAVING FUN DURING HARD TIMES

To forget life's troubles, people went to the movies. At first, the Depression caused attendance to decline. But audiences soon grew as hard times made people eager for entertainment.

Viewers flocked to escapist movies such as *The Wizard of Oz*. People also saw realistic movies about the times, such as *The Grapes of Wrath*, based on John Steinbeck's novel.

Reading comic books about superheroes also was a popular pastime. Comic books were first published in 1933. *Superman* was introduced in 1938.

▼ *The Grapes of Wrath*

▼ *Gone with the Wind*

◀ *The Wizard of Oz*

Photographers also captured Depression-era suffering. Dorothea Lange was one of several photographers whom the government hired to document the times. Her pictures show the hard lives of poor people during the Depression. (See pages 343 and 349.)

Women in the New Deal

The first lady, **Eleanor Roosevelt,** worked to help poor Americans. Because her husband had a disability, Mrs. Roosevelt acted as his "eyes and ears." She toured the country, visiting coal mines, work camps, and hospitals to find out how programs were working. Then she told the president what she learned and made suggestions.

In March 1933, Eleanor Roosevelt began to hold regular press conferences for women reporters. At these, the first lady introduced the women who ran New Deal programs. During Roosevelt's presidency, more women held positions with the government than ever before.

In 1933, the president named Frances Perkins secretary of labor, which made her the first female cabinet officer. Years earlier, Perkins had assisted Jane Addams at Chicago's Hull House. As secretary of labor, she supported laws granting a minimum wage, a limit on child employment, and unemployment compensation.

Minorities and the Depression

Mary McLeod Bethune was one of several African Americans who played a role in the government. They were called FDR's "Black Cabinet." This group included William Hastie and Robert C. Weaver. Hastie was a brilliant young lawyer who worked in the Department of the Interior. Weaver, an economist who had graduated from Harvard, became the president's adviser on racial issues.

Though he included more African Americans in government, FDR failed to back civil rights laws. For example, he did not support an antilynching bill. FDR opposed lynching but feared upsetting Southern white congressmen. Roosevelt said, "If I come out for the antilynching bill now, [the Southerners] will block every bill I ask Congress to pass to keep America from collapsing." In spite of this, African Americans remained loyal to the president because of his efforts to help the poor.

The Depression also greatly affected Mexican Americans. Many lived in rural areas, especially in the Southwest. Increasingly, migrants from other areas competed with them for jobs. Mexican Americans living in cities also had difficulty finding scarce jobs. While many Mexican Americans did benefit from New Deal programs, in general they received less aid than other groups.

*Reading*History
C. Making Inferences Why do you think Eleanor Roosevelt publicized the women who worked in government?

*Reading*History
D. Contrasting How did African Americans and Mexican Americans benefit differently from the New Deal?

During the 1930s, immigration from Mexico declined. In addition, many immigrants returned to Mexico. Some left on their own; the federal government deported others. Some of those who were forced to leave were U.S. citizens whose rights were ignored. Because they feared deportation, many Mexican Americans stopped applying for aid.

Life improved somewhat for Native Americans. In 1934, Congress passed the Indian Reorganization Act, which restored some reservation lands to Indian ownership. It also created the Indian Arts and Crafts Board to promote native arts.

Unions Gain Strength

Background
John L. Lewis had been president of the United Mine Workers of America since 1920.

Some minorities joined a new labor organization. The country's largest labor organization was the American Federation of Labor (AFL). It was open only to skilled workers, such as plumbers and electricians. Labor leader John L. Lewis wanted industrywide unions that included both skilled and unskilled workers. He and other leaders founded the **Congress of Industrial Organizations (CIO),** which broke from the AFL in 1938. It was more open to women and minorities than the AFL.

In the 1930s, the labor movement used an effective bargaining tactic called the **sit-down strike.** Instead of walking off their jobs, striking workers remained idle inside the plant. As a result, factory owners could not hire strikebreakers to do the work.

The Wagner Act, passed in 1935, gave unions the ability to negotiate better working conditions. Union membership jumped from 2.7 million in 1933 to 7.0 million in 1937. The growing strength of labor unions was just one legacy of the New Deal. Section 4 discusses other legacies of the Great Depression and the New Deal.

In early 1939, a women's group refused to rent a hall for opera star Marian Anderson's performance because of her race. So Mrs. Roosevelt asked her to sing at the Lincoln Memorial.

Section 3 Assessment

1. Terms & Names
Explain the significance of:
- Dust Bowl
- Eleanor Roosevelt
- Congress of Industrial Organizations (CIO)
- sit-down strike

2. Taking Notes
Use a cluster diagram like the one below to record details about life during the Depression.

3. Main Ideas
a. How did storms in the Dust Bowl contribute to economic problems?

b. What effect did the Depression have on families?

c. How did Eleanor Roosevelt help her husband, the president?

4. Critical Thinking
Recognizing Effects What were some positive and negative results of the government's policies toward minorities during the Depression?

THINK ABOUT
- African Americans
- Mexican Americans
- Native Americans

ACTIVITY OPTIONS

SPEECH

ART

You have been asked to teach young children about life during the Depression. Write and perform a **monologue** or create a **comic strip** about it.

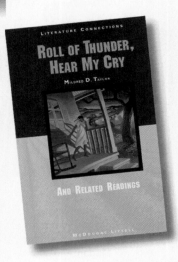

from
ROLL OF THUNDER, HEAR MY CRY

by Mildred D. Taylor

Even before the Depression, many African Americans struggled with poverty. When the Depression began, hard times made it more difficult for them to get ahead— or to keep what they had. Because the Logan family owns land in Mississippi, they are better off than their sharecropper neighbors. But they also have more to lose.

"Little Man, would you come on? You keep it up and you're gonna make us late."

My youngest brother paid no attention to me. Grasping more firmly his newspaper-wrapped notebook and his tin-can lunch of cornbread and oil sausages, he continued to concentrate on the dusty road. He lagged several feet behind my other brothers, Stacey and Christopher-John, and me, attempting to keep the rusty Mississippi dust from swelling with each step and drifting back upon his shiny black shoes and the cuffs of his corduroy pants by lifting each foot high before setting it gently down again. Always meticulously neat, six-year-old Little Man never allowed dirt or tears or stains to mar anything he owned. Today was no exception.

"You keep it up and make us late for school, Mama's gonna wear you out," I threatened, pulling with exasperation at the high collar of the Sunday dress Mama had made me wear for the first day of school—as if that event were something special. It seemed to me that showing up at school at all on a bright August-like October morning made for running the cool forest trails and wading barefoot in the forest pond was concession enough; Sunday clothing was asking too much. Christopher-John and Stacey were not too pleased about the clothing or school either. Only Little Man, just beginning his school career, found the prospects of both intriguing.

"Y'all go ahead and get dirty if y'all wanna," he replied without even looking up from his studied steps. "Me, I'm gonna stay clean."

"I betcha Mama's gonna 'clean' you, you keep it up," I grumbled.

"Ah, Cassie, leave him be," Stacey admonished, frowning and kicking testily at the road.

"I ain't said nothing but—"

Stacey cut me a wicked look and I grew silent. His disposition had been irritatingly sour lately. If I hadn't known the cause of it, I could have forgotten very easily that he was, at twelve, bigger than I, and that I had promised Mama to arrive at school looking clean and ladylike. "Shoot," I mumbled finally, unable to restrain myself from further comment, "it ain't my fault you gotta be in Mama's class this year."

Stacey's frown deepened and he jammed his fists into his pockets, but said nothing.

Christopher-John, walking between Stacey and me, glanced uneasily at both of us but did not interfere. A short, round boy of seven, he took little interest in troublesome things, preferring to remain on good terms with everyone. Yet he was always sensitive to others and now, shifting the handle of his lunch can from his right hand to his right wrist and his smudged notebook from his left hand to his left armpit, he stuffed his free hands into his pockets and attempted to make his face as moody as Stacey's and as cranky as mine. But after a few moments he seemed to forget that he was supposed to be grouchy and began whistling cheerfully. There was little that could make Christopher-John unhappy for very long, not even the thought of school.

I tugged again at my collar and dragged my feet in the dust, allowing it to sift back onto my socks and shoes like gritty red snow. I hated the dress. And the shoes. There was little I could do in a dress, and as for shoes, they imprisoned freedom-loving feet accustomed to the feel of the warm earth.

"Cassie, stop that," Stacey snapped as the dust billowed in swirling clouds around my feet. I looked up sharply, ready to protest. Christopher-John's whistling increased to a raucous, nervous shrill, and grudgingly I let the matter drop and trudged along in moody silence, my brothers growing as pensively quiet as I.

Before us the narrow, sun-splotched road wound like a lazy red serpent dividing the high forest bank of quiet, old trees on the left from the cotton field, forested by giant green-and-purple stalks, on the right. A barbed-wire fence ran the length of the deep field, stretching eastward for over a quarter of a mile until it met the sloping green pasture that signaled the end of our family's four hundred acres. An ancient oak tree on the slope, visible even now, was the official dividing mark between Logan land and the beginning of a dense forest. Beyond the protective fencing of the forest, vast farming fields, worked by a multitude of sharecropping families, covered two thirds of a ten-square-mile plantation. That was Harlan Granger land.

Once our land had been Granger land too, but the Grangers had sold it during Reconstruction to a Yankee for tax money. In 1887, when the land was up for sell again, Grandpa had bought two hundred acres of it, and in 1918, after the first two hundred acres had been paid off, he had bought another two hundred. It was good rich land, much of it still virgin forest, and there was no debt on half of it. But there was a **mortgage**[1] on the two hundred acres bought in 1918 and there were taxes on the full four hundred, and for the past three years there had not been enough money from the cotton to pay both and live on too.

That was why Papa had gone to work on the railroad.

In 1930 the price of cotton dropped. And so, in the spring of 1931, Papa set out looking for work, going as far north as Memphis and as far south as the Delta country. He had gone west too, into Louisiana. It was there he found work laying track for the railroad. He worked the remainder of the year away from us, not returning until the deep winter when the ground was cold and barren. The following spring after the planting was finished, he did the same. Now it was 1933, and Papa was again in Louisiana laying track.

I asked him once why he had to go away, why the land was so important. He took my hand and said in his quiet way: "Look out there, Cassie girl. All that belongs to you. You ain't never had to live on nobody's place but your own and long as I live and the family survives, you'll never have to. That's important. You may not understand that now, but one day you will. Then you'll see."

I looked at Papa strangely when he said that, for I knew that all the land did not belong to me. Some of it belonged to Stacey, Christopher-John, and Little Man, not to mention the part that belonged to Big Ma, Mama, and Uncle Hammer, Paper's older brother who lived in Chicago. But Papa never divided the land in his mind; it was simply Logan land. For it he would work the long, hot summer pounding steel; Mama would teach and run the farm; Big Ma, in her sixties, would work like a woman of twenty in the fields and keep the house; and the boys and I would wear threadbare clothing washed to dishwater color; but always, the taxes and the mortgage would be paid.

---

1. mortgage: the transfer of a deed to property, usually in exchange for a loan.

This Dorothea Lange photograph shows sharecroppers like the Logans' neighbors.

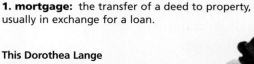

CONNECT TO HISTORY

1. **Analyzing Causes** Which of the economic problems shown in the graphs on page 328 has been making life hard for the Logan family?

   S See Skillbuilder Handbook, page R11.

CONNECT TO TODAY

2. **Researching** What are current interest rates on mortgages?

For more about the Great Depression . . .

RESEARCH LINKS
CLASSZONE.COM

4 The Effects of the New Deal

TERMS & NAMES
Securities and
  Exchange
  Commission
liberal
conservative

MAIN IDEA	WHY IT MATTERS NOW
The Depression and the New Deal had many long-term effects on U.S. government and society.	Politicians still debate how large a role government should play in American life.

ONE AMERICAN'S STORY

Until 1935, Ward James worked as a writer for a New York publisher. Then he lost his job. His wife and son went to Ohio to live with her parents. James moved in with a friend and applied for government relief. Even after he got a steady writing job with the WPA, Ward James continued to worry about what would happen next.

The fear and despair described by Ward James was felt by many unemployed people during the Depression.

> *A VOICE FROM THE PAST*
>
> Everyone was emotionally affected. We developed a fear of the future which was very difficult to overcome. Even though I eventually went into some fairly good jobs, there was still this constant dread: everything would be cut out from under you and you wouldn't know what to do. It would be even harder, because you were older.
>
> **Ward James,** quoted in *Hard Times*

Years after the Depression, James still had "a little fear . . . that it might happen again." As this section explains, both the Depression and the New Deal had lasting effects on Americans and their government.

Lasting Effects of the Depression

Americans like Ward James who lived through the Depression often saw themselves as the survivors of a terrible battle. For the rest of their lives, many feared losing their money and property again. One elderly government worker bought land whenever she could afford it so that if the Depression returned, she would "have something to live off."

Virginia Durr, who had worked for the federal government under FDR, said that the Depression affected people in two ways. "The great majority reacted by thinking money is the most important thing in the world. . . . And there was a small number of people who felt the whole system was lousy. You have to change it."

The New Deal did not end the Depression. Even with all the new programs, the government still wasn't spending enough money to jump-start a stalled economy. Then, in the 1940s, World War II changed the situation. To fight in that war, the government had to purchase guns, tanks, ships, airplanes, and other military equipment. The defense industry hired many people, who then had more money to spend. The U.S. economy started growing again.

Although the New Deal didn't end the Depression, it forever changed the U.S. government. As Supreme Court justice John Clarke told FDR, "You have put a new face upon the social and political life of our country."

> *"We developed a fear of the future."*
>
> **Ward James**

A Larger Role for Government

*Reading*History
A. Recognizing Effects How did FDR increase the president's power?

President Roosevelt increased the president's power. Under FDR, the White House became the center of government. More than other early-20th-century presidents, Roosevelt proposed bills and programs for Congress to consider instead of waiting for Congress to act.

Other nations also saw the rise of strong leaders. But at the same time, those nations saw a loss of freedom. For example, during the Depression, Germany elected Adolf Hitler, who became a dictator. The United States did have some leaders who abused power—such as Huey Long—but they never became president. FDR's leadership and his concern for the poor helped Americans keep their faith in democracy.

As well as increasing the president's power, Roosevelt also expanded the federal government. Because of the New Deal, the federal government became directly responsible for people's well-being in a way it had not

---

CONNECTIONS TO MATH

Effects of the New Deal, *1929–1941*

Although Franklin Roosevelt's New Deal programs did not end the Depression, they did make some economic conditions better. Use these graphs to determine how the New Deal—begun in 1933—affected the unemployment rate, the number of bank closings, and the number of business failures.

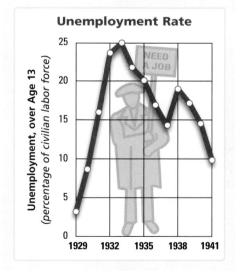

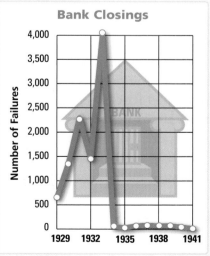

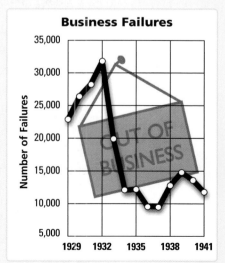

Sources: *Historical Statistics of the United States*

SKILLBUILDER Interpreting Graphs

1. *Judging from these graphs, did the Depression's negative effects on business improve after FDR took office in 1933? Explain.*
2. *In which area was there the biggest change for the better?*

HISTORY through ART

The Works Progress Administration (WPA) created many jobs. One of the WPA's most enduring legacies is the art that it commissioned. Much WPA art was used to decorate public places, such as post offices and government buildings. This mural by William Gropper shows the building of a dam.

What attitude did Gropper want to convey about laborers?

been before. It now made relief payments, served school lunches, and ran a program providing pensions. People came to see the federal government, not their state or local governments, as the protector of their welfare.

The federal government went into debt to provide this aid. FDR used deficit spending both to fund the New Deal and to pay for the war. Since then, deficit spending has often been part of the federal budget.

New Deal Programs Today

Several of FDR's New Deal programs continue to help Americans today. Some of the more important programs that still exist offer the following benefits and protections.

1. **A National Pension System.** The Social Security system pays out old-age pensions (and has been expanded to include aid to other groups). It is funded through taxes on employers and employees.

2. **Oversight of Labor Practices.** Created by the Wagner Act, the National Labor Relations Board (NLRB) oversees labor unions. It also investigates disputes between management and labor.

3. **Agricultural Price Supports.** This program pays farmers to raise crops for domestic use rather than export. To receive payments, farmers must agree to limit the space they devote to certain crops.

4. **Protection for Savings.** After the bank holiday of 1933, the Federal Deposit Insurance Corporation (FDIC) was created. The FDIC insures bank deposits up to $100,000. It replaces the deposits of individuals if banks close.

5. **Regulation of the Stock Market.** A federal agency called the **Securities and Exchange Commission** watches the stock market. It makes sure companies follow fair practices for trading stocks.

Reading History

B. Analyzing Causes Why do you think FDR wanted to create an agency to oversee the stock market?

An Ongoing Political Debate

The issues that came out of the New Deal continue to shape American politics. For example, Democrats and Republicans still argue about whether federal or local government should be responsible for various programs. In addition, Democrats are more likely to be liberal and Republicans are more likely to be conservative in their political beliefs. A **liberal** in politics favors government action to bring about social and economic reform. A **conservative** favors fewer government controls and more individual freedom in economic matters.

Despite these lingering disagreements, some New Deal programs are still so popular that everyone supports them. For example, neither party wants to end Social Security, even though the system is in trouble. The amounts that people pay in through payroll taxes today do not completely pay for pensions. The system may run out of money sometime in the future.

In early 1999, President Bill Clinton announced a plan to save Social Security by using extra money from the federal budget. The Republicans accepted his plan. They knew that saving Social Security is a priority for Americans and that voters might grow angry if they made a political fight of the issue.

FDR probably would have approved. "The great public," Roosevelt said, "is interested more in government than in politics." Roosevelt felt that party labels mattered little as long as politicians "did the big job that their times demanded to be done."

In the 1940s, President Roosevelt would face another big job. He had to lead the country in fighting a world war. Chapter 13 discusses World War II and America's role in it.

Reading **History**

C. Analyzing Points of View How would you summarize FDR's view of government's role?

Now and then

SOCIAL SECURITY

Today, many young people worry that the Social Security trust fund won't have enough money for their pensions. For one thing, people live longer now than they did in the 1930s. Also, the percentage of people receiving benefits keeps increasing compared to the number paying into the system. Last, Social Security benefits have been expanded since the 1930s.

Section 4 Assessment

1. Terms & Names

Explain the significance of:
• Securities and Exchange Commission
• liberal
• conservative

2. Taking Notes

Use a bulleted list like the one shown below to list the legacy of the Depression and New Deal.

Legacy of the Depression and New Deal
• _____
• _____
• _____
• _____

What part of the legacy affects politics today?

3. Main Ideas

a. What psychological impact did the Depression have on many Americans?

b. What finally pulled the United States out of its economic depression?

c. How do today's political differences date back to the Depression?

4. Critical Thinking

Drawing Conclusions Of the following New Deal programs, which one do you think affects your life the most? Explain.

THINK ABOUT
• Social Security
• Federal Deposit Insurance Corporation
• Securities and Exchange Commission

ACTIVITY OPTIONS

LANGUAGE ARTS

TECHNOLOGY

Ask your grandparents or other older relatives what they think the legacy of the Depression and New Deal is. Prepare a **written interview** or an **audio recording**.

The Great Depression and New Deal

CAUSES

- problems in agriculture and some industries
- unequal income distribution
- too much inventory
- too much debt
- stock market speculation

BROOKLYN DAILY EAGLE   LATE NEWS
And Complete Long Island News
WALL ST. IN PANIC AS STOCKS CRASH

DEPRESSION

- stock market crash
- bank and business failures
- high unemployment
- hunger and homelessness

NEW DEAL

- relief for the hungry and jobless
- recovery for agriculture and industry
- reforms to change the way the economy worked

SWEEPING THE DEPRESSION OUT

LONG-TERM EFFECTS

- fear of future
- more influence by federal government
- more presidential power
- long-term government programs
- debate between conservatives and liberals

TERMS & NAMES

Briefly explain the significance of each of the following.

1. Herbert Hoover
2. Crash of 1929
3. Great Depression
4. Franklin Delano Roosevelt
5. New Deal
6. deficit spending
7. Dust Bowl
8. Eleanor Roosevelt
9. liberal
10. conservative

REVIEW QUESTIONS

Hoover and the Crash (pages 327–331)

1. Why did stock prices fall so quickly during the stock market crash?
2. Who did President Hoover think should help the needy?
3. How did MacArthur's attack on the Bonus Army affect the 1932 election?

Roosevelt and the New Deal (pages 332–336)

4. What was the "brain trust"?
5. What were fireside chats, and how did they affect the country?
6. Why didn't Roosevelt propose many new programs during his second term?

Life During the Depression (pages 337–343)

7. How did writers and filmmakers respond to the hard times?
8. What new bargaining tactic did labor unions use, and how did it work?

The Effects of the New Deal (pages 344–347)

9. How did the New Deal change the role of the federal government in American life?
10. What New Deal program remains popular even though it is in financial trouble?

CRITICAL THINKING

1. USING YOUR NOTES

Using your completed chart, answer the questions below.

GREAT DEPRESSION

Hoover's Responses	FDR's Responses	Citizens' Responses
Effectiveness	Effectiveness	Effectiveness

a. What do you think was Hoover's most successful response to the Depression?
b. Judging from his responses to the Depression, do you think that FDR was one of our greatest presidents? Explain.

2. ANALYZING LEADERSHIP

During the Depression, many countries turned to strong leaders. How did the Depression-era leadership of Germany differ from that of the United States?

3. ANALYZING CAUSES

Review the economic problems that led to the Depression. What similar problems exist in the economy today?

4. THEME: ECONOMICS IN HISTORY

What reforms did FDR make to ensure that the United States would never again experience such a severe depression?

5. APPLYING CITIZENSHIP SKILLS

How were each of the following citizenship skills important during the Depression: voting, staying informed about issues, and community service?

Interact with History

Now that you have read the chapter, would you give the same answer to the question, "Who do you think should help the poor?" Explain why or why not.

HISTORY SKILLS

1. INTERPRETING CHARTS

Study the chart. Then answer the questions.

Roosevelt's Presidential Elections		
ELECTION YEAR	TOTAL VOTES	VOTES FOR FDR
1932	39,749,382	22,825,016
1936	45,642,303	27,747,636
1940	49,840,443	27,263,448
1944	47,974,819	25,611,936

Source: *New York Times Almanac*

Basic Chart Elements

a. What presidential elections does this chart cover?

b. Who won each of the elections?

Interpreting the Chart

c. What percentage of the vote did FDR win in each election?

d. Most of FDR's programs were proposed in 1933 and 1935. Based on the election numbers, did his programs make him more or less popular?

2. INTERPRETING PRIMARY SOURCES

This photograph, taken by Dorothea Lange, is one of the most famous images of the Great Depression. It shows a mother and her children in a camp for migrant workers in 1936.

a. How would you describe this woman's expression?

b. Why do you think this photograph is often used to illustrate the effects of the Depression on individuals?

ALTERNATIVE ASSESSMENT

1. INTERDISCIPLINARY ACTIVITY: Science

Diagramming a Dam Find out how hydroelectric dams, such as those built by the TVA, turn the energy of flowing water into electricity. Draw a diagram or illustration explaining this process.

2. COOPERATIVE LEARNING ACTIVITY

Debating Government Policy Working in a small group, have each group member take on the role of a Depression-era leader and hold a panel discussion in which you debate the following question: Should the government go into debt to help the poor? Before holding the discussion, do further research on your leader's beliefs. Possible leaders to choose include the following.

• Herbert Hoover

• Franklin Delano Roosevelt

• Eleanor Roosevelt

• Huey Long

• Father Coughlin

• Francis Townshend

• a conservative Republican

3. TECHNOLOGY ACTIVITY

Preparing a Multimedia Presentation Choose an aspect of the Great Depression that you would like to learn more about. Using books, the Internet, and software, research your topic. Then prepare a multimedia presentation. Consider including oral histories, quotations from FDR's speeches, Depression-era photographs and art, excerpts from literature, and videotaped interviews with older relatives.

For more about the Great Depression . . .

INTERNET ACTIVITY
CLASSZONE.COM

4. HISTORY PORTFOLIO

Option 1 Review your section and chapter assessment activities. Select one that you think is your best work. Then use comments made by your teacher or classmates to improve your work and add it to your portfolio.

Option 2 Review the questions that you wrote for What Do You Want to Know? on page 326. Then write a short report in which you explain the answers to your questions. If any questions were not answered, do research to answer them. Add your answers to your portfolio.

Additional Test Practice, pp. S1–S33

TEST PRACTICE
CLASSZONE.COM

Paint a WPA Mural

Franklin Roosevelt once remarked that "the very soundness of our democratic institutions depends on the determination of our government to give employment to idle [people]." Indeed, one of Roosevelt's New Deal programs, the Works Progress Administration's (WPA) Federal Art Project (FAP), provided creative work for artists during the Great Depression. These artists created more than 2,500 murals and 100,000 paintings. Many of the works celebrate American workers. The paintings mainly appeared in schools, post offices, and other public buildings.

ACTIVITY Create your own WPA mural, as artists did during the Great Depression. Then write an exhibit note that tells viewers about your mural. Finally, give a speech dedicating your mural to your school.

A man shoes a horse in part of the mural shown above.

TOOLBOX

Each group will need:

pencils

drawing paper

newspapers to protect desks and floor

yardstick

poster-sized/oversized sheets of art paper

water-based paints

paintbrushes

STEP BY STEP

1 **Form artist groups.** Meet with three or four other students to discuss your new art project. Imagine that you have all signed a work contract with the WPA. Your job is to create a mural to show Americans at work during the Great Depression.

2 **Research the WPA and the FAP.** Use the Internet, encyclopedias, or books about the Great Depression to brainstorm ideas for your mural. Jot down the types of work people were doing, the structures they were building, and the machinery they were using. With your group, discuss these ideas and answer these questions to help plan your mural:

• Who should be in the mural?

• What should they look like?

• What should they be doing?

• What colors would best represent the subject of your mural?

3 **Sketch your mural.** Using a pencil, accurately sketch your mural on drawing paper. This drawing should be a much smaller version of the mural you will paint later.

Warren Hunter painted this mural in 1939 on the wall of the post office in Alice, Texas.

4 **Draw a grid over the sketch.** A grid consists of lines drawn across and down a drawing to form squares. Like individual puzzle pieces, each square contains a part of the picture. Use a yardstick to make your grid lines straight.

5 **Transfer the design to larger paper.** Draw another grid on over-sized paper that has the same number of squares as the scale drawing. This time, though, the grid should be much larger—as large as the oversized paper. Make sure the grid lines are faint. Now copy the original drawing one square at a time.

6 **Paint the mural.** Each group member can paint one grid area at a time. This process is like filling in the outlines of a gigantic coloring book. When your mural is completed, hang it on a wall along with the other groups' paintings.

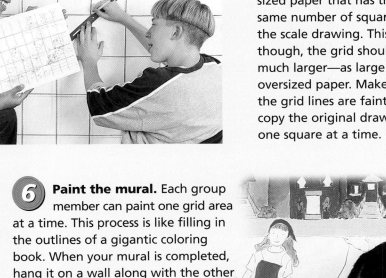

WRITE AND SPEAK

Write an exhibit note about how the mural reflects the type of work people did during the Great Depression. Attach the explanation to the back of the mural. Then, in a classroom dedication ceremony, deliver a speech dedicating your mural to your school.

HELP DESK

For related information, see page 346 in Chapter 12.

Researching Your Project

• *Life During the Great Depression* by Dennis Nishi
• *The New Deal* by Gail Stewart

For more about the Great Depression . . .

RESEARCH LINKS
CLASSZONE.COM

Did You Know?

Between 1935 and 1943, the WPA employed 8.5 million people and spent $11 billion. The average wage was $55 a month. The government poverty level at the time was $100 a month.

The agency built

• 651,087 miles of roads
• 125,110 public buildings
• 8,192 parks
• 853 airports

Among these projects were New York City's famed Lincoln Tunnel and the Fort Knox gold depository, located in Kentucky.

REFLECT & ASSESS

• Compare and contrast your image with those of the other groups.
• Why did you choose the particular image in your mural?
• How well does your mural represent the history, social issues, and culture of the time?

CHAPTER
13

The Rise of Dictators and World War II

1931–1945

The battleship U.S.S. *West Virginia* burns in Pearl Harbor in Hawaii after the Japanese attack on December 7, 1941.

Adolf Hitler, leader of Nazi Germany, is shown carving up the world for the dictators to devour.

Benito Mussolini, Italy's leader, takes his slice of the world.

General Tojo, the prime minister of Japan, awaits his portion.

The year is 1941, and the American naval base at Pearl Harbor has been bombed. Now the United States has joined the Allies in World War II. The Allies face dangerous opponents in leaders such as Hitler, Mussolini, and Tojo. You must do your part to help defeat them.

What Do You Think?

- What threat do dictators pose to the world?
- What would you be willing to sacrifice to defeat dictators?

Would you risk your life to fight against dictators?

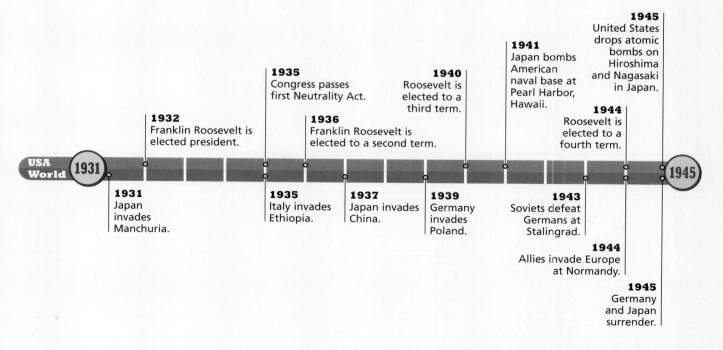

1931
Japan invades Manchuria.

1932
Franklin Roosevelt is elected president.

1935
Congress passes first Neutrality Act.

1935
Italy invades Ethiopia.

1936
Franklin Roosevelt is elected to a second term.

1937
Japan invades China.

1940
Roosevelt is elected to a third term.

1939
Germany invades Poland.

1941
Japan bombs American naval base at Pearl Harbor, Hawaii.

1943
Soviets defeat Germans at Stalingrad.

1944
Roosevelt is elected to a fourth term.

1944
Allies invade Europe at Normandy.

1945
United States drops atomic bombs on Hiroshima and Nagasaki in Japan.

1945
Germany and Japan surrender.

USA
World
1931 — 1945

BEFORE YOU READ

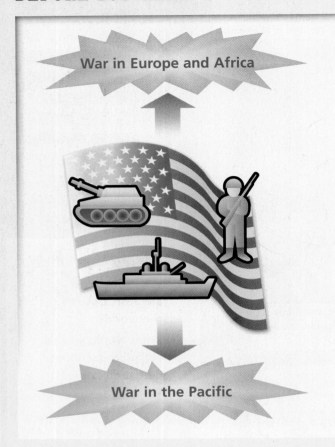

War in Europe and Africa

War in the Pacific

Previewing the Theme

America in the World The United States tried to stay out of World War II. But after the attack on Pearl Harbor, the United States entered the war. Chapter 13 describes U.S. participation in the war. It also explains how the war changed the role of the United States in the world.

What Do You Know?

What do you think of when you hear the word *dictator* and the phrase *World War II*? Where did the fighting take place in this war?

THINK ABOUT

• what you've heard about dictators from the news
• what you have learned about World War II from books, movies, or television

What Do You Want to Know?

 What questions do you have about World War II? Record these questions in your notebook before you read the chapter.

READ AND TAKE NOTES

Reading Strategy: Sequencing Events
Sequencing means putting events in the order in which they occurred. In learning about World War II, you will find it useful to list important events in order. For example, you might record important

battles and their dates in a graphic organizer such as the one shown below. Copy this organizer in your notebook. Fill it in as you read the chapter.

S **See Skillbuilder Handbook, page R4.**

IMPORTANT BATTLES IN EUROPE, AFRICA, AND THE PACIFIC

September 1, 1939—Germany invades Poland

April 1945—U.S. Marines invade Okinawa

① Steps to War

TERMS & NAMES
fascism
Adolf Hitler
Nazi Party
Joseph Stalin
Axis
appeasement
Lend-Lease Act
Pearl Harbor

MAIN IDEA	WHY IT MATTERS NOW
The rise of dictators in Europe and Asia led to World War II.	Aggressive rulers still threaten peace today.

ONE AMERICAN'S STORY

One of George Messersmith's duties as a U.S. diplomat in Austria in the 1930s was to watch events in Central Europe closely. What he saw happening in Germany worried him. Although Germany had been devastated after its defeat in World War I, it was again on the rise. In March 1936, Messersmith described what he saw.

A VOICE FROM THE PAST

The National Socialist [Nazi] regime in Germany is based on a program of ruthless force, which program has for its aim, first, the enslavement of the German population to a National Socialist social and political program, and then to use the force of these 67 million people for the extension of German political and economic sovereignty over South-Eastern Europe—thus putting it into a position to dominate Europe completely.

George Messersmith, quoted in *The Making of the Second World War*

Adolf Hitler greets a crowd of more than one million people at a Harvest Festival in 1937.

Messersmith's predictions would soon prove true. In the coming years, Germany and its allies threw the world into war, as you will read in this section.

The Rise of Dictators

By the mid-1930s, dictators, or absolute rulers, had seized control in several countries—Italy, Germany, Japan, and the Soviet Union. Their rise to power was due to economic and political factors that dated back to the end of World War I.

The treaties that ended the war had left many nations feeling betrayed. Japan and Italy, for example, had helped to win the war. However, both were dissatisfied by the peace treaties. Italy gained less territory than it wanted. Japan felt ignored by the European powers. Of the losing countries, Germany was treated the most severely. The winners stripped Germany of more than 10 percent of its territory and all of its overseas colonies. The winners also forced Germany to disarm. And they made Germany pay for war damages and accept responsibility for the war.

GERMAN SCIENTISTS

Many scientists left Germany or gave up their German citizenship after the Nazis took power. The most famous German scientist to do so was the physicist Albert Einstein (below).

Einstein, a German Jew, was visiting the United States when Hitler took control of Germany in 1933. Einstein announced he would not return home. "I shall live only in a country where civil liberty, tolerance, and equality of all citizens before the law prevail," he said. Einstein played a key role in convincing President Roosevelt to support research that would lead to the development of nuclear weapons.

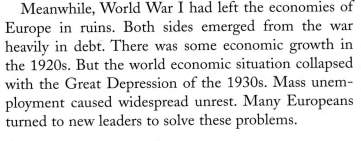

Meanwhile, World War I had left the economies of Europe in ruins. Both sides emerged from the war heavily in debt. There was some economic growth in the 1920s. But the world economic situation collapsed with the Great Depression of the 1930s. Mass unemployment caused widespread unrest. Many Europeans turned to new leaders to solve these problems.

Reading History

A. Finding Main Ideas What factors led to the rise of dictators after World War I?

Mussolini, Hitler, and Stalin

One new leader was Benito Mussolini of Italy. Shortly after World War I, Mussolini began a political movement known as **fascism** (FASH•IZ•uhm). Fascists preached an extreme form of patriotism and nationalism that was often linked to racism. They oppressed people who did not share their views. In 1922, Mussolini became prime minister of Italy. In 1925, he established a dictatorship and took the title *Il Duce* (eel DOO•chay), or "the Leader."

In Germany, **Adolf Hitler** led the fascist National Socialist German Workers' Party, or **Nazi Party**. Throughout the early 1930s, the Nazis gained power by preaching German racial superiority. They also promised to avenge the nation's defeat in World War I. In 1933, the Nazis won control of the government. Hitler then overthrew the constitution. He called himself *der Führer* (duhr FYUR•uhr), or "the Leader."

In the Soviet Union, the Communists tightened their grip on power during the 1920s and 1930s. V.I. Lenin, who led the Communist takeover of Russia in 1917, died in 1924. His successor was **Joseph Stalin.** Under Stalin, the government tried to control every aspect of life in the nation. It crushed any form of opposition.

Vocabulary
avenge: to get revenge

Background
In theory, Communists and fascists have opposing ideas about government and society. Despite these differences, Stalin and Hitler were both brutal dictators.

Dictators Seek to Expand Territory

While dictators were gaining power in Europe, the military was gaining increasing power in Japan. By 1931, the Japanese military pushed the island nation to grab more land and resources. That year, the Japanese attacked Manchuria, a province in northern China rich in natural resources. They conquered the region within months.

Both Italy and Germany also sought new territory. In 1935, Italy attacked Ethiopia, one of the few independent African nations. Italian troops roared in with machine guns, tanks, and airplanes. By the spring of 1936, *Il Duce* had his first conquest.

That same year, Hitler moved troops into the Rhineland, a region of Germany along the French border. Under the Treaty of Versailles, the Rhineland was to remain free of German forces. The French government was outraged by the treaty violation. However, it took no action. Nor did the League of Nations.

Spanish artist Pablo Picasso expresses the horrors of war in his painting *Guernica* (GUAHR•nih•keh), shown above. Picasso created this work after German planes destroyed much of the Spanish town of Guernica in April 1937, during the Spanish Civil War. Through Picasso's painting, the town became a symbol of the destructiveness of air warfare.

What characteristics of war does the painting bring out?

In 1936, Hitler and Mussolini formed an alliance known as the Rome-Berlin Axis. After this treaty, Germany, Italy, and their allies became known as the **Axis.** That year, a civil war erupted in Spain. The conflict pitted Spain's fascist-style military against the country's elected government. Hitler and Mussolini supplied the fascist forces with troops, weapons, and aircraft. In April 1939, Spain's army declared victory over the government and established a dictatorship.

In 1938, Hitler invaded Austria, home to mostly German-speaking peoples. He insisted that the Austrians wanted to be part of Germany. Many residents of Austria and Germany welcomed the unification.

Appeasement at Munich

After taking over Austria, Hitler set his sights on the Sudetenland. This was a region of Czechoslovakia where many people of German descent lived. Czechoslovakia, though, did not want to give up the region.

France and Russia pledged their support to Czechoslovakia if Germany attacked. Suddenly, Europe teetered on the brink of another war. Britain's prime minister, Neville Chamberlain, stepped in. He met with Hitler in an attempt to calm the situation. But their talks made little progress.

On September 29, 1938, Hitler and Chamberlain met in Munich, Germany. By the next day, the two sides had made a breakthrough and signed an agreement. Germany gained control of the Sudetenland. In return, Hitler promised to stop seeking any more territory.

The Munich Agreement was an example of the British and French policy known as **appeasement.** Under this policy, they met Germany's demands in order to avoid war. Chamberlain returned home from Munich and triumphantly announced that he had achieved "peace in our time."

Others, however, disagreed with appeasement. Winston Churchill reportedly wrote of the agreement: "[Britain and France] had to choose between war and shame. They chose shame. They will get war, too."

*Reading***History**
B. Analyzing Points of View What were the different points of view about the policy of appeasement?

Germany Starts the War

Hitler soon broke the promise he had made in Munich. In March 1939, his troops moved in and conquered the rest of Czechoslovakia. The *Führer* then declared his intent to seize territory from Poland. Britain and France warned that an attack on Poland would mean war.

Britain and France assumed they had an ally in Stalin. After all, the Soviet Union and Germany were bitter enemies. However, in August 1939, Germany and the Soviet Union signed a nonaggression pact. In it, they agreed not to declare war on each other. On September 1, 1939, Germany invaded Poland. Great Britain and France declared war on Germany two days after the invasion of Poland. World War II had begun.

The Germans introduced a new method of warfare known as *blitzkrieg* ("lightning war"). It stressed speed and surprise in the use of tanks, troops, and planes. German forces drove deep into Poland. As Germany conquered western Poland, the Soviet Union invaded from the east. In less than a month, Poland fell to the invading armies.

In April 1940, Hitler conquered Denmark and overran Norway. A month later, Germany launched a *blitzkrieg* against Belgium, Luxembourg, and the Netherlands. British and French troops could do little to stop the advancing Germans.

Reading **History**

C. Making Inferences Why do you think Stalin signed a nonaggression pact with Hitler?

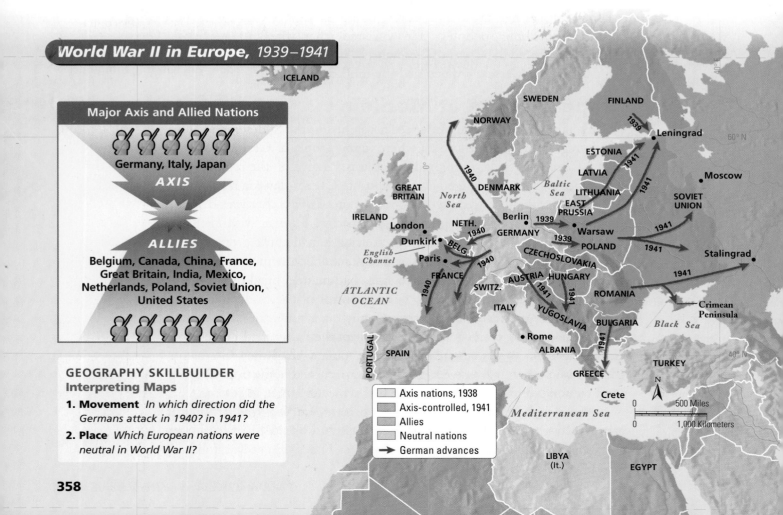

World War II in Europe, 1939–1941

Major Axis and Allied Nations

AXIS
Germany, Italy, Japan

ALLIES
Belgium, Canada, China, France, Great Britain, India, Mexico, Netherlands, Poland, Soviet Union, United States

Axis nations, 1938
Axis-controlled, 1941
Allies
Neutral nations
→ German advances

GEOGRAPHY SKILLBUILDER
Interpreting Maps

1. **Movement** In which direction did the Germans attack in 1940? in 1941?

2. **Place** Which European nations were neutral in World War II?

358

As each nation surrendered, British soldiers retreated to the French seaport of Dunkirk on the English Channel. Under heavy German bombardment, British vessels evacuated nearly 340,000 British, French, and Belgian troops.

In June 1940, the Germans launched a major offensive against France. In less than two weeks, they reached Paris. Days later, France surrendered. Hitler believed that Great Britain would seek peace after France fell.

Even though France had fallen, the British had no intention of quitting. Churchill, the new British prime minister, declared, "We shall defend every village, every town, and every city." Hitler soon made plans to invade Britain. To do so, however, he needed to destroy Britain's Royal Air Force, often called the RAF. In the summer of 1940, the German air force, or Luft-waffe (LUFT•VAHF•eh), and the RAF fought in the skies over Britain.

German planes also unleashed massive bombing attacks on London and other civilian targets. By September, however, the Battle of Britain had left Hitler frustrated. The RAF was holding off the Luftwaffe. And despite constant bombing, the British people did not surrender.

British civilians sleep in a subway station being used as an air raid shelter during the Battle of Britain in 1940.

Germany Attacks the Soviet Union

While Hitler's forces conquered Western Europe, Stalin's troops invaded Finland in November 1939. The Soviets then seized the countries of Estonia, Latvia, and Lithuania along the Baltic Sea. Despite their partnership, Hitler and Stalin distrusted each other. Hitler feared Soviet ambitions in Europe. He also wanted Soviet wheat and oil fields.

As a result, Hitler invaded the Soviet Union in June 1941. German forces moved easily through the giant country. They inflicted heavy casualties on Soviet troops. Then Hitler made a major mistake. He decided not to concentrate all his forces against Moscow. Instead, he reinforced his armies heading north toward Leningrad and south toward the Crimean Peninsula. The Germans tried to capture Leningrad from September 1941 to January 1944. About one million citizens died, many from starvation. But the city never fell to the Germans.

As German troops approached Moscow in December 1941, they ran into the harshest Russian winter in decades. Many German soldiers suffered frostbite. German tanks and weapons broke down in the cold. The Nazi advance had ground to a halt, and Soviet forces drove the Germans back.

Reading **History**
D. Making Inferences Why did Hitler attack the Soviet Union just months after signing the non-aggression pact?

The United States Aids the Allies

While the Nazis advanced, President Roosevelt tried to help the Allies by supplying them with arms and other materials. "We must be the great arsenal of democracy," he declared. He proposed the **Lend-Lease Act** to address this issue. This measure allowed the United States to lend or lease raw materials, equipment, and weapons to the Allied nations. Congress approved the act in 1941. Under Lend-Lease, the United States sent about $50 billion worth of war goods to the Allies.

Japan Attacks Pearl Harbor

In 1940, Japan joined the alliance with Germany and Italy. In 1941, an even more warlike government came to power in Japan. Its leader was Hideki Tojo (HEE•deh•kee TOH•JOH), an army general. The Tojo government made plans to invade the Dutch East Indies—a source of oil—and Asian territories.

In the eyes of Japan's rulers, only one thing stood in their way—the United States Navy. On December 7, 1941, Japanese warplanes bombed the huge American naval base at **Pearl Harbor** in Hawaii. Before the day was over, about 2,400 Americans—both servicemen and civilians—died. Many of the American warplanes and ships were destroyed or damaged.

President Roosevelt asked Congress to declare war on Japan. He called December 7, 1941, "a date which will live in infamy." The nation quickly united behind him. On December 11, Germany and Italy declared war on the United States. In the next section, you will read about U.S. participation in the war in Europe.

America's HERITAGE

U.S.S. *ARIZONA* MEMORIAL

The U.S.S. *Arizona* suffered extensive damage during the attack on Pearl Harbor. The ship sank, and 1,177 of its crew died. The nation chose not to raise the ship. Instead, officials created a memorial (shown below) that sits above the sunken hull.

The names of all the crewmen who perished aboard the ship are carved on the memorial. To commemorate the 50th anniversary of the attack, President George Bush visited the site and dropped flowers in the water above the ship.

*Reading*History
E. Analyzing Causes What was the main source of conflict between Japan and the United States?

Section 1 Assessment

1. Terms & Names

Explain the significance of:
- fascism
- Adolf Hitler
- Nazi Party
- Joseph Stalin
- Axis
- appeasement
- Lend-Lease Act
- Pearl Harbor

2. Taking Notes

Use a diagram to review events that led to American participation in World War II.

Event 1 → Event 2
Event 3 → Event 4

Which of these events do you think was the most important? Why?

3. Main Ideas

a. Who were the main Axis powers? Who were the main Allied powers?

b. Why was Hitler unable to conquer Great Britain?

c. What event prompted U.S. entry into the war?

4. Critical Thinking

Analyzing Causes Why do you think dictators such as Hitler and Mussolini were able to gain such power in the years before World War II?

THINK ABOUT
- the peace treaties of World War I
- the worldwide depression

ACTIVITY OPTIONS

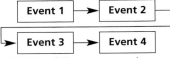

Imagine that you are a citizen of one of the countries invaded by Germany. Write a **journal entry** describing the invasion or draw a **map** of the invasion route.

② **War in Africa and Europe**

TERMS & NAMES
Dwight D. Eisenhower
D-Day
Battle of the Bulge
Yalta Conference
Holocaust

MAIN IDEA	WHY IT MATTERS NOW
The Allies defeated the Axis powers in Europe and Africa.	During World War II, the United States assumed a leading role in world affairs that continues today.

ONE AMERICAN'S STORY

Private First Class Richard Courtney could hardly believe it. Rumors had been circulating for weeks that his 26th Infantry Division was heading overseas to fight the Nazis in Europe. Now it was finally happening. His ship pulled out of New York harbor on a late summer morning in 1944. As the ship started down the river and headed out to sea, Courtney, a 19-year-old native of Altoona, Pennsylvania, described his feelings.

A VOICE FROM THE PAST

I was eager to see all the ships in the harbor and to look up at the *Statue of Liberty,* which I had seen two years before on a trip to New York with my father. . . . For a moment I considered missing Mass and staying on deck with the others to see the statue. Then my better sense took over, and I headed down the stairs to Mass. As soon as Mass ended, I hurried up the stairs and rushed out on deck to see water, nothing but water. Well, Old Girl [Statue of Liberty], I will just have to wait for the return trip to see you again.

Richard Courtney, *Normandy to the Bulge*

U.S. troops stand beside their train as they wait to travel overseas for duty in World War II.

Courtney was just one of millions of soldiers who left American shores to fight around the world. In this section, you will learn how American troops, along with those of its allies, defeated Germany and Italy and freed Europe.

Mobilizing for War

The Japanese attack on Pearl Harbor pulled the United States into World War II. Now, there was little time to waste. The nation quickly had to build up its armed forces. Millions of Americans volunteered for duty. Millions more were drafted, or selected for military service. Under the Selective Service Act, all men between the ages of 18 and 38 had to register for military service.

Those who served represented many of the nation's ethnic and racial groups. For example, more than 300,000 Mexican Americans fought in Europe as well as Asia. Nearly one million African Americans served in the armed forces. Native Americans and Asian Americans also took part in the struggle. African-American and some Japanese-American soldiers fought in segregated, or separate, units. For example, the 99th Fighter Squadron, known as the Tuskegee Airmen, consisted of African-American pilots. They served in North Africa and Italy.

More than 300,000 women also served in the U.S. armed forces. Many worked for the Women's Army Corps (WAC) as mechanics, drivers, and clerks. Others joined the Army and Navy Nurse Corps. Thousands of women also joined the U.S. Navy and Coast Guard, where they performed important noncombat duties.

Battles in Africa and Italy

The Allies began making plans to invade Europe. The Americans wanted to land in France as soon as possible. Stalin agreed. But Churchill believed the Allies were not prepared for such an invasion. He convinced the Americans that the Allies should first drive the Germans out of North Africa. This action would help the Allies gain control of the Mediterranean and open the way to invade Europe through Italy.

Since the summer of 1940, Britain had been battling Axis forces for control of northern Africa—especially Egypt. Without Egypt, the British would lose access to the Suez Canal. The canal was the shortest sea route to Asia and the Middle Eastern oil fields.

Reading **History**

A. Making Decisions Why did the Allies decide to attack the Nazis in North Africa before invading France?

World War II in Europe and Africa, 1942–1945

The Tuskegee Airmen were an all-black unit of pilots that fought in North Africa and Italy.

GEOGRAPHY SKILLBUILDER
Interpreting Maps

1. **Movement** Which Allied power captured Berlin?

2. **Place** What was the last territory in North Africa held by the Axis?

Axis nations, 1938
Axis-controlled, 1941
Allies
Neutral nations
→ Allied advances

0   500 Miles
0   1,000 Kilometers

British troops in northern Africa faced a tough opponent in Germany's General Erwin Rommel. Rommel's skills had earned him the nickname "The Desert Fox." He commanded Germany's Afrika Korps, including two powerful tank divisions. In June 1942, Rommel's tanks pushed the British lines to the Egyptian town of El Alamein. The Desert Fox was just 200 miles from the Suez Canal.

He would go no further, however. The British stopped the German advance at El Alamein and then forced them to retreat. A wave of Allied troops, led by American General **Dwight D. Eisenhower,** landed in northern Africa in November 1942. They advanced toward Rommel's army in Tunisia. In February 1943, the two sides clashed. The inexperienced Americans fell to Rommel's forces. However, the Allies regrouped and continued attacking. In May, the Axis powers in northern Africa surrendered. The Allies now could establish bases from which to attack southern Europe.

The invasion of Italy got under way with an attack on the island of Sicily in July 1943. Allied and German forces engaged in a month of bitter fighting. American nurse June Wandrey recalled trying to help the wounded.

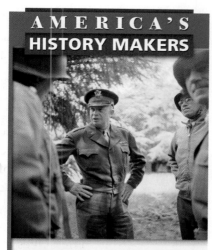

AMERICA'S HISTORY MAKERS

DWIGHT D. EISENHOWER
1890–1969

If ever there was a general who cared about his troops, it was General Dwight Eisenhower. As Allied forces battled in Italy, Eisenhower learned that he and another general were scheduled to stay in two large villas. He was not happy. He exploded.

That's *not* my villa! And that's not General Spaatz' villa! None of those will belong to any general as long as I'm Boss around here. This is supposed to be a rest center—for combat men—not a playground for the Brass!

How might Eisenhower's concern for the common soldier have affected his standing with the troops?

A VOICE FROM THE PAST

Many wounded soldiers' faces still haunt my memory. I recall one eighteen year old who had just been brought in from the ambulance to the shock ward. I went to him immediately. He looked up at me trustingly, sighed and asked, "How am I doing, Nurse?" . . . I put my hands around his face, kissed his forehead and said, "You are doing just fine, soldier." He smiled sweetly and said, "I was just checking up." Then he died. Many of us shed tears in private.

June Wandrey, quoted in *We're in This War, Too*

The Allies forced the Germans out of Sicily and then swept into Italy. By this time, the Italians had turned on Mussolini. Officials had imprisoned their leader. However, he escaped. The new Italian government surrendered to the Allies in September 1943.

The Allied Advance and D-Day

Meanwhile, Germany's difficulties in the Soviet Union had grown worse. In September 1942, German forces attacked the Russian city of Stalingrad, an important industrial center. A brutal battle took place. The Soviet army fiercely defended the city. As winter approached, the German commander begged Hitler to let him retreat. The *Führer* refused.

Fighting continued through the winter. The trapped Germans had no food or supplies. Many thousands of Nazi soldiers froze or starved to death. In February 1943, the remaining German troops surrendered.

Reading **History**
B. Summarizing What prevented the Germans from conquering the Soviet Union?

American troops storm Omaha Beach in Normandy in northern France on June 6, 1944.

Each side had suffered staggering losses. With Germany's defeat at Stalingrad, its hopes of conquering the Soviet Union appeared gone.

Hitler soon had other things to worry about in the West. In June 1944, the Allies' plan to invade France got under way. On the morning of June 6, more than 5,000 ships and landing craft carried more than 130,000 soldiers across the English Channel to a region in northern France called Normandy. The attackers included American, British, and Canadian forces. The day of this historic assault became known as **D-Day**. It was the largest seaborne invasion in history.

The attack surprised the German forces positioned along the beach. Nonetheless, they defended the region fiercely. As Allied troops hit the shore, they endured a hail of gun and mortar fire. More than 10,000 Allied soldiers were killed or wounded as they attempted to move inland. By the end of the day, however, the Allies had secured the beaches.

By the end of June 1944, 850,000 Allied troops had poured into France. They moved inland toward Paris, battling German troops along the way. On August 25, Allied forces liberated, or freed, the French capital. As they continued fighting to recapture the rest of France from the Germans, numerous American heroes emerged. One of them was Audie Murphy, the most decorated U.S. soldier of World War II. In January 1945, German troops attacked Murphy's unit in France. The 20-year-old Murphy climbed on a burning tank destroyer and used its machine gun to kill about 50 enemy troops. The U.S. government awarded him the Medal of Honor, the nation's highest military award.

As Allied forces advanced through Europe from the west, Soviet troops were beating back Hitler's army in the East. In December 1944, the German leader launched one final assault. In what became known as the **Battle of the Bulge,** German troops attacked Allied forces in the Ardennes region in Belgium and Luxembourg. The Nazi troops overwhelmed the Allies and pushed them back. U.S. forces regrouped and defeated the Germans. The Battle of the Bulge was costly. German casualties totalled 120,000. Meanwhile, nearly 80,000 Americans were killed, captured, or wounded.

Background
The Germans were surprised by the attack at Normandy because many, including Hitler, thought it would occur at Calais—150 miles away—where the English Channel is narrowest.

Victory in Europe

By February 1945, the Germans were retreating everywhere. That month, Allied leaders met in the Soviet resort of Yalta. Attending the **Yalta Conference** were the "Big Three" as they were called—Roosevelt, Churchill, and Stalin. During the conference, these leaders made plans for the end of the war and the future of Europe.

Reading **History**

C. Finding Main Ideas What was the purpose and outcome of the Yalta Conference?

Stalin promised to declare war on Japan after Germany surrendered. The three leaders also agreed to establish a postwar international peace-keeping organization. In addition, they discussed the type of governments that would be set up in Eastern Europe after the war.

By the time of the Yalta Conference, President Roosevelt was in poor health. In April 1945, just months after being sworn in for a fourth term, the president died. Roosevelt's vice-president, Harry S. Truman, succeeded him. As the nation mourned Roosevelt's death, the new president continued the war effort.

Churchill, Roosevelt, and Stalin meet during the Yalta Conference in 1945.

In late April 1945, the Russians reached Berlin. Deep inside his air-raid bunker, Adolf Hitler sensed the end was near. On April 30, the man who had conquered much of Europe committed suicide.

On May 2, the Soviet Army captured Berlin. Five days later, German leaders officially signed an unconditional surrender at General Eisenhower's headquarters in France. The Allies declared the next day, May 8, as V-E Day, or Victory in Europe Day. The war in Europe was finally over.

The Horrors of the Holocaust

Vocabulary
concentration camp: place where Germans held persecuted groups during World War II

As the Allies fought toward Berlin, they made a shocking discovery. Scattered throughout German-occupied Europe were concentration camps where Jews and people of other persecuted groups had been murdered. The world would soon learn of the horrifying events that took place behind German lines during the war. In what has become known as the **Holocaust,** the Nazis killed about 6 million Jewish men, women, and children—more than two-thirds of the Jews in Europe. The Nazis also killed millions of people of other ethnic groups, including Gypsies, Russians, and Poles. An estimated 11 million people were killed in all.

The roots of the Holocaust lay in Adolf Hitler's intense racism. He preached that other groups, particularly the Jews, were inferior to Germans. As he rose to power in the 1930s, Hitler blamed the Jews for many of Germany's troubles. After becoming leader of Germany, Hitler enforced anti-Semitism, prejudice against Jews, in numerous ways. He denied Jews many of their rights and possessions.

Survivors of the concentration camp at Buchenwald in central Germany stand behind a fence in April 1945.

Soon after war broke out, Germany's anti-Semitic policies took an even darker turn. In a policy decision labeled "The Final Solution," Nazi leaders set out to murder every Jew under German rule. To accomplish this evil scheme, the Germans built huge facilities known as concentration camps. Officials crammed Jews into railroad boxcars and sent them to these camps. They forced able-bodied people to work. All others were slaughtered. The Germans carried out their killings with terrible efficiency. For example, they killed hundreds of people at a time in gas chambers disguised as showers. They then burned the bodies in large ovens or open pits. The largest concentration camp was Auschwitz in Poland. More than 1 million people are thought to have been murdered there.

On reaching the camps, the advancing Allies were outraged by what they saw. The Allies would battle this type of hate and bias by bringing German leaders to trial for what they had done. First, however, they had to defeat the Japanese. In the next section, you will read about the war in the Pacific.

Section ❷ Assessment

1. Terms & Names

Explain the significance of:
- Dwight D. Eisenhower
- D-Day
- Battle of the Bulge
- Yalta Conference
- Holocaust

2. Taking Notes

Use a cluster diagram like the one shown below to identify the key battles and events that led to the Allies' victory in Europe.

Victory in Europe

3. Main Ideas

a. How did the United States build an army for the war?

b. Why did the Allies try to conquer North Africa before attacking southern Europe?

c. Why was the Battle of Stalingrad considered the turning point of the war in the east?

4. Critical Thinking

Supporting Opinions How might the war have been different if Hitler had decided to fight alongside the Soviet Union instead of against it?

THINK ABOUT
- the difficulties of fighting a two-front war
- the resources of Germany and the Soviet Union

ACTIVITY OPTIONS

GEOGRAPHY
TECHNOLOGY

Research the El Alamein battle. Draw a **map** of the battle or make a **database** showing the resources, such as the weapons and troops, of each side.

A Voice from the Holocaust

Setting the Stage Elie Wiesel (EHL•ee vee•ZEHL) was a Jewish boy from Romania. In 1944, when Wiesel was just 15, the Nazis sent the Jews of his town to Auschwitz in Poland. Wiesel's mother and one of his sisters died there. Wiesel and his father were sent to the Buchenwald concentration camp, where Wiesel's father died just a few months before the camp was liberated. In this excerpt from *Night,* Wiesel describes the terror he experienced on his way to Auschwitz. **See Primary Source Explorer** 🔘

The train stopped at Kaschau, a little town on the **Czechoslovak frontier.**[1] We realized then that we were not going to stay in Hungary. Our eyes were opened, but too late.

The door of the car slid open. A German officer, accompanied by a Hungarian lieutenant-interpreter, came up and introduced himself.

"From this moment, you come under the authority of the German army. Those of you who still have gold, silver, or watches in your possession must give them up now. Anyone who is later found to have kept anything will be shot on the spot. Secondly, anyone who feels ill may go to the hospital car. That's all."

The Hungarian lieutenant went among us with a basket and collected the last possessions from those who no longer wished to taste the bitterness of terror. "There are eighty of you in this wagon," added the German officer. "If anyone is missing, you'll all be shot, like dogs. . . ."

They disappeared. The doors were closed. We were caught in a trap, right up to our necks. The doors were nailed up; the way back was finally cut off. The world was a cattle wagon **hermetically**[2] sealed.

—*Elie Wiesel*

1. **Czechoslovak frontier:** the border of Czechoslovakia, a former European country occupied by Germany during World War II.

2. **hermetically:** thoroughly.

A CLOSER LOOK

A REIGN OF TERROR

The Germans attempt to rule their captives with a combination of brutality and terror.

1. What does the narrator mean when he describes "those who no longer wished to taste the bitterness of terror"?

A CLOSER LOOK

A CLOSED WORLD

The Jews as well as others were transported to the death camps in railway wagons.

2. What might be the effect of sealing people up in railway cars?

Interactive Primary Source Assessment

1. Main Ideas

a. What does the narrator mean when he says, "Our eyes were opened, but too late"?

b. What would be the effect on people of uprooting them from their homes?

c. This excerpt is from a book called *Night.* What might be the meaning of the title?

2. Critical Thinking

Analyzing Causes The horrors of the Holocaust followed from viewing and treating other people as less than human. What elements in this excerpt show the Germans treating the Jews this way?

THINK ABOUT

• the words and images used, both by the narrator and those he quotes

• the relations between those with power and those without

3 War in the Pacific

TERMS & NAMES
Bataan Death
 March
Battle of Midway
island hopping
Manhattan Project
Hiroshima

MAIN IDEA	WHY IT MATTERS NOW
After early losses, the Allies defeated the Japanese in the Pacific.	Since the war, the United States has continued to play a major role in Asia.

ONE AMERICAN'S STORY

In April 1942, more than 70,000 Filipino and American troops surrendered to the Japanese on the Bataan Peninsula in the Philippines. From there, the Japanese marched the starving, exhausted soldiers about 60 miles to a prison camp. Along the way, about 10,000 prisoners lost their lives to shootings, beatings, and starvation. Sergeant Sidney Stewart was an American soldier in the **Bataan Death March**.

A VOICE FROM THE PAST

   The sun beat down on my throbbing head. I thought only of bringing my feet up, putting them down, bringing them up. Along the road the jungle was a misty green haze, swimming before my sweat-filled eyes.
   The hours dragged by, and a great many of the prisoners reached the end of their endurance. The drop-outs became more numerous. They fell by the hundreds in the road. . . .
   There was a crack of a pistol and the shot rang out across the jungle. There was another shot, and more shots, and I knew that, straggling along behind us, was a clean-up squad of Japanese, killing their helpless victims on the white dusty road. . . . The shots continued, goading us on. I gritted my teeth. "Oh, God, I've got to keep going. I can't stop. I can't die like that."

Sidney Stewart, *Give Us This Day*

Thousands of American prisoners endure the Bataan Death March.

Allied and Japanese forces fought for more than three years in the Pacific. As you will read in this section, the fighting was brutal before the Allies emerged victorious.

Japan Expands Its Empire

At the same time as the attack on Pearl Harbor, Japanese forces launched attacks throughout the Pacific. By Christmas, Japan controlled Hong Kong, Thailand, and the U.S. islands of Guam and Wake.

   The Japanese also pushed further into Southeast Asia, attacking Malaya and Burma. Great Britain, which ruled these lands and Hong Kong, fought back. But British forces proved to be no match for the Japanese invaders. Japan conquered the region within a few months.

But it took Japan longer to conquer the Philippines. They invaded the islands in December 1941 and pushed the Allied forces from the capital city of Manila onto the Bataan Peninsula. American and Filipino troops, led by U.S. General Douglas MacArthur, then fought the Japanese to a standstill for several months.

As fighting raged in the Philippines, the Allies feared that the Japanese might invade Australia. President Roosevelt ordered MacArthur to withdraw to Australia in March 1942. But MacArthur promised, on reaching Australia, "I shall return." Shortly after MacArthur left, the Japanese mounted an offensive. The U.S. troops on Bataan surrendered and endured the brutal Bataan Death March. The situation looked bleak for the Allies. But the momentum would soon turn.

> ## "I shall return."
> Gen. Douglas MacArthur

The Allies Turn the Tide at Midway

In the spring of 1942, the Allies began to turn the tide against the Japanese. The push began in April, with a daring air raid on Japanese cities, including Tokyo. Lieutenant Colonel James Doolittle led 16 bombers in the attack. Doolittle's raid caused little damage. But it shocked Japan's leaders and boosted the Allies' morale.

Reading **History**

A. Evaluating What was the significance of the Battle of the Coral Sea?

In May, the U.S. Navy clashed with Japanese forces in the Coral Sea off Australia. For the first time in naval history, enemy ships fought a battle without seeing each other. Instead, war planes launched from aircraft carriers fought the battle. Neither side won a clear victory in the Battle of the Coral Sea. However, the Americans had successfully blocked Japan's push toward Australia.

The opposing navies clashed again in June off the island of Midway in the central Pacific. The U.S. Navy destroyed four Japanese carriers and at least 250 planes. America lost one carrier and about 150 planes. The **Battle of Midway,** in June 1942, was a turning point in the war.

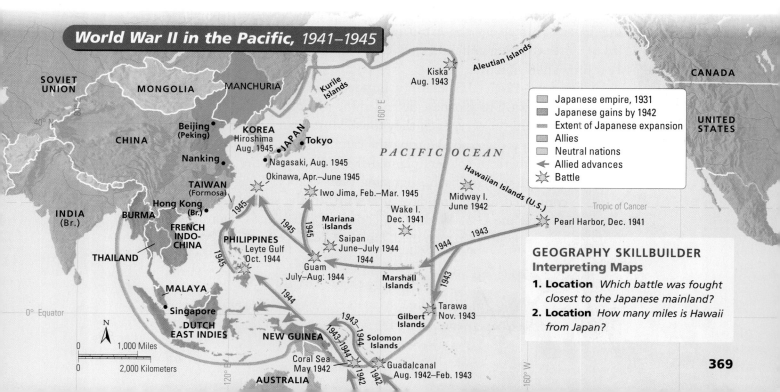

World War II in the Pacific, 1941–1945

SOVIET UNION
MONGOLIA
MANCHURIA
Kurile Islands
Kiska Aug. 1943
Aleutian Islands
CANADA
40° N
CHINA
Beijing (Peking)
KOREA
Hiroshima Aug. 1945
JAPAN
Tokyo
160° E
PACIFIC OCEAN
UNITED STATES
Nanking
Nagasaki, Aug. 1945
Okinawa, Apr.–June 1945
TAIWAN (Formosa)
Iwo Jima, Feb.–Mar. 1945
Midway I. June 1942
Hawaiian Islands (U.S.)
Tropic of Cancer
INDIA (Br.)
BURMA
Hong Kong (Br.)
FRENCH INDO-CHINA
1945
PHILIPPINES
Leyte Gulf Oct. 1944
Mariana Islands
Saipan June–July 1944
Wake I. Dec. 1941
1943
Pearl Harbor, Dec. 1941
1944
THAILAND
1945
Guam July–Aug. 1944
1944
Marshall Islands
1943

Legend:
- Japanese empire, 1931
- Japanese gains by 1942
- Extent of Japanese expansion
- Allies
- Neutral nations
- ← Allied advances
- ✶ Battle

MALAYA
Singapore
DUTCH EAST INDIES
NEW GUINEA
1944
Gilbert Islands
Tarawa Nov. 1943
Solomon Islands
1943–1944
0° Equator
0 1,000 Miles
0 2,000 Kilometers
N
Coral Sea May 1942
1942
Guadalcanal Aug. 1942–Feb. 1943
AUSTRALIA
120° E
180° W

GEOGRAPHY SKILLBUILDER
Interpreting Maps

1. **Location** Which battle was fought closest to the Japanese mainland?
2. **Location** How many miles is Hawaii from Japan?

The Allies Advance

After the Battle of Midway, the Allies went on the attack to liberate the lands Japan had conquered. Rather than attempt to retake every Japanese-held island, the Allies decided to invade islands that were not heavily defended by the Japanese. The Allies could then use the captured islands to stage further attacks. This strategy was known as **island hopping**.

The two sides fought an important battle on the island of Guadalcanal. U.S. Marines marched ashore in August 1942. Six months of bitter fighting followed. In February 1943, the Allies finally won. They had gained their first major land victory against the Japanese.

Playing a role in this victory—and many others throughout the Pacific—was a group of Navajo Indians. To keep Japanese intelligence from breaking its codes, the U.S. military had begun using the Navajo language to transmit important messages. The marines recruited about 400 Navajos to serve as Code Talkers. They accompanied troops into battle and helped them communicate safely.

In October 1944, Allied forces invaded the Philippines. The effort included a massive naval battle off the Philippine island Leyte (LAY•tee). About 280 ships participated. The Allies won the three-day battle. Japan's navy was so badly damaged that it was no longer a threat. Allied forces came ashore. They liberated Manila in March 1945. General MacArthur, three years after leaving the Philippines, had returned.

Although they lost the fight in the Philippines, the Japanese increased their use of a new weapon—the *kamikaze* (KAH•mih• KAH•zee), or suicide pilot. *Kamikazes* filled their planes with explosives and crashed them into Allied warships. Japanese pilots volunteered for these suicide missions. But they couldn't stop Allied advances.

*Reading*History

B. Finding Main Ideas What was the Allies' strategy in the Pacific?

U.S. Marines raise a flag atop Mount Suribachi on Iwo Jima.

Iwo Jima and Okinawa

By early 1945, with Japan's defenses weakened, the Allies began bombing Japan. To step up the campaign, however, they had to establish bases closer to the mainland. They chose the Japanese-held islands of Iwo Jima and Okinawa.

In February 1945, U.S. marines invaded Iwo Jima. In April, they invaded Okinawa. The Japanese defended the islands fiercely. The Allies had to fight hard for every inch they took. More than 23,000 U.S. soldiers were killed or wounded during the campaign for Iwo Jima. In late February, American soldiers planted the U.S. flag at the top of the island's Mount Suribachi, signaling their victory, though fighting continued for several days afterward. In the several months it took the U.S. Marines to conquer both islands, more than 18,000 U.S. men died. Japanese deaths exceeded 120,000.

*Reading*History

C. Summarizing What happened during the battles for Iwo Jima and Okinawa?

Atomic Weapons End the War

In the summer of 1945, Japan continued to fight. The Allies planned to invade Japan in November 1945. American military leaders feared that an invasion of mainland Japan might cost 200,000 American casualties. Therefore, American officials considered the use of an atomic bomb.

Shortly after entering the war, the United States set up the **Manhattan Project** in 1942. This was a top-secret program to build an atomic bomb. Led by American scientist J. Robert Oppenheimer, the project team worked for three years to construct the weapon.

INTERNET ACTIVITY
CLASSZONE.COM

Soon after officials successfully tested the bomb, Truman told Japan that if it did not surrender, it faced destruction. The Japanese refused to give in. On August 6, 1945, the B-29 bomber *Enola Gay* dropped an atomic bomb on the city of **Hiroshima.** The explosion killed more than 70,000 people and turned five square miles into a wasteland. Still, the Japanese refused to surrender. On August 9, the United States dropped a second atomic bomb on Nagasaki, killing another 40,000. On August 14, Japan surrendered.

The Japanese city of Hiroshima was leveled by the atomic bomb.

Background
By the end of 1945, another 70,000 people had died due to injuries and radiation caused by the atomic bomb dropped on Hiroshima.

On September 2, 1945, Japanese and Allied leaders met aboard the U.S. battleship *Missouri* in Tokyo Bay. There, Japanese officials signed an official letter of surrender.

The war changed forever the lives of the soldiers who fought in it. In the next section, you will learn about how the war affected Americans back home.

Section 3 Assessment

1. Terms & Names

Explain the significance of:
- Bataan Death March
- Battle of Midway
- island hopping
- Manhattan Project
- Hiroshima

2. Taking Notes

Use a diagram like the one shown to list events that led to the defeat of Japan.

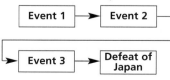

Which event do you think was most important, and why?

3. Main Ideas

a. Why was the Battle of Midway considered such an important victory for the Allies?

b. Why did the Allies want to conquer the islands of Iwo Jima and Okinawa?

c. What event finally prompted Japan to surrender?

4. Critical Thinking

Forming Opinions What might be the arguments for and against using the atomic bomb on Japan?

THINK ABOUT
- the consequences of invading Japan
- the bomb's destructive power

ACTIVITY OPTIONS

LANGUAGE ARTS

SCIENCE

Research the Manhattan Project. Write a **biography** of one of the scientists on the project or draw a **diagram** explaining how the atomic bomb worked.

4 The Home Front

TERMS & NAMES
War Production
 Board
rationing
Rosie the Riveter
A. Philip Randolph
bracero program
Japanese-American
 internment

MAIN IDEA	WHY IT MATTERS NOW
Americans at home made great contributions to the Allied victory.	World War II caused lasting changes in the lives of civilians.

ONE AMERICAN'S STORY

Margaret "Peggy" Hooper of San Pedro, California, was 17 years old when the United States entered the war. Her father went off to fight. Eventually, Hooper took a job as an "incoming inspector" at an aircraft plant. Her duties included keeping time sheets and inspecting materials. She often described her work in her letters to a friend serving with the Pacific fleet.

A VOICE FROM THE PAST

Gosh, we have been working hard at work lately. Just rushed to death and never getting through. Our production schedule has been doubled and still we work harder and put out more all the time. . . .

You had better be careful how you talk to me 'cause I have developed a big muscle in my right arm and a good strong one in my left arm, so take it easy, kid.

Margaret Hooper, quoted in *Since You Went Away*

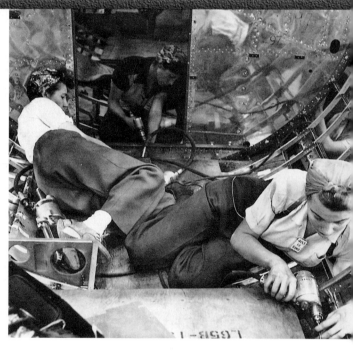

Women factory workers rivet the interior of an airplane during World War II.

World War II created jobs for thousands of citizens such as Peggy Hooper. Americans on the home front worked together to help achieve an Allied victory, as you will read in this section.

Wartime Production

The effort to defeat the Axis powers took more than just soldiers. American forces needed planes, tanks, weapons, parachutes, and other supplies. Under the guidance of the **War Production Board** (WPB), factories churned out materials around the clock. By 1945, the country had built about 300,000 aircraft and 75,000 ships. The United States was producing 60 percent of all Allied ammunition.

With so many factories in need of workers, jobs became easy to find. In effect, the war ended the Great Depression. Shortly after the war began, the nation's unemployment rate fell. The country's yearly gross national product (GNP) rose to new heights during the war. The GNP is the total value of all the goods and services produced by a nation during a year. Between 1939 and 1945, the U.S. GNP soared from $90.5 billion to nearly $212 billion.

Reading **History**

A. Recognizing Effects How did World War II affect the U.S. economy?

Because the armed forces needed so many materials, some of the items Americans took for granted became scarce. For example, American auto makers did not produce any cars between 1942 and 1945. Instead, they built tanks, jeeps, and airplanes. Items such as gasoline, tires, shoes, meat, and sugar were also in short supply. To divide these scarce goods among its citizens, the government established a system of **rationing**. Under this system, families received a fixed amount of a certain item.

The war was expensive. To help pay the cost, the government raised income taxes and sold war bonds. These bonds were loans that the government promised to repay with interest. Movie stars urged people to buy war bonds. Americans bought billions of dollars worth of bonds.

Opportunities for Women and Minorities

With so many men fighting overseas, the demand for women workers rose sharply. In 1940, about 14 million women worked—about 25 percent of the nation's labor force. By 1945, that number had climbed to more than 19 million—roughly 30 percent of the work force. Women worked in munitions factories, shipyards, and offices.

Much of the nation welcomed the growing numbers of women into the workplace. The country promoted "**Rosie the Riveter**"—an image of a strong woman hard at work at an arms factory—as its cherished symbol for its new group of wage earners.

The war also created new job opportunities for minorities. More than 1 million African Americans worked in the defense industry during the war years. Many of these jobs were along the West Coast and in the North. As a result, more than 1 million African Americans migrated from the South during the war. Many traveled to California and such Northern cities as Detroit and Chicago. The inflow of African Americans often inflamed racial tensions. In 1943, a terrible race riot broke out in Detroit. Federal troops had to restore order after 34 people were killed.

On paper, at least, African Americans enjoyed equal rights in some workplaces. **A. Philip Randolph,** an African-American labor leader, had helped achieve these rights in 1941. Randolph had threatened to lead an African-American protest march for better jobs through Washington, D.C. President Roosevelt sought to avoid such a march. As a result, he issued Executive Order 8802. It outlawed job discrimination in defense industries working for the federal government.

Background
A. Philip Randolph was the leader of the Brotherhood of Sleeping Car Porters, a powerful African-American labor union.

A. Philip Randolph and Eleanor Roosevelt chat at a labor rally in 1946.

Other minorities lent their hand to the home-front effort. Some 46,000 Native Americans left their reservations to work in the nation's war industries. Tens of thousands of Hispanics—people with ancestors from Spanish-speaking lands—also joined the ranks of the country's war-related laborers. Included in this group were thousands of Mexicans who migrated to the United States at the government's request. During the war years, the nation faced a serious shortage of farm workers. The government responded by hiring Mexicans to perform the much-needed labor. This policy was known as the ***bracero* program.** By mid-1945, more than 120,000 *braceros* worked on farms throughout the country.

Meanwhile, Mexican Americans struggled against prejudice and sometimes violence. In Los Angeles, for example, U.S. sailors often fought with "zoot suiters." These were young Mexican-American men who wore zoot suits—an outfit consisting of a broad-brimmed hat, a knee-length jacket, and baggy-legged pants. In what became known as the zoot-suit riots, groups of American servicemen attacked Mexican Americans. Beginning the night of June 3, 1943, the violence lasted 10 days before it was brought under control by police.

Reading **History**

B. Comparing and Contrasting What did the African-American and Hispanic-American experiences during World War II have in common?

The Internment of Japanese Americans

In the aftermath of Pearl Harbor, a growing number of Americans began to direct their anger toward people of Japanese ancestry. Many Americans saw Asian immigrants as a threat to their jobs. Many also believed that Asians could never fit into American society. As a result,

CITIZENSHIP TODAY

Writing to Government Officials

In the late 1970s, Japanese Americans asked the government to redress, or make up for, the injustice of the World War II internment. A letter-writing campaign by Japanese Americans helped secure passage of the Civil Liberties Act of 1988. This act included a formal apology and authorized payments of $20,000 each to Japanese Americans who were interned. The act also established a public-education program to prevent such discrimination in the future.

President Ronald Reagan signs the Civil Liberties Act of 1988.

How Do You Write to Government Officials?

1. Think about public issues that are important to you.

2. Choose one issue about which you would like the government to adopt a certain policy or take a certain action.

3. Gather information about the issue.

4. Refine your position on the issue in terms of a specific policy or action that you would like the government to follow.

5. Write a letter to your congressional representative or senator in which you urge him or her to take a particular stand on the issue.

 See Citizenship Handbook, page 106.

For more about contacting elected officials . . .

RESEARCH LINKS
CLASSZONE.COM

Congress banned practically all immigrants from Asia in 1942.

In the days and weeks after Pearl Harbor, several newspapers declared Japanese Americans to be a security threat. President Roosevelt eventually responded to the growing anti-Japanese hysteria. In February 1942, he signed an order that allowed for the removal of Japanese and Japanese Americans from the Pacific Coast. This action came to be known as the **Japanese-American internment**. More than 110,000 men, women, and children were rounded up. They had to sell their homes and possessions and leave their jobs.

These citizens were placed in internment camps, areas where they were kept under guard. In these camps, families lived in single rooms with little privacy. About two-thirds of the people interned were *Nisei* (NEE•say), Japanese Americans born in the United States.

Soldiers stand by as Japanese Americans in San Francisco board a bus to take them to an internment camp.

Background
Daniel Inouye later became a U.S. senator from the state of Hawaii.

The nation's fear of disloyalty from Japanese Americans was unfounded. Many of the camp internees raised the American flag each morning. In addition, thousands of young men in the camps volunteered to fight for the United States. The all-*Nisei* units, the 442nd Infantry and the 100th Infantry, fought in Europe. They were among the most highly decorated units in the war. One member, Daniel Inouye, showed extreme courage. After being severely wounded, he continued to lead his platoon in an attack in Italy. He lost his right arm, but earned the Distinguished Service Cross. In the next section, you will learn about other effects that World War II had on both the United States and the world.

Section 4 Assessment

1. Terms & Names

Explain the significance of:
- War Production Board
- rationing
- Rosie the Riveter
- A. Philip Randolph
- *bracero* program
- Japanese-American internment

2. Using Graphics

Use a cluster diagram like the one shown to review the ways in which Americans at home contributed to the war effort.

3. Main Ideas

a. How did the war lift the nation out of the Great Depression?

b. How did the war spur an African-American migration at home?

c. What action did the U.S. government take against many Japanese Americans during the war?

4. Critical Thinking

Comparing and Contrasting How were the war years a time of both opportunity and struggle for American women and minorities?

THINK ABOUT
- Rosie the Riveter
- African-American migrants
- zoot-suit riots

ACTIVITY OPTIONS

LANGUAGE ARTS

ART

Research the wartime life of one of the groups mentioned in this section. Write a **report** or design a **mural** about its members' experiences during the war.

Build Morale on the Home Front

You are an American helping to fight the war from the home front. You have friends and family stationed in Europe and the Pacific. You worry about them every day. To help them and the rest of your family and friends through the war, you do everything you can to keep morale high.

COOPERATIVE LEARNING On this page are three challenges you face as an American on the home front during World War II. Working with a small group, decide how to meet each challenge. Choose an option, assign a task to each group member, and do the activity. You will find useful information in the Data File. Be prepared to present your solutions to the class.

MUSIC CHALLENGE

"Jukebox Saturday Night"

Everybody loves the Andrews Sisters and Glenn Miller's big band sound. People whistle tunes like "Jukebox Saturday Night," a favorite of jitterbugging bobbysoxers. You want to write a snappy song with catchy lyrics to brighten people's moods in these tough times. Present your song using one of these options:

- Sing your song in an audition for the bandleader.
- Tape record your song to send to the bandleader.

HOME ECONOMICS CHALLENGE

"Make it do, or do without"

It's up to you to help with the war effort. How will you do it? You know that factories need certain materials to manufacture supplies for the war effort. And the troops need food. What can you do to help the troops fighting overseas? Use the Data File for help. Then present your ideas using one of these options:

- Create a list of activities that you and your friends can participate in to help the war effort, both by collecting materials and saving food.
- Write a letter to a relative serving in the armed forces explaining how the activities of you and your friends have helped him and his fellow soldiers.

DATA FILE

Life on the Home Front

- People collect tinfoil, old tools, scrap metal, lard, and bacon grease for making arms and ammunition.
- Rationed gas and tires force workers to rise early and take buses, trolleys, and trains to work. People stay home at night.
- People share housing to cut costs and provide child care for working mothers. Neighbors use one another's appliances.
- Bobby pins, can openers, flashlight batteries, boxed candy, lawn mowers, alarm clocks, and other everyday items are scarce.
- People save fuel by keeping houses at 65 degrees.

Victory Gardens

- Americans plant gardens on rooftops, in backyards, and on vacant lots, producing beans, radishes, carrots, squash, corn, and tomatoes.
- Housewives preserve corn relish, stewed tomatoes, and fruit jams.

Popular Music

Big Bands The Glenn Miller Orchestra is one of the most popular bands. It creates a special sound, mixing a clarinet and saxophones. The band's hits include "Don't Sit Under the Apple Tree (With Anyone Else But Me)," "When Johnny Comes Marching Home," "My Prayer," "Moonlight Serenade," and "A String of Pearls."

Andrews Sisters These three sisters harmonize on songs, including "I'll Be with You in Apple Blossom Time" and "Boogie Woogie Bugle Boy of Company B."

For more about the home front . . .

RESEARCH LINKS
CLASSZONE.COM

ART CHALLENGE

"POW!". . . "OW!!"

These days, battle stories crackle over the radio and fill the daily papers, bringing worry into every waking hour. The comic book adventures of Captain America help you cope with all the frightening news. This bold superpatriot and his pal Bucky find and defeat Nazis working in American factories, radio stations, and transportation systems. A recent Captain America tale gave you the idea for a super-spy character who helps the troops fighting overseas. You decide to send your idea to Joe Simon and Jack Kirby, creators of Captain America. Present your idea using one of these options:

- Create a short comic book of your hero's exploits.
- Design a cover illustrating your comic superhero.

ACTIVITY WRAP-UP

Present to the class As a group, review your methods of boosting wartime morale. Evaluate which of your solutions is the best.

Present your solutions to the class.

The Legacy of the War

MAIN IDEA	WHY IT MATTERS NOW
World War II had deep and lasting effects on the United States and the world.	As a result of World War II, the United States became the dominant power in the world.

ONE AMERICAN'S STORY

When the end of the war came, Elliot Johnson was excited. He was finally going home. At an army dismissal parade, however, one of his captains told the troops that it might not be so easy to put the war behind them.

A VOICE FROM THE PAST

When it was over, we all threw our hats in the air and screamed and yelled and cheered. . . . I recall very well one of the captains standing and looking at us without cheering. "You guys are anxious to get home and put this all behind you," he said. "But you don't understand how big a part of your life this has been. "You'll put it all behind you for about ten years, and then someday you'll hear a marching band. You'll pick up the beat and it will all come back to you and you'll be right back here on the parade ground marching again." And he was right.

Elliot Johnson, quoted in *The Homefront*

Soldiers celebrate being discharged from the service on May 12, 1945, at Fort Dix, New Jersey.

From the soldiers who survived it to the families who lost a loved one, World War II affected millions of Americans. The great struggle also touched the United States and the world in many other ways, as you will read in this section.

The War's Human Cost

No war has claimed so many lives or caused so much destruction as World War II. The human cost on both sides was immense. About 20 million soldiers were killed, and millions more were wounded. The Soviet Union suffered the greatest losses, with at least 7.5 million military deaths and another 5 million people wounded. More than 400,000 American soldiers died and more than 600,000 were wounded.

Civilian casualties also numbered in the millions. Both the Allied and Axis powers had fought a war without boundaries. They bombed cities, destroyed villages, and brought destruction to civilian life. Again, the Soviet Union experienced the worst losses. All told, about 20 million

Soviet citizens died in the struggle. China, which also endured years of attack from Japan in the 1930s, lost about 10 million civilians.

The war also created an enormous wave of refugees. They included orphans, prisoners of war, survivors of Nazi concentration camps, and those who fled advancing armies. After the war, 21 million refugees, most starving and homeless, tried to put their lives back together amid the ruins of Europe and Asia.

World War II Military Casualties, *1939–1945*		
NATION	DEAD	WOUNDED
Soviet Union	7,500,000	5,000,000
Germany	3,500,000	7,250,000
China	2,200,000	1,762,000
Japan	1,219,000	295,247
United States	405,399	671,278
Great Britain	329,208	348,403
France	210,671	390,000
Italy	77,494	120,000

Source: *World Book*

SKILLBUILDER Interpreting Charts
1. *Which two nations suffered the most casualties in World War II?*
2. *Which of the major combatants suffered the fewest casualties?*

Economic Winners and Losers

*Reading*History
A. Finding Main Ideas Why did the United States emerge from World War II so strong?

The war left many of the world's economies in ruins. Bombing campaigns had destroyed factories, transportation centers, and other important buildings. Only the United States—where no major battles were fought (except for Pearl Harbor)—came out of the war with a strong economy. The boom in industry during the war had pulled the nation out of the Great Depression. After the war, the U.S. economy continued to grow.

With the world's strongest economy, the United States set out to help rebuild the shattered economies of Europe and Japan. U.S. forces occupied Japan for several years after the war. During that time, they introduced programs that put Japan on the road to recovery. In 1948, Congress approved the **Marshall Plan** to help boost the economies of Europe. The plan was named after the man who came up with it, Secretary of State George C. Marshall. Under the plan, the United States gave more than $13 billion to help the nations of Europe get back on their feet.

Changes in American Society

The nation faced important social changes in the years following the war. For one thing, the country had to deal with the return of millions of soldiers. With so many servicemen suddenly back home, the competition for jobs and education was great. The government responded by passing a law that is commonly known as the **G.I. Bill of Rights** or G.I. Bill. This measure provided educational and economic help to veterans. The government paid for returning soldiers' schooling and provided them with a living allowance. More than 7.8 million World War II veterans attended school under the G.I. Bill.

The return of so many fighting men also created a great demand for housing. The Truman administration took steps to address the country's housing shortage. However, many Americans had to live in crowded urban slums or in country shacks.

The U.S. soldiers who returned home found an America that had changed. During the war, millions of Americans had moved to find war-related jobs in California and in the cities. Included in this group was a large number of African Americans. By war's end, hundreds of thousands of African Americans had moved from the South to various Northern cities and California. There, they lived in overcrowded ghettos and experienced prejudice. However, many also found economic opportunity.

Now and then

WAR CRIMES

More than 40 years after the Nuremberg trials (shown below), the world community once again brought army officials to trial for war crimes. These crimes were committed during brutal civil wars in the former Yugoslavia from 1991 to 1999. An international tribunal met in The Hague in 1996 to begin trying persons for their role in the conflicts.

These civil wars pitted Serbs, Croats, Bosnians, and Albanians against each other. Many people, especially Serbs, were accused of undertaking a policy of "ethnic cleansing"—the systematic attempt to rid a region of people from certain ethnic groups, often by killing them.

The Nuremberg Trials

As the United States dealt with important matters at home, the nation also joined the world in dealing with war crimes. The international community put together a court to try Nazi leaders for their role in World War II.

The trial opened in November 1945 in Nuremberg, Germany. The original 24 defendants included some of Hitler's top officials. The charges against them included crimes against humanity. These crimes referred to the Nazis' murder of millions of Jews and others. In his opening argument, the U.S. chief counsel at Nuremberg spelled out why a trial was necessary.

A VOICE FROM THE PAST

What makes this inquest significant is that these prisoners represent sinister influences that will lurk in the world long after their bodies have returned to dust. They are living symbols of racial hatreds, of terrorism and violence, and of the arrogance and cruelty of power.

Robert H. Jackson, *The Nürnberg Case*

After nearly a year-long trial, 19 of the defendants were found guilty. Twelve were sentenced to death. About 185 other Nazi leaders were found guilty in later trials. The **Nuremberg trials** upheld an important idea: People are responsible for their actions, even in wartime.

Creation of the United Nations

The war helped to establish another principle—nations must work together in order to secure world peace. The outbreak of World War II demonstrated the weakness of the League of Nations, the international peacekeeping body created after the First World War. The League was weak in large part because the United States had refused to join out of a strong desire to stay out of foreign affairs. Toward the end of World War II, President Roosevelt urged his fellow Americans not to turn their backs on the world again.

The country listened. In April 1945, delegates from 50 nations—including the United States—met in San Francisco to discuss creating a new international peace organization. In June, all 50 nations approved

Reading **History**

B. Solving Problems Why did President Roosevelt support U.S. participation in the United Nations?

the charter creating the new peacekeeping body known as the **United Nations,** or UN.

International Tensions

The horrors of World War II had caused many countries to work together toward lasting peace. However, tensions still arose among nations in the wake of the war. For example, in 1948 the United Nations helped found the nation of Israel to create a homeland for the Jews in Palestine. Fighting immediately broke out as neighboring Arab nations attacked Israel. In addition, colonies around the world began fighting for their independence.

*Reading*History

C. Reading a Map Look at the map on page R33 to find out where Israel is.

The United States, however, was more concerned with the rise of the Soviet Union. Despite suffering so much damage and loss of life, the Soviet Union emerged from World War II as a great power. It had conquered much of Eastern Europe.

Background
An important reason for U.S. leaders to drop the atomic bombs on Japan was to make the Soviets fear U.S. power.

During the war, the United States and the Soviet Union had been uneasy partners. After the war, Stalin angered the United States by breaking a wartime promise to promote democracy in the nations he had occupied in Eastern Europe. Instead, Stalin forced the countries to live under Communist regimes. The Soviet Union wanted to spread communism. The United States wanted to halt it. This led to future conflict.

Finally, the end of the war marked the beginning of the atomic age. The atomic bombs dropped on Japan showed the world a powerful new weapon. In the next chapter, you will learn how atomic weapons increased tensions between the United States and the Soviet Union.

D.R. Fitzpatrick drew this cartoon, entitled " . . . Shall Not Have Died in Vain." He hoped the memory of U.S. losses would push Americans to support the UN and preserve peace.

Section 5 Assessment

1. Terms & Names

Explain the significance of:
- Marshall Plan
- G.I. Bill of Rights
- Nuremberg trials
- United Nations

2. Taking Notes

Use a cluster diagram like the one shown to review the effects of World War II.

Effects of W.W. II

Which effect seems the most important to you?

3. Main Ideas

a. What was the Marshall Plan?

b. How did the G.I. Bill of Rights help World War II veterans?

c. What principles did the Nuremberg trials establish?

4. Critical Thinking

Analyzing Causes Why did the United States emerge from the war so much better off than other nations?

THINK ABOUT
- the geographic location of the United States
- the role of American industry

ACTIVITY OPTIONS

LANGUAGE ARTS

SPEECH

As a reporter, research and write a **news article** on a defendant at the Nuremberg trials or, as a lawyer, deliver a closing **speech** against a defendant.

The Rise of Dictators and World War II

■ Asia and the Pacific ■ Europe and Africa

1931–1941

■ 1931 Japan invades Manchuria.

■ 1933 Hitler comes to power in Germany.

■ 1936 Germany and Italy form Axis.

■ 1938 Germany takes over Austria.

■ 1939 Germany invades Poland. World War II begins.

■ 1940 Germany invades France. Battle of Britain fought.

■ 1941 Japanese attack Pearl Harbor.

1942

■ Japanese stopped at Battle of Coral Sea.

■ Japanese defeated at Battle of Midway.

1943

■ Soviets defeat Germans at Stalingrad.

■ Allies stop Axis advance in North Africa.

■ Allies invade Italy. Italy surrenders.

1944

■ Allies invade Europe at Normandy.

■ Allies invade the Philippines.

1945

■ Allies invade Iwo Jima and Okinawa.

■ Germany surrenders.

■ United States drops atomic bombs on Hiroshima and Nagasaki.

■ Japan surrenders.

TERMS & NAMES

Briefly explain the significance of each of the following.

1. Adolf Hitler
2. Pearl Harbor
3. D-Day
4. Holocaust
5. Battle of Midway
6. Hiroshima
7. rationing
8. Japanese-American internment
9. G.I. Bill of Rights
10. Nuremberg trials

REVIEW QUESTIONS

Steps to War (pages 355–360)

1. Why did Hitler attack the Soviet Union?
2. What was the Lend-Lease program?

War in Africa and Europe (pages 361–367)

3. What role did women play in the war?
4. What was D-Day and why was it significant?

War in the Pacific (pages 368–371)

5. What was the strategy of island hopping?
6. What was the Manhattan Project?

The Home Front (pages 372–377)

7. In what ways did Americans at home contribute to the war effort?
8. Why did the nation put thousands of Japanese Americans in internment camps during the war?

The Legacy of the War (pages 378–381)

9. Which nation lost the most soldiers and civilians in the war?
10. What international tensions arose after World War II?

CRITICAL THINKING

1. USING YOUR NOTES

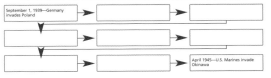

IMPORTANT BATTLES IN EUROPE, AFRICA, AND THE PACIFIC

Use your chart to answer these questions.

a. Which battle that you listed occurred first?
b. Which battle was the most important?

2. ANALYZING LEADERSHIP

Do you agree or disagree with Neville Chamberlain's policy of appeasement? Explain.

3. APPLYING CITIZENSHIP SKILLS

Imagine you are a Japanese American in an internment camp. If you were to write a letter of protest to the government, what violations of your rights would you describe in the letter?

4. THEME: AMERICA IN THE WORLD

Why do you think the United States joined the United Nations after World War II, when it had refused to join the League of Nations after World War I?

5. COMPARING AND CONTRASTING

What role did racism play in the Holocaust and the internment of Japanese Americans? How was the level of racism different?

Interact with History

After reading the chapter, would you make the same choice about whether to risk your life to fight against dictators that you made at the beginning of the chapter? Explain.

HISTORY SKILLS

1. INTERPRETING MAPS: Movement

Study the map and answer the questions.

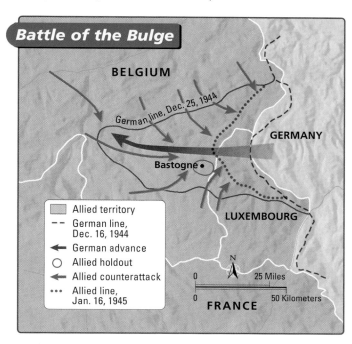

Battle of the Bulge

BELGIUM

German line, Dec. 25, 1944

GERMANY

Bastogne

Allied territory

German line,
Dec. 16, 1944

German advance

Allied holdout

Allied counterattack

Allied line,
Jan. 16, 1945

LUXEMBOURG

N

0   25 Miles

0   50 Kilometers

FRANCE

Basic Map Elements

a. In what countries was the Battle of the Bulge fought?

b. During what time period was the battle fought?

Interpreting the Map

c. About how many miles westward had the Germans advanced by Christmas 1944?

d. Why was this battle called the Battle of the Bulge?

2. INTERPRETING PRIMARY SOURCES

This poster shows a woman factory worker during World War II.

a. What does this poster reveal about women's roles in the war?

b. What does this image suggest about the abilities of women?

ALTERNATIVE ASSESSMENT

1. INTERDISCIPLINARY ACTIVITY: Language Arts

Writing a Diary Imagine you are a woman who has found a job as a welder in a shipyard during the war. Write a diary entry describing the changes the war has brought to your life.

2. COOPERATIVE LEARNING ACTIVITY

Creating a News Broadcast With a group of three to five students, create a news show about the experiences of Americans at home or abroad during World War II. Choose a specific year between 1941 and 1945 and a specific location, such as a hospital, factory, or battle front.

• Take on the roles of anchor, reporter, or interviewees.

• Write a script for your role.

• Conduct your "broadcast" in front of the class.

3. 💿 PRIMARY SOURCE EXPLORER

Making a Class Presentation Using the Internet, library, and the CD-ROM, do further research on the Holocaust and present your findings to the class. Some suggested topic ideas are given below.

• Examine in more depth one of the Nazi camps in Europe.

• Research individual experiences of the Holocaust, such as those of Elie Wiesel, Anne Frank, or Gerda Weissman Klein.

• Build a Holocaust collage, using photographs and other visuals along with corresponding captions.

• Create a map depicting the location of all of the Nazi concentration camps in Europe.

• Examine U.S. response to the Holocaust from 1942 to 1945.

4. HISTORY PORTFOLIO

Option 1 Review your section and chapter assessment activities. Select one that you think is your best work. Then use comments made by your teacher or classmates to improve your work and add it to your portfolio.

Option 2 Review the questions that you wrote for What Do You Want to Know? on page 354. Then write a short report in which you explain the answers to your questions. Add your answers to your portfolio.

Additional Test Practice, pp. S1–S33

TEST PRACTICE
CLASSZONE.COM

CHAPTER 14

The Cold War and the American Dream 1945–1960

Section 1 **Peacetime Adjustments and the Cold War**
Section 2 **The Korean War and McCarthyism**
Section 3 **The Fifties**

The photograph above shows the window of an Edsel showroom. The new car was introduced in 1957. Shown at right is the Edsel.

Interact *with* History

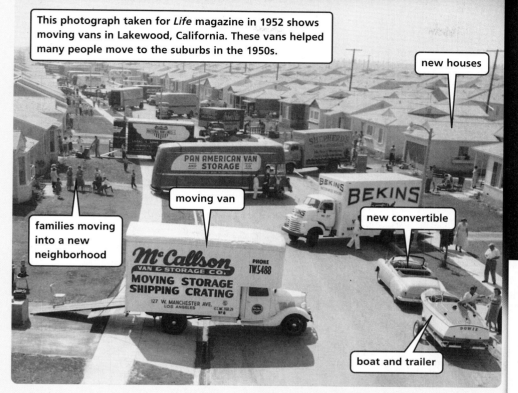

This photograph taken for *Life* magazine in 1952 shows moving vans in Lakewood, California. These vans helped many people move to the suburbs in the 1950s.

new houses

moving van

new convertible

families moving into a new neighborhood

boat and trailer

In the 1950s, American technology produced a flood of consumer goods. These included cars and houses in suburbs springing up across the country. You and your family have moved to a new house in a growing suburb—which some people think of as the American Dream.

What Do You Think?

- How might the American Dream be connected to prosperity?
- How might the American Dream involve helping others?
- How might the American Dream be connected to democracy, equality, and justice?

What is the American Dream to you?

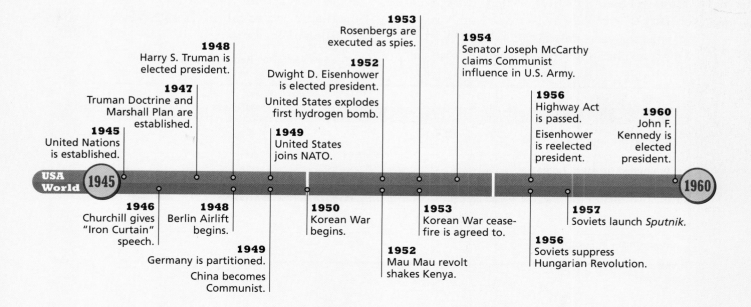

1953
Rosenbergs are executed as spies.

1954
Senator Joseph McCarthy claims Communist influence in U.S. Army.

1948
Harry S. Truman is elected president.

1952
Dwight D. Eisenhower is elected president.
United States explodes first hydrogen bomb.

1947
Truman Doctrine and Marshall Plan are established.

1956
Highway Act is passed.
Eisenhower is reelected president.

1960
John F. Kennedy is elected president.

1945
United Nations is established.

1949
United States joins NATO.

USA
World 1945 ———————————————————— 1960

1946
Churchill gives "Iron Curtain" speech.

1948
Berlin Airlift begins.

1950
Korean War begins.

1953
Korean War cease-fire is agreed to.

1957
Soviets launch *Sputnik*.

1949
Germany is partitioned.
China becomes Communist.

1952
Mau Mau revolt shakes Kenya.

1956
Soviets suppress Hungarian Revolution.

BEFORE YOU READ

Previewing the Theme

Economics in History After more than 15 years of depression and war, the United States entered a time of economic prosperity and rapid change. This chapter explains how the United States came into conflict with the Soviet Union.

(Right) Eisenhower campaign glasses. (Top) Drive-in restaurant in the 1950s.

What Do You Know?

What do you think of when you hear the phrase *the American Dream*? What sorts of dreams might a people and a nation have?

THINK ABOUT

• what you have learned about the 1950s from television and movies

• hopes and dreams that might be achieved both through and outside of politics

What Do You Want to Know?

 What additional information do you want to know about the Cold War and the American Dream? Record the sort of information you want in your notebook before you read the chapter.

READ AND TAKE NOTES

Reading Strategy: Categorizing The presidencies of Harry S. Truman and Dwight D. Eisenhower spanned the years between 1945 and 1960. There were a number of important issues, foreign and domestic, that both presidents had to deal with. Use the chart below to categorize each president's policy or action on the issues.

S See Skillbuilder Handbook, page R6.

ISSUES	PRESIDENTS	
Domestic	Truman	Eisenhower
Labor unions and big business		
Communist threat at home		
Foreign		
Korea		
Communism in Europe		

TERMS & NAMES
Harry S. Truman
Fair Deal
Cold War
containment
Truman Doctrine
NATO
Marshall Plan

MAIN IDEA	WHY IT MATTERS NOW
Americans looked for prosperity after World War II. They also fought communism in the Cold War.	The U.S. economy grew rapidly, and the nation's role in the world expanded after World War II.

ONE AMERICAN'S STORY

Harold Russell was a soldier, not an actor. Even so, in 1946 he won an Academy Award for best supporting actor in the Hollywood film *The Best Years of Our Lives.* Russell played an amputee struggling to adjust to civilian life after World War II. It was a role he knew well. As a paratrooper, Sergeant Russell had lost both hands in a grenade explosion. He was then fitted with hooks. Russell had to teach himself and others to accept his disability.

A VOICE FROM THE PAST

I was all right. My problem was to make the people I met feel at ease. I just acted myself and didn't sulk in corners hiding the hooks. When my neighborhood friends saw I was okay and laughing they said to themselves, "Why should we feel sorry for him? He's getting along better than we are."

Harold Russell, quoted in *Life,* December 16, 1946

Sergeant Harold Russell demonstrates to other disabled veterans how to drink a cup of coffee.

Russell won a second special Academy Award for "bringing hope and courage to his fellow veterans." As you will read in this section, millions of returning soldiers like Russell were preparing to restart their lives at the end of World War II.

Adjusting to Peace

The United States had spent the years 1941–1945 fighting World War II. Now, the country was at peace. The aircraft industry and other defense plants were changing over to making goods for peacetime. As part of this process, most industries reduced their work force. Factories shut down, and more than 10 million returning war veterans were looking for work.

Returning servicemen flooded the job market. Veterans won out over female workers in the competition for jobs in the first years after the war. In the aircraft industry, more than 800,000 workers—mostly women— were laid off. Several years after the war ended, as the economy boomed, employment rates for women began to return to wartime peaks. However, often these jobs were in traditional women's fields, such as office work and teaching.

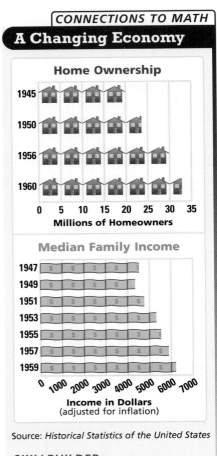

Home Ownership

1945

1950

1956

1960

0   5   10   15   20   25   30   35
Millions of Homeowners

Median Family Income

1947
1949
1951
1953
1955
1957
1959

0   1000 2000 3000 4000 5000 6000 7000
Income in Dollars
(adjusted for inflation)

Source: *Historical Statistics of the United States*

SKILLBUILDER
Interpreting Charts
1. *What period showed the biggest increase in home ownership?*
2. *About how much did family income increase in the years 1947 to 1959?*

The Postwar Economy

Instead of slowing down, as many had feared, the nation's economy boomed. During the war years, few consumer goods had been produced. After the war, people were starting families and buying new homes. They wanted cars, washing machines, toasters, and all the other goods they had put off buying during wartime. American factories were fitted out with new machinery and tools to make different products.

The spending spree led to inflation, or a rise in prices. During the war, the government had put controls on prices and wages. After the war, in 1946, the controls on prices were lifted. Consumer goods were still in short supply. People had plenty of money to spend, but few goods to buy. As a result, the demand for goods increased, and prices skyrocketed.

After the war, the number of marriages increased. At first, a housing shortage forced many newlyweds to move in with relatives. Government-guaranteed housing loans for veterans under the G.I. Bill spurred the demand for new houses. Businessman William Levitt saw a way to meet this demand. He applied assembly-line techniques to home building. His mass-produced houses were so cheap that many people could afford them. He built Levittown in 1947 on Long Island, New York. Three years later, 17,500 homes had turned the farmland into an instant suburb. However, not everyone benefited from the postwar boom.

Reading **History**
A. Making Inferences Why did Levitt's houses become so popular?

Labor Unrest and Civil Rights

During the war, unions had agreed to give up pay raises. When the government put controls on wages, the unions agreed not to strike. But with the war over, workers faced with rising prices demanded better pay. In 1946, the United States entered one of the most strike-torn years in its history. More than one million workers joined strikes in the automobile, steel, meatpacking, and electrical industries.

Later that year, both miners and railway workers also went out on strike. Although President **Harry S. Truman** was a friend of labor, he feared these strikes would cripple the nation. During the railroad strike, he threatened to draft all railroad workers into the army. He said he would have the army run the trains. But the strike was settled before Truman could carry out his threat.

African Americans were still excluded from prosperity and full equality in the postwar world. World War II had raised the hopes of African Americans for greater equality. Many African-American veterans expected their wartime service to be recognized. Particularly in the

South, however, little had changed. In many Southern states, African Americans who attempted to vote were threatened, fired from their jobs, and even murdered.

To deal with these problems, President Truman created a commission on civil rights. He issued an executive order in July 1948 ending racial segregation and discrimination in the armed forces. Truman also asked Congress for an anti-lynching law and an end to the poll tax as a requirement for voting. However, when Southern Democrats in Congress balked at the proposals, Truman backed off. Nonetheless, he was the first president to make equal rights a national issue. The action he took began the federal government's effort to deal with racial issues.

The Fair Deal

In 1946, fears about the economy hurt the Democrats. Voters sent a Republican majority to Congress. The new Congress wanted to block Truman's programs. Congress turned down his plans to provide federal funds for housing, education, and health care. Congress also limited the power of unions by passing the 1947 Taft-Hartley Act. This act outlawed the closed shop, a workplace that hired only union members. The act also gave the president the power to require an 80-day cooling-off period before a strike.

As the 1948 presidential election campaign opened, few political experts believed President Truman would keep his job. Polls showed the Republican candidate, New York governor Thomas E. Dewey, to be the clear favorite. Even within his own party, few of Truman's supporters thought that he could win.

Ignoring politicians and pollsters, Truman took his campaign to the people. Hiring a special train, he made a tour through hundreds of cities and small towns. Wherever his train stopped, Truman blasted the "do-nothing" Republican Congress because it passed little legislation. His strategy worked. When the votes were counted, he had won an upset victory over Dewey. The Democrats had also regained control of Congress.

After his victory, Truman presented Congress with a package of reforms he called the Fair Deal. He hoped to extend the social programs begun with FDR's New Deal. The **Fair Deal** called for new projects to create jobs, build public housing, and end racial discrimination in hiring. Many Republicans and Southern Democrats worked together to block his plans. Congress passed few of his proposals. Only his low-cost public housing measure became law. In addition to problems at home, Truman faced major problems abroad.

AMERICA'S HISTORY MAKERS

HARRY S. TRUMAN
1884–1972
During Harry Truman's 1948 whistle-stop campaign, he traveled many thousands of miles in eight weeks. He was often accompanied by his daughter and wife.

Audiences enjoyed his straightforward manner and his spirited attacks on the Republicans. He blamed the Republicans for the nation's problems. When the votes were counted, Truman won an upset victory over his opponent, Thomas Dewey. A Chicago newspaper (above) mistakenly declared Dewey the winner in the close contest.

What might Truman's whistle-stop campaign suggest about his character?

Origins of the Cold War

After World War II, the capitalist Western democracies came into increasing conflict with the communist Soviet Union. Their differing economic and political systems resulted in misunderstandings. During the war, the Western democracies were allied with the Soviet Union. They were united in the struggle to defeat Nazi Germany. However, as victory grew nearer, the West and the Soviet Union distrusted each other.

The most difficult issue was the political future of Eastern Europe. In the final battles of the war, the Soviets freed Eastern European states from Nazi rule. Then Soviet forces occupied those states, including the eastern sector of Germany. The Soviet leader Joseph Stalin promised free elections to the nations of Eastern Europe. However, when the war ended, Stalin installed pro-Soviet governments throughout Eastern Europe.

Stalin feared that free elections in Eastern Europe might result in the election of anti-Soviet governments on its borders. The Western democracies saw Stalin's occupation of Eastern Europe differently. President Truman believed that Stalin intended to spread communism worldwide.

Truman was determined to protect Western Europe from the threat of Soviet expansion. As the gap between the Soviet Union and the Western democracies widened, tensions developed. The resulting **Cold War** was a conflict that pitted the United States against the Soviet Union. The two nations never directly confronted each other on the battlefield. However, the threat of deadly conflict lasted for decades.

Reading **History**

B. Comparing and Contrasting How did the Soviet Union and the West view Eastern Europe?

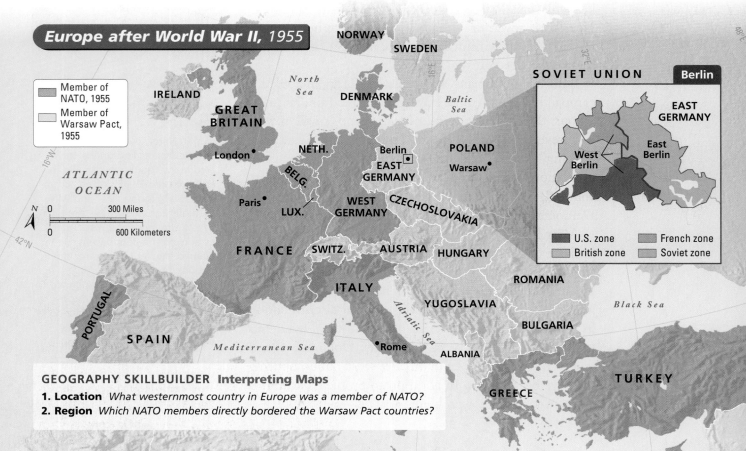

Europe after World War II, 1955

- Member of NATO, 1955
- Member of Warsaw Pact, 1955

Berlin

- U.S. zone
- British zone
- French zone
- Soviet zone

GEOGRAPHY SKILLBUILDER Interpreting Maps

1. **Location** *What westernmost country in Europe was a member of NATO?*
2. **Region** *Which NATO members directly bordered the Warsaw Pact countries?*

Containing Communism Abroad

As tensions between the United States and the Soviet Union were increasing, Britain's Winston Churchill visited the United States in 1946. He warned the world of Soviet aims.

> ## A VOICE FROM THE PAST
>
> From Stettin in the Baltic to Trieste in the Adriatic, an iron curtain has descended across the continent. Behind that line lie all the . . . states of Central and Eastern Europe. . . . All these . . . populations . . . lie in the Soviet sphere and all are subject . . . not only to Soviet influence but to . . . increasing . . . control from Moscow.
>
> **Winston Churchill,** "Iron Curtain" speech, Fulton, Missouri

"An iron curtain has descended across the continent."
Winston Churchill

Background
Truman's containment policy was first announced in 1947 in response to Soviet pressure on Greece and Turkey.

The Truman Administration's main strategy in the Cold War was its containment policy. The goal of **containment** was to stop the spread of communism. This meant that the United States would work in military and nonmilitary ways to contain communism. Next, Truman announced the **Truman Doctrine,** which promised aid to people struggling to resist threats to democratic freedom.

In 1948, there was alarm over communist control of Eastern Europe. This led to formation of the North Atlantic Treaty Organization (NATO). The **NATO** alliance included the United States, Canada, and ten Western European nations. In response, the Soviet Union and Eastern European nations formed the Warsaw Pact (see map on page 390).

Marshall Plan and Berlin Airlift

Hoping to prevent the spread of communism, the United States came up with a plan to revive the war-torn economies of Europe. The plan was named for Truman's Secretary of State, George C. Marshall. The **Marshall Plan** offered $13 billion in aid to western and southern Europe. The plan helped the nations of Europe rebuild.

Reading **History**

C. Reading a Map Use the map on page 390 to see how Berlin was divided among the four nations.

The European nation in which the Cold War almost turned hot was Germany. In June of 1945, the Allies had agreed to a temporary division of Germany into four zones. These were controlled by the Soviet Union, France, Great Britain, and the United States. The Western powers merged their zones and made plans to unite them as West Germany. Stalin feared a united Germany might threaten the Soviet Union.

Berlin, Germany's former capital, lay within the eastern zone, still held by the Soviet Union. Like Germany, it too had been divided into East and West Berlin. In 1948, Stalin hoped to force the Western powers to abandon the city. His forces blocked access to Berlin.

Truman responded by approving a huge airlift of food, fuel, and equipment into the city. For nearly a year,

An American plane brings supplies to Berlin during the airlift.

391

Ethel and Julius Rosenberg were executed despite numerous pleas to spare their lives.

U.S. and British cargo planes made 275,000 flights into Berlin. They carried supplies to the city's residents. In 1949, Stalin called off the blockade. By May 1949, Germany had been divided into communist East Germany and democratic West Germany.

Fear of Communism at Home

After World War II, a growing number of Americans feared that communism would gain strength within the United States. In part this was a response to the Soviet occupation of Eastern Europe. At first, attention focused on Americans who belonged to the U.S. Communist Party who, it was feared, might spy for Russia.

Two famous spy trials made such fears believable. Alger Hiss was a former State Department official. He was accused of passing military information to the Soviet Union. Tried for lying under oath, he was sentenced to five years in prison in 1950. Ethel and Julius Rosenberg were members of the American Communist Party. In 1951, they were convicted of passing atomic secrets to the Russians. They were executed in 1953.

Truman fought Republican charges that his administration was soft on communism. He issued an executive order requiring 3 million government workers to undergo loyalty checks. Federal workers who objected to signing loyalty oaths lost their jobs. Between 1947 and 1951, loyalty boards forced over 3,000 government workers to resign.

The anticommunist crusade gave new life to the House Un-American Activities Committee (HUAC). In 1947, HUAC began targeting actors, directors, and writers in the movie industry for suspected communist ties. Within the entertainment industry, lists of names circulated among the Hollywood movie studios. These were blacklists—unofficial lists of people thought to be communists. The careers of the people on these lists were ruined. As you will read in the next section, fear of communism dominated American life in the early 1950s.

Section 1 Assessment

1. Terms & Names

Explain the significance of:

- Harry S. Truman
- Fair Deal
- Cold War
- containment
- Truman Doctrine
- NATO
- Marshall Plan

2. Taking Notes

In a chart, explain the goals of these Cold War programs.

Program	Goal
Containment policy	
Truman Doctrine	
Marshall Plan	
NATO	

3. Main Ideas

a. Why was inflation a concern in the early postwar period?

b. What were the causes of the Cold War?

c. Why did the United States experience fear of communism after the war?

4. Critical Thinking

Forming Opinions Do you think an exaggerated fear of communism could occur again? Explain.

THINK ABOUT

- relations between the United States and Russia today
- American attitudes toward opposing views
- beliefs about communism

ACTIVITY OPTIONS

LANGUAGE ARTS

ART

Imagine that you were a child in Berlin during the airlift. Write a **letter** to a pen pal in the United States, or draw a **picture** describing your experiences.

The Korean War and McCarthyism

MAIN IDEA

The Cold War and the Korean War produced a far-reaching form of anticommunism.

WHY IT MATTERS NOW

Reckless charges damaged personal lives and set up a climate of suspicion that affected Americans for years.

ONE AMERICAN'S STORY

John Stewart Service was one of thousands of Americans whose lives were turned upside down by the anticommunism of the postwar era. Service was born in China of missionary parents. He spent his childhood and teenage years there before coming to the United States for college. His firsthand knowledge of China made him a respected member of the Foreign Service. As a China expert, he warned the State Department of the weakness of China's anticommunist Nationalist Party.

In 1949, the Communists took control of China. Angry Americans wanted someone to blame. Service's good advice was forgotten. He became one of the first State Department officials blamed for the loss of China to the Communists. Although a loyalty board cleared him of charges of disloyalty, he lost his job. The Supreme Court later ruled that he had been unfairly dismissed. As you will read in this section, many innocent Americans suffered a similar fate.

John Stewart Service defends himself before the Senate Foreign Relations Committee against charges that he worked with Communists.

Origins of the Korean War

In September 1949, the Communists defeated the anticommunist Nationalists in a civil war in China. The Nationalists were supported by the United States. **Mao Zedong** became head of the new Communist state. The Nationalist government, headed by Chiang Kai-shek, fled to the island of Taiwan, formerly Formosa, off the coast of the Chinese mainland. Many Americans were shocked by the fall of the Nationalist government. They viewed the takeover as part of a Communist plot to rule the world. They blamed the State Department for failing to stop the Communist revolution. American fear of communism grew. Events in Korea contributed to this fear.

Korea had been a Japanese colony for half a century when Japan surrendered to the Allies at the end of World War II. In 1945, Soviet troops occupied Korea north of the **38th parallel,** or line of latitude. American forces took control south of this line. Aided by the Soviets, a Communist government came to power in North Korea. In South Korea, a noncommunist leader supported by the United States governed.

Fighting Breaks Out in Korea

In June 1950, North Korean forces crossed the 38th parallel into South Korea. The conflict that followed became known as the **Korean War**. President Truman viewed Korea as a test case for his containment policy. He responded promptly. The United States appealed to the United Nations (UN) to stop the Communist move into South Korea. Sixteen nations provided soldiers for a UN force. However, U.S. troops made up most of the force and did most of the fighting. General Douglas MacArthur, former World War II hero in the Pacific, served as commander of all UN forces.

In early fighting, the North Koreans pushed the South Koreans back almost to Pusan. This city was on the southeastern tip of the Korean peninsula. MacArthur reversed the situation by landing his troops at Inchon. This was a port city behind the North Korean lines. It was a daring, dangerous plan, but it worked.

Squeezed between enemy troops coming at them from the north and south, the North Koreans soon retreated across the 38th parallel. General MacArthur requested permission of his superiors to pursue the enemy into North Korea. The UN and President Truman agreed. The president hoped the invasion might lead to a reunion of the two Koreas. The UN forces pushed northward beyond the 38th parallel (latitude) toward the Yalu

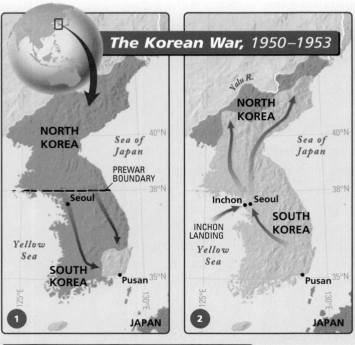

The Korean War, 1950–1953

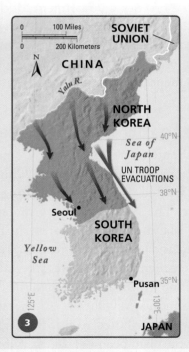

1. North Korea Invasion, 1950
2. UN Offensive, 1950
3. Chinese Offensive, 1951
4. Stalemate and Armistice, 1953

Area occupied by Communist forces
Area occupied by UN forces
← Movement of Communist forces
← Movement of UN forces

GEOGRAPHY SKILLBUILDER Interpreting Maps

1. **Movement** In map 1, which forces moved south almost to Pusan?
2. **Region** Compare the prewar boundary in map 1 with the armistice line in map 4. Which side gained slightly more territory?

River, the boundary separating China from North Korea. The Chinese warned them to stop.

China Enters the Conflict

Reading **History**
A. Reading a Map Find the 38th parallel on the maps on page 394. Notice the movement of Communist and UN forces back and forth across this parallel.

Communist China saw the movement of UN forces into North Korea as a threat to China's security. Chinese leaders warned that a further advance would force them to enter the war. Ignoring this warning, UN forces pushed on toward the Yalu River. On November 25, 1950, hundreds of thousands of Chinese Communist troops attacked in human waves across the Yalu River into North Korea. They drove UN troops back to South Korea. By early 1951, the two sides were deadlocked along the 38th parallel.

American and South Korean troops search prisoners after the Inchon landing.

General MacArthur requested permission to blockade China's coastline and bomb China. Truman refused. The president feared that such action would draw the Soviet Union in and make the conflict a world war. The general went over the president's head to win support for his war aims. He spoke and wrote to newspaper and magazine publishers. He also wrote to Republican leaders.

Reading **History**
B. Making Inferences What effect might MacArthur's actions have had on the idea of civilian control of the military?

As president, Truman was commander in chief of the armed forces. He viewed MacArthur's public criticism of his orders as undermining civilian control of the military. As a result, Truman fired MacArthur and ordered him home. When MacArthur returned to the United States, his admirers treated him as a hero. His farewell speech to Congress won the sympathy of many. "I now close my military career and just fade away—an old soldier who tried to do his duty as God gave him the light to see that duty. Good-bye." Despite support for MacArthur, Truman refused to back down. Most Americans came to agree with the president's actions.

War Ends in Stalemate

As the war dragged on, it became more unpopular. In July 1951, Truman accepted a Soviet suggestion that truce talks begin. The talks dragged on for two years. They continued through the 1952 presidential campaign. When Truman decided not to run again, the Democrats chose Illinois governor Adlai Stevenson as their candidate. The Republicans picked World War II hero General Dwight D. Eisenhower. Ike, as voters liked to call him, criticized the unpopular war. He promised to go to Korea to seek a speedy end to the conflict.

Eisenhower made good on his promise when he won a landslide victory. During talks with the North Koreans and Chinese, he agreed to compromise to end the war. But he also warned privately that he was ready to use nuclear weapons and carry the war into China. A cease-fire ended the fighting in July 1953. The two Koreas were left more or less where they had been in 1950 with a border near the 38th parallel. Communism had been contained in Korea. However, Americans felt frustrated by the indecisive war. Some politicians selfishly made use of this frustration.

McCarthy and Communism

Senator Joseph McCarthy during the 1954 Army-McCarthy hearings

One such politician was **Joseph McCarthy,** a Republican senator from Wisconsin. He used the Korean War to fan Americans' fears of communism. In February 1950, McCarthy declared that he had a list of 205 State Department officials who belonged to the Communist Party. These charges were never proven. Nonetheless, McCarthy's claim launched a hunt for Communists that wrecked the careers of thousands of people. The term *McCarthyism* came to stand for reckless charges against innocent citizens.

In the spring of 1954, the Senate held hearings. During these nationally televised Army-McCarthy hearings, McCarthy accused the U.S. Army of "coddling Communists." Army spokesmen then charged McCarthy's staff with improper conduct. McCarthy responded with unsupported charges against a young lawyer helping to represent the Army. Joseph Welch, the Army counsel, spoke out against McCarthy.

A VOICE FROM THE PAST

Until this moment, Senator, I think I never really gauged your cruelty or your recklessness. . . . Senator. You have done enough. Have you no sense of decency, sir, at long last? Have you left no sense of decency?

Joseph Welch, Army-McCarthy hearings, April 22, 1954

Reading **History**

C. Summarizing What were some of McCarthy's charges?

Americans watching the exchange between McCarthy and Welch were shocked by McCarthy's conduct. After the Senate issued a statement censuring, or criticizing, his conduct, he faded from public view.

Eisenhower and the Cold War

Like Truman, President Eisenhower waged the Cold War. Eisenhower's Secretary of State was John Foster Dulles. Dulles rejected Truman's containment policy. He favored a more aggressive stand. He urged the overthrow of Communist governments. In 1956, Dulles announced that the United States would go to the brink of war to combat communism. This approach was known as **brinksmanship.**

In August 1949, Americans learned that the Soviet Union had produced an atomic bomb, in part by using information stolen by Soviet spies. The two superpowers were soon locked in an **arms race**, developing weapons with more destructive power. In 1952, the United States built a hydrogen bomb, or **H-bomb.** Three years later the Soviets tested their H-bomb. Fear led both sides to build up huge nuclear stockpiles.

In the 1950s, both the United States and the Soviet Union helped allies and weakened enemies around the world. In 1953 in Iran, the U.S. government's Central Intelligence Agency (CIA) helped topple a leader whom they thought might seek Soviet aid. In 1954, the CIA trained an army that succeeded in overthrowing Guatemala's President Jacobo Arbenz Guzmán. The United States believed he favored communism.

During Eisenhower's presidency, the Suez Canal in Egypt, which connected the Mediterranean Sea and the Red Sea, was at the center of another Cold War conflict. In 1955, Egypt's ties with the Soviet Union angered Britain and the United States. The two Western powers withdrew aid to Egypt. Gamal Abdel Nasser, Egypt's leader, reacted by seizing the canal, which was owned by France and Britain. France, Britain, and Israel jointly attacked Egypt. The Soviet Union threatened to support Egypt. The United States, along with the Soviets and the rest of the UN, pressured France, Britain, and Israel to withdraw from Egypt. The UN imposed a cease-fire.

In 1957, the superpowers began a **space race**. The Soviet Union stunned the world by launching the world's first space satellite. They sent *Sputnik* into orbit around the earth. This meant that the Soviet Union had a missile powerful enough to reach the United States. American scientists raced to launch a satellite. Congress set aside billions of dollars for space research.

Eisenhower suggested easing tensions through face-to-face talks. A setback to such efforts occurred in May 1960. The president was to meet in Paris with Soviet Premier Nikita Khrushchev. Two weeks before the meeting, the Soviets shot down an American U-2 plane. The spy plane had been flying over the Soviet Union. Eisenhower denied the aircraft was a spy plane until the pilot was captured. Khrushchev demanded an apology. When the president refused, the talks collapsed. Meanwhile, America was changing at home, as you will read in the next section.

Connections TO SCIENCE

SPUTNIK

The 184-pound *Sputnik 1* (shown below), whose name means "traveling companion," was the first man-made object to orbit the Earth. Circling every 96 minutes, it remained in orbit until early 1958. *Sputnik 2* carried a dog into space.

In 1961, the Soviet Union sent Yuri Gagarin into space to orbit the earth. The Americans lagged behind because the rockets that carried U.S. satellites were smaller and less powerful. The early Soviet lead disappeared, however, as American scientists and engineers found ways to improve rocket design, construction, and testing.

Section 2 Assessment

1. Terms & Names

Explain the significance of:

- Mao Zedong
- 38th parallel
- Korean War
- Joseph McCarthy
- brinksmanship
- arms race
- H-bomb
- space race

2. Taking Notes

Create a time line of up to five events that played a part in the Korean War from its beginning to end.

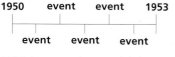

Which event do you think was most important? Why?

3. Main Ideas

a. Why did war break out in Korea? How did it end?

b. Why was McCarthy able to wield so much power during the 1950s?

c. How did Eisenhower's approach to the Cold War differ from Truman's?

4. Critical Thinking

Drawing Conclusions
How was U.S. involvement in Korea an example of the Truman Doctrine in action?

THINK ABOUT

- U.S. concerns about North Korean leadership
- U.S. goals for ending conflict
- the conflict's outcome

ACTIVITY OPTIONS

SCIENCE

ART

Research the problems of putting a satellite in orbit. Prepare a **report** explaining how these problems were solved, or draw a **design** of a rocket.

MAIN IDEA

While the United States was locked in a Cold War, social and economic changes took place in American life.

WHY IT MATTERS NOW

The American economy and popular culture continue to spread their influence around the globe.

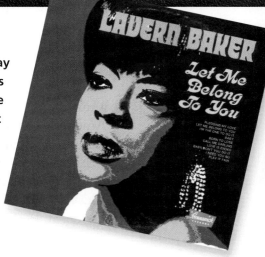

This is the cover of a long-playing record album by LaVern Baker.

ONE AMERICAN'S STORY

LaVern Baker was one of many talented African-American artists to play a part in the popular music of the 1950s. Among her best known songs are "Tweedlee Dee," "Jim Dandy," and "See See Rider." As was the case with many other black rhythm-and-blues musicians, her records at first sold mostly to African-American teenagers. White singers covered, or copied, her songs. These remakes became hits. Disk jockeys played them over and over for their white radio audiences. Baker was annoyed that remakes of her songs by white singers outsold her originals. She made the following comment about one such singer.

A VOICE FROM THE PAST

When I went to Australia with Bill Haley, Big Joe Turner, the Platters, and Freddy Bell and the Bellboys, I left her my [flight] insurance policy. I sent it to her with a letter, "Since I'll be away and you won't have anything new to copy, you might as well take this."

LaVern Baker, quoted in *USA Today,* March 12, 1997

In 1990, Baker's importance as a recording artist was confirmed. The Rock and Roll Hall of Fame honored Baker by making her a member. The following section describes social, political, and cultural changes during the 1950s.

The Domestic Scene in the Fifties

Not everyone prospered in the 1950s. In 1957, nearly one out of every five Americans lived in poverty. Many of the nation's poorest were in cities. In his book *The Other America* (1962), Michael Harrington called attention to the forgotten poor. They were the people left behind as more well-to-do Americans headed for the **suburbs**—residential areas surrounding a city. Shops and businesses moved to suburbia as well.

Fewer people remained in the city to pay taxes for such services as garbage collection, firefighting, and road repair. Often those most affected by urban decay were African Americans and Latinos. Many could not afford homes in the suburbs.

In the 1950s, immigration from Mexico increased greatly. Many people crossed the border illegally. Others came through the government-sponsored *bracero,* or temporary worker, program. The *braceros* found jobs on farms in the Southwest and Midwest. There they often earned low wages and endured difficult living and working conditions.

Despite this, when the program ended, many stayed on illegally. Employers took advantage of them. Fearful of being sent back to Mexico, workers were forced to work longer hours for lower pay.

When Eisenhower ran for president, he promised to steer a middle course. Once elected, Eisenhower pleased business leaders and conservatives without upsetting moderates and liberals. Although he disliked big government spending programs, Eisenhower kept most New Deal programs. He agreed to expand Social Security. He increased the minimum wage for workers. He also created the Department of Health, Education, and Welfare. He even backed some new spending. For example, Congress passed the Highway Act of 1956. This act provided $32 billion to build 41,000 miles of highway.

Changes Sweep America

In the postwar period, Americans began to feel more prosperous. The Depression and World War II had led many couples to put off marrying and starting a family. Now with the economy booming, Americans were getting married and having children. During the 1950s, the United States grew by almost 30 million people. This increase was mostly because of the **baby boom,** a sharp increase in the U.S. birthrate following World War II (from about 1946 through 1961). The number of families with three or four children increased dramatically.

The baby boom also spurred the growth of suburbs. Growing families left crowded city apartments for a house in the suburbs. Irving, Texas, a suburb of Dallas, was typical. In 1950, it had around 2,600 residents. Ten years later, 45,000 people lived there. To serve the suburbs, shopping centers, movie theaters, and restaurants sprouted up on what was once farmland. As suburbs grew, car sales exploded. In the suburbs, owning a car was a necessity. Few buses or other forms of public transportation existed.

In the 1950s, Americans not only moved from city to suburb. They also moved from the north and east to the south and west. The movement of people to the **sunbelt** increased the population of the warmer states of the South and Southwest. In the 1960s, California surpassed New York as the nation's most populous state.

STRANGE *but* True

FROM AUTOBAHN TO INTERSTATE

In the 1930s, Germany began to build a vast network of limited access, four-lane highways called *autobahns.* Germans believed these roads would have great military value.

During World War II, General Eisenhower saw the German road system firsthand. He was impressed by the way these highways enabled Germans to quickly move troops and supplies. President Eisenhower remembered Germany's *autobahns* when he called on Congress to pass the Highway Act of 1956. This act created the nation's first interstate highway system. A cloverleaf interchange is shown below.

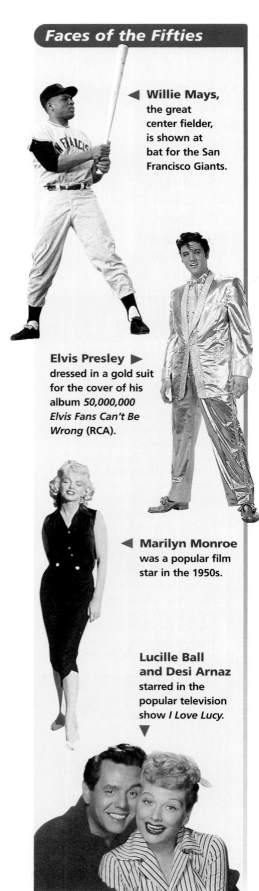

◀ **Willie Mays,** the great center fielder, is shown at bat for the San Francisco Giants.

Elvis Presley ▶ dressed in a gold suit for the cover of his album *50,000,000 Elvis Fans Can't Be Wrong* (RCA).

◀ **Marilyn Monroe** was a popular film star in the 1950s.

Lucille Ball and Desi Arnaz starred in the popular television show *I Love Lucy.* ▼

The American Dream in the Fifties

For millions of mainly white Americans, life in the suburbs was the American dream. They were happy to live in affordable, single-family houses. People welcomed the chance to send their children to good schools. Americans shopped in malls where parking was free and easy to find. They didn't care if their houses looked alike. Parents wanted a safe place in which to raise their children.

Many critics worried that Americans were being forced to fit into suburban life. Some argued that in business offices and suburbs, people felt pressured to conform—that is, to agree with the beliefs and ideas of the majority. Yet most Americans seemed willing to conform for the rewards of a comfortable life.

In the 1950s, popular magazines, films, and television programs praised women for their roles as homemakers. *Time* magazine called women the "keeper[s] of the suburban dream." But not all women felt fulfilled in this role. Some felt bored or isolated. Those working outside the home had limited job choices. Openings were largely in nursing, teaching, and office work.

By the mid-1950s, American industry was churning out goods for consumers to buy. The economy was booming. Americans filled their houses with dishwashers, washing machines, clothes dryers, and vacuum cleaners. The suburban living room or den showed off the family's television, tape recorder, and high-fidelity record player. The garage held a lawn mower. Barbecue equipment and patio furniture filled the backyard. Owning the latest car or appliance came to be a symbol of social standing and success. The advertising industry encouraged consumers to join the spending spree. Television helped advertisers lure buyers to stores and car showrooms.

Pop Culture and Rock 'n' Roll

In the 1950s, Hollywood cranked out westerns, musicals, and romances. However, movie attendance plummeted as more and more people stayed home to watch TV. By 1960, nine out of ten households owned a set. One of the most popular shows of the decade was the situation comedy (sitcom) *I Love Lucy.* It starred Lucille Ball as the zany wife of bandleader Desi Arnaz. In *Father Knows Best* and many other Fifties sitcoms,

Reading **History**

A. Drawing Conclusions What might be some of the advantages and disadvantages of fitting in?

cheerful moms kept the house spotless. The dads worked to support the family. On *Father Knows Best*, Mr. Anderson exercised kindly but firm control over his children, who seldom rebelled.

Young children watched *Lassie, The Lone Ranger, The Howdy Doody Show*, and the *Mickey Mouse Club*. Their teenage sisters and brothers had fallen head over heels for another form of entertainment—**rock 'n' roll** music. In 1955, Bill Haley and His Comets hit it big with "Rock Around the Clock." By the mid-1950s, Chuck Berry, Little Richard, Fats Domino, and other black musicians held the spotlight with white rockers like Jerry Lee Lewis. But the largest fan club belonged to Elvis Presley. With such songs as "Heartbreak Hotel" and "Don't Be Cruel," he became the king of rock 'n' roll. His onstage bumps and shakes delighted teenagers.

In the mid-1950s, Allen Ginsberg and Jack Kerouac led a group of poets and writers. They protested what they saw as the shallowness and conformity of American society. Known as "beatniks," their followers filled coffeehouses to hear their heated attacks on "square" society. A Democratic presidential candidate, John F. Kennedy, also wanted to shake up the dullness of the Eisenhower years.

The Election of 1960

The 1960 presidential election was one of the closest in U.S. history. John Fitzgerald Kennedy, Democratic senator from Massachusetts, defeated Richard M. Nixon, Eisenhower's vice president. At age 43, Kennedy was the nation's youngest elected president. He was also the first Catholic president. Kennedy had campaigned to "get this country moving again" after the Eisenhower years. Kennedy and Nixon staged the first televised presidential debates. Kennedy's youthful energy and confidence helped him to win. In the next chapter, you will read about Kennedy's role in setting domestic policy, including civil rights.

Section 3 Assessment

1. Terms & Names

Explain the significance of:
• suburb
• baby boom
• sunbelt
• rock 'n' roll

2. Taking Notes

Create a web like the one below to examine the way life was changing the United States in the 1950s.

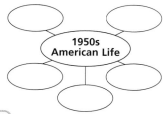

1950s American Life

3. Main Ideas

a. How did the movement to the suburbs affect the urban poor?

b. What caused the 1950s baby boom? How did the baby boom contribute to suburban growth?

c. How did television affect American life in the 1950s?

4. Critical Thinking

Contrasting Do you think the American Dream for most Americans today would be the same as it was in the 1950s? Why?

THINK ABOUT
• expectations about suburban/urban living
• changes in transportation and workplace

ACTIVITY OPTIONS

TECHNOLOGY
MUSIC

Research one aspect of music in the 1950s, and either plan a **Web page** to share your information, or write your own **song** that fits this time period.

Route 66

America was changing, and few things contributed more to that change than U.S. Highway Route 66. Completed in the summer of 1926, this road connected small towns from Chicago to Los Angeles. Its course across the Heartland enabled farmers to move grain and produce to the big cities.

In the 1930s, farmers escaping the Great Plains' Dust Bowl fled westward along this highway. The first service stations—full-service gas stations—were built along Route 66. In the 1940s, it became an important route for the movement of troops and supplies. By the 1950s, a culture had developed along the highway. This roadside culture included the motor hotel (or motel), roadside diners, and tourist traps.

So many people were on the road that bigger, faster, wider highways were needed. These highways didn't go through the small towns connected by Route 66. With the new superhighways bypassing them, many of the well-known sights along Route 66 vanished.

WYOMING

COLORADO

CALIFORNIA

NEVADA

ARIZONA

SANTA MONICA, CA

SAN BERNARDINO, CA

ROUTE 66

LOS ANGELES, CA

NEEDLES, CA

FLAGSTAFF, AZ

ALBUQUERQUE, NM

NEW MEXICO

PACIFIC OCEAN

ARTIFACT FILE

America's Main Street
Many of the towns, tourist traps, and beauty spots along Route 66 became popular destinations. Route 66 was often called "America's Main Street" because it ran through the centers of the small towns it connected.

Roadside Drive-In
Roadside food stands such as this one in Seligman, Arizona, were found all along Route 66.

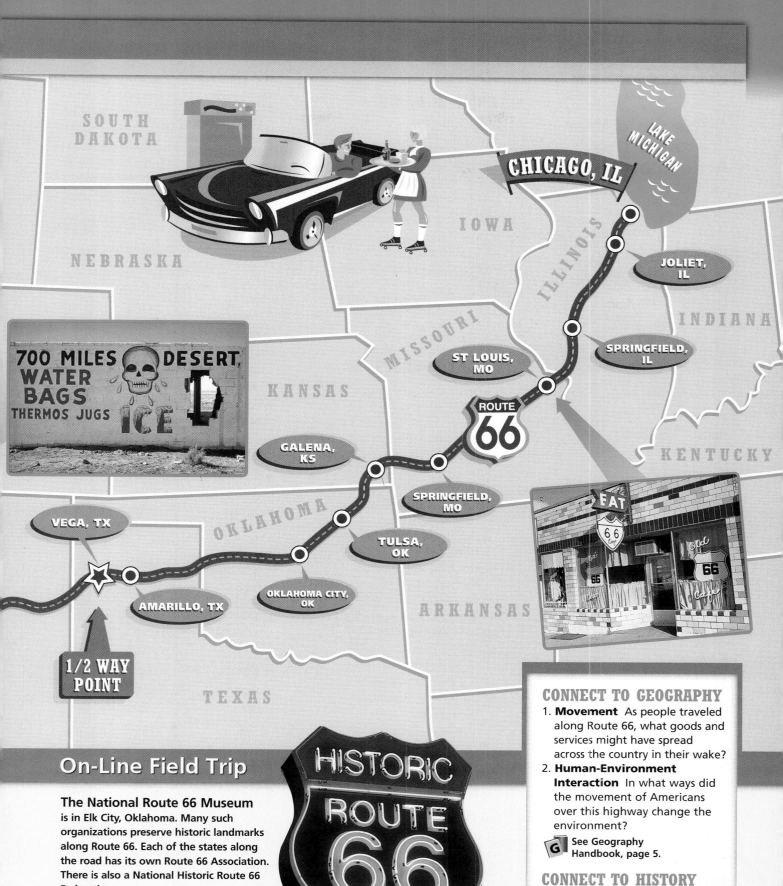

700 MILES DESERT
WATER
BAGS
THERMOS JUGS
ICE

SOUTH DAKOTA

NEBRASKA

IOWA

CHICAGO, IL

LAKE MICHIGAN

ILLINOIS

INDIANA

JOLIET, IL

SPRINGFIELD, IL

MISSOURI

ST LOUIS, MO

KANSAS

ROUTE 66

KENTUCKY

GALENA, KS

SPRINGFIELD, MO

EAT

OKLAHOMA

TULSA, OK

VEGA, TX

OKLAHOMA CITY, OK

ARKANSAS

AMARILLO, TX

1/2 WAY POINT

TEXAS

On-Line Field Trip

The National Route 66 Museum is in Elk City, Oklahoma. Many such organizations preserve historic landmarks along Route 66. Each of the states along the road has its own Route 66 Association. There is also a National Historic Route 66 Federation.

For more about Route 66 . . .

HISTORIC ROUTE 66

CONNECT TO GEOGRAPHY

1. **Movement** As people traveled along Route 66, what goods and services might have spread across the country in their wake?

2. **Human-Environment Interaction** In what ways did the movement of Americans over this highway change the environment?

See Geography Handbook, page 5.

CONNECT TO HISTORY

3. **Drawing Conclusions** In what ways did Route 66 contribute to the American Dream?

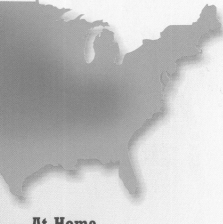

VISUAL SUMMARY

The Cold War and the American Dream

At Home

1940s:
- Truman faces labor unrest.
- Fear of communism spreads.
- Fair Deal is proposed.
- Equal rights for all remains a problem.

1950s:
- The economy booms under Eisenhower.
- McCarthy gains and loses power.
- Billions are spent on space research.
- Rock 'n' roll transforms popular culture.

Abroad

1940s:
- Truman Doctrine is announced.
- Marshall Plan offers aid to Europe.
- Berlin airlift takes place.
- NATO is formed.

1950s:
- Korean War ends in stalemate.
- Dulles practices brinksmanship.
- *Sputnik* is launched.
- Arms race takes place between superpowers.

TERMS & NAMES

Briefly explain the significance of each of the following.

1. Cold War
2. containment
3. Truman Doctrine
4. NATO
5. Korean War
6. brinksmanship
7. space race
8. baby boom
9. sunbelt
10. rock 'n' roll

REVIEW QUESTIONS

Peacetime Adjustments and the Cold War (pages 387–392)

1. How did the federal government help veterans?
2. Why was inflation a bigger problem than recession in the postwar period?
3. Why was the fate of Eastern Europe an issue that divided the Soviet Union from its former allies?
4. How did the Marshall Plan and the formation of NATO reflect Truman's containment policy?

The Korean War and McCarthyism (pages 393–397)

5. Why did the United States become involved in the Korean War?
6. Why were Americans frustrated by the outcome of the Korean War?
7. How was McCarthy able to gain such a powerful hold on the government and the American public?

The Fifties (pages 398–403)

8. What groups were left out of postwar prosperity?
9. What factors boosted the growth of suburbs?
10. Why did Americans become bigger consumers in the 1950s?

CRITICAL THINKING

1. USING YOUR NOTES

ISSUES	PRESIDENTS	
Domestic	Truman	Eisenhower
Labor unions and big business		
Communist threat at home		
Foreign		
Korea		
Communism in Europe		

Using your completed chart, answer the questions below.

a. Which policy or action might have increased the chances of war?
b. What policies or actions might have led to a stalemate?
c. In your opinion, could anything have been done to end the Korean War sooner?

2. APPLYING CITIZENSHIP SKILLS

Was McCarthyism or communism a greater threat to the American way of life? Explain (or support) your opinion.

3. THEME: ECONOMICS IN HISTORY

What factors contributed most strongly to the economic prosperity of the 1950s?

4. ANALYZING LEADERSHIP

Why did Truman consider it his duty as president to fire MacArthur? What might have been the consequences of allowing him to remain in Korea?

5. RECOGNIZING EFFECTS

Soviet and American leaders had different views of the events of war and the challenges of the postwar period. How did these different views contribute to the mistrust and fear of the Cold-War era?

Interact *with* History

How did the American Dream you discussed before you read the chapter compare with the dreams that people actually pursued?

HISTORY SKILLS

1. INTERPRETING GRAPHS

Gross National Product (GNP) means the total value of all goods and services produced by a nation. Study the graph and then answer the questions.

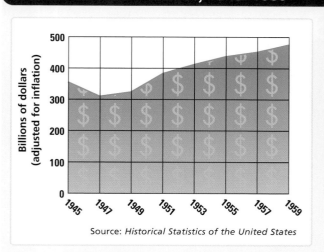

Gross National Product, *1945–1959*

Source: *Historical Statistics of the United States*

a. In dollars, approximately how much did the GNP increase between 1945 and 1951?

b. About how much did the GNP increase between 1951 and 1959?

2. INTERPRETING PRIMARY SOURCES

The following cartoon shows a buyer or perhaps salesman discussing cars with Uncle Sam. Study the cartoon and then answer the questions that follow.

So Russia Launched a Satellite, but Has It Made a Car with Fins Yet?

a. Which is more important for a country's security—consumer goods or space technology?

b. In the opinion of the cartoonist, how might the American Dream be rooted in technology?

ALTERNATIVE ASSESSMENT

1. INTERDISCIPLINARY ACTIVITY: Speech

Debating NATO's Role Since the collapse of the Soviet Union, many former Warsaw Pact nations have wanted to become NATO members. Research and debate the question: What are some of the advantages and disadvantages of expanding NATO?

2. COOPERATIVE LEARNING ACTIVITY

Examining Images of the 1950s Examine images of the American family and family life in the media of the 1950s. Working in groups, look at advertisements in magazines and books of the era, and if possible view TV reruns of 1950s sitcoms. Present your findings as a short TV show about a 1950s family. Groups can prepare for the presentations using these suggestions.

• Make a list of media images you want to present.

• Assign group members roles as writers, actors, directors, and narrator.

• Identify any props or costumes needed.

3. TECHNOLOGY ACTIVITY

Making a Class Presentation Popular culture in the 1950s included music, television, and movies. Using the library and the Internet, find articles and pictures about popular shows, music, and celebrities of the period.

For more about the Fifties . . .

INTERNET ACTIVITY
CLASSZONE.COM

Prepare an electronic presentation about one aspect of popular culture of the Fifties. Use these suggestions or a topic of your own.

• Music: lyrics, bands, performers, record companies

• Movies: stars, popular films, drive-ins

• Fashion: clothing, dress, hairstyles, teen life

• Television: stars, shows, viewing habits

4. HISTORY PORTFOLIO

Option 1 Review your section and chapter assessment activities. Select one that you think was your best work. Then use comments made by your teacher or classmates to improve your work, and add it to your portfolio.

Option 2 Review the information that you hoped to acquire for What Do You Want to Know? on page 386. Then write a short report in which you explain the information. If any information seems incomplete, do research to expand it. Add your report to your portfolio.

Additional Test Practice, pp. S1–S33

TEST PRACTICE
CLASSZONE.COM

Tensions at Home and Abroad

Dr. Martin Luther King, Jr., waves to demonstrators at the March on Washington in 1963.

"I have a dream that my four little children . . . will not be judged by the color of their skin, but by the content of their character."

—Dr. Martin Luther King, Jr.

CHAPTER
15

The Civil Rights Era 1954–1975

Section 1 **Origins of the Civil Rights Movement**
Section 2 **Kennedy, Johnson, and Civil Rights**
Section 3 **The Equal Rights Struggle Expands**

Civil rights marchers sing at the March on Washington in 1963.

Before the civil rights era, it was legal in many American states for businesses to deny service to African Americans.

Employees were not permitted to serve the students.

In February 1960, four African-American college students began protesting this "whites-only" policy at a lunch counter in Greensboro, North Carolina.

It is 1960, and you live in a Southern city. For decades, African Americans in the South have endured racial segregation. Now they are protesting against it—in spite of the risk of being attacked. You must decide whether or not you will participate in the protests and in what way.

What Do You Think?

- What policy do the students in the picture hope to change?
- How far would you be willing to go to help the protesters?
- In what ways, besides protesting, could you help to end segregation?

How would you stop injustice in society?

1955
Montgomery bus boycott begins.

1954
The Supreme Court decides *Brown v. Board of Education of Topeka.*

1957
Federal troops are sent to desegregate Little Rock Central High School.

1963
The March on Washington takes place.

Kennedy is assassinated, and Johnson becomes president.

1964
Congress passes Civil Rights Act of 1964.

1965
Congress passes the Voting Rights Act.

1968
Dr. Martin Luther King, Jr., is assassinated.

1970
La Raza Unida is founded.

1972
Members of AIM occupy the Bureau of Indian Affairs.

USA
World

1954

1975

1957
African nation of Ghana wins independence.

1962
African National Congress leader Nelson Mandela is imprisoned.

1967
Civil war rages in Nigeria.

1971
India and Pakistan go to war.

BEFORE YOU READ

Previewing the Theme

Democratic Ideals For a century after the Civil War, the United States refused to provide equal rights for African Americans. Chapter 15 tells about the African-American struggle for equality. It also explains how African-American protests for equal rights spread to other groups, including Hispanics, Native Americans, and women.

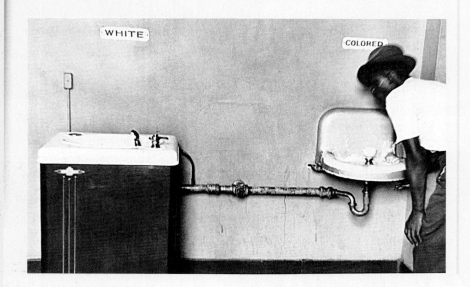

What Do You Know?

What do you think of when people talk about civil rights? Why have some people in the United States been denied their civil rights? Why are civil rights important in a democratic society?

THINK ABOUT

• what you have learned about racism, segregation, and discrimination in earlier chapters
• what you have learned about famous civil rights leaders from your parents or teachers

What Do You Want to Know?

What questions do you have about civil rights? Write those questions in your notebook before you read the chapter.

READ AND TAKE NOTES

Reading Strategy: Analyzing Causes Copy the chart below in your notebook. Use it to take notes on the cause of each event listed in the chart.

S **See Skillbuilder Handbook, page R11.**

Causes	Events
	Brown v. *Board of Education of Topeka*
	Montgomery bus boycott
	Civil Rights Act of 1964
	Voting Rights Act of 1965
	La Raza Unida
	Publication of *The Feminine Mystique*, by Betty Friedan
	The federal government ends its "termination policy."

① Origins of the Civil Rights Movement

TERMS & NAMES
Thurgood Marshall
Brown v. Board of Education of Topeka
Montgomery bus boycott
Dr. Martin Luther King, Jr.
SCLC
sit-in
SNCC

MAIN IDEA	WHY IT MATTERS NOW
Changes after World War II helped African Americans make progress in their struggle for equality.	The African-American struggle for equality became a model for modern protest movements.

ONE AMERICAN'S STORY

On December 1, 1955, Rosa Parks, an African-American woman from Montgomery, Alabama, boarded a bus to go home after work. Along the way, a group of white people climbed aboard. The bus driver told Parks and a few other African Americans to give up their seats for the whites and move to the back of the bus. All of them except Parks got up to move. She described what happened next.

A VOICE FROM THE PAST

The driver of the bus saw me still sitting there, and he asked was I going to stand up. I said, "No." He said, "Well, I'm going to have you arrested." Then I said, "You may do that."

Rosa Parks, *Rosa Parks: My Story*

Rosa Parks rides a bus in Montgomery, Alabama, in 1956.

The bus driver called the police, who arrested Parks. The arrest angered Montgomery's African-American community. They respected Parks for her long history of fighting for civil rights. She had been an officer in the local chapter of the NAACP. She had also been put off buses in the past for defying segregation. As Section 1 explains, her arrest would spark a movement that began to tear down segregation in America.

Postwar Changes Strengthen Protests

Since the Civil War, African Americans had fought for equality. Their goals included full political rights, better job opportunities, and an end to segregation. But before World War II, they had had little success. Several changes made their efforts more successful after the war.

First, more Americans began to see racism as evil. Racist attitudes had supported the discrimination that oppressed African Americans. Many white Americans saw that racist beliefs had contributed to the rise of Adolf Hitler and the Holocaust. As a result, they began to recognize that racism had no place in the United States.

In addition, the war made African Americans more determined than ever to win equality at home. Having fought for freedom in Europe, African Americans wanted a share of it in the United States, too.

African Americans also gained important resources to help them fight segregation. More blacks had moved into cities to work. They made more money and formed more contacts with one another at work, on the street, and in churches. These changes helped to make the civil rights protests successful.

Brown Overturns *Plessy*

The NAACP, the oldest civil rights organization in the United States, benefited from these changes. Before the war, it had established a fund to pay for legal challenges to segregation. Even so, the "separate but equal" doctrine remained in effect well into the 1950s. This doctrine had been established by *Plessy* v. *Ferguson* in 1896.

In the early 1950s, African Americans in several states sued to end segregation in, or integrate, public schools. Up to this point, white-controlled school boards had provided white children with better schoolhouses and newer books and equipment than they provided to black children. **Thurgood Marshall,** the NAACP counsel, led the attorneys who challenged the segregation laws in the courts.

In the early 1950s, the Supreme Court heard these cases under the name ***Brown v. Board of Education of Topeka***. On May 17, 1954, Chief Justice Earl Warren delivered the Court's historic opinion on these cases.

In 1954, Thurgood Marshall persuaded the Supreme Court that racial segregation in public schools was not constitutional.

A VOICE FROM THE PAST

We conclude that in the field of public education the doctrine of "separate but equal" has no place. Separate educational facilities are inherently unequal.

Chief Justice Earl Warren, *Brown* v. *Board of Education of Topeka*

The *Brown* decision was limited to public schools. But many people hoped that it would eventually end segregation in other public facilities. In the meantime, civil rights supporters hoped that black children would receive the same educational opportunities as white children. But the Supreme Court did not say how desegregation was to occur until a year later.

At that time, the Court ordered public schools to desegregate "with all deliberate speed." This ruling, which was known as *Brown II*, actually gave segregated school districts *more* time to desegregate. A few places, such as Washington, D.C., desegregated quickly. But in most places, white-controlled schools resisted desegregation.

Montgomery Bus Boycott

In 1955, about six months after the *Brown II* decision, Rosa Parks was arrested, as you read in One American's Story on page 411. News of her arrest quickly reached the other members of her church. The church members issued a notice to other African-American churches and local groups. It said, "If Negroes did not ride the buses, they [the buses] could not operate. We are, therefore, asking every Negro to stay off the buses Monday in protest of the arrest and trial." This protest, called the **Montgomery bus boycott,** began that day.

That evening, local NAACP leaders held a meeting to decide whether to continue the boycott. A 26-year-old Baptist minister from Atlanta, Georgia, named **Dr. Martin Luther King, Jr.,** spoke to the group.

> *A VOICE FROM THE PAST*
>
> There comes a time that people get tired. We are here this evening to say to those who have mistreated us so long that we are tired—tired of being segregated and humiliated; tired of being kicked about by the brutal feet of oppression.
>
> **Martin Luther King, Jr.,** quoted in *Stride Toward Freedom*

The church members vowed to continue the boycott. It went on for 13 months. Boycotters, including some whites, organized car pools, rode bikes, or walked to their jobs and schools. King and other leaders endured death threats, bombings, and jailings. The violent reactions of whites to the nonviolent boycott gained the attention of the national media.

Meanwhile, the Montgomery bus segregation law had been challenged in court. On November 13, 1956, the Supreme Court ruled that the law was unconstitutional. African Americans once again boarded the buses in Montgomery. This time they sat wherever they pleased.

The boycott had several important results. First, it ended segregation on Montgomery buses. Second, it led to the founding of the Southern Christian Leadership Conference (**SCLC**). SCLC coordinated civil rights protests across the South. Third, the boycott made Dr. King one of the best-known civil rights leaders in the nation.

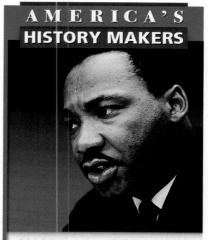

AMERICA'S HISTORY MAKERS

MARTIN LUTHER KING, JR.
1929–1968

Fresh out of school, King had been in Montgomery about a year when he became leader of the bus boycott. But his courage and brilliant speaking abilities made him the ideal leader for the civil rights movement.

King learned about nonviolence by studying writers and thinkers such as Mohandas Gandhi. He came to believe that only love could convert people to the side of justice. He described the power of nonviolent resisters: "We will wear you down by our capacity to suffer. And in winning our freedom . . . we will win you in the process."

Why do you think King was well-suited to lead a nonviolent protest?

Massive Resistance

Civil rights victories upset many Southern whites. Polls showed that more than 80 percent opposed school desegregation. Segregationists fought back against African Americans and civil rights organizations. The Ku Klux Klan used beatings, arson, and murder to threaten African Americans who pursued their civil rights.

Many whites, especially among the middle class, organized groups known as White Citizens Councils to prevent desegregation. The opposition of whites to desegregation became known as massive resistance. It was very effective in delaying desegregation.

Showdown in Little Rock

Massive resistance threatened the desegregation of schools in Little Rock, Arkansas, in 1957. Following the *Brown* case, the Little Rock school board made plans to integrate. It called for nine African-American students to enroll at Central High School in September 1957.

As the start of the school year neared, segregationists tried to block the integration of the school. Arkansas governor Orval Faubus sided with the segregationists. On September 3, he ordered National Guard troops to prevent the African-American students from entering the school the next morning.

Eight of the students had received phone calls saying someone would drive them to the high school for their safety. When they arrived, the National Guard troops turned them away. The family of the ninth student, Elizabeth Eckford, had no telephone. She took a bus to school alone that morning. When she arrived, a mob of angry whites followed her toward the school's doors.

She saw a guard let some white students pass, so she went up to him. But he did not move out of the way. Later Eckford wrote, "When I tried to squeeze past him, he raised his bayonet. . . . Somebody started yelling, 'Lynch her! Lynch her!'" Finally, a white woman guided Eckford away from the mob and took her home.

For three weeks, Faubus refused to allow the African-American students into the school—even after meeting with President Dwight Eisenhower. The president did not want to force the governor to obey the law, but he eventually realized that it was his only choice.

Background
The nine African-American students chosen to integrate Central High School became known as the Little Rock Nine.

Vocabulary
lynch: to execute illegally, especially by hanging

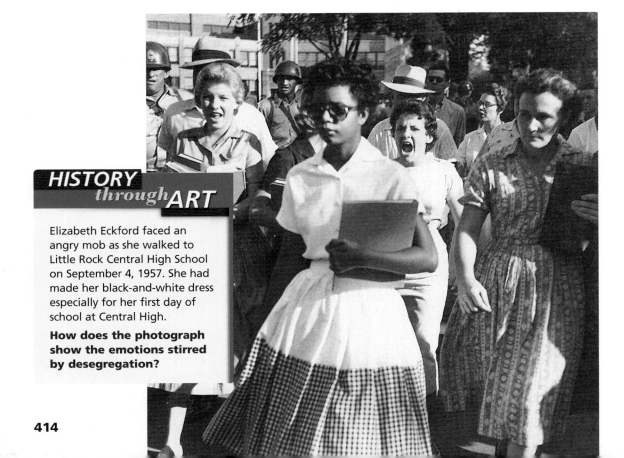

HISTORY *through* ART

Elizabeth Eckford faced an angry mob as she walked to Little Rock Central High School on September 4, 1957. She had made her black-and-white dress especially for her first day of school at Central High.

How does the photograph show the emotions stirred by desegregation?

On September 24, Eisenhower ordered the 101st Airborne Division into Little Rock. The Little Rock Nine rode to school, escorted by jeeps armed with machine guns. Paratroopers lined the streets and protected the students as they entered Central High.

Sit-Ins Energize the Movement

Victories like the one in Little Rock encouraged civil rights supporters to continue their fight. In February 1960, four African-American college students began a sit-in to desegregate a lunch counter at a store in Greensboro, North Carolina. A **sit-in** is a protest in which people sit in a place and refuse to move until their demands are met. The students sat down at the lunch counter and ordered coffee. The waitress refused to serve them because they were African Americans.

> *"The doctrine of 'separate but equal' has no place."*
> From *Brown v. Board of Education*

That first day, the students stayed for 45 minutes. They came back each day that week with more protesters. By Thursday, there were more than 100 protesters, including some whites. Over the following weeks, thousands of protesters took part in sit-ins across the South.

As the sit-ins spread, segregationists began to abuse the protesters. They covered the protesters with ammonia and itching powder. They yelled at them, beat them, and burned them with cigarettes. Some protesters went to jail. But other protesters replaced them at the counters. The sit-ins were an effective protest tactic. They forced many stores with lunch counters to serve African Americans.

Many civil rights leaders saw the success of the sit-ins and supported an organization for young people. Out of this movement, the Student Nonviolent Coordinating Committee (**SNCC**) was formed. Through SNCC, SCLC, and other groups, the civil rights movement increased the pressure for change in the 1960s, as you will read in the next section.

*Reading*History
C. Solving Problems How did African Americans end discrimination at many lunch counters?

Section 1 Assessment

1. Terms & Names

Explain the significance of:
- Thurgood Marshall
- *Brown* v. *Board of Education of Topeka*
- Montgomery bus boycott
- Dr. Martin Luther King, Jr.
- SCLC
- sit-in
- SNCC

2. Taking Notes

Use a cluster diagram to record details about the early civil rights movement.

Brown v. Board of Education

Early Civil Rights Movement

3. Main Ideas

a. How did World War II help lead to the civil rights movement?

b. What role did Thurgood Marshall play in challenging segregation?

c. How did Martin Luther King, Jr., become a well-known civil rights leader?

4. Critical Thinking

Contrasting How did the tactics used by civil rights protesters differ from the response of many Southern whites?

THINK ABOUT
- the Montgomery bus boycott
- the events in Little Rock
- the nature of sit-ins

ACTIVITY OPTIONS

ART

TECHNOLOGY

You have been asked to honor people in the civil rights movement. Create a **wall of fame**, or plan a **Web page** that pays tribute to several of them.

2 Kennedy, Johnson, and Civil Rights

MAIN IDEA	WHY IT MATTERS NOW
The civil rights movement led to the end of legal segregation.	African Americans still face discrimination but now have more opportunities than before.

ONE AMERICAN'S STORY

Jim Zwerg, a white student from Wisconsin, joined a Freedom Ride in May 1961. **Freedom Rides** were protests against segregation on interstate busing in the South. During the rides, whites would sit in the back of a bus. African Americans would sit in the front and refuse to move. At bus terminals along the route, black riders would try to use "whites only" facilities.

Zwerg and the other freedom riders expected trouble from segregationists on the journey. In Montgomery, Alabama, segregationists savagely attacked the freedom riders.

Zwerg was beaten unconscious. But he was not the only victim. Black or white, man or woman, few freedom riders were spared. In this section, you will read how the Freedom Rides and other protests helped African Americans win support for civil rights.

John Lewis (left) and Jim Zwerg of SNCC are covered with blood after being beaten in Montgomery.

Kennedy and Civil Rights

In 1960, Americans elected a new president. Although civil rights was not the main issue in the campaign, it played an important role. The Democrats nominated John F. Kennedy, a senator from Massachusetts. The Republicans nominated Vice-President Richard Nixon. During the campaign, the candidates had similar positions on most issues. But many Americans thought that Kennedy was more dynamic.

Late in the campaign, police arrested Martin Luther King, Jr., in Georgia. Kennedy called King's wife, and Robert Kennedy, the candidate's brother, arranged for King's release. That one act dramatically increased African-American support for Kennedy. The election was one of the closest in U.S. history, and Kennedy won.

As president, Kennedy had to work with a Congress that was reluctant to act on civil rights issues. In the early 1960s, Southern Democrats supported segregation. Kennedy did not want to anger Southern Democrats because they could weaken his presidency.

Even so, activists continued to pressure the federal government. In May 1961, the Congress of Racial Equality (**CORE**) planned Freedom Rides to desegregate interstate buses, or buses that travel between states.

Despite attacks on the freedom riders by segregationists along the route, the riders would not give up. Kennedy had to do something. Finally, he sent a group of federal marshals to protect the riders. Four months later, the federal government issued an order integrating interstate bus facilities. The riders had achieved their goal.

Protests in Birmingham

Reading **History**
A. Drawing Conclusions Why did civil rights leaders choose to protest in cities where they were likely to face violence?

In the early 1960s, the civil rights movement gained strength across the South. African Americans in Birmingham, Alabama, wanted to integrate public facilities and gain better job and housing opportunities. Local civil rights leaders invited King and SCLC to join the protests.

Birmingham was a great opportunity for protesters to expose the evils of segregation. They knew that Eugene "Bull" Connor, the city's Public Safety commissioner, was likely to use violence to stop the protests. They also knew that the sight of segregationists attacking nonviolent protesters would increase the pressure for change.

The protests began in April 1963. After about a week, the police arrested King, who had traveled to Birmingham for the protests. From jail, King wrote an eloquent defense of the protests.

A VOICE FROM THE PAST

I guess it is easy for those who have never felt the stinging darts of segregation to say, "Wait." . . . [But] there comes a time when the cup of endurance runs over, and men are no longer willing to be plunged into an abyss [a bottomless pit] of injustice.

Martin Luther King, Jr., "Letter from Birmingham Jail"

SCLC recruited children for the Birmingham marches. The police used dogs and firehoses on the marchers. People across the nation saw this on television and were horrified. Soon, Birmingham's white leaders agreed to

The firehoses used on Birmingham protesters had enough force to tear people's clothes and send small children skidding down the street.

desegregate lunch counters, remove segregation signs, and employ more African Americans in downtown stores.

The March on Washington

The events in Birmingham caused many Americans to support passage of new laws to protect the civil rights of all people. Civil rights organizations planned a huge demonstration in Washington, D.C., to build support for civil rights legislation.

On August 28, 1963, about 250,000 people took part in the **March on Washington,** as the demonstration became known. The march ended at the Lincoln Memorial. The high point of the march came when King delivered his "I Have a Dream" speech. (For a section from King's speech, see page 426.) During this speech, King spoke these famous words.

Reading **History**
B. Making Inferences Why might marchers have chosen the Lincoln Memorial as the place to end their march?

> *A VOICE FROM THE PAST*
>
> I have a dream that my four little children will one day live in a nation where they will not be judged by the color of their skin but by the content of their character.
>
> **Martin Luther King, Jr.,** from "I Have a Dream"

The March on Washington united many groups that called for passage of civil rights laws. President Kennedy promised support.

New Civil Rights Laws

Tragically, though, President Kennedy did not live long enough to fulfill this promise. On November 22, 1963, Kennedy and Vice-President Lyndon Baines Johnson went to Texas to campaign. As the presidential motorcade passed through Dallas, thousands of people greeted the president. Suddenly, shots rang out. Kennedy slumped forward; he'd been hit. The president died within an hour.

The tragedy deeply saddened the nation. Schools, factories, and businesses closed as citizens mourned their slain leader. The assassination of President Kennedy would remain a central event in the memories of many Americans in the decades to come.

Lyndon Johnson became president after Kennedy's death. He promised to continue Kennedy's policies. Johnson moved quickly on civil rights. He argued that "no memorial oration or eulogy could more eloquently honor President Kennedy's memory than the earliest possible passage of the civil rights bill." The nation's grief led to broad support for the bill.

Background The man accused of shooting Kennedy, Lee Harvey Oswald, was killed two days later by another assassin.

In July, the **Civil Rights Act of 1964** was signed into law. The law banned segregation in public places, such as hotels, restaurants, and theaters. It also created the Equal Employment Opportunity Commission to prevent job discrimination. At long last, segregation was officially illegal throughout the United States.

Kennedy's flag-draped casket is drawn through the streets of Washington, D.C., during the slain leader's funeral procession.

Fighting for Voting Rights

White Southerners had long used literacy tests, poll taxes, and violence to keep African Americans from voting. The Civil Rights Act of 1964 barred states from using different voting standards for blacks and whites. In the same year, the states ratified the Twenty-Fourth Amendment. It outlawed poll taxes. Even so, African Americans in the South still found it difficult to vote. As a result, they lobbied Congress to pass a strong voting rights law.

In 1964, SNCC organized a voter-registration drive for Southern blacks. The program was called **Freedom Summer.** It brought Northern college students into Mississippi to work with SNCC organizers. The young volunteers endured bombings, beatings, arrests, and murder while performing their work. Even so, they managed to add about 1,200 African Americans to voter registration rolls.

Early in 1965, King and SCLC organized voter-registration drives in Selma, Alabama, including a protest march to Montgomery. On March 7, as the marchers crossed a bridge at the edge of Selma, state troopers on horseback attacked them. Americans watched as the violence was broadcast on national television. Pressure for federal action rose.

President Johnson told Alabama Governor George Wallace that he would not tolerate any more violence. When the march to Montgomery resumed, the president sent troops to protect it. He also used the public's anger at the incident to push for action on voting rights.

Johnson used the considerable political skills he had acquired when he was a senator to push a voting rights bill through Congress. On August 6, 1965, he signed the **Voting Rights Act** into law. It banned literacy tests and other laws that kept blacks from registering to vote. It also sent federal officials to register voters. Within weeks, the percentage of African Americans in Selma who registered to vote increased from 10 percent to 60 percent.

Reading **History**

C. Drawing Conclusions How did television help to advance the civil rights movement?

Reading **History**

D. Reading a Map Use the map below to see how the registration of African-American voters increased throughout the South.

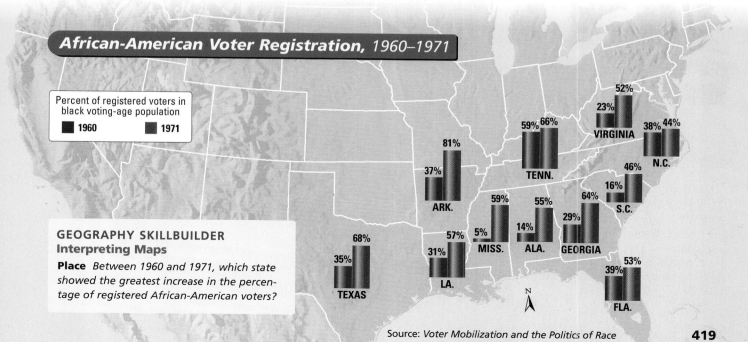

African-American Voter Registration, 1960–1971

Percent of registered voters in black voting-age population
■ 1960 ■ 1971

ARK. 37% 81%
TENN. 59% 66%
VIRGINIA 23% 52%
N.C. 38% 44%
S.C. 16% 46%
MISS. 5% 59%
ALA. 14% 55%
GEORGIA 29% 64%
TEXAS 35% 68%
LA. 31% 57%
FLA. 39% 53%

GEOGRAPHY SKILLBUILDER
Interpreting Maps

Place Between 1960 and 1971, which state showed the greatest increase in the percentage of registered African-American voters?

Source: *Voter Mobilization and the Politics of Race*

President Johnson signs the Medicare bill into law on July 30, 1965.

Johnson and the Great Society

The Civil Rights Act and the Voting Rights Act were important parts of the reform plan supported by President Johnson. Shortly after taking office, Johnson asked Americans to seek a "great society [that] demands an end to poverty and racial injustice." His program was called the **Great Society**. It provided a series of programs to help the disenfranchised, the poor, the elderly, and women. It also included legislation to promote education, end discrimination, and protect the environment.

Many of the programs were passed and still exist today, such as Medicare and Medicaid. Medicare provides health insurance for senior citizens, while Medicaid provides medical care for the poor.

In addition, Congress passed the Elementary and Secondary School Act, which provided new federal funds for education. Laws were also passed to protect the environment. Congress strengthened the 1960 Clean Water and 1963 Clean Air acts. And it passed legislation to protect endangered species and to preserve millions of acres of wilderness.

Vocabulary
disenfranchised: people deprived of the rights of citizenship, especially the right to vote

Divisions in the Civil Rights Movement

In the late 1960s, with the civil rights laws of Johnson's Great Society already passed, civil rights leaders disagreed about what steps to take next. The SCLC and other organizations wanted to expand the nonviolent struggle. But some groups wanted the movement to become more aggressive.

In 1966, King and the SCLC joined protests in Chicago. In the North, there were no laws that denied African Americans their civil rights—white people simply discriminated against them. Whites would not sell property in certain areas to African Americans, and some white employers refused to hire black workers.

In spite of the protests, most white Chicagoans were no more interested in desegregation than Southern whites had been. Chicago mayor Richard J. Daley made only a few minor changes before SCLC abandoned its campaign.

African Americans in Chicago and other U.S. cities were frustrated with their lack of political power and economic opportunity. This frustration led to a series of

The Great Society

Civil Rights Act (1964)
Outlawed discrimination in public places, created the Equal Employment Opportunity Commission, and barred states from using different standards for voter registration for whites and blacks

Voting Rights Act (1965)
Banned literacy tests and used federal registrars to register voters

Medical Care Act (1965)
Established Medicare and Medicaid programs to assist the aged and the poor with medical care

Elementary and Secondary School Act (1965)
Provided federal aid to education

SKILLBUILDER
Interpreting Charts
1. *What act created the Equal Employment Opportunity Commission?*
2. *What acts helped to increase the number of African-American voters?*

riots in the late 1960s. Nationwide, 164 riots broke out in the first 9 months of 1967. Then, on April 4, 1968, Martin Luther King, Jr., was assassinated in Memphis, Tennessee. As the nation mourned the slain civil rights leader, African-American neighborhoods across the country exploded in anger. Over 45 people died in the rioting.

Reading **History**
E. Forming Opinions Why did race riots take place in Northern cities?

Some African Americans had begun to reject nonviolence and cooperation with whites. In 1966, SNCC's black members forced white members out of the organization. Stokely Carmichael, the new leader of SNCC, began to call for "black power." Carmichael and others wanted blacks to create their own organizations under their own control to fight white racism.

The Nation of Islam, a branch of Islam founded in the United States, also urged African Americans to separate from whites. In the 1960s, the Nation was led by Elijah Muhammad, but the group's most popular personality was **Malcolm X**.

Malcolm X speaks at a rally in Harlem in 1963.

Background
Mecca is the holiest city for Muslims.

By the mid-1960s, Malcolm X rejected the separatist ideas of the Nation of Islam and left the group. During a trip to Mecca, in Saudi Arabia, he had met Muslims of all races. He began to picture a world where all races could live together in peace. But he had little time to spread his new message. In 1965, he was gunned down by members of the Nation of Islam.

From the late 1960s on, civil rights progress came slowly for African Americans. But the African-American struggle for equality encouraged civil rights movements among other oppressed groups, as you will read in the next section.

Section 2 Assessment

1. Terms & Names

Explain the significance of:
• Freedom Ride
• CORE
• March on Washington
• Civil Rights Act of 1964
• Freedom Summer
• Voting Rights Act
• Great Society
• Malcolm X

2. Taking Notes

Use a time line like the one shown to record important events of the civil rights movement.

In what year was the voter registration drive in Selma?

3. Main Ideas

a. Why did civil rights workers believe that Birmingham was a good place to protest?

b. How did civil rights workers fight to improve African-American voting rights?

c. Why did the movement begin to break apart?

4. Critical Thinking

Making Inferences Why do you think African Americans placed so much importance on the right to vote?

THINK ABOUT
• who and what they might want to vote for
• what they were willing to endure to win voting rights
• how Southern whites kept them from voting

ACTIVITY OPTIONS

ART

SPEECH

Imagine that you are taking part in the March on Washington. Design a **poster** you could carry, or deliver a **speech** in favor of civil rights.

③ The Equal Rights Struggle Expands

TERMS & NAMES
Cesar Chavez
National Congress of American Indians
Betty Friedan
NOW
ERA

MAIN IDEA	WHY IT MATTERS NOW
The African-American struggle for equality inspired other groups to fight for equality.	Nonwhites and women continue to fight for equality today.

ONE AMERICAN'S STORY

<u>Cesar Chavez</u> was born in Yuma, Arizona, in 1927. In the 1940s, he and his family worked as migrant laborers in the California fields. (Migrant workers travel from place to place in search of work.) One time, they found work picking peas. The whole family, parents and six children, worked. Chavez described the poor pay for such hard work.

A VOICE FROM THE PAST

They [the managers] would take only the peas they thought were good, and they only paid you for those. The pay was twenty cents a hamper, which had to weigh in at twenty-five pounds. So in about three hours, the whole family made only twenty cents.

Cesar Chavez, *Cesar Chavez: Autobiography of* La Causa

Cesar Chavez, head of the National Farm Workers Association, marches with striking grape pickers in the 1960s. (*Huelga* is the Spanish word for strike.)

In 1962, Chavez decided to start a union for farm workers. But the owners refused to recognize the union. Chavez used the example set by Martin Luther King, Jr., to change their minds.

Responding to Chavez's call, workers went on strike. Then Chavez asked people not to buy produce harvested by nonunion workers. The tactics worked. In 1970, 26 major California growers signed a contract with the union. It gave the workers higher wages and new benefits. The victory of Chavez and his union showed how the fight for equal rights spread beyond African Americans, as you will read in this section.

Mexican Americans Organize

The farm workers' struggle inspired other Mexican Americans. By the 1960s, most Mexican Americans lived in cities in the Southwest and California. In 1970, Mexican Americans formed *La Raza Unida* (lah RAH•sah oo•NEE•dah)—"the united people." *La Raza* fought for better jobs, pay, education, and housing. It also worked to elect Mexican Americans to public office.

Mexican-American students also began to organize. They wanted reform in the school system. The students demanded such changes as

Background
Many Mexican Americans prefer to be called Chicanos, or Chicanas if they are female.

better facilities, more courses on the Mexican-American experience, and more Mexican-American teachers.

In 1968, students in Los Angeles walked out of classes to press their demands. At first, school authorities reacted harshly to the walkouts and arrested many of the protesters. Even so, they eventually admitted to the poor conditions of many schools and met with protesters to discuss solutions. By the early 1970s, many of the reforms that the students demanded had been made.

Hispanic Diversity

Hispanics, including Mexican Americans, trace their roots to Spanish-speaking countries and cultures. Because these countries are commonly known as Latin America, some people from these areas refer to themselves as Latinos.

Because Hispanic Americans come from many different countries, they sometimes have little in common. For example, among Mexican Americans, immigration and citizenship are important issues. Puerto Ricans, however, are already U.S. citizens and are not troubled by such issues.

*Reading*History
A. Summarizing What are the factors that unite and separate Hispanics?

Similarly, many Cubans came to the United States as political refugees after Communists took power in Cuba. They tend to be more politically conservative than other Hispanics. Such differences make it difficult for Hispanic Americans to achieve political unity.

Native Americans Unite

Native Americans, like Hispanics, often had difficulty uniting to address common problems. But in the 1950s, that began to change. In 1953, the federal government began a "termination policy" that ended federal protection of land and other assets held by Native American tribes. One result of this policy was the decline of traditional Native American cultures.

Native Americans protested against these policies. The **National Congress of American Indians** (NCAI)—founded in 1944 to promote the "common welfare" of Native Americans—led the protests. Under pressure, the federal government changed the policy in 1958.

The success of these protests inspired a new generation of Native American activists to fight for their rights. In 1961, more than 400 Native Americans from dozens of tribes met in Chicago. They issued a statement they titled the Declaration of Indian Purpose. In it, they demanded the "right to choose our own way of life" and the "responsibility of preserving precious heritage."

In 1968, a group of Native Americans founded the American Indian Movement (AIM). AIM was more aggressive than other organizations in demanding rights for people on reservations and greater recognition of

America's HERITAGE

CINCO DE MAYO

During the civil rights era, many Americans learned to appreciate the variety of cultural traditions that make their nation unique.

For example, many Americans now join in the celebration of the Mexican holiday Cinco de Mayo (5th of May). This holiday commemorates the 1862 victory of Mexican troops over the French Army in Puebla, Mexico.

The holiday reflects the national pride of Mexicans over the defeat of a superior fighting power. But the holiday has also taken on a broader meaning for all Americans as a celebration of the right of all people to self-determination. A Cinco de Mayo gathering is shown below.

Reading **History**

B. Comparing Did any African-American organizations during the civil rights era have goals similar to AIM's?

tribal laws. In 1972, members of AIM occupied the Bureau of Indian Affairs in Washington, D.C., for seven days. Russell Means, one of the group's leaders, declared, "We don't want civil rights in the white man's society—we want our own sovereign rights."

In the early 1970s, Native Americans protested to force the government to provide them with more federal aid. In addition, the Indian Self-Determination Act of 1975 gave tribal governments more control over social programs, law enforcement, and education. Other victories came through winning court cases. Native Americans won back some of their lands. They have also gone to court over rights to water, hunting, and fishing.

Native Americans petition for the return of tribal artifacts at the state capital in Albany, New York, in 1970.

The Women's Movement

In the 1960s, women also demanded equal rights. Early in the decade, women were kept out of many jobs. They faced discrimination in many male-dominated businesses. For example, there were few female police officers. The military also limited the jobs open to women.

Women also had limited legal rights. Married women, for example, faced problems in signing contracts, selling property, and getting credit. A woman could lose her job if she became pregnant. In addition, society pressured women to quit their jobs when they married. Women who wanted to work at jobs outside their homes were seen as "unnatural." **Betty Friedan** described the problems women faced in her 1963 book, *The Feminine Mystique*.

> *A VOICE FROM THE PAST*
>
> We can no longer ignore that voice within women that says: "I want something more than my husband and my children and my home."
>
> **Betty Friedan**, *The Feminine Mystique*

Friedan's words helped give direction to a movement for women's liberation. In 1966, Friedan helped to found the National Organization for Women (**NOW**). Some of NOW's major goals were to help women get good jobs and equal pay for their work.

In response to women's groups, Congress passed the Equal Rights Amendment (**ERA**) in 1972 and sent it to the states for ratification. The proposed amendment stated, "Equality of rights under the law shall not be denied or abridged by the United States or any State on account of sex." Supporters of the amendment argued that it would protect women against discrimination. They also said it would help women achieve equality with men, including such things as equal opportunity for jobs and education as well as equal pay for equal work.

Background

An Equal Rights Amendment was initially proposed in 1923, after women gained the right to vote.

In July 1972, women's rights leaders met in Washington, D.C., to demand that women play a larger role in the upcoming presidential conventions.

1 **Bella Abzug** was a U.S. representative from New York.

2 **Gloria Steinem** was the founding editor of *Ms.* magazine.

3 **Shirley Chisholm** was a U.S. representative from New York and ran for president in 1972.

4 **Betty Friedan** wrote *The Feminine Mystique* and was the cofounder and first president of NOW.

For the amendment to be added to the Constitution, 38 of the 50 states had to ratify it. Within months, 22 states had done so. But by the 1982 deadline, only 35 states had ratified the amendment, and it died despite support by a majority of Americans. The amendment failed because it faced well-organized opposition, even from some women. Phyllis Schlafly, ERA's most famous opponent, argued that it would destroy American families and that the problems of women were not the government's business.

Other reforms, however, reduced the inequality between women and men. The Civil Rights Act of 1964 and the Higher Education Act of 1972 outlawed discrimination against women. These two laws helped to expand opportunities for women in education, sports, and the workplace.

The civil rights movements that followed World War II greatly changed life in the United States. As you will read in the next chapter, the war in Vietnam also changed the nation.

Reading **History**

C. Analyzing Causes Why wasn't the ERA added to the Constitution even though it was passed in 1972?

Section 3 Assessment

1. Terms & Names

Explain the significance of:
- Cesar Chavez
- National Congress of American Indians
- Betty Friedan
- NOW
- ERA

2. Taking Notes

Use a chart like the one shown to record important details about the struggle for equal rights.

Mexican Americans	Native Americans	Women

How do the positions women hold today reflect changes won in the civil rights era?

3. Main Ideas

a. What was *La Raza Unida*, and what did it do?

b. What was the Declaration of Indian Purpose?

c. How did Betty Friedan help to launch the women's liberation movement?

4. Critical Thinking

Analyzing Points of View
What were the different opinions about the ERA?

THINK ABOUT
- what NOW and other women's groups would have thought of it
- what Phyllis Schlafly thought of it

ACTIVITY OPTIONS

TECHNOLOGY

LANGUAGE ARTS

Plan part of a **multimedia presentation** focusing on one of the groups mentioned in this section, or write a **pamphlet** explaining that group's goals.

I Have a Dream

Setting the Stage On August 28, 1963, Martin Luther King, Jr., gave his most famous speech at the March on Washington. In it, he shared his dream of equality for all. **See Primary Source Explorer**

A CLOSER LOOK

ABRAHAM LINCOLN

In his speech, King made references to Abraham Lincoln. He specifically referred to the Emancipation Proclamation and used the phrase "Five score years ago" to remind his listeners of the opening of the Gettysburg Address.

1. Why do you think King would refer to Lincoln's speeches?

A CLOSER LOOK

THE AMERICAN DREAM

The American dream can mean different things to different people. Usually, however, it refers to the freedom and opportunity for Americans to lead their own lives.

2. How do civil rights fit into the American dream?

A CLOSER LOOK

GOING TO JAIL

Dr. King—who was arrested 30 times for civil rights activities—said that, with the faith that some day all men will be treated as equals, people will be ready to go to jail together.

3. Why do you think civil rights workers were willing to go to jail?

I am happy to join with you today in what will go down in history as the greatest demonstration for freedom in the history of our nation.

Five score years ago, a great American, in whose symbolic shadow we stand today, signed the Emancipation Proclamation. . . . But one hundred years later, the Negro still is not free. One hundred years later, the life of the Negro is still sadly crippled by the **manacle**[1] of segregation and the chains of discrimination.

So we've come here today to dramatize a shameful condition. . . .

I say to you today, my friends, that even though we face the difficulties of today and tomorrow, I still have a dream. It is a dream deeply rooted in the American dream.

I have a dream that one day this nation will rise up and live out the true meaning of its **creed**[2] —we hold these truths to be self-evident that all men are created equal.

I have a dream that my four little children will one day live in a nation where they will not be judged by the color of their skin but by the content of their character.

I have a dream today!

This is our hope. This is the faith that I will go back to the South with. . . . With this faith we will be able to work together, to pray together, to struggle together, to go to jail together, to stand up for freedom together, knowing that we will be free one day. This will be the day, this will be the day when all of God's children will be able to sing with new meaning "My country 'tis of thee, sweet land of liberty, of thee I sing. Land where my fathers died, land of the Pilgrim's pride, from every mountainside, let freedom ring!" And if America is to be a great nation, this must become true.

And when this happens, when we allow freedom to ring, when we let it ring from every tenement and every hamlet, from every state and every city, we will be able to speed up that day when all of God's children, black men and white men, Jews and **Gentiles,**[3] Protestants and Catholics, will be able to join hands and sing in the words of the old Negro spiritual, "Free at last, free at last. Thank God Almighty, we are free at last."

Martin Luther King, Jr.

1. **manacle:** handcuff.   2. **creed:** statement of belief.   3. **Gentile:** Non-Jewish person.

An Open Letter

Setting the Stage In 1969, Cesar Chavez wrote a letter in which he denied accusations that he had used violence to win decent wages and better benefits for farm workers. **See Primary Source Explorer**

Today . . . we remember the life and sacrifice of Martin Luther King, Jr., who gave himself totally to the nonviolent struggle for peace and justice. In his letter from Birmingham Jail, Dr. King describes better than I could our hopes for the strike and boycott: "Injustice must be exposed, with all the tension its exposure creates, to the light of human conscience and the air of national opinion before it can be cured." For our part, I admit that we have seized upon every tactic and strategy consistent with the morality of our cause to expose that injustice and thus to heighten the sensitivity of the American conscience so that farmworkers will have without bloodshed their own union and the dignity of bargaining with their **agribusiness**[1] employers. . . .

Our strikers here in **Delano**[2] and those who represent us throughout the world are well trained for this struggle. . . . They have been taught not to lie down and die or to flee in shame, but to resist with every ounce of human endurance and spirit. To resist not with retaliation in kind but to overcome with love and compassion, with **ingenuity**[3] and creativity, with hard work and longer hours, with stamina and patient **tenacity**[4], with truth and public appeal, with friends and allies, with mobility and discipline, with politics and law, and with prayer and fasting. They were not trained in a month or even a year; after all, this new harvest season will mark our fourth full year of strike and even now we continue to plan and prepare for the years to come. . . .

We shall overcome and change it not by retaliation or bloodshed but by a determined nonviolent struggle carried on by those masses of farmworkers who intend to be free and human.

Cesar E. Chavez

A CLOSER LOOK

AGRIBUSINESS

Farm workers were excluded from the National Labor Relations Act of 1935—the law that gives most Americans the right to organize a union. By 1975, pressure from Chavez had convinced lawmakers in California to allow farm workers in the state to organize unions.

1. Why do you think farm workers wanted to organize a union?

A CLOSER LOOK

TRAINING FOR PROTESTS

During the civil rights era, protesters often received extensive training before participating in marches, demonstrations, and sit-ins. Chavez explains that farm workers were also trained for the struggle.

2. Why do you think that training for nonviolent protest might be necessary?

1. **agribusiness:** farming as a large-scale business operation.

2. **Delano:** a farming city in California.

3. **ingenuity:** imagination or cleverness.

4. **tenacity:** persistence.

Interactive Primary Sources Assessment

1. Main Ideas

a. Why does King declare that the United States is not living up to its creed?

b. What does King say must happen before America can be considered a truly great nation?

c. Why do you think Cesar Chavez refers to King in his speech?

2. Critical Thinking

Comparing and Contrasting In what ways were the problems that King and Chavez wrote about similar and different?

THINK ABOUT

• the kinds of discrimination they faced

• their hopes for the future

VISUAL SUMMARY

The Civil Rights Era

1954

1954
Brown v. Board of Education of Topeka

1955
The Montgomery bus boycott begins.

1957
Federal troops are sent to desegregate Little Rock Central High School.

1960
John F. Kennedy is elected president.

1961
Native Americans issue the Declaration of Indian Purpose.

1962
Cesar Chavez starts a union for farm workers.

1963
March on Washington

Kennedy is assassinated, and Johnson becomes president.

1964
Civil Rights Act

1965
Voting Rights Act

Malcolm X is assassinated.

1968
Martin Luther King, Jr., is assassinated.

1970
La Raza Unida is founded.

1972
Congress passes the Equal Rights Amendment, but it is never ratified by the states.

ERA YES

1975

TERMS & NAMES

Briefly explain the significance of each of the following.

1. *Brown* v. *Board of Education of Topeka*
2. Montgomery bus boycott
3. Martin Luther King, Jr.
4. March on Washington
5. Civil Rights Act of 1964
6. Voting Rights Act
7. Great Society
8. Cesar Chavez
9. National Congress of American Indians
10. ERA

REVIEW QUESTIONS

Origins of the Civil Rights Movement (pages 411–415)

1. What factors helped to give strength to the demands of the civil rights movement?
2. What were the immediate and long-term effects of *Brown* v. *Board of Education of Topeka?*
3. How did white people react to civil rights protests?

Kennedy, Johnson, and Civil Rights (pages 416–421)

4. What factors made it difficult for Kennedy to act on civil rights?
5. Why did Congress eventually pass civil rights legislation?
6. What effects did Johnson's Great Society legislation have?

The Equal Rights Struggle Expands (pages 422–427)

7. How did farm workers participate in the equal rights movement?
8. What challenges did Hispanics face in their civil rights struggle?
9. Why did Native Americans protest U.S. government policy?
10. What kinds of discrimination did women challenge during the civil rights era?

CRITICAL THINKING

1. USING YOUR NOTES

Using your completed chart, answer the questions below.

Causes	Events
	Brown v. *Board of Education of Topeka*
	Montgomery bus boycott
	Civil Rights Act of 1964
	Voting Rights Act of 1965
	La Raza Unida
	Publication of *The Feminine Mystique,* by Betty Friedan
	The federal government ends its "termination policy."

a. What causes resulted in the Supreme Court decision *Brown* v. *Board of Education of Topeka?*
b. What forces led Betty Friedan to write *The Feminine Mystique?*

2. ANALYZING LEADERSHIP

What qualities do you think made Martin Luther King, Jr., an effective leader?

3. THEME: DEMOCRATIC IDEALS

How did participants in the civil rights movement advance the democratic ideals of the United States?

4. APPLYING CITIZENSHIP SKILLS

How did the nonviolent methods used by protesters during the civil rights movement demonstrate good citizenship?

5. MAKING GENERALIZATIONS

In what ways do you think the lives of Americans today might differ from the lives of Americans who lived before the civil rights movement?

Interact *with* History

How has your study of the civil rights era influenced your decision about the ways in which you would act to change injustices in society?

HISTORY SKILLS

1. INTERPRETING GRAPHS

Study the graph. Answer the questions.

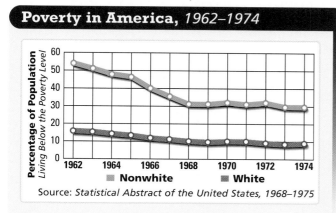

Poverty in America, *1962–1974*

Source: *Statistical Abstract of the United States, 1968–1975*

Basic Graph Elements

a. What does the graph show?

Interpreting the Graph

b. Which group of people does the chart show as having a lower rate of poverty?

c. What was the difference between the poverty rates of whites and nonwhites in 1974?

2. INTERPRETING PRIMARY SOURCES

In 1976, Anthony Gauthier painted *Freedom*. Examine the painting and answer the questions.

a. Why do you think the artist showed a Native American with Martin Luther King, Jr.?

b. How did the artist change the U.S. flag to make a statement?

ALTERNATIVE ASSESSMENT

1. INTERDISCIPLINARY ACTIVITY: Language Arts

Writing Your Representative The House of Representatives is considering the Voting Rights Act. Your representative is against the act because it will reduce his or her chances for reelection. Write a letter trying to persuade your representative to support the bill.

2. COOPERATIVE LEARNING ACTIVITY

Organizing a March With a small group, think of a way in which you could make your community a better place for everyone to live. Then organize a march that will raise awareness of the group's plan. Remember to consider the following:

- How will you recruit and organize marchers?
- What would be the best route for the march?
- Is permission from local officials required to march?
- Will you need to consider food and sanitation?

3. 💿 PRIMARY SOURCE EXPLORER

Creating a Radio Special Many people say that the civil rights movement reached its climax on August 28, 1963. On that day, about 250,000 people arrived in Washington, D.C., to peacefully protest racial discrimination and show support for civil rights legislation. Use the CD-ROM, Internet, books, and other resources to create a special radio broadcast on the March on Washington. Consider including the following content:

- descriptions of and sound bytes from marchers
- the recollections of participants in the march
- recordings of speeches made at the gathering
- different newspaper accounts of the march

4. HISTORY PORTFOLIO

Option 1 Review your section and chapter assessment activities. Select one that you think is your best work. Then use comments made by your teacher or classmates to improve your work, and add it to your portfolio.

Option 2 Review the questions that you wrote for What Do You Want to Know? on page 410. Then write a short report in which you explain the answers to your questions. If any questions were not answered, do research to answer them. Add your answers to your portfolio.

Additional Test Practice, pp. S1–S33

TEST PRACTICE
CLASSZONE.COM

CHAPTER 16

The Vietnam War Years 1954–1975

Visitors honor the dead at the Vietnam Veterans Memorial in Washington, D.C.

Interact *with* History

Prowar rally in New York in 1970

Antiwar rally in Washington in 1969

WITH AMERICANS LIKE JOHN LINDSAY... HANOI CAN'T LOSE

GOD BLESS AMERICA

IMPEACH THE RED MA...

END THE WAR IN VIETNAM NOW

You are a young person in 1969. Your country is at war to stop Communists from taking over South Vietnam. College students have organized huge protests against the war and the draft. Many people think such protests are unpatriotic and an insult to the soldiers who are fighting.

What Do You Think?

- Should the United States try to stop the spread of communism in Vietnam?
- Why are so many people against the war?
- Is it unpatriotic to criticize the government? To refuse army service?

Would you support the war?

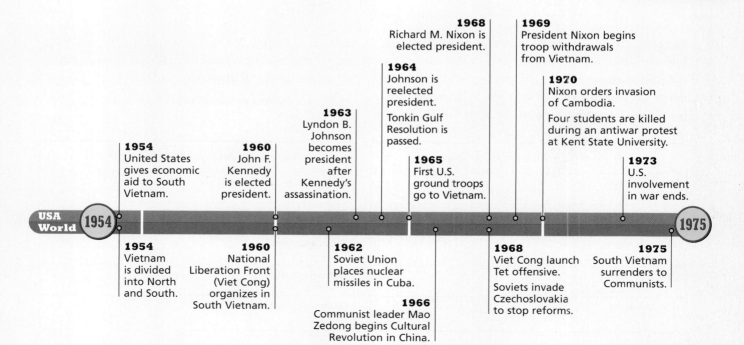

1954
United States gives economic aid to South Vietnam.

1960
John F. Kennedy is elected president.

1963
Lyndon B. Johnson becomes president after Kennedy's assassination.

1964
Johnson is reelected president.

Tonkin Gulf Resolution is passed.

1965
First U.S. ground troops go to Vietnam.

1968
Richard M. Nixon is elected president.

1969
President Nixon begins troop withdrawals from Vietnam.

1970
Nixon orders invasion of Cambodia.

Four students are killed during an antiwar protest at Kent State University.

1973
U.S. involvement in war ends.

USA
World

1954

1975

1954
Vietnam is divided into North and South.

1960
National Liberation Front (Viet Cong) organizes in South Vietnam.

1962
Soviet Union places nuclear missiles in Cuba.

1966
Communist leader Mao Zedong begins Cultural Revolution in China.

1968
Viet Cong launch Tet offensive.

Soviets invade Czechoslovakia to stop reforms.

1975
South Vietnam surrenders to Communists.

BEFORE YOU READ

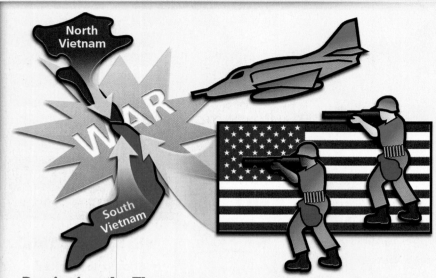

What Do You Know?

What images spring to mind when you hear the word *Vietnam*? What have you learned about the Vietnam War from movies, books, or relatives' stories? Have you seen the Vietnam Veterans Memorial or any other Vietnam memorials?

THINK ABOUT

• whether Americans seem proud of or ashamed of the war
• how this war differed from World War II or other wars you know about

Previewing the Theme

America in the World The United States became involved in the Vietnam War to stop the spread of communism in Asia. As more U.S. troops were sent there, doubts grew about whether they could achieve their mission. Eventually, the United States withdrew its soldiers and became more cautious about fighting foreign wars. Chapter 16 explains the history and legacy of the war in Vietnam.

What Do You Want to Know?

In your notebook, write down any questions you have about the war. Later, note the answers if you learn them in this chapter.

READ AND TAKE NOTES

Reading Strategy: Analyzing Points of View The Vietnam War bitterly divided Americans. Presidents, military strategists, ordinary soldiers, and college students, among others, all had their reasons for supporting or opposing the war. On a chart like the one below, note these reasons as you read. This will help you understand how the war split the country and why Americans still argue over it today.

 See Skillbuilder Handbook, page R9.

Reasons for Involvement in Vietnam
French alliance
Domino theory
Nation-building
Cold War crises
U.S. weaponry

Reasons Against Involvement in Vietnam
U.S. interests
Draft
Social programs
Vietnamese civilians
Domestic unrest

TERMS & NAMES
Ngo Dinh Diem
French Indochina
Ho Chi Minh
domino theory
Viet Cong
Ho Chi Minh Trail
Cuban missile crisis

1 Cold War Roots of the Conflict

MAIN IDEA	WHY IT MATTERS NOW
The United States entered the Vietnam War to stop the spread of communism.	The United States still becomes involved in foreign struggles for political reasons.

ONE AMERICAN'S STORY

Edward Lansdale, a U.S. military officer, went to South Vietnam in June 1954. His mission: to stop the spread of communism in Vietnam. He would try to do this by helping the non-Communist government of South Vietnam resist being taken over by Communist North Vietnam. Lansdale believed that the United States could defeat communism by "exporting the American way" and "winning the hearts and minds of the people" with generous economic and military aid.

Lansdale became a trusted adviser to **Ngo Dinh Diem** (uhng•oh dihn zih•ehm), the leader of South Vietnam. At Lansdale's urging, the United States helped support Diem's unpopular government. Within a year, Lansdale reported, "The Free Vietnamese are now becoming unified and learning how to cope with the Communist enemy."

Lansdale was too optimistic. U.S. involvement in Vietnam grew into the longest war the United States ever fought—and one in which it failed. The war would deeply divide not only the Vietnamese but also Americans. In this section, you will learn how the United States first became involved in Vietnam.

Edward Lansdale was one of the earliest U.S. military advisers sent to Vietnam.

Vietnam After World War II

From the late 1800s until World War II, France ruled Vietnam as part of its colony of **French Indochina**. The colony also included neighboring Laos (LAH•ohs) and Cambodia. (See the map on page 435.) During this colonial period, France increased its wealth by exporting rice and rubber from Vietnam. But Vietnamese peasants lost their land and grew poor.

The Vietnamese never accepted French rule. Various groups of nationalists, who wanted Vietnam to become an independent nation, staged revolts against the French. In 1930, a revolutionary leader named **Ho Chi Minh** (hoh chee mihn) united three Communist groups to form the Indochinese Communist Party (ICP). This new party called for an independent Vietnam controlled by peasants and other workers.

Ho Chi Minh speaks to a French audience in 1946.

The Indochinese Communist Party organized protests by peasants against the French government. The French responded by arresting suspected Communists and executing a number of leaders. Ho Chi Minh, who was living in China, was sentenced to death without being present.

In 1940, during World War II, Japan took over Indochina. The next year, Ho Chi Minh secretly returned to Vietnam and hid in a jungle camp. Under his direction, the ICP joined with other nationalists to form an organization called the Viet Minh. The Viet Minh trained soldiers to fight to make Vietnam independent of all foreign rulers. Because Japan was an enemy of the United States in World War II, the U.S. government aided Ho Chi Minh and the Viet Minh in their fight against the Japanese.

After the Japanese surrendered to the Allies in August 1945, Ho Chi Minh declared Vietnam's independence before a cheering crowd in Hanoi. But France soon tried to regain control of Vietnam. Ho Chi Minh sought a peaceful solution to the conflict with France.

Reading **History**

A. Analyzing Causes What was the original source of the conflict in Vietnam?

> **A VOICE FROM THE PAST**
>
> If they force us into war, we will fight. The struggle will be atrocious [terrible], but the Vietnamese people will suffer anything rather than renounce [give up] their freedom.
>
> **Ho Chi Minh,** quoted in *Vietnam: A History* by Stanley Karnow

Reading **History**

B. Reading a Map Use the map on page 435 to find Haiphong and Hanoi.

In 1946, war broke out between the Viet Minh and France. The French bombed Haiphong, and the Viet Minh attacked Hanoi.

Truman and Eisenhower Aid the French

As France fought to hold on to power in Vietnam, the United States struggled against the Soviet Union in the Cold War. President Truman followed a policy of containment, working to prevent the spread of communism in Western Europe.

In the fall of 1949, Communists gained control of China. This event made American leaders worry about the spread of communism in Asia. When France asked the United States for aid to help them fight the Viet Minh, the United States agreed. One reason was that U.S. leaders needed French support in opposing the Soviets in Europe. Another reason was that the United States did not want Vietnam to become Communist.

The United States entered the conflict in Vietnam in 1950, when President Truman offered $10 million in military aid to the French. After Dwight D. Eisenhower became president in 1953, he continued aiding the French war effort in Vietnam.

Reading History
C. Analyzing Points of View
Why did Truman and Eisenhower support the French in Vietnam?

Both Truman and Eisenhower used the **domino theory** to explain the need to support anti-Communists in Vietnam. According to this theory, if a country fell to communism, nearby countries would also topple, like a row of dominoes standing on end. U.S. leaders feared that if Vietnam became Communist, the rest of Southeast Asia would follow.

Dividing North and South

Even with limited U.S. support, France could not defeat the Viet Minh. In 1954, the Viet Minh overran French forces at Dien Bien Phu, in northwestern Vietnam. In May 1954, France met with the Viet Minh for peace talks in Geneva, Switzerland. The two sides reached an agreement called the Geneva Accords. This agreement divided Vietnam into North and South along the 17th parallel, or at 17°N latitude. Surrounding this line was a demilitarized zone, or DMZ. The split was meant to be temporary, however. The two sides agreed to hold elections in 1956 for a single government that would reunify the country.

Until then, the Geneva Accords allowed for separate governments in the North and the South. Ho Chi Minh and the Communists controlled North Vietnam. Ngo Dinh Diem, an anti-Communist, became prime minister and, later, president of South Vietnam. Thousands of anti-Communists from the North fled to the South. The United States provided ships for their transportation.

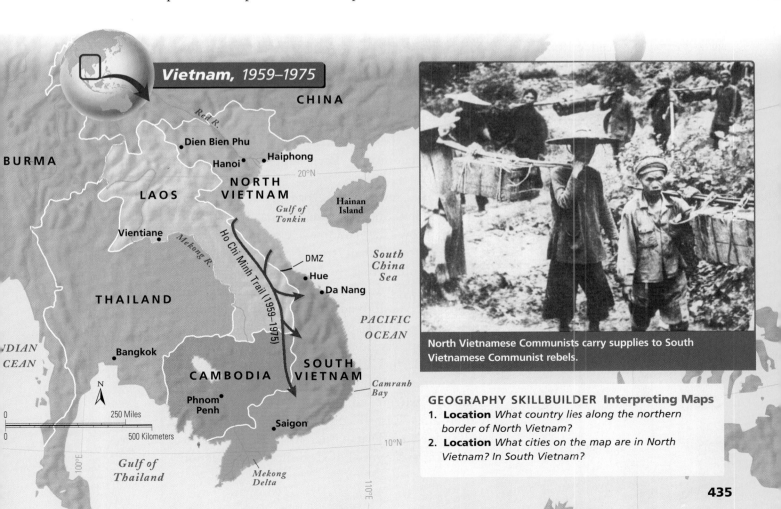

Vietnam, 1959–1975

North Vietnamese Communists carry supplies to South Vietnamese Communist rebels.

GEOGRAPHY SKILLBUILDER Interpreting Maps
1. **Location** What country lies along the northern border of North Vietnam?
2. **Location** What cities on the map are in North Vietnam? In South Vietnam?

Ho Chi Minh enjoyed great popularity in North Vietnam, while Diem had little support from the people of South Vietnam. As a result, Diem refused to hold national elections in 1956. President Eisenhower supported him, later saying, "If the elections had been held in 1956, Ho Chi Minh would have won 80% of the vote."

Instead, Eisenhower sent more aid and advisers to South Vietnam to help the Diem government. U.S. advisers described their mission as "nation-building."

The Viet Cong Oppose Diem

In spite of U.S. aid, Diem did not establish a democratic government in South Vietnam. Instead, his government was corrupt. In the countryside, for example, he let landlords take back land given to peasants. In addition, he jailed, tortured, and killed opponents.

Reading **History**
D. Making Inferences Why was the Diem government unpopular?

Diem's opponents included South Vietnamese Communists. In 1960, they joined with other dissatisfied South Vietnamese to form the National Liberation Front. Diem ridiculed the group by calling them the **Viet Cong,** for Vietnamese Communists. This name became the commonly used term for the group.

The Viet Cong fought to overthrow the Diem government and reunite the country under Communist rule. North Vietnam supported the Viet Cong, sending soldiers and supplies along a network of paths called the **Ho Chi Minh Trail**. This supply line wove through the jungles and mountains of neighboring Laos and Cambodia. By 1963, when John F. Kennedy was in the White House, the Viet Cong were close to victory.

Reading **History**
E. Reading a Map Find the Ho Chi Minh Trail on the map on page 435.

Kennedy Faces Communist Threats

President Kennedy continued to send military advisers and equipment to South Vietnam. By late 1963, the United States had more than 16,000 military personnel there. Kennedy faced a number of Cold War crises that influenced him to keep supporting the fight against communism in Vietnam.

The first was the Bay of Pigs invasion in April 1961. An army of Cuban exiles, trained by the United States, invaded Cuba. They planned to overthrow the country's Communist leader, Fidel Castro. Cuban troops easily crushed the invasion, humiliating the United States.

Then in June 1961, the Soviet Union threatened to close off Western access to West Berlin because so many East Germans were fleeing there to escape communism. Tensions rose when Kennedy insisted on West Berlin's independence. The Soviets and East Germans then built the Berlin Wall, a heavily guarded barrier dividing West Berlin from Communist East Berlin and East Germany. The wall, which made it harder for East Germans to flee, became a symbol of Communist oppression.

A woman in West Berlin talks across the Berlin Wall to her mother in East Berlin.

The **Cuban missile crisis** in October 1962 was Kennedy's most serious confrontation with the Soviets. Fidel Castro, believing the United States planned another attack on Cuba, had asked for more Soviet military aid. The United States learned that the Soviets had put nuclear missiles in Cuba. These missiles could reach U.S. cities within minutes. Kennedy weighed his choices. "The greatest danger of all," he told the country, "would be to do nothing." In a frightening showdown between the two superpowers, the Soviets agreed to remove the missiles, and the United States promised not to invade Cuba.

These Cold War crises fed American fears that the Soviet Union might become the strongest world power. In this climate of fear and suspicion, the United States made a greater effort to contain communism in Asia by sending more money and military advisers to South Vietnam.

Reading **History**
F. Analyzing Causes What Cold War crises made Kennedy increase his commitment to fight communism in Asia?

The Diem Government Falls

As U.S. aid increased, so did South Vietnamese opposition to Diem. American officials told Diem to make political, economic, and military reforms. But he refused.

The Kennedy administration lost faith in Diem. With U.S. support, a military coup overthrew Diem on November 1, 1963. Against Kennedy's wishes, the coup's leaders killed Diem. In a terrible and unrelated turn of events, President Kennedy was assassinated three weeks later. Vice-President Lyndon Johnson became president. He deepened U.S. involvement in the Vietnam War, as you will see in the next section.

Vocabulary
coup (koo): a sudden takeover by a small group

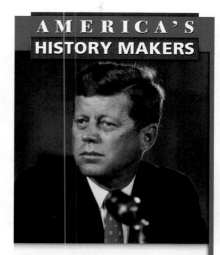

AMERICA'S HISTORY MAKERS

JOHN F. KENNEDY
1917–1963

In 1960, at age 43, John F. Kennedy became the youngest U.S. president ever elected. Handsome and energetic, he inspired belief in the country's capabilities.

Many Americans regard the Cuban missile crisis as Kennedy's finest moment of leadership. This conflict brought the United States to the brink of nuclear war. Kennedy considered bombing the Soviet missile sites in Cuba and invading the country before deciding it was safer to blockade Cuba and keep bargaining with Soviet leader Nikita Khrushchev.

How did the missile crisis show Kennedy's leadership?

 Section 1 Assessment

1. Terms & Names
Explain the significance of:
- Ngo Dinh Diem
- French Indochina
- Ho Chi Minh
- domino theory
- Viet Cong
- Ho Chi Minh Trail
- Cuban missile crisis

2. Taking Notes
Review the section and identify a key event for each year on the time line.

1930   1945   1950   1960

1940   1946   1954   1963

What event brought the United States into the Vietnam conflict?

3. Main Ideas
a. What were Ho Chi Minh's goals for Vietnam?

b. How did the Cold War affect American decisions regarding Vietnam?

c. What level of involvement did the Truman, Eisenhower, and Kennedy administrations have in Vietnam?

4. Critical Thinking
Evaluating How did U.S. support of the Diem government involve a conflict of values?

THINK ABOUT
- American beliefs in democracy and individual rights
- the actions of the Diem government

ACTIVITY OPTIONS

SPEECH
ART

Record imaginary **radio interviews** with Ho Chi Minh and Ngo Dinh Diem about Vietnam, or construct **signs** that their supporters might carry in a demonstration.

TERMS & NAMES
Gulf of Tonkin
  Resolution
escalation
William
  Westmoreland
guerrilla warfare
napalm
Agent Orange
Tet offensive

② War Expands in Vietnam

MAIN IDEA	WHY IT MATTERS NOW
America sent ground troops to Vietnam expecting victory, but soldiers soon grew frustrated.	The Vietnam War taught Americans that superior military strength does not always ensure victory.

ONE AMERICAN'S STORY

Reginald Edwards landed in Vietnam in 1965, the first year American combat troops were sent there. Despite two years of training, he was unprepared for the experience. It was nothing like his dream of "landing on this beach like they did in World War II." On night patrols through the dark countryside, Edwards and his fellow marines shot at whatever moved. Their first large-scale attack on the enemy proved disastrous.

A VOICE FROM THE PAST

We had received fire. All of a sudden we could see people in front of us. Instead of waiting for air [support], we returned the fire, and you could see people fall. . . . Come to find out it was Bravo Company. What the VC [Viet Cong] had done was [lure] Bravo Company in front of us. . . . It was our own people. That's the bodies we saw falling. . . . I think we shot up maybe 40 guys in Bravo Company.

Private Reginald "Malik" Edwards, quoted in *Bloods: An Oral History of the Vietnam War by Black Veterans*

American soldiers take aim in the Vietnamese jungle.

In this section, you will learn why the Vietnam War created such confusion and why people questioned how the war was conducted.

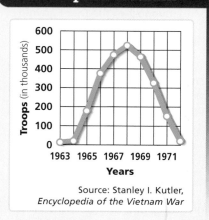

U.S. Troops in Vietnam

Troops (in thousands)

600
500
400
300
200
100
0

1963 1965 1967 1969 1971
Years

Source: Stanley I. Kutler,
Encyclopedia of the Vietnam War

Johnson Sends Combat Troops

The assassination of President Diem in 1963 brought chaos to South Vietnam. One ineffective leader after another headed the government. Meanwhile, the North Vietnamese kept shipping more aid to the Viet Cong. By late 1964, combined Viet Cong and North Vietnamese forces controlled much of the South Vietnamese countryside.

Like earlier presidents, Lyndon Johnson did not want to lose Vietnam to communism. As a result, he increased U.S. efforts in Vietnam.

In the summer of 1964, Johnson's military advisers made plans to bomb North Vietnam. They wanted to pressure Ho Chi Minh to stop supporting the Viet Cong. But no bombing could start unless Congress approved the plan. A shooting incident off the coast of North Vietnam spurred Congress to give its approval.

The U.S. destroyer *Maddox* had been patrolling in the Gulf of Tonkin when North Vietnamese torpedo boats fired on it. Two days later, on August 4, the *Maddox* and another destroyer reported a second attack. However, no one could confirm this attack. There had been thunderstorms that night, and the weather could have affected the radar screens. U.S. jet pilots flying overhead said they had seen no North Vietnamese boats.

Reading History

A. Finding Main Ideas What did the Gulf of Tonkin Resolution do?

Despite doubts about the second attack, Johnson asked Congress to pass the **Gulf of Tonkin Resolution**. This gave the president the power to use military force in Vietnam. All but two senators voted for the resolution. The "yes" vote in the House was unanimous.

In March 1965, Johnson began bombing North Vietnam. At about the same time, he sent the first combat ground troops to Vietnam. Their numbers grew from 75,000 in the middle of 1965 to 184,000 by the end of 1965.

This policy of **escalation,** or increasing military involvement in Vietnam, continued over the next few years. General **William Westmoreland,** the commander of U.S. forces in South Vietnam, asked for more and more troops. By the end of 1968, there were more than 536,000 American military personnel in South Vietnam.

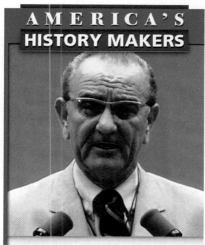

AMERICA'S HISTORY MAKERS

LYNDON JOHNSON

1908–1973

Lyndon Johnson wanted people to remember him as a social reformer. The Great Society was the name for his wide-ranging domestic programs, which included reforms in education, medical care for the elderly, aid to cities, and support for civil rights.

The Vietnam War overshadowed Johnson's achievements. He was tormented by the deaths and the social divisions the war brought. His goals for the country were blocked by the war, which still had not ended when he died.

How would you describe Johnson's presidency?

A Frustrating War

Many Americans thought that, with their superior weapons, U.S. ground forces would quickly defeat the Viet Cong and drive them out of the villages. Many conditions frustrated American soldiers, however. First of all, they could wage only a limited war, partly because the government feared drawing China into the conflict.

Background
The average World War II soldier was 26 and served for three years. Many soldiers in Vietnam had fathers who had fought in World War II.

Also, most U.S. soldiers in Vietnam were young and inexperienced. The average soldier was 19 and served a one-year tour of duty. Officers served even shorter tours, on average six months. The short tours meant that by the time soldiers and officers had gained enough experience, their tours of duty were over.

The Vietnam War differed from World War II in that there was no frontline. The Viet Cong mixed with the general population and operated everywhere, attacking U.S. troops in the countryside and in the cities. Even a shoeshine boy on a city street corner might toss a grenade into an army bus carrying American soldiers. Marine captain E. J. Banks described his frustration: "You never knew who was the enemy and who was the friend. . . . The enemy was all around you."

Booby Traps
The Viet Cong hid deadly booby traps made of sharpened sticks.

Guerrilla Warfare
In the jungles, surprise attacks could come at any moment. Helicopters quickly took the wounded to hospitals.

The style of fighting in Vietnam also differed from that in World War II. Because they could not match American firepower, the Viet Cong relied on **guerrilla warfare,** surprise attacks by small bands of fighters. Viet Cong guerrillas would suddenly emerge from networks of underground tunnels to fight. Then they would disappear back into the tunnels. They riddled the countryside and jungles with land mines and booby traps, such as bamboo stakes hidden in covered pits. They hung grenades from trees and hid them in bushes. Every day, U.S. Army and Navy nurses treated young soldiers with gruesome wounds.

Even the land and climate of Vietnam proved difficult. The heat was suffocating and the rain almost constant. Soldiers sweated through tangled jungles. After wading through flooded rice paddies, they had to pick leeches off their feet and legs. American soldier Warren Wooten said, "It seemed like the whole country was an enemy. The animals, the reptiles, the insects, the plants. And the people."

Finally, the Viet Cong were a very dedicated enemy. They took heavy losses, built up their ranks again, and kept on fighting year after year because they believed in their cause. An American who interviewed Viet Cong prisoners noted, "They see the war entirely as one of defense of their country against the invading Americans, who, in turn, are seen merely as successors to the French."

Background
Nearly 7,500 women served in Vietnam as nurses.

Reading **History**
B. Analyzing Causes Why was the war so hard for the United States to win?

Stripping the Jungle

One of the strengths of the Viet Cong was their ability to hide in the jungle and in underground tunnels. To reveal and destroy Viet Cong hideouts, American troops used chemicals that ruined the landscape.

Search-and-Destroy Missions
U.S. soldiers destroyed villages
suspected of hiding Viet Cong.

Napalm
U.S. planes dropped fiery napalm
bombs to wipe out Viet Cong
bases. Napalm is jellied gasoline.

Over wide areas, U.S. planes dropped bombs of **napalm,** jellied gasoline that burns violently. Planes also sprayed **Agent Orange,** a chemical that kills plants, over the jungles.

Such chemicals helped destroy the hideouts and food supplies of the Viet Cong. But in the process, they also harmed innocent Vietnamese villagers. This undermined the villagers' support for the United States. Later, people learned that Agent Orange harmed U.S. soldiers as well. Veterans exposed to it have suffered from skin diseases and cancers.

Search-and-Destroy Missions

Search-and-destroy missions were another American war tactic that terrorized Vietnamese villagers. In such missions, soldiers hunted Viet Cong and burned or bombed villages thought to be sheltering them. Marine sergeant William Ehrhart described how search-and-destroy missions affected South Vietnamese peasants.

A VOICE FROM THE PAST

Their homes had been wrecked, their chickens killed, their rice confiscated [taken away]—and if they weren't pro-Vietcong before we got there, they sure . . . were by the time we left.

William Ehrhart, quoted in *Vietnam: A History* by Stanley Karnow

*Reading*History

C. Drawing Conclusions Why did Americans fail in "winning the hearts and minds" of the people in Vietnam?

These destructive methods defeated the purpose of "winning the hearts and minds" of the villagers and turning them against communism. Furthermore, even if the tactics did clear a village of Viet Cong temporarily, the Viet Cong usually returned later.

The Surprise Tet Offensive

By the end of 1967, the war had caused great destruction, but neither side was close to victory. Still, U.S. military officials claimed that they would soon win. Then, on January 30 and 31, 1968, the Communists launched the **Tet offensive**. This was a surprise attack on U.S. military bases and more than 100 cities and towns in South Vietnam. It came during Tet, the Vietnamese celebration of the lunar New Year.

In preparation for the Tet offensive, the Viet Cong hid weapons in vegetable trucks, food trucks, peddlers' carts, and even coffins. They smuggled these weapons into South Vietnamese cities. Soldiers dressed in civilian clothes entered the cities on buses, on motorcycles, and on foot. No one could tell them apart from the war refugees who streamed into the cities from the countryside or from visitors coming for the holiday.

The Viet Cong fought to take over the cities during the offensive. They killed not only enemy soldiers but also government officials, schoolteachers, doctors, and priests.

The Tet offensive was a military defeat for the Communists. They gained no cities and lost 45,000 soldiers, while the South Vietnamese lost 2,300 soldiers and the United States 1,100.

But the attack stunned Americans. General Westmoreland had recently declared, "We have turned the corner," suggesting that victory was in sight. The Tet offensive raised doubts that this was true. Many government and business leaders began to think that the United States could not win the war, except at too high a price.

The Tet offensive also made many Americans ask whether the U.S. mission in Vietnam was wise. To retake some cities, troops had to almost level them with bombing and shelling. Speaking of the city of Ben Tre, a U.S. major said, "It became necessary to destroy the town in order to save it." The quote became an example of what many considered the senselessness of the war.

Because of the doubts it raised, the Tet offensive became a turning point in the war. Afterward, President Johnson changed his war policy. When General Westmoreland asked for 206,000 more troops, to take advantage of the enemy's weakness, President Johnson said no. Then, on March 31, 1968, Johnson said that he would stop bombing most of North Vietnam and would seek to

Background
In the Tet offensive, enemy forces invaded the U.S. embassy compound in Saigon, killing five Americans.

Reading **History**

D. Drawing Conclusions How was the Tet offensive both a failure and a success for the Viet Cong?

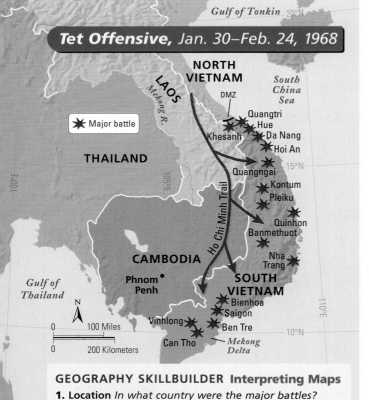

Tet Offensive, *Jan. 30–Feb. 24, 1968*

Gulf of Tonkin

NORTH VIETNAM

LAOS

Mekong R.

DMZ

South China Sea

★ Major battle

Quangtri
Hue
Khesanh
Da Nang
Hoi An

THAILAND

Ho Chi Minh Trail

Quangngai

Kontum
Pleiku

Quinhon
Banmethuot

CAMBODIA

Nha Trang

Gulf of Thailand

Phnom Penh

SOUTH VIETNAM

Bienhoa
Saigon
Vinhlong
Ben Tre
Can Tho
Mekong Delta

0   100 Miles
0   200 Kilometers

GEOGRAPHY SKILLBUILDER Interpreting Maps
1. **Location** *In what country were the major battles?*
2. **Location** *What did the number and location of attacks suggest about the country's security?*

bargain for peace. In the same speech, he announced that he would not run for another term as president.

U.S. Morale Sinks

As the Vietnam War went on, it wore down American soldiers. They fought hard and bravely, but many were losing faith that the United States could win the war. The South Vietnamese government did not have the loyalty of the people. In addition, the South Vietnamese army often avoided fighting. American soldiers asked why they were fighting a war the Vietnamese did not want to fight themselves.

The low morale of American forces in Vietnam became clear when news of the My Lai (mee ly) massacre broke in 1969. The incident happened on March 16, 1968. A U.S. platoon led by Lieutenant William Calley, Jr., rounded up and shot between 175 and 500 unarmed civilians, mostly women, children, and old men. A U.S. helicopter pilot rescued some civilians by threatening to fire on the soldiers. To Americans, My Lai represented a horrifying breakdown in morality and discipline in the armed forces. In 1971, a colonel warned that U.S. forces were "in a state approaching collapse."

In the next section, you'll learn how the United States withdrew from the Vietnam War.

Background
Calley was jailed briefly, but many saw him as a scapegoat because charges were dropped against higher-ranking officers.

"I DON'T KNOW IF EITHER SIDE IS WINNING, BUT I KNOW WHO'S LOSING."

This 1968 cartoon by Herblock comments on the war's cost to civilians.

Section 2 Assessment

1. Terms & Names

Explain the significance of:
- Gulf of Tonkin Resolution
- escalation
- William Westmoreland
- guerrilla warfare
- napalm
- Agent Orange
- Tet offensive

2. Taking Notes

On a chart like the one below, note the war's effects on Vietnamese villagers and on U.S. soldiers.

Effects of War

Villagers	U.S. Soldiers

3. Main Ideas

a. How did President Johnson escalate U.S. involvement in the Vietnam War?

b. What made fighting the war so frustrating for American soldiers?

c. How was the Tet offensive a turning point in the war?

4. Critical Thinking

Analyzing Points of View
Were the Viet Cong right to see the Americans "merely as successors to the French"?

THINK ABOUT
- the goals of the French in Vietnam
- the goals of the Americans in Vietnam
- the actions of the French and the Americans

ACTIVITY OPTIONS

SCIENCE

HEALTH

Investigate the health effects of Agent Orange reported by Vietnam veterans. Design a science **exhibit** or create a **warning label** to share your findings.

TERMS & NAMES
doves
hawks
Richard Nixon
Vietnamization
Cambodia
Twenty-sixth
  Amendment
War Powers Act

MAIN IDEA

The Vietnam War divided Americans and had lasting effects in the United States and Southeast Asia.

WHY IT MATTERS NOW

Lessons of the Vietnam War still influence the United States whenever it gets involved in a foreign conflict.

ONE AMERICAN'S STORY

Mary Ann Vecchio was just 14 years old when she suddenly became a symbol of the anguish that the Vietnam War caused Americans. A student journalist snapped Vecchio's picture as she knelt over a dead student at Kent State University in Ohio. The youth was Jeffrey Glenn Miller, one of four students killed by the National Guard during an antiwar demonstration on May 4, 1970. Looking back 25 years later, Vecchio described her feelings of disbelief.

Mary Ann Vecchio cries out in horror after the Kent State shootings in May 1970.

A VOICE FROM THE PAST

I couldn't believe that people would kill people over what they thought, just because he demonstrated against the Vietnam War—that they would shoot you over it. I couldn't believe . . . . There was nothing I could do for Jeffrey or any of the other students. And that's part of history and that'll remain with me for the rest of my life.

Mary Ann Vecchio Gillum, conference at Emerson College, April 23, 1995

In this section, you will learn how growing opposition to the war eventually led the United States to pull its troops out of Vietnam.

A Growing Antiwar Movement

As the war escalated in the mid-1960s, antiwar feeling grew among Americans at home. Religious leaders, civil rights leaders, teachers, students, journalists, and others protested the war for a variety of reasons. Some believed that the United States had no business involving itself in another country's civil war. Others believed that the methods of fighting the war were immoral. Still others thought that the costs to American society were too high.

College students formed a large and vocal group of protesters. They particularly opposed the draft, which required young men to serve in the military. In demonstrations around the country, young men burned their draft cards. About 50,000 people staged such a protest in front of the Pentagon on October 21, 1967.

Opponents of the draft pointed out its unfairness. Most draftees were poor. Middle- and upper-class youths could delay being drafted by enrolling in college. They also sought advice from draft counselors, doctors, and lawyers to help them avoid service. Certain medical conditions or religious beliefs, for example, could keep them out of the military.

Reading**History**
A. Analyzing Points of View
Why did people think the draft was unfair?

Another unfair aspect of the draft was the high number of African Americans called to serve. African Americans made up about 20 percent of combat troops in Vietnam. In 1965, they accounted for 24 percent of U.S. Army combat deaths. Yet they were only 11 percent of the male population in the United States.

For this and other reasons, the antiwar movement became linked with the civil rights movement. In 1967, civil rights leader Martin Luther King, Jr., spoke out against the Vietnam War. Noting that the war took money away from antipoverty programs, he declared, "I was increasingly compelled to see the war as an enemy of the poor."

By 1967, it was clear that the Vietnam War was dividing Americans into two camps. Even within families, people took opposite sides. Those who opposed the war were called **doves**. Those who supported it were known as **hawks**. Supporters of the war staged marches of their own. Believing that antiwar protesters were unpatriotic, they popularized such slogans as "America—love it or leave it."

1968—A Turning Point

As you learned in Section 2, the Tet offensive in January 1968 made Americans doubt that they could win the war. Walter Cronkite, a respected TV news anchorman, visited Vietnam in February. After returning, he ended a special report with his own opinion of the war. He concluded that the United States was not winning but was in a deadlock.

A VOICE FROM THE PAST

[T]he only rational way out, then, will be to negotiate, not as victors, but as an honorable people who lived up to their pledge to defend democracy, and did the best they could.

Walter Cronkite, *A Reporter's Life*

President Johnson took Cronkite's words to heart. "If I've lost Cronkite, I've lost middle America," he reportedly said.

That summer, the Democratic National Convention in Chicago reflected the country's turmoil. Democrats chose Hubert Humphrey, Johnson's vice-president, as their nominee. Outside the convention hall, TV

daily *life*

THE "TELEVISION WAR"

The Vietnam War was the first "television war," broadcast each night on the evening news. Reports rarely showed actual battles, partly because much of the fighting occurred off and on and at night, between small units.

Networks also tried to avoid gruesome scenes because they did not want to offend viewers. In addition, the networks agreed not to show any American dead or wounded so that their families would not see them on the screen. Still, the images of war shocked TV audiences.

cameras showed police clubbing antiwar demonstrators and bystanders. The chaos helped Republican candidate **Richard Nixon** win the presidency in 1968. In his campaign, Nixon promised to "bring an honorable end to the war in Vietnam."

Nixon's Vietnam Strategy

In July 1969, Nixon announced his strategy of **Vietnamization.** It called for gradually withdrawing U.S. forces and turning the ground fighting over to the South Vietnamese. Nixon promised to withdraw 25,000 of the 543,000 U.S. ground troops in Vietnam by the end of the year. However, Nixon had already begun secret bombing raids of **Cambodia,** a country bordering Vietnam. This bombing was meant to stop North Vietnamese troops and supplies from moving along the Ho Chi Minh Trail. Many people grew angry when they learned that the government had widened the war and hidden its actions.

Public anger and distrust of the government grew after Daniel Ellsberg released the Pentagon Papers to the *New York Times* in 1971. Ellsberg had helped research and write these secret Defense Department papers. They showed that the four previous presidential administrations had not been honest with the public about U.S. involvement and goals in Vietnam.

Background
In 1970, a U.S. invasion of Cambodia sparked protests at Kent State and many other colleges.

Withdrawal from Vietnam

Thousands try to escape during the fall of Saigon.

Promising that peace was at hand, Nixon was reelected by a landslide in 1972. On January 27, 1973, the United States and South Vietnam signed a peace agreement with North Vietnam and the Viet Cong. The United States agreed to withdraw all its troops, and North Vietnam agreed not to invade South Vietnam. On March 29, the last U.S. troops left Vietnam. For the United States, the war was over.

But for the Vietnamese, the war continued. In 1975, North Vietnam launched a massive invasion of South Vietnam. On April 30 of that year, Communist forces captured Saigon, which they renamed Ho Chi Minh City. The war then ended.

*Reading*History
B. Making Inferences Why did fighting begin again after the peace agreement?

Legacy of the Vietnam War

The Vietnam War caused terrible destruction and suffering in Southeast Asia. More than 1.2 million North and South Vietnamese died in the conflict. American bombing and chemical spraying caused lasting damage to farmland and forests. The war ruined Vietnam's economy, leaving many in poverty. After the North Vietnamese set up Communist rule in the reunited country, many Vietnamese fled. By 1980, almost 173,000 had come to the United States.

The Vietnam War also took a heavy toll on American soldiers. About 58,000 died, and more than 300,000 were wounded. Many suffered permanent, disabling injuries. Returning soldiers often had recurring nightmares and other stress-related problems. To make things worse, they came home to a public that treated them coldly.

Background
Although there is no draft now, 18-year-old men must still register with the Selective Service in case Congress orders a draft in the future.

The Vietnam War had far-reaching political effects in the United States. The **Twenty-sixth Amendment,** passed in 1971, lowered the voting age from 21 to 18. Its supporters argued persuasively that anyone old enough to be drafted should be allowed to vote. The government ended the draft in 1973 because so many people opposed it. The nation now relies on an all-volunteer military.

Another legacy of Vietnam is that Americans have been less willing to get involved in overseas wars. In 1973, Congress passed the **War Powers Act,** which limits the president's war-making powers. The president must report to Congress within 48 hours if troops have been sent into a hostile situation without a declaration of war. They can remain for no more than 90 days unless Congress permits them to.

Reading **History**
C. Making Inferences Why did the Vietnam War influence Congress to pass the War Powers Act?

Finally, the war made many Americans distrust government leaders, who sometimes misled the public about actions in Vietnam. In Chapter 17, you will read about the Watergate scandal, which further shook confidence in government and brought down Nixon's presidency.

America's HERITAGE

VIETNAM VETERANS MEMORIAL

The public finally honored those who served in Vietnam with the Vietnam Veterans Memorial, designed by Maya Lin and unveiled in Washington, D.C., on November 13, 1982. Etched into this V-shaped black granite wall are the names of all Americans killed in the war.

At the Wall, as it is known, visitors leave letters, flowers, and mementos. Many believe that the monument has helped heal the divisions created by the war. As the father of a veteran noted, "It doesn't say whether the war was right or wrong. . . . It just says, 'Here is the price we paid.'"

Section 3 Assessment

1. Terms & Names

Explain the significance of:
- doves
- hawks
- Richard Nixon
- Vietnamization
- Cambodia
- Twenty-sixth Amendment
- War Powers Act

2. Taking Notes

Use a chart like this one to review information about the antiwar movement.

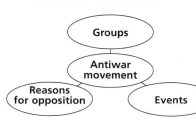

Groups

Antiwar movement

Reasons for opposition

Events

3. Main Ideas

a. Why did more and more Americans oppose the war after 1968?

b. How did the Vietnam War end?

c. In what major ways did the war affect Southeast Asia and the United States?

4. Critical Thinking

Forming and Supporting Opinions What is your opinion of the way the United States ended its involvement in the Vietnam War?

THINK ABOUT
- what happened to South Vietnam
- what options the United States had

ACTIVITY OPTIONS

LITERATURE

MATH

Compare the Vietnam War to World War II by writing an **essay** on two pieces of war literature or by presenting comparable **statistics.**

Chapter 16 ASSESSMENT

The Vietnam War Years

1946

1946
Communist-led Vietnamese nationalists struggle for independence from France.

1950
United States sends aid to the French.

1954
French are defeated. Vietnam divides into Communist North and non-Communist South.

1965
United States bombs North Vietnam and sends combat ground troops to South Vietnam.

1973
United States withdraws its troops.

1975
South Vietnam surrenders to the Communists.

TERMS & NAMES

Briefly explain the significance of each of the following.

1. Ho Chi Minh
2. domino theory
3. Viet Cong
4. Ho Chi Minh Trail
5. guerrilla warfare
6. Agent Orange
7. Tet offensive
8. Richard Nixon
9. Vietnamization
10. Twenty-sixth Amendment

REVIEW QUESTIONS

Cold War Roots of the Conflict (pages 433–437)

1. Why did the United States decide to support France in its fight against the Viet Minh?
2. What decisions about Vietnam were laid out in the 1954 Geneva Accords?
3. What Cold War crises made President Kennedy continue to aid Ngo Dinh Diem's government in South Vietnam?

War Expands in Vietnam (pages 438–443)

4. How was President Johnson's Vietnam policy different from President Kennedy's?
5. What kept U.S. troops from defeating the Viet Cong quickly?
6. How did American war tactics affect Vietnamese villagers?
7. How was the Tet offensive both a defeat and a victory for the Communists?

The Vietnam War Ends (pages 444–447)

8. Why did many Americans protest against the war?
9. What policies did President Nixon pursue in Vietnam?
10. What long-term political effects did the Vietnam War have on the United States?

CRITICAL THINKING

1. USING YOUR NOTES

Reasons for involvement in Vietnam
French alliance
Domino theory
Nation building
Cold War crises
U.S. weaponry

Reasons against involvement in Vietnam
U.S. interests
Draft
Social programs
Vietnamese civilians
Domestic unrest

Using your completed chart from the beginning of this chapter, answer the questions.

a. Which do you consider the strongest reason in support of American involvement in the Vietnam War?
b. Which do you consider the strongest reason against American involvement in the Vietnam War?
c. Which side do you think is more persuasive? Why?

2. ANALYZING LEADERSHIP

How would you evaluate President Johnson's leadership during the Vietnam War and his decision not to seek a second term as president?

3. APPLYING CITIZENSHIP SKILLS

During the Vietnam War, many Americans had to choose between obeying laws and following their consciences. In your opinion, what is the right thing to do in such a situation?

4. THEME: AMERICA IN THE WORLD

How do you think involvement in the Vietnam War affected the reputation of the United States among other nations? Why?

5. DRAWING CONCLUSIONS

Would the United States have become involved in the Vietnam War if the Cold War had not been going on? Explain your opinion.

Interact *with* History

If you had lived during the Vietnam War, what would have determined whether you supported or opposed the war?

HISTORY SKILLS

1. INTERPRETING CHARTS

Read the chart and then answer the questions.

U.S. Deaths in Four Wars		
WAR	BATTLE DEATHS	OTHER DEATHS*
World War I	53,513	63,195
World War II	292,131	115,185
Korean War	33,629	20,617
Vietnam War	47,244	10,446

*accidents, diseases, etc.

Source: Harry G. Summers, Jr., *Vietnam War Almanac*

Basic Chart Elements

a. What is the subject of the chart?

b. What is the difference between the second and third columns?

Interpreting the Chart

c. Which war or wars caused more battle deaths than the Vietnam War?

d. Which war had the lowest ratio of nonbattle deaths to battle deaths?

2. INTERPRETING PRIMARY SOURCES

Read this passage by a Vietnamese woman, addressed to an American veteran of the Vietnam War. Then answer the questions.

> You came to Vietnam, willingly or not, because your country demanded it. Most of you did not know, or fully understand, the different wars my people were fighting when you got here. For you, it was a simple thing: democracy against communism. For us, that was not our fight at all. How could it be? We knew little of democracy and even less about communism. For most of us it was a fight for independence—like the American Revolution.
>
> **Le Ly Hayslip,** *When Heaven and Earth Changed Places*

a. What did American soldiers misunderstand, according to Hayslip?

b. What seems to be Hayslip's attitude toward Americans?

ALTERNATIVE ASSESSMENT

1. INTERDISCIPLINARY ACTIVITY: Music

Analyzing Antiwar Songs Research antiwar songs of the late 1960s and early 1970s. Choose one song, play it for the class, and talk about the meaning of its lyrics. Explain what the song adds to your understanding of the Vietnam era.

2. COOPERATIVE ACTIVITY

Making a Video Documentary Work in a group to create and present a video documentary about the Vietnam War and its impact on the country or your town. As part of your research, talk to adults who lived through the Vietnam era and who have different perspectives on the war. You might try to locate a soldier or nurse who served, someone who faced the draft but was not called to serve, an antiwar demonstrator, or someone who lost a loved one in the war.

3. TECHNOLOGY ACTIVITY

Planning a Web Site Most Americans still know little about the country of Vietnam. Plan a Web site that will give future classes geographical, historical, and cultural background on Vietnam before they study the war. Use the library and the Internet, or contact colleges, museums, or Vietnamese organizations to get started.

For more about Vietnam . . .

INTERNET ACTIVITY
CLASSZONE.COM

Your site might include the following things.

- Detailed maps of Vietnam and its major cities
- Photographs of people, landscapes, and art objects
- A listing of products grown or made in Vietnam
- Biographies of important people in Vietnamese history
- Excerpts from stories, poetry, or memoirs by Vietnamese writers
- Internet links to other sites

4. HISTORY PORTFOLIO

Option 1 Review your section and chapter assessment activities. Select one that you think is your best work. Use comments made by your teacher or classmates to improve your work, then add it to your portfolio.

Option 2 Review the questions that you wrote for What Do You Want to Know? on page 432. Then write a short report in which you explain the answers to your questions. If any questions were not answered, do research to answer them.

Additional Test Practice, pp. S1–S33

TEST PRACTICE
CLASSZONE.COM

Years of Doubt
1969–1981

NUCLEAR ACCIDENT AT THREE MILE ISLAND

IRANIANS TAKE AMERICANS HOSTAGE

NATION SUFFERS ENERGY CRISIS

SORRY NO GAS
Save our Water

WATERGATE BREAK-IN LEADS TO PRESIDENTIAL SCANDAL

Nixon Resigns

Ford Assumes Presidency Today

It is the evening of August 8, 1974. You are watching television when your favorite program is interrupted by a speech from President Richard M. Nixon. Looking grim and tired, Nixon says that he will resign the next day. You wonder how the country will cope with the crisis.

What Do You Think?

- What happens when a president resigns from office? Has a president resigned before?

- How has the government functioned when a president has died?

- What other crises has the country faced?

How is America able to survive a crisis and move on?

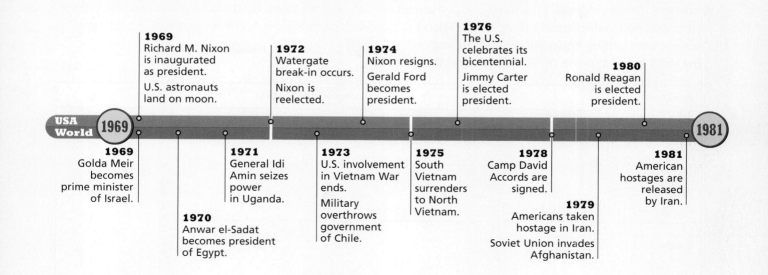

USA
World 1969 — 1981

1969
Richard M. Nixon is inaugurated as president.
U.S. astronauts land on moon.

1972
Watergate break-in occurs.
Nixon is reelected.

1974
Nixon resigns.
Gerald Ford becomes president.

1976
The U.S. celebrates its bicentennial.
Jimmy Carter is elected president.

1980
Ronald Reagan is elected president.

1969
Golda Meir becomes prime minister of Israel.

1971
General Idi Amin seizes power in Uganda.

1970
Anwar el-Sadat becomes president of Egypt.

1973
U.S. involvement in Vietnam War ends.
Military overthrows government of Chile.

1975
South Vietnam surrenders to North Vietnam.

1978
Camp David Accords are signed.

1979
Americans taken hostage in Iran.
Soviet Union invades Afghanistan.

1981
American hostages are released by Iran.

BEFORE YOU READ

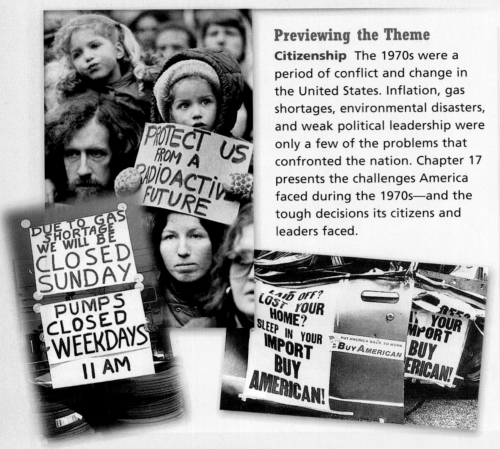

Previewing the Theme

Citizenship The 1970s were a period of conflict and change in the United States. Inflation, gas shortages, environmental disasters, and weak political leadership were only a few of the problems that confronted the nation. Chapter 17 presents the challenges America faced during the 1970s—and the tough decisions its citizens and leaders faced.

What Do You Know?

What do you already know about the problems of the 1970s, such as inflation and the energy crisis? Were they different from problems the country faced at other times in its history?

THINK ABOUT

• what you have learned about the 1970s from books, movies, television, and popular music
• how the nation has reacted to economic, political, and social problems in the past

What Do You Want to Know?

What would you like to know about Watergate and other crises of the 1970s? In your notebook, record what you hope to learn from this chapter.

READ AND TAKE NOTES

Reading Strategy: Taking Notes To help you remember what you read, take notes about the major issues and events discussed in this chapter. Taking notes means writing down important information. The chart below lists the three presidents of the 1970s—Richard Nixon, Gerald Ford, and Jimmy Carter. As you read, use a chart like the one below to take notes on the issues and events of their presidencies.

 See Skillbuilder Handbook, page R3.

President	Issues and Events
Nixon	
Ford	
Carter	

Nixon Confronts Problems

TERMS & NAMES
Richard M. Nixon
Henry Kissinger
revenue sharing
détente
SALT

MAIN IDEA

President Richard M. Nixon faced the challenge of governing a deeply divided America.

WHY IT MATTERS NOW

Social, economic, and political divisions are still part of American life.

ONE AMERICAN'S STORY

Shortly after his election as president in November 1968, **Richard M. Nixon** began selecting his cabinet and closest advisers. Most of his choices were wealthy business executives or lawyers. But one who did not fit this description was **Henry Kissinger**. Kissinger was a professor at Harvard University and a Jewish refugee from Nazi Germany. He had become a well-known foreign-policy expert.

Nixon picked Kissinger to be his national security adviser because he felt that Kissinger had great intelligence, insight, and experience. Nixon also found that he and Kissinger had very similar ideas about politics. Both men were practical politicians who did not let their ideologies, or beliefs, get in the way of their actions.

President Richard Nixon (left) walks with Henry Kissinger, his national security adviser.

A VOICE FROM THE PAST

The statesman manipulates [shrewdly manages] reality; his first goal is survival. . . . He is conscious of many great hopes which have failed, of many good intentions that could not be realized.

Henry A. Kissinger, *American Foreign Policy*

That statement might just as easily have been written by President Nixon. In this section, you will learn how Nixon used a practical approach to try to solve problems at home and, with Kissinger's help, abroad.

A Divided America

As president, Richard M. Nixon would have liked to focus on foreign policy and leave domestic issues to his cabinet. But he became president at a time when America was being torn apart by inflation, racial problems, and conflict over the war in Vietnam. Also, he had won the presidency in 1968 by only a narrow margin. His major support came from conservatives. They wanted him to shrink the federal government and end Lyndon Johnson's Great Society programs.

Nixon hoped to cut the cost of running the federal government and turn some of its activities over to the states. But both houses of Congress were controlled by the Democrats. As a result, he took a more moderate

DESTINATION MOON

On July 20, 1969, with 600 million people viewing on television, Apollo 11 astronaut Neil Armstrong stepped onto the moon and said, "That's one small step for a man, one giant leap for mankind." Edwin Aldrin (shown below) soon joined him. The excitement of the first moon landing gave Americans a sense of unity during a troubled time.

On July 31, 1999, an American space probe was sent crashing into the moon's surface. Its purpose was to see whether there was water on the moon. This flight took place almost 30 years to the day after the historic first landing.

approach at first. But he did veto many spending bills passed by the Democratic Congress. Included were cuts in funds for education and low-income housing—Great Society programs.

In 1969, President Nixon attempted to change the existing welfare system, which had been criticized by conservatives. But he could not get congressional agreement. He was more successful in starting **revenue sharing**. Under revenue sharing, the federal government gave back some tax money it collected to state and local governments. These governments could spend the money on any number of different programs. The plan was supported by both parties and passed Congress in 1972.

*Reading*History
A. Recognizing Effects How did Nixon try to shrink the size of the federal government?

Law-and-Order Politics

During the presidential campaign, Nixon had said that he would restore law and order. He promised an end to the social unrest and rioting of the late 1960s. Nixon also promised a return to traditional values.

One way to his goal, Nixon thought, was to appoint more conservative justices to the Supreme Court. He believed that these justices would rule against loose interpretations of the law. Such interpretations, Nixon and his supporters felt, were partly to blame for rising crime. During his first term, he appointed four new justices.

Nixon also used all the powers of the federal government to "crack down" on crime and protest. He directed the Central Intelligence Agency and the Federal Bureau of Investigation to investigate some of his political enemies. Nixon would later excuse any illegal acts by claiming they were needed for the nation's security.

A Troubled Economy

Civil unrest and crime were not the only problems President Nixon had to face. He inherited serious economic troubles. Under the Johnson administration, the government began spending huge amounts of money on programs to aid the poor *and* on fighting the Vietnam War. But taxes were not raised to cover these expenses. As a result, the government spent more money than it collected in taxes. This practice is called deficit spending.

Deficit spending put a great deal of money into circulation in the late 1960s. At the same time, the economy began to slow down. By 1970, the economy had gone into a recession. With the recession, fewer goods were produced. The increase in the money supply and the decrease in products to buy caused inflation. (See Economics in History on the next page.)

Inflation caused problems for all Americans, but especially the poor. One mother said, "I used to be able to go to the store with $50 and come back with six or seven bags of groceries. Now I'm lucky if I come back

*Reading*History
B. Analyzing Causes What were causes of the nation's troubled economy?

with three." When Nixon took office in 1969, the inflation rate was about 5 percent. That was twice the rate it had been earlier in the decade. Increasing unemployment was another problem. It doubled from about 3 percent in 1969 to 6 percent in 1971.

Nixon tried different ways to help the economy. He cut spending. He also placed a temporary freeze on wage and price increases. Inflation dropped but only temporarily. Then, in 1973, the economy was jolted by the actions of the Organization of Petroleum Exporting Countries (OPEC).

OPEC raised its prices and cut its shipments of oil to the United States. OPEC, which was made up mainly of Arab nations, took these actions in part to protest America's support of Israel in the Yom Kippur War of 1973. That war was fought between Israel and its Arab neighbors. In a few months, gas prices quadrupled. Inflation and unemployment soared to new heights.

Vocabulary
quadrupled: multiplied by four

Besides these serious economic problems at home, Nixon also faced tough challenges in foreign policy.

Economics *in* History

Inflation

Inflation is a rise in prices across the economy. When the price of milk goes up, that's a price increase. When the prices of gasoline, clothing, food, housing, and health care all go up, that's inflation.

Sometimes prices rise because there's more demand for goods than there are goods available to buy. This happened after World War II. During the war years, factories had produced weapons and supplies for the war effort. After the war, it took a while for factories to produce enough peacetime goods to meet consumer demand.

Sometimes prices rise because businesses increase their prices to cover their rising costs. This was the case in the 1970s, when the rising price of oil sent up the prices of many different goods and services.

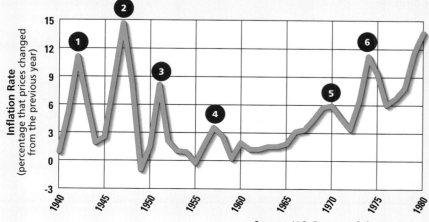

Source: *U.S. Bureau of the Census*

CONNECT TO HISTORY

1. **Making Inferences** Why do you think oil price increases had such a widespread effect on the economy?

   [S] See Skillbuilder Handbook, page R12.

CONNECT TO TODAY

2. **Researching** Find out what the rate of inflation has been in the most recent two years. How does today's inflation rate compare with that when Nixon came to office and when he left?

For more about inflation . . .

RESEARCH LINKS
CLASSZONE.COM

1 World War II

2 Postwar boom

3 Korean War

4 Suez crisis

5 Vietnam War

6 Arab oil embargo— oil prices increase

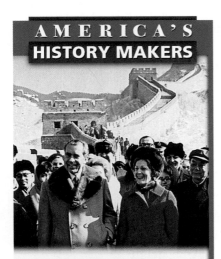

AMERICA'S HISTORY MAKERS

RICHARD M. NIXON

1913–1994

Richard Nixon entered politics in 1946 when he ran as a Republican for Congress. He was bright and ambitious. Some opponents, though, said that he would do anything to gain political power. Within seven years, he was vice-president of the United States.

In 1960, Nixon lost the presidential election to John Kennedy. In 1962, he was defeated for governor of California. Most thought his career over. But he battled back and was elected president in 1968. He is shown here in China in 1972 with his wife, Pat.

What characteristics did Nixon show as a leader?

Nixon Eases the Cold War

Nixon's main foreign-policy goal was world stability. During his 1968 presidential campaign, Nixon pledged to end the Vietnam War quickly and honorably. As you learned in Chapter 16, it took four years to negotiate a cease-fire with the North Vietnamese.

Nixon's most important triumph came in dealings with the People's Republic of China. He had long opposed the Communists, who took power in China in 1949. But Nixon believed a nation of a billion people could not be ignored. He asked Henry Kissinger to find a way to improve relations with China, even though they knew many Americans would be opposed. Kissinger arranged for Nixon to visit China in February 1972. This trip led to the opening of diplomacy and trade with the Chinese.

Nixon's China trip affected American relations with the Soviet Union, which was having conflicts with China. The Soviets feared closer relations between the United States and China. So they invited Nixon to Moscow in May 1972. As a result, Soviet-American relations improved. This easing of tensions between rivals is called **détente**—a French word. The policy of détente led the two nations to sign the Strategic Arms Limitation Treaty of 1972 (**SALT**). This pact limited the number of each country's nuclear weapons, easing fears of nuclear war.

Nixon's triumphs in foreign policy helped make him look like a sure winner for reelection in 1972. But, as you will read in the next section, events that occurred in that campaign eventually destroyed his presidency.

*Reading*History
C. Making Inferences
What effect did improved American-Chinese relations have on Soviet-American relations?

Section 1 Assessment

1. Terms & Names

Explain the significance of:
• Richard M. Nixon
• Henry Kissinger
• revenue sharing
• détente
• SALT

2. Taking Notes

Use a spider diagram to describe problems Nixon faced in his first term.

```
        Problems
   Nixon Faced During
     His First Term
```

Which problems were linked?

3. Main Ideas

a. How did Nixon try to show support for law-and-order politics?

b. What economic problems developed during Nixon's first term as president?

c. How did Nixon change the country's relationship with China? with Russia?

4. Critical Thinking

Making Inferences Nixon often surprised Americans in the policies that he supported. Which do you think was most surprising? Why?

THINK ABOUT
• his economic policies, such as deficit spending
• his appointment of conservative justices
• the policy of détente

ACTIVITY OPTIONS

Draw a **political cartoon** or write a **press release** describing one of Nixon's policies or achievements from his first term as president.

② Watergate Brings Down Nixon

MAIN IDEA	**WHY IT MATTERS NOW**
Nixon's involvement in the Watergate scandal caused a political crisis that forced him to resign.	Watergate led many Americans to have less confidence in government and politicians.

ONE AMERICAN'S STORY

Barbara Jordan grew up in a poor home in Houston, Texas, in the 1940s. Early on, she realized that her voice was one of her greatest assets. She had a strong, deep, beautiful voice and a gift for reciting dramatic poetry. Jordan was also highly intelligent. After graduating from Boston University Law School in 1959, she became interested in politics. She began her career as a volunteer worker for John Kennedy in his 1960 presidential campaign against Richard Nixon.

Jordan went on to become the first African-American woman from the South elected to the U.S. Congress. The 1972 election that sent her to the House of Representatives also saw Nixon's reelection as president. Two years later, at impeachment hearings in the House Judiciary Committee, Jordan warned that Nixon's actions during that campaign and his presidency were threats to the Constitution.

As a member of the House Judiciary Committee, Representative Barbara Jordan of Texas recommended the impeachment of President Nixon.

A VOICE FROM THE PAST

My faith in the Constitution is whole, it is complete, it is total, and I am not going to sit here and be an idle spectator to the diminution [lessening], the subversion [undermining], the destruction of the Constitution.

Barbara Jordan, speech in House Judiciary Committee, July 25, 1974

In this section, you will read about the events that led Nixon, Jordan, and the nation into the political nightmare that ended his presidency.

The 1972 Presidential Election

The 1972 presidential campaign did not appear to be much of a race for President Nixon. His diplomatic successes in China and the Soviet Union and Kissinger's negotiations to end the Vietnam War were triumphs for the president. The Republicans nominated him overwhelmingly for reelection.

Nixon's Democratic opponent was George McGovern. McGovern was a liberal senator from South Dakota who spoke out against the Vietnam War. McGovern had strong support from young people, African Americans, and members of the women's movement. But Nixon won with the largest victory of any Republican candidate to that time.

The Watergate scandal was the subject of thousands of political cartoons. Here, cartoonist Paul Conrad shows Nixon attempting to tap the telephones at the Democratic Party headquarters in the Watergate building.

What do you think the cartoon suggests about Nixon's involvement in the Watergate scandal?

"HE SAYS HE'S FROM THE PHONE COMPANY..."

The Watergate Scandal

An almost certain victory in the 1972 presidential election had not been enough for Nixon. He had wanted to win big. By doing so, he would help Republicans take control of Congress, and he would gain more power. To ensure this landslide victory, many people working for him engaged in various illegal activities.

These activities started coming to light on June 17, 1972. Five men were caught breaking into Democratic Party headquarters in the Watergate office-apartment complex in Washington, D.C. The burglars had cameras and listening devices for the telephones. They were linked to Nixon's reelection campaign staff, called the **Committee to Reelect the President**. Nixon may not have known in advance about the break-in. But in less than a week, he was talking to his aides about covering up any White House connection to the Watergate burglary to avoid a scandal.

The cover-up involved lies told by President Nixon and his aides. It involved payments to the Watergate burglars and others to lie. It involved using the CIA to halt an FBI investigation of Watergate. These illegal actions by Nixon and his aides to cover up Watergate and other related crimes came to be called the **Watergate scandal**.

The Watergate break-in stayed on the back pages of most newspapers in the 1972 campaign. But some reporters kept investigating. They found more evidence tying Nixon to Watergate. In February 1973, the Senate began an investigation. The threat to Nixon's presidency was building.

Nixon Resigns

The Senate Watergate investigation began with the questioning of members of the reelection committee and the White House staff. Within six weeks, the investigation was closing in on the president's closest advisers—H. R. Haldeman, John Ehrlichman, former Attorney-General John Mitchell, and John Dean. On March 21, 1973, Dean, one of the president's attorneys, spoke to Nixon about the worsening situation.

> *A VOICE FROM THE PAST*
>
> I think that there is no doubt about the seriousness of the problem we've got. We have a cancer within, close to the Presidency, that is growing. It is growing daily.
>
> **John Dean,** quoted in *The White House Transcripts*

Dean was warning about money needed to keep the burglars quiet. Nixon agreed to pay the "hush money." He now clearly had committed a crime.

As more Watergate information was being uncovered, Dean decided to tell all to the Senate. He said that the president had been involved in the

*Reading*History
A. Making Inferences Why did Nixon want a big win in the 1972 presidential election?

Background
Eventually, 25 members of the Nixon administration were convicted and served prison terms for crimes connected to Watergate.

cover-up for months. But Nixon denied any knowledge. It was Dean's word against Nixon's until mid-July. Then a White House aide revealed that Nixon had been taping conversations in his office. A long battle over the tapes began in the courts.

Meanwhile, more bad news came for Nixon. It was revealed that Vice-President Spiro Agnew had accepted bribes as governor of Maryland and continued taking them as vice-president. Not wanting to face impeachment, Agnew resigned in October 1973. Nixon then nominated Congressman Gerald Ford of Michigan as the new vice-president.

President Nixon put on an upbeat face as he left Washington after resigning on August 9, 1974.

Evidence of the president's role in the cover-up continued to grow, but he told the country that he had done nothing wrong. He said, "I am not a crook." Then, in January 1974, the House Judiciary Committee began an impeachment investigation. It reviewed court testimony, Senate transcripts, and documents from special prosecutors. Nixon did not give them his tapes but released edited transcripts. The committee felt it had a strong case even without the tapes. In July, both Democrats and Republicans on the committee approved impeachment charges.

On August 5, Nixon was forced by a court order to release full transcripts of the tapes. The evidence that he had been involved in the cover-up from the beginning—what investigators called "a smoking gun"—had been recorded on the tapes. On August 9, 1974, Richard Nixon resigned. Vice-President Gerald Ford was then sworn in as the next president.

Reading **History**

B. Recognizing Effects How did the Watergate scandal change many Americans' view of their government?

Watergate was one of the worst political scandals in the nation's history. Many Americans lost faith in the government and its leaders. This lack of confidence weakened the government, especially the president. As you will read in the following section, the next two presidents—Gerald Ford and Jimmy Carter—worked hard to try to restore the presidency.

Section 2 Assessment

1. Terms & Names

Explain the significance of:
• Committee to Reelect the President
• Watergate scandal

2. Taking Notes

Use a time line like the one below to trace the events of the Watergate scandal.

Which event made Nixon's downfall almost certain?

3. Main Ideas

a. Why did Nixon want a big win in the 1972 election?

b. What kinds of illegal activities was Nixon involved with in the Watergate scandal?

c. What was the outcome of the Watergate scandal?

4. Critical Thinking

Forming and Supporting Opinions What do you think would have happened if President Nixon had apologized for Watergate rather than trying to cover it up?

THINK ABOUT
• when the break-in occurred
• how the nation reacted to past scandals

ACTIVITY OPTIONS

TECHNOLOGY
LANGUAGE ARTS

Interview someone who remembers Watergate. Either create a **radio broadcast** of the interview or write it as a **question-and-answer magazine feature.**

TERMS & NAMES
Gerald Ford
Jimmy Carter
Camp David
   Accords
environmentalism
Rachel Carson
Iran hostage crisis

MAIN IDEA	WHY IT MATTERS NOW
Presidents Ford and Carter had a difficult time solving the nation's problems after Watergate.	These problems helped lead to a conservative mood in the United States.

ONE AMERICAN'S STORY

On August 9, 1974, Vice-President **Gerald Ford** became president after Richard Nixon resigned. A year earlier, Nixon had chosen Ford as his vice-president. He replaced Spiro Agnew, who had resigned in disgrace. During 25 years as a congressman from Michigan, Ford had gained a reputation for integrity and openness.

As president, Ford inherited a nation that had suffered through the years of Vietnam and Watergate. He tried to reassure Americans that the turmoil of the Nixon years was behind them in his first speech.

President Gerald Ford speaks to the nation from the White House.

A VOICE FROM THE PAST

My fellow Americans, our long national nightmare is over. Our Constitution works; our great Republic is a Government of laws and not of men. Here the people rule. . . . As we bind up the internal wounds of Watergate, more painful and more poisonous than those of foreign wars, let us restore the golden rule to our political process, and let brotherly love purge our hearts of suspicion and of hate.

Gerald Ford, speech on August 9, 1974

As part of the healing process, Ford decided to pardon former President Nixon. Ford's pardon of Nixon brought him much criticism and added to the divisions in the country.

In this section, you will learn more about the difficulties Presidents Ford and Jimmy Carter faced as they tried to govern in the 1970s.

Ford Takes Over

In his first weeks in office, Ford set out to restore confidence in the presidency. He soothed the nation with his plain speaking, openness, and willingness to talk to the press and to work with Congress.

However, within a month, Ford lost the support of many Americans when he pardoned Richard Nixon for any crimes he might have committed during the Watergate scandal. It had been Ford's hope to spare the country the spectacle of a former president being brought to trial. But

Reading History

A. Drawing Conclusions Why were many Americans upset with President Ford over Nixon's pardon?

many people felt strongly that Nixon should be charged with crimes because of the Watergate cover-up. Ford's popularity dropped sharply.

Making life even tougher for Ford was the fact that the economy was not in good shape. Inflation was spiraling higher while a recession was throwing more people out of work. Many Americans were having a hard time making ends meet. Ford proposed a voluntary campaign to "Whip Inflation Now." He asked Americans to cut spending and energy use. The WIN plan received much publicity but failed to help the economy.

In foreign affairs, Ford had mixed success. He asked Congress to help South Vietnam when the cease-fire in the Vietnam War broke down in 1974. But Congress refused. In 1975, he negotiated a treaty with European nations and Canada called the Helsinki Accords. This pact spelled out basic human rights for the citizens of the signer nations.

Vocabulary

human rights: basic rights and freedoms to which all human beings are entitled, such as freedom of speech

Ford's pardon of Nixon and his difficulty in improving the economy caused him problems in the 1976 presidential campaign. He only narrowly won his party's nomination over California governor Ronald Reagan. Then he lost the presidency in a close election to Democrat **Jimmy Carter**.

Carter was a former peanut farmer and governor of Georgia. He had run for president as a Washington outsider and one who would "never lie" to the American people. He promised honesty in government and support for human rights throughout the world.

Carter as President

Reading History

B. Making Inferences How did Jimmy Carter benefit from the Watergate scandal?

Many Americans were still suspicious of their government as Carter took office in 1977. Since Carter had never served in Washington, Americans hoped that he would bring fresh ideas to the presidency.

Carter immediately tried to show that he was one of the people. On inauguration day, he and his family walked from the Capitol to the White House rather than take the traditional limousine. However, being a Washington outsider would make political life difficult for Carter.

Carter and Congress often clashed. One point of conflict was the energy crisis. Early in 1977, shortages of oil and natural gas forced many schools and businesses to close. In response, Carter asked Americans to conserve energy. He also sent a national energy program to Congress. It would cut oil imports, increase production of oil and natural gas at home, and promote alternative energy sources like coal and nuclear and solar energy.

After months of debate, Congress passed some of the measures. But they were of little help when OPEC again sharply raised oil prices. Inflation surged beyond 10 percent. Unemployment rose. Like Nixon and Ford, Carter could not solve the nation's economic problems.

America's HERITAGE

THE BICENTENNIAL

On July 4, 1976, the United States celebrated the 200th anniversary of the Declaration of Independence. The Bicentennial, as it was called, was a year-long birthday party. People in every corner of the nation celebrated with special events.

Americans also used the time to reflect on the nation's progress. Women, African Americans, Hispanic Americans, Native Americans, and others still faced discrimination. Yet Americans were proud of what had been achieved, and the celebration helped the nation move beyond the turmoil of the early 1970s.

MIDDLE EAST PEACE PROCESS

The signing of the Camp David Accords in 1978 by (left to right) Prime Minister Menachem Begin of Israel, President Carter, and President Anwar el-Sadat of Egypt was the first important step in the attempt to bring peace to the Middle East.

In 1998, another step was taken when President Bill Clinton brought Palestinian leader Yasir Arafat and Israeli Prime Minister Benjamin Netanyahu together to sign a peace agreement called the Wye River Accords.

Carter had more success in accomplishing his foreign-policy goals. He wanted to end the long-standing conflict with Panama over the Panama Canal. As you read in Chapter 9 the Panama Canal was built and controlled by the United States. Most Americans wanted it to stay that way. But Carter thought winning the good will of Latin America was worth losing control of the canal. Under treaties signed in 1977, the United States agreed to give the canal to Panama in 2000.

Carter also tried to reduce tensions in the Middle East. In 1978, he helped to negotiate the **Camp David Accords**. Under these agreements, Egypt and Israel signed the first peace treaty between Israel and an Arab nation, thus ending 30 years of conflict.

The Environmental Movement Begins

Protection of the environment was also a goal of Carter's. He supported a movement to save the environment that had gained momentum in the 1970s. Actually, the first laws to protect the nation's natural environment had been passed in the late 1800s. But **environmentalism,** or work toward protecting the environment, only began to attract wide public attention in the 1960s. In 1962, biologist **Rachel Carson** wrote of the dangers of heavy pesticide use in her bestseller, *Silent Spring*. She warned that some of these chemicals could kill animals, cause disease, and destroy the environment unless their use was limited or stopped.

In 1969, a huge oil spill near Santa Barbara, California, polluted miles of beaches and killed many marine animals. The cry for tougher laws to protect the environment grew. In the 1970s, Nixon, Ford, and Carter all proposed laws to restrict pesticide use, to regulate the cleanup of oil spills, and to curb air and water pollution. With these laws in effect, many polluted lakes began to recover, and high levels of some air pollutants began to drop. But environmental disasters continued to occur.

In 1979, an accident occurred at the Three Mile Island nuclear power plant in Pennsylvania. Radioactive water leaked out of the plant, causing

Reading **History**
C. Finding Main Ideas What role did Rachel Carson play in the environmental movement?

fears that the nuclear reactor might explode. Within a week, the reactor was shut down. Disaster was averted. To assure people it was safe, Carter visited Three Mile Island. But not long after, he faced another disaster—a political one—in Iran.

Reagan and the Conservatives Win

Reading **History**
D. Reading a Map
Locate Tehran, the capital of Iran, in the map on this page.

For decades, the United States had supported the Shah (king) of Iran. In 1979, Muslim leaders overthrew his government. When Carter allowed the Shah to come to the United States for medical treatment, Iranians struck back at the United States. On November 4, 1979, they overran the American embassy in Iran's capital of Tehran and took 52 Americans hostage. The **Iran hostage crisis** had begun.

Carter tried negotiating to get Iran's leaders to release the hostages but without success. He approved a secret military mission, but it failed. The continuing crisis affected the election in 1980. Americans blamed Carter for the plight of the hostages, for the nation's economic ills, and for making America look weak to the world.

Meanwhile, support for conservative ideas had been growing for more than a decade. The Republicans chose a conservative—Ronald Reagan, a former actor and California governor—to be their candidate in 1980. He vowed that, if elected president, he would not allow the United States to be pushed around. Reagan's get-tough talk appealed to many voters.

Carter eventually won release of the hostages. But the majority of voters had already decided that it was time for a change and elected Reagan president. The hostages left Iran on January 20, 1981, the day Reagan was inaugurated. In the next chapter, you will read how Ronald Reagan took the nation in a more conservative direction.

Section ③ Assessment

1. Terms & Names
Explain the significance of:
- Gerald Ford
- Jimmy Carter
- Camp David Accords
- environmentalism
- Rachel Carson
- Iran hostage crisis

2. Taking Notes
Use a chart to list the high and low points of both the Ford and Carter presidencies.

Presidency	High points	Low points
Gerald Ford		
Jimmy Carter		

Which do you think was the highest point of each? Why?

3. Main Ideas
a. Why did Carter win the 1976 election over Ford?

b. What were some problems related to energy use that occurred during Carter's term?

c. What progress did the environmental movement make during the 1960s and the 1970s?

4. Critical Thinking
Comparing How would you compare the strengths and weaknesses of Ford and Carter? Use events from their presidencies to support your answer.

THINK ABOUT
- actions each took to draw Americans together
- response to economic and foreign-policy issues

ACTIVITY OPTIONS

MATH

ART

Research inflation in the 1970s. Make a **graph** to show the annual rate change or create a **political cartoon** about inflation's effect on people's lives.

Save the Environment!

You are a citizen of the 1970s who has joined the fight against pollution, waste, and the destruction of the Earth's natural resources. Each year on Earth Day, you help out with community clean-ups. You are interested in finding ways to rally public opinion and help save the planet.

COOPERATIVE LEARNING On this page are three challenges you face as an American concerned about the environment. Working with a small group, decide how to deal with each challenge. Select an option, assign a task to each group member, and do the activity. You will find useful information in the Data File. Present your solutions to the class.

Renew the Earth

LANGUAGE ARTS CHALLENGE

"the community of living things"

You are worried that lack of concern about the environment may result in a permanently damaged world. The destruction of natural resources by individuals and industry continues. You decide to promote a campaign to save the environment. Present your ideas using one of these options:

• Write an editorial describing environmental dangers and promoting conservation.
• Make a speech to rally people in support of conservation.

Take Public Transportation

ART CHALLENGE

"the air we breathe for life"

Ozone alert! TV announcers warn families to keep small children at home. The elderly, especially those with lung and heart problems, must stay inside. You wish that people understood the terrible effects of air pollution better so they might start demanding cleaner air. You decide to take action. Present your ideas using one of these options:

• Design a public service ad for magazines explaining how air pollutants harm the body.

• Draw a cartoon asking people to use public transportation.

SCIENCE CHALLENGE

"the lakes and rivers and oceans"

News of an oil spill off California's shores has sparked your concern for the environment. You are sickened by pictures of oil-soaked beaches and thousands of injured and dead animals. You want to help rid the oceans of this menace. Use the Data File for information. Then present your ideas, using one of these options:

• Create a labeled diagram for your local paper showing why oil pollution harms most sea life.

• Role-play a community meeting in which you explain how offshore oil pollution damages sea life.

Prevent Pollution

ACTIVITY WRAP-UP

Present to the class Meet with the group to review your methods of helping to save the environment. Select a solution that best meets each challenge and then present it to the class.

DATA FILE

ENVIRONMENTAL PROBLEMS

Air and water pollution, acid rain, destruction of the ozone layer, toxic chemical disposal, extinction of wildlife, oil spills, destruction of forests, overpopulation

OCEAN LIFE ZONES

• Shorelines support crabs, oysters, shore birds, and other marine life.

• Open ocean over the continental shelf supports the largest amount of sea life, including algae, lobsters, thousands of fish species, turtles, seals, sharks, and whales.

• Deep ocean supports a smaller variety.

SOURCES OF OCEAN OIL POLLUTION

Offshore oil production, vessel accidents, natural seepage, non-tanker and tanker shipping operations, waste car oil

AIR POLLUTANTS

• sources—fossil fuels, cars, power plants, industry, ozone

• effects—smog; eye irritation; impaired judgment; chest pains; lung, nerve, and kidney damage; cancer; birth defects

WAYS TO CLEAN WATER

• Install oil pollution prevention equipment on ships.

• Car owners, cities, and industry recycle used oil.

REDUCE AIR POLLUTION

• Burn fewer fossil fuels.

• Take public transportation.

• Improve car efficiency.

• Use sun and wind power.

For more about the environment . . .

RESEARCH LINKS
CLASSZONE.COM

TERMS & NAMES

Briefly explain the significance of each of the following.

1. Richard M. Nixon
2. Henry Kissinger
3. revenue sharing
4. détente
5. Watergate scandal
6. Gerald Ford
7. Jimmy Carter
8. Camp David Accords
9. environmentalism
10. Iran hostage crisis

REVIEW QUESTIONS

Nixon Confronts Problems (pages 453–456)

1. What kinds of government programs did Nixon propose to deal with America's social problems?
2. How did Nixon try to promote "law and order"?
3. What were the economic problems Nixon faced?
4. How was Nixon's foreign policy toward China different from that of previous presidents?

Watergate Brings Down Nixon (pages 457–459)

5. What were the chief causes of the Watergate scandal?
6. What did reporters and others find when they looked more deeply into the Watergate burglary?
7. What were the events that caused Nixon to resign?

Issues of the Seventies (pages 460–465)

8. What were the main reasons people did not vote for Gerald Ford in the 1976 election?
9. What successes did Carter have with foreign policy and what problems did he have at home?
10. What appealed to voters about Ronald Reagan in the 1980 election?

CRITICAL THINKING

1. USING YOUR NOTES

President	Issues and Events
Nixon	
Ford	
Carter	

Use your completed chart to answer these questions.

a. What issues did all three presidents have to deal with during their terms? Which were the most frequently occurring issues of their presidencies?

b. Which of the presidents do you think faced the most difficult issues? Explain.

2. ANALYZING LEADERSHIP

What characteristics did Nixon, Ford, and Carter have that made them good leaders? Poor leaders?

3. THEME: CITIZENSHIP

What could Americans do to help their country during the 1970s?

4. FORMING AND SUPPORTING OPINIONS

Do you think Nixon's actions showed that his main goal was to survive during the events of Watergate? Explain your answer.

5. EVALUATING

Do you think that Ford made a good decision in pardoning Nixon? Explain why or why not.

Interact with History

Did your ideas about how the nation survives a crisis agree or disagree with what you read?

VISUAL SUMMARY

Years of Doubt

The Nixon Administration

- Revenue sharing
- Law-and-order politics
- Inflation, recession, and unemployment
- Opening to China
- Détente with the Soviet Union
- Watergate scandal
- Nixon resignation

The Ford Administration

- Unelected president
- Nixon pardon
- Whip Inflation Now program
- Helsinki Accords

The Carter Administration

- Energy crisis
- Worsening inflation
- Panama Canal Treaties
- Camp David Accords
- Environmental protection
- Iran hostage crisis

HISTORY SKILLS

1. INTERPRETING GRAPHS

Study the graph and then answer the questions.

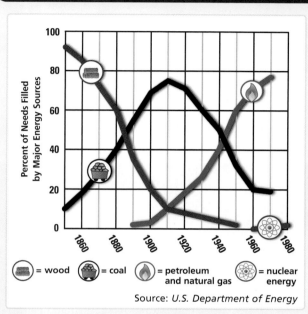

Major Energy Sources, *1850–1980*

Percent of Needs Filled by Major Energy Sources

= wood   = coal   = petroleum and natural gas   = nuclear energy

Source: *U.S. Department of Energy*

a. What fuel supplied most of the nation's energy between 1850 and 1880?

b. When did petroleum and natural gas begin being used as fuel?

c. What was the percentage increase in the use of coal from 1850 to 1910?

2. INTERPRETING PRIMARY SOURCES

The following excerpt was written by a citizens' group after a 1970 oil spill off the coast of Santa Barbara, California. Read the excerpt and then answer the questions.

> Centuries of careless neglect of the environment have brought [hu]mankind to a final crossroads. The quality of our lives is eroded and our very existence threatened by our abuse of the natural world. . . . We, therefore, resolve to act. We propose a revolution in conduct toward an environment which is rising in revolt against us. Granted that ideas and institutions long established are not easily changed; yet today is the first day of the rest of our life on this planet. We will begin anew.
>
> Santa Barbara Declaration of Environmental Rights, 1970

a. What kinds of problems does this excerpt from the *Santa Barbara Declaration* discuss?

b. What is the general solution that it proposes?

ALTERNATIVE ASSESSMENT

1. INTERDISCIPLINARY ACTIVITY: Geography

Making a Map Research the territory that was the subject of the negotiations at Camp David in 1979. Make a three-dimensional map that shows the land, including its location relative to Egypt, Israel, and the other countries of the Middle East. Use your map to identify the resources of the territory.

2. COOPERATIVE LEARNING ACTIVITY

Performing a Play The fall of President Richard Nixon was one of the most dramatic events of modern American history. Working in a small group, research Nixon's last two years in office. Pick one event from this time and write a one-act play about the incident. Use primary sources, such as diaries or tape transcripts, to create your dialogue. Present your play and ask for comments from your classmates.

3. TECHNOLOGY ACTIVITY

Designing a Bicentennial Web Site The 200th anniversary of independence was a cause for celebration for Americans everywhere. President Ford told the nation to "break out the flag, strike up the band, light up the sky." It was a time to reflect on how the nation began, where it was then, and what might happen next. Use the library and the Internet to find information about the celebration. Also make use of what you have learned about the nation's history from your textbook.

For more about the U.S. Bicentennial celebration . . .

INTERNET ACTIVITY
CLASSZONE.COM

Design a Bicentennial Web site. Use the suggestions below to get started.

- Locate images showing Bicentennial highlights.
- Choose music that captures the spirit of the celebration.
- Highlight important events in the nation's history.
- Include the words and images of historic figures.
- Select Web sites that would be good links for visitors to your site.

4. PORTFOLIO ACTIVITY

Review your section and chapter assessment activities. Select one that you think is your best work. Then use comments made by your teacher or classmates to improve your work and add it to your portfolio.

Additional Test Practice, pp. S1–S33

TEST PRACTICE
CLASSZONE.COM

CHAPTER 18

Entering a New Millennium

1981–present

Section 1 **Conservatives Reshape Politics**

Section 2 **Technological and Economic Changes**

Section 3 **The New Americans**

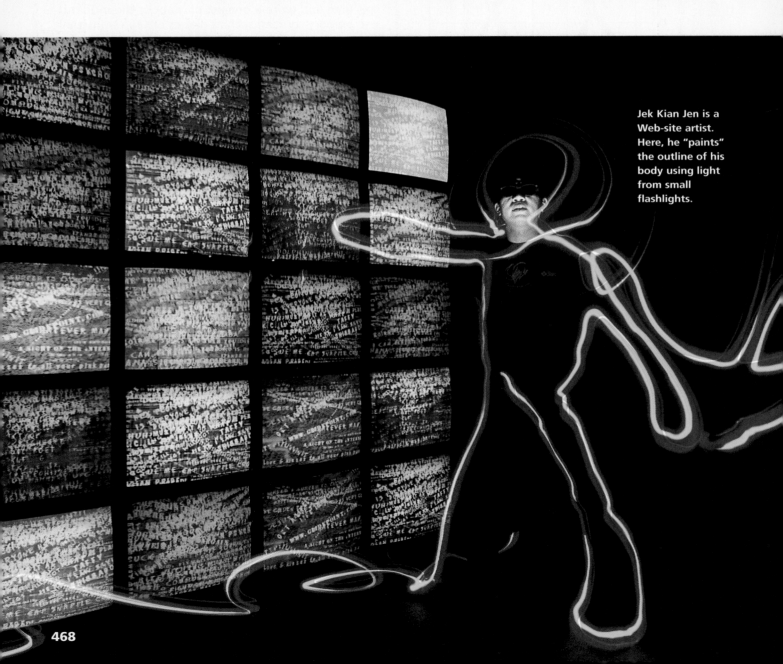

Jek Kian Jen is a Web-site artist. Here, he "paints" the outline of his body using light from small flashlights.

Interact *with* History

Sixteen-year-old Andre McGregor is already a high-tech businessman.

Shown holding a computer board, he designs Web pages. He also tutors adults in how to use technology.

The time is four years from now, and you're about to finish high school. Your friends ask about your plans for the future. At graduation, the speaker urges your class not just to focus on earning money but also to care about making the world a better place. How can you do that?

What can you contribute to the future?

What Do You Think?
- What are your talents, and how could you use them to benefit both yourself and society?
- What things do you really enjoy doing?
- What do you think the United States and the world need most from your generation?

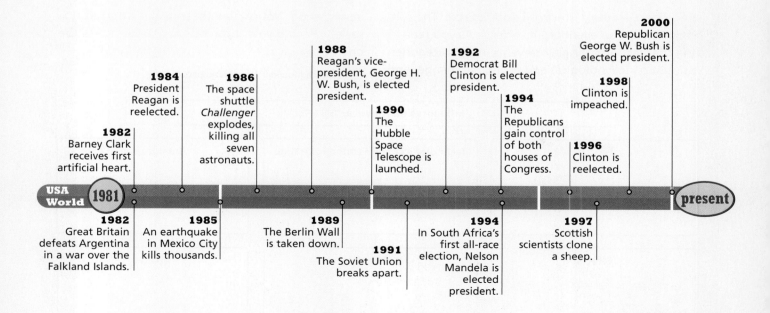

1982
Barney Clark receives first artificial heart.

1984
President Reagan is reelected.

1986
The space shuttle *Challenger* explodes, killing all seven astronauts.

1988
Reagan's vice-president, George H. W. Bush, is elected president.

1990
The Hubble Space Telescope is launched.

1992
Democrat Bill Clinton is elected president.

1994
The Republicans gain control of both houses of Congress.

2000
Republican George W. Bush is elected president.

1998
Clinton is impeached.

1996
Clinton is reelected.

USA World **1981**

1982
Great Britain defeats Argentina in a war over the Falkland Islands.

1985
An earthquake in Mexico City kills thousands.

1989
The Berlin Wall is taken down.

1991
The Soviet Union breaks apart.

1994
In South Africa's first all-race election, Nelson Mandela is elected president.

1997
Scottish scientists clone a sheep.

present

BEFORE YOU READ

SPECIAL ISSUE
TIME

Take a good look at this woman. She was created by a computer from a mix of several races. What you see is a remarkable preview of . . .

THE NEW FACE OF AMERICA
How Immigrants Are Shaping the World's
First Multicultural Society

This magazine cover is symbolic of U.S. diversity. To create it, *Time* used a computer to blend the features of people of many different races.

Previewing the Theme

Diversity and Unity As this chapter explains, during the 1980s and 1990s, Republicans and Democrats fought for control of the national government. World events also affected U.S. politics. At the same time, technology changed daily life, and U.S. society became more diverse as immigrants from around the world continued to come to America.

What Do You Know?

How closely do you follow current events? What do you think are the major trends in the United States today?

THINK ABOUT
• political events in the news
• the latest changes in technology
• how immigration is affecting the United States

What Do You Want to Know?

 What would you like to know about our most recent presidents? What questions do you have about technology? What do you want to learn about recent patterns of immigration? Record your questions in your notebook before you read this chapter.

READ AND TAKE NOTES

Reading Strategy: Recognizing Effects The consequences of an event are its effects. As you read the chapter, look for major events in the categories of politics, technological and economic change, and immigration. Notice how these events affected U.S. society. Record your information on a chart like the one below.

S See Skillbuilder Handbook, page R11.

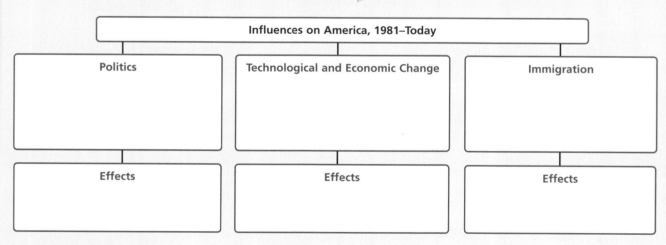

Influences on America, 1981–Today

Politics	Technological and Economic Change	Immigration
Effects	Effects	Effects

Conservatives Reshape Politics

Ronald Reagan

supply-side
  economics

Iran-Contra affair

George H. W. Bush

Persian Gulf War

Bill Clinton

NAFTA

George W. Bush

MAIN IDEA	WHY IT MATTERS NOW
The country became more conservative, leading to Republican political victories.	In response, the Democratic Party became less liberal and even adopted some conservative ideas.

ONE AMERICAN'S STORY

As the owner of a popular restaurant, Mike Savic knew the mood in his working-class Chicago neighborhood. In the fall of 1980, most of his customers were frightened. Unemployment and inflation were rising. President Jimmy Carter seemed to have no answers. Yet, Carter was asking the American people to reelect him. Most of Savic's neighbors had supported Carter in 1976, but now they turned to Carter's Republican opponent, former California governor **Ronald Reagan**.

A VOICE FROM THE PAST

People have been talking. . . . Some of them in this neighborhood have been laid off four, six months. Or their neighbor is out of work. People don't like to see their neighbors out of work. And they've been scared. . . . The ones who'd been talking that they were for Carter, well, they changed. They were talking different. They were going for Reagan.

Mike Savic, quoted in the *Chicago Tribune,* November 6, 1980

This campaign button is from the 1980 debate between Jimmy Carter and Ronald Reagan.

In 1980, millions of Democrats voted for Reagan in the hope that he could fix the economy. With their help, Reagan won the election. This section covers the presidencies of Reagan and his successors.

Reagan's Conservative Goals

President Reagan was a conservative. In his 1981 inaugural address, he declared, "Government is not the solution to our problem. . . . It is time to check the growth of government." Reagan pursued the following conservative goals.

1. **Lower Taxes.** Reagan preached **supply-side economics.** This theory held that if taxes were lower, people would save more money. Banks could loan that money to businesses, which could invest in ways to improve productivity. The supply of goods would increase, driving down prices. At Reagan's urging, Congress lowered income taxes by 25 percent over three years.
2. **Deregulation.** The president deregulated, or eased restrictions on, many industries. Reagan believed that business would grow more rapidly if government interfered with it less.

3. **Fewer Government Programs.** Reagan fought to end or weaken many government programs, from affirmative action to environmental regulations.

4. **A Conservative Supreme Court.** Reagan named three conservative judges to the Supreme Court. One of them, Sandra Day O'Connor, was the first woman to sit on the nation's highest court.

At first, inflation rose, and unemployment stayed high. But by 1983, inflation decreased, and more people found jobs. Business boomed. Even so, Reagan's policies created a problem. Because of the tax cut, the federal government took in less money and had to resort to deficit spending. As a result, the national debt doubled from 1981 to 1986.

Vocabulary
deficit spending: using borrowed money to fund government programs

A Tough Anti-Communist Stand

Reagan opposed communism. To compete militarily with the Soviet Union, he began the most expensive arms buildup in history. It cost more than $2 trillion.

In 1985, Mikhail Gorbachev became the leader of the Soviet Union. He and Reagan met four times to discuss improving U.S.-Soviet relations and easing the threat of nuclear war. They signed the Intermediate-Range Nuclear Forces (INF) Treaty in 1987. Under that treaty, the two countries agreed to destroy all of their medium-range missiles.

The Reagan administration also decided to support the anti-Communist side in several conflicts, including two Central American civil wars. In El Salvador, the United States backed the government against Communist-led rebels. In Nicaragua, the United States provided aid to anti-Communist rebels known as Contras.

This aid resulted in a scandal, known as the **Iran-Contra affair.** In 1986, Americans learned that the U.S. government had sold weapons to Iran in return for help in freeing American hostages in the Middle East. The money from these sales went to the Contras. This action violated a law that barred the U.S. government from funding the rebels. President Reagan claimed he never knew about the deal. But investigators concluded that he should have kept track of what his administration was doing.

*Reading*History
A. Analyzing Causes Why did investigators hold Reagan responsible for the Iran-Contra affair?

Bush and a Changing World

Despite the scandal, Reagan and his administration remained popular. In 1988, Reagan's vice-president, **George H. W. Bush,** ran for president and won. During his presidency, dramatic foreign events took place.

In 1989, several Eastern European countries ended Communist rule. This angered old-time Communists in the Soviet Union. In August 1991, a group of them tried to take over the Soviet government. Boris Yeltsin, a Russian reform leader, fought the takeover attempt and won.

Unlike Gorbachev, who wanted to reform communism, Yeltsin and others wanted to get rid of it. One by one, the republics that made up the Soviet Union declared their independence from it. In December 1991, Yeltsin and the leaders of these nations joined in a loose alliance called the Commonwealth of Independent States (CIS). The Soviet Union, once a superpower, was gone. Its breakup marked the end of the Cold War.

A crisis also erupted in the Middle East. In August 1990, Iraq invaded its neighbor Kuwait—a major supplier of oil. The United States, led by Bush, and the United Nations (UN) organized a group of 39 nations to free Kuwait by fighting the **Persian Gulf War**. In mid-January 1991, UN forces began bombing Iraqi military targets. A month later, UN ground forces moved into Kuwait and drove the Iraqis out of that country.

The war's success boosted George Bush's popularity, and he seemed certain to win reelection in 1992. Then the economy stalled. By the spring of 1992, the U.S. unemployment rate had climbed to around 7 percent—a six-year high. Americans began to think that Bush was good at foreign policy but ineffective with problems at home. In November, they elected his Democratic opponent, Arkansas governor **Bill Clinton**.

Clinton's Fights with Congress

One of President Clinton's first acts was to try to reform the health-care system. Clinton asked his wife, Hillary Rodham Clinton, to design a health-care plan. Opponents criticized the plan as costing too much, and Congress chose not to vote on it. But it did pass a law allowing workers to keep their insurance when they change jobs.

Clinton did win passage of the North American Free Trade Agreement (NAFTA) in 1993. NAFTA lifted tariffs in an effort to increase trade among Mexico, Canada, and the United States.

In 1994, Republicans won control of both houses of Congress. Clinton and the new Congress could not agree on a budget for 1995 and government agencies shut down twice in late 1995. Finally, Clinton and Congress reached a compromise on the budget.

The two sides did work together to pass a welfare reform bill, a long time conservative goal. The bill ended a guarantee of aid to needy families. It also cut the length of time people could receive benefits.

In 1996, Clinton was reelected. But his second term in office was marked by scandal. Clinton was investigated for a land deal he took part in during the 1970s. During that investigation, information emerged that Clinton had had an improper relationship with a White House intern. And he allegedly had lied about it under oath.

Reading **History**

B. Summarizing
What were two major world events that happened during George H. W. Bush's presidency?

Background
Most developed countries have nationalized health insurance, a government program that pays for the health care of most citizens. The United States does not.

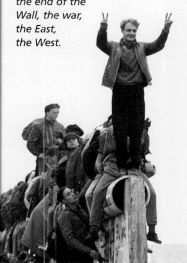

Connections TO WORLD HISTORY

THE BERLIN WALL FALLS
Communists built the Berlin Wall in 1961 to separate Communist East Berlin from West Berlin. In November 1989, as communism began to fall, East Germans tore down the wall. The photograph below shows Germans celebrating the opening of the wall. Andreas Ramos witnessed the event.

The final slab was moved away. A stream of East Germans began to pour through. . . . Looking around, I saw an indescribable joy in people's faces. It was the end of the government telling people what not to do, it was the end of the Wall, the war, the East, the West.

The Washington Post

Weather
Today: *Variably cloudy, showers. High 53. Low 44.*
Monday: *Variably cloudy, warmer. High 62. Low 45.*
Details, Page 82.

SUNDAY, DECEMBER 20, 1998

122ND YEAR No. 15 ··· ··· A B C F O K

$1.50

Clinton Impeached
House Approves Articles Charging Perjury, Obstruction

When the charges became public in January 1998, Clinton denied them. Later, he admitted to the relationship but denied lying under oath. In December 1998, the House of Representatives impeached President Clinton. In general, Republicans voted for impeachment while Democrats voted against it. In spite of the charges, Clinton remained popular. In January 1999, the Senate held its trial of President Clinton and acquitted him. Clinton remained in office to finish his second term.

Background
Clinton was the second president to be impeached, or formally charged with wrongdoing. The first was Andrew Johnson. (See Chapter 4.)

War in Kosovo

Despite his troubles at home, Clinton still had to act as a world leader. In 1999, he led a group of nations dealing with a crisis in Yugoslavia. The European country of Yugoslavia was created after World War I. Yugoslavia contained many ethnic and religious groups. Often, these groups fought with one another.

The Yugoslav republic of Serbia has a region called Kosovo (KAW-suh-VOH) inhabited mostly by people of Albanian descent. The Kosovars sought independence, but the Serbs opposed them. A vicious war broke out over Kosovo. The Serbian government tried to drive the Albanians out of Kosovo by using violence and murder.

In March 1999, the North Atlantic Treaty Organization (NATO) began bombing Serbia. In June 1999, the Serbs withdrew from Kosovo. After the troops pulled out, UN peacekeepers moved in. The United Nations has run Kosovo since then. In February 2003, Yugoslavia became a federation called Serbia and Montenegro. In 2006, both republics will vote on independence.

Reading **History**
C. Analyzing Causes What caused the violence in Kosovo?

The 2000 Presidential Campaign

In 2000, the nation turned its attention to a presidential election as Clinton finished his second term. The Democrats nominated Vice-President Al Gore as their candidate. The Republicans chose Texas governor George W. Bush, the son of the former president. Other candidates included Ralph Nader of the Green Party and Pat Buchanan of the Reform Party. It was clear, however, that Bush and Gore were the leaders in the race.

In the campaign, Gore emphasized his experience as vice-president. Bush attacked Gore's connection with Clinton's administration. On the issue of taxes, Bush proposed a large income tax cut, which he said would stimulate economic growth. Gore argued that Bush's plan would mainly benefit wealthy Americans. Gore called for a smaller tax cut aimed to help lower- and middle-class Americans.

Reading **History**
D. Drawing Conclusions How was it helpful and harmful to Al Gore to be Clinton's vice-president?

A Close Election

On Election Day, November 7, 2000, most people expected a very close race. The election ended up being one of the closest in U.S. history. As the day moved into night, it became clear that whichever candidate won Florida would win the presidency.

The next morning, Gore led the nationwide popular vote by more than 300,000 votes and also had a lead in electoral votes. But Bush led in Florida by a few hundred votes, which could still win the election for him.

The vote was so close in Florida that recounts were required. In addition, many Floridians claimed there were problems with the voting process. Some voters were confused by the way the names were listed on the ballots. They claimed this may have caused them to vote for the wrong candidate. In some cases, the voting machines did not work correctly.

The Gore campaign asked for manual, or hand, recounts of ballots in four Florida counties. The Bush campaign opposed manual recounts and sued to stop them. The legal battles reached the U.S. Supreme Court. On December 12, the Court voted five to four to stop the recounts. The majority argued that there was no way to be sure the votes would be recounted in exactly the same way in all counties. This situation, they said, would be unfair to some voters. With the recounts stopped, Florida's electoral votes, and the presidency, went to George W. Bush.

The 2000 election raised issues about how elections are conducted in the United States. For example, Gore won the popular vote but lost the election. This led to renewed efforts to abolish the Electoral College. Americans also looked to improve the ways votes are cast and counted.

*Reading*History

E. Analyzing Causes Why did Bush win the presidency even though he had fewer popular votes than Gore?

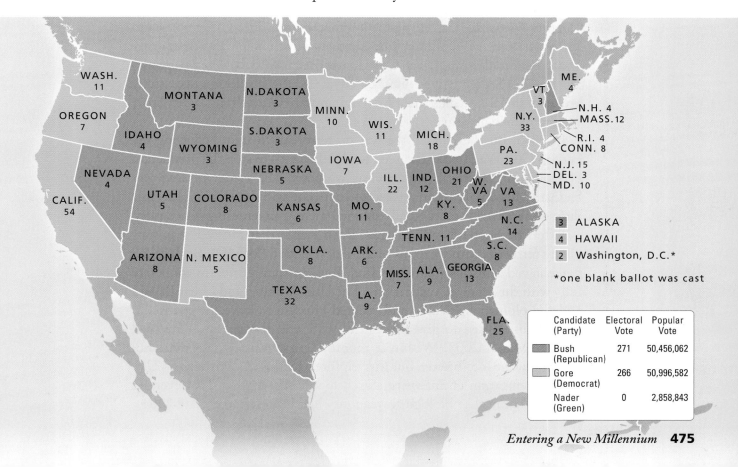

Candidate (Party)	Electoral Vote	Popular Vote
Bush (Republican)	271	50,456,062
Gore (Democrat)	266	50,996,582
Nader (Green)	0	2,858,843

3 ALASKA
4 HAWAII
2 Washington, D.C.*

*one blank ballot was cast

Bush Fights Terrorism

The Pentagon after the September 11 attack

Bush tried to put the controversial election behind him and to begin governing. On September 11, 2001, however, Bush and the world faced a new challenge. A series of terrorist attacks against the United States cost thousands of people their lives and dramatically changed the world. The Bush administration, now with the overwhelming support of Congress and the American people, shifted its energy and attention to combating terrorism. (For a special report, see pages 892–897.)

In October 2001, Bush signed an antiterrorism bill into law. The law allowed the government to detain foreigners suspected of terrorism for seven days without charging them with a crime. Bush also created the Department of Homeland Security, a government body to coordinate national efforts to combat terrorism. In addition, the federal government increased its involvement in aviation security.

The Bush Administration also began a war against terrorism. In October 2001, the United States led forces from different countries in an attack on Afghanistan. The Afghan government was harboring Osama bin Laden and his al-Qaeda terrorist network believed responsible for the September 11 attacks. In 2002, the coalition successfully broke up the al-Qaeda network in Afghanistan. Osama bin Laden, however, remained at large.

In 2003, Bush expanded the war on terrorism to Iraq. Following the Persian Gulf War, Iraq had agreed to UN demands to stop the production of biological, chemical, and nuclear weapons. The leader of Iraq was Saddam Hussein. Hussein refused to cooperate with UN arms inspectors during the 1990s and eventually stopped them from entering his country.

After the September 11 attacks, Bush feared that Hussein was supplying terrorists with weapons of mass destruction (WMD). Bush called for renewed arms inspections in Iraq. But Hussein refused to cooperate fully with the renewed inspections. The United States and Great Britain ended diplomacy with Iraq and ordered Hussein to leave the country.

Hussein refused to give up control. U.S. and British forces invaded Iraq in March 2003. Within a month, Iraq's military was defeated. Hussein went into hiding, but was captured by the end of the year. U.S. forces then began an intensive search for WMD in Iraq. However, no trace of chemical or biological weaponry had been found by late 2004.

The Bush Presidency at Home

During his first months as president, Bush began to work on his domestic policies. He signed into law an education reform plan entitled No Child Left Behind. This plan called for more accountability by states for students' success, mandatory achievement testing, and more school options for parents.

Bush also wanted to improve a slowing economy. But corporate scandals further damaged the economy. In the 1990s, Enron had established itself as one of the most successful companies in the world. In October 2001, the Security Exchange Commission began investigating Enron's financial records. Several months later, the company was charged with using illegal accounting practices and was fined $3 million. Enron's accounting firm, Arthur Andersen, was charged with obstruction of justice.

Political opinion remained deeply divided through Bush's first term. While Bush's antiterrorism policies initially gained wide support, many Americans began to question his handling of the invasion of Iraq.

In 2004, Massachusetts senator John Kerry challenged Bush. After both sides waged one of the most expensive campaigns in history, Bush was able to win a majority of the popular vote, but once again the electoral vote came down to one state. In Ohio, Bush held a lead of more than 130,000 votes, which would give him the state's 20 electoral votes and the presidency. After deciding that the uncounted absentee and paper ballots would not be enough to take the lead, Kerry conceded the race to Bush the day after the election.

In Bush's victory speech, he promised to revise the nation's tax code and reform Social Security in order to improve the economy. In the next section you will read more about the U.S. economy, including the impact of technology on it, at the start of the 21st century.

President George W. Bush campaigning for Republican candidates in 2002

Section 1 Assessment

1. Terms & Names

Explain the significance of:
- Ronald Reagan
- supply-side economics
- Iran-Contra affair
- George H. W. Bush
- Persian Gulf War
- Bill Clinton
- NAFTA
- George W. Bush

2. Using Graphics

Use a chart like the one shown to record important details about the terms of three presidents.

Reagan	
Bush	
Clinton	

What do you think was the greatest achievement by any of these presidents?

3. Main Ideas

a. What were the positive and negative effects of Reagan's economic policies?

b. Why did Clinton win the 1992 presidential election?

c. Why did it take five weeks to decide the winner of the 2000 presidential election?

4. Critical Thinking

Drawing Conclusions
What do you think was the stronger force shaping U.S. politics from 1981 to 2000—economics or foreign affairs?

THINK ABOUT
- Reagan's goals and actions
- the events of George H. W. Bush's presidency
- the events of Clinton's presidency

ACTIVITY OPTIONS

ART

TECHNOLOGY

You have been asked to summarize the politics of the years 1981–2001. Create an **illustrated time line,** or plan part of a **multimedia presentation.**

TERMS & NAMES
Internet
e-commerce
service economy
information
  revolution
downsizing

② Technological and Economic Changes

MAIN IDEA	WHY IT MATTERS NOW
Advances in science and technology have improved daily life and created a global economy.	Technology continues to change American homes, leisure activities, and workplaces.

ONE AMERICAN'S STORY

In the late 1990s, technology transformed business. One reason was the **Internet**, a worldwide computer network. Some enterprising people developed **e-commerce**, business that is conducted over the Internet.

Jeff Bezos was a pioneer of e-commerce. In 1994, he decided to open a bookstore on-line. The idea caught on quickly. From 1997 to 1999, the number of customers using his bookstore grew from 2 million to 16.9 million. Bezos doesn't define his job as selling books but as giving buyers more choice.

A VOICE FROM THE PAST

Our business is helping customers make purchasing decisions. . . . It all has to do with the balance of power shifting away from companies and toward consumers.

Jeff Bezos, quoted in "Companies Wired for the Bottom Line," *Newsweek,* September 20, 1999

Jeff Bezos revolutionized the bookselling industry by putting it on-line.

Bezos' company did not make a profit in 1999 or 2000. But he remained confident in his business. In late 2000, however, many people lost confidence in Internet companies. Many Internet companies went out of business, or like Bezos's company, laid off workers. Section 2 explains more about the ways technology has affected American life and the U.S. economy.

Technology and Daily Life

As the 20th century drew to a close, thousands of institutions, from hospitals to airports to banks, relied on computers to perform essential tasks. Computer use also grew in homes and schools. By 2001, more than half of all U.S. households had a personal computer. And from 1985 to 1998, the number of computers in classrooms leaped from 630,000 to more than 8 million.

Computers and the Internet revolutionized communication and research. Using the Internet, a person can track down information on nearly any subject. Internet users can also send and receive electronic messages called e-mail. In addition, they can shop at on-line stores.

Other forms of new technology have also transformed American life. One popular example is the battery-powered cellular telephone. People can carry these phones with them anywhere. Between 1990 and 2001, the number of cellular phone subscribers in the United States grew dramatically from 5.3 million to more than 110 million.

A Changing Economy

For much of the 20th century, manufacturing made up a major share of the U.S. economy. By the year 2000, that had changed drastically. The computer age fueled the growth of the service economy. In a **service economy**, most jobs provide services instead of producing goods. By 1996, about 71 percent of all workers had jobs in the service industry. Many of these jobs—such as lawyers, teachers, engineers, and Web-site designers—focused on providing knowledge and information.

Some experts said the United States was going through an **information revolution**. This meant that technology had radically changed the way information was delivered—and gave people access to far more information than ever before. This improved the productivity of many industries.

Computers changed not just industries but also the lives of most individual workers. For example, engineers began to use computers to test new car designs. In large companies, workers from many departments were able to share information through computer networks. Filmmakers used computers to create animated characters that would react on-screen with live actors.

Economic Change Affects Workers

The dramatic changes in the economy were both good news and bad news for U.S. workers. During the 1990s, high-tech industries created many new, high-paying jobs for skilled workers.

Yet other workers faced hard times. The decline of manufacturing meant the loss of factory jobs. The newly unemployed workers faced an uncertain future. They had earned good wages in the factory, although many of them were not highly skilled or educated. Most new jobs required specialized skills. As a result, job seekers had to obtain education and training, or they had to settle for lower-paying jobs.

Highly skilled workers also lost jobs. Many corporations engaged in **downsizing**—reducing the number of workers to increase company profits. During the mid-1990s, companies let go of hundreds of thousands of workers. In addition, many mergers—in which two companies

STRANGE *but* **True**

INTERNET 911
In April 1997, 12-year-old Sean Redden was using the Internet at his home in Texas when he saw a startling message: "Hello, help me."

The message was from 20-year-old Tarja Laitinen of Finland. While using the Internet, she'd had a severe attack of asthma.

Sean's mother called 911. This led to a series of phone calls that ended up with Tarja's being rushed to a Finnish hospital. Sean, with the help of the Internet, had saved Tarja's life!

Reading **History**
A. Drawing Conclusions Why is the Internet an important part of the information revolution?

Background Downsizing most often occurs during hard times but also can take place when the economy is strong.

The Computer Revolution

Would you be impressed if a scientist came to you and said, "I can take a machine, reduce it to one-thousandth of its present size, and yet increase its power"? That is exactly what happened with computers during the last half of the 20th century. Today, personal computers can perform more operations more quickly than the first giant computers did. In addition, the first computers were very expensive and difficult to maintain. The development of inexpensive personal computers made it possible for small businesses and ordinary families to use the latest technology.

1970s

Commodore PET Computer chips made the personal computer possible. The Commodore PET was the first personal computer designed to be sold to the public. It cost only $595—but had just 12K of memory.

Computer Chip Vacuum tubes were replaced first by transistors and later by tiny computer chips. By the 1970s, all of a computer's operations were contained on a small number of chips, wired to a control board.

1940s

ENIAC One of the first general-purpose electronic computers, the ENIAC used 18,000 vacuum tubes (which looked a bit like light bulbs). ENIAC took up 1,500 square feet, about one-third of a basketball court. It was used for mathematical calculations and could do 5,000 additions a second.

1990s

Virtual Reality The personal computers of the 1990s grew increasingly powerful and were able to perform sophisticated jobs. Here, an interior designer uses a virtual-environment program to recreate a room. Computers were also used in engineering and film animation.

FUTURE

CONNECT TO HISTORY

1. **Recognizing Effects** Do you think the development of the personal computer had a positive or negative effect on the economy? Explain.

   See Skillbuilder Handbook, page R11.

CONNECT TO TODAY

2. **Identifying Problems** What problem might the computer industry try to solve next?

For more information about computers . . .

RESEARCH LINKS CLASSZONE.COM

join—took place. When two companies merge, it creates a situation in which people hold duplicate jobs, so mergers usually lead to layoffs.

Most laid-off workers found other jobs. But in an effort to cut costs, many companies hired people for part-time or temporary jobs. Such jobs generally offer lower pay and fewer benefits than full-time jobs.

In the late 1990s, however, many more jobs were created when the economy boomed. By late summer of 2000, the unemployment rate dipped below 4 percent—its lowest level in 30 years. In addition, the economy grew by a robust 5 percent in 2000. The growth of Internet companies contributed greatly to these numbers.

By the end of 2000, however, many Internet companies that had not made profits went out of business. Others laid off workers. Technology stocks collapsed. In March 2001, the nation fell into a recession. Unemployment climbed to 5.7 percent in November 2001. But the economy still managed to grow early in the year.

A More Global Economy

Technology helped to build a more global economy—in which countries around the world are linked through business. Through the Internet, companies on different continents could do business as if they were in the same city. Trade and investment among nations expanded.

Corporations also built factories and offices in other countries. By 1995, for example, more than 3 million Japanese cars were made at U.S. plants. And businesses in different countries merged to form multinational corporations. For example, in May 1998, the German company Daimler-Benz AG bought the Chrysler Corporation. This created a worldwide auto giant, DaimlerChrysler AG.

President Clinton saw the growth of world trade as a chance for America to sell more goods and create more jobs. This was why he urged Congress to pass NAFTA.

The global economy caused problems for some U.S. workers. To cut costs, some businesses moved their operations from the United States to countries where wages were lower. In the mid-1990s, for example, a large U.S. clothing maker moved many of its sewing operations to Mexico, the Caribbean, and Central America. Thousands of U.S. workers lost their jobs.

Because of global trade, the economies of various countries had become more closely linked. Nations were more likely to suffer from each other's financial woes. For example, in October 1997, Hong Kong's stock market fell, which caused stock markets from Europe to North America to drop. In the summer of 1998, Russia temporarily experienced a financial crisis, which also caused markets to fall.

*Reading*History
B. Analyzing Causes Why did Americans fear that the U.S. economy was headed for a recession in 2001?

Background
NAFTA is the North American Free Trade Agreement. (See Section 1.)

Now and **then**

PREPARING FOR TOMORROW'S JOBS

In the past, many workers spent their entire careers at one company. By the 1990s, workers were changing jobs often to gain more pay or more challenging assignments.

Workers today also have more chances to work overseas. For example, 27-year-old Anne Larlarb has already worked in England and Thailand. In the photo above, she uses e-mail to keep in touch with friends.

If these trends continue, future workers will need to be flexible, quick learners and be open to other cultures.

Scientific Breakthroughs

In the last decades of the 20th century, the world of medicine saw many breakthroughs. Engineers developed smaller, more precise surgical instruments. These and new technologies such as lasers allowed doctors to perform surgery through tiny incisions in the body, which heal more quickly than large cuts. New tests helped doctors to make better diagnoses.

Scientists developed new drugs that offer greater hope for a cure for cancer. New drugs and treatments also slowed the rate at which AIDS (acquired immune deficiency syndrome) kills infected people.

In 1997, Scottish scientists cloned the first mammal—a sheep. This set off a furious debate. Many feared that cloning human beings could be next. Some insisted that cloning would help to improve the human species. Others argued that the process is unethical.

This firefighter has received an artificial arm with the ability to sense heat.

Vocabulary
clone: to make a genetic duplicate of a living being

Reading **History**
C. Identifying Facts and Opinions Is Representative Ehlers expressing a fact or an opinion? Explain.

A VOICE FROM THE PAST

Creating life in the laboratory is totally inappropriate and so far removed from the process of marriage and parenting that . . . we must rebel against the very concept of human cloning. It is simply wrong to experiment with the creation of human life in this way.

U.S. Representative Vernon Ehlers, statement to U.S. Congress

In nonmedical science, the United States and other nations began to build an international space station. The station was scheduled to be finished in the early 2000s. Nations will use it to research the stars, planets, and galaxies. While technology and science shape the years to come, so too will people. Section 3 discusses the nation's diverse population and how these many groups are shaping American society.

Section **2** *Assessment*

1. Terms & Names

Explain the significance of:
- Internet
- e-commerce
- service economy
- information revolution
- downsizing

2. Taking Notes

Use a cluster diagram like the one shown to list changes in technology, the economy, and science.

3. Main Ideas

a. How did the information revolution change jobs?

b. Why did the rise of the global economy cause some workers to worry?

c. What advances did scientists make in the field of medicine?

4. Critical Thinking

Forming and Supporting Opinions What job skills do you think you will need for the future? Why?

THINK ABOUT
- the changes in technology and science
- the changes in the economy

ACTIVITY OPTIONS

TECHNOLOGY / **DRAMA**

What technological marvel would you like to see invented? Design a **Web page** advertising the new technology, or perform a **skit** showing someone using it.

③ The New Americans

MAIN IDEA

Due to immigration, the United States grew more diverse.

WHY IT MATTERS NOW

Americans of all backgrounds share common goals: the desire for equal rights and economic opportunity.

ONE AMERICAN'S STORY

Born in the Dominican Republic, Junot Díaz came to the United States with his family when he was seven. He started writing when he was just 13. In 1996, at the age of 28, he published his first book of stories. Díaz writes about being Dominican but believes his stories are universal; that is, they have meaning for everyone.

A VOICE FROM THE PAST

I am Dominican and that for me is important, but I also know that there is this whole idea that if you are a Dominican that's not universal, that's not American. But, I argue that [my stories] are universal and American.

Junot Díaz, quoted in *Frontera*

Junot Díaz won praise for his stories about being Dominican.

Díaz and millions of other recent immigrants have made important contributions to the nation's growth. This section discusses how these new Americans are making the United States a more diverse nation.

Immigrants Affect American Society

From 1981 to 1996, nearly 13.5 million legal immigrants came to the United States. These immigrants increased U.S. diversity. Most of the immigrants who came to America during earlier periods had come from Europe. Nearly 85 percent of the arrivals since 1981 came from either Latin America or Asia. The Census Bureau predicts that the Hispanic population in the United States will increase from 12.5 percent in 2000 to 17 percent by 2020. The Asian population is expected to climb from 3.6 percent in 2000 to about 6 percent in 2020.

Changes to immigration laws passed in 1965 have contributed to the recent surge in immigration. These changes allowed people from a greater variety of countries to enter the United States. The lure of America also plays a role. As earlier immigrants did, many of the newcomers came to the United States seeking economic opportunity and, in some cases, political freedom.

U.S. citizens have mixed feelings about immigration. Some argue that immigrants take jobs from citizens. Many Americans also worry about the number of immigrants who enter the United States illegally. Officials

The American People

Ancestry of Americans, 1990	(descendants, in thousands)	Origins of Immigrants, 1981–1996	(immigrants, in thousands)
1. German	58,000	1. Mexico	3,300
2. Irish	39,000	2. Philippines	840
3. English	33,000	3. China*	730
4. African	24,000	4. Vietnam	720
5. Italian	15,000	5. Dominican Republic	510
6. Mexican	12,000	6. India	500
7. French	10,000	7. Korea	450
8. Native American	9,000	8. Soviet Union†	420
9. Polish	9,000	9. El Salvador	360
10. Dutch	6,000	10. Jamaica	320

SKILLBUILDER Interpreting Charts

1. *Compare the origins of recent immigrants to the ancestry of Americans overall. Are any the same?*
2. *How might the list of top ten ancestry groups change in the future?*

* China includes Taiwan.
† The Soviet Union broke apart in 1991. This figure includes the former Soviet republics.

Source: *U.S. Bureau of the Census*

estimate that in 1996, about 5 million illegal immigrants lived in the United States. Roughly 2.7 million were thought to be from Mexico.

Because illegal immigrants are here secretly, they do not pay income taxes. However, they do pay sales taxes and often work for low wages in poor conditions because they fear being sent away. Even so, they receive some government services, such as education for their children. As a result, some people feel that they are a drain on the U.S. economy. Congress passed the **Immigration Reform and Control Act of 1986** to strengthen immigration laws and enforcement measures. But illegal immigrants continued to come to the United States.

Background
An illegal immigrant is someone who enters the United States secretly and without filling out the appropriate government forms.

Immigrant Contributions

Recent immigrants have brought, and continue to bring, many talents to the United States. The National Science Foundation estimates that 23 percent of all U.S. residents with doctorate degrees in engineering and science are foreign-born. High-tech industries, such as those located in Silicon Valley, California, have benefited from their skills.

In addition, immigrants are an important source of labor. Some studies indicate that without immigrants, the workforce might actually begin to shrink by 2015. In other words, U.S. businesses wouldn't be able to hire enough people to maintain their productivity.

Immigrants also make sports much more exciting. In 1998 and 1999, Dominican-born Sammy Sosa thrilled baseball fans by battling Mark McGwire for the home run record. Immigrants have also starred in other sports such as basketball, football, soccer, and golf.

Many immigrants enrich American arts and culture. Latin music, for example, has become very popular. Chinese-born author Bette Bao

*Reading*History
A. Drawing Conclusions What have immigrants contributed to the economy?

Lord has written popular books for children and adults. In addition, immigrants, and their sons and daughters, are acting in a greater number of movies. "When immigrants come to America they bring their culture, and that culture becomes part of a new country," noted Cuban-born singer Gloria Estefan. "It makes everyone stronger."

What Americans Have in Common

While immigrants bring their culture to America, many of them also have embraced American ways. They wear American clothes, adopt American customs, and learn English.

They also share the American belief in democracy and freedom. Ken Burns, a documentary filmmaker, explained that these beliefs make America unique in the world.

*Reading*History

B. Making Inferences
Judging from this quotation, how do you think Ken Burns views the future of the United States?

A VOICE FROM THE PAST

There is no other country on Earth that is configured like ours. Every other nation is there because of race, religion, language, ethnicity, or geography. We are here only because we agreed to subscribe to the words on four pieces of paper—the U.S. Constitution. Unlike every other country which sees itself as an end unto itself, we see ourselves as evolving. We're not satisfied. We're not willing to rest on our laurels. We think we can do better. We think we have got someplace to go.

Ken Burns, quoted in *The West*

Today the United States is a very different nation from the one founded in 1776. Democratic rights have expanded to include more and more people. As the United States moves into the future, it will no doubt continue to change. Tolerance and cooperation will be essential.

Citizens of all backgrounds will play a vital role in shaping what America will be. So will today's students. You have a part to play in helping the United States embrace people from every culture and land. You are the generation that will create the America of the future.

Section **3** Assessment

1. Terms & Names

Explain the significance of:
• Immigration Reform and Control Act of 1986

2. Using Graphics

Use a diagram like the one shown to record the effects of recent immigration on the United States.

Immigration

Effect   Effect   Effect

How has immigration affected your life?

3. Main Ideas

a. How did changes to immigration laws in 1965 help create a more diverse population?

b. In which areas of American society have immigrants made contributions?

c. What ideals do both immigrant and native-born Americans believe in?

4. Critical Thinking

Comparing and Contrasting How was the immigration that occurred in the years 1981–2000 similar to and different from earlier waves of immigration?

THINK ABOUT
• the immigration you read about in Chapter 14
• the immigration you read about in Chapter 21

ACTIVITY OPTIONS

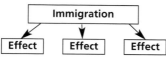

MATH

SPEECH

Survey ten people outside your class to learn their ethnic background. Present your findings as a **table** like the one on page 886 or in a **speech**.

Entering a New Millennium

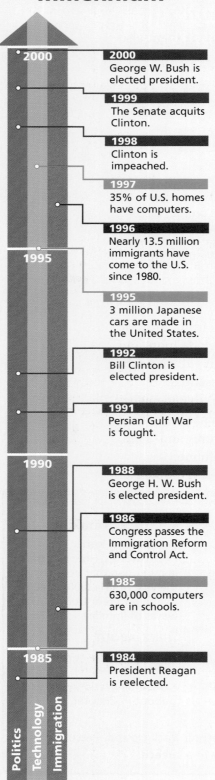

2000
George W. Bush is elected president.

1999
The Senate acquits Clinton.

1998
Clinton is impeached.

1997
35% of U.S. homes have computers.

1996
Nearly 13.5 million immigrants have come to the U.S. since 1980.

1995
3 million Japanese cars are made in the United States.

1992
Bill Clinton is elected president.

1991
Persian Gulf War is fought.

1988
George H. W. Bush is elected president.

1986
Congress passes the Immigration Reform and Control Act.

1985
630,000 computers are in schools.

1984
President Reagan is reelected.

Politics   Technology   Immigration

486

TERMS & NAMES

Briefly explain the significance of each of the following.

1. Ronald Reagan
2. supply-side economics
3. Iran-Contra affair
4. George H. W. Bush
5. Persian Gulf War
6. Bill Clinton
7. Internet
8. service economy
9. information revolution
10. Immigration Reform and Control Act of 1986

REVIEW QUESTIONS

Conservatives Reshape Politics (pages 471–477)

1. How did Reagan try to improve the economy?
2. What happened in the Iran-Contra affair?
3. What role did the United States play during the Persian Gulf War?
4. What happened during the 2000 presidential election?

Technological and Economic Changes (pages 478–482)

5. What did the Internet allow its users to do?
6. How did corporate mergers affect individuals?
7. What were the different reactions to cloning?

The New Americans (pages 483–485)

8. Why did the recent wave of immigrants come to the United States?
9. What do immigrants contribute to the economy?
10. Why do experts think the United States will become more diverse?

CRITICAL THINKING

1. USING YOUR NOTES

Using your completed chart, answer the questions below.

a. What were the effects of recent political events?
b. What were the main technological and economic changes?

2. ANALYZING LEADERSHIP

Judging from what you read in this chapter, what issues will a U.S. president face in the 21st century?

3. APPLYING CITIZENSHIP SKILLS

In what ways have recent immigrants demonstrated good citizenship here in the United States?

4. THEME: DIVERSITY AND UNITY

What ideas and goals help to unify Americans of different racial and ethnic backgrounds?

5. MAKING INFERENCES

Are U.S. citizens likely to be more or less welcoming to immigrants in good economic times? Explain.

Interact *with* History

Now that you have read about recent changes in the United States, what new ideas do you have about how you can contribute to the future?

HISTORY SKILLS

1. INTERPRETING MAPS: Movement

Study the map. Then answer the questions.

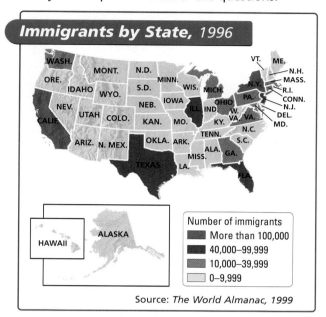

Immigrants by State, 1996

Number of immigrants
- More than 100,000
- 40,000–99,999
- 10,000–39,999
- 0–9,999

Source: *The World Almanac, 1999*

Basic Map Elements

a. Which year's statistics does this map show?

b. What do the various colors of the states indicate?

Interpreting the Map

c. Which states have the highest numbers of immigrants?

d. How would you describe what those states have in common?

2. INTERPRETING PRIMARY SOURCES

This photograph shows a robot that was designed to play a keyboard instrument.

a. What are some of the separate skills that humans need to play keyboard instruments? Think of both physical and mental skills.

b. If a robot can play a keyboard instrument, what else might it be able to do? Consider how else it might use the separate skills involved in the task.

ALTERNATIVE ASSESSMENT

1. INTERDISCIPLINARY ACTIVITY: Science

Explaining a Medical Advance Research a recent advance in medical science, such as a new medicine, treatment, or diagnostic test. Give a brief speech explaining the advance to the class.

2. COOPERATIVE LEARNING ACTIVITY

Creating a Front Page With three other students, create a newspaper front page that reports on the major events of the late 20th century. Three of the students will each write an article. The fourth student will be responsible for finding images for each story. Possible story topics are

- the arrival of a new device, the computer
- the number of recent immigrants to America reaches 13 million
- the most recent presidential election

Type and print out the stories and arrange them with their images on a large piece of paper. Show the front page to the class and have each student read his or her story aloud.

3. TECHNOLOGY ACTIVITY

Designing a Web Page What do you think the United States will be like in ten years? Design a Web page that presents your vision. Your Web page may include pictures and descriptions that portray your ideas. It should also include links to other sites that discuss technology, politics, or social issues. Draw a design of what the page will look like. Also provide written descriptions and addresses of other Web sites that are linked to yours.

For more information on sample Web pages . . .

INTERNET ACTIVITY
CLASSZONE.COM

4. HISTORY PORTFOLIO

Option 1 Review your section and chapter assessment activities. Select one that you think is your best work. Then use comments by your teacher or classmates to improve your work, and add it to your portfolio.

Option 2 Review the questions that you wrote for What Do You Want to Know? on page 470. Then write a short report in which you explain the answers to your questions. If any questions were not answered, do research to answer them. Add your answers to your portfolio.

Additional Test Practice, pp. S1–S33

TEST PRACTICE
CLASSZONE.COM

Make a Time Capsule

A time capsule is a sealed container that preserves records and artifacts from the present for people in the future. Ancient Babylonians and Egyptians began this custom by carving messages inside their temples. These records give people today an idea of what life was like thousands of years ago. One of the first modern time capsules is in Oglethorpe, Georgia. Sealed in 1940, it is not due to be opened until 8113. It contains such things as a Donald Duck doll and 640,000 pages on microfilm.

ACTIVITY With a group, construct a time capsule. Write an explanation of the contents and your predictions or dreams for the future. Then record this explanation on a cassette tape.

A family from the 1960s poses in front of their house.

TOOLBOX

Each group will need:

posterboard	stapler
aluminum foil	markers
cellophane	3 x 5 notecards
scissors	blank cassette tape
duct or masking tape	cassette recorder

STEP BY STEP

1 **Form groups.** Meet with three to four students to create a time capsule. To complete this project, groups will be expected to

- do research on a particular decade
- identify artifacts from that decade to place in a time capsule
- construct a time capsule
- write an explanation of the contents, and record it on an audio cassette

2 **Choose the 1950s, 1960s, 1970s, 1980s, or 1990s.** Use the Internet, encyclopedias, or books about that decade to brainstorm ideas for the contents of your time capsule. Each person should jot down items on a piece of paper. A sample is shown below. With your group, discuss these items and decide which ones you'd like to use. Be sure to include enough items so that people opening the capsule many years from now will have a complete picture of your decade.

Hairstyles and fashions in the 1970s were very different from those in the 1950s.

1960s items

photo of Vietnam war

Beatles record

peace sign

3 **Build the time capsule.** First, cut a small square out of the middle of the posterboard to make a window. Using tape or a stapler, place the cellophane over the hole. Then roll the posterboard so that it forms a large cylinder. Tape or staple the ends of the posterboard together. Place aluminum foil over one end of your time capsule—using tape to secure it.

4 **Decorate the time capsule.** Use markers to decorate the outside of the time capsule. These decorations should reflect your decade. Also, include a message that is connected with your decade. Be sure to explain when the capsule should be opened.

5 **Select your items.** Use the actual item, or a picture. On each 3 x 5 card, write an explanation of the items you've selected and explain their purpose. Attach a card to each picture or item. Be sure to include the year the item was first used.

6 **Present the contents to the class.** Using your notecards, explain to the class why you chose these items. Place the notecards inside the time capsule. Wait until you make your audio cassette to seal the time capsule—and be sure to include it.

WRITE AND SPEAK

Write a paragraph describing your time capsule. Include your predictions and dreams for future generations. Then record your message on an audio cassette and place it inside the time capsule. After sealing the time capsule, put it on display with the other time capsules.

HELP DESK

For related information, see Chapters 15, 16, 17, and 18.

Researching Your Project

"Time Immemorial," *Popular Mechanics,* February 1999.

For more about time capsules . . .

 **RESEARCH LINKS**
CLASSZONE.COM

Did You Know?

Westinghouse Electric Company coined the term *time capsule.* The company built one for the New York World's Fair of 1939–1940. The capsule is due to be opened in 6939. To preserve the capsule's contents, the company formed a new metal alloy called Cupaloy. It combined the durability of steel with the ability of copper to prevent corrosion.

The designers figured people living in the 70th century may not know the time capsule exists. So they created *The Book of Record.* It gives the time capsule's location and was placed in libraries all over the world.

REFLECT & ASSESS

- Why did you choose the particular artifacts in your time capsule?
- How do you think future generations might react to the articles in your time capsule?
- How well do your items represent the history, social issues, and culture of your decade?

The Attack: September 11, 2001

Terrorism is the use of violence against people or property to force changes in societies or governments. Acts of terrorism are not new. Throughout history, individuals and groups have used terror tactics to achieve political or social goals.

In recent decades, however, terrorist groups have carried out increasingly destructive and high-profile attacks. The growing threat of terrorism has caused many people to feel vulnerable and afraid. However, it also has prompted action from many nations, including the United States.

Many of the terrorist activities of the late 20th century occurred far from U.S. soil. As a result, most Americans felt safe from such violence. All that changed, however, on the morning of September 11, 2001.

A Surprise Strike

As the nation began another workday, 19 terrorists hijacked four airplanes heading from East Coast airports to California. The hijackers crashed two of the jets into the twin towers of the World Trade Center in New York City. They slammed a third plane into the Pentagon outside Washington, D.C. The fourth plane crashed into an empty field in Pennsylvania after passengers apparently fought the hijackers.

The attacks destroyed the World Trade Center and badly damaged a section of the Pentagon. In all, some 3,000 people died. Life for Americans would never be the same after that day. Before, most U.S. citizens viewed terrorism as something that happened in other countries. Now they knew it could happen on their soil as well.

Officials soon learned that those responsible for the attacks were part of a largely Islamic terrorist network known as al-Qaeda. Observers, including many Muslims, accuse al-Qaeda of preaching a false and extreme form of Islam. Its members believe, among other things, that the United States and other Western nations are evil.

U.S. president George W. Bush vowed to hunt down all those responsible for the attacks. In addition, he called for a greater international effort to combat global terrorism. "This battle will take time and resolve," the president declared. "But make no mistake about it: we will win."

Securing the Nation

As the Bush Administration began its campaign against terrorism, it

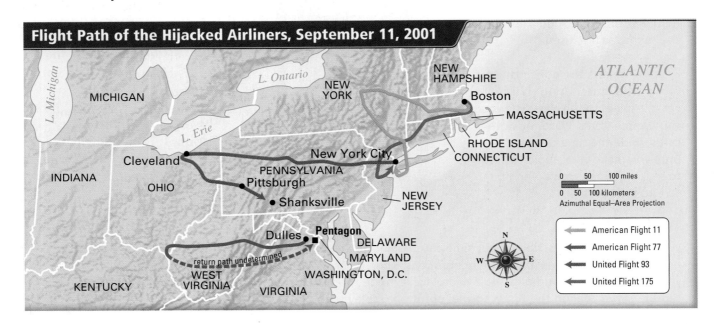

Flight Path of the Hijacked Airliners, September 11, 2001

ATLANTIC OCEAN

L. Michigan

MICHIGAN

L. Ontario

L. Erie

NEW HAMPSHIRE

NEW YORK

Boston

MASSACHUSETTS

RHODE ISLAND
CONNECTICUT

Cleveland

New York City

INDIANA

OHIO

PENNSYLVANIA

Pittsburgh

Shanksville

NEW JERSEY

0   50   100 miles
0   50   100 kilometers
Azimuthal Equal–Area Projection

return path undetermined

Dulles   **Pentagon**

DELAWARE

MARYLAND

WASHINGTON, D.C.

KENTUCKY   WEST VIRGINIA

VIRGINIA

N   W   E   S

American Flight 11
American Flight 77
United Flight 93
United Flight 175

also sought to prevent any further attacks on America. In October 2001, the president signed into law the USA Patriot Act. The law gave the federal government a broad range of new powers to strengthen national security.

The new law enabled officials to detain foreigners suspected of terrorism for up to seven days without charging them with a crime. Officials could also monitor all phone and Internet use by suspects, and prosecute terrorist crimes without any time restrictions or limitations.

In addition, the government created a new cabinet position, the Department of Homeland Security, to coordinate national efforts against terrorism. President Bush named former Pennsylvania governor Tom Ridge as the first Secretary of Homeland Security.

Underneath a U.S. flag posted amid the rubble of the World Trade Center, rescue workers search for survivors of the attack.

Some critics charged that a number of the government's new anti-terrorism measures violated people's civil rights. Supporters countered that occasionally limiting some civil liberties was justified in the name of greater national security.

The federal government also stepped in to ensure greater security at the nation's airports. The September 11 attacks had originated at several airports, with four hijackings occurring at nearly the same time. In November 2001, President Bush signed the Aviation and Transportation Security Act into law. The law put the federal government in charge of airport security. Before, individual airports had been responsible for security. The new law created a federal security force to inspect passengers and carry-on bags. It also required the screening of checked baggage.

While the September 11 attacks shook the United States, they also strengthened the nation's unity and resolve. In 2003, officials approved plans to rebuild on the World Trade Center site and construct a memorial. Meanwhile, the country has grown more unified as Americans recognize the need to stand together against terrorism.

Stunned bystanders look on as smoke billows from the twin towers of the World Trade Center moments after an airplane slammed into each one.

Fighting Back

The attack against the United States on September 11, 2001, represented the single most deadly act of terrorism in modern history. By that time, however, few regions of the world had been spared from terrorist attacks. Today, America and other nations are responding to terrorism in a variety of ways.

The Rise of Terrorism

The problem of modern international terrorism first gained world attention during the 1972 Summer Olympic Games in Munich, Germany. Members of a Palestinian terrorist group killed two Israeli athletes and took nine others hostage. Five of the terrorists, all the hostages, and a police officer were later killed in a bloody gun battle.

Since then, terrorist activities have occurred across the globe. In Europe, the Irish Republican Army (IRA) used terrorist tactics for decades against Britain. The IRA has long opposed British control of Northern Ireland. Since 1998, the two sides have been working toward a peaceful solution to their conflict. In South America, a group known as the Shining Path terrorized the residents of Peru throughout the late 20th century. The group sought to overthrow the government and establish a Communist state.

Africa, too, has seen its share of terrorism. Groups belonging to the al-Qaeda terrorist organization operated in many African countries. Indeed, officials have linked several major attacks against U.S. facilities in Africa to al-Qaeda. In 1998, for example, bombings at the U.S. embassies in Kenya and Tanzania left more than 200 dead and 5,000 injured.

Most terrorists work in a similar way: targeting high profile events or crowded places where people normally feel safe. They include such places as subway stations, bus stops, restaurants, or shopping malls. Terrorists choose these spots carefully in order to gain the most attention and to achieve the highest level of intimidation.

Terrorists use bullets and bombs as their main weapons. In recent years, however, some terrorist groups have used biological and chemical agents in their attacks. These actions involve the release of bacteria or poisonous gas into the air. Gas was the weapon of choice for a radical Japanese religious cult, Aum Shinrikyo. In 1995, cult members released sarin, a deadly nerve gas, in subway stations in Tokyo. Twelve people were killed and more than 5,700 injured. The possibility of this type of terrorism is particularly worrisome, because biochemical agents are relatively easy to acquire.

Terrorism: A Global Problem

PLACE	YEAR	EVENT
Munich, Germany	1972	Palestinians take Israeli hostages at Summer Olympics; hostages and terrorists die in gun battle with police
Beirut, Lebanon	1983	Terrorists detonate truck bomb at U.S. marine barracks, killing 241
Tokyo, Japan	1995	Religious extremists release lethal gas into subway stations, killing 12 and injuring thousands
Omagh, Northern Ireland	1998	Faction of Irish Republican Army sets off car bomb, killing 29
Beslan, North Ossetia, Russia	2004	Separatists from Chechnya take over a school and hold more than 1,000 people hostage; more than 300 people killed.

Hunting Down Terrorists

Most governments have adopted an aggressive approach to tracking down and punishing terrorist groups. This approach includes spying on the groups to gather information on membership and future plans. It also includes striking back harshly after a terrorist attack, even to the point of assassinating known terrorist leaders.

Another approach that governments use is to make it more difficult for terrorists to act. This involves eliminating a terrorist group's source of funding. President Bush issued an executive order freezing the U.S. assets of alleged terrorist organizations as well as various groups accused of supporting terrorism. President Bush asked other nations to freeze such assets as well. By the spring of 2002, the White House reported, the United States and other countries had blocked nearly $80 million in alleged terrorist assets.

Battling al-Qaeda

In one of the more aggressive responses to terrorism, the United States quickly took military action against those it held responsible for the September 11 attacks.

U.S. officials had determined that members of the al-Qaeda terrorist group had carried out the assault under the direction of the group's leader, Osama bin Laden. Bin Laden was a Saudi Arabian millionaire who lived in Afghanistan. He directed his terrorist activities under the protection of the country's extreme Islamic government, known as the Taliban.

The United States demanded that the Taliban turn over bin Laden. The Taliban refused. In October 2001, U.S. forces began bombing Taliban air defenses, airfields, and command centers. They also struck numerous al-Qaeda training camps. On the ground, the United States provided assistance to rebel groups opposed to the Taliban. By December, the United States had driven the Taliban from power and severely weakened the al-Qaeda network. However, as of November, 2004, Osama bin Laden was still believed to be at large.

Osama bin Laden delivers a videotaped message from a hidden location shortly after the U.S.-led strikes against Afghanistan began.

Troops battling the Taliban in Afghanistan await transport by helicopter.

The War in Iraq

In the ongoing battle against terrorism, the United States confronted the leader of Iraq, Saddam Hussein. The longtime dictator had concerned the world community for years. During the 1980s, Hussein had used chemical weapons to put down a rebellion in his own country. In 1990, he had invaded neighboring Kuwait—only to be pushed back by a U.S.-led military effort. In light of such history, many viewed Hussein as an increasing threat to peace and stability in the world. As a result, the Bush Administration led an effort in early 2003 to remove Hussein from power.

The Path to War

One of the main concerns about Saddam Hussein was his possible development of so-called weapons of mass destruction. These are weapons that can kill large numbers of people. They include chemical and biological agents as well as nuclear devices.

Bowing to world pressure, Hussein allowed inspectors from the United Nations to search Iraq for such outlawed weapons. Some investigators, however, insisted that the Iraqis were not fully cooperating with the inspections.

U.S. and British officials soon threatened to use force to disarm Iraq. During his State of the Union address in January 2003, President Bush declared Hussein too great a threat to ignore in an age of increased terrorism. Reminding Americans of the September 11 attacks, Bush stated, "Imagine those 19 hijackers with other weapons and other plans—this time armed by Saddam Hussein. It would take one vial, one canister, one crate slipped into this country to bring a day of horror like none we have ever known. We will do every-thing in our power to make sure that day never comes."

Operation Iraqi Freedom

In the months that followed, the UN Security Council debated what action to take. Some countries, such as France and Germany, called for letting the inspectors continue searching for weapons. British prime minister Tony Blair, however, accused the Iraqis of "deception and evasion" and insisted inspections would never work.

On March 17, President Bush gave Saddam Hussein and his top aides 48 hours to leave the country or face a military strike. The Iraqi leader refused. On March 19, a coalition led by the United States and Britain launched air strikes in and around the Iraqi capital, Baghdad. The next day, coalition forces marched into Iraq though Kuwait. The invasion of Iraq to remove Saddam Hussein, known as Operation Iraqi Freedom, had begun.

The military operation met with strong opposition from numerous countries. Russian president Vladimir Putin claimed the invasion could "in no way be justified." He and others criticized the policy of attacking a nation to prevent it from future misdeeds. U.S. and British officials, however, argued that they would not wait for Hussein to strike first.

As coalition troops marched north to Baghdad, they met pockets of stiff resistance and engaged in fierce fighting in several southern cities. Meanwhile, coalition forces parachuted into northern Iraq and began moving south toward the capital city. By early April, Baghdad had fallen and the regime of Saddam Hussein had collapsed. After less than four weeks of fighting, the coalition had won the war.

U.S. Army Specialist Shoshana Johnson was one of several Americans held prisoner and eventually released during the war in Iraq.

As the regime of Saddam Hussein collapsed, statues of the dictator toppled.

The Struggle Continues

Despite the coalition victory, much work remained in Iraq. The United States installed a civil administrator, retired diplomat L. Paul Bremer, to help oversee the rebuilding of the nation. With the help of Bremer and others, the Iraqis established their own interim government several months after the war. The new governing body went to work creating a constitution and planning democratic elections.

Meanwhile, intelligence officials searched for clues of Saddam Hussein's whereabouts. The defeated dictator was captured near his hometown of Tikrit on December 13, 2003. Despite Hussein's capture, numerous U.S. troops had to remain behind to help maintain order and battle pockets of Iraqi insurgents—different groups made up of Hussein loyalists, followers of rebel Islamic clerics, and terrorists with links to al-Qaeda.

Finally, inspectors were not able to find any weapons of mass destruction in the months after major combat had ended. The governments of the United States and Britain issued reports in 2004 saying that pre-war intelligence regarding such weapons was flawed.

Despite the unresolved issues, coalition leaders declared the defeat of Saddam Hussein to be a victory for global security. In a post-war speech to U.S. troops aboard the aircraft carrier *USS Abraham Lincoln*, President Bush urged the world community to keep moving forward in its battle against terrorism. "We do not know the day of final victory, but we have seen the turning of the tide," declared the president. "No act of the terrorists will change our purpose, or weaken our resolve, or alter their fate. Their cause is lost. Free nations will press on to victory."

President George W. Bush and British prime minister Tony Blair stood together throughout the war.

Special Report Assessment

1. Main Ideas

a. What steps did the U.S. government take to make the nation more secure after the attacks on September 11, 2001?

b. Why did the United States take military action against the Taliban in Afghanistan?

c. What was the result of Operation Iraqi Freedom?

2. Critical Thinking

Analyzing Issues Is it important for the U.S. government to respect people's civil rights as it wages a war against terrorism? Why or why not?

THINK ABOUT
- what steps are necessary to protect the nation
- a government that grows too powerful

The Supreme Court

The task of the Supreme Court, according to Chief Justice John Marshall, is "to say what the law is." The Court reviews appeals of decisions by lower courts. It judges whether federal laws or government actions violate the Constitution. And it settles conflicts between state and federal laws.

By interpreting the law, the Supreme Court wields great power, for its decisions affect practically every aspect of life in the United States. In the following pages, you'll learn about some of the Supreme Court's landmark cases—decisions that altered the course of history or brought major changes to American life.

> *"When we have examined . . . the Supreme Court and the [rights] which it exercises, we shall readily admit that a more imposing judicial power was never constituted by any people."*
>
> — ALEXIS DE TOCQUEVILLE, *DEMOCRACY IN AMERICA* (1835)

Chief Justice John Marshall established the principle of judicial review.

The development of steamships led to Supreme Court decisions on interstate commerce.

McCulloch v. *Maryland* decided if a state had the power to tax a federal agency.

1803
Marbury v. *Madison*
Judicial Review

1819
McCulloch v. *Maryland*
Powers of Congress and States' Rights

1824
Gibbons v. *Ogden*
State Versus Federal Authority

1857
Dred Scott v. *Sandford*
Citizenship

1896
Plessy v. *Ferguson*
Segregation

Landmark decisions on school desegregation helped give rise to the civil rights movement.

Opinions written by Justice Oliver Wendell Holmes, Jr., helped to set standards for free speech.

TABLE OF CONTENTS

BEFORE YOU READ

Think About It Why is there a need for a judicial authority "to say what the law is"? How might the history of the United States have been different if the Supreme Court had not taken on this role?

Find Out About It Use library resources or the Internet to find out what issues the Supreme Court is presently reviewing. How might the Court's decisions on these issues affect you?

For more information on the Supreme Court . . .

RESEARCH LINKS CLASSZONE.COM

The Supreme Court has reviewed several affirmative-action cases in recent years.

1919
Schenck v. **United States**
Freedom of Speech

1954
Brown v. **Board of Education of Topeka**
School Desegregation

1964
Reynolds v. **Sims**
One Person, One Vote

1978
Regents of the University of California v. **Bakke**
Affirmative Action

Marbury v. Madison (1803)

THE ISSUE Judicial Review

ORIGINS OF THE CASE In 1801, just before he left office, President John Adams appointed dozens of Federalists as judges. Most of these "midnight justices" took their posts before Thomas Jefferson, Adams's Democratic-Republican successor, took office. Jefferson ordered his secretary of state, James Madison, to block the remaining appointees from taking their posts. One of these appointees, William Marbury, asked the Supreme Court to issue an order forcing Madison to recognize the appointments.

THE RULING The Court ruled that the law under which Marbury had asked the Supreme Court to act was unconstitutional.

LEGAL Sources

U.S. CONSTITUTION/LEGISLATION

Article 3, Section 2 (1789)
"In all cases affecting ambassadors, other public ministers and consuls, and those in which a state shall be party, the Supreme Court shall have original jurisdiction. In all the other cases . . . the Supreme Court shall have appellate jurisdiction."

Judiciary Act, Section 13 (1789)
"The Supreme Court shall . . . have power to issue . . . writs of *mandamus,* in cases warranted by the principles and usages of law."

RELATED CASES

Fletcher v. Peck (1810)
For the first time, the Supreme Court ruled a state law unconstitutional.

Cohens v. Virginia (1821)
For the first time, the Court overturned a state court decision.

The Legal Arguments

Chief Justice John Marshall wrote the Court's opinion, stating that Marbury had every right to receive his appointment. Further, Marshall noted, the Judiciary Act of 1789 gave Marbury the right to file his claim directly with the Supreme Court. But Marshall questioned whether the Court had the power to act. The answer, he argued, rested on the kinds of cases that could be argued directly in the Supreme Court without first being heard by a lower court.

Article 3 of the Constitution clearly identified those cases that the Court could hear directly. A case like Marbury's was not one of them. The Judiciary Act, therefore, was at odds with the Constitution. Which one should be upheld? Marshall's response was clear:

> . . . [T]he particular phraseology of the Constitution of the United States confirms and strengthens the principle . . . that a law repugnant to the Constitution is void; and that *courts* . . . are bound by that instrument.

Since Section 13 of the Judiciary Act violated the Constitution, Marshall concluded, it could not be enforced. The Court, therefore, could not issue the order. With this decision, Marshall appeared to limit the powers of the Supreme Court. In fact, the decision increased the Court's power because it established the principle of judicial review. This holds that the courts—most notably the Supreme Court—have the power to decide if laws are unconstitutional.

William Marbury received his appointment as a reward for his loyal support of John Adams in the 1800 presidential election.

Why Did It Matter Then?

The principle of judicial review had been set down in earlier state and lower federal court decisions. However, Marshall did not refer to those cases in *Marbury*. Rather, he based his argument on logic.

For a written constitution to have any value, Marshall stated, it is logical that any "legislative act [that is] contrary to the Constitution is not law." Only then could the Constitution be—as Article VI calls it—"the supreme law of the land." Who, then, decides that a law is invalid? Marshall declared that this power rests only with the courts:

> It is, emphatically, the province and duty of the judicial department to say what the law is. Those who apply the rule to particular cases must of necessity expound and interpret that rule. If [the Constitution and a law] conflict with each other, the courts must decide on the operation of each.

Not only did the courts have this power, Marshall said, it was "the very essence of judicial duty" for them to exercise it.

Why Does It Matter Now?

Over the years, judicial review has become a cornerstone of American government. The principle plays a vital role in the system of checks and balances that limits the powers of each branch of the federal government. For example, since 1803 the Court has struck down more than 125 acts of Congress as unconstitutional.

The Court has cited *Marbury* more than 250 times to justify its decisions. In *Clinton* v. *Jones* (1997), for example, the Court found that presidents are not protected by the Constitution from lawsuits involving actions in their private lives. The Court supported this finding by pointing to its power "to say what the law is." More recently, in *United States* v. *Morrison* (2000), the Court ruled that Congress went beyond its constitutional bounds by basing a federal law banning violence against women on the Fourteenth Amendment and the Commerce Clause of the Constitution. The opinion pointed out that "ever since *Marbury* this Court has remained the ultimate [explainer] of the constitutional text."

John Marshall, a Federalist, was practically a "midnight justice." John Adams appointed him chief justice in January 1801, just two months before Thomas Jefferson took office.

CONNECT TO HISTORY

1. **Making Decisions** Marshall was a Federalist, and many people expected him to act quickly on Marbury's case. What do you think might have been the consequences if Marshall had found for Marbury?

 See Skillbuilder Handbook, page R14.

CONNECT TO TODAY

2. **Researching** Find a recent instance of a law or administrative action that was ruled unconstitutional by the Supreme Court. What were the Court's reasons for the ruling, and what impact did the decision have? Prepare a summary of your findings.

For more information on judicial review . . .

RESEARCH LINKS
CLASSZONE.COM

McCulloch v. Maryland
(1819)

THE ISSUES Balance of power between the federal and state governments

ORIGINS OF THE CASE The second Bank of the United States (BUS) was established by an act of Congress in 1816. It set up branches nationwide. But many states objected to the bank's policies and wanted to limit its operations. In fact, Maryland set a tax on the currency issued by the Baltimore branch. The bank could avoid the tax by paying an annual fee of $15,000. However, James McCulloch, the branch cashier, refused to pay either the tax or the fee. The state sued McCulloch, and the Maryland courts ordered him to pay. McCulloch appealed the case to the Supreme Court.

THE RULING The Court ruled that Congress had the power to establish a national bank and that the Maryland tax on that bank was unconstitutional.

The Legal Arguments

The Court first addressed Maryland's argument that the act establishing the BUS was unconstitutional. Chief Justice John Marshall wrote that the Constitution listed the specific powers of Congress. These included collecting taxes, borrowing money, and regulating commerce. In addition, the Elastic Clause gave Congress the authority to make all "necessary and proper" laws needed to exercise those powers. Establishing a bank, he concluded, was necessary for Congress to carry out its powers. The BUS, then, was constitutional.

Next, Marshall addressed whether Maryland had the power to tax the BUS. Marshall acknowledged that the states had the power of taxation. But he said:

> [T]he constitution and the laws made in pursuance thereof are supreme . . . they control the constitution and laws of the respective states, and cannot be controlled by them.

So, to give a state the power to tax a federal agency created under the Constitution would turn the Supremacy Clause, Article 6, Section 2, on its head. Further, Marshall observed, "the power to tax involves the power to destroy." If a state could tax one federal agency, it might tax others. This eventually "would defeat all the ends of government." He added that the framers of the Constitution certainly did not intend to make the national government subject to the states:

> [T]he States have no power, by taxation or otherwise, to retard, impede, burden, or in any manner control, the operations of the constitutional laws enacted by Congress to carry [out its] powers.

The Maryland tax, therefore, was unconstitutional.

LEGAL Sources

U.S. CONSTITUTION/LEGISLATION

Article 1, Section 8 (1789)
"The Congress shall have the power to . . . make all laws which shall be necessary and proper for carrying into execution the [specific powers given to Congress]."

Article 6, Section 2 (1789)
"This Constitution, and the laws of the United States . . . shall be the supreme law of the land; . . . anything in the Constitution or laws of any state to the contrary notwithstanding."

RELATED CASES

Fletcher v. Peck (1810)
Noting that the Constitution was the supreme law of the land, the Supreme Court ruled a state law unconstitutional.

Gibbons v. Ogden (1824)
The Court ruled that the federal Congress—not the states—had the power to regulate interstate commerce.

Why Did It Matter Then?

At the time of the *McCulloch* case, there was considerable debate over what powers Congress held. Some people took a very limited view. They suggested that Congress's powers should be restricted to those named in the Constitution. Others pointed out that the Elastic Clause implied that Congress had much broader powers.

The *McCulloch* opinion followed this second view. Marshall wrote:

> Let the end be [lawful], let it be within the scope of the Constitution, and all means which are appropriate, which are plainly adapted to that end, which are not prohibited, but consist with the letter and spirit of the Constitution, are constitutional.

In other words, Congress could exercise the powers it considered appropriate to achieve its lawful goals.

Marshall's broad view of congressional power strengthened the federal government. And this stronger government reflected and encouraged the growing nationalist spirit in the early 1800s.

Why Does It Matter Now?

Since Marshall's time, the United States has undergone many changes. Over the course of the 19th and 20th centuries, the country has grown dramatically. The population has increased and moved. In Marshall's day, the United States was predominantly rural. Today, most people live in urban areas, where economic and leisure activities abound.

The economy of the United States, too, has changed. The country has moved from an agricultural economy to one based on industry and, later, service and information.

During this time, the federal government has stretched its powers to meet the needs of the ever-changing American society. Programs like Franklin Roosevelt's New Deal and Lyndon Johnson's Great Society came about through this expanding of powers. Marshall's broad reading of the Elastic Clause in the *McCulloch* opinion, in large part, laid the groundwork for this growth in the size and power of the federal government.

The Bank of the United States had branches throughout the country, including this one in Philadelphia.

CONNECT TO HISTORY

1. **Forming and Supporting Opinions** Chief Justice John Marshall considered the *McCulloch* decision the most important that he made. Why do you think he considered it such an important decision? Give reasons for your answer.

 See Skillbuilder Handbook, page R17.

CONNECT TO TODAY

2. **Researching** One issue addressed in *McCulloch* was states' rights and federal authority. Do research to find a recent Supreme Court case that has dealt with this issue. Write a paragraph describing the basis of the case and the Court's decision.

For more information on states' rights and federal authority . . .

RESEARCH LINKS
CLASSZONE.COM

Gibbons v. Ogden (1824)

THE ISSUE Federal power to regulate interstate commerce

ORIGINS OF THE CASE Aaron Ogden ran steamboats between New York City and New Jersey. The New York state legislature granted him a monopoly—the right to operate this service without any competition. However, Thomas Gibbons ran a competing service. He had a license to sail under the federal Coasting License Act of 1793. Ogden sued Gibbons for violating his monopoly. When the New York state courts found in Ogden's favor, Gibbons appealed to the United States Supreme Court.

THE RULING In a unanimous decision, the Court ruled that when state and federal laws on interstate commerce conflict, federal laws are superior.

The Legal Arguments

Chief Justice John Marshall wrote the Court's unanimous opinion, which found for Gibbons. Since the Constitution gave Congress the power to regulate commerce among the states, Marshall began, it would be useful to decide what the word *commerce* meant. In arguments before the Court, Ogden's lawyers had said that it simply referred to the buying and selling of goods. Marshall disagreed, suggesting that it also included the navigation necessary to move goods from one place to another. He wrote:

> **The word used in the constitution comprehends . . . navigation within its meaning; and a power to regulate navigation is as expressly granted as if that term had been added to the word "commerce."**

Marshall then pointed to the Supremacy Clause of the Constitution. This is Article 6, Section 2, which states, "This Constitution, and the laws of the United States . . . shall be the supreme law of the land."

The New York monopoly law denied Gibbons the right to sail in New York waters. The federal Coasting License Act, however, gave him the right to sail *all* U.S. waters. According to the Supremacy Clause, the Constitution and federal laws were the supreme law of the land. So, Marshall concluded, the Coasting License Act was "the supreme law of the land," and the New York monopoly was void.

LEGAL *Sources*

U.S. CONSTITUTION/LEGISLATION

Article 1, Section 8 (1789)
"The Congress shall have power to . . . regulate commerce with foreign nations, and among the several states, and with the Indian tribes."

Coasting License Act (1793)
All ships licensed under this act, "and no others, shall be deemed ships or vessels of the United States, entitled to the privileges of ships or vessels employed in the coasting trade or fisheries."

RELATED CASES

Fletcher v. Peck (1810)
Citing the Supremacy Clause, the Court ruled that a state law was unconstitutional.

McCulloch v. Maryland (1819)
The Court established that states had no authority to tax federal agencies.

Aaron Ogden obtained a monopoly on steamship operation between New York and New Jersey in 1815.

Why Did It Matter Then?

At the time of the *Gibbons* case, navigation of the waters around New York was difficult. To encourage companies to provide water transportation, New York granted monopolies to the companies. Some states set up their own. Other states passed laws preventing New York steamboats from entering their waters. Obviously, such a situation was not good for trade among the states. By making it clear that the federal government regulated commerce among the states, the *Gibbons* decision brought order to interstate commerce. And this helped the national economy to grow.

Unlike other decisions of the Marshall Court that strengthened the federal government, *Gibbons* proved popular. Most Americans—even New Yorkers—were opposed to the New York steamboat monopoly. They saw any kind of monopoly as a limit to economic competition. As a result, the *Gibbons* decision was well received throughout the country. One newspaper reported the following incident:

Yesterday the Steamboat *United States*, [commanded by] Capt. Bunker, from New Haven, entered New York in triumph, with streamers flying and a large company of passengers [celebrating] the decision of the United States Supreme Court against the New York monopoly. She fired a salute which was loudly returned by [cheers] from the wharves.

Why Does It Matter Now?

Marshall defined "commerce" very broadly in the *Gibbons* decision. Over the years, Congress has used Marshall's definition to expand its authority over interstate commerce. Today, Congress regulates practically every activity that affects or is connected to commerce.

In 1964, for example, Congress used the Commerce Clause to justify the passage of the Civil Rights Act. This law banned racial discrimination in hotels, restaurants, theaters, and other public places.

The Supreme Court rejected two challenges to the Civil Rights Act—in *Heart of Atlanta Motel, Inc.* v. *United States* (1964) and *Katzenbach* v. *McClung* (1964). In both cases, the Court noted that racial discrimination could harm interstate commerce.

After the first voyage of Robert Fulton's *Clermont* in 1807, it soon became clear that operating steamships could be a profitable business.

CONNECT TO HISTORY

1. **Drawing Conclusions** Many of Chief Justice John Marshall's opinions contributed to the growth of the nationalist spirit in the early 1800s. How do you think the *Gibbons* v. *Ogden* decision might have helped to build national unity?

 See Skillbuilder Handbook, page R13.

CONNECT TO TODAY

2. **Researching** Use library resources and the Internet to find recent Supreme Court cases that involved interstate commerce. Write a brief summary of one of these cases, noting whether it expanded or contracted Congress's power to regulate commerce.

For more information on interstate commerce . . .

RESEARCH LINKS
CLASSZONE.COM

Dred Scott v. Sandford (1857)

THE ISSUE The definition of citizenship

ORIGINS OF THE CASE Dred Scott was an enslaved African American who had lived for a while in Illinois and in the Wisconsin Territory, both of which banned slavery. Scott sued for his freedom, arguing that since he had lived in a free state and a free territory, he was a free man. In 1854, a federal court found against Scott, ruling that he was still a slave. Scott's lawyers appealed to the Supreme Court, which heard arguments in 1856 and delivered its decision the following year.

THE RULING The Court ruled that no African American could be a citizen and that Dred Scott was still a slave. The Court also ruled that the Missouri Compromise of 1820 was unconstitutional.

The Legal Arguments

Chief Justice Roger Taney wrote the majority opinion for the Court. He began by addressing the issue of citizenship. He pointed out that since colonial times African Americans had been looked on as inferior and "had no rights which the white man was bound to respect." Taney added that where African Americans were mentioned in the Constitution, they were referred to as property—slaves. African Americans, whether enslaved or free, he continued:

> . . . are not included, and were not intended to be included, under the word 'citizens' in the Constitution, and can therefore claim none of the rights and privileges which that instrument provides for and secures to citizens of the United States.

Since Scott was not a citizen, Taney concluded, he had no right to use the courts to sue for his freedom.

Taney then went further, claiming Scott was still a slave because he had never been free. Congress had gone beyond its power when it passed the Missouri Compromise, he argued. The Constitution guaranteed the right to own property, and slaves were property. By banning slavery from the territories, Congress was, in effect, taking away private property without due process of the law. This action violated the Fifth Amendment. The Missouri Compromise was, Taney charged, "not warranted by the Constitution, and . . . therefore void." As a result, Scott remained a slave, regardless of where he lived.

Two justices disagreed with the majority on both grounds. They pointed to precedents—earlier legal rulings—that indicated that African Americans could, indeed, be citizens. They also argued that the Constitution gave Congress the power to establish rules and regulations for the territories.

LEGAL Sources

U.S. CONSTITUTION/LEGISLATION

Article 4, Section 3 (1789)
"No person held to service or labor in one state, . . . escaping into another, shall, in consequence of any law or regulation therein, be discharged from such service or labor. . . ."

Fifth Amendment (1791)
"No person shall be . . . deprived of life, liberty, or property, without due process of law."

Missouri Enabling Act (1820)
"[I]n all that territory . . . north of 36° 30' N latitude, . . . slavery . . . shall be . . . forever prohibited." Also known as the Missouri Compromise.

RELATED CASE

Ableman v. Booth (1858)
The Court ruled that laws passed in Northern states that prohibited the return of fugitive slaves were unconstitutional.

Why Did It Matter Then?

Dred Scott contributed to the growing dispute over slavery that led to the Civil War. White Southerners praised the ruling, seeing it as a spirited defense of their right to own slaves. Many Northerners, however, viewed it with alarm. They feared that if Congress could not ban slavery in the territories, slavery would spread. If this happened, slave states eventually would outnumber free states and would control Congress.

Stephen A. Douglas, a Northern Democrat, disagreed with the Court's finding. He favored leaving the issue of slavery to the voters in each territory. Most Southern Democrats, however, did not agree with him. As a result, the Democratic Party divided along sectional lines in the 1860 presidential election. Northern Democrats supported Douglas, while Southern Democrats backed a pro-slavery candidate. Because of this split, Abraham Lincoln of the anti-slavery Republican Party won the election. Soon after, many slave states seceded, and the Civil War began.

Northern abolitionists held meetings to show their support for Scott (shown here) and their opposition to the Supreme Court decision.

Why Does It Matter Now?

The issues addressed by *Dred Scott* were resolved by the Thirteenth and Fourteenth amendments to the Constitution. The Thirteenth Amendment, which was ratified in 1865, abolished slavery in the United States. The Fourteenth Amendment, ratified three years later, made it very clear who was a citizen:

> **All persons born or naturalized in the United States, and subject to the jurisdiction thereof, are citizens of the United States and of the state wherein they reside.**

This amendment went on to guarantee all citizens "equal protection of the laws" and the right to due process. These amendments meant the rulings in *Dred Scott* no longer had the force of law.

Today, *Dred Scott* is not used as a precedent. Instead, it is pointed to as an example of how the Supreme Court can make mistakes. In fact, many legal scholars think it is the worst decision the Court has ever handed down.

CONNECT TO HISTORY

1. **Forming and Supporting Opinions** The *Dred Scott* decision was just one in a long line of events that led to the Civil War. Write an editorial about the case in which you evaluate its importance in bringing about the war.

 See Skillbuilder Handbook, page R17.

CONNECT TO TODAY

2. **Researching** Use library sources and the Internet to research a contemporary Court decision that affects civil rights. Use newspaper indices, periodical guides, and library catalogs, for example, to locate sources of this information. Create a public service brochure to report your findings.

For more information on citizenship . . .

RESEARCH LINKS
CLASSZONE.COM

Plessy v. Ferguson (1896)

THE ISSUE Segregation

ORIGINS OF THE CASE By the 1890s, most Southern states had begun to pass laws enforcing segregation—the separation of the races—in public places. One Louisiana law called for "equal but separate accommodations for the white and colored races" on trains. On June 7, 1892, Homer Plessy, who was part African American, took a seat in a train car reserved for whites. When a conductor told him to move, Plessy refused. Plessy was convicted of breaking the "separate car" law. He appealed the case, saying that the law violated his rights under the Thirteenth and Fourteenth amendments.

THE RULING The Court ruled that "separate but equal" facilities for blacks and whites did not violate the Constitution.

The Legal Arguments

The Court's opinion, written by Justice Henry Billings Brown, rejected Plessy's appeal. Brown first answered Plessy's claim that the separate car law created a relationship between whites and blacks similar to that which existed under slavery. The Thirteenth Amendment simply ended the ownership of one person by another, Brown wrote. Louisiana's law did not reestablish this system of ownership.

Brown then turned to Plessy's claim that the Fourteenth Amendment was designed to ensure the equality of the races before the law. Brown wrote that the amendment "could not have been intended to abolish distinctions based on color." A law that treated the races differently did not brand one race as inferior. If a law made people feel inferior, it was because they chose to see it that way. Summing up, Brown stated:

> A [law] which implies merely a legal distinction between the white and colored races . . . has no tendency to destroy the legal equality of the two races.

Justice John Marshall Harlan strongly disagreed with the majority view. In a bitter dissent, he wrote that the "thin disguise" of separate but equal facilities would fool no one, "nor atone for the wrong this day done."

In his dissent, Justice Harlan stated that "our constitution is color-blind, and neither knows nor tolerates classes among citizens."

LEGAL Sources

U.S. CONSTITUTION/LEGISLATION

Thirteenth Amendment (1865)
"Neither slavery nor involuntary servitude . . . shall exist within the United States, or any place subject to their jurisdiction."

Fourteenth Amendment (1868)
"No state shall make or enforce any law which shall abridge the privileges or immunities of citizens of the United States; nor shall any state deprive any person of life, liberty, or property, without due process of law; nor deny to any person within its jurisdiction the equal protection of the laws."

RELATED CASE

Cumming v. Board of Education of Richmond County (1899)
The Court ruled that because education is a local issue, the federal government could not stop school districts from having separate facilities for black and white students.

Why Did It Matter Then?

Plessy was one of several cases in the late 1800s involving the civil rights of African Americans. In these cases, the Court misread the Fourteenth Amendment and let stand state laws that denied African Americans their rights. *Plessy* has come to stand for all of these decisions because it said that "separate but equal" facilities for blacks and whites did not violate the Constitution.

Although the *Plessy* decision dealt only with public transportation, state governments across the South applied it to all areas of life. In time, "Jim Crow" laws forced African Americans to use separate restaurants, hotels, train cars, parks, schools, and hospitals. Signs reading "For Colored Only" and "Whites Only" ruled everyday life in the South for years to come.

Why Does It Matter Now?

After *Plessy,* many African Americans and some whites looked for ways to fight segregation. Some of these people helped to found the National Association for the Advancement of Colored People (NAACP).

Throughout the first half of the 20th century, lawyers working for the NAACP chipped away at segregation laws. Their greatest victory came in 1954, in *Brown* v. *Board of Education of Topeka.* In this decision, the Supreme Court ruled that separate educational facilities were "inherently unequal" and, therefore, unconstitutional. Southern state and local governments had used the *Plessy* decision to build a system of legal segregation. In the same way, civil rights workers used the *Brown* ruling to dismantle it.

After the *Plessy* decision, signs designating separate facilities for whites and African Americans became a common sight throughout the South.

CONNECT TO HISTORY

1. **Drawing Conclusions** Read the section of the Fourteenth Amendment reprinted in the "Legal Sources" section on page 506. Based on that passage, what do you think "equal protection of the laws" means? How does it apply to the *Plessy* case?

S See Skillbuilder Handbook, page R13.

CONNECT TO TODAY

2. **Researching** Use library resources and the Internet to find information on Supreme Court cases that dealt with segregation. Present your findings in a three-column chart. Use "Case," "Brief Description of Issues Involved," and "Decision" as column headings.

For more information on segregation and the law . . .

RESEARCH LINKS
CLASSZONE.COM

Schenck v. United States
(1919)

THE ISSUE Freedom of Speech

ORIGINS OF THE CASE In August 1917, Charles Schenck, a Socialist Party official, distributed several thousand antiwar leaflets throughout the city of Philadelphia. The leaflets called the draft a crime and urged people to work for the repeal of the Selective Service Act. Schenck was found guilty of violating the Espionage Act of 1917 and sentenced to prison. He appealed his conviction, arguing that the language in the leaflets was protected by the First Amendment.

THE RULING The Court upheld the verdict against Schenck, noting that the leaflets presented "a clear and present danger" to the country during wartime.

LEGAL *Sources*

U.S. CONSTITUTION/LEGISLATION

First Amendment (1791)
"Congress shall make no law . . . abridging the freedom of speech, or of the press."

The Espionage Act (1917)
"[Anyone who] shall wilfully obstruct . . . the recruiting or enlistment service of the United States . . . shall be punished by . . . fine . . . or imprisonment . . . or both."

RELATED CASES

Debs v. United States (1919)
Upheld the conviction of Socialist Party leader Eugene V. Debs for violating the Espionage Act.

Frohwerk v. United States (1919)
Confirmed the guilty verdict against a newspaper publisher for printing articles opposing U. S. involvement in World War I.

Abrams v. United States (1919)
Upheld convictions of five people under the Espionage Act. Holmes dissented, arguing that their action did not present "a clear and imminent danger."

The Legal Arguments

Justice Oliver Wendell Holmes, Jr., wrote the Court's unanimous opinion. In ordinary times, Holmes noted, Schenck's claim of First Amendment rights might well be valid. "But the character of every act depends upon the circumstances in which it is done," Holmes added. Schenck distributed the leaflets during wartime, when "many things that might be said in time of peace . . . will not be endured." Holmes suggested that Schenck's "impassioned" appeal for people to oppose the draft was just like someone "falsely shouting fire in a theatre and causing a panic." The First Amendment certainly did not protect such behavior.

Holmes then went on to offer a guide for judging when speech is protected by the First Amendment:

> The question in every case is whether the words used are used in such circumstances and are of such a nature as to create a clear and present danger that they will bring about the . . . evils that Congress has a right to prevent.

Schenck's words, Holmes charged, did pose "a clear and present danger" to the United States war effort. Therefore, they did not merit protection under the First Amendment.

Justice Holmes's opinions in the Espionage Act cases set the standard for free speech.

Why Did It Matter Then?

The Supreme Court decisions in *Schenck* and other Espionage Act cases considered the limits of free speech during wartime. In *Schenck,* Justice Holmes stated that speech that presented "a clear and present danger" to the country's well being was not protected. As he looked at other cases, however, Holmes began to refine this view.

In *Frohwerk* v. *United States* (1919), decided just a week after *Schenck,* the Court again upheld a conviction under the Espionage Act. However, Holmes noted that anti-government speech uttered during wartime is not always a crime. "We do not lose our right to condemn either measures or men because the country is at war," he wrote.

Holmes broadened this statement in his dissent to the majority opinion in *Abrams* v. *United States* (1919). The government's power to limit speech during wartime undoubtedly is greater, he noted, "because war opens dangers that do not exist at other times." However, the basic principles of free speech are the same in war as in peace:

> **It is only the present danger of immediate evil or an intent to bring it about that warrants Congress in setting a limit to the expression of opinion.**

All opinions, even ones we find hateful, should be heard, Holmes concluded.

Why Does It Matter Now?

The Supreme Court has been asked to decide on free speech issues dozens of times since *Schenck.* In making these decisions, the Court has attempted to heed Justice Holmes's words and strike a balance between protecting free speech and maintaining political and social order.

Over the years, the Court has applied this balance test to free speech questions in many settings, including schools. In *Tinker* v. *Des Moines Independent Community School District* (1969), the Court upheld students' right to protest in school. However, the Court added that in certain circumstances school officials might limit the exercise of such rights—if the students' actions disrupt the work of the school, for example.

In two later cases, *Bethel School District No. 403* v. *Fraser* (1986) and *Hazelwood School District* v. *Kuhlmeier* (1988), the Court felt that such circumstances existed. In *Bethel,* the Court upheld the suspension of a student who, during a school assembly, gave a speech that included inappropriate language. The Court ruled that the school could punish behavior that "interferes with the educational process." In *Hazelwood,* the Court ruled that school officials could censor the content of a student newspaper if it was "inconsistent with [the school's] educational mission."

During the Vietnam War, some Americans vigorously challenged government policies.

CONNECT TO HISTORY

1. **Making Inferences** The Supreme Court decided *Schenck* and other Espionage Act cases during the Red Scare. Do you think the timing of the cases influenced the Court's decisions? Why or why not?

 See Skillbuilder Handbook, page R12.

CONNECT TO TODAY

2. **Researching** Working with a group of two or three other students, identify and research recent court cases involving free speech issues. Present your findings in a brief oral report to the class.

For more information on free speech . . .

RESEARCH LINKS
CLASSZONE.COM

Brown v. Board of Education of Topeka (1954)

THE ISSUE School desegregation

ORIGINS OF THE CASE In September 1950, Oliver Brown tried to enroll his seven-year-old daughter, Linda, at the neighborhood grade school. The school principal rejected Brown's request because Linda was an African American. The school was for white students only. Linda ended up attending a school farther away from her home. Brown filed suit against the school board, demanding that Linda be allowed to go to the neighborhood school. The Supreme Court heard arguments in the *Brown* case in 1952 and 1953.

THE RULING A unanimous court ruled that segregation in education was unconstitutional.

The Legal Arguments

Chief Justice Earl Warren wrote the Court's decision. He began by reviewing the history of the Fourteenth Amendment. Its equal protection clause was the basis for the decision. The Court had ruled in *Plessy* v. *Ferguson* (1896) that "separate but equal" facilities for blacks and whites did not violate this amendment. However, Warren pointed out that *Plessy* involved transportation, not education. He then stressed the importance of education for society:

> It is doubtful that any child may reasonably be expected to succeed in life if he is denied the opportunity of an education.

Warren went on to suggest that segregation denied African-American children that opportunity. He concluded with *Brown's* most famous statement:

> . . . [I]n the field of public education the doctrine of "separate but equal" has no place. Separate educational facilities are inherently unequal.

The Court expected whites in the South, where segregation was dominant, to resist the ruling. Therefore, it delayed orders on how to put the decision into action for several months.

Thurgood Marshall was one of the team of lawyers that represented Oliver Brown. In 1967, Marshall became the first African American appointed as a Supreme Court justice.

LEGAL Sources

U.S. CONSTITUTION/LEGISLATION

Fourteenth Amendment (1868)
"No state shall . . . deprive any person of life, liberty, or property, without due process of law; nor deny to any person within its jurisdiction the equal protection of the laws."

RELATED CASES

Plessy v. Ferguson (1896)
Upheld Louisiana laws that segregated railroad passenger cars according to race. Established the doctrine of "separate but equal."

Brown v. Board of Education of Topeka (May, 1955)
Ordered that desegregation take place "with all deliberate speed." Often called "*Brown II.*"

Why Did It Matter Then?

The Fourteenth Amendment had guaranteed African Americans equal rights as citizens. In the late 1800s, however, many Southern states passed "Jim Crow" laws, which enforced separation of the races in public places. In 1896, the Supreme Court upheld a "Jim Crow" law in *Plessy* v. *Ferguson.* In the Court's view, "separate but equal" rail cars did not violate the Fourteenth Amendment.

Brown, however, stated that segregated schools denied African Americans the "equal protection of the laws" guaranteed by the Fourteenth Amendment. Segregation, therefore, had no place in school systems.

As the Court expected, the decision met opposition. One Southern politician accused the Court of "a flagrant abuse of judicial power." Even after *Brown II,* many school districts, particularly in the South, dragged their feet on desegregation. Some 10 years later, segregation was still the rule in most Southern school districts. Even so, the impact of the *Brown* decision on American society was immense. It marked the beginning of the civil rights movement, which you read about in Chapter 29.

The *Brown* decision was a front-page story in newspapers across the United States.

Why Does It Matter Now?

Throughout the 1960s and 1970s, the Supreme Court continued to review the issue of school segregation. In *Green* v. *New Kent County* (1968), the Court called for the end of the dual school system—one white and one black. This involved integrating not only students, but also teachers, support staff, and services.

In *Swann* v. *Charlotte-Mecklenburg Board of Education* (1971), the Court ruled that busing could be used to achieve school desegregation. Later, in *Milliken* v. *Bradley* (1974), the Court ruled that students might be bused between school districts to achieve this goal. However, this step could be taken only in very exceptional circumstances.

In recent years, the Court has moved away from enforcing desegregation. Still, the *Brown* decision brought about far-reaching changes. The statement that separate facilities are "inherently unequal" proved a powerful weapon against segregation in all areas of American life. Indeed, the Court's opinion in *Brown* provided the basis for most of the civil rights laws passed in the late 1950s and 1960s.

CONNECT TO HISTORY

1. **Analyzing Points of View** Chief Justice Earl Warren wanted the *Brown* opinion to be unanimous. He even pressured Justice Stanley Reed, a southerner, not to file a dissenting opinion. Why do you think Warren insisted that all the justices agree to the *Brown* decision?

 See Skillbuilder Handbook, page R9.

CONNECT TO TODAY

2. **Researching** Working with a group of two or three other students, conduct research to find out about efforts to desegregate another part of American society, such as the military, the workplace, or colleges. Report your findings to the class.

For more information on civil rights today . . .

Reynolds v. Sims (1964)

THE ISSUE One Person, One Vote

ORIGINS OF THE CASE Most state constitutions require a redrawing of legislative districts every 10 years, based on the latest U.S. Census figures. By the 1960s, however, many states had not redrawn their districts for decades. For example, Alabama's last redrawing—in 1901—did not reflect the great population changes that had taken place. In 1962, a group of Alabama voters sued to have their legislative map redrawn. When a federal court found for the voters, the Alabama state legislature appealed to the Supreme Court.

THE RULING The Court firmly established the principle of "one person, one vote." It ruled that Alabama must redraw its legislative districts so that each district had about the same number of people.

LEGAL Sources

U.S. CONSTITUTION/LEGISLATION

Fourteenth Amendment (1868)
"No state shall . . . deprive any person of life, liberty, or property, without due process of law; nor deny to any person within its jurisdiction the equal protection of the laws."

Alabama Constitution, Article 9, Section 198 (1901)
"The members of the house of representatives shall be apportioned by the legislature among the several counties of the state, according to the number of inhabitants in them, respectively, as ascertained by the decennial census of the United States."

RELATED CASES

Baker v. Carr (1962)
Ruled that federal courts could intervene in state legislative districting issues.

Gray v. Sanders (1963)
Ruled that when counting votes in primary elections, states should follow the principle of "one person, one vote."

The Legal Arguments

The Court's ruling, written by Chief Justice Earl Warren, clearly stated the issue:

> The right to vote freely for the candidate of one's choice is of the essence of a democratic society, and any restrictions on that right strike at the heart of representative government.

Weakening the power of an individual's vote, Warren added, was as much a restriction as preventing that individual from voting.

"Legislators represent people, not trees or acres," Warren continued. Population, therefore, had to be the determining factor in redrawing legislative districts. Warren based his argument squarely on the Fourteenth Amendment:

Chief Justice Earl Warren considered *Reynolds* v. *Sims* one of the most important opinions he had written.

> We hold that as a basic constitutional standard, the Equal Protection Clause requires that seats in . . . a . . . state legislature must be apportioned on a population basis. . . . [T]he Equal Protection Clause requires that a State make an honest and good faith effort to construct districts . . . as nearly of equal population as is practicable.

John Marshall Harlan—the grandson of the justice who wrote the famous dissent to *Plessy* v. *Ferguson*—dissented. He claimed that the Constitution did not give the Court the power to interfere in how states decide on their legislative districts.

Why Did It Matter Then?

Reynolds was one of several voting rights cases that the Court heard in the 1960s. In the first, *Baker* v. *Carr* (1962), the Court broke with past decisions and said that federal courts had the power to make sure that states drew legislative districts fairly. A year later, in *Gray* v. *Sanders* (1963), the Court applied the principle of "one person, one vote" for the first time. The Court observed that the vote of someone living in one part of a state should count as much as that of someone living in another part.

In *Reynolds,* the court extended the "one person, one vote" principle to the drawing of state legislative districts. In time, the *Reynolds* ruling forced most states to draw new district boundaries. As a result, there was a shift in political power in state legislatures. The number of state representatives from cities, which had larger populations, increased. In contrast, the number from rural areas, where fewer people lived, declined.

Why Does It Matter Now?

During the 1990s, the Court faced a new redistricting issue. The Voting Rights Act of 1965 urged states to increase minority representation in the legislatures. To do so, many states created districts where minorities made up a voting majority. However, some white voters challenged these districts under the Fourteenth Amendment.

In several cases—*Bush* v. *Vera* (1996), for example—the Court ruled that such districts were unconstitutional. Since these districts were drawn *solely* based on race, the Court said, they violated the Fourteenth Amendment's equal protection clause. In *Lawyer* v. *Department of Justice* (1997), the Court upheld a Florida district drawn to include several African-American communities. The Court found that in this case, race was only one of several factors used to draw district boundary lines.

After the U.S. Census of 2000, the states began a new round of redistricting. As a result, the Supreme Court probably will revisit this issue over the next few years.

Representation in the Alabama State Legislature, 1962		
COUNTY	**POPULATION**	**NUMBER OF HOUSE REPRESENTATIVES**
Bullock	*13,462*	*2*
Henry	*15,286*	*2*
Mobile	*314,301*	*3*
Jefferson	*634,864*	*7*

Source: *U.S. Supreme Court,* Reynolds v. Sims, *377 U.S. 533 (1964)*

In 1962, the rural counties of Bullock and Henry had less than one-thirtieth of the population of the urban counties of Mobile and Jefferson. Even so, they returned close to half as many state representatives as did the two urban counties.

CONNECT TO HISTORY

1. **Finding Main Ideas** Use library or Internet resources to locate a copy of the majority opinion in *Reynolds* v. *Sims.* Make a chart listing the main idea and details for each part of the opinion. Make a similar chart for Harlan's dissenting opinion in this case.

 See Skillbuilder Handbook, page R5.

CONNECT TO TODAY

2. **Researching** Conduct research to find news stories about a recent Supreme Court decision on the issue of redistricting. Write a summary of the background of the case, the ruling the Court made, and the legal reasoning behind that ruling.

For more information on the Supreme Court and redistricting . . .

RESEARCH LINKS
CLASSZONE.COM

Regents of the University of California v. Bakke (1978)

THE ISSUE Affirmative action

ORIGINS OF THE CASE In 1970, the medical school of the University of California at Davis adopted an "affirmative action" admissions policy. The policy set a quota calling for 16 percent of each year's incoming students to be minority students. Allan Bakke, a white applicant, had better test scores and grades than most of the students accepted under the affirmative-action plan. However, he was not admitted. Bakke sued, arguing that he had been rejected because of his race. The California Supreme Court ordered the school to admit Bakke. The school appealed the case to the U.S. Supreme Court.

THE RULING The Court ruled that the school could use race as one of several factors in making admissions decisions but that setting racial quotas was unconstitutional.

LEGAL Sources

U.S. CONSTITUTION/LEGISLATION

Fourteenth Amendment (1868)
"No state shall . . . deprive any person of life, liberty, or property, without due process of law; nor deny to any person within its jurisdiction the equal protection of the laws."

Civil Rights Act, Title VI (1964)
"No person in the United States shall, on the ground of race, color, or national origin, be excluded from participation in . . . any program or activity receiving Federal financial assistance."

RELATED CASE

Fullilove v. Klutznick (1980)
The Court upheld the Public Works Employment Act of 1977, which required that minority-owned businesses receive 10 percent of all federal funds for public works projects.

The Legal Arguments

The Court upheld the California Supreme Court decision in a 5–4 vote. Four of the five majority justices maintained that holding a set number of admission slots for minority students violated the Civil Rights Act of 1964. The fifth justice, Justice Lewis Powell, noted that racial quotas violated the Fourteenth Amendment. Powell wrote:

> The guarantee of equal protection cannot mean one thing when applied to one individual and something else when applied to a person of another color. If both are not accorded the same protection, then it is not equal.

However, the Court did not reject affirmative action completely. By a different 5-4 majority, the Court ruled that race could be used as one of several factors in college admissions. Powell, who again provided the deciding vote, thought that race should be considered in order to promote a "diverse student body."

Allan Bakke graduated from the University of California at Davis with a medical degree in 1982.

Why Did It Matter Then?

African Americans made many gains in civil rights during the 1950s and 1960s. President Lyndon Johnson, however, thought more needed to be done. He explained why:

> You do not take a person who for years has been hobbled by chains and . . . bring him up to the starting line of a race and then say, "you are free to compete with all the others" and still justly believe that you have been completely fair.

In 1965, Johnson urged companies to increase the hiring and promoting of minorities.

In time, many businesses, colleges, and other organizations set up affirmative-action programs. Not everyone was happy with this development, however. Some whites felt that affirmative action amounted to little more than "reverse discrimination." That is, they felt that they would be denied jobs or college places because of their race.

With the Bakke ruling, the Supreme Court took a compromise position on affirmative-action programs. They were acceptable, the Court said, as long as they did not use strict racial quotas.

Why Does It Matter Now?

Since *Bakke,* the Court has ruled on several affirmative-action cases. In *Metro Broadcasting* v. *Federal Communications Commission* (1990), for example, the Court upheld a policy that gave preference to minority broadcasters. However, in *Adarand Constructors, Inc.* v. *Peña* (1995), the Court struck down a similar affirmative-action program.

The standing of affirmative action in college admissions is somewhat clearer, however. Some states have abandoned the policy altogether. In California, for example, voters approved a 1996 referendum banning the state's universities from using affirmative action in admissions.

Washington voters passed a similar measure in 1998. These and other states are looking for new ways to help minority students attend college. One method—adopted by California, Florida, and Texas—guarantees admission to state universities for the top students from each high school graduating class.

The affirmative-action debate, at times, has been quite bitter. Here, supporters and opponents of affirmative action confront each other at a demonstration on the campus of the University of California at Berkeley.

CONNECT TO HISTORY

1. **Making Inferences** In the *Bakke* case, the Supreme Court issued six separate opinions. Also, the voting on the two issues in the case was 5-4. From this information, what inferences can you draw on the Court's attitudes on affirmative action?

 See Skillbuilder Handbook, page R12.

CONNECT TO TODAY

2. **Researching** The state university system of Michigan recently has faced court challenges to its affirmative-action program. Track the progress of these challenges and write a few paragraphs comparing the arguments and court findings in Michigan to those in the *Bakke* case.

For more information on affirmative action . . .

RESEARCH LINKS
CLASSZONE.COM

RAND M^CNALLY
World Atlas

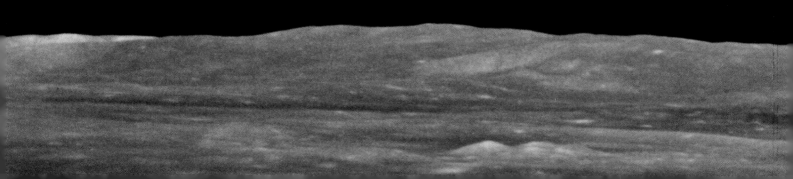

CONTENTS

Complete Legend for Physical and Political Maps

Symbols

	Lake
	Salt Lake
	Seasonal Lake
～～	River
\	Waterfall
——	Canal
△	Mountain Peak
▲	Highest Mountain Peak

Cities

▪ Los Angeles	City over 1,000,000 population
▣ Calgary	City of 250,000 to 1,000,000 population
• Haifa	City under 250,000 population
✪ Paris	National Capital
★ Vancouver	Secondary Capital (State, Province, or Territory)

Type Styles Used to Name Features

CHINA	Country
ONTARIO	State, Province, or Territory
PUERTO RICO (U.S.)	Possession
ATLANTIC OCEAN	Ocean or Sea
Alps	Physical Feature
Borneo	Island

Boundaries

	International Boundary
	Secondary Boundary

Land Elevation and Water Depths

Land Elevation

Meters		Feet
3,000 and over --		-- 9,840 and over
2,000 - 3,000 --		-- 6,560 - 9,840
500 - 2,000 --		-- 1,640 - 6,560
200 - 500 --		-- 656 - 1,640
0 - 200 --		-- 0 - 656

Water Depth

Less than 200 --		-- Less than 656
200 - 2,000 --		-- 656 - 6,560
Over 2,000 --		-- Over 6,560

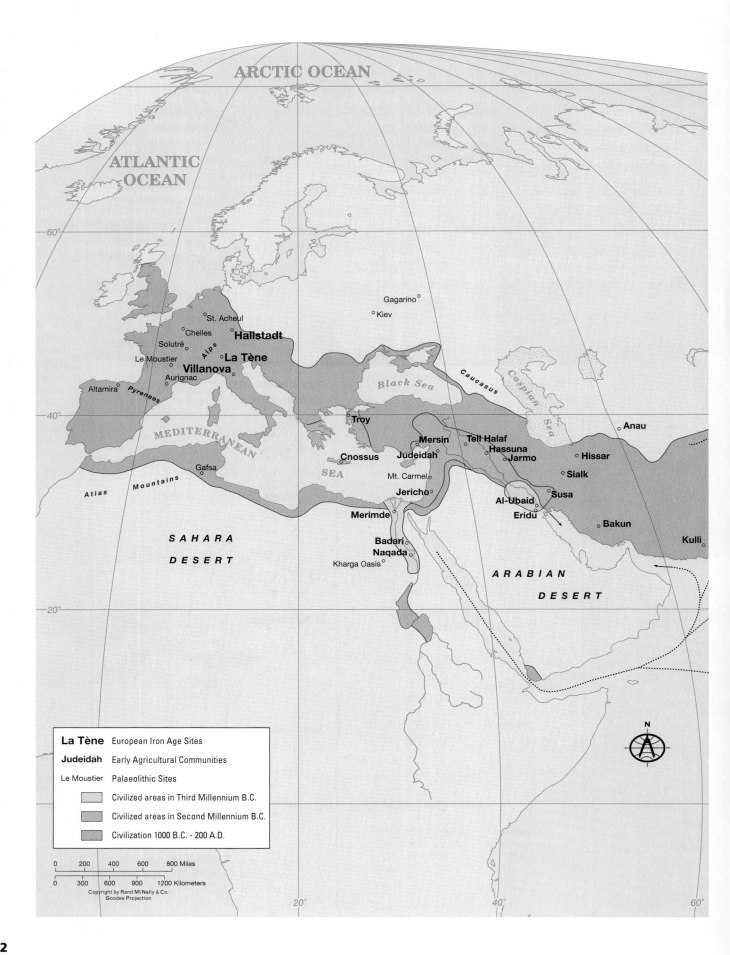

ARCTIC OCEAN

ATLANTIC
OCEAN

60°

Gagarino

Kiev

St. Acheul

Chelles   **Hallstadt**

Solutré   Caucasus   *Caspian Sea*

Le Moustier   *Alps*   **La Tène**

Villanova   *Black Sea*

Aurignac

Altamira   *Pyrenees*   **Anau**

40°   *Troy*

Mersin   **Tell Halaf**   **Hissar**

MEDITERRANEAN   **Hassuna**

Cnossus   **Judeidah**   **Jarmo**

Gafsa   **Sialk**

SEA   Mt. Carmel

Atlas   *Mountains*   **Susa**

Jericho   **Al-Ubaid**   **Bakun**

Merimde   **Eridu**   **Kulli**

SAHARA   **Badari**
                        Naqada
DESERT   Kharga Oasis   *ARABIAN*

DESERT

20°

N

La Tène   European Iron Age Sites

Judeidah   Early Agricultural Communities

Le Moustier   Palaeolithic Sites

Civilized areas in Third Millennium B.C.

Civilized areas in Second Millennium B.C.

Civilization 1000 B.C. - 200 A.D.

0   200   400   600   800 Miles

0   300   600   900   1200 Kilometers

Copyright by Rand McNally & Co.
Goodes Projection

20°   40°   60°

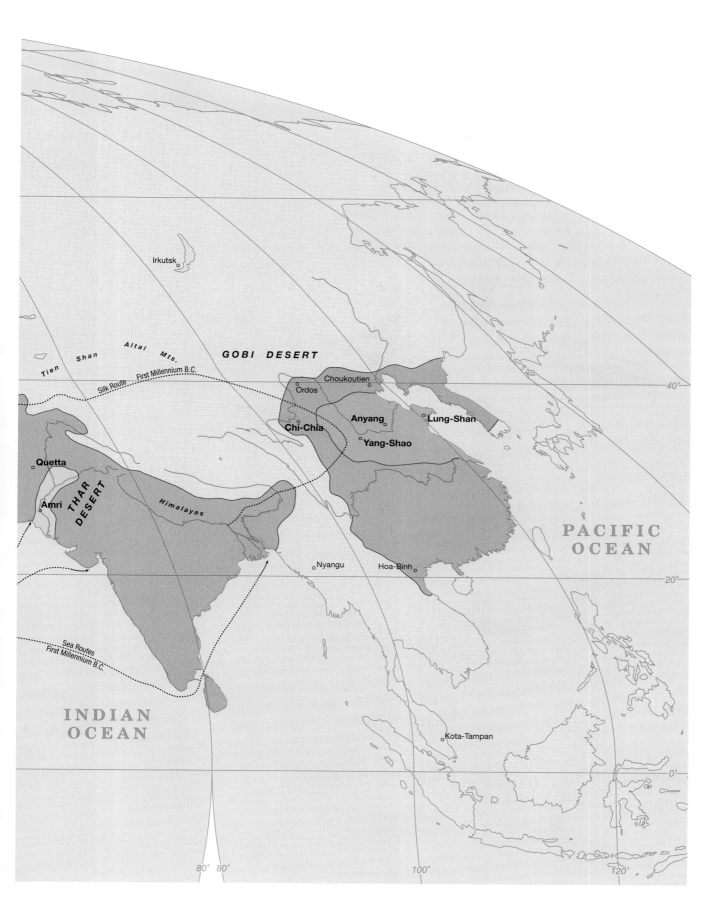

Irkutsk

Tien Shan *Altai Mts.*

GOBI DESERT

Silk Route   First Millennium B.C.

Choukoutien

Ordos

Anyang   **Lung-Shan**

Chi-Chia

Yang-Shao

Quetta

THAR DESERT

Himalayas

Amri

Nyangu   Hoa-Binh

PACIFIC OCEAN

Sea Routes
First Millennium B.C.

Kota-Tampan

INDIAN OCEAN

40°

20°

0°

80° 80°   100°   120°

ARCTIC OCEAN

Baffin
Bay

GREENLAND
(Den.)

Arctic Circle

RUSSIA   ALASKA
Yukon (U.S.)   ICELAND   FARØE IS.
                                                                                                      (Den.)
Anchorage   UNITED
60°   KINGDOM
Aleutian Islands   IRELAND
                    CANADA   Hudson   London
                                                     Bay
Vancouver   FRANCE
                 Missouri   Newfoundland
45°   Montréal   Madrid
                          Ottawa   Azores   PORTUGAL
            Chicago   (Port.)   SPAIN
UNITED STATES
                         New York   Casablanca
Los Angeles   Colorado   Washington D.C.   MOROCCO
                                                         ATLANTIC   Canary
            Houston   Islands
30°   (Sp.)
MIDWAY IS.   Gulf of Mexico   BAHAMAS
(U.S.)
Tropic of Cancer   MEXICO   MAURITANIA   MALI
Hawaiian   CUBA
Islands   Mexico City   BELIZE   HAITI DOM. REP.   SENEGAL
(U.S)   GUAT. HOND.   JAMAICA PUERTO RICO (U.S.)   GAMBIA   BURK.
15°   EL. SAL. NIC.   Caribbean   GUINEA-BISSAU FASO
                                    COSTA   Sea   GUINEA
PACIFIC   RICA   Caracas TRINIDAD AND TOBAGO   SIERRA LEONE CÔTE
                               PANAMA   VENEZUELA   GUYANA   D'IVOIRE
                                       COLOMBIA   SURINAME   LIBERIA
                                                   FRENCH GUIANA
KIRIBATI
0° Equator   Galapagos Islands   ECUADOR   Amazon
                      (Ecuador)
                                       PERU   BRAZIL
OCEAN   Lima   OCEAN
SAMOA
15°
AMERICAN   BOLIVIA   ST. HELENA
SAMOA   COOK   (U.K.)
TONGA   ISLANDS (N.Z.)   PARAGUAY Rio de Janeiro
Tropic of Capricorn   FRENCH POLYNESIA
                                               ARGENTINA
                      Easter Island   URUGUAY   N
30°   (Chile)
                                       Santiago Buenos
                                                  Aires

45°

         0   1000   2000 Miles
         0   1000   2000   3000 Kilometers   FALKLAND IS.   South
         Copyright by Rand McNally & Co.   (U.K.)   Georgia
         Robinson Projection   (U.K.)

60°   South
                                               South   Orkney Is.
Antarctic Circle   Shetland Is.   (U.K.)
                                               (U.K.)   Weddell
                                                               Sea
75°

15° 30° 45° 60° 75° 90° 105° 120° 135° 150° 165° 180°

ARCTIC OCEAN

Spitsbergen (Nor.)

Franz Josef Land

Novaya Zemlya

75°

Ob' *Yenisey* *Lena*

NORWAY FINLAND

SWEDEN

North Sea DEN.

EST.

LAT.

LITH.

Volga

⊛ Moscow

R U S S I A

60° *Sea of Okhotsk* *Bering Sea*

NETH.

GERMANY

BEL.

POLAND

BELARUS

CZ.

SWITZ. AUS. SLVK. HUNG.

UKRAINE

MOLD.

KAZAKHSTAN

• Novosibirsk

M O N G O L I A

45°

ITALY

SLO. CRO. ROM.

BOS. SER.

ALB. MA. BUL.

Black Sea

GEO.

ARM. AZER.

UZBEKISTAN

KYRG.

NORTH KOREA

Sea of Japan

JAPAN

• Rome ⊛

GREECE

TURKEY

TURKMENISTAN

TAJIK.

C H I N A

Beijing ⊛

SOUTH KOREA

• Tokyo

P A C I F I C

Crete

CYPRUS SYRIA

LEB.

ISRAEL IRAQ

JORDAN

IRAN

AFGHANISTAN

Chang Jiang *(Yangtze)*

• Shanghai

30°

Mediterranean Sea

• Cairo ⊛

KUWAIT

PAKISTAN

NEPAL BHU.

Tropic of Cancer

TUNISIA

ALGERIA

LIBYA

EGYPT

SAUDI

ARABIA

QATAR

U.A.E.

OMAN

Red Sea *Nile*

Ganges

I N D I A

Kolkata (Calcutta)•

BNGL.

MYANMAR

Guangzhou•

LAOS

TAIWAN

NORTHERN MARIANA ISLANDS (U.S.)

WAKE ISLAND (U.S.)

15°

NIGER

CHAD

SUDAN

YEMEN

ERITREA DJIBOUTI

Mumbai (Bombay)•

Arabian Sea

THAILAND

Bay of Bengal

Bangkok•

South China Sea

VIETNAM

CAMBODIA

PHILIPPINES

GUAM (U.S.)

O C E A N

BENIN

NIGERIA

Lagos•

CAMEROON

CENTRAL AFRICAN REPUBLIC

Addis Ababa•

ETHIOPIA

SRI LANKA

SOMALIA

BRUNEI

MALAYSIA

PALAU

FED. STATES OF MICRONESIA

MARSHALL ISLANDS

EQUATORIAL GUINEA

GABON

Congo

REP. OF CONGO

DEM. REP. OF CONGO

UGANDA

RWANDA

BURUNDI

KENYA

TANZANIA

MALDIVES

Singapore•

Borneo

SEYCHELLES

Sumatra

⊛ Jakarta

I N D O N E S I A

Java

EAST TIMOR

New Guinea

PAPUA NEW GUINEA

SOLOMON ISLANDS

Equator

0°

I N D I A N

COMOROS

ANGOLA

ZAMBIA

MALAWI

MOZAMBIQUE

MADAGASCAR

MAURITIUS

•Darwin

Coral Sea

VANUATU

NEW CALEDONIA (Fr.)

FIJI

15°

NAMIBIA

ZIMBABWE

BOTSWANA

REUNION (Fr.)

O C E A N

A U S T R A L I A

Tropic of Capricorn

SWAZILAND

SOUTH AFRICA

LESOTHO

Perth•

Darling

•Sydney

30°

Cape Town ⊛

Melbourne•

NEW ZEALAND

Kerguelen Islands (Fr.)

Tasmania

Wellington ⊛

45°

60°

Antarctic Circle

A N T A R C T I C A

75°

15° 30° 45° 60° 75° 90° 105° 120° 135° 150° 165° 180°

⊛ National Capital

• Major Cities

ARCTIC OCEAN

Greenland

Jan Mayen

Baffin
Island

Baffin
Bay

Arctic Circle

Iceland

Faroe Is.

Mt. McKinley △
20,320 Ft.
6,194m

Yukon

Mackenzie

Canadian Shield

Hudson
Bay

British
Isles

London

Vancouver

NORTH

Rocky Mountains

Great Plains

St. Lawrence

Newfoundland

AMERICA

Appalachian Mts.

Washington D.C.

Azores

Iberian
Peninsula

Los Angeles

Colorado

Mississippi

Cape Hatteras

Atlas
Mts.

ATLANTIC

Baja
California

Gulf of Mexico

Yucatan
Peninsula

Cuba

Hispaniola

Puerto Rico

Canary
Islands

Tropic of Cancer

Midway Is.

Hawaiian
Islands

Jamaica

Caribbean
Sea

Cape
Verde
Islands

Cape Verde

Niger

PACIFIC

Trinidad

OCEAN

Orinoco

Palmyra

Equator

Kiribati

OCEAN

Galapagos Islands

Amazon

Amazon

SOUTH

St. Helena

Samoa
Islands

Marquesas Is.

Andes

Basin

AMERICA

Mato Grosso
Plateau

Tonga
Is.

Cook
Islands

Tahiti

Rio de Janeiro

Tropic of Capricorn

Easter Island

Andes

Paraná

30°

Mt. Aconcagua
22,831 Ft.
6,959m

Buenos Aires

N

Chatham Is.

Archipiélago
Juan Fernández

Patagonia

Falkland Is.

South
Georgia

0   1000   2000 Miles

0   1000   2000   3000 Kilometers

Tierra del Fuego

South
Sandwich Is.

Copyright by Rand McNally & Co.
Robinson Projection

Cape Horn

South
Orkney Is.

Antarctic Circle

South
Shetland Is.

Antarctic
Peninsula

Weddell
Sea

Ross
Sea

Marie
Byrd
Land

△ Vinson Massif
16,066 Ft.
4,897m

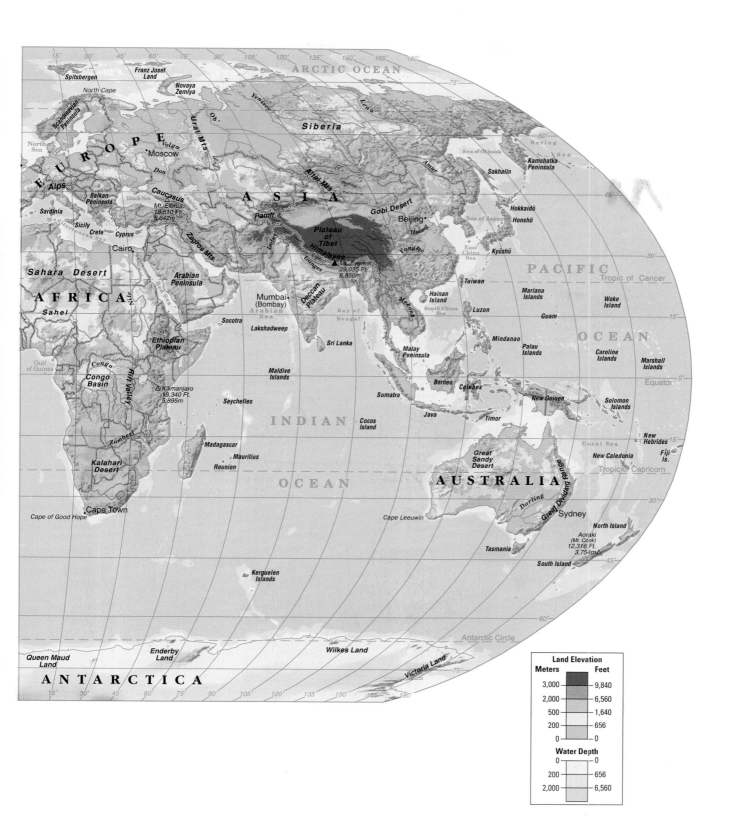

15° 30° 45° 60° 75° 90° 105° 120° 135° 150° 165° 180°

ARCTIC OCEAN

75°

Spitsbergen

Franz Josef
Land

North Cape

Novaya
Zemlya

Scandinavian
Peninsula

Yenisey

Lena

Siberia

60°

Bering
Sea

North
Sea

EUROPE

Volga

Moscow

Ob'

Ural Mts.

Sea of Okhotsk

Kamchatka
Peninsula

Alps

Don

Balkan
Peninsula

Caucasus

Black Sea

Altai Mts.

ASIA

Amur

Sakhalin

45°

Sardinia

Mt. Elbrus
18,510 Ft.
5,642m

Aral

Pamir

Gobi Desert

Beijing

Hokkaidō

Honshū

Sicily

Crete

Mediterranean Sea

Cyprus

Zagros Mts.

Plateau
of
Tibet

Huang

Sea of Japan

Cairo

Indus

Himalayas

Mt. Everest
29,035 Ft.
8,850m

Ganges

Yangtze

East
China
Sea

Kyūshū

30°

PACIFIC

Tropic of Cancer

Sahara Desert

Arabian
Peninsula

Mumbai
(Bombay)

Deccan
Plateau

Bay of
Bengal

Taiwan

Hainan
Island

Mariana
Islands

Wake
Island

AFRICA

Nile

Red Sea

Arabian
Sea

South China
Sea

Luzon

Guam

15°

Sahel

Socotra

Lakshadweep

Sri Lanka

Malay
Peninsula

Mindanao

Palau
Islands

Caroline
Islands

Marshall
Islands

OCEAN

Ethiopian
Plateau

Maldive
Islands

Borneo

Celebes

Equator

0°

Gulf
of Guinea

Congo

Congo
Basin

Rift Valley

Kilimanjaro
19,340 Ft.
5,895m

Seychelles

Sumatra

Java

Timor

New Guinea

Solomon
Islands

INDIAN

Cocos
Island

Zambezi

Madagascar

Mauritius

Reunion

New
Hebrides

Coral Sea

New Caledonia

Fiji
Is.

15°

Kalahari
Desert

OCEAN

Great
Sandy
Desert

AUSTRALIA

Tropic of Capricorn

Cape Town

Cape of Good Hope

Cape Leeuwin

Darling

Great Dividing Range

Sydney

30°

Aoraki
(Mt. Cook)
12,316 Ft.
3,754m

North Island

Tasmania

South Island

45°

Kerguelen
Islands

60°

Antarctic Circle

Queen Maud
Land

Enderby
Land

Wilkes Land

Victoria Land

75°

ANTARCTICA

15° 30° 45° 60° 75° 90° 105° 120° 135° 150° 165° 180°

Land Elevation		
Meters		Feet
3,000		9,840
2,000		6,560
500		1,640
200		656
0		0

Water Depth		
0		0
200		656
2,000		6,560

RAND MCNALLY

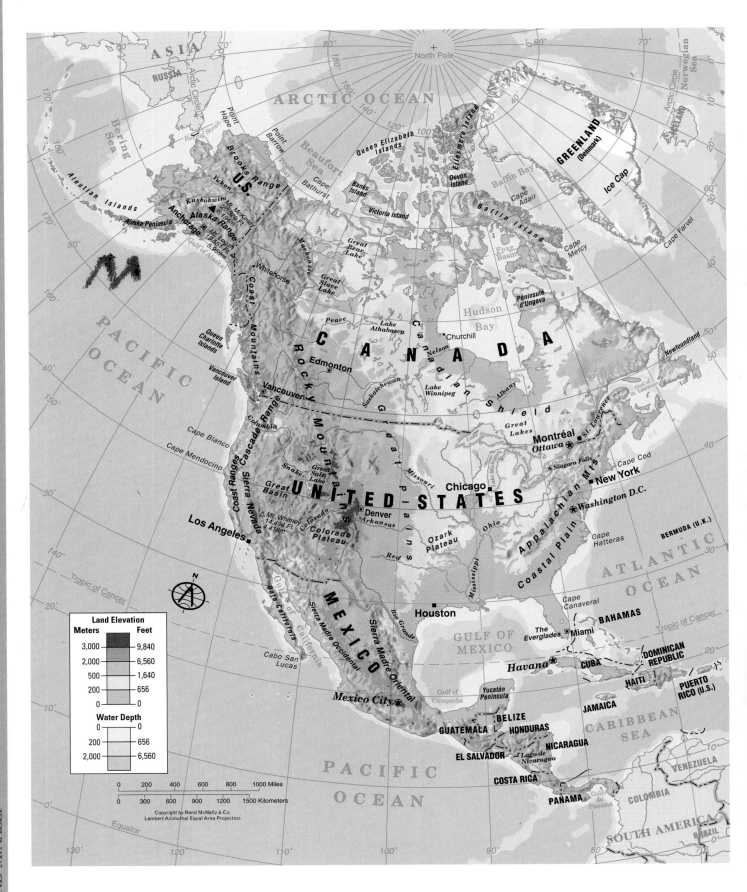

ASIA
RUSSIA
Arctic Circle
Bering Strait
Point Hope
Point Barrow
Prudhoe Bay
BEAUFORT SEA
Cape Bathurst
ARCTIC OCEAN
North Pole
Queen Elizabeth Islands
Banks Island
Victoria Island
Devon Island
Ellesmere Island
Baffin Bay
Cape Adair
Cape Mercy
Baffin Island
Foxe Basin
GREENLAND (Denmark)
Ice Cap
Cape Farvel
Arctic Circle
ICELAND
Norwegian Sea

Bering Sea
Aleutian Islands
Alaska Peninsula
Brooks Range
U.S.
Yukon
Kuskokwim
Mt. McKinley 20,320 Ft. 6,194m
Anchorage
Alaska Range
Mt. Logan 19,551 Ft. 5,959m
Gulf of Alaska
Mackenzie
Whitehorse
Great Bear Lake
Great Slave Lake
Péninsule d'Ungava
Hudson Bay
Churchill
Foxe Basin
Newfoundland

PACIFIC OCEAN

Coast Mountains
Queen Charlotte Islands
Vancouver Island
Vancouver
Rocky Mountains
Peace
Lake Athabasca
Edmonton
Saskatchewan
Nelson
Lake Winnipeg
Canadian Shield
Albany
James Bay
CANADA
Great Lakes
Lake Superior
Montréal
Ottawa
St. Lawrence
Gulf of St. Lawrence

Cape Blanco
Cape Mendocino
Columbia
Cascade Range
Snake
Great Salt Lake
Great Basin
Sierra Nevada
Mt. Whitney 14,494 Ft. 4,418m
Los Angeles
Colorado Plateau
Denver
Colorado
Arkansas
Great Plains
Missouri
Chicago
Lake Michigan
Ontario
Niagara Falls
Appalachian Mts.
New York
Cape Cod
Washington D.C.
ATLANTIC OCEAN
Ozark Plateau
Red
Ohio
Mississippi
Coastal Plain
Cape Hatteras
BERMUDA (U.K.)

UNITED STATES

N

Baja California
Gulf of California
Sierra Madre Occidental
Rio Grande
Houston
Cape Canaveral
The Everglades
Miami
GULF OF MEXICO
Tropic of Cancer
BAHAMAS

Land Elevation
Meters		Feet
3,000		9,840
2,000		6,560
500		1,640
200		656
0		0

Water Depth
0		0
200		656
2,000		6,560

Cabo San Lucas
MEXICO
Sierra Madre Oriental
Mexico City
Gulf of Campeche
Yucatán Peninsula
Havana
CUBA
DOMINICAN REPUBLIC
HAITI
PUERTO RICO (U.S.)
JAMAICA
CARIBBEAN SEA

0   200   400   600   800   1000 Miles
0   300 600 900 1200 1500 Kilometers
Copyright by Rand McNally & Co.
Lambert Azimuthal Equal Area Projection

BELIZE
GUATEMALA
EL SALVADOR
HONDURAS
NICARAGUA
Lago de Nicaragua
COSTA RICA
PANAMA
Golfo de Panama
VENEZUELA
COLOMBIA
SOUTH AMERICA
BRAZIL

PACIFIC OCEAN
Equator

GULF OF MEXICO

NORTH AMERICA

MEXICO

GUATEMALA
BELIZE
Gulf of Honduras
HONDURAS

EL SALVADOR

NICARAGUA

COSTA RICA

PANAMA
Gulf of Panama

CUBA

JAMAICA

HAITI
DOMINICAN REPUBLIC

PUERTO RICO (U.S.)

Greater Antilles

Lesser Antilles

CARIBBEAN SEA

TRINIDAD AND TOBAGO

ATLANTIC OCEAN

Cristóbal Colón Peak △
18,948 Ft.
5,775m

Caracas ⊛

VENEZUELA

Orinoco

Llanos

GUYANA

SURINAME
FRENCH GUIANA

Cape Orange

Magdalena

Bogotá ⊛

COLOMBIA

Galapagos Islands (Ec.)

ECUADOR

△ Chimborazo
20,703 Ft.
6,310m

Putumayo

Japurá

Amazon

Amazon

Amazon

Basin

Manaus ■

Negro

Ilha de Marajó

Belém ■

Equator

Tocantins

Juruá

Madeira

Tapajós

BRAZIL

Selvas

PERU

Andes

Ucayali

Mt. Huascarán △
22,133 Ft.
6,746m

Lima ⊛

Mato Grosso Plateau

Recife ■

Lake Titicaca

Mt. Illampu △
21,066 Ft.
6,421m

BOLIVIA

Brasília ⊛

Serra do Espinhaço

São Francisco

Cordillera Oriental

△ Mt. Sajama
21,463 Ft.
6,542m

Atacama Desert

Gran Chaco

PARAGUAY

Paraná

São Paulo ■

Rio de Janeiro ■

Tropic of Capricorn

Tropic of Capricorn

Isla San Ambrosio (Chile)

Mt. Ojos del Salado △
22,615 Ft.
6,893m

Isla San Félix (Chile)

Andes

CHILE

Paraná

PACIFIC OCEAN

Archipiélago Juan Fernández (Chile)

Santiago ⊛

△ Mt. Aconcagua
22,831 Ft.
6,959m

Buenos Aires ⊛

Pampas

URUGUAY

Rio de la Plata

N

ARGENTINA

Land Elevation

Meters		Feet
3,000		9,840
2,000		6,560
500		1,640
200		656
0		0

Water Depth

0		0
200		656
2,000		6,560

San Matías Gulf

Península Valdés

Chiloé

Patagonia

San Jorge Gulf

Point Medanoso

ATLANTIC OCEAN

0   200   400   600   800   1000 Miles
0   300   600   900   1200   1500 Kilometers

Copyright by Rand McNally & Co.
Lambert Azimuthal Equal Area Projection

Grand Bay

FALKLAND ISLANDS (U.K.)

West Falkland

East Falkland

Strait of Magellan

Tierra del Fuego

Cape Horn

South Georgia (U.K.)

Drake Passage

South Shetland Islands (U.K.)

South Orkney Islands (U.K.)

South Sandwich Islands (U.K.)

A9

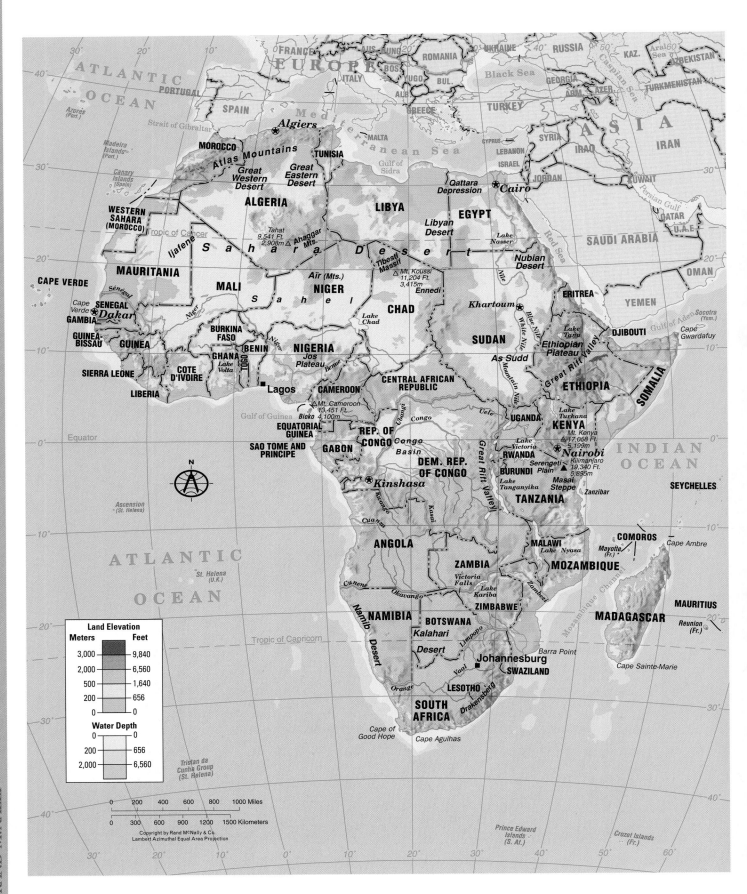

Land Elevation

Meters		Feet
3,000		9,840
2,000		6,560
500		1,640
200		656
0		0

Water Depth

0		0
200		656
2,000		6,560

0   200   400   600   800   1000 Miles

0   300   600   900   1200   1500 Kilometers

Copyright by Rand McNally & Co.
Lambert Azimuthal Equal Area Projection

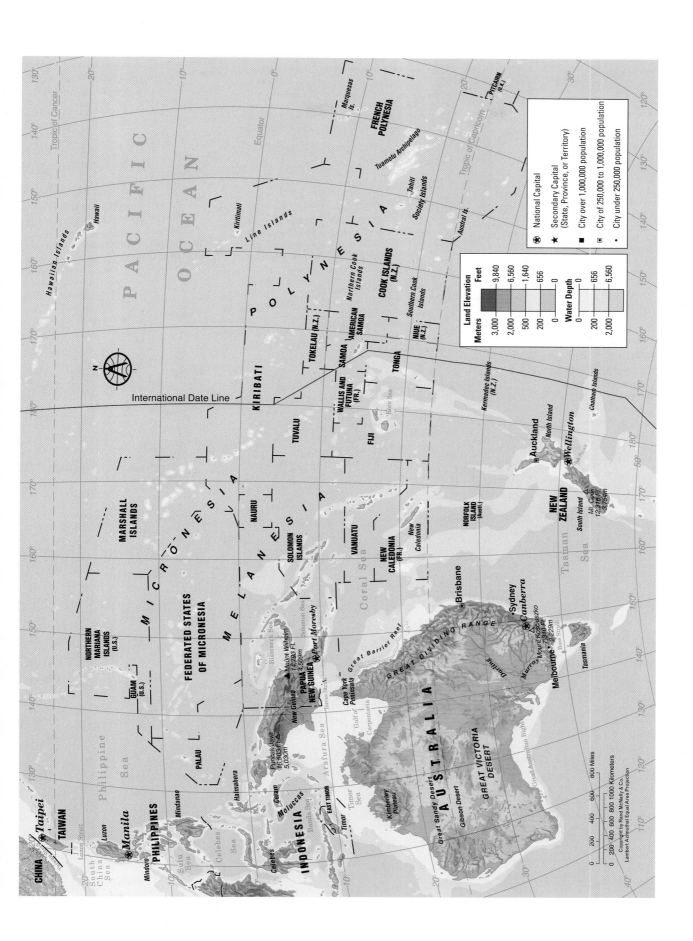

International Date Line

N

PACIFIC OCEAN

Tropic of Cancer

Equator

Tropic of Capricorn

Hawaiian Islands

Hawaii

Kiritimati

Line Islands

Marquesas Is.

FRENCH POLYNESIA

Tuamotu Archipelago

Tahiti

Society Islands

Austral Is.

PITCAIRN (U.K.)

P O L Y N E S I A

Northern Cook Islands

COOK ISLANDS (N.Z.)

Southern Cook Islands

NIUE (N.Z.)

TOKELAU (N.Z.)

AMERICAN SAMOA

SAMOA

TONGA

WALLIS AND FUTUNA (FR.)

Kermadec Islands (N.Z.)

Chatham Islands

KIRIBATI

TUVALU

FIJI

Koro Sea

Auckland

North Island

Wellington

NEW ZEALAND

South Island

Mt. Cook 12,316 Ft. 3,754m

MARSHALL ISLANDS

NAURU

M E L A N E S I A

M I C R O N E S I A

SOLOMON ISLANDS

Bismarck Sea

Solomon Sea

VANUATU

NEW CALEDONIA (FR.)

New Caledonia

NORFOLK ISLAND (Aust.)

NORTHERN MARIANA ISLANDS (U.S.)

FEDERATED STATES OF MICRONESIA

GUAM (U.S.)

PALAU

Mount Wilhelm 14,793 Ft. 4,509m

PAPUA NEW GUINEA

New Guinea

Port Moresby

Torres Strait

Cape York Peninsula

Gulf of Carpentaria

Great Barrier Reef

Coral Sea

Tasman Sea

Brisbane

Sydney

Canberra

GREAT DIVIDING RANGE

Mount Kosciuszko 7,310 Ft. 2,229m

Melbourne

Darling

Murray

Bass Strait

Tasmania

A U S T R A L I A

GREAT VICTORIA DESERT

Great Sandy Desert

Gibson Desert

Kimberley Plateau

Great Australian Bight

CHINA

Taipei

TAIWAN

Luzon Strait

South China Sea

Manila

PHILIPPINES

Luzon

Mindoro

Mindanao

Philippine Sea

Celebes Sea

Sulu Sea

Halmahera

Celebes

Banda Sea

Moluccas

Ceram

INDONESIA

EAST TIMOR

Timor

Timor Sea

Arafura Sea

Puncak Jaya 16,503 Ft. 5,030m

0 200 400 600 800 1000 Kilometers

0 200 400 600 800 Miles

Land Elevation

Meters	Feet
3,000	9,840
2,000	6,560
500	1,640
200	656
0	0

Water Depth

0	0
200	656
2,000	6,560

⊛ National Capital

★ Secondary Capital (State, Province, or Territory)

■ City over 1,000,000 population

▣ City of 250,000 to 1,000,000 population

· City under 250,000 population

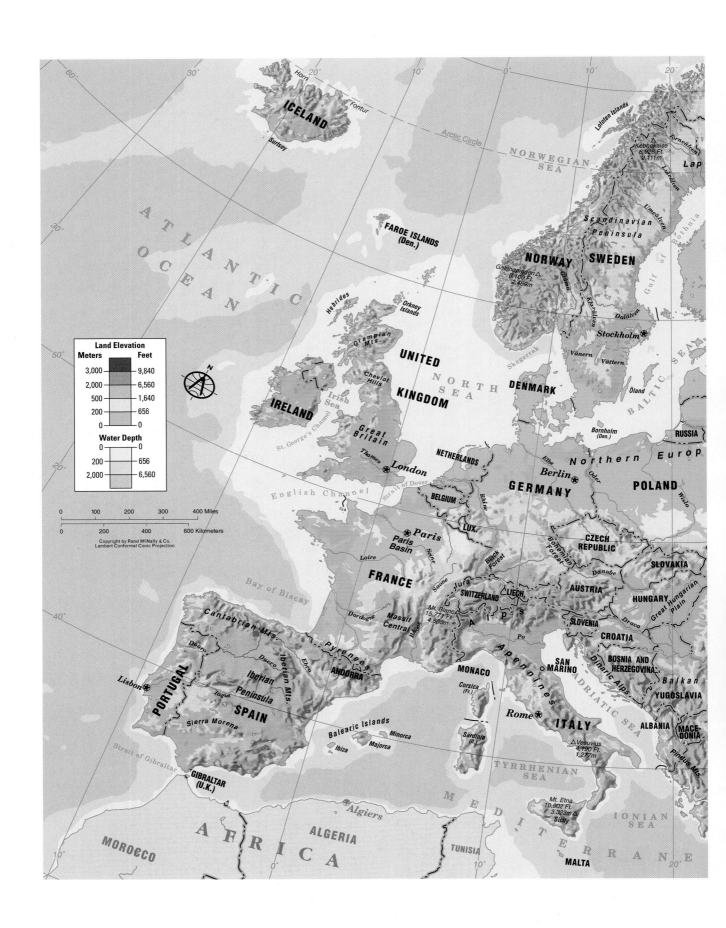

Land Elevation

Meters		Feet
3,000		9,840
2,000		6,560
500		1,640
200		656
0		0

Water Depth

0		0
200		656
2,000		6,560

0	100	200	300	400 Miles
0	200		400	600 Kilometers

Copyright by Rand McNally & Co.
Lambert Conformal Conic Projection

ICELAND
Horn
Fontur
Surtsey

ATLANTIC
OCEAN

NORWEGIAN
SEA

Arctic Circle

Lofoten Islands
Kebnekaise
6,926 Ft.
2,111m
Torneälven
Lap

FAROE ISLANDS
(Den.)

Scandinavian
Peninsula

NORWAY
SWEDEN
Galdhøpiggen
8,100 Ft.
2,469m
Glåma
Klarälven
Dalälven
Stockholm
Vänern
Vättern

Gulf of Bothnia

Hebrides
Orkney
Islands

Grampian
Mts.

UNITED
KINGDOM

Cheviot
Hills

NORTH
SEA

DENMARK

Skagerrak

Öland

BALTIC SEA

IRELAND

Irish
Sea

Great
Britain

Bornholm
(Den.)

RUSSIA

St. George's Channel

Thames

London

NETHERLANDS

Berlin

Northern Europ

Elbe
Oder

GERMANY

POLAND

English Channel

Strait of Dover

BELGIUM

Rhine

Wisla

LUX.

Paris
Paris
Basin

Loire

Seine

Black
Forest

Bohemian
Forest

CZECH
REPUBLIC

SLOVAKIA

Danube

Great Hungarian
Plain

FRANCE

Saône

Jura

SWITZERLAND

LIECH.

AUSTRIA

HUNGARY

Bay of Biscay

Cantabrian Mts.

Dordogne

Massif
Central

Pyrenees

Mt. Blanc
15,771 Ft.
4,808m

Rhône

A L P S

SLOVENIA

Drava

Po

Apennines

CROATIA

BOSNIA AND
HERZEGOVINA

Dinaric Alps

Balkan

Duero

Iberian Mts.

ANDORRA

MONACO

SAN
MARINO

ADRIATIC SEA

YUGOSLAVIA

Lisbon

PORTUGAL

Douro

Iberian
Peninsula

Ebro

Corsica
(Fr.)

Rome

ITALY

ALBANIA

MACE-
DONIA

Tagus

SPAIN

Sierra Morena

Balearic Islands

Minorca

Sardinia
(It.)

Pindus Mts.

Ibiza

Majorca

Vesuvius
4,190 Ft.
1,277m

TYRRHENIAN
SEA

IONIAN
SEA

Strait of Gibraltar

GIBRALTAR
(U.K.)

Mt. Etna
10,902 Ft.
3,323m
Sicily

Algiers

MEDITERRANE

MOROCCO

AFRICA

ALGERIA

TUNISIA

MALTA

20° E

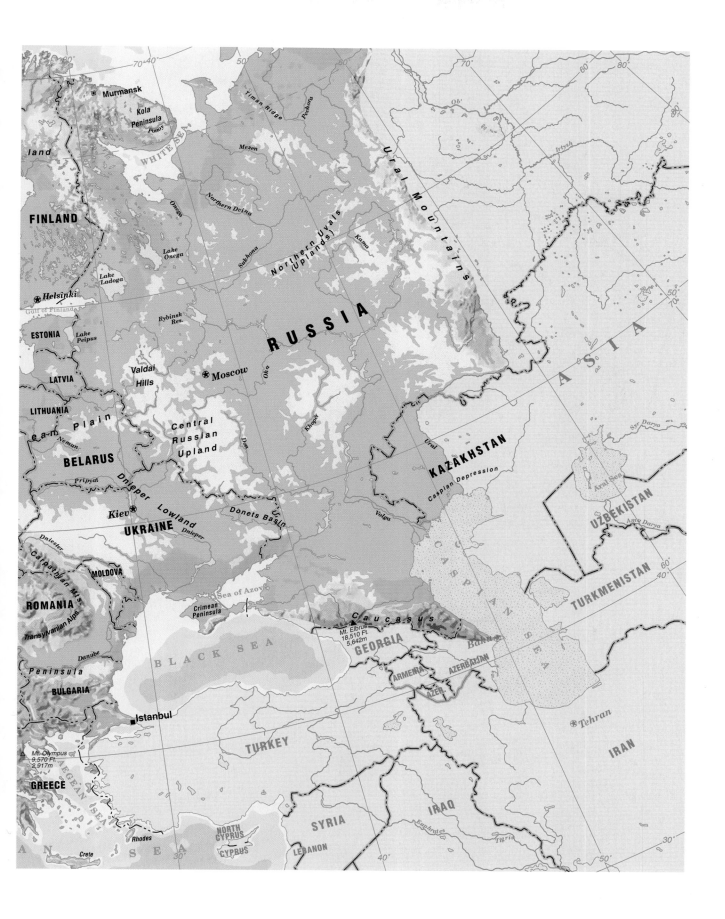

Murmansk

Kola
Peninsula
Ponoy

land

WHITE SEA

Timan Ridge

Pechora

FINLAND

Mezen

Northern Dvina

Onega

Sukhona

Northern Uvals
(Uplands)

Kama

Lake
Onega

U
r
a
l

M
o
u
n
t
a
i
n
s

Ob'

Irtysh

Lake
Ladoga

Helsinki

Gulf of Finland

Rybinsk
Res.

R U S S I A

A
S
I
A

ESTONIA

Lake
Peipus

Moscow

Oka

LATVIA

Valdai
Hills

Irtysh

Syr Darya

LITHUANIA

e a n   Plain

Neman

Central
Russian
Upland

Don

Khopër

KAZAKHSTAN

BELARUS

Pripyat

Dnieper Lowland

Ural

Caspian Depression

Aral Sea

UZBEKISTAN

Kiev

Dniester

UKRAINE

Dnieper

Donets Basin

Volga

Amu Darya

Carpathian Mts.

MOLDOVA

Sea of Azov

Crimean
Peninsula

C
A
S
P
I
A
N
S
E
A

TURKMENISTAN

ROMANIA

Transylvanian Alps

Danube

Caucasus

Mt. Elbrus
18,510 Ft.
5,642m

Baku

Peninsula

B L A C K   S E A

GEORGIA

ARMENIA

AZERBAIJAN

BULGARIA

AZER.

Istanbul

Tehran

Mt. Olympus
9,570 Ft.
2,917m

TURKEY

IRAN

GREECE

A
E
G
E
A
N
S
E
A

A N   S E A

Rhodes

30°

Crete

NORTH
CYPRUS

CYPRUS

SYRIA

LEBANON

IRAQ

Euphrates

Tigris

40°

50°

30°

70° 40°

50°

60°

70°

60°

80°

50°

70°

60°

40°

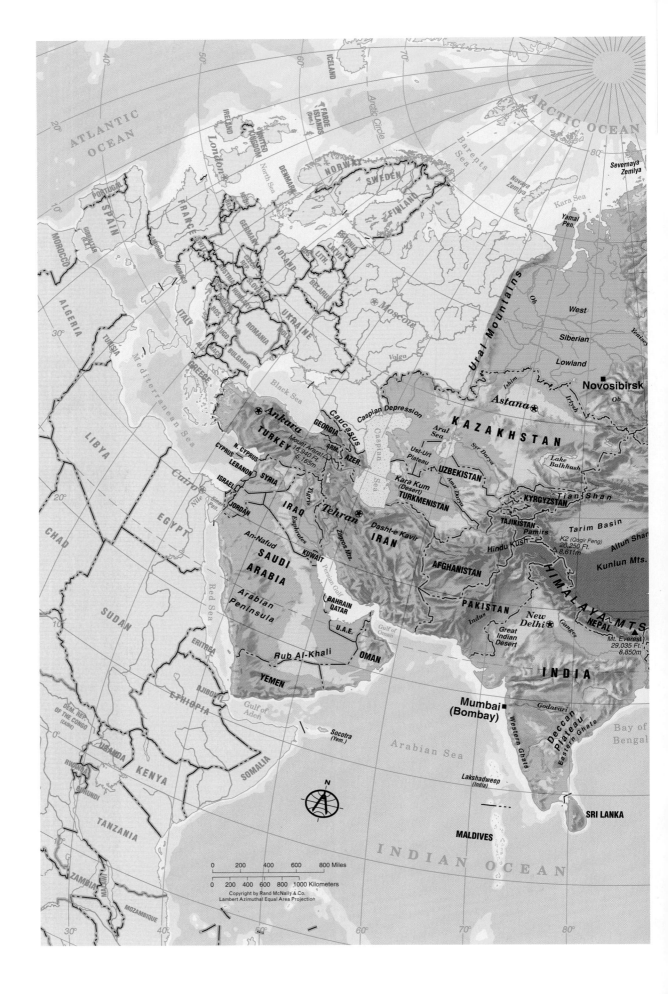

ATLANTIC OCEAN

ARCTIC OCEAN

ICELAND

IRELAND

UNITED KINGDOM

London

FAROE ISLANDS (Den.)

NORWAY

SWEDEN

FINLAND

ESTONIA

LATVIA

LITH.

Arctic Circle

Barents Sea

Novaya Zemlya

Kara Sea

Yamal Pen.

Severnaya Zemlya

PORTUGAL

SPAIN

MOROCCO

GIBRALTAR (U.K.)

ALGERIA

TUNISIA

FRANCE

ITALY

DENMARK

North Sea

GERMANY

POLAND

BELARUS

UKRAINE

ROMANIA

BULGARIA

Moscow

Volga

Ob

Ural Mountains

West Siberian Lowland

Yenisey

Novosibirsk

Ob

Irtysh

Ishim

Astana

KAZAKHSTAN

Lake Balkhash

Tian Shan

Mediterranean Sea

GREECE

Black Sea

Ankara

GEORGIA

Caucasus

TURKEY

Mount Ararat 16,940 Ft. 5,165m

ARM.

AZER.

Caspian Depression

Aral Sea

Caspian Sea

Ust-Urt Plateau

Syr Darya

UZBEKISTAN

Amu Darya

KYRGYZSTAN

TAJIKISTAN

Pamirs

Tarim Basin

Altun Shan

LIBYA

CYPRUS

N. CYPRUS

LEBANON

ISRAEL

SYRIA

Tigris

JORDAN

IRAQ

Euphrates

Tehran

Dasht-e Kavir

IRAN

Zagros Mts.

Kara Kum (Desert)

TURKMENISTAN

Hindu Kush

K2 (Qogir Feng) 28,250 Ft. 8,611m

Kunlun Mts.

HIMALAYA MTS.

CHAD

EGYPT

Cairo

Nile

Sinai Pen.

An-Nafud

SAUDI ARABIA

KUWAIT

Persian Gulf

BAHRAIN

QATAR

AFGHANISTAN

PAKISTAN

Indus

New Delhi

Ganges

Great Indian Desert

NEPAL

Mt. Everest 29,035 Ft. 8,850m

SUDAN

Red Sea

Arabian Peninsula

Rub Al-Khali

U.A.E.

Gulf of Oman

OMAN

ERITREA

YEMEN

Gulf of Aden

INDIA

Godavari

Mumbai (Bombay)

Western Ghats

Deccan Plateau

Eastern Ghats

Bay of Bengal

DJIBOUTI

ETHIOPIA

DEM. REP. OF THE CONGO (ZAIRE)

UGANDA

SOMALIA

Socotra (Yem.)

Arabian Sea

Lakshadweep (India)

SRI LANKA

RWANDA

BURUNDI

KENYA

N

MALDIVES

TANZANIA

INDIAN OCEAN

ZAMBIA

MALAWI

MOZAMBIQUE

0   200   400   600   800 Miles

0   200 400 600 800 1000 Kilometers

Copyright by Rand McNally & Co.
Lambert Azimuthal Equal Area Projection

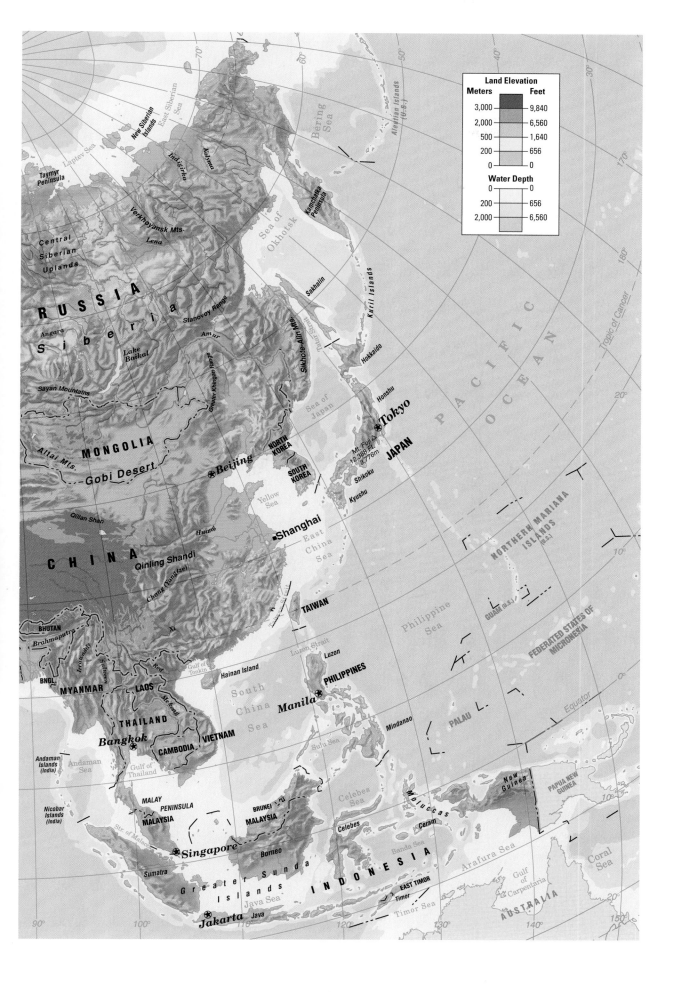

Land Elevation

Meters		Feet
3,000		9,840
2,000		6,560
500		1,640
200		656
0		0

Water Depth

0		0
200		656
2,000		6,560

Taymyr Peninsula

New Siberian Islands

East Siberian Sea

Laptev Sea

Indigirka

Kolyma

Central Siberian Uplands

Angara

RUSSIA

Siberia

Verkhoyansk Mts.

Lena

Lake Baikal

Stanovoy Range

Amur

Sayan Mountains

Altai Mts.

MONGOLIA

Gobi Desert

Greater Khingan Range

Sikhote-Alin Mts.

Sea of Okhotsk

Kamchatka Peninsula

Bering Sea

Aleutian Islands (U.S.)

Sakhalin

Tatar Strait

Kuril Islands

Sea of Japan

Hokkaido

Honshu

Tokyo

Mt. Fuji △ 12,388 ft. 3,776m

JAPAN

Shikoku

Kyushu

PACIFIC OCEAN

Tropic of Cancer

NORTH KOREA

SOUTH KOREA

Beijing

Yellow Sea

Qilian Shan

Huang

CHINA

Qinling Shandi

Chang (Yangtze)

Shanghai

East China Sea

NORTHERN MARIANA ISLANDS (U.S.)

GUAM (U.S.)

BHUTAN

Brahmaputra

Irrawaddy

Salween

Xi

TAIWAN

Philippine Sea

FEDERATED STATES OF MICRONESIA

BNGL.

MYANMAR

LAOS

Red

Mekong

Gulf of Tonkin

Hainan Island

Luzon Strait

Luzon

PHILIPPINES

South China Sea

Manila

Mindanao

PALAU

Equator

THAILAND

Bangkok

CAMBODIA

VIETNAM

Sulu Sea

Andaman Islands (India)

Andaman Sea

Gulf of Thailand

MALAY PENINSULA

MALAYSIA

Str. of Malacca

BRUNEI

MALAYSIA

Celebes Sea

Celebes

Ceram

Moluccas

Banda Sea

New Guinea

PAPUA NEW GUINEA

Nicobar Islands (India)

Singapore

Borneo

Greater Sunda Islands

Sumatra

Jakarta

Java

Java Sea

INDONESIA

EAST TIMOR

Timor

Timor Sea

Arafura Sea

Gulf of Carpentaria

Coral Sea

AUSTRALIA

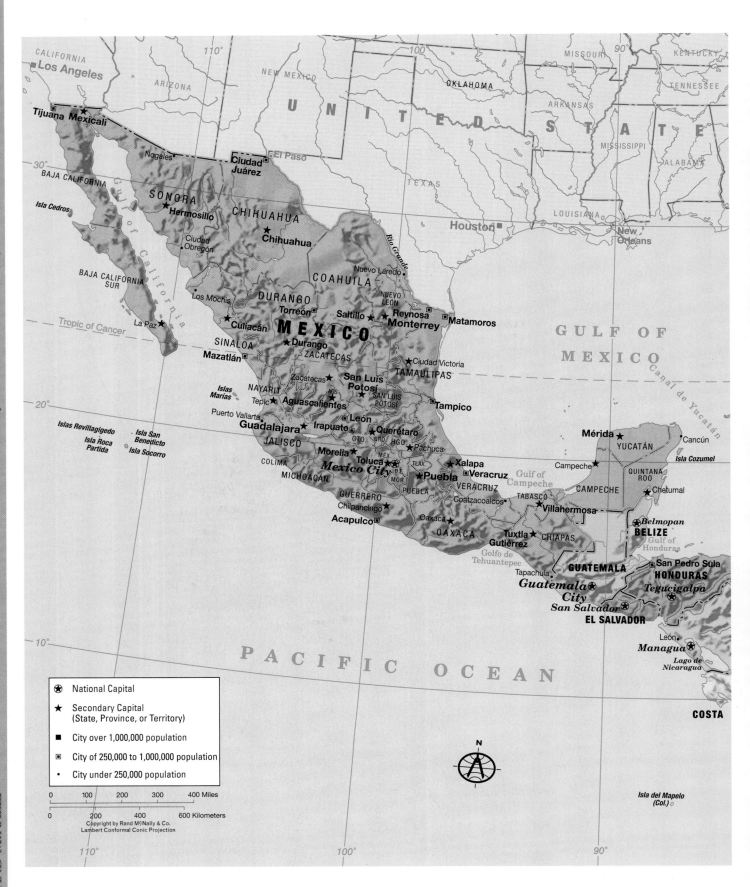

CALIFORNIA
Los Angeles

ARIZONA

NEW MEXICO

OKLAHOMA

MISSOURI

KENTUCKY

TENNESSEE

MISSISSIPPI

ALABAMA

U N I T E D   S T A T E

Tijuana Mexicali

Nogales

El Paso

Ciudad
Juárez

TEXAS

ARKANSAS

LOUISIANA

Houston

New
Orleans

BAJA CALIFORNIA

Isla Cedros

SONORA

Hermosillo

CHIHUAHUA

Chihuahua

Ciudad
Obregón

BAJA CALIFORNIA
SUR

Los Mochis

COAHUILA

DURANGO

Torreón

Nuevo Laredo

Rio Grande

NUEVO
LEÓN

Saltillo

Reynosa
Monterrey

Matamoros

GULF OF

MEXICO

Tropic of Cancer

La Paz

Culiacán

M E X I C O

Durango
ZACATECAS

Ciudad Victoria

Mazatlán

SINALOA

TAMAULIPAS

Canal de Yucatán

Islas
Marías

NAYARIT

Zacatecas

San Luis
Potosí

SAN LUIS
POTOSÍ

Tampico

GULF OF
MEXICO

30°

110°

100°

90°

Tepic

AGS

Aguascalientes

Mérida

YUCATÁN

Cancún

Puerto Vallarta

León

Irapuato

Querétaro

Pachuca

Campeche

Isla Cozumel

Islas Revillagigedo

Isla San
Benedicto

Isla Roca
Partida

Isla Socorro

Guadalajara

JALISCO

GTO

ORO

HGO

QUINTANA
ROO

20°

COLIMA

Morelia

Toluca

MEX

Mexico City

TLAX

D.F.

MOR

Xalapa

Veracruz

Gulf of
Campeche

Chetumal

CAMPECHE

MICHOACÁN

Puebla

PUEBLA

VERACRUZ

TABASCO

Villahermosa

GUERRERO

Chilpancingo

Coatzacoalcos

Belmopan

BELIZE

Acapulco

Oaxaca

OAXACA

Tuxtla
Gutiérrez

CHIAPAS

Gulf of
Honduras

Golfo de
Tehuantepec

San Pedro Sula

HONDURAS

P A C I F I C   O C E A N

Tapachula

GUATEMALA

Guatemala
City

San Salvador

EL SALVADOR

Tegucigalpa

León

Managua

Lago de
Nicaragua

10°

COSTA

N

National Capital

Secondary Capital
(State, Province, or Territory)

City over 1,000,000 population

City of 250,000 to 1,000,000 population

City under 250,000 population

Isla del Mapelo
(Col.)

0   100   200   300   400 Miles

0   200   400   600 Kilometers

Copyright by Rand McNally & Co.
Lambert Conformal Conic Projection

110°

100°

90°

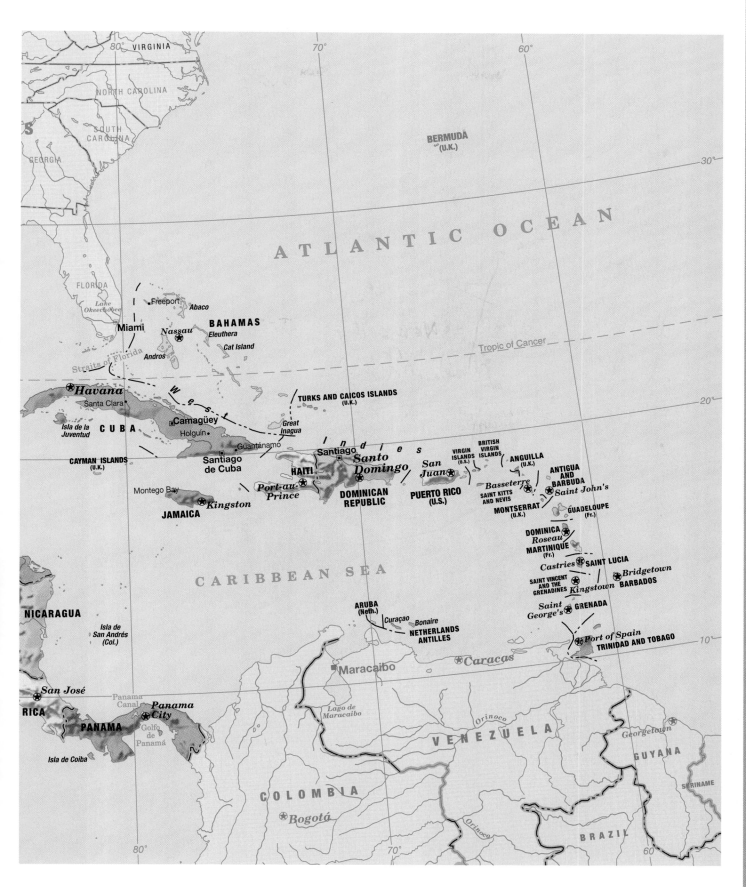

RAND McNALLY

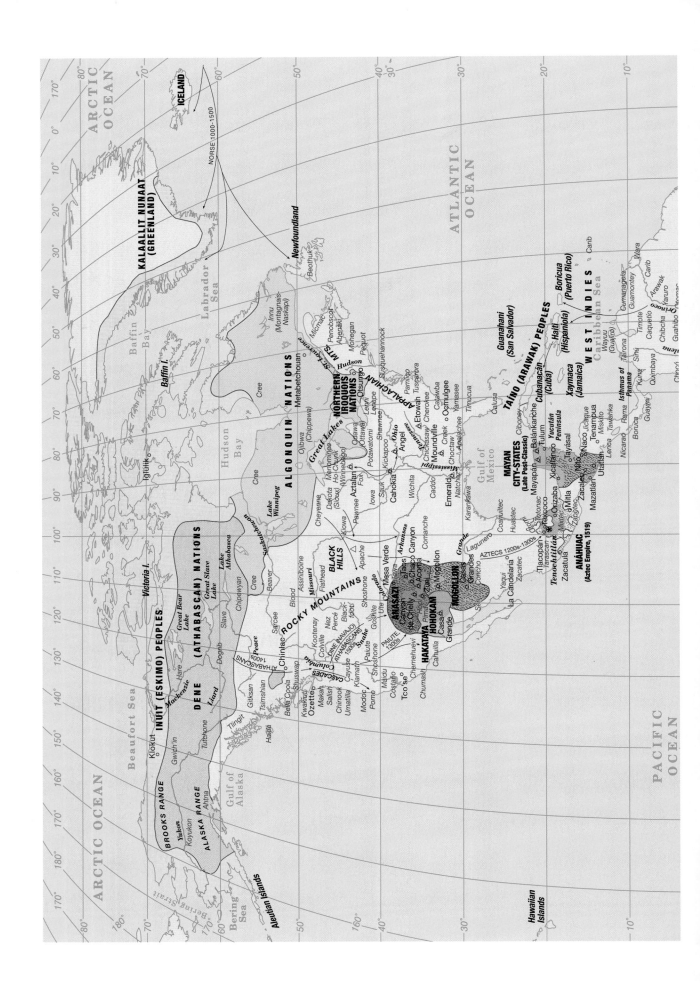

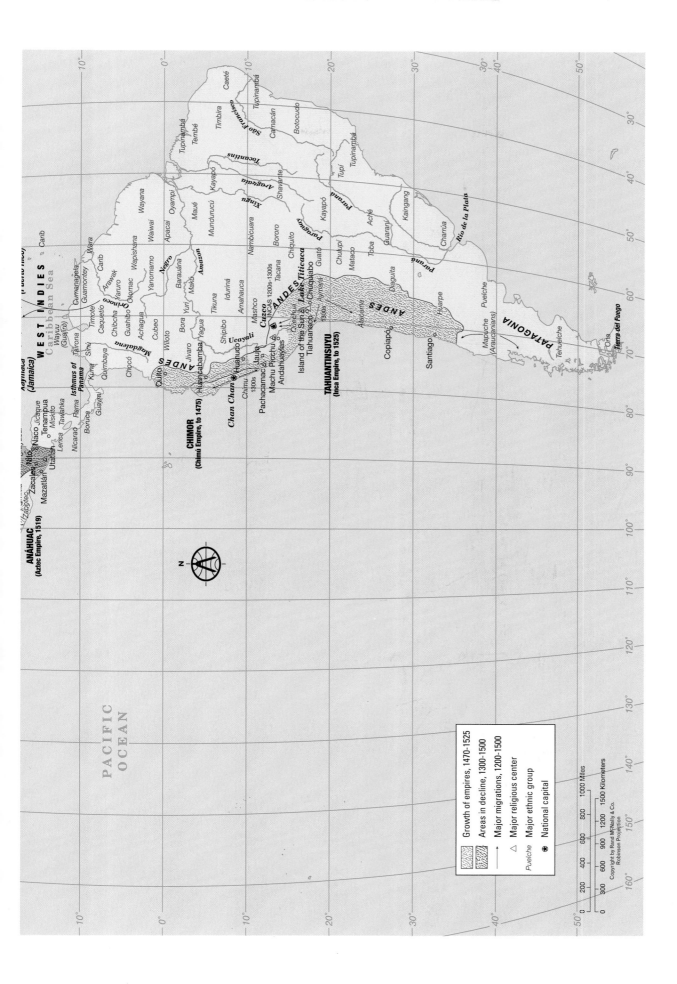

ANÁHUAC
(Aztec Empire, 1519)

PACIFIC
OCEAN

WEST INDIES

Caribbean Sea

Isthmus of
Panama

ANDES

CHIMOR
(Chimú Empire, to 1475)

Chan Chan

TAHUANTINSUYU
(Inca Empire, to 1525)

ANDES

ANDES

PATAGONIA

Tierra del Fuego

Growth of empires, 1470-1525
Areas in decline, 1300-1500
Major migrations, 1200-1500
△ Major religious center
Puelche Major ethnic group
Major national capital

0   200   400   600   800   1000 Miles
0   300   600   900   1200   1500 Kilometers

Copyright by Rand McNally & Co.
Robinson Projection

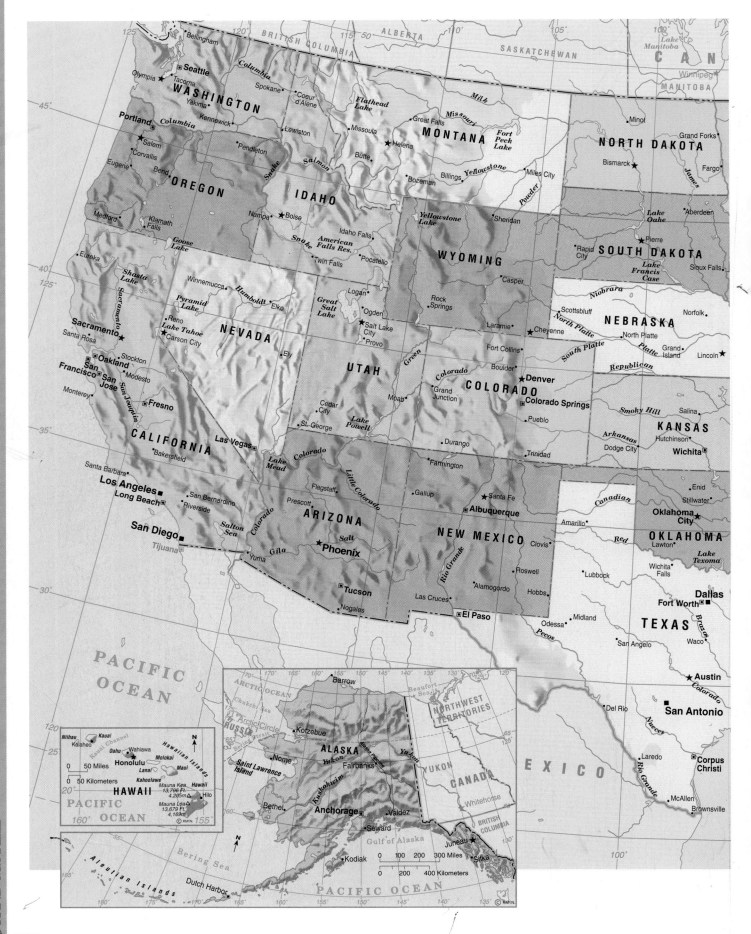

PACIFIC OCEAN

PACIFIC OCEAN

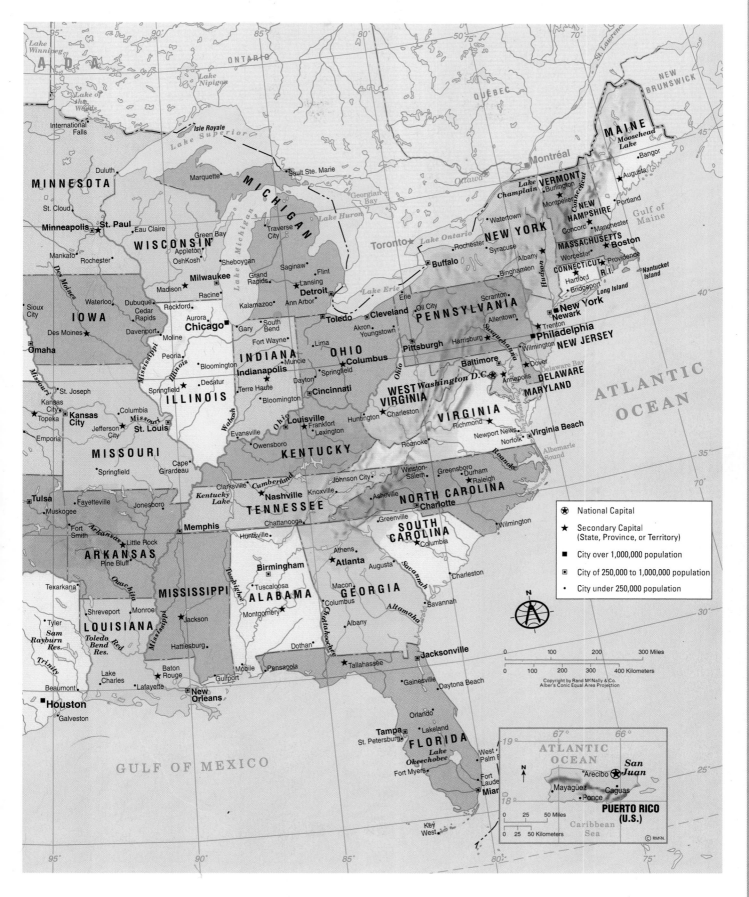

Legend

⊛ National Capital

★ Secondary Capital
(State, Province, or Territory)

■ City over 1,000,000 population

▣ City of 250,000 to 1,000,000 population

• City under 250,000 population

0   100   200   300 Miles

0   100   200   300   400 Kilometers

Copyright by Rand McNally & Co.
Alber's Conic Equal Area Projection

**PUERTO RICO
(U.S.)**

RAND McNALLY

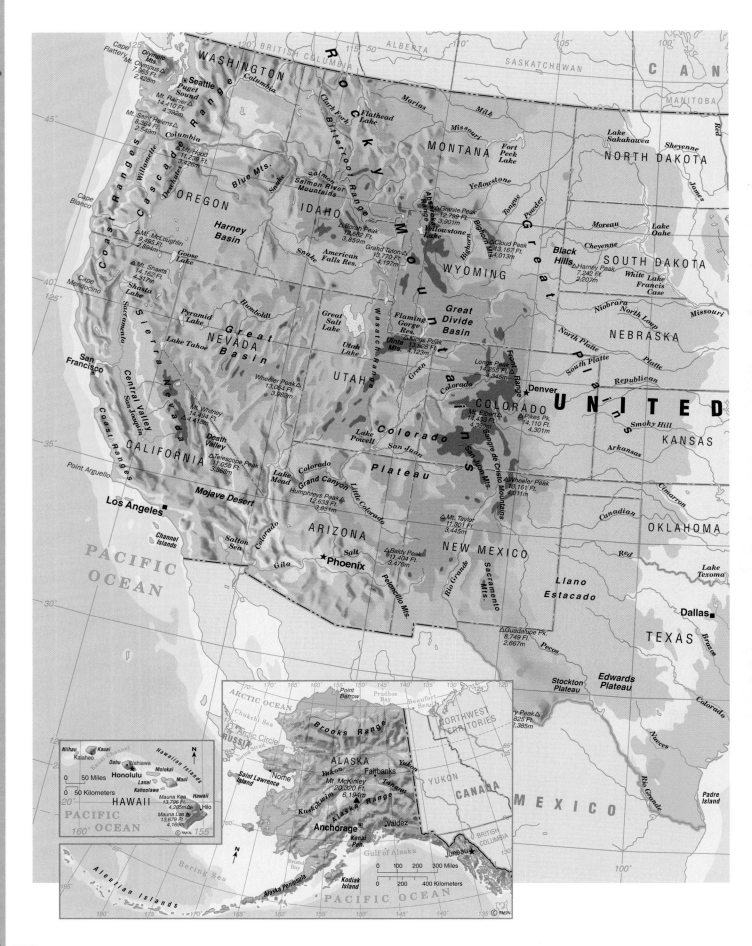

RAND M^cNALLY

WASHINGTON
Cape Flattery
Olympic Mts.
Mt. Olympus △ 7,965 Ft. 2,428m
Seattle
Puget Sound
Mt. Rainier △ 14,410 Ft. 4,392m
Columbia
BRITISH COLUMBIA
ALBERTA
SASKATCHEWAN
C A N
MANITOBA

Mt. Saint Helens △ 8,364 Ft. 2,549m
Columbia
Blue Mts.
Clark Fork
Flathead Lake
Marias
Milk
Missouri
Fort Peck Lake
NORTH DAKOTA
Lake Sakakawea
Sheyenne
Red
James

Mt. Hood 11,239 Ft. 3,426m
OREGON
Deschutes
Snake
Salmon Mountains
Salmon River Mountains
Bitterroot Range
MONTANA
Yellowstone
Tongue
Powder
Moreau
Lake Oahe

Cape Blanco
Mt. McLoughlin △ 9,495 Ft. 2,894m
Harney Basin
IDAHO
Snake
△ Borah Peak 12,662 Ft. 3,859m
Absaroka Range
△ Granite Peak 12,799 Ft. 3,901m
Yellowstone Lake
Bighorn
Bighorn Mts.
△ Cloud Peak 13,167 Ft. 4,013m
Black Hills
△ Harney Peak 7,242 Ft. 2,207m
SOUTH DAKOTA
White River
Lake Francis Case
Cheyenne

Mt. Shasta △ 14,162 Ft. 4,317m
Goose Lake
American Falls Res.
Grand Teton 13,770 Ft. 4,197m
WYOMING
Niobrara
North Loup
Missouri

Cape Mendocino
Shasta Lake
Sacramento
Pyramid Lake
Humboldt
Great Salt Lake
Flaming Gorge Res.
Great Divide Basin
Uinta Mts.
△ Kings Peak 13,528 Ft. 4,123m
Longs Peak 14,255 Ft. 4,345m
Front Range
NEBRASKA
North Platte
South Platte
Platte

San Francisco
Sierra Nevada
Lake Tahoe
Great NEVADA Basin
Utah Lake
UTAH
Green
Wasatch Range
Colorado
COLORADO
Denver
Mt. Elbert 14,433 Ft. 4,399m
Pikes Pk. 14,110 Ft. 4,301m
U N I T E D
Republican
Smoky Hill
KANSAS

Wheeler Peak △ 13,064 Ft. 3,982m
Mt. Whitney △ 14,494 Ft. 4,418m
Death Valley
Central Valley
San Joaquin
CALIFORNIA
Coast Ranges
Death Valley
△ Telescope Peak 11,050 Ft. 3,368m
Lake Powell
Colorado Plateau
San Juan
Sangre de Cristo Mountains
San Juan Mts.
△ Wheeler Peak 13,161 Ft. 4,011m
Arkansas
Cimarron

Mojave Desert
Los Angeles
Channel Islands
Salton Sea
Colorado
Lake Mead
Grand Canyon
Colorado
Little Colorado
Humphreys Peak 12,633 Ft. 3,851m
△ Mt. Taylor 11,301 Ft. 3,445m
NEW MEXICO
OKLAHOMA
Red
Lake Texoma

PACIFIC OCEAN
Point Arguello
Gila
Phoenix
Salt
ARIZONA
△ Baldy Peak 11,404 Ft. 3,476m
Peloncillo Mts.
Sacramento Mts.
Rio Grande
Llano Estacado
Canadian
Dallas
TEXAS

Stockton Plateau
Edwards Plateau
Pecos
△ Guadalupe Pk. 8,749 Ft. 2,667m
ry Peak 825 Ft. 2,385m
Colorado
Nueces
Rio Grande
MEXICO
Padre Island

ARCTIC OCEAN
Point Barrow
Prudhoe Bay
Beaufort Sea
Chukchi Sea
NORTHWEST TERRITORIES
Arctic Circle
RUSSIA
Bering Strait
Brooks Range
ALASKA
Nome
Saint Lawrence Island
Yukon
Fairbanks
Tanana
Yukon
YUKON
CANADA
Mt. McKinley 20,320 Ft. 6,194m
Kuskokwim
Alaska Range
Anchorage
Valdez
Kenai Pen.
BRITISH COLUMBIA
Juneau

Niihau
Kauai
Kalaheo
Oahu
Wahiawa
Honolulu
Molokai
Lanai
Maui
Kahoolawe
HAWAII
Mauna Kea 13,796 Ft. 4,205m
Mauna Loa 13,679 Ft. 4,169m
Hawaii
Hilo
Hawaiian Islands
Kauai Channel
PACIFIC OCEAN
0 50 Miles
0 50 Kilometers

Bering Sea
Aleutian Islands
Bristol Bay
Alaska Peninsula
Kodiak Island
Gulf of Alaska
PACIFIC OCEAN
0 100 200 300 Miles
0 200 400 Kilometers

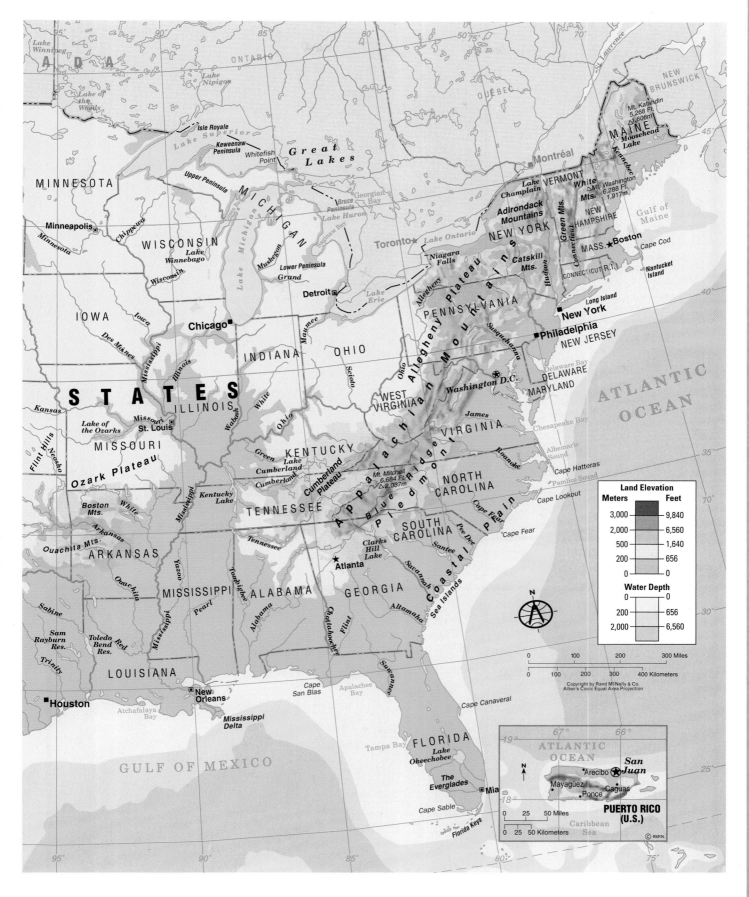

Guam

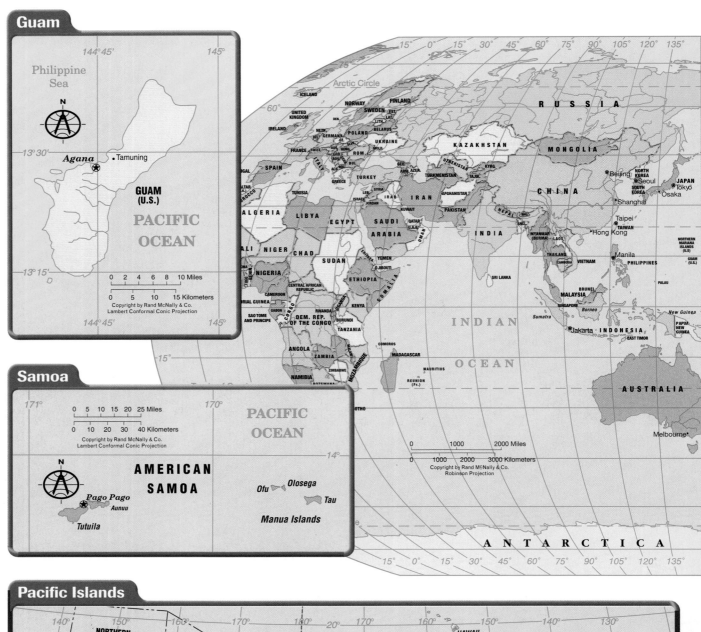

Philippine
Sea

N

144° 45'   145°

13° 30'

Agana ⊛   • Tamuning

GUAM
(U.S.)

PACIFIC
OCEAN

13° 15'

```
0   2   4   6   8   10 Miles
0    5      10     15 Kilometers
```
Copyright by Rand McNally & Co.
Lambert Conformal Conic Projection

144° 45'   145°

Samoa

```
0   5   10  15  20  25 Miles
0    10    20    30    40 Kilometers
```
Copyright by Rand McNally & Co.
Lambert Conformal Conic Projection

171°   170°

PACIFIC
OCEAN

14°

N

AMERICAN
SAMOA

Pago Pago ⊛
Aunuu
Tutuila

Ofu 🝛 🝛 Olosega
🝛 Tau

Manua Islands

Pacific Islands

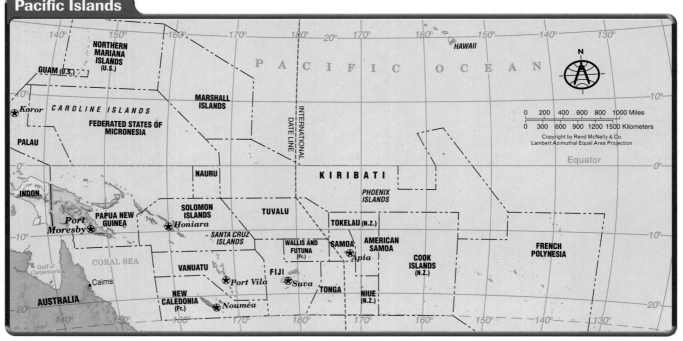

140°   150°   160°   170°   180°   20°   170°   160°   150°   140°   130°

PACIFIC OCEAN

HAWAII

N

NORTHERN
MARIANA
ISLANDS
(U.S.)

GUAM (U.S.)

CAROLINE ISLANDS

⊛ Koror

FEDERATED STATES OF
MICRONESIA

PALAU

MARSHALL
ISLANDS

10°

```
0   200   400   600   800  1000 Miles
0  300  600  900 1200 1500 Kilometers
```
Copyright by Rand McNally & Co.
Lambert Azimuthal Equal Area Projection

Equator

0°

INTERNATIONAL DATE LINE

NAURU

KIRIBATI

PHOENIX
ISLANDS

INDON.

Port
Moresby ⊛

PAPUA NEW
GUINEA

SOLOMON
ISLANDS
⊛ Honiara

SANTA CRUZ
ISLANDS

TUVALU

TOKELAU (N.Z.)

10°

CORAL SEA

VANUATU

WALLIS AND
FUTUNA
(Fr.)

SAMOA
⊛ Apia

AMERICAN
SAMOA

COOK
ISLANDS
(N.Z.)

FRENCH
POLYNESIA

Gulf of
Carpentaria

Cairns

⊛ Port Vila

FIJI
⊛ Suva

TONGA

NIUE
(N.Z.)

AUSTRALIA

NEW
CALEDONIA
(Fr.)
⊛ Nouméa

20°

140°   150°   160°   180°   170°   160°   150°   140°   130°

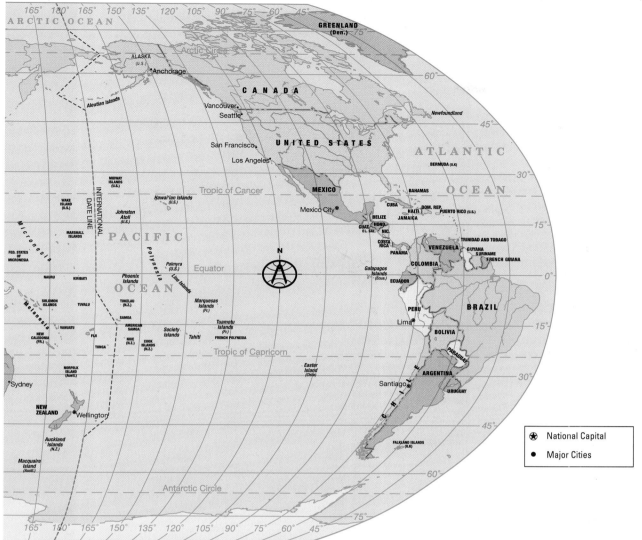

National Capital

Major Cities

Puerto Rico and the U.S. Virgin Islands

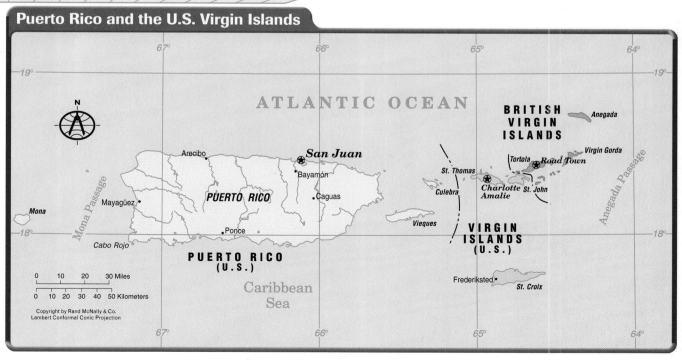

Copyright by Rand McNally & Co.
Lambert Conformal Conic Projection

0 10 20 30 Miles

0 10 20 30 40 50 Kilometers

RAND McNALLY

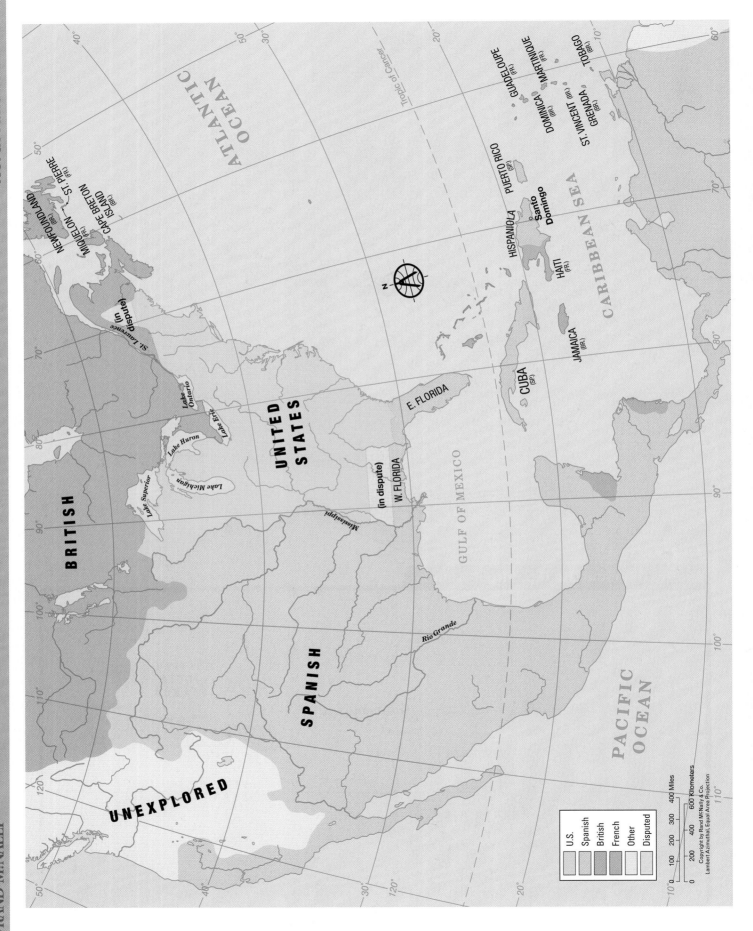

ATLANTIC OCEAN

Tropic of Cancer

GUADELOUPE (FR.)

DOMINICA (BR.)

MARTINIQUE (FR.)

ST. VINCENT (BR.)

GRENADA (BR.)

TOBAGO (BR.)

PUERTO RICO (SP.)

HISPANIOLA

Santo Domingo

HAITI (FR.)

CARIBBEAN SEA

NEWFOUNDLAND (BR.)

ST. PIERRE (FR.)

MIQUELON (FR.)

CAPE BRETON ISLAND (BR.)

(in dispute)

St. Lawrence

Lake Ontario

Lake Erie

Lake Huron

Lake Superior

Lake Michigan

BRITISH

UNITED STATES

E. FLORIDA

CUBA (SP.)

JAMAICA (BR.)

(in dispute)

W. FLORIDA

Mississippi

GULF OF MEXICO

SPANISH

Rio Grande

PACIFIC OCEAN

UNEXPLORED

U.S.

Spanish

British

French

Other

Disputed

400 Miles

600 Kilometers

Copyright by Rand McNally & Co.
Lambert Azimuthal, Equal Area Projection

0   100   200   300   400

0   200   400   600

A26

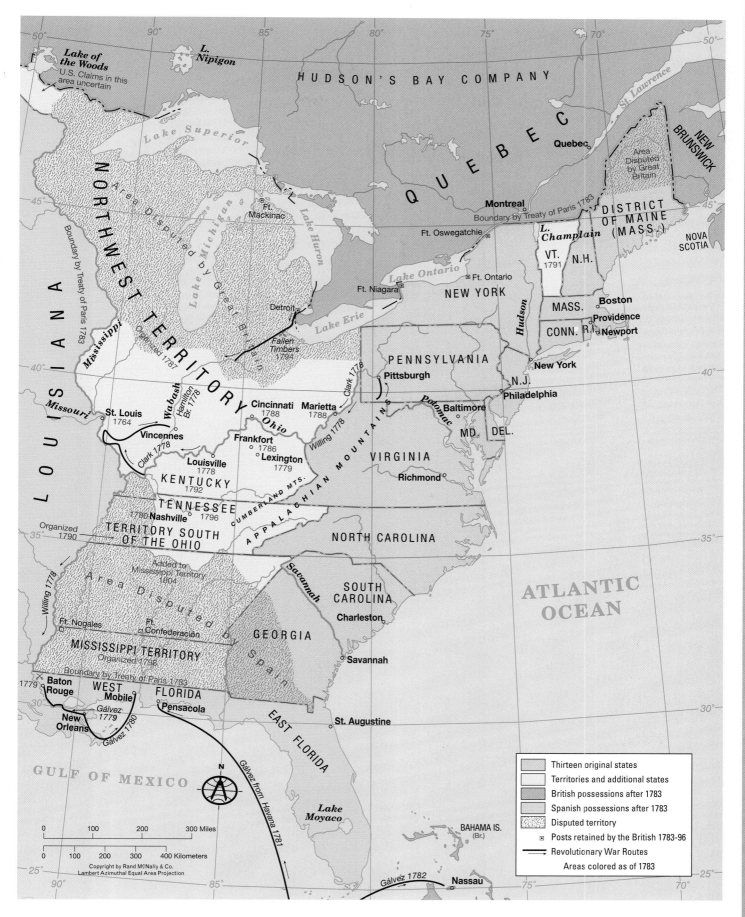

Lake of the Woods
U.S. Claims in this area uncertain

L. Nipigon

HUDSON'S BAY COMPANY

Lake Superior

Ft. Mackinac

QUEBEC

St. Lawrence

Quebec

NEW BRUNSWICK

NORTHWEST TERRITORY

Area Disputed by Great Britain

Lake Michigan

Lake Huron

Montreal
Boundary by Treaty of Paris 1783

Ft. Oswegatchie

DISTRICT OF MAINE (MASS.)

Area Disputed by Great Britain

NOVA SCOTIA

Boundary by Treaty of Paris 1783

Mississippi

Organized 1787

Detroit

Fallen Timbers 1794

Lake Erie

Lake Ontario

Ft. Niagara

Ft. Ontario

L. Champlain

VT. 1791

N.H.

NEW YORK

Hudson

MASS.

Boston

CONN.

R.I.

Providence
Newport

PENNSYLVANIA

Pittsburgh

Clark 1778

New York

N.J.

Philadelphia

Wabash

Hamilton Br. 1778

Missouri

St. Louis 1764

Vincennes

Clark 1778

Cincinnati 1788

Marietta 1788

Ohio

Frankfort 1786

Willing 1778

Lexington 1779

Louisville 1778

KENTUCKY 1792

APPALACHIAN MOUNTAINS

Potomac

Baltimore

MD.

DEL.

VIRGINIA

Richmond

LOUISIANA

Organized 1790

TENNESSEE 1796

Nashville 1780

TERRITORY SOUTH OF THE OHIO

CUMBERLAND MTS.

NORTH CAROLINA

Willing 1778

Area Disputed by Spain

Added to Mississippi Territory 1804

Savannah

SOUTH CAROLINA

Charleston

Ft. Nogales

Ft. Confederación

GEORGIA

MISSISSIPPI TERRITORY
Organized 1798

Boundary by Treaty of Paris 1783

1779

Baton Rouge

WEST

FLORIDA

Mobile

Savannah

ATLANTIC OCEAN

New Orleans

Gálvez 1779

Pensacola

Gálvez 1780

EAST FLORIDA

St. Augustine

GULF OF MEXICO

N

Gálvez from Havana 1781

Lake Moyaco

BAHAMA IS. (Br.)

0   100   200   300 Miles

0 100 200 300 400 Kilometers

Copyright by Rand McNally & Co.
Lambert Azimuthal Equal Area Projection

Gálvez 1782   Nassau

	Thirteen original states
	Territories and additional states
	British possessions after 1783
	Spanish possessions after 1783
	Disputed territory
□	Posts retained by the British 1783-96
▬	Revolutionary War Routes
	Areas colored as of 1783

RAND McNALLY

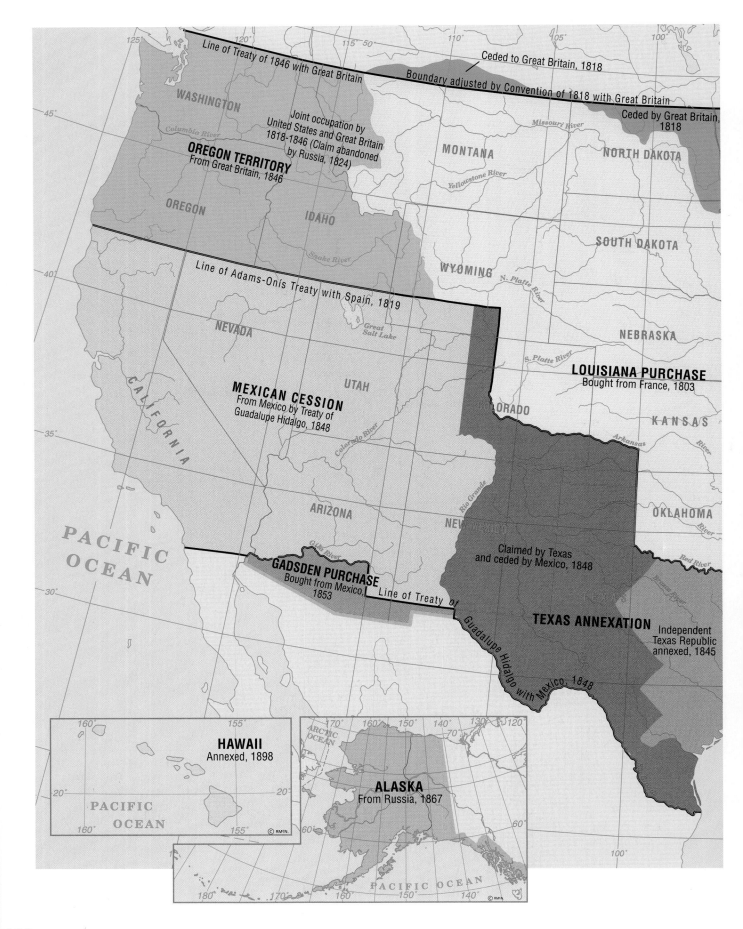

Line of Treaty of 1846 with Great Britain

Ceded to Great Britain, 1818

Boundary adjusted by Convention of 1818 with Great Britain

Ceded by Great Britain, 1818

WASHINGTON

Columbia River

MONTANA

Missouri River

NORTH DAKOTA

Joint occupation by
United States and Great Britain
1818-1846 (Claim abandoned
by Russia, 1824)

OREGON TERRITORY
From Great Britain, 1846

OREGON

IDAHO

Yellowstone River

SOUTH DAKOTA

Snake River

WYOMING

N. Platte River

Line of Adams-Onís Treaty with Spain, 1819

NEVADA

Great
Salt Lake

NEBRASKA

S. Platte River

LOUISIANA PURCHASE
Bought from France, 1803

UTAH

COLORADO

K A N S A S

Arkansas

River

MEXICAN CESSION
From Mexico by Treaty of
Guadalupe Hidalgo, 1848

C A L I F O R N I A

Colorado River

ARIZONA

NEW MEXICO

Rio Grande

OKLAHOMA

Red River

PACIFIC
OCEAN

Gila River

GADSDEN PURCHASE
Bought from Mexico,
1853

Line of Treaty of

Claimed by Texas
and ceded by Mexico, 1848

Brazos River

Guadalupe Hidalgo with Mexico, 1848

TEXAS ANNEXATION

Independent
Texas Republic
annexed, 1845

160°   155°

HAWAII
Annexed, 1898

20°   20°

PACIFIC

160°   155°

OCEAN

© RMcN.

170°   160° 150° 140° 130° 120°
ARCTIC
OCEAN
70°

ALASKA
From Russia, 1867

60°   60°

180°   170°   160°   150°   140°

PACIFIC OCEAN

© rmcn.

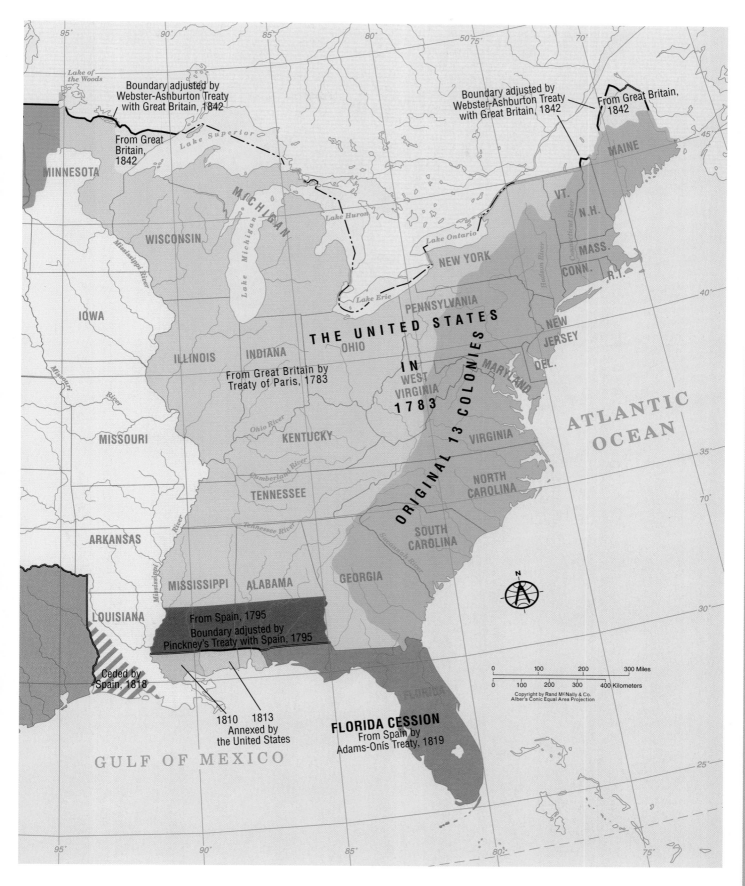

Lake of
the Woods

Boundary adjusted by
Webster-Ashburton Treaty
with Great Britain, 1842

From Great
Britain,
1842

Boundary adjusted by
Webster-Ashburton Treaty
with Great Britain, 1842

From Great Britain,
1842

MINNESOTA

Lake Superior

MICHIGAN

MAINE

WISCONSIN

Lake Michigan

Lake Huron

VT.

N.H.

Mississippi River

IOWA

Lake Ontario

Connecticut River

MASS.

NEW YORK

CONN.

R.I.

Lake Erie

PENNSYLVANIA

Hudson River

ILLINOIS

INDIANA

OHIO

THE UNITED STATES

NEW
JERSEY

Missouri River

From Great Britain by
Treaty of Paris, 1783

IN

DEL.

WEST
VIRGINIA
1783

MARYLAND

ORIGINAL 13 COLONIES

Ohio River

MISSOURI

KENTUCKY

VIRGINIA

ATLANTIC
OCEAN

Cumberland River

NORTH
CAROLINA

TENNESSEE

Tennessee River

ARKANSAS

Savannah River

SOUTH
CAROLINA

Mississippi River

MISSISSIPPI

ALABAMA

GEORGIA

N

LOUISIANA

From Spain, 1795
Boundary adjusted by
Pinckney's Treaty with Spain, 1795

FLORIDA

Ceded by
Spain, 1818

0   100   200   300 Miles

0   100   200   300   400 Kilometers

Copyright by Rand McNally & Co.
Alber's Conic Equal Area Projection

1810   1813
Annexed by
the United States

FLORIDA CESSION
From Spain by
Adams-Onís Treaty, 1819

GULF   OF   MEXICO

RAND MᶜNALLY

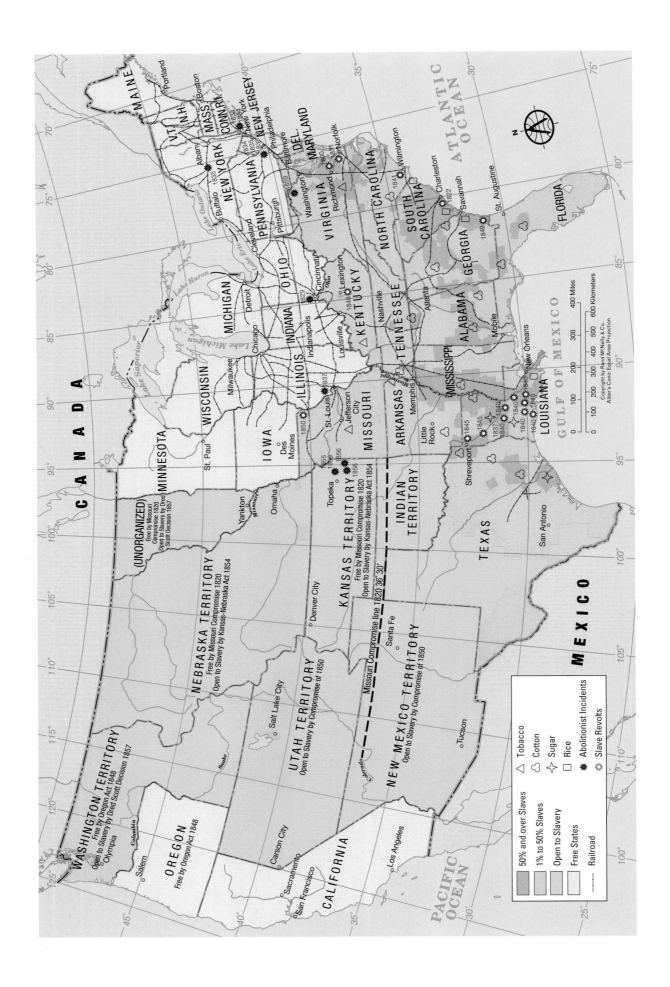

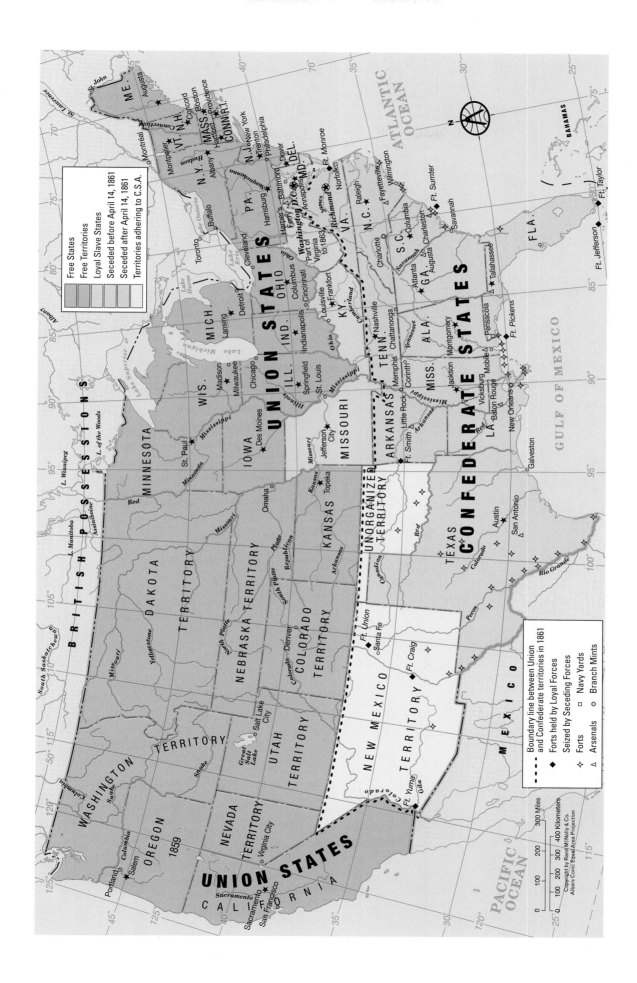

Free States
Free Territories
Loyal Slave States
Seceded before April 14, 1861
Seceded after April 14, 1861
Territories adhering to C.S.A.

- - - Boundary line between Union and Confederate territories in 1861
◆ Forts held by Loyal Forces
★ Seized by Seceding Forces
✦ Forts
△ Arsenals
◎ Navy Yards
◎ Branch Mints

Copyright by Rand McNally & Co.
Albers Conic Equal Area Projection

0   100   200   300 Miles
0   100 200 300 400 Kilometers

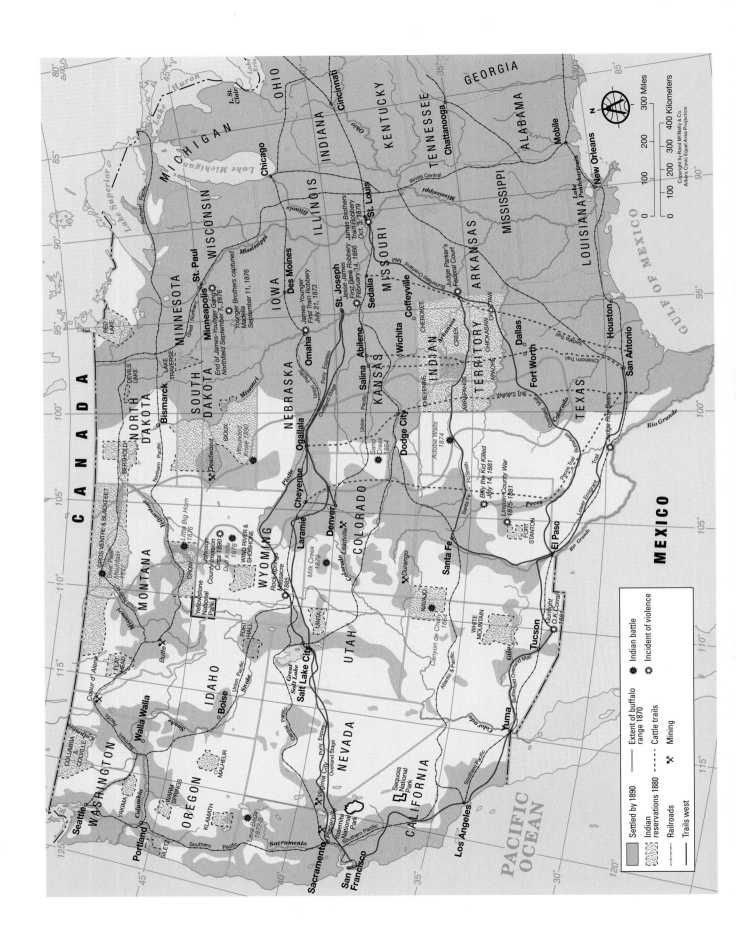

N

300 Miles
400 Kilometers

Copyright by Rand McNally & Co.
Albers Conic Equal Area Projection

0 100 200 300
0 100 200 300 400

CANADA

MEXICO

GULF OF MEXICO

PACIFIC OCEAN

GEORGIA

ALABAMA

MISSISSIPPI

LOUISIANA

TENNESSEE

KENTUCKY

OHIO

INDIANA

ILLINOIS

MICHIGAN

WISCONSIN

MINNESOTA

IOWA

MISSOURI

ARKANSAS

TEXAS

NORTH DAKOTA

SOUTH DAKOTA

NEBRASKA

KANSAS

OKLAHOMA

INDIAN TERRITORY

MONTANA

WYOMING

COLORADO

NEW MEXICO

IDAHO

UTAH

ARIZONA

NEVADA

CALIFORNIA

OREGON

WASHINGTON

Mobile
New Orleans
Houston
San Antonio
Dallas
Fort Worth
El Paso
Tucson
Yuma
Los Angeles
San Francisco
Sacramento
Portland
Seattle
Walla Walla
Boise
Salt Lake City
Denver
Santa Fe
Durango
Leadville
Laramie
Cheyenne
Ogallala
Omaha
Des Moines
St. Joseph
St. Louis
Sedalia
Coffeyville
Wichita
Salina
Abilene
Dodge City
Chicago
St. Paul
Minneapolis
Bismarck
Butte
Cincinnati
Chattanooga

Chicago

New Orleans

Houston

San Antonio

Dallas

Fort Worth

Little Big Horn 1876

Johnson County Invasion Circa 1890

Dull Knife 1876

WIND RIVER & SHOSHONE

CROW

Wounded Knee 1890

SIOUX

Deadwood

Sand Creek 1864

Adobe Walls 1874

Billy the Kid Killed July 14, 1881

Lincoln County War 1875–1881

Gunfight O.K. Corral 1881

Milk Creek 1879

Rock Springs Massacre 1885

Lava Beds 1872–3

Legend:
Settled by 1890
Indian reservations 1880
Railroads
Trails west
Extent of buffalo range 1870
Cattle trails
Indian battle
Incident of violence
Mining

Yellowstone National Park

Yosemite National Park

Sequoia National Park

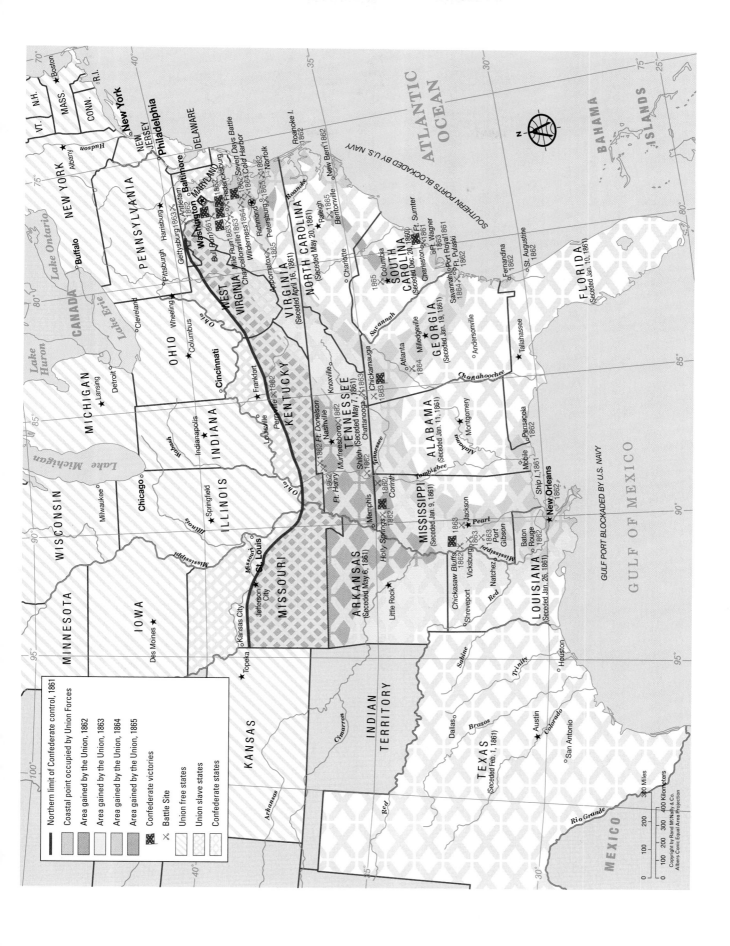

Map Legend

- Northern limit of Confederate control, 1861
- Coastal point occupied by Union Forces
- Area gained by the Union, 1862
- Area gained by the Union, 1863
- Area gained by the Union, 1864
- Area gained by the Union, 1865
- Confederate victories
- × Battle Site
- Union free states
- Union slave states
- Confederate states

SOUTHERN PORTS BLOCKADED BY U.S. NAVY

GULF PORT BLOCKADED BY U.S. NAVY

ATLANTIC OCEAN

GULF OF MEXICO

BAHAMA ISLANDS

States and territories:

CANADA

MAINE

VT. N.H. MASS. R.I. CONN.

NEW YORK

PENNSYLVANIA

NEW JERSEY

DELAWARE

MARYLAND

WEST VIRGINIA

VIRGINIA (Seceded April 16, 1861)

NORTH CAROLINA (Seceded May 20, 1861)

SOUTH CAROLINA (Seceded Dec. 20, 1860)

GEORGIA (Seceded Jan. 19, 1861)

FLORIDA (Seceded Jan. 10, 1861)

ALABAMA (Seceded Jan. 11, 1861)

MISSISSIPPI (Seceded Jan. 9, 1861)

LOUISIANA (Seceded Jan. 26, 1861)

TEXAS (Seceded Feb. 1, 1861)

ARKANSAS (Seceded May 6, 1861)

TENNESSEE (Seceded May 7, 1861)

KENTUCKY

MISSOURI

KANSAS

INDIAN TERRITORY

OHIO

INDIANA

ILLINOIS

MICHIGAN

WISCONSIN

MINNESOTA

IOWA

Cities and places:

Boston, Albany, Buffalo, New York, Philadelphia, Baltimore, Washington, Harrisburg, Pittsburgh, Cleveland, Columbus, Cincinnati, Frankfort, Louisville, Indianapolis, Springfield, Chicago, Milwaukee, Lansing, Detroit, Des Moines, Topeka, Kansas City, St. Louis, Jefferson City, Little Rock, Memphis, Nashville, Knoxville, Chattanooga, Raleigh, Charlotte, Columbia, Charleston, Savannah, Milledgeville, Atlanta, Andersonville, Montgomery, Mobile, Pensacola, New Orleans, Baton Rouge, Natchez, Jackson, Vicksburg, Port Gibson, Shreveport, Houston, Dallas, Austin, San Antonio, Tallahassee, Fernandina, St. Augustine, Norfolk, Richmond, Wheeling

Battles / events (with dates):

Gettysburg 1863, Antietam 1862, Bull Run 1861, Fredericksburg, Chancellorsville 1863, Wilderness 1864, Seven Days Battle 1862, Cold Harbor 1864, Petersburg 1864-1865, Appomattox 1865, Roanoke I. 1862, New Bern 1862, Bentonville 1865, Ft. Sumter, Ft. Wagner 1863, Port Royal 1861, Ft. Pulaski 1862, Perryville 1862, Ft. Donelson 1862, Murfreesboro 1862, Ft. Henry 1862, Shiloh 1862, Corinth 1862, Chickamauga 1863, Holly Springs 1862, Chickasaw Bluffs 1862, Vicksburg 1863, Port Gibson 1863, Ship I. 1861

Rivers:

Hudson, Ohio, Wabash, Illinois, Mississippi, Missouri, Tennessee, Tombigbee, Chattahoochee, Savannah, Roanoke, Pearl, Red, Sabine, Trinity, Brazos, Colorado, Rio Grande, Cimarron, Arkansas

Lake Ontario, Lake Erie, Lake Huron, Lake Michigan

MEXICO

Scale: 0 100 200 300 400 Kilometers / 0 100 200 300 Miles

Albers Conic Equal Area Projection

Copyright by Rand McNally & Co.

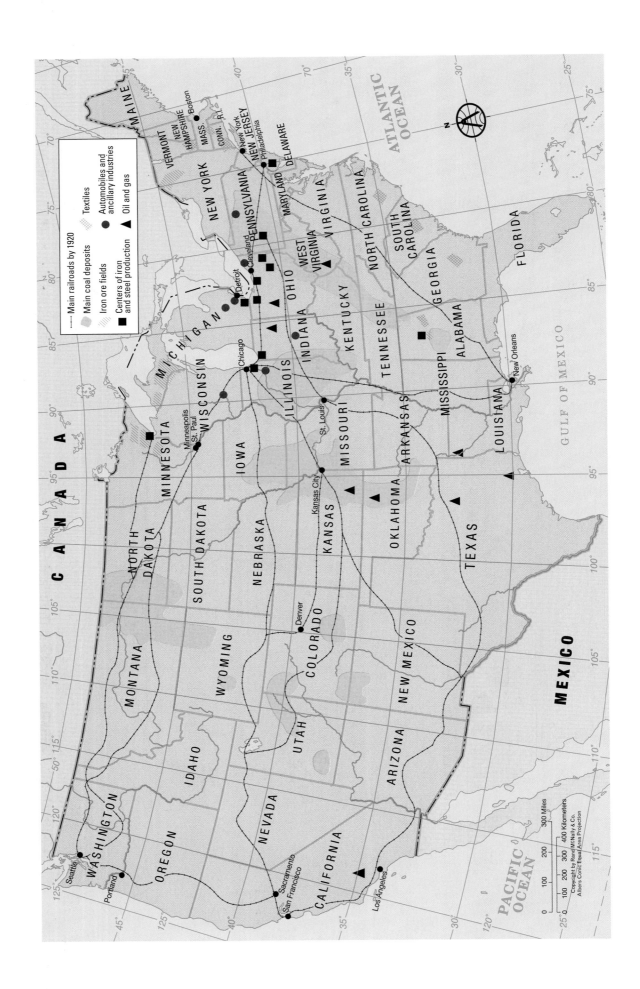

Main railroads by 1920
Main coal deposits
Iron ore fields
Centers of iron
and steel production

Textiles
Automobiles and
ancillary industries
Oil and gas

Copyright by Rand McNally & Co.
Albers Conic Equal Area Projection

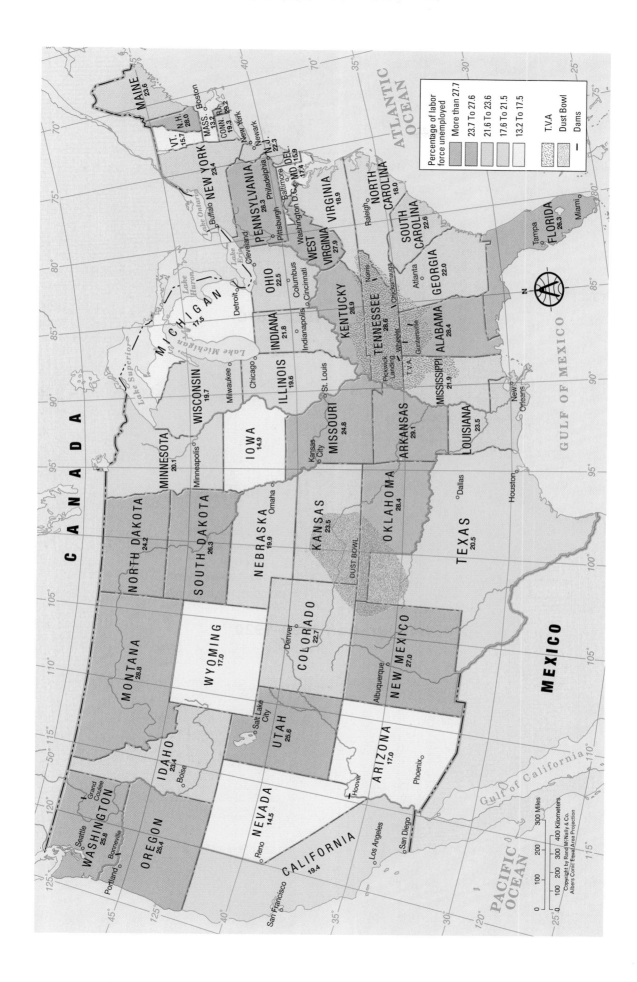

Percentage of labor force unemployed

More than 27.7
23.7 To 27.6
21.6 To 23.6
17.6 To 21.5
13.2 To 17.5

T.V.A
Dust Bowl
Dams

MAINE 23.6
VT. 15.7
N. H. 28.0
MASS. 13.2
CONN. 19.3
R.I. 29.2
Boston
NEW YORK 23.4
New York
Newark
N.J. 22.3
Buffalo
PENNSYLVANIA 28.3
Philadelphia
Pittsburgh
Baltimore
Washington D.C.
DEL. 15.9
MD. 17.4
WEST VIRGINIA 27.9
VIRGINIA 18.9
Raleigh
NORTH CAROLINA 18.0
SOUTH CAROLINA 22.6
GEORGIA 22.0
Atlanta
FLORIDA 26.3
Miami
Tampa

Cleveland
Columbus
Cincinnati
Detroit
OHIO 22.5
MICHIGAN 17.5
INDIANA 21.8
Indianapolis
KENTUCKY 28.9
TENNESSEE 28.6
Norris
Chickamauga
Wheeler
Guntersville
ALABAMA 28.4
Pickwick Landing
T.V.A.
MISSISSIPPI 21.9
New Orleans
LOUISIANA 23.5

WISCONSIN 19.7
Milwaukee
Chicago
ILLINOIS 19.6
St. Louis
MISSOURI 24.8
ARKANSAS 29.1
Kansas City
IOWA 14.9
MINNESOTA 20.1
Minneapolis
Omaha
NEBRASKA 19.9
KANSAS 23.5
OKLAHOMA 28.4
Dallas
Houston
TEXAS 20.5
DUST BOWL

NORTH DAKOTA 24.2
SOUTH DAKOTA 26.3
WYOMING 17.0
COLORADO 22.7
Denver
NEW MEXICO 27.0
Albuquerque

MONTANA 28.8
Grand Coulee
Seattle
Bonneville
Portland
WASHINGTON 25.8
OREGON 25.4
IDAHO 23.4
Boise
Salt Lake City
UTAH 25.6
NEVADA 14.5
Reno
ARIZONA 17.0
Phoenix
Hoover
San Diego
Los Angeles
San Francisco
CALIFORNIA 19.4

C A N A D A

M E X I C O

ATLANTIC OCEAN

GULF OF MEXICO

PACIFIC OCEAN

Gulf of California

Lake Superior
Lake Michigan
Lake Huron
Lake Erie
Lake Ontario

0 100 200 300 Miles
0 100 200 300 400 Kilometers
Copyright by Rand McNally & Co.
Albers Conic Equal Area Projection

N

RAND McNALLY

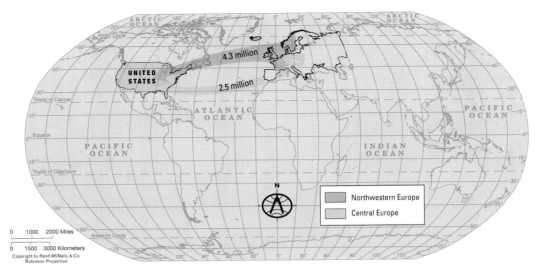

Immigration 1820–1870

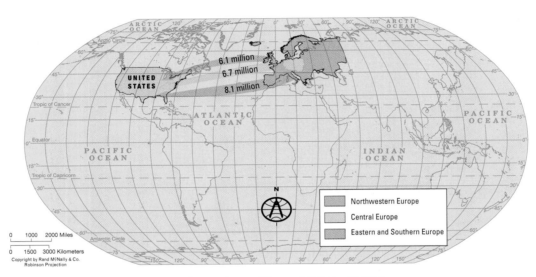

Immigration 1880–1920

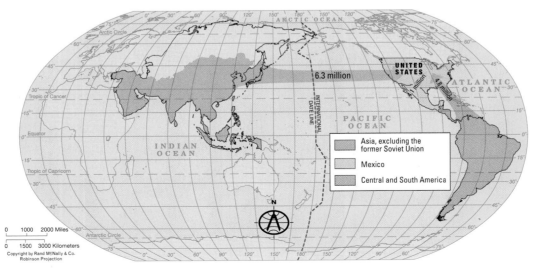

Immigration 1960s–1990s

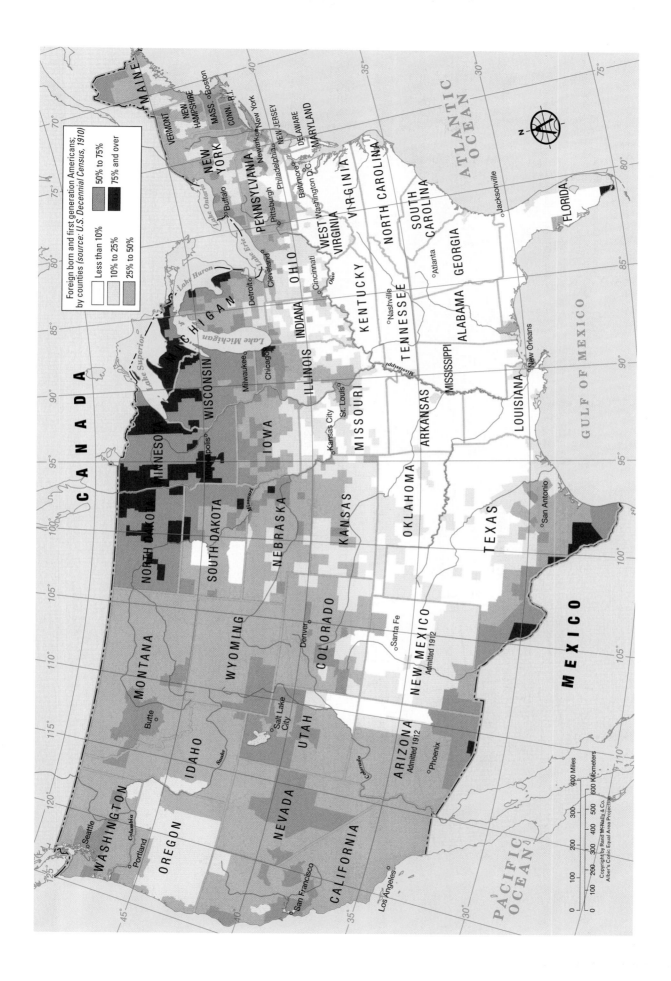

Foreign born and first generation Americans;
by counties (source: *U.S. Decennial Census, 1910*)

Less than 10%
10% to 25%
25% to 50%
50% to 75%
75% and over

ATLANTIC OCEAN

PACIFIC OCEAN

GULF OF MEXICO

CANADA

MEXICO

0   100   200   300   400 Miles
0   100   200   300   400   500   600 Kilometers

RAND MCNALLY

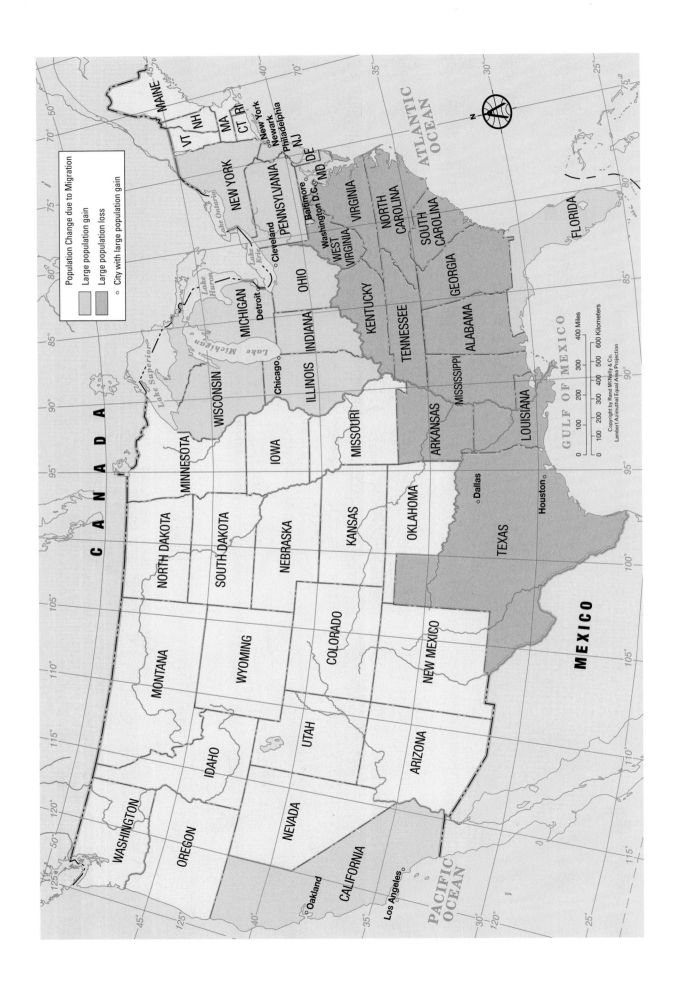

African-American Migration 1940–1970

Population Change due to Migration

Large population gain

Large population loss

○ City with large population gain

ATLANTIC OCEAN

MAINE

VT
NH
MA
CT RI

New York
Newark
Philadelphia
NJ
DE
MD
Baltimore
Washington D.C.

NEW YORK

PENNSYLVANIA

WEST VIRGINIA
VIRGINIA

NORTH CAROLINA

SOUTH CAROLINA

GEORGIA

FLORIDA

Lake Ontario

Cleveland

OHIO

KENTUCKY

TENNESSEE

ALABAMA

Lake Erie

MICHIGAN
Detroit

INDIANA

Lake Huron

Lake Michigan

Lake Superior

WISCONSIN

Chicago

ILLINOIS

MISSOURI

ARKANSAS

MISSISSIPPI

LOUISIANA

GULF OF MEXICO

CANADA

MINNESOTA

IOWA

NORTH DAKOTA

SOUTH DAKOTA

NEBRASKA

KANSAS

OKLAHOMA

Dallas

Houston

TEXAS

MEXICO

NEW MEXICO

COLORADO

WYOMING

MONTANA

IDAHO

UTAH

ARIZONA

NEVADA

WASHINGTON

OREGON

CALIFORNIA

Oakland

Los Angeles

PACIFIC OCEAN

0   100   200   300   400 Miles
0   100   200   300   400   500   600 Kilometers

Copyright by Rand McNally & Co.
Lambert Azimuthal Equal Area Projection

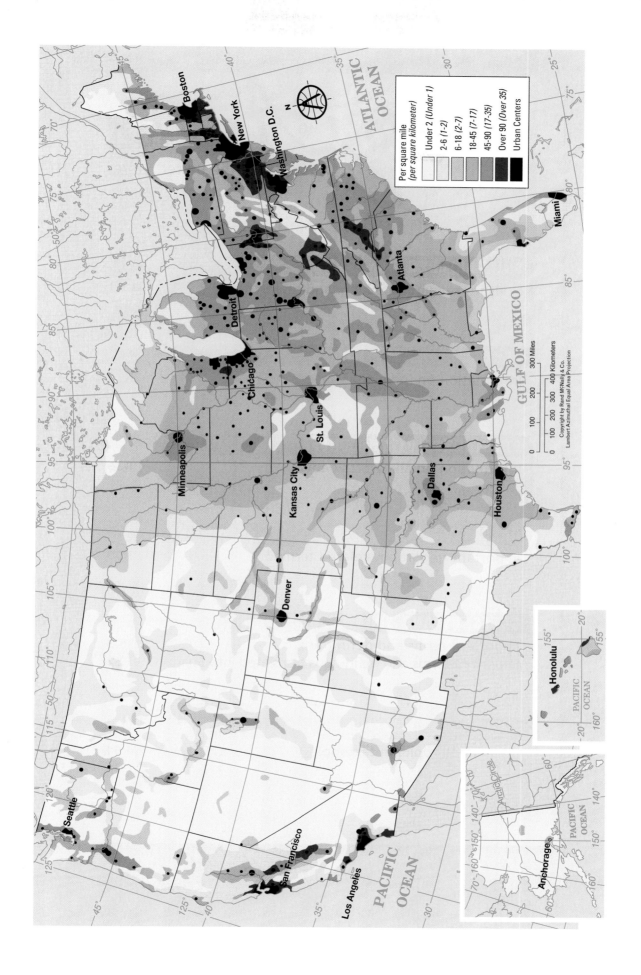

ATLANTIC OCEAN

Boston
New York
Washington D.C.

Miami

Atlanta

Detroit

Chicago

St. Louis

Minneapolis

Kansas City

Dallas

Houston

GULF OF MEXICO

Denver

Seattle

San Francisco

Los Angeles

PACIFIC OCEAN

Per square mile
(per square kilometer)

Under 2 (Under 1)
2-6 (1-2)
6-18 (2-7)
18-45 (7-17)
45-90 (17-35)
Over 90 (Over 35)
Urban Centers

300 Miles
400 Kilometers

Copyright by Rand McNally & Co.
Lambert Azimuthal Equal Area Projection

Honolulu
PACIFIC OCEAN

Anchorage
Arctic Circle
PACIFIC OCEAN

RAND McNALLY

A39

Creating America

A History of the United States

Table of Contents

1.1 Summarizing

Defining the Skill

When you **summarize,** you restate a paragraph, passage, or chapter in fewer words. You include only the main ideas and most important details. It is important to use your own words when summarizing.

Applying the Skill

The passage below tells about Harriet Tubman, a prominent member of the Underground Railroad. She helped runaway slaves to freedom. Use the strategies listed below to help you summarize the passage.

How to Summarize

Strategy ① Look for topic sentences stating the main idea. These are often at the beginning of a section or paragraph. Briefly restate each main idea—in your own words.

Strategy ② Include key facts and any numbers, dates, amounts, or percentages from the text.

Strategy ③ After writing your summary, review it to see that you have included only the most important details.

HARRIET TUBMAN

① One of the most famous conductors on the Underground Railroad was Harriet Tubman. ② Born into slavery in Maryland, the 13-year-old Tubman once tried to save another slave from punishment. The angry overseer fractured Tubman's skull with a two-pound weight. She suffered fainting spells for the rest of her life but did not let that stop her from working for freedom. When she was 25, Tubman learned that her owner was about to sell her. Instead, ② she escaped.

After her escape, ② Harriet Tubman made 19 dangerous journeys to free enslaved persons. The tiny woman carried a pistol to frighten off slave hunters and medicine to quiet crying babies. Her enemies offered $40,000 for her capture, but ② no one caught her. "I never run my train off the track and I never lost a passenger," she proudly declared. Among the people she saved were her parents.

Write a Summary

You can write your summary in a paragraph. The paragraph at right summarizes the passage you just read.

③ Harriet Tubman was one of the most famous conductors on the Underground Railroad. She had been a slave, but she escaped. She later made 19 dangerous journeys to free other slaves. She was never captured.

Practicing the Skill

Turn to Chapter 5, Section 1, "Miners, Ranchers, and Cowhands." Read "The Rise of the Cattle Industry" and write a paragraph summarizing the passage.

1.2 Taking Notes

Defining the Skill

When you **take notes,** you write down the important ideas and details of a paragraph, passage, or chapter. A chart or an outline can help you organize your notes to use in the future.

Applying the Skill

The following passage describes President Washington's cabinet. Use the strategies listed below to help you take notes on the passage.

How to Take and Organize Notes

Strategy ❶ Look at the title to find the main topic of the passage.

Strategy ❷ Identify the main ideas and details of the passage. Then summarize the main idea and details in your notes.

Strategy ❸ Identify key terms and define them. The term *cabinet* is shown in boldface type and underlined; both techniques signal that it is a key term.

Strategy ❹ In your notes, use abbreviations to save time and space. You can abbreviate words such as *department (dept.), secretary (sec.), United States (U.S.),* and *president (pres.)* to save time and space.

> **❶ WASHINGTON'S CABINET**
>
> **❷** The Constitution gave Congress the task of creating departments to help the president lead the nation. The **❷** president had the power to appoint the heads of these departments, which became his **❸** **cabinet.**
>
> Congress created three departments. Washington chose talented people to run them. **❷** For secretary of war, he picked Henry Knox, a trusted general during the Revolution. **❷** For secretary of state, Washington chose Thomas Jefferson. He had been serving as ambassador to France. The State Department oversaw U.S. foreign relations. For secretary of the treasury, Washington turned to the brilliant **❷** Alexander Hamilton.

Make a Chart

Making a chart can help you take notes on a passage. The chart below contains notes from the passage you just read.

❷ Item	Notes
1. ❸ cabinet	heads of ❹ depts.; ❹ pres. appoints heads
a. War Dept.	Henry Knox; ❹ sec. of war; former Revolutionary War general
b. State Dept.	Thomas Jefferson; sec. of state; oversees relations between ❹ U.S. and other countries
c. Treasury Dept.	Alexander Hamilton; sec. of the treasury

Practicing the Skill

Turn to Chapter 10, Section 1, "War Breaks Out in Europe." Read "America's Path to War" and use a chart to take notes on the passage.

1.3 Sequencing Events

Defining the Skill

Sequence is the order in which events follow one another. By being able to follow the sequence of events through history, you can get an accurate sense of the relationship among events.

Applying the Skill

The following passage describes the sequence of events involved in Britain's plan to capture the Hudson River Valley during the American Revolution. Use the strategies listed below to help you follow the sequence of events.

How to Find the Sequence of Events

Strategy ① Look for specific dates provided in the text. If several months within a year are included, the year is usually not repeated.

Strategy ② Look for clues about time that allow you to order events according to sequence. Words such as *day, week, month,* or *year* may help to sequence the events.

> **BRITAIN'S STRATEGY**
>
> Burgoyne captured Fort Ticonderoga in ① July 1777. From there, it was 25 miles to the Hudson River, which ran to Albany. ② Burgoyne took three weeks to reach the Hudson. On ① August 3, Burgoyne received a message from Howe. He would not be coming north, Howe wrote, because he had decided to invade Pennsylvania to try to capture Philadelphia and General Washington. "Success be ever with you," Howe's message said. But General Burgoyne needed Howe's soldiers, not his good wishes. Howe did invade Pennsylvania. In ① September 1777, he defeated —but did not capture—Washington at the Battle of Brandywine.

Make a Time Line

Making a time line can help you sequence events. The time line below shows the sequence of events in the passage you just read.

July 1777: Burgoyne captures Fort Ticonderoga.

Three weeks after the capture of Fort Ticonderoga: Burgoyne reaches the Hudson.

August 3, 1777: Howe writes that he will not join Burgoyne.

September 1777: Howe defeats Washington at Brandywine.

Practicing the Skill

Turn to Chapter 15, Section 2, "Kennedy, Johnson, and Civil Rights." Read "Fighting for Voting Rights" and make a time line showing the sequence of events in that passage.

1.4 Finding Main Ideas

Defining the Skill

The **main idea** is a statement that summarizes the main point of a speech, an article, a section of a book, or a paragraph. Main ideas can be stated or unstated. The main idea of a paragraph is often stated in the first or last sentence. If it is the first sentence, it is followed by sentences that support that main idea. If it is the last sentence, the details build up to the main idea. To find an unstated idea, you must use the details of the paragraph as clues.

Applying the Skill

The following paragraph describes the role of women in the American Revolution. Use the strategies listed below to help you identify the main idea.

How to Find the Main Idea

Strategy ① Identify what you think may be the stated main idea. Check the first and last sentences of the paragraph to see if either could be the stated main idea.

Strategy ② Identify details that support that idea. Some details explain the main idea. Others give examples of what is stated in the main idea.

> ### WOMEN IN THE REVOLUTION
>
> ① Many women tried to help the army. Martha Washington and other wives followed their husbands to army camps. ② The wives cooked, did laundry, and nursed sick or wounded soldiers. ② A few women even helped to fight. ② Mary Hays earned the nickname "Molly Pitcher" by carrying water to tired soldiers during a battle. ② Deborah Sampson dressed as a man, enlisted, and fought in several engagements.

Make a Chart

Making a chart can help you identify the main idea and details in a passage or paragraph. The chart below identifies the main idea and details in the paragraph you just read.

Main Idea: Women helped the army during the Revolution.

Detail: They cooked and did laundry.
Detail: They nursed the wounded and sick soldiers.
Detail: They helped to fight.
Detail: One woman, Molly Pitcher, carried water to soldiers during battles.

Practicing the Skill

Turn to Chapter 7, Section 1, "Cities Grow and Change." Read "Technology Changes City Life" and create a chart that identifies the main idea and the supporting details.

1.5 Categorizing

Defining the Skill

To **categorize** is to sort people, objects, ideas, or other information into groups, called categories. Historians categorize information to help them identify and understand patterns in historical events.

Applying the Skill

The following passage contains information about the reasons people went west during the mid-1800s. Use the strategies listed below to help you categorize information.

How to Categorize

Strategy ① First, decide what kind of information needs to be categorized. Decide what the passage is about and how that information can be sorted into categories.
   For example, find the different motives people had for moving west.

Strategy ② Then find out what the categories will be. To find why many different groups of people moved west, look for clue words such as *some, other,* and *another.*

Strategy ③ Once you have chosen the categories, sort information into them. Of the people who went west, which ones had which motives?

THE LURE OF THE WEST

① People had many different motives for going west. ② One motive was to make money. ② *Some* people called speculators bought huge areas of land and made great profits by selling it to thousands of settlers. ② *Other* settlers included farmers who dreamed of owning their own farms in the West because land was difficult to acquire in the East. ② *Another* group to move west was merchants. They hoped to earn money by selling items that farmers needed. Finally, ② *some* people went west for religious reasons. These people included ② missionaries, who wanted to convert the Native Americans to Christianity, and Mormons, who wanted a place where they could practice their faith without interference.

Make a Chart

Making a chart can help you categorize information. You should have as many columns as you have categories. The chart below shows how the information from the passage you just read can be categorized.

③

Motives	Money	Land	Religion
Groups	• speculators • merchants	• farmers	• missionaries • Mormons

Practicing the Skill

Turn to Chapter 12, Section 3, "Life During the Depression." Read "Minorities and the Depression" and make a chart in which you categorize the experience of African Americans, Mexican Americans, and Native Americans during the Depression.

1.6 Making Public Speeches

Defining the Skill

A speech is a talk given in public to an audience. Some speeches are given to persuade the audience to think or act in a certain way, or to support a cause. You can learn how to **make public speeches** effectively by analyzing great speeches in history.

Applying the Skill

The following is an excerpt from the "I Have a Dream" speech delivered by Martin Luther King, Jr., in 1963 in Washington, D.C. Use the strategies listed below to help you analyze King's speech and prepare a speech of your own.

How to Analyze and Prepare a Speech

Strategy ❶ Choose one central idea or theme and organize your speech to support it. King organized his speech around his dream of equality.

Strategy ❷ Use words or images that will win over your audience. King referred to the Declaration of Independence when he used the words "all men are created equal."

Strategy ❸ Repeat words or images to drive home your main point—as if it is the "hook" of a pop song. King repeats the phrase "I have a dream."

> **I HAVE A DREAM**
>
> ❶ I have a dream that one day this nation will rise up and live out the true meaning of its creed—we hold these truths to be ❷ self-evident that all men are created equal.
>
> ❸ I have a dream that one day on the red hills of Georgia the sons of former slaves and the sons of former slave owners will be able to sit down together at the table of brotherhood.
>
> ❸ I have a dream that my four little children will one day live in a nation where they will not be judged by the color of their skin but by the content of their character.
>
> ❸ I have a dream today!

Make an Outline

Making an outline like the one to the right will help you make an effective public speech.

Practicing the Skill

Turn to Chapter 8, Section 1, "Roosevelt and Progressivism." Read the section and choose a topic for a speech. First, make an outline like the one to the right to organize your ideas. Exchange your outline with a partner. Organize and interpret information from that outline to write a speech.

Title: I Have a Dream

I. *Introduce Theme:* I have a dream
　A. This nation will live up to its creed
　B. Quote from the Declaration of Independence: that all men are created equal

II. *Repeat theme:* I have a dream
　A. Sons of former slaves and slave owners will sit together in brotherhood
　B. My four children will be judged by their character, not by their skin color

III. *Conclude:* I have a dream

1.7 Writing for Social Studies

Defining the Skill

Writing for social studies requires you to describe an idea, situation, or event. Often, social studies writing takes a stand on a particular issue or tries to make a specific point. To successfully describe an event or make a point, your writing needs to be clear, concise, and factually accurate.

Applying the Skill

The following passage describes Stephen A. Douglas. Notice how the strategies below helped the writer explain Douglas's historical importance.

How to Write for Social Studies

Strategy ❶ Focus on your topic. Be sure that you clearly state the main idea of your piece so that your readers know what you intend to say.

Strategy ❷ Collect and organize your facts. Collect accurate information about your topic to support the main idea you are trying to make. Use your information to build a logical case to prove your point.

Strategy ❸ To express your ideas clearly, use standard grammar, spelling, sentence structure, and punctuation when writing for social studies. Proofread your work to make sure it is well organized and grammatically correct.

STEPHEN A. DOUGLAS, 1813–1861

❶ Stephen A. Douglas was one of the most powerful members of Congress in the 1850s. In fact, ❷ he was called the "Little Giant" because he commanded great respect even though he was only five feet four inches tall. The most important issue that Douglas faced in his career was slavery in the territories. ❷ He played a key role in the passage of the Compromise of 1850 as well as the Kansas–Nebraska Act, which addressed this issue. In 1858, his famous debates with Abraham Lincoln also focused on slavery in the territories. ❷ When Douglas ran for president in 1860, his position on slavery was critical to his defeat.

Practicing the Skill

Turn to Chapter 9, Section 3, "U.S. Involvement Overseas." Read the section and use the strategies above to write your answer to Question 4 on page 271.

2.1 Analyzing Points of View

Defining the Skill

Analyzing points of view means looking closely at a person's arguments to understand the reasons behind that person's beliefs. The goal of analyzing a point of view is to understand a historical figure's thoughts, opinions, and biases about a topic.

Applying the Skill

The following passage describes the Panic of 1837 and two politicians' points of view about it. Use the strategies listed below to help you analyze their points of view.

How to Analyze Points of View

Strategy ❶ Look for statements that show you a person's view on an issue. For example, Van Buren said he believed the economy would improve if he took no action. Clay thought the government should do something to help the people.

Strategy ❷ Use information about people to validate them as sources and understand why they might disagree. What do you know about Clay and Van Buren that might explain their own biases and disagreements with each other?

Strategy ❸ Write a summary that explains why different people took different positions on the issue.

> ### THE PANIC OF 1837
>
> The Panic of 1837 caused severe hardship. People had little money, so manufacturers had few customers for their goods. Almost 90 percent of factories in the East closed. Jobless workers could not afford food or rent. Many people went hungry.
>
> ❶ Whig senator Henry Clay wanted the government to do something to help the people. ❶ President Van Buren, a Democrat, disagreed. He believed that the economy would improve if left alone. He argued that "the less government interferes with private pursuits the better for the general prosperity." Many Americans blamed Van Buren for the Panic, though he had taken office only weeks before it started. The continuing depression made it difficult for him to win reelection in 1840.

Make a Diagram

Using a diagram can help you analyze points of view. The diagram below analyzes the views of Clay and Van Buren in the passage you just read.

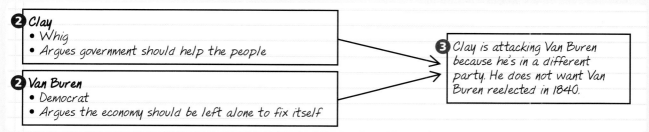

❷ **Clay**
- Whig
- Argues government should help the people

❷ **Van Buren**
- Democrat
- Argues the economy should be left alone to fix itself

❸ Clay is attacking Van Buren because he's in a different party. He does not want Van Buren reelected in 1840.

Practicing the Skill

Turn to Chapter 5, Section 4, "Farming and Populism." Read "The Election of 1896," paying attention to the positions of William McKinley and William Jennings Bryan. Use their language, information from other sources, and information about each man to validate them as sources. Then make a chart to analyze their different points of view on the gold and silver.

2.2 Comparing and Contrasting

Defining the Skill

Comparing means looking at the similarities and differences between two or more things. **Contrasting** means examining only the differences between them. Historians compare and contrast events, personalities, behaviors, beliefs, and situations in order to understand them.

Applying the Skill

The following paragraph describes the American and British troops during the Revolutionary War. Use the strategies listed below to help you compare and contrast these two armies.

How to Compare and Contrast

Strategy ① Look for two aspects of the subject that may be compared and contrasted. This passage compares the British and American troops to show why the Americans won the war.

Strategy ② To contrast, look for clue words that show how two things differ. Clue words include *by contrast, however, except,* and *yet.*

Strategy ③ To find similarities, look for clue words indicating that two things are alike. Clue words include *both, like, as,* and *similarly.*

> **WHY THE AMERICANS WON**
>
> ① By their persistence, the Americans defeated the British even though they faced many obstacles. The Americans lacked training and experience. They were often short of supplies and weapons. ② *By contrast,* the British forces ranked among the best trained in the world. They were experienced and well-supplied professional soldiers. ② *Yet,* the Americans also had advantages that enabled them to win. These advantages over the British were better leadership, foreign aid, a knowledge of the land, and motivation. Although ③ *both* the British and the Americans were fighting for their lives, ② the Americans were also fighting for their property and their dream of liberty.

Make a Venn Diagram

Making a Venn diagram will help you identify similarities and differences between two things. In the overlapping area, list characteristics shared by both subjects. Then, in the separate ovals, list the characteristics of each subject not shared by the other. This Venn diagram compares and contrasts the British and American soldiers.

American Soldiers:
- lacked experience and training
- short of supplies and weapons
- had better leadership
- received foreign aid
- had knowledge of the land
- fought for liberty and property

Both: fought for their lives

British Soldiers:
- best trained in the world
- experienced
- well-supplied

Practicing the Skill

Turn to Chapter 5, Section 3, "Life in the West." Read "The Real West" and make a Venn diagram showing the similarities and differences between the real West and the myth of the West.

2.3 Analyzing Causes; Recognizing Effects

Defining the Skill

A **cause** is an action in history that makes something happen. An **effect** is the historical event that is the result of the cause. A single event may have several causes. It is also possible for one cause to result in several effects. Historians identify cause-and-effect relationships to help them understand why historical events took place.

Applying the Skill

The following paragraph describes events that caused changes in Puritan New England. Use the strategies listed below to help you identify the cause-and-effect relationships.

How to Analyze Causes and Recognize Effects

Strategy ❶ Ask why an action took place. Ask yourself a question about the title and topic sentence, such as, "What caused changes in Puritan society?"

Strategy ❷ Look for effects. Ask yourself, "What happened?" (the effect). Then ask, "Why did it happen?" (the cause). For example, What caused the decline of Puritan religion in New England?

Strategy ❸ Look for clue words that signal causes, such as *cause* and *led to.*

Strategy ❹ One way to practice recognizing effects is to make predictions about the consequences that will result from particular actions. Then, as you read, look to see if your predictions were accurate.

❶ **CHANGES IN PURITAN SOCIETY**

❶ The early 1700s saw many changes in New England society. ❷ One of the most important changes was the gradual decline of the Puritan religion in New England. There were a number of reasons for that decline.

❸ One *cause* of this decline was the increasing competition from other religious groups. Baptists and Anglicans established churches in Massachusetts and Connecticut, where Puritans had once been the most powerful group. ❸ Political changes also *led to* a weakening of the Puritan community. In 1691, a new royal charter for Massachusetts granted the vote based on property ownership instead of church membership.

Make a Diagram

Using a diagram can help you understand causes and effects. The diagram below shows two causes and an effect for the passage you just read.

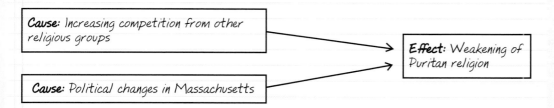

Cause: Increasing competition from other religious groups

Cause: Political changes in Massachusetts

Effect: Weakening of Puritan religion

Practicing the Skill

Turn to Chapter 10, Section 1, "War Breaks Out in Europe." Read "America's Path to War" and make a diagram about the causes that led the United States to enter World War I.

2.4 Making Inferences

Defining the Skill

Inferences are ideas that the author has not directly stated. **Making inferences** involves reading between the lines to interpret the information you read. You can make inferences by studying what is stated and using your common sense and previous knowledge.

Applying the Skill

The passage below describes the strengths and weaknesses of the North and the South as the Civil War began. Use the strategies listed below to help you make inferences from the passage.

How to Make Inferences

Strategy ① Read to find statements of facts and ideas. Knowing the facts will give you a good basis for making inferences.

Strategy ② Use your knowledge, logic, and common sense to make inferences that are based on facts. Ask yourself, "What does the author want me to understand?" For example, from the facts about population, you can make the inference that the North would have a larger army than the South. See other inferences in the chart below.

> ### ADVANTAGES OF THE NORTH AND THE SOUTH
>
> The North had more people and resources than the South. ① The North had about 22 million people. ① The South had roughly 9 million, of whom about 3.5 million were slaves. In addition, ① the North had more than 80 percent of the nation's factories and almost all of the shipyards and naval power. The South had some advantages, too. ① It had able generals, such as Robert E. Lee. ① It also had the advantage of fighting a defensive war. Soldiers defending their homes have more will to fight than invaders do.

Make a Chart

Making a chart will help you organize information and make logical inferences. The chart below organizes information from the passage you just read.

① Stated Facts and Ideas	② Inferences
The North had about 22 million people. The Confederacy had about 9 million.	The North would have a larger army than the South.
The North had more factories, naval power, and shipyards.	The North could provide more weapons, ammunition, and ships for the war.
The Confederacy had excellent generals.	The Confederacy had better generals, which would help it overcome other disadvantages.
The Confederacy was fighting a defensive war.	Confederate soldiers would fight harder because they were defending their homes and families.

Practicing the Skill

Turn to Chapter 14, Section 3, "The Fifties." Read "The American Dream in the Fifties" and use a chart like the one above to make inferences about suburban life in the 1950s.

2.5 Drawing Conclusions

Defining the Skill

Drawing conclusions means analyzing what you have read and forming an opinion about its meaning. To draw conclusions, look at the facts and then use your own common sense and experience to decide what the facts mean.

Applying the Skill

The following passage presents information about the Intolerable Acts and the colonists' reactions to them. Use the strategies listed below to help you draw conclusions about those acts.

How to Draw Conclusions

Strategy ❶ Read carefully to identify and understand all the facts, or statements, that can be proven true.

Strategy ❷ List the facts in a diagram and review them. Use your own experiences and common sense to understand how the facts relate to each other.

Strategy ❸ After reviewing the facts, write down the conclusion you have drawn about them.

> ### THE INTOLERABLE ACTS
>
> ❶ In 1774, Parliament passed a series of laws to punish the Massachusetts colony and serve as a warning to other colonies.
>
> ❶ These laws were so harsh that colonists called them the **Intolerable Acts.** One of the acts closed the port of Boston. Others banned committees of correspondence and allowed Britain to house troops wherever necessary.
>
> In 1773, Sam Adams had written, "I wish we could arouse the continent." ❶ The Intolerable Acts answered his wish. Other colonies immediately offered Massachusetts their support.

Make a Diagram

Making a diagram can help you draw conclusions. The diagram below shows how to organize facts and inferences to draw a conclusion about the passage you just read.

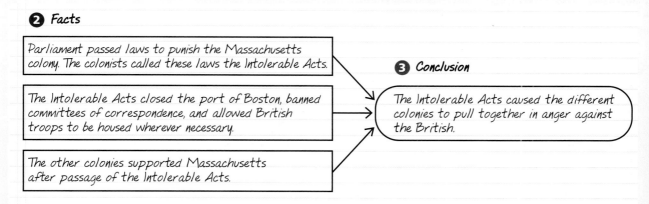

❷ Facts

- Parliament passed laws to punish the Massachusetts colony. The colonists called these laws the Intolerable Acts.
- The Intolerable Acts closed the port of Boston, banned committees of correspondence, and allowed British troops to be housed wherever necessary.
- The other colonies supported Massachusetts after passage of the Intolerable Acts.

❸ Conclusion

The Intolerable Acts caused the different colonies to pull together in anger against the British.

Practicing the Skill

Turn to Chapter 14, Section 1, "Peacetime Adjustments and the Cold War." Read "Fear of Communism at Home" and use the diagram above as a model to draw conclusions about Americans' attitudes toward communism.

2.6 Making Decisions

Defining the Skill

Making decisions involves choosing between two or more options, or courses of action. In most cases, decisions have consequences, or results. Sometimes decisions may lead to new problems. By understanding how historical figures made decisions, you can learn how to improve your decision-making skills.

Applying the Skill

The following passage describes Lincoln's decisions regarding federal forts after the Southern states seceded. Use the strategies listed below to help you analyze his decisions.

How to Make Decisions

Strategy ① Identify a decision that needs to be made. Think about what factors make the decision difficult.

Strategy ② Identify possible consequences of the decision. Remember that there can be more than one consequence to a decision.

Strategy ③ Identify the decision that was made.

Strategy ④ Identify actual consequences that resulted from the decision.

FIRST SHOTS AT FORT SUMTER

① Lincoln had to decide what to do about the forts in the South that remained under federal control. A Union garrison still held **Fort Sumter**, but it was running out of supplies. ② If Lincoln supplied the garrison, he risked war. ② If he withdrew the garrison, he would be giving in to the rebels. ③ Lincoln informed South Carolina that he was sending supply ships to Fort Sumter. ④ Confederate leaders decided to prevent the federal government from holding on to the fort by attacking before the supply ships arrived. No one was killed, but ④ the South's attack on Fort Sumter signaled the beginning of the Civil War.

Make a Flow Chart

A flow chart can help you identify the process of making a decision. The flow chart below shows the decision-making process in the passage you just read.

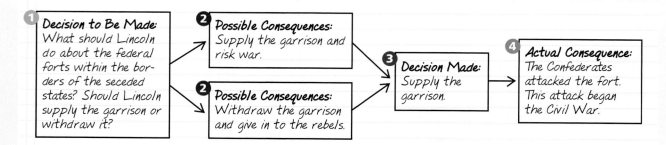

① Decision to Be Made: What should Lincoln do about the federal forts within the borders of the seceded states? Should Lincoln supply the garrison or withdraw it?

② Possible Consequences: Supply the garrison and risk war.

② Possible Consequences: Withdraw the garrison and give in to the rebels.

③ Decision Made: Supply the garrison.

④ Actual Consequence: The Confederates attacked the fort. This attack began the Civil War.

Practicing the Skill

Turn to Chapter 13, Section 3, "War in the Pacific." Read "Atomic Weapons End the War" and make a flow chart to identify a decision and its consequences described in that section.

2.7 Recognizing Propaganda

Defining the Skill

Propaganda is communication that aims to influence people's opinions, emotions, or actions. Propaganda is not always factual. Rather, it uses one-sided language or striking symbols to sway people's emotions. Modern advertising often uses propaganda. By thinking critically, you will avoid being swayed by propaganda.

Applying the Skill

The following political cartoon shows Andrew Jackson dressed as a king. Use the strategies listed below to help you understand how it works as propaganda.

How to Recognize Propaganda

Strategy ❶ Identify the aim, or purpose, of the cartoon. Point out the subject and explain the point of view.

Strategy ❷ Identify those images on the cartoon that viewers might respond to emotionally and identify the emotions.

Strategy ❸ Think critically about the cartoon. What facts has the cartoon ignored?

Make a Chart

Making a chart will help you think critically about a piece of propaganda. The chart below summarizes the information from the anti-Jackson cartoon.

❶	Identify Purpose	The cartoon portrays Jackson negatively by showing him as a king.
❷	Identify Emotions	The cartoonist knows that Americans like democracy. So he portrays Jackson as a king because kings are not usually supporters of democracy. He also shows Jackson standing on a torn U.S. Constitution—another thing that Americans love.
❸	Think Critically	The cartoon shows Jackson vetoing laws. But it ignores the fact that those actions were not against the Constitution. The president has the power to veto legislation. In this case, Jackson was exercising the power of the presidency, not acting like a king.

Practicing the Skill

Turn to Chapter 10, Section 3, "Life on the Homefront," and look at the war bond poster on page 290. Use a chart like the one above to think critically about the poster as an example of propaganda.

2.8 Identifying Facts and Opinions

Defining the Skill

Facts are events, dates, statistics, or statements that can be proved to be true. **Opinions** are the judgments, beliefs, and feelings of a writer or speaker. By identifying facts and opinions, you will be able to think critically when a person is trying to influence your own opinion.

Applying the Skill

The following passage tells about the Virginia Plan for legislative representation offered at the Constitutional Convention of 1787. Use the strategies listed below to help you distinguish facts from opinions.

How to Recognize Facts and Opinions

Strategy ① Look for specific information that can be proved or checked for accuracy.

Strategy ② Look for assertions, claims, and judgments that express opinions. In this case, one speaker's opinion is expressed in a direct quote.

Strategy ③ Think about whether statements can be checked for accuracy. Then, identify the facts and opinions in a chart.

ANTIFEDERALIST VIEWS

① Antifederalists published their views about the Constitution in newspapers and pamphlets. ① They thought the Constitution took too much power away from the states and did not protect the rights of the people. They charged that the Constitution would destroy American liberties. As one Antifederalist wrote, ② "It is truly astonishing that a set of men among ourselves should have had the [nerve] to attempt the destruction of our liberties."

Make a Chart

The chart below analyzes the facts and opinions from the passage above.

Statement	③ Can It Be Proved?	③ Fact or Opinion
Antifederalists published their views in newspapers and pamphlets.	Yes. Check newspapers and other historical documents.	Fact
They thought the Constitution took too much power away from the states.	Yes. Check newspapers and other historical documents.	Fact
It is astonishing that some Americans would try to destroy American liberties.	No. This cannot be proved. It is what one speaker believes.	Opinion

Practicing the Skill

Turn to Chapter 12, Section 4, "The Effects of the New Deal." Read the section entitled "Lasting Effects of the Depression." Make a chart in which you analyze key statements to determine whether they are facts or opinions.

2.9 Forming and Supporting Opinions

Defining the Skill

When you **form opinions,** you interpret and judge the importance of events and people in history. You should always **support your opinions** with facts, examples, and quotes.

Applying the Skill

The following passage describes events that followed the gold rush. Use the strategies listed below to form and support your opinions about the events.

How to Form and Support Opinions

Strategy ❶ Look for important information about the events. Information can include facts, quotations, and examples.

Strategy ❷ Form an opinion about the event by asking yourself questions about the information. For example, How important was the event? What were its effects?

Strategy ❸ Support your opinions with facts, quotations, and examples. If the facts do not support the opinion, then rewrite your opinion so it is supported by the facts.

THE IMPACT OF THE GOLD RUSH

By 1852, the gold rush was over. ❶ While it lasted, about 250,000 people flooded into California. ❶ This huge migration caused economic growth that changed California. ❶ The port city San Francisco grew to become a center of banking, manufacturing, shipping, and trade. ❶ However, the gold rush ruined many *Californios. Californios* are the Hispanic people of California. The newcomers did not respect *Californios,* their customs, or their legal rights. ❶ In many cases, Americans seized their property.

Native Americans suffered even more. ❶ Thousands died from diseases brought by the newcomers. ❶ Miners hunted down and killed thousands more. ❶ By 1870, California's Native American population had fallen from 150,000 to only about 30,000.

Make a Chart

Making a chart can help you organize your opinions and supporting facts. The following chart summarizes one possible opinion about the impact of the gold rush.

❷ Opinion	The effects of the gold rush were more negative than positive.
❸ Facts	Californios were not respected, and their land was stolen.
	Many Native Americans died from diseases, and others were killed by miners. Their population dropped from 150,000 to about 30,000.

Practicing the Skill

Turn to Chapter 15, Section 3, "The Equal Rights Struggle Expands." Read "The Women's Movement" and form your own opinion about the Equal Rights Amendment. Make a chart like the one above to summarize your opinion and the supporting facts and examples.

2.10 Identifying and Solving Problems

Defining the Skill

Identifying problems means finding and understanding the difficulties faced by a particular group of people during a certain time. **Solving problems** means understanding how people tried to remedy those problems. By studying how people solved problems in the past, you can learn ways to solve problems today.

Applying the Skill

The following paragraph describes problems that the Constitutional Convention faced on the issues of taxation, representation, and slavery. Use the strategies listed below to help you see how the Founders tried to solve these problems.

How to Identify Problems and Solutions

Strategy ❶ Look for the difficulties, or problems, people faced.

Strategy ❷ Consider how the problem affected people with different points of view. For example, the main problem described here was how to count the population of each state.

Strategy ❸ Look for solutions people tried to deal with each problem. Think about whether the solution was a good one for people with differing points of view.

> **SLAVERY AND THE CONSTITUTION**
>
> Because the House of Representatives would have members according to the population of each state, ❶ the delegates had to decide who would be counted in the population of each state. The Southern states had many more slaves than the Northern states had. ❷ Southerners wanted the slaves to be counted as part of the general population for representation but not for taxation. ❷ Northerners argued that slaves were not citizens and should not be counted for representation, but that slaves should be counted for taxation. ❸ The delegates decided that three-fifths of the slave population would be counted in the population to determine both representation and taxes.

Make a Chart

Making a chart will help you identify and organize information about problems and solutions. The chart below shows problems and solutions included in the passage you just read.

❶ Problem	❷ Differing Points of View	❸ Solution
Northerners and Southerners couldn't agree on how to count population because of slavery in the South.	Southerners wanted slaves counted for representation but not for taxation. Northerners wanted slaves counted for taxation but not for representation.	Delegates decided that three-fifths of the slave population should be counted.

Practicing the Skill

Turn to Chapter 9, Section 3, "U.S. Involvement Overseas." Read "The Panama Canal." Then make a chart that summarizes the problems faced by the United States and the solutions to those problems.

2.11 Evaluating

Defining the Skill

To **evaluate** is to make a judgment about something. Historians evaluate the actions of people in history. One way to do this is to examine both the positives and negatives of a historical action, then decide which is stronger—the positive or the negative.

Applying the Skill

The following passage describes Susan B. Anthony's fight for women's rights. Use the strategies listed below to evaluate how successful she was.

How to Evaluate

Strategy ❶ Before you evaluate a person's actions, first determine what that person was trying to do. In this case, think about what Anthony wanted to accomplish.

Strategy ❷ Look for statements that show the positive, or successful, results of her actions. For example, Did she achieve her goals?

Strategy ❸ Also look for statements that show the negative, or unsuccessful, results of her actions. Did she fail to achieve something she tried to do?

Strategy ❹ Write an overall evaluation of the person's actions.

SUSAN B. ANTHONY

❶ Susan B. Anthony was a skilled organizer who fought for women's rights. ❷ She successfully built the women's movement into a national organization. Anthony believed that a woman must have money of her own. To this end, she supported laws that would give married women rights to control their own property and wages. ❷ Mississippi passed the first such law in 1839. New York passed a property law in 1848 and a wages law in 1860. ❸ Anthony also wanted to win the vote for women but failed to convince lawmakers to pass this reform in her lifetime. This reform did go through in 1920, 14 years after her death.

Make a Diagram for Evaluating

Using a diagram can help you evaluate. List the positives and negatives of the historical person's actions and decisions. Then make an overall judgment. The diagram below shows how the information from the passage you just read can be diagrammed.

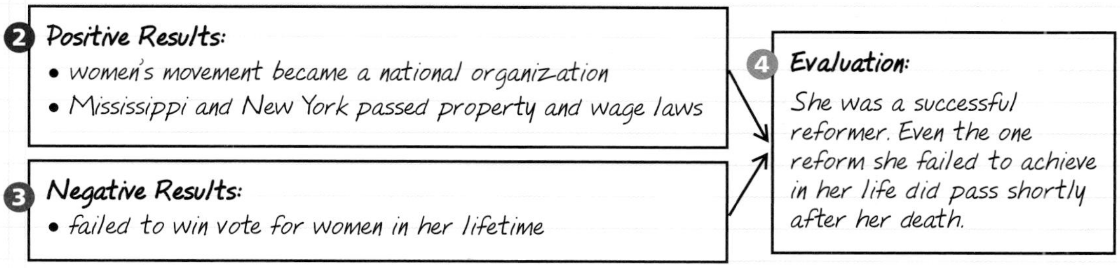

❷ *Positive Results:*
- *women's movement became a national organization*
- *Mississippi and New York passed property and wage laws*

❸ *Negative Results:*
- *failed to win vote for women in her lifetime*

❹ *Evaluation:*
She was a successful reformer. Even the one reform she failed to achieve in her life did pass shortly after her death.

Practicing the Skill

Turn to Chapter 17, Section 3, "Issues of the Seventies." Read "Carter as President" and make a diagram in which you evaluate whether Carter was an effective president.

2.12 Making Generalizations

Defining the Skill

To **make generalizations** means to make broad judgments based on information. When you make generalizations, you should gather information from several sources.

Applying the Skill

The following three passages contain different views on George Washington. Use the strategies listed below to make a generalization about these views.

How to Make Generalizations

Strategy ① Look for information that the sources have in common. These three sources all discuss George Washington's ability as a military leader.

Strategy ② Form a generalization that describes Washington in a way that all three sources would agree with. State your generalization in a sentence.

> ### WASHINGTON'S LEADERSHIP
>
> ① Washington learned from his mistakes. After early defeats, he developed the strategy of dragging out the war to wear down the British. ① Despite difficulties, he never gave up.
>
> —*Creating America*
>
> ① [Washington] was no military genius. . . . But he was a great war leader. Creating an army out of unpromising material, he kept it in being against great odds.
>
> —*The Limits of Liberty*
>
> ① [Washington] certainly deserves some merit as a general, that he . . . can keep General Howe dancing from one town to another for two years together, with such an army as he has.
>
> —*The Journal of Nicholas Cresswell, July 13, 1777*

Make a Chart

Using a chart can help you make generalizations. The chart below shows how the information you just read can be used to generalize about people's views of Washington.

① Washington kept the army together against great odds.

① Washington kept the enemy guessing by moving his army quickly.

② Generalization: Although Washington made mistakes, he was a good military leader.

① Washington learned from his mistakes and never gave up.

Practicing the Skill

Turn to Chapter 7, Section 3, "Segregation and Discrimination." After reading this section, use a chart like the one above to make a generalization about minority rights around the turn of the 20th century.

3.1 Using Primary and Secondary Sources

Defining the Skill

Primary sources are materials written or made by people who lived during historical events and witnessed them. Primary sources can be letters, journal entries, speeches, autobiographies, or artwork. Other kinds of primary sources are government documents, census surveys, and financial records. **Secondary sources** are materials written by people who did not participate in an event. History books are secondary sources.

Applying the Skill

The following passage contains both a primary source and a secondary source. Use the strategies listed below to help you read them.

How to Read Primary and Secondary Sources

Strategy ① Distinguish sec-ondary sources from primary sources. The first paragraph is a secondary source. The Declaration of Independence is a primary source. The secondary source explains something about the pri-mary source.

Strategy ② Analyze the pri-mary source and consider why the author produced it. Consider what the document was supposed to achieve and who would read it.

Strategy ③ Identify the author of the primary source and note when and where it was written.

> ① The core idea of the Declaration is based on the philosophy of John Locke. This idea is that people have unalienable rights, or rights that government cannot take away. Jefferson stated this belief in what was to become the Declaration's best-known passage.
>
> ② We hold these truths to be self-evident, that all men are created equal, that they are endowed by their Creator with certain unalienable Rights, that among these are Life, Liberty and the pursuit of Happiness.
>
> ③ —Thomas Jefferson, *The Declaration of Independence*, 1776

Make a Chart

Making a chart will help you summarize information from primary sources and secondary sources. The chart below summarizes the information from the passage you just read.

Author	Thomas Jefferson
Document	The Declaration of Independence
Notes on Primary Source	The Declaration says that "all men are created equal." It also says that people have "unalienable rights." These rights include the right to life and the right to liberty, as well as a right to pursue happiness.
Notes on Secondary Source	Jefferson based his ideas on those of John Locke. Locke had written about rights that governments could not take away from the people.

Practicing the Skill

Turn to Chapter 15, Section 1, "Origins of the Civil Rights Movement." Read "Montgomery Bus Boycott" and make a chart like the one above to summarize the information in the primary source and the secondary source.

3.2 Interpreting Graphs

Defining the Skill

Graphs use pictures and symbols, instead of words, to show information. Graphs are created by taking information and presenting it visually. The graph on this page takes numerical information on immigration and presents it as a bar graph. There are many different kinds of graphs. Bar graphs, line graphs, and pie graphs are the most common. Bar graphs compare numbers or sets of numbers. The length of each bar shows a quantity. It is easy to see how different categories compare on a bar graph.

Applying the Skill

The bar graph below shows numbers of immigrants coming to the United States between 1821 and 1860. Use the strategies listed below to help you interpret the graph.

How to Interpret a Graph

Strategy ❶ Read the title to identify the main idea of the graph. Ask yourself what kinds of information the graph shows. For example, does it show chronological information, geographic patterns and distributions, or something else?

Strategy ❷ Read the vertical axis (the one that goes up and down) on the left side of the graph. This one shows the number of immigrants in thousands. Each bar represents the number of immigrants during a particular decade.

Strategy ❸ Read the horizontal axis (the one that runs across the bottom of the graph). This one shows the four decades from 1821 to 1860.

Strategy ❹ Summarize the information shown in each part of the graph. Use the title to help you focus on what information the graph is presenting.

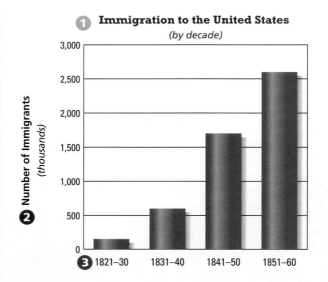

❶ **Immigration to the United States**
(by decade)

❷ Number of Immigrants *(thousands)*

❸ 1821–30   1831–40   1841–50   1851–60

Write a Summary

Writing a summary will help you understand the information in the graph. The paragraph to the right summarizes the information from the bar graph.

Practicing the Skill

Turn to Chapter 10, Section 2, "America Joins the Fight." Look at the graph entitled "Military Deaths in World War I" and write a paragraph in which you summarize what you learned from it.

❹ Immigration to the United States increased between 1821 and 1860. Between 1821 and 1830, fewer than 200,000 immigrants arrived. In the next decade, more than 500,000 immigrants came. During the 1840s, more than 1.5 million immigrants arrived, and that number increased to more than 2.5 million in the 1850s.

3.3 Interpreting Charts

Defining the Skill

Charts, like graphs, present information in a visual form. Charts are created by organizing, summarizing, and simplifying information and presenting it in a format that makes it easy to understand. Tables and diagrams are examples of commonly used charts.

Applying the Skill

The chart below shows the number of slaves who were imported to the Americas between 1601 and 1810. Use the strategies listed below to help you interpret the information in the chart.

How to Interpret a Chart

Strategy ❶ Read the title. It will tell you what the chart is about. Ask yourself what kinds of information the chart shows. For example, does it show chronological information, geographic patterns and distributions, or something else?

Strategy ❷ Read the labels to see how the information in the chart is organized. In this chart, it is organized by region and years.

Strategy ❸ Study the data in the chart to understand the facts that the chart intends to show.

Strategy ❹ Summarize the information shown in each part of the chart. Use the title to help you focus on what information the chart is presenting.

1601–1810

❶ **Slaves Imported to the Americas** *(in thousands)*

❷ REGION/COUNTRY	1601–1700	1701–1810
❸ British N. America	*	348
British Caribbean	263.7	1,401.3
French Caribbean	155.8	1,348.4
Spanish America	292.5	578.6
Dutch Caribbean	40	460
Danish Caribbean	4	24
Brazil (Portugal)	560	1,891.4

*= less than 1,000

Source: Philip D. Curtin, *The Atlantic Slave Trade*

Write a Summary

Writing a summary can help you understand the information given in a chart. The paragraph to the right summarizes the information in the chart "Slaves Imported to the Americas, 1601–1810."

❹ *The chart shows how many slaves were imported to the Americas between 1601 and 1810. It divides the Americas into seven regions. It also divides the time period into two parts: 1601–1700 and 1701–1810. The number of slaves imported increased greatly from the 1600s to the 1700s. More slaves were imported to Brazil than to any other region.*

Practicing the Skill

Turn to Chapter 13, Section 5, and look at the chart entitled "World War II Military Casualties, 1939–1945." Study the chart and ask yourself what geographic patterns and distributions are shown in it. Then write a paragraph in which you summarize what you learned from the chart.

3.4 Interpreting Time Lines

Defining the Skill

A **time line** is a visual list of events and dates shown in the order in which they occurred. Time lines can be horizontal or vertical. On horizontal time lines, the earliest date is on the left. On vertical time lines, the earliest date is often at the top.

Applying the Skill

The time line below lists dates and events during the presidencies of John Adams, Andrew Jackson, and Martin Van Buren. Use the strategies listed below to help you interpret the information.

How to Read a Time Line

Strategy ❶ Read the dates at the beginning and end of the time line. These will show the period of history that is covered. The time line below is a dual time line. It includes items related to two topics. The labels show that the information covers U.S. events and world events.

Strategy ❷ Read the dates and events in sequential order, beginning with the earliest one. Pay particular attention to how the entries relate to each other. Think about which events caused later events.

Strategy ❸ Summarize the focus, or main idea, of the time line. Try to write a main idea sentence that describes the time line.

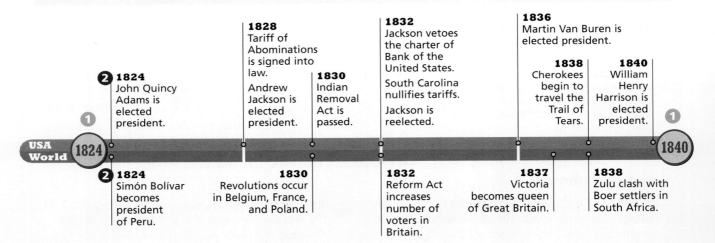

1828
Tariff of Abominations is signed into law.

1832
Jackson vetoes the charter of Bank of the United States.

South Carolina nullifies tariffs.

Jackson is reelected.

1836
Martin Van Buren is elected president.

❷ **1824**
John Quincy Adams is elected president.

1830
Andrew Jackson is elected president.

1830
Indian Removal Act is passed.

1838
Cherokees begin to travel the Trail of Tears.

1840
William Henry Harrison is elected president.

❶

USA
World (1824)

(1840) ❶

❷ **1824**
Simón Bolívar becomes president of Peru.

1830
Revolutions occur in Belgium, France, and Poland.

1832
Reform Act increases number of voters in Britain.

1837
Victoria becomes queen of Great Britain.

1838
Zulu clash with Boer settlers in South Africa.

Write a Summary

Writing a summary can help you understand information shown on a time line. The summary to the right states the main idea of the time line and tells how the events are related.

Practicing the Skill

Turn to Chapter 7, page 205, and write a summary of the information shown on the time line.

❸ *The time line covers the period between 1824, when John Quincy Adams was elected president, and 1840, when William Henry Harrison was elected president. During that period of time, Andrew Jackson and Martin Van Buren also served as president. The time line shows that the important issues in the United States were tariffs, banking, and relations with Native Americans.*

3.5 Reading a Map

Defining the Skill

Maps are representations of features on the earth's surface. Some maps show political features, such as national borders. Other maps show physical features, such as mountains and bodies of water. By learning to use map elements and math skills, you can better understand how to read maps.

Applying the Skill

The following map shows the Battle of Yorktown during the Revolution. Use the strategies listed below to help you identify the elements common to most maps.

How to Read a Map

Strategy 1 Read the title. This identifies the main idea of the map.

Strategy 2 Look for the grid of lines that forms a pattern of squares over the map. These numbered lines are the lines of latitude (horizontal) and longitude (vertical). They indicate the location of the area on the earth.

Strategy 3 Read the map key. It is usually in a box. This will give you the information you need to interpret the symbols or colors on the map.

Strategy 4 Use the scale and the pointer, or compass rose, to determine distance and direction.

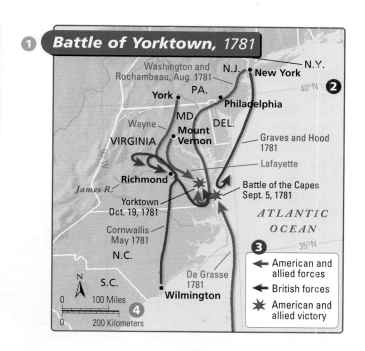

1 **Battle of Yorktown,** *1781*

Make a Chart

A chart can help you organize information given on maps. The chart below summarizes information about the map you just studied.

Title	Battle of Yorktown, 1781
Location	between latitude 40° N and 35° N, just east of longitude 80° W
Map Key Information	blue = American and allied forces, red = British forces
Scale	7/16 in. = 100 miles, 9/16 in. = 200 km
Summary	British commanders Graves and Hood sailed south from New York. They were defeated by De Grasse at the Battle of the Capes. British commander Cornwallis marched north from Wilmington, North Carolina, to Virginia, where he was defeated by American forces.

Practicing the Skill

Turn to Chapter 6, Section 2, "Railroads Transform the Nation." Read the map entitled "Railroads of the Transcontinental Era, 1865–1900" and make a chart to identify information on the map.

3.6 Reading a Special-Purpose Map

Defining the Skill

Special-purpose maps help people focus on a particular aspect of a region, such as economic development in the South. These kinds of maps often use symbols to indicate information.

Applying the Skill

The following special-purpose map indicates the products of the Southern colonies. Use the strategies listed below to help you identify the information shown on the map.

How to Read a Special-Purpose Map

Strategy ❶ Read the title. It tells you what the map is intended to show.

Strategy ❷ Read the legend. This tells you what each symbol stands for. This legend shows the crops that were grown in various Southern colonies.

Strategy ❸ Look for the places on the map where the symbols appear. These tell you the places where each crop was grown.

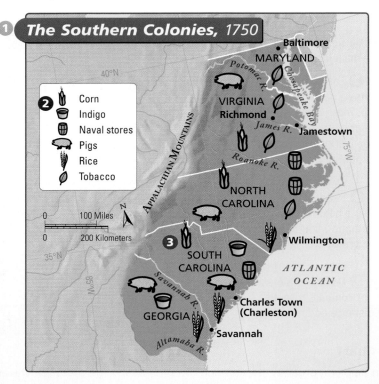

❶ The Southern Colonies, 1750

Legend:
- Corn
- Indigo
- Naval stores
- Pigs
- Rice
- Tobacco

Make a Chart

A chart can help you understand special-purpose maps. The chart below shows information about the special-purpose map you just studied.

	Corn	Indigo	Naval stores	Pigs	Rice	Tobacco
Maryland						x
Virginia	x			x		x
North Carolina	x		x	x	x	x
South Carolina	x	x	x	x	x	
Georgia		x		x	x	

Practicing the Skill

Turn to Chapter 6, Section 3, "The Rise of Big Business." Look at the special-purpose map entitled "Industry in the Midwest" and make a chart that shows information about industries in the Midwest.

3.7 Creating a Map

Defining the Skill

Creating a map involves representing geographical information. When you draw a map, it is easiest to use an existing map as a guide. On the map you draw, you can show geographical information. You can also show other kinds of information, such as data on climates, population trends, resources, or routes. Often, this data comes from a graph or a chart.

Applying the Skill

Below is a map that a student created to show information about the number of slaves in 1750. Read the strategies listed below to see how the map was created.

How to Create a Map

Strategy ① Select a title that identifies the geographical area and the map's purpose. Include a date in your title.

Strategy ② Draw the lines of latitude and longitude using short dashes.

Strategy ③ Create a key that shows the colors.

Strategy ④ Draw the colors on the map to show information.

Strategy ⑤ Draw a compass rose and scale.

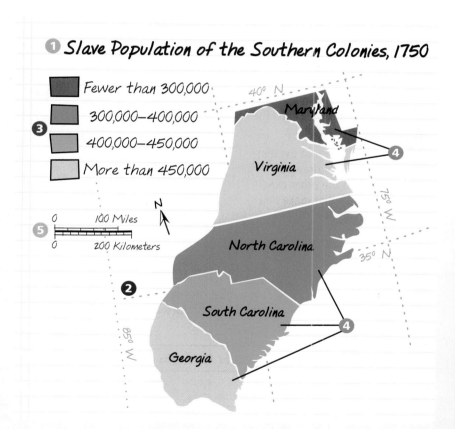

① **Slave Population of the Southern Colonies, 1750**

③
- Fewer than 300,000
- 300,000–400,000
- 400,000–450,000
- More than 450,000

⑤ 0   100 Miles
0   200 Kilometers

N

40° N
Maryland
Virginia
75° W
North Carolina
35° N
②
South Carolina
85° W
Georgia
④

Practicing the Skill

Make your own map. Turn to page 167 in Chapter 5 and study the chart entitled "Population of Western Cities." Use the strategies described above to create a map that shows the 4 cities and their populations. You can use the map on page 190 of Chapter 6 to help locate the cities.

3.8 Interpreting Political Cartoons

Defining the Skill

Political cartoons are cartoons that use humor to make a serious point. Political cartoons often express a point of view on an issue better than words do. Understanding signs and symbols will help you to interpret political cartoons.

Applying the Skill

The cartoon below shows Abraham Lincoln and the other candidates running for the presidency in 1860. Use the strategies listed below to help you understand the cartoon.

How to Interpret a Political Cartoon

Strategy ❶ Identify the subject by reading the title of the cartoon and looking at the cartoon as a whole.

Strategy ❷ Identify important symbols and details. The cartoonist uses the image of a running race to discuss a political campaign. The White House is the finish line.

Strategy ❸ Interpret the message. Why is Lincoln drawn so much taller than the other candidates? How does that make him the fittest candidate?

Make a Chart

Making a chart will help you summarize information from a political cartoon. The chart below summarizes the information from the cartoon above.

Subject	"A Political Race" (The Election of 1860)
Symbols and Details	Running is a symbol for a political campaign. Lincoln is the tallest and fastest candidate.
Message	❸ Lincoln is pulling ahead of the other candidates in the campaign for the presidency.

Practicing the Skill

Turn to Chapter 12, Section 2, "Roosevelt and the New Deal." Look at the political cartoon on page 336. It shows a cartoonist's view of Roosevelt's New Deal policies. Use a chart like the one above and the strategies outlined to interpret the cartoon.

3.9 Creating a Model

Defining the Skill

When you **create a model,** you use information and ideas to show an event or a situation in a visual way. A model might be a poster or a diagram that explains how something happened. Or, it might be a three-dimensional model, such as a diorama, that depicts an important scene or situation.

Applying the Skill

The following sketch shows the early stages of a model of three ways that people could have traveled from the eastern United States to California during the gold rush. Use the strategies listed below to help you create your own model.

How to Create a Model

Strategy ❶ Gather the information you need to understand the situation or event. In this case, you need to be able to show the three routes and their dangers.

Strategy ❷ Visualize and sketch an idea for your model. Once you have created a picture in your mind, make an actual sketch to plan how it might look.

Strategy ❸ Think of symbols you may want to use. Since the model should give information in a visual way, think about ways you can use color, pictures, or other visuals to tell the story.

Strategy ❹ Gather the supplies you will need and create the model. For example, you will need a globe and art supplies, such as yarn, for this model.

Strategy ❺ Write and answer a question about the California gold rush, as shown in this model.

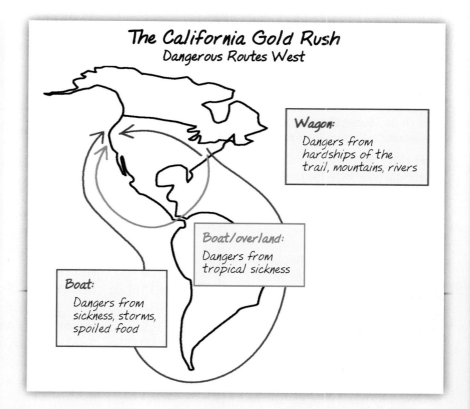

The California Gold Rush
Dangerous Routes West

Wagon:
Dangers from hardships of the trail, mountains, rivers

Boat/overland:
Dangers from tropical sickness

Boat:
Dangers from sickness, storms, spoiled food

Practicing the Skill

Read the Interdisciplinary Challenge called "Stage a Wild West Show" on pages 572–573. Use the Art Challenge to create a poster for the show.

4.1 Using an Electronic Card Catalog

Defining the Skill

An **electronic card catalog** is a library's computerized search program that will help you find information about the books and other materials in the library. You can search the catalog by entering a book title, an author's name, or a subject of interest to you. The electronic card catalog will give you information about the materials in the library. This information is called bibliographic information. You can use an electronic card catalog to create a bibliography (a list of books) on any topic you are interested in.

Applying the Skill

The screen shown below is from an electronic search for information about Thomas Jefferson. Use the strategies listed below to help you use the information on the screen.

How to Use an Electronic Card Catalog

Strategy ❶ Begin searching by choosing either subject, title, or author, depending on the topic of your search. For this search, the user chose "Subject" and typed in the words "Jefferson, Thomas."

Strategy ❷ Once you have selected a book from the results of your search, identify the author, title, city, publisher, and date of publication.

Strategy ❸ Look for any special features in the book. This book is illustrated, and it includes bibliographical references and an index.

Strategy ❹ Locate the call number for the book. The call number indicates the section in the library where you will find the book. You can also find out if the book is available in the library you are using. If not, it may be in another library in the network.

```
Search Request:
❶ Subject          Title          Author
  ─────────────────────────────────────────
  Find Options Locations Backup Startover Help

❷ Miller, Douglas T. Thomas Jefferson and the
  creation of America. New York: Facts on File,
  1997.
❷        AUTHOR:  Miller, Douglas T.
         TITLE:   Thomas Jefferson and the
                  creation of America/Douglas T.
                  Miller.
❷ PUBLISHED:  New York: Facts on File, ©1997.
❸    PAGING:  vi, 122p. : ill ; 24 cm.
      SERIES:  Makers of America.
❸     NOTES:  Includes bibliographical
              references (p. 117-118) and index.
❹ CALL NUMBER:  1. 973.46 N61T 1997—Book Available—
```

Practicing the Skill

Turn to Chapter 14, "The Cold War and the American Dream," and find a topic that interests you, such as the Cold War, the Berlin Airlift, the space race, or Elvis. Use the SUBJECT search on an electronic card catalog to find information about your topic. Make a bibliography of books about the subject. Be sure to include the author, title, city, publisher, and date of publication for all the books included.

4.2 Creating a Database

Defining the Skill

A **database** is a collection of data, or information, that is organized so that you can find and retrieve information on a specific topic quickly and easily. Once a computerized database is set up, you can search it to find specific information without going through the entire database. The database will provide a list of all information in the database related to your topic. Learning how to use a database will help you learn how to create one.

Applying the Skill

The chart below is a database for the significant battles of the Civil War. Use the strategies listed below to help you understand and use the database.

How to Create a Database

Strategy ❶ Identify the topic of the database. The keywords, or most important words, in this title are *Civil War* and *Battles*. These words were used to begin the research for this database.

Strategy ❷ Ask yourself what kind of data you need to include. For example, what geographic patterns and distributions will be shown? Your choice of data will provide the column headings for your database. The key words *Battle, Date, Location,* and *Significance* were chosen to focus the research.

Strategy ❸ Identify the entries included under each heading.

Strategy ❹ Use the database to help you find information quickly. For example, in this database you could search for "Union victories" to find a list of significant battles won by the North.

❶ LOCATION OF SIGNIFICANT CIVIL WAR BATTLES			
❷ BATTLE	DATE	❷ LOCATION	SIGNIFICANCE
❸ Fort Sumter	April 12, 1861	Charleston, SC	Beginning of the Civil War
First Battle of Bull Run (Manassas)	July 21, 1861	Virginia	Confederate victory
Shiloh	April 6–7, 1862	Tennessee (near Shiloh Church)	❹ Union victory
Antietam	September 17, 1862	Sharpsburg, MD	No clear victory; considered bloodiest battle of war
Gettysburg	July 1–3, 1863	Gettysburg, PA	Retreat of Confederacy
Vicksburg	Three-month siege ending July 3, 1863	Vicksburg, MS	Union gained control of Mississippi River
Chattanooga	November 23–25, 1863	Chattanooga, TN	❹ Union victory
Atlanta	September 2, 1864	Atlanta, GA	❹ Union victory; helped convince Confederacy of defeat

Practicing the Skill

Create a database for U.S. presidents from Abraham Lincoln through Franklin Roosevelt that shows each president's home state, political party, and years served as president. Use the information in "Presidents of the United States" on pages R36–R38 to provide the data. Use aformat like the one above for your database.

4.3 Using the Internet

Defining the Skill

The Internet is a computer network that connects to universities, libraries, news organizations, government agencies, businesses, and private individuals throughout the world. Each location on the Internet has a home page with its own address, or URL (universal resource locator). With a computer connected to the Internet, you can reach the home pages of many organizations and services. The international collection of home pages, known as the World Wide Web, is a good source of up-to-date information about current events as well as research on subjects in history.

Applying the Skill

The Web page below shows the links for Chapter 15 of *Creating America*. Use the strategies listed below to help you understand how to use the Web page.

How to Use the Internet

Strategy ❶ Go directly to a Web page. For example, type classzone.com in the box at the top of the screen and press ENTER (or RETURN). The Web page will appear on your screen. Then click on ClassZone and find the link to *Creating America*.

Strategy ❷ Explore the *Creating America* links. Click on any one of the links to find out more about a specific subject. These links take you to other pages at this Web site. Some pages include links to related information that can be found at other places on the Internet.

Strategy ❸ When using the Internet for research, you should confirm the information you find. Web sites set up by universities, government agencies, and reputable news sources are more reliable than other sources. You can often find information about the creator of a site by looking for copyright information.

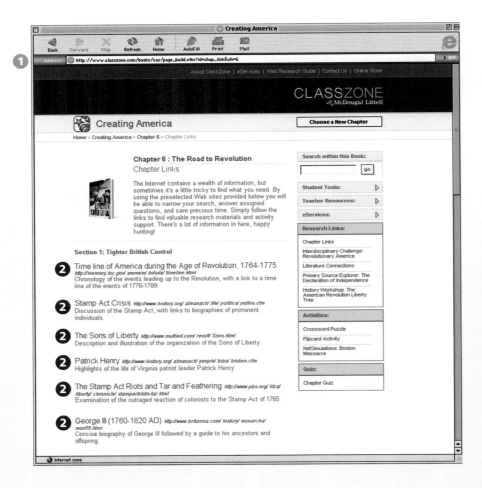

Practicing the Skill

Turn to Chapter 11, Section 3, "The Jazz Age and the Harlem Renaissance." Read the section and make a list of topics you would like to research. If you have Internet access, go to classzone.com. There you will find links that provide more information about the topics in the section.

4.4 Creating a Multimedia Presentation

Defining the Skill

Movies, CD-ROMs, television, and computer software are different kinds of media. To **create a multimedia presentation,** you need to collect information in different media and organize them into one presentation.

Applying the Skill

The scene below shows students using computers to create a multimedia presentation. Use the strategies listed below to help you create your own multimedia presentation.

How to Create a Multimedia Presentation

Strategy ❶ Identify the topic of your presentation and decide which media are best for an effective presentation. For example, you may want to use slides or posters to show visual images of your topic. Or, you may want to use CDs or audiotapes to provide music or spoken words.

Strategy ❷ Research the topic in a variety of sources. Images, text, props, and background music should reflect the historical period of the event you choose.

Strategy ❸ Write the script for the oral portion of the presentation. You could use a narrator and characters' voices to tell the story. Primary sources are an excellent source for script material. Make sure the recording is clear so that the audience will be able to understand the oral part of the presentation.

Strategy ❹ Videotape the presentation. Videotaping the presentation will preserve it for future viewing and allow you to show it to different groups of people.

Practicing the Skill

Turn to Chapter 10, "World War I." Choose a topic from the chapter and use the strategies listed above to create a multimedia presentation about it.

Alabama
4,486,508 people
52,218 sq. mi.
Rank in area: 30
Entered Union in 1819

Alaska
643,786 people
616,240 sq. mi.
Rank in area: 1
Entered Union in 1959

Arizona
5,456,453 people
113,998 sq. mi.
Rank in area: 6
Entered Union in 1912

Arkansas
2,710,079 people
53,178 sq. mi.
Rank in area: 28
Entered Union in 1836

California
35,116,033 people
158,854 sq. mi.
Rank in area: 3
Entered Union in 1850

Colorado
4,506,542 people
104,093 sq. mi.
Rank in area: 8
Entered Union in 1876

Connecticut
3,460,503 people
5,543 sq. mi.
Rank in area: 48
Entered Union in 1788

Delaware
807,385 people
2,396 sq. mi.
Rank in area: 49
Entered Union in 1787

District of Columbia
570,898 people
68 sq. mi.

Florida
16,713,149 people
59,909 sq. mi.
Rank in area: 23
Entered Union in 1845

Georgia
8,560,310 people
58,970 sq. mi.
Rank in area: 24
Entered Union in 1788

Hawaii
1,244,898 people
6,641 sq. mi.
Rank in area: 47
Entered Union in 1959

Idaho
1,341,131 people
83,570 sq. mi.
Rank in area: 14
Entered Union in 1890

Illinois
12,600,620 people
57,914 sq. mi.
Rank in area: 25
Entered Union in 1818

Indiana
6,159,068 people
36,418 sq. mi.
Rank in area: 38
Entered Union in 1816

Iowa
2,936,760 people
56,271 sq. mi.
Rank in area: 26
Entered Union in 1846

Kansas
2,715,884 people
82,276 sq. mi.
Rank in area: 15
Entered Union in 1861

Kentucky
4,092,891 people
40,409 sq. mi.
Rank in area: 37
Entered Union in 1792

Louisiana
4,482,646 people
49,650 sq. mi.
Rank in area: 31
Entered Union in 1812

Maine
1,294,464 people
33,738 sq. mi.
Rank in area: 39
Entered Union in 1820

Maryland
5,458,137 people
12,297 sq. mi.
Rank in area: 42
Entered Union in 1788

Massachusetts
6,427,801 people
9,240 sq. mi.
Rank in area: 45
Entered Union in 1788

Michigan
10,050,446 people
96,716 sq. mi.
Rank in area: 11
Entered Union in 1837

Minnesota
5,019,720 people
86,938 sq. mi.
Rank in area: 12
Entered Union in 1858

Mississippi
2,871,782 people
48,282 sq. mi.
Rank in area: 32
Entered Union in 1817

Missouri
5,672,579 people
69,704 sq. mi.
Rank in area: 21
Entered Union in 1821

Montana
909,453 people
147,042 sq. mi.
Rank in area: 4
Entered Union in 1889

Sources: U.S. Bureau of the Census, July 1 2002 population estimates.
World Almanac and Book of Facts, 2003
Statistical Abstract of the United States, 2002

Nebraska
1,729,180 people
77,353 sq. mi.
Rank in area: 16
Entered Union in 1867

Ohio
11,421,267 people
44,825 sq. mi.
Rank in area: 34
Entered Union in 1803

Texas
21,779,893 people
267,256 sq. mi.
Rank in area: 2
Entered Union in 1845

Nevada
2,173,491 people
110,560 sq. mi.
Rank in area: 7
Entered Union in 1864

Oklahoma
3,493,714 people
69,898 sq. mi.
Rank in area: 20
Entered Union in 1907

Utah
2,316,256 people
84,898 sq. mi.
Rank in area: 13
Entered Union in 1896

New Hampshire
1,275,056 people
9,282 sq. mi.
Rank in area: 44
Entered Union in 1788

Oregon
3,521,515 people
97,126 sq. mi.
Rank in area: 10
Entered Union in 1859

Vermont
616,592 people
9,614 sq. mi.
Rank in area: 43
Entered Union in 1791

New Jersey
8,590,300 people
8,214 sq. mi.
Rank in area: 46
Entered Union in 1787

Pennsylvania
12,335,091 people
46,055 sq. mi.
Rank in area: 33
Entered Union in 1787

Virginia
7,293,542 people
42,328 sq. mi.
Rank in area: 35
Entered Union in 1788

New Mexico
1,855,059 people
121,589 sq. mi.
Rank in area: 5
Entered Union in 1912

Rhode Island
1,069,725 people
1,231 sq. mi.
Rank in area: 50
Entered Union in 1790

Washington
6,068,996 people
70,634 sq. mi.
Rank in area: 19
Entered Union in 1889

New York
19,157,532 people
54,077 sq. mi.
Rank in area: 27
Entered Union in 1788

South Carolina
4,107,183 people
31,190 sq. mi.
Rank in area: 40
Entered Union in 1788

West Virginia
1,801,873 people
24,230 sq. mi.
Rank in area: 41
Entered Union in 1863

North Carolina
8,320,146 people
52,670 sq. mi.
Rank in area: 29
Entered Union in 1789

South Dakota
761,063 people
77,116 sq. mi.
Rank in area: 17
Entered Union in 1889

Wisconsin
5,441,196 people
65,498 sq. mi.
Rank in area: 22
Entered Union in 1848

North Dakota
634,110 people
70,699 sq. mi.
Rank in area: 18
Entered Union in 1889

Tennessee
5,797,289 people
42,143 sq. mi.
Rank in area: 36
Entered Union in 1796

Wyoming
498,703 people
97,813 sq. mi.
Rank in area: 9
Entered Union in 1890

United States: *Major Dependencies*

- American Samoa—68,688 people; 90 sq. mi.
- Guam—160,796 people; 217 sq. mi.
- Commonwealth of Puerto Rico—3,957,988 people; 5,324 sq. mi.
- Virgin Islands of the United States—123,498 people; 171 sq. mi.
- Midway Atoll—no indigenous inhabitants; 2 sq. mi.
- Wake Atoll—no indigenous inhabitants; 3 sq. mi.

Here are some little-known facts about the presidents of the United States:

- Only former president to serve in Congress: John Quincy Adams
- First president born in the new United States: Martin Van Buren (eighth president)
- Only president who was a bachelor: James Buchanan
- First left-handed president: James A. Garfield
- Largest president: William H. Taft (6 feet 2 inches, 326 pounds)
- Youngest president: Theodore Roosevelt (42 years old)
- Oldest president: Ronald Reagan (77 years old when he left office in 1989)
- First president born west of the Mississippi River: Herbert Hoover (born in West Branch, Iowa)
- First president born in the 20th century: John F. Kennedy (born May 29, 1917)

1 George Washington
1789–1797
No Political Party
Birthplace: Virginia
Born: February 22, 1732
Died: December 14, 1799

2 John Adams
1797–1801
Federalist
Birthplace: Massachusetts
Born: October 30, 1735
Died: July 4, 1826

3 Thomas Jefferson
1801–1809
Democratic-Republican
Birthplace: Virginia
Born: April 13, 1743
Died: July 4, 1826

4 James Madison
1809–1817
Democratic-Republican
Birthplace: Virginia
Born: March 16, 1751
Died: June 28, 1836

5 James Monroe
1817–1825
Democratic-Republican
Birthplace: Virginia
Born: April 28, 1758
Died: July 4, 1831

6 John Quincy Adams
1825–1829
Democratic-Republican
Birthplace: Massachusetts
Born: July 11, 1767
Died: February 23, 1848

7 Andrew Jackson
1829–1837
Democrat
Birthplace: South Carolina
Born: March 15, 1767
Died: June 8, 1845

8 Martin Van Buren
1837–1841
Democrat
Birthplace: New York
Born: December 5, 1782
Died: July 24, 1862

9 William H. Harrison
1841
Whig
Birthplace: Virginia
Born: February 9, 1773
Died: April 4, 1841

10 John Tyler
1841–1845
Whig
Birthplace: Virginia
Born: March 29, 1790
Died: January 18, 1862

11 James K. Polk
1845–1849
Democrat
Birthplace: North Carolina
Born: November 2, 1795
Died: June 15, 1849

12 Zachary Taylor
1849–1850
Whig
Birthplace: Virginia
Born: November 24, 1784
Died: July 9, 1850

13 Millard Fillmore
1850–1853
Whig
Birthplace: New York
Born: January 7, 1800
Died: March 8, 1874

14 Franklin Pierce
1853–1857
Democrat
Birthplace: New Hampshire
Born: November 23, 1804
Died: October 8, 1869

15 James Buchanan
1857–1861
Democrat
Birthplace: Pennsylvania
Born: April 23, 1791
Died: June 1, 1868

16 Abraham Lincoln
1861–1865
Republican
Birthplace: Kentucky
Born: February 12, 1809
Died: April 15, 1865

17 Andrew Johnson
1865–1869
National Union
Birthplace: North Carolina
Born: December 29, 1808
Died: July 31, 1875

18 Ulysses S. Grant
1869–1877
Republican
Birthplace: Ohio
Born: April 27, 1822
Died: July 23, 1885

19 Rutherford B. Hayes
1877–1881
Republican
Birthplace: Ohio
Born: October 4, 1822
Died: January 17, 1893

20 James A. Garfield
1881
Republican
Birthplace: Ohio
Born: November 19, 1831
Died: September 19, 1881

21 Chester A. Arthur
1881–1885
Republican
Birthplace: Vermont
Born: October 5, 1829
Died: November 18, 1886

22 24 Grover Cleveland
1885–1889, 1893–1897
Democrat
Birthplace: New Jersey
Born: March 18, 1837
Died: June 24, 1908

23 Benjamin Harrison
1889–1893
Republican
Birthplace: Ohio
Born: August 20, 1833
Died: March 13, 1901

25 William McKinley
1897–1901
Republican
Birthplace: Ohio
Born: January 29, 1843
Died: September 14, 1901

26 Theodore Roosevelt
1901–1909
Republican
Birthplace: New York
Born: October 27, 1858
Died: January 6, 1919

27 William H. Taft
1909–1913
Republican
Birthplace: Ohio
Born: September 15, 1857
Died: March 8, 1930

28 Woodrow Wilson
1913–1921
Democrat
Birthplace: Virginia
Born: December 28, 1856
Died: February 3, 1924

29 Warren G. Harding
1921–1923
Republican
Birthplace: Ohio
Born: November 2, 1865
Died: August 2, 1923

30 **Calvin Coolidge**
1923–1929
Republican
Birthplace: Vermont
Born: July 4, 1872
Died: January 5, 1933

31 **Herbert C. Hoover**
1929–1933
Republican
Birthplace: Iowa
Born: August 10, 1874
Died: October 20, 1964

32 **Franklin D. Roosevelt**
1933–1945
Democrat
Birthplace: New York
Born: January 30, 1882
Died: April 12, 1945

33 **Harry S. Truman**
1945–1953
Democrat
Birthplace: Missouri
Born: May 8, 1884
Died: December 26, 1972

34 **Dwight D. Eisenhower**
1953–1961
Republican
Birthplace: Texas
Born: October 14, 1890
Died: March 28, 1969

35 **John F. Kennedy**
1961–1963
Democrat
Birthplace: Massachusetts
Born: May 29, 1917
Died: November 22, 1963

36 **Lyndon B. Johnson**
1963–1969
Democrat
Birthplace: Texas
Born: August 27, 1908
Died: January 22, 1973

37 **Richard M. Nixon**
1969–1974
Republican
Birthplace: California
Born: January 9, 1913
Died: April 22, 1994

38 **Gerald R. Ford**
1974–1977
Republican
Birthplace: Nebraska
Born: July 14, 1913

39 **James E. Carter, Jr.**
1977–1981
Democrat
Birthplace: Georgia
Born: October 1, 1924

40 **Ronald W. Reagan**
1981–1989
Republican
Birthplace: Illinois
Born: February 6, 1911
Died: June 5, 2004

41 **George H. W. Bush**
1989–1993
Republican
Birthplace: Massachusetts
Born: June 12, 1924

42 **William J. Clinton**
1993–2001
Democrat
Birthplace: Arkansas
Born: August 19, 1946

43 **George W. Bush**
2001–
Republican
Birthplace: Connecticut
Born: July 6, 1946

The Gazetteer identifies important places and geographical features in this book. Entries include a short description, often followed by two page numbers. The first number refers to a text page on which the entry is discussed, and the second, in italics, refers to a map where the place appears. (The reference *Atlas* is to the section of U.S. and world maps on pages A1–A21.) In addition, some entries include rounded-off geographical coordinates. There are entries for all U.S. states (with capital cities).

Africa world's second largest continent. *Atlas*

Alabama 22nd state. Capital: Montgomery. *Atlas*

Alamo Texas mission in San Antonio captured by Mexico in 1836. (29°N 98°W), 125

Alaska 49th state. Capital: Juneau. *Atlas*

Antarctica continent at the South Pole. *Atlas*

Antietam Maryland creek; site of bloodiest day's fighting in the Civil War. (39°N 77°W), 140

Appalachian Mountains mountain range running from Alabama into Canada. *m33,* 36

Arizona 48th state. Capital: Phoenix. *Atlas*

Arkansas 25th state. Capital: Little Rock. *Atlas*

Asia world's largest continent. *Atlas*

Atlantic Ocean ocean forming east boundary of the United States. *Atlas*

Australia island country between Indian and Pacific oceans; also the world's smallest continent. *Atlas*

Austria-Hungary one of the Central Powers in World War I; after the war, divided into smaller countries. 278, *m278*

Bay of Pigs (Bahía de Cochinos) inlet on south coast of Cuba; site of 1961 ill-fated, U.S.-backed Cuban invasion attempt. (22°N 81°W), 436

Beringia former land bridge connecting Asia with North America and now under waters of Bering Strait. (66°N 169°W), 27

Berlin capital of Germany; divided into East and West Berlin, 1948–1989. (53°N 13°E), 391, *m392*

Boston capital of Massachusetts; site of early colonial unrest and conflict. (42°N 71°W), *m33,* 38

Bull Run stream 30 miles southwest of Washington, D.C.; site of first land battle of Civil War. (39°N 78°W), 139

Bunker Hill hill now part of Boston; its name misidentifies Revolutionary War battle fought at nearby Breed's Hill. (42°N 71°W), 39

California 31st state. Capital: Sacramento. *Atlas*

Canada nation sharing northern U.S. border. *Atlas*

Caribbean Sea expanse of the Atlantic Ocean between the Gulf of Mexico and South America. *Atlas*

Central America area of North America between Mexico and South America. *Atlas*

Charleston as Charles Town, largest Southern colonial city; South Carolina site of first Civil War shots, at offshore Fort Sumter. (33°N 80°W), *m33,* 41

Chicago large Illinois city on Lake Michigan. (42°N 88°W), 200, *Atlas*

China large nation in Asia. *Atlas*

Colorado 38th state. Capital: Denver. *Atlas*

Concord Massachusetts city and site of second battle of the Revolutionary War. (42°N 71°W), 39

Confederate States of America nation formed by 11 Southern states during the Civil War. Capital: Richmond, Virginia. 136

Connecticut 5th state. Capital: Hartford. *Atlas*

Cuba Caribbean island south of Florida. 260, *m263*

Delaware 1st state. Capital: Dover. *Atlas*

District of Columbia (D.C.) self-governing federal district between Virginia and Maryland, made up entirely of the city of Washington, the U.S. capital. (39°N 77°W), *Atlas*

Dominican Republic nation sharing the island of Hispaniola with Haiti. 271, *m270*

England southern part of Great Britain. *Atlas*

English Channel narrow waterway separating Great Britain from France. *m362*

Erie Canal all-water channel dug to connect the Hudson River with Lake Erie. *i110,* 124

Florida 27th state. Capital: Tallahassee. *Atlas*

Fort McHenry fort in Baltimore harbor where 1814 British attack inspired U.S. national anthem. (39°N 77°N), 116

Fort Sumter fort in Charleston, South Carolina, harbor where 1861 attack by Confederates began the Civil War. (33°N 80°W), 137

France nation in western Europe; it aided America in the Revolutionary War. *Atlas*

Gadsden Purchase last territory (from Mexico, 1853) added to continental United States. *m126*

Georgia 4th state. Capital: Atlanta. *Atlas*

Germany nation in central Europe; once divided into West and East Germany, 1949–1990. *Atlas*

Gettysburg Pennsylvania town and site of 1863 Civil War victory for the North that is considered war's turning point. (40°N 77°W), 141

Ghana first powerful West African trading empire. 29

Great Britain European island nation across from France; it consists of England, Scotland, and Wales. *Atlas*

Gulf of Mexico body of water forming southern U.S. boundary from east Texas to west Florida. *Atlas*

Haiti nation sharing the island of Hispaniola with Dominican Republic. *Atlas*

Harpers Ferry village today in extreme eastern West Virginia where John Brown raided stored U.S. weapons in 1859. (39°N 78°W), 136

Hawaii 50th state. Capital: Honolulu. *Atlas*

Hiroshima Japanese city destroyed by U.S. atomic bomb dropped to end World War II. (34°N 132°E), 369, *m369*

Hudson River large river in eastern New York. 31

Idaho 43rd state. Capital: Boise. *Atlas*

Illinois 21st state. Capital: Springfield. *Atlas*

Indiana 19th state. Capital: Indianapolis. *Atlas*

Indian Territory area, mainly of present-day Oklahoma, that in the 1800s became land for relocated Native Americans. 119

Iowa 29th state. Capital: Des Moines. *Atlas*

Iran Middle East nation. 463, *m463*

Iraq Middle East nation whose 1990 invasion of Kuwait led to the Persian Gulf War. 473, *m463*

Ireland island country west of England whose mid-1800s famine caused more than one million people to emigrate to America. *Atlas*

Israel Jewish nation in the Middle East. 462, *Atlas*

Italy nation in southern Europe. *Atlas*

Jamestown community in Virginia that was the first permanent English settlement in North America. 32–33, *m33*

Japan island nation in east Asia. *Atlas*

Kansas 34th state. Capital: Topeka. *Atlas*

Kentucky 15th state. Capital: Frankfort. *Atlas*

Kosovo province of the Yugoslavian republic of Serbia. 474, *m475*

Kuwait tiny, oil-rich Middle East nation. 473, *m463*

Latin America region made up of Mexico, Caribbean Islands, and Central and South America, where Latin-based languages of Spanish, French, or Portuguese are spoken. *m270*

Lexington Massachusetts city and site of first Revolutionary War battle in 1775. (42°N 71°W), 39

Little Bighorn River Montana site of Sioux and Cheyenne victory over Custer. (46°N 108°W), 163, *m161*

Little Rock capital of Arkansas and site of 1957 school-desegregation conflict. 414, *Atlas*

Los Angeles 2nd largest U.S. city, on California's coast. 422, *m402*

Louisiana 18th state. Capital: Baton Rouge. *Atlas*

Louisiana Purchase land west of the Mississippi River purchased from France in 1803. 115

Lowell Massachusetts city built in early 1800s as planned factory town. (43°N 71°W), 123

Maine 23rd state. Capital: Augusta. *Atlas*

Mali early West African trading empire succeeding Ghana empire. 29

Maryland 7th state. Capital: Annapolis. *Atlas*

Massachusetts 6th state. Capital: Boston. *Atlas*

Mexico nation sharing U.S. southern border. *Atlas*

Michigan 26th state. Capital: Lansing. *Atlas*

Middle East eastern Mediterranean region that includes countries such as Iran, Iraq, Syria, Kuwait, Jordan, Saudi Arabia, Israel, and Egypt. 462, *m362*, *m463*

Minnesota 32nd state. Capital: St. Paul. *Atlas*

Mississippi 20th state. Capital: Jackson. *Atlas*

Mississippi River second longest U.S. river, south from Minnesota to the Gulf of Mexico. 115

Missouri 24th state. Capital: Jefferson City. *Atlas*

Montana 41st state. Capital: Helena. *Atlas*

Montgomery Alabama capital and site of 1955 African-American bus boycott. (32°N 86°W), 411

Nagasaki Japanese port city, one-third of which was destroyed by U.S. atomic bomb dropped to end World War II. (33°N 130°E), 371, *m369*

Nebraska 37th state. Capital: Lincoln. *Atlas*

Nevada 36th state. Capital: Carson City. *Atlas*

New England northeast U.S. region made up of Maine, New Hampshire, Vermont, Massachusetts, Rhode Island, and Connecticut. 33, *m33*

New Hampshire 9th state. Capital: Concord. *Atlas*

New Jersey 3rd state. Capital: Trenton. *Atlas*

New Mexico 47th state. Capital: Santa Fe. *Atlas*

New Netherland early Dutch colony that became New York in 1664. 31, 34

New Orleans Louisiana port city at mouth of the Mississippi River. *Atlas*

New York 11th state. Capital: Albany. *Atlas*

New York City largest U.S. city, at the mouth of the Hudson River; temporary U.S. capital, 1785–1790. *Atlas*

Normandy region of northern France where Allied invasion in 1944 turned tide of World War II. 364, *m364*

North America continent of Western Hemisphere north of Panama-Colombia border. *Atlas*

North Carolina 12th state. Capital: Raleigh. *Atlas*

North Dakota 39th state. Capital: Bismarck. *Atlas*

North Korea Communist country in Asia, bordering eastern China. 393, *m394*

North Vietnam northern region of Vietnam, established in 1954; reunified with South Vietnam in 1975 after Vietnam War. 435, *m435*

Northwest Territory U.S. land north of the Ohio River to the Great Lakes and west to the Mississippi River; acquired in 1783. 56, *m56*, 114

Ohio 17th state. Capital: Columbus. *Atlas*

Ohio River river that flows from western Pennsylvania to the Mississippi River. *Atlas*

Oklahoma 46th state. Capital: Oklahoma City. *Atlas*

Oregon 33rd state. Capital: Salem. *Atlas*

Oregon Country former region of northwest North America claimed jointly by Britain and the United States until 1846. 125

Oregon Trail pioneer wagon route from Missouri to the Oregon Territory in the 1840s and 1850s. 125

Pacific Ocean world's largest ocean, on the west coast of the United States. *Atlas*

Panama Canal ship passageway cut through Panama in Central America, linking Atlantic and Pacific oceans. (8°N 80°W), 268, *m268*

Pearl Harbor naval base in Hawaii; site of surprise Japanese aerial attack in 1941. (21°N 158°W), 259, *m258*

Pennsylvania 2nd state. Capital: Harrisburg. *Atlas*

Persian Gulf waterway between Saudi Arabia and Iran, leading to Kuwait and Iraq. 473, *m463*

Philadelphia large port city in Pennsylvania; U.S. capital, 1790–1800. (40°N 76°W), 53, *Atlas*

Philippine Islands Pacific island country off the southeast coast of China. 260, *m263*

Plymouth town on Massachusetts coast and site of Pilgrim landing and colony. (42°N 76°W), 33

Puerto Rico Caribbean island that has been U.S. territory since 1898. 265, *m263*

Quebec major early Canadian city, also a province of eastern Canada. 31

Rhode Island 13th state. Capital: Providence. *Atlas*

Rio Grande river that forms part of the border between the United States and Mexico. *Atlas*

Roanoke Island island off the coast of North Carolina; 1585 site of the first English colony in the Americas. (36°N 76°W), 32, *m33*

Rocky Mountains mountain range in the western United States and Canada. *Atlas*

Russia large Eurasian country, the major republic of the former Soviet Union (1922–1991). 278, *m278*

St. Louis Missouri city at the junction of the Missouri and Mississippi rivers. (39°N 90°W), *Atlas*

San Francisco major port city in northern California. (38°N 123°W), *m190*

Santa Fe Trail old wagon route from Missouri to Santa Fe in Mexican province of New Mexico. 125

Songhai early West African trading empire succeeding Mali empire. 29

South America continent of Western Hemisphere south of Panama-Colombia border. *Atlas*

South Carolina 8th state. Capital: Columbia. *Atlas*

South Dakota 40th state. Capital: Pierre. *Atlas*

South Korea East Asian country bordering North Korea. 393, *m394*

South Vietnam southern region of Vietnam, established in 1954; reunified with North Vietnam in 1975 after Vietnam War. 435, *m435*

Soviet Union country created in 1922 by joining Russia and other republics; in 1991, broken into independent states. 355, *m358*

Tennessee 16th state. Capital: Nashville. *Atlas*

Texas 28th state. Capital: Austin. *Atlas*

Utah 45th state. Capital: Salt Lake City. *Atlas*

Valley Forge village in southeast Pennsylvania and site of Washington's army camp during winter of 1777–1778. (40°N 75°W), 40, *m40*

Vermont 14th state. Capital: Montpelier. *Atlas*

Vicksburg Mississippi River site of major Union victory (1863) in Civil War. (32°N 91°W), 141

Vietnam country in Southeast Asia; divided into two regions (1954–1975), North and South, until end of Vietnam War. 433, *m435*

Virginia 10th state. Capital: Richmond. *Atlas*

Washington 42nd state. Capital: Olympia. *Atlas*

Washington, D.C. capital of the United States since 1800; makes up whole of District of Columbia (D.C.). (39°N 77°W), *Atlas*

West Virginia 35th state. Capital: Charleston. *Atlas*

Wisconsin 30th state. Capital: Madison. *Atlas*

Wounded Knee South Dakota site that was scene of 1890 massacre of Sioux. (43°N 102°W), 164, *m161*

Wyoming 44th state. Capital: Cheyenne. *Atlas*

Yorktown Virginia village and site of American victory that sealed British defeat in Revolutionary War. (37°N 77°W), *m40*, 41

GLOSSARY

abolition (AB uh LIHSH uhn) *n.* the movement to end slavery. (p. 121)

AEF *n.* the American Expeditionary Force, U.S. forces during World War I. (p. 284)

Agent Orange *n.* a chemical that kills plants. (p. 441)

allies (AL yz) *n.* an alliance of Serbia, Russia, France, Great Britain, Italy, and seven other countries during World War I. (p. 278)

Antifederalist (AN tee FED uh uh list) *n.* a person who opposed the ratification of the U.S. Constitution. (p. 58)

American Federation of Labor (AFL) *n.* a national organization of labor unions founded in 1886. (p. 201)

Angel Island *n.* the first stop in the United States for most immigrants coming from Asia. (p. 213)

Anti-Imperialist (AN tee im PEER y uh LIZT) **League** *n.* a group of well-known Americans that believed the United States should not deny other people the right to govern themselves. (p. 265)

appeasement (uh PEEZ muhnt) *n.* the granting of concessions to a hostile power in order to keep the peace. (p. 355)

Appomattox (AP uh MAT uhks) **Court House** *n.* the place where Confederate general Robert E. Lee finally surrendered to Union general Ulyssess S. Grant in 1865, ending the Civil War. (p. 142)

armistice (AHR mi stis) *n.* an end to fighting. (p. 288)

arms race *n.* from the late 1940s to the late 1980s, the United States and the Soviet Union tried to top each other by developing weapons with great destructive power. (p. 396)

Articles of Confederation *n.* a document, adopted by the Continental Congress in 1777 and approved by the states in 1781, that outlined the form of government of the new United States. (p. 51)

assimilation (uh SIM uh LAY shuhn) *n.* the process of blending into society. (p. 214)

Axis (AK sis) *n.* Germany, Italy, and their allies during World War II. (p. 355)

baby boom *n.* the term for the generation born between 1946 and 1961, when the U.S. birthrate sharply increased following World War II. (p. 399)

Bataan (buh TAN) **Death March** *n.* in 1942, the Japanese marched 70,000 Filipino and American soldiers 60 miles to a prison camp. (p. 366)

Battle of Gettysburg (GET eez BURG) *n.* an 1863 battle in the Civil War in which the Union defeated the Confederacy, ending hopes for a Confederate victory in the North. (p. 141)

Battle of Midway *n.* a victory for the United States over the Japanese in a 1942 naval battle that was a turning point of World War II. (p. 368)

Battle of the Bulge *n.* a month-long battle of World War II in which the Allies turned back the last major German offensive of the war. (p. 362)

Battle of the Little Bighorn *n.* an 1876 battle in which the Sioux and the Cheyenne wiped out an entire force of U.S. troops. (p. 163)

Bessemer (BES uh muhr) **steel process** *n.* a new way of making steel that was developed in the 1850s and caused steel production to soar. (p. 185)

Bill of Rights *n.* the first ten amendments to the U.S. Constitution, added in 1791, and consisting of a formal list of citizens' rights and freedoms. (p. 61)

Black Tuesday *n.* a name given to October 29, 1929, when stock prices fell sharply. (p. 329)

Bonus Army *n.* in 1932, thousands of veterans streamed into Washington demanding bonuses that they never received. (p. 331)

boomtown *n.* a town that has a sudden burst of economic or population growth. (p. 156)

Boxer Rebellion *n.* in 1900, Chinese resentment toward foreigners' attitude of cultural superiority resulted in this violent uprising. (p. 267)

bracero (bruh SAIR oh) **program** *n.* the hiring of Mexicans to perform much-needed labor during World War II. (p. 372)

brinksmanship (BRINGKS muhn SHIP) *n.* in international politics, the act of pushing a dangerous situation to the limits; for example, the United States going to the brink of war to stop Communism. (p. 396)

Brown v. Board of Education of Topeka, Kansas *n.* a 1954 case in which the Supreme Court ruled that "separate but equal" education for black and white students was unconstitutional. (p. 412)

buffalo soldier *n.* a name given by Native Americans to African Americans serving in the U.S. army in the West. (p. 169)

business cycle *n.* the pattern of good times and bad times in the economy. (p. 184)

buy on margin *v.* to pay a small part of a stock's price and then borrow money to pay for the rest. (p. 328)

California gold rush *n.* movement of large numbers of people to California in 1849 after gold was discovered there. (p. 127)

Cambodia (kam BOW dee uh) *n.* a country bordering Vietnam. (p. 446)

Camp David Accords *n.* in 1979, under these agreements, Egypt and Israel signed a peace treaty that ended 30 years of conflict. (p. 462)

Centennial (sen TEN ee uhl) **Exhibition** *n.* an exhibition in Philadelphia in 1876 that celebrated America's 100th birthday. (p. 186)

Central Powers *n.* an alliance of Austria-Hungary, Germany, the Ottoman Empire, and Bulgaria during World War I. (p. 278)

Chinese Exclusion Act *n.* enacted in 1882, this law banned Chinese immigration for ten years. (p. 215)

Civil Rights Act of 1964 *n.* this act banned segregation in public places and created the Equal Employment Opportunity Commission. (p. 418)

Clayton Antitrust Act *n.* a law passed in 1914 that laid down rules forbidding business practices that lessened competition; it gave the government more power to regulate trusts. (p. 246)

Cold War *n.* the state of hostility, without direct military conflict, that developed between the United States and the Soviet Union after World War II. (p. 390)

Columbian (kuh LUM bee uhn) **Exchange** *n.* the transfer of plants, animals, and diseases between the Western and the Eastern hemispheres. (p. 31)

Committee to Reelect the President *n.* an organization linked to the break-in at the Democratic National Committee headquarters that set off the Watergate scandal. (p. 458)

Compromise of 1850 *n.* a series of Congressional laws intended to settle the major disagreements between free states and slave states in 1850. (p. 134)

Confederate States of America *n.* the confederation formed in 1861 by the Southern states that seceded from the Union. (p. 136)

Congress of Industrial Organizations (CIO) *n.* a labor organization that broke away from the American Federation of Labor in 1938. (p. 341)

conquistador (kon KWIS tuh DAWR) *n.* a Spaniard who traveled to the Americas as an explorer and a conqueror in the 16th century. (p. 30)

conservative *n.* a person who favors fewer government controls and more individual freedom in economic matters. (p. 347)

Constitutional Convention *n.* a meeting held in 1787 to consider changes to the Articles of Confederation; resulted in the drafting of the Constitution. (p. 53)

containment (kuhn TAYN muhnt) *n.* the blocking by one nation of another nation's attempts to spread influence—especially the efforts of the United States to block the spread of Soviet Communism during the late 1940s and early 1950s. (p. 391)

convoy system *n.* a heavy guard of destroyers that escorts merchant ships during wartime. (p. 285)

cooperative (koh OP uhr uh tiv) *n.* an organization owned and run by its members. (p. 175)

CORE *n.* the Congress of Racial Equality, a group that planned Freedom Rides to desegregate interstate buses. (p. 416)

corporation *n.* a business owned by investors who buy part of the company through shares of stock. (p. 192)

cotton gin *n.* a machine invented in 1793 that cleaned cotton much faster and far more efficiently than human workers. (p. 120)

Crash of 1929 *n.* the plunge in stock market prices. (p. 329)

Cuban Missile Crisis *n.* in 1962, the United States and the Soviet Union almost went to war because the Soviets had placed nuclear missiles in Cuba. (p. 437)

D

Dawes (dawz) **Act** *n.* a law, enacted in 1887, that distributed reservation land to individual owners. (p. 165)

D-Day *n.* June 6, 1944, the day the Allies invaded France during World War II. (p. 362)

Declaration of Independence *n.* the document, written in 1776, in which the colonies declared independence from Britain. (p. 39)

deficit (DEF i sit) **spend** *v.* to use borrowed money to fund government programs. (p. 336)

department store *n.* a store that sells everything from clothing to furniture to hardware. (p. 225)

détente (day TAHNT) *n.* an easing of tensions between the United States and the Soviet Union during the Cold War. (p. 356)

direct primary *n.* voters, rather than party conventions, choose candidates to run for public office. (p. 238)

domino (DOM uh NOH) **theory** *n.* a theory stating that if a country fell to communism, nearby countries would also fall to communism. (p. 435)

dove *n.* a person opposed to war. (p. 445)

downsize *v.* to reduce the number of workers in order to increase company profits. (p. 479)

dust bowl *n.* the area of dust-damaged farms across a 150,000-square-mile region during the early 1930s. (p. 337)

E

e-commerce *n.* business that is conducted over the Internet. (p. 478)

Ellis Island *n.* the first stop in the United States for most immigrants coming from Europe. (p. 212)

Emancipation (i MAN suh PAY shuhn) **Proclamation** *n.* an executive order issued by Abraham Lincoln on January 1, 1863, freeing the slaves in all regions in rebellion against the Union. (p. 140)

environmentalism (en VY ruhn MEN tl IZ uhm) *n.* work toward protecting the environment. (p. 462)

ERA *n.* the Equal Rights Amendment, a proposed amendment that would give equality of rights regardless of sex; the amendment died in 1982. (p. 424)

escalation (ES kuh LAY shuhn) *n.* the policy of increasing military involvement, as in Vietnam. (p. 439)

Espionage (ES pee uh NAHZH) **Act** *n.* passed in 1917, this law set heavy fines and long prison terms for antiwar activities and for encouraging draft resisters. (p. 290)

exoduster (EKS suh duhs tuhr) *n.* an African American who left the South for the West and compared himself or herself to Biblical Hebrews who left slavery in Egypt. (p. 173)

expatriate (ek SPAY tree it) *n.* a citizen of one country who takes up residence in another country. (p. 319)

Fair Deal *n.* a program under Harry Truman that called for new projects to create jobs, new public housing, and an end to racial discrimination in hiring. (p. 389)

fascism (FASH iz uhm) *n.* a political philosophy that advocates a strong, centralized, nationalistic government headed by a powerful dictator. (p. 354)

federalism *n.* a system of government where power is shared among the central (or federal) government and the states. (p. 58)

Federalists *n.* supporters of the Constitution. (p. 58)

Federalist Papers *n.* a series of essays defending and explaining the Constitution. (p. 59)

Federal Reserve Act *n.* a law passed in 1913 that "created" the nation's banking system and instituted a flexible currency system. (p. 246)

Fifteenth Amendment *n.* passed in 1870, this amendment to the U.S. Constitution stated that citizens could not be stopped from voting "on account of race, color, or previous condition of servitude." (p. 146)

fireside chat *n.* the name of Franklin Roosevelt's radio broadcasts in which he explained his policies. (p. 333)

flapper *n.* a young woman who embraced the fashions and urban attitudes of the 1920s. (p. 312)

Fort Sumter *n.* a federal fort located in the harbor of Charleston, South Carolina; the Southern attack on Fort Sumter marked the beginning of the Civil War. (p. 137)

Fourteen Points *n.* President Woodrow Wilson's goals for peace after World War I. (p. 293)

Fourteenth Amendment *n.* an amendment to the U.S. Constitution, passed in 1868, that made all persons born or naturalized in the United States—including former slaves—citizens of the country. (p. 145)

Freedom Ride *n.* a protest against segregation on interstate busing in the South. (p. 416)

Freedom Summer *n.* in 1964, the SNCC organized a voter-registration drive. (p. 419)

French and Indian War *n.* a conflict in North America from 1754 to 1763 that was part of a worldwide struggle between France and Britain; Britain defeated France and gained French Canada. (p. 36)

French Indochina (IN doh CHY nuh) *n.* a French colony that included present-day Vietnam, Laos, and Cambodia. (p. 433)

frontier (frun TEER) *n.* unsettled or sparsely settled area occupied largely by Native Americans. (p. 155)

fundamentalist *n.* a person who believes in a literal, or word-for-word, interpretation of the bible. (p. 314)

generator *n.* a machine that produces electric current. (p. 185)

Ghana (GAH nuh) *n.* a West African empire in the 8th–11th centuries A.D. (p. 29)

G.I. Bill of Rights *n.* passed in 1944, this bill provided educational and economic help to veterans. (p. 377)

Gilded (gil did) **Age** *n.* an era during the late 1800s of fabulous wealth. (p. 194)

gold standard *n.* a policy under which the government backs every dollar with a certain amount of gold. (p. 175)

Grange (graynj) *n.* formed in 1867, the Patrons of Husbandry tried to meet the social needs of farm families. (p. 175)

Great Compromise *n.* the Constitutional Convention's agreement to establish a two-house national legislature, with all states having equal representation in one house and each state having representation based on its population in the other house. (p. 54)

Great Depression *n.* a period, lasting from 1929 to 1941, in which the U.S. economy was in severe decline and millions of Americans were unemployed. (p. 329)

Great Migration *n.* the movement of African Americans between 1910 and 1920 to northern cities from the South. (p. 291)

Great Plains *n.* the area from the Missouri River to the Rocky Mountains. (p. 155)

Great Society *n.* a program started by President Lyndon Johnson that provided help to the poor, the elderly, and women, and also promoted education and outlawed discrimination. (p. 420)

guerrilla warfare *n.* surprise attacks by small bands of fighters. (p. 440)

Gulf of Tonkin Resolution *n.* congressional resolution that gave the president power to use military force in Vietnam. (p. 439)

Harlem Renaissance *n.* a flowering of African-American artistic creativity during the 1920s, centered in the Harlem community of New York City. (p. 318)

hawk *n.* a person who supports war. (p. 445)

Haymarket affair *n.* in 1886, a union protest resulted in about 100 dead after an unknown person threw a bomb, and police opened fire on the crowd. (p. 200)

H-bomb *n.* a hydrogen bomb. (p. 396)

Hiroshima (HEER uh SHEE muh) *n.* the first city in Japan that was hit by an atomic bomb on August 6, 1945. (p. 369)

Ho Chi Minh (HOH CHEE MIN) **Trail** *n.* a network of paths that the Viet Cong used to move soldiers and supplies during the Vietnam War. (p. 436)

Holocaust (HOL uh KAWST) *n.* the systematic killing by Germany during World War II of about six million Jews as well as millions from other ethnic groups. (p. 363)

homestead *n.* land to settle on and farm. (p. 166)

Homestead Act *n.* passed in 1862, this law offered 160 acres of land free to anyone who agreed to live on and improve the land for five years. (p. 172)

House of Burgesses *n.* created in 1619, the first representative assembly in the American colonies. (p. 33)

Hull House *n.* founded in 1889, a model for other settlement houses of the time. (p. 211)

Hundred Days *n.* in his first hundred days, from March 9 to mid-June 1933, Franklin Roosevelt sent Congress many new bills. (p. 333)

Immigration Reform and Control Act of 1986 *n.* a law that is designed to strengthen immigration laws and enforcement measures. (p. 484)

imperialism *n.* the policy by which stronger nations extend their economic, political, or military control over weaker nations or territories. (p. 257)

impressment *n.* the act of seizing by force. (p. 116)

Indian Removal Act *n.* this 1830 act called for the government to negotiate treaties that would require Native Americans to relocate west. (p. 119)

Industrial Revolution *n.* in late 18th-century Britain, factory machines began to replace hand tools and manufacturing began to replace farming as the main form of work. (p. 123)

information revolution *n.* a time when technology has radically changed how much information and the way information is delivered. (p. 479)

initiative (i NISH uh tiv) *n.* the procedure that allows voters to propose a law directly. (p. 238)

installment buy *v.* to buy something by making small monthly payments. (p. 310)

Internet *n.* a worldwide computer network. (p. 478)

Iran-Contra affair *n.* in 1986, the U.S. government sold weapons to Iran for help in freeing American hostages in the Middle East, and the money from the sale went to the Contra rebels in El Salvador. (p. 472)

Iran hostage crisis *n.* on November 4, 1979, a group of Iranians overran the American embassy in Iran's capital of Tehran and took 52 Americans hostage. (p. 463)

island hopping *n.* a World War II strategy in which the Allies invaded islands that the Japanese weakly defended in order to stage further attacks. (p. 368)

isolationist *n.* a person who believed that the United States should stay out of other nations' affairs except in self-defense. (p. 309)

Jacksonian Democracy *n.* the idea of spreading political power to more of the people. (p. 118)

Jamestown *n.* the first permanent English settlement in North America. (pp. 32–33)

jazz *n.* a new kind of music in the 1920s that captured the carefree spirit of the times. (p. 315)

Jim Crow *n.* laws meant to enforce separation of white and black people in public places in the South. (p. 219)

Kellogg-Briand Pact *n.* in 1928, this pact was signed by many nations who pledged not to make war against each other except in self-defense. (p. 309)

Knights of Labor *n.* an organization of workers from all different trades formed after the Civil War. (p. 199)

Korean War *n.* a conflict between North Korea and South Korea, lasting from 1950 to 1953; the United States, along with other UN countries, fought on the side of the South Koreans, and China fought on the side of the North Koreans. (p. 394)

Ku Klux Klan *n.* a group formed in 1866 that wanted to restore white control of the South and to keep former slaves powerless. (pp. 146, 314)

L

laissez faire (LES ay FAIR) *n.* a theory that stated that business, if unregulated, would act in a way that would benefit the nation. (p. 308)

League of Nations *n.* an organization set up after World War I to settle international conflicts. (p. 293)

leisure (LEE zhuhr) *n.* free time. (p. 225)

Lend-Lease *n.* a 1941 law that allowed the United States to ship arms and supplies, without immediate payment, to nations fighting the Axis powers. (p. 358)

liberal *n.* a person who favors government action to bring about social and economic reform. (p. 347)

lode *n.* a deposit of mineral buried in rock. (p. 156)

long drive *n.* taking cattle by foot to a railway. (p. 158)

Lost Generation *n.* the generation of the 1920s after World War I, when men and women saw little hope for the future. (p. 318)

Louisiana (loo EE zee AN uh) **Purchase** *n.* the 1803 purchase of the Louisiana Territory from France. (p. 115)

Loyalist *n.* an American colonist who supported the British in the American Revolution. (p. 39)

M

mail-order catalog *n.* a publication that contains pictures and descriptions of items so that people can order by mail. (p. 225)

Manhattan Project *n.* the top-secret program set up in 1942 to build an atomic bomb. (p. 369)

manifest destiny *n.* the belief that the United States was destined to stretch across the continent from the Atlantic Ocean to the Pacific Ocean. (p. 125)

Marbury v. Madison *n.* an 1803 case in which the Supreme Court ruled that it had the power to abolish laws by declaring them unconstitutional. (p. 115)

March on Washington *n.* a huge civil rights demonstration in Washington, D.C., in 1963. (p. 418)

Marshall Plan *n.* approved in 1948, the United States gave more than $13 billion to help the nations of Europe after World War II. (p. 377)

mass culture *n.* a common culture experienced by large numbers of people. (p. 224)

mass media *n.* communications that reach a large audience. (p. 316)

Mayflower Compact *n.* an agreement established by the men who sailed to America on the *Mayflower,* which called for laws for the good of the colony and helped establish the idea of self-government. (p. 33)

melting pot *n.* a place where cultures blend. (p. 214)

Mexicano (may hi KAH noh) *n.* a person of Spanish descent whose ancestors had come from Mexico and settled in the Southwest. (p. 168)

militarism *n.* the belief that a nation needs a large military force. (p. 277)

mission *n.* a settlement created by the Roman Catholic Church in order to convert Native Americans to Christianity. (p. 31)

monopoly *n.* a company that eliminates its competitors and controls an industry. (p. 193)

Monroe Doctrine *n.* a policy of U.S. opposition to any European interference in the Western Hemisphere, announced by President James Monroe in 1823. (p. 31)

Montgomery bus boycott *n.* in 1955, African Americans boycotted the public buses in Montgomery, Alabama, in response to the arrest of Rosa Parks, who refused to give up her seat to a white person. (p. 413)

Mound Builder *n.* an early Native American who built large earthen structures. (p. 28)

muckraker *n.* around 1900, the term for a journalist who exposed corruption in American society. (p. 238)

Muslim (MUZ luhm) *n.* a followers of Islam. (p. 29)

N

NAACP *n.* formed in 1909, the National Association for the Advancement of Colored People. (pp. 220, 313)

NAFTA *n.* passed in 1993, the North American Free Trade Agreement created a free trade block among the United States, Mexico, and Canada. (p. 473)

napalm (NAY PAHM) *n.* a jellied gasoline that burns violently. (p. 441)

NATO *n.* the North Atlantic Treaty Organization is a military alliance formed in 1949 by ten Western European countries, the United States, and Canada. (p. 391)

naturalization *n.* a way to give full citizenship to a person born in another country. (p. 43)

Nazi (NAHT see) **Party** *n.* the National Socialist German Workers' Party; came to power under Adolf Hitler in the 1930s. (p. 354)

NCAI *n.* the National Congress of American Indians was founded in 1944 and aimed to promote the "common welfare" of Native Americans. (p. 423)

neutral (NOO truhl) *adj.* not siding with one country or the other. (p. 114)

neutrality (noo TRAL i tee) *n.* refusing to take sides in a war. (p. 280)

New Deal *n.* President Franklin Roosevelt's programs to fight the Great Depression. (p. 333)

new immigrant *n.* a person from southern or eastern Europe who entered the United States after 1900. (p. 212)

New Jersey Plan *n.* a plan of government proposed at the Constitutional Convention in 1787 that called for a one-house legislature in which each state would have one vote. (p. 54)

Nineteenth Amendment *n.* an amendment to the U.S. Constitution, ratified in 1920, which gave women full voting rights. (p. 251)

Nisei (NEE say) *n.* a Japanese American born in the United States. (p. 373)

NOW *n.* founded in 1966, the National Organization for Women pushed to get women good jobs at equal pay. (p. 424)

nullification *n.* the idea that states can reject federal laws that they oppose. (p. 120)

Nuremberg (NOOR uhm BURG) **Trials** *n.* the court proceedings held in Nuremberg, Germany, after World War II, in which Nazi leaders were tried for war crimes. (p. 378)

O

Open Door Policy *n.* in 1899, the United States asked nations involved in Asia to follow a policy in which no one country controlled trade with China. (p. 267)

Oregon Trail *n.* a trail that ran westward from Independence, Missouri, to the Oregon Territory. (p. 125)

P

Palmer raids *n.* in 1920, federal agents and police raided the homes of suspected radicals. (p. 295)

Panama (PAN uh MAH) **Canal** *n.* a shortcut through Panama that connects the Atlantic and the Pacific oceans. (p. 268)

patent *n.* a government document giving an inventor the exclusive right to make or sell his or her invention for a specific number of years. (p. 184)

Patriot *n.* an American colonist who sided with the rebels in the American Revolution. (p. 39)

Pearl Harbor *n.* a naval base in Hawaii that was hit in a surprise attack by Japan on December 7, 1941. (p. 358)

Persian (PUR zhen) **Gulf War** *n.* in 1990–1991, the United States and the UN drove Iraq out of Kuwait, a country the Iraqis had invaded in 1990. (p. 473)

petroleum *n.* an oily, flammable liquid. (p. 183)

philanthropist (fil LAN thruh pist) *n.* a person who gives large sums of money to charities. (p. 194)

Pilgrim *n.* a member of the group that rejected the Church of England, sailed to America, and founded the Plymouth Colony in 1620. (p. 33)

Platt Amendment *n.* a result of the Spanish-American War, which gave the United States the right to intervene in Cuban affairs when there was a threat to "life, property, and individual liberty." (p. 264)

Plessy v. Ferguson *n.* an 1896 case in which the Supreme Court ruled that separation of the races in public accommodations was legal. (p. 219)

political machine *n.* an organization that influences enough votes to control a local government. (p. 211)

popular culture *n.* items such as music, fashion, and movies that are popular among a large number of people. (p. 316)

Populist Party *n.* also known as the People's Party and formed in the 1890s, this group wanted a policy that would raise crop prices. (p. 175)

progressivism (pruh GREHS ih VIHZ uhm) *n.* an early 20th-century reform movement seeking to return control of the government to the people, to restore economic opportunities, and to correct injustices in American life. (p. 237)

prohibition (PROH uh BIHSH uhn) *n.* the banning of the manufacture, sale, and possession of alcoholic beverages. (p. 313)

propaganda (PRAHP uh GAN duh) *n.* an opinion expressed for the purpose of influencing the actions of others. (p. 290)

public works project *n.* a government-funded project to build public resources such as roads and dams. (p. 330)

Pullman Strike *n.* a nationwide railway strike that spread throughout the rail industry in 1894. (p. 201)

Puritan *n.* a member of a group from England that settled the Massachusetts Bay Colony in 1630 and sought to reform the practices of the Church of England. (pp. 33–34)

R

racial (RAY shuhl) **discrimination** (dih SKRIHM uh NAY shuhn) *n.* different treatment based on a person's race. (p. 218)

ragtime *n.* a blend of African-American songs and European musical forms. (p. 227)

ration (RASH uhn) *v.* to distribute a fixed amount of a certain item. (p. 371)

recall *v.* to vote an official out of office. (p. 238)

Reconstruction *n.* the process the U.S. government used to readmit the Confederate states to the Union after the Civil War. (p. 144)

Red Scare *n.* in 1919–1920, a wave of panic from fear of a Communist revolution. (p. 295)

referendum (REHF uh REHN duhm) *n.* when a proposed law is submitted to a vote of the people. (p. 238)

reservation *n.* land set aside by the U.S. government for Native American tribes. (p. 160)

revenue sharing *n.* the distribution of federal money to state and local governments with few or no restrictions on how it is spent. (p. 454)

robber baron *n.* a business leader who became wealthy through dishonest methods. (p. 192)

rock 'n' roll *n.* a form of popular music, characterized by heavy rhythms and simple melodies, that developed from rhythm and blues in the 1950s. (p. 401)

Roosevelt Corollary (KAWR uh lehr ee) *n.* a 1904 addition to the Monroe Doctrine allowing the United States to be the "policeman" in Latin America. (p. 270)

Rosie the Riveter (RIHV iht uhr) *n.* an image of a strong woman hard at work at an arms factory during World War II. (p. 371)

Rough Rider *n.* a member of the First United States Volunteer Cavalry, organized by Theodore Roosevelt during the Spanish-American War. (p. 263)

S

SALT *n.* the Strategic Arms Limitation Treaty, a treaty signed in 1972 between the United States and the Soviet Union; it limited nuclear weapons. (p. 456)

Sand Creek Massacre (MAS uh kuhr) *n.* an 1864 attack in which more than 150 Cheyenne men, women, and children were killed by the Colorado militia. (p. 162)

SCLC *n.* the Southern Christian Leadership Conference, a group that coordinated civil rights protests across the South. (p. 413)

secede (sih SEED) *v.* to withdraw. (pp. 136–137)

Second Battle of the Marne (mahrn) *n.* a 1918 battle during World War I that marked the turning point in the war; allied troops along with Americans halted the German advance into France. (p. 287)

Second New Deal *n.* a set of programs passed in 1935 to fight the Great Depression. (p. 334)

Securities and Exchange Commission *n.* an agency that watches the stock market and makes sure companies follow fair practices for trading stocks. (p. 346)

Sedition (sih DIHSH uhn) **Act** *n.* a 1918 law that made it illegal to criticize the war; it set heavy fines and long prison terms for those who engaged in anti-war activities. (p. 290)

segregation (SEHG rih GAY shuhn) *n.* separation, especially of races. (p. 219)

Seneca (SEHN ih kuh) **Falls Convention** *n.* a women's rights convention held in Seneca Falls, New York, in 1848. (p. 122)

service economy *n.* an economy in which most jobs provide services instead of producing goods. (p. 479)

Seventeenth Amendment *n.* an amendment to the U.S. Constitution, ratified in 1913, that provided for the direct election of U.S. senators. (p. 246)

Sherman Antitrust Act *n.* a law passed in 1890 that made it illegal for corporations to gain control of industries by forming trusts. (p. 239)

sit-down strike *n.* a strike in which workers remain idle inside the plant or factory. (p. 341)

Sixteenth Amendment *n.* an amendment to the U.S. Constitution, ratified in 1913, that gave Congress the power to create income taxes. (p. 245)

slavery *n.* the practice of holding a person in bondage for labor. (p. 31)

slum *n.* a neighborhood with overcrowded and dangerous housing. (p. 210)

SNCC *n.* formed in 1960, the Student Nonviolent Coordinating Committee was created to give young people a larger role in the civil rights movement. (p. 415)

social gospel (GAHS puhl) *n.* a movement aimed at improving the lives of the poor. (p. 210)

socialism *n.* an economic system in which all members of a society are equal owners of all businesses; members share the work and the profits. (p. 200)

Social Security Act *n.* a law, passed in 1935, that requires workers and employers to make payments into a fund, from which they draw a pension after they retired. (p. 334)

sodbuster *n.* a farmer on the frontier. (p. 173)

space race *n.* a competition, beginning in 1957, between the Soviet Union and the United States in the exploration of space. (p. 397)

Spanish-American War *n.* a war in 1898 that began when the United States demanded Cuba's independence from Spain. (p. 262)

speculation (SPEHK yuh LAY shuhn) *n.* buying and selling of a stock in the hope of making a quick profit. (p. 328)

sphere of influence *n.* an area where foreign nations claim special rights and economic privileges. (p. 267)

standard time *n.* a system adopted in 1918 that divided the United States into four time zones. (p. 190)

suburb *n.* a residential area that surrounds a city. (p. 398)

sunbelt *n.* the warmer states of the South and Southwest. (p. 399)

supply-side economics *n.* the idea that lowering taxes will lead to increases in jobs, savings, investments, and so lead to an increase in government revenue. (p. 471)

sweatshop *n.* a place where workers labored long hours under poor conditions for low wages. (p. 198)

Tammany (TAM uh nee) **Hall** *n.* a famous political machine, located in New York City in the late 19th century. (p. 211)

tariff *n.* a tax on imported goods. (p. 113)

Teapot Dome Scandal *n.* episode caused by Secretary of the Interior Albert B. Fall's leasing of oil-rich public land to private companies for money and land. (p. 308)

tenement *n.* an apartment building that is usually run-down and overcrowded. (p. 209)

Tet (tet) **offensive** *n.* in 1968, a surprise attack by the Viet Cong on U.S. military bases and more than 100 cities and towns in South Vietnam during Tet, the Vietnamese celebration of the lunar New Year. (p. 442)

Thirteenth Amendment *n.* an amendment to the U.S. Constitution, adopted in 1865, banning slavery and involuntary servitude in the United States. (p. 143)

38th parallel *n.* the area north of this latitude in Korea occupied by Soviet troops in 1945. (p. 393)

Three-Fifths Compromise *n.* the Constitutional Convention's agreement to count three-fifths of a state's slaves as population for purposes of representation and taxation. (p. 55)

Trail of Tears *n.* the journey of the Cherokee people from their homeland to Indian Territory between 1838 and 1839; thousands of Cherokee died. (p. 119)

transcontinental (TRANS kon tuh NEN tl) **railroad** *n.* a railroad that spanned the entire continent. (p. 188)

Treaty of Guadalupe Hidalgo (GWAHD loop hi DAH goh) *n.* the 1848 treaty ending the U.S. war with Mexico; Mexico ceded nearly one-half of its land to the United States. (p. 126)

Treaty of Paris *n.* the 1763 treaty that ended the French and Indian War; Britain gained all of North America east of the Mississippi River. (p. 36)

Treaty of Paris of 1783 *n.* the treaty that ended the Revolutionary War, confirming the independence of the United States and setting the boundaries of the new nation. (p. 41)

Treaty of Versailles (vuhr SY) *n.* the 1919 treaty that ended World War I. (p. 294)

trench warfare *n.* a kind of warfare during World War I in which troops huddled at the bottom of trenches and fired artillery and machine guns at each other. (p. 278)

triangular trade *n.* the transatlantic system of trade in which goods, including slaves, were exchanged between Africa, England, Europe, the West Indies, and the colonies in North America. (p. 35)

Truman Doctrine *n.* a policy that promised aid to people struggling to resist threats to democratic freedom. (p. 391)

trust *n.* a legal body created to hold stock in many companies, often in the same industry. (p. 193)

Twenty-sixth Amendment *n.* an amendment to the U.S. Constitution, adopted in 1971 and lowering the voting age from 21 to 18. (p. 447)

United Nations *n.* an international peacekeeping organization to which most nations in the world belong, founded in 1945 to promote world peace, security, and economic development. (p. 379)

urbanization *n.* growth of cities resulting from industrialization. (p. 207)

U.S.S. *Maine* *n.* a U.S. warship that mysteriously exploded and sank in the harbor of Havana, Cuba, on February 15, 1898. (p. 261)

vaquero (vah KAIR oh) *n.* a cowhand that came from Mexico with the Spaniards in the 1500s. (p. 158)

vaudeville (VAWD vil) *n.* a form of live stage entertainment with a mixture of songs, dance, and comedy. (p. 227)

Viet Cong *n.* a Vietnamese Communist. (p. 436)

Vietnamization (vee ET nuh mi ZAY shuhn) *n.* a strategy of gradually withdrawing U.S. forces and turning the ground fighting over to the South Vietnamese during the Vietnam War. (p. 446)

vigilante (vij uh LAN tee) *n.* a person willing to take the law into his or her own hands. (p. 159)

Virginia Plan *n.* a plan proposed at the 1787 Constitutional Convention to create a government with three branches and a two-house legislature in which representation would be based on a state's population or wealth. (p. 53)

Voting Rights Act of 1965 *n.* this law banned literacy tests and other laws that kept African Americans from registering to vote. (p. 419)

war bond *n.* a low-interest loan by civilians to the government, meant to be repaid in a number of years. (p. 289)

War Powers Act *n.* passed in 1973, this limits the president's war-making powers without consulting Congress. (p. 447)

War Production Board *n.* an agency established during World War II to coordinate the production of military supplies by U.S. industries. (p. 370)

War with Mexico *n.* war between the United States and Mexico fought between 1846 and 1848. (p. 126)

Watergate scandal *n.* a scandal resulting from the Nixon administration's attempt to cover up its involvement in the 1972 break-in at the Democratic National Committee headquarters in the Watergate apartment complex in Washington, D.C. (p. 458)

Wounded Knee Massacre *n.* the massacre by U.S. soldiers of 300 unarmed Native Americans at Wounded Knee Creek, South Dakota, in 1890. (p. 164)

Y2K *n.* a computer problem caused by computer programs using only the last two digits of a year and complicated by the arrival of the year 2000. (p. 476)

Yalta (YAWL tuh) **Conference** *n.* in 1945, Franklin Roosevelt, Winston Churchill, and Joseph Stalin discussed plans for the end of World War II and the future of Europe. (p. 363)

yellow journalism *n.* a style of journalism that exaggerates and sensationalizes the news. (p. 261)

Zimmermann telegram *n.* a message sent in 1917 by the German foreign minister to the German ambassador in Mexico, proposing a German-Mexican alliance and promising to help Mexico regain Texas, New Mexico, and Arizona if the United States entered World War I. (p. 280)

abolition [abolición] *s.* movimiento para eliminar la esclavitud. (p. 120)

AEF *s.* Fuerza Expedicionaria Estadounidense, fuerzas de EE. UU. durante la primera guerra mundial. (p. 284)

Agent Orange [agente naranja] *s.* herbicida que mata las plantas. (p. 441)

allies [aliados] *s.* alianza de Serbia, Rusia, Francia, Gran Bretaña, Italia y otros siete países durante la primera guerra mundial. (p. 278)

American Federation of Labor (AFL) [Federación Norteamericana del Trabajo] *s.* organización nacional de sindicatos obreros fundada en 1886. (p. 201)

Angel Island [isla del Ángel] *s.* primera parada en Estados Unidos para la mayoría de los inmigrantes que venían de Asia. (p. 213)

Antifederalist [antifederalista] *s.* persona que se oponía a la ratificación de la Constitución de los Estados Unidos. (p. 58)

Anti-Imperialist League [Liga Antiimperialista] *s.* grupo de estadounidenses importantes que creían que Estados Unidos no debía negarle a otras personas el derecho de gobernarse a sí mismas. (p. 265)

appeasement [apaciguamiento] *s.* otorgamiento de concesiones a una potencia hostil con el fin de mantener la paz. (p. 355)

Appomattox [Appomattox] **Court House** *s.* pueblo de Virginia donde Robert E. Lee se rindió a Ulysses S. Grant en 1865, finalizando así la guerra civil. (p. 142)

armistice [armisticio] *s.* suspensión de la lucha en una guerra. (p. 288)

arms race [carrera de armamento] *s.* desde fines de los años cuarenta hasta fines de los años ochenta, Estados Unidos y la Unión Soviética trataron de superarse una a la otra desarrollando armas de mayor poder destructivo. (p. 396)

Articles of Confederation [Artículos de Confederación] *s.* documento, adoptado por el Congreso Continental en 1777 y finalmente aprobado por los estados en 1781, que delineaba la forma de gobierno de los nuevos Estados Unidos. (p. 51)

assimilation [asimilación] *s.* proceso de integrarse a una sociedad. (p. 214)

Axis [Eje] *s.* Alemania, Italia y sus aliados durante la segunda guerra mundial. (p. 355)

baby boom *s.* término para la generación que nació en Estados Unidos entre 1946 y 1961, cuando el índice de natalidad aumentó marcadamente después de la segunda guerra mundial. (p. 399)

Bataan Death March [Marcha de la Muerte de Bataan] *s.* en 1942 los japoneses forzaron a 70,000 soldados filipinos y estadounidenses a marchar 60 millas a un campo de prisioneros. (p. 366)

Battle of Gettysburg [batalla de Gettysburg) *s.* batalla de 1863 de la guerra civil en que la Unión derrotó a la Confederación, poniendo fin a la esperanza de una victoria confederada en el Norte. (p. 141)

Battle of Midway *s.* victoria de Estados Unidos sobre los japoneses en una batalla naval de 1942 que señaló un cambio decisivo en la segunda guerra mundial. (p. 368)

Battle of the Bulge [batalla del Bolsón] *s.* batalla de la segunda guerra mundial de un mes de duración en que los aliados lograron rechazar la última gran ofensiva alemana de la guerra. (p. 362)

Battle of the Little Bighorn [batalla del Little Bighorn] *s.* batalla de 1876 en que los sioux y los cheyennes aniquilaron toda una partida militar estadounidense. (p. 163)

Bessemer steel process [proceso siderúrgico Bessemer] *s.* manera nueva de producir acero desarrollada hacia 1850 que causó un gran incremento en la producción siderúrgica. (p. 40)

Bill of Rights [Carta de Derechos] *s.* diez primeras enmiendas a la Constitución de Estados Unidos, adoptadas en 1791, que consisten en una lista formal de los derechos y libertades de los ciudadanos. (p. 61)

Black Tuesday [martes negro] *s.* nombre que se le da al 29 de octubre de 1929, cuando se desplomó el precio de las acciones. (p. 329)

Bonus Army [Ejército de la Prima] *s.* en 1932 miles de veteranos marcharon a Washington demandando el pago de una prima que nunca habían recibido. (p. 331)

boomtown [pueblo en auge] *s.* pueblo que tiene una explosión repentina de crecimiento económico o demográfico. (p. 156)

Boston Massacre [Matanza de Boston] *s.* choque en 1770 entre soldados británicos y colonos de Boston en que perecieron cinco de los colonistas, incluso Crispus Attucks. (p. 38)

Boxer Rebellion [Rebelión bóxer] *s.* en 1900 el resentimiento chino contra la actitud de superioridad cultural de los extranjeros resultó en este violento levantamiento. (p. 267)

***bracero* program** [programa bracero] *s.* uso de trabajadores mexicanos en la época de escasez de labriegos durante la segunda guerra mundial. (p. 372)

brinksmanship *s.* política internacional, el acto de empujar al límite una situación peligrosa; por ejemplo: los Estados Unidos yendo al borde de la guerra para parar el comunismo. (p. 396)

Brown v. Board of Education of Topeka, Kansas [Brown contra el Consejo de Educación de Topeka, Kansas] *s.* caso de 1954 en que la Corte Suprema declaró que la doctrina educativa de "iguales pero separados" para los blancos y los afroamericanos no era constitucional. (p. 412)

buffalo soldier [soldado búfalo] *s.* apodo que los amerindios les dieron a los afroamericanos que servían en el ejército estadounidense del oeste. (p. 169)

business cycle [ciclo económico] *s.* serie de períodos de la economía buenos y malos. (p. 184)

buy on margin [comprar valores a crédito] *s.* pagar una pequeña parte del precio de una acción y pagar el resto con un préstamo. (p. 328)

C

Cambodia [Camboya] *s.* país fronterizo de Vietnam. (p. 446)

Camp David Accords [acuerdos de Camp David] *s.* en 1979, basados en estos acuerdos, Egipto e Israel firmaron un tratado de paz que puso fin a 30 años de conflicto. (p. 462)

Centennial Exhibition [Exposición del Centenario] *s.* exposición de 1876 en Filadelfia que celebró el centésimo cumpleaños de Estados Unidos. (p. 186)

Central Powers [Potencias Centrales] *s.* alianza de Austria-Hungría, Alemania, el Imperio otomano y Bulgaria durante la primera guerra mundial. (p. 278)

Chinese Exclusion Act [ley de Exclusión para chinos] *s.* aprobada en 1882, esta ley prohibía la inmigración china por diez años. (p. 215)

Civil Rights Act of 1964 [ley de Derechos Civiles de 1964] *s.* esta ley prohibía la segregación racial en los lugares públicos y creó la Comisión para la Igualdad de Oportunidades de Empleo. (p. 418)

Clayton Antitrust Act [ley Anti-trust Clayton] *s.* ley aprobada en 1914 que establecía reglas que prohibían prácticas comerciales que disminuyeran la competencia y le daba al gobierno más poder para reglamentar los trusts. (p. 246)

Cold War [guerra fría] *s.* estado de hostilidad, sin conflicto militar directo, que se desarrolló entre Estados Unidos y la Unión Soviética después de la segunda guerra mundial. (p. 390)

Columbian Exchange [transferencia colombina] *s.* transferencia de plantas, animales y enfermedades entre el hemisferio occidental y el oriental. (p. 31)

Committee to Reelect the President [Comité de Reelección del Presidente] *s.* organización cuya conexión con el allanamiento de la Sede Central del Partido Demócrata hizo estallar el escándalo Watergate. (p. 458)

Compromise of 1850 [Acuerdo de 1850] *s.* serie de medidas del Congreso para resolver los desacuerdos principales entre los estados libres y los esclavistas. (p. 134)

Confederate States of America [Estados Confederados de América] *s.* confederación constituida en 1861 por los estados sureños después de separarse de la Unión. (p. 136)

Congress of Industrial Organizations (CIO) [Congreso de Organizaciones Industriales] *s.* organización sindical que en 1938 se separó de la Federación Norteamericana del Trabajo. (p. 341)

conquistador [conquistador] *s.* español que en el siglo XVI viajó a las Américas para explorar y conquistar. (p. 30)

conservative [conservador] *s.* persona que está a favor de menos controles gubernamentales y más libertad individual en cuestiones de la economía. (p. 347)

Constitutional Convention [Convención Constitucional] *s.* reunión realizada en 1787 para considerar cambios a los Artículos de Confederación, que resultó en la redacción de la Constitución. (p. 53)

containment [contención] *s.* bloqueo de una nación en la expansión de la influencia de otras naciones, especialmente los esfuerzos de Estados Unidos por bloquear la expansión de la influencia soviética hacia fines de los años cuarenta y comienzos de los cincuenta. (p. 391)

convoy system [sistema de convoyes] *s.* fuerte flotilla de destructores que escolta a los barcos mercantes durante épocas de guerra. (p. 285)

cooperative [cooperativa] *s.* organización propiedad de los asociados que la dirigen. (p. 175)

CORE [Congreso para la Igualdad Racial] *s.* grupo que planeó freedom rides o viajes en autobús por todo el Sur para eliminar la segregación racial en los autobuses interestatales. (p. 416)

corporation [corporación] *s.* empresa propiedad de inversionistas que compran parte de la compañía mediante acciones. (p. 192)

cotton gin [desmontadora de algodón] *s.* máquina inventada en 1793 que limpiaba el algodón con mucha más rapidez y eficiencia que los obreros humanos. (p. 120)

Crash of 1929 [Crack de 1929] *s.* el desplome de los precios de las acciones. (p. 329)

Cuban Missile Crisis [crisis de los misiles cubanos] *s.* en 1962 casi estalló la guerra entre Estados Unidos y la Unión Soviética porque ésta había instalado misiles nucleares en Cuba. (p. 437)

D

Dawes Act [ley Dawes] *s.* ley, aprobada en 1887, que distribuía la tierra de las reservas amerindias a dueños individuales. (p. 165)

D-Day [día D] *s.* 6 de junio de 1944, día en que los aliados invadieron a Francia durante la segunda guerra mundial. (p. 362)

Declaration of Independence [Declaración de Independencia] *s.* documento, escrito en 1776, en que las colonias declararon su independendia de Gran Bretaña. (p. 39)

deficit [déficit] spend *v.* usar dinero prestado para financiar programas del gobierno. (p. 336)

department store [almacén departamental] *s.* tienda que vende de todo, desde ropa a muebles a artículos de ferretería. (p. 225)

détente [distensión] *s.* disminución de las tensiones entre EE. UU. y la Unión Soviética durante la guerra fría. (p. 456)

direct primary [elecciones primarias directas] *s.* el electorado, y no las convenciones de partido, eligen a los candidatos para los cargos públicos. (p. 238)

domino theory [teoría del dominó] *s.* teoría que sostenía que si un país caía en la órbita comunista, los países vecinos también caerían en el comunismo. (p. 435)

dove [paloma] *s.* persona opuesta a la guerra. (p. 445)

downsize [reducir el tamaño] *v.* disminuir una empresa el número de sus empleados para incrementar las ganancias. (p. 479)

dust bowl [cuenca de polvo] *s.* fincas arruinadas por el polvo a comienzos de los años treinta, en una región de unas 150,000 millas cuadradas. (p. 337)

e-commerce [comercio electrónico] *s.* negocios que se realizan por Internet. (p. 478)

Ellis Island [isla Ellis] *s.* para la mayoría de los inmigrantes que vienen de Europa, la primera parada en Estados Unidos. (p. 212)

English Bill of Rights [Carta de Derechos Ingleses] *s.* acuerdo firmado por Guillermo y María por el que prometían respetar los derechos del Parlamento y los ciudadanos ingleses, incluso el derecho a elecciones libres. (p. 35)

environmentalism [ecologismo] *s.* trabajo dedicado a proteger el medio ambiente. (p. 462)

ERA *s.* Enmienda para la Igualdad de Derechos, enmienda constitucional propuesta para dar igualdad de derechos sin consideración de sexo; la propuesta murió en 1982. (p. 424)

escalation [escalada] *s.* política de aumentar la intervención militar en Vietnam. (p. 439)

Espionage Act [ley sobre el Espionaje] *s.* aprobada en 1917, esta ley establecía multas severas y muchos años de prisión para quienes participaran en actividades contra la guerra o alentaran a los que resistían la conscripción. (p. 290)

exodusters *s.* afroamericanos que abandonaron el Sur para irse al Oeste y se comparaban a los hebreos bíblicos que habían escapado la esclavitud de Egipto. (p. 173)

expatriate [expatriado] *s.* ciudadano de un país que establece su residencia en otro país. (p. 319)

Fair Deal [Trato Justo] *s.* programa presentado por Harry Truman que proponía proyectos nuevos para crear trabajos, construir viviendas públicas y acabar con la discriminación racial en el empleo. (p. 389)

fascism [fascismo] *s.* filosofía política que propugna un fuerte gobierno nacionalista centralizado, con un dictador poderoso a la cabeza. (p. 354)

federalism [federalismo] *s.* sistema de gobierno en que el poder está dividido entre el gobierno central (o federal) y los estados. (p. 58)

Federalists [federalistas] *s.* partidarios de la Constitución. (p. 58)

Federalist Papers [*El federalista*] *s.* serie de ensayos que defienden y explican la Constitución, escritos por Alexander Hamilton, James Madison y John Jay. (p. 59)

Federal Reserve Act [ley de la Reserva Federal] *s.* ley aprobada en 1913 que creó el sistema bancario de la nación e instituyó un sistema monetario flexible. (p. 246)

fireside chats [charlas al calor de la lumbre] *s.* nombre dado a las radioemisiones de Franklin Roosevelt en las que explicaba sus medidas. (p. 333)

flapper *s.* jovencita librepensadora que abrazaba las modas y actitudes urbanas nuevas de los años veinte. (p. 312)

Fort Sumter [fuerte Sumter] *s.* fuerte federal ubicado en el puerto de Charleston, Carolina del Sur; el ataque sureño al fuerte Sumter marcó el comienzo de la guerra civil. (p. 137)

Fourteen Points [Catorce puntos] *s.* los objetivos del presidente Woodrow Wilson para la paz que siguió a la primera guerra mundial. (p. 293)

Fourteenth Amendment [Enmienda Decimocuarta] *s.* enmienda a la Constitución de Estados Unidos, aprobada en 1868, que hizo ciudadanos del país a todas las personas nacidas en Estados Unidos o naturalizadas, incluso a los antiguos esclavos. (p. 145)

First Continental Congress [primer Congreso Continental] *s.* reunión en 1774 de delegados de todas las colonias, excepto Georgia, para defender los derechos coloniales. (p. 38)

Freedom Ride [Viaje por la Libertad] *s.* protesta contra la segregación racial en los autobuses interestatales del Sur. (p. 416)

Freedom Summer [Verano de la Libertad] *s.* en 1964 el Comité de Estudiantes no Violentos organizó una campaña de registro de votantes. (p. 419)

French and Indian War [guerra Francesa y Amerindia] *s.* conflicto en Norteamérica, entre 1754 y 1763, que fue parte de una lucha mundial entre Francia y Gran Bretaña y que terminó con la derrota de Francia y el traspaso del Canadá francés a Gran Bretaña. (p. 36)

French Indochina [Indochina Francesa] *s.* colonia francesa que incluía lo que es hoy Vietnam, Laos y Camboya. (p. 433)

frontier [frontera] *s.* región sin o con muy pocos asentamientos ocupada mayormente por amerindios. (p. 155)

fundamentalist [fundamentalista] *s.* persona que cree en la interpretación textual, o palabra por palabra, de la Biblia. (p. 314)

generator [generador] *s.* máquina que produce corriente eléctrica. (p. 185)

Ghana [Ghana] *s.* imperio del África Occidental entre los siglos VIII y XI d.de C. (p. 29)

G.I. Bill of Rights [Carta de Derechos del Soldado] *s.* aprobada en 1944, esta ley ofrecía ayuda educacional y económica a los veteranos. (p. 377)

Gilded Age [Edad Dorada] *s.* época de fines del siglo XIX de fabulosa riqueza. (p. 194)

gold standard [patrón oro] *s.* sistema en que el gobierno garantiza cada dólar con una cierta cantidad de oro. (p. 175)

Grange [La Quinta] *s.* creada en 1867 por un grupo de agricultores para tratar de satisfacer las necesidades sociales de las familias granjeras. (p. 175)

Great Compromise [Gran Compromiso] *s.* acuerdo en la Convención Constitucional que estableció una legislatura nacional de dos cámaras; en una de estas cámaras, todos los estados tendrían representación igual, en la otra, cada estado tendría representación basada en su población. (p. 54)

Great Depression [gran depresión] *s.* período que duró desde 1929 hasta 1941, en que la economía de Estados Unidos declinó severamente y millones de estadounidenses estaban sin empleo. (p. 329)

Great Migration [Gran Emigración] *s.* el movimiento de afroamericanos entre 1910 y 1920 del Sur hacia las ciudades del Norte. (p. 291)

Great Plains [Grandes Llanuras] *s.* región desde el río Missouri hasta las montañas Rocosas. (p. 155)

Great Society [gran sociedad] *s.* programa iniciado por Lyndon Johnson para ayudan a los pobres, los ancianos y las mujeres y también promovía la educación, prohibía la discriminación racial y protegía el medio ambiente. (p. 420)

guerrilla warfare [guerra de guerrillas] *s.* ataques inesperados por bandas pequeñas de guerrilleros. (p. 440)

Gulf of Tonkin Resolution [Resolución del golfo de Tonkín] *s.* resolución del Congreso que dio al presidente el poder de usar fuerza militar en Vietnam. (p. 439)

Harlem Renaissance [renacimiento de Harlem] *s.* florecimiento de la creatividad artística afroamericana durante los años veinte, centrada en la comunidad de Harlem de la ciudad de Nueva York. (p. 318)

hawk [halcón] *s.* persona que apoya la guerra. (p. 445)

Haymarket affair [asunto Haymarket] *s.* mitín de protesta sindicalista que resultó aproximadamente en un centenar de muertes después de que un desconocido tiró una bomba y la policía abrió fuego contra la multitud. (p. 200)

H-bomb [bomba H] *s.* bomba de hidrógeno. (p. 396)

Hiroshima [Hiroshima] *s.* primera ciudad del Japón contra la cual se lanzó la bomba atómica el 6 de agosto de 1945 durante la segunda guerra mundial. (p. 369)

Ho Chi Minh Trail [ruta de Ho Chi Minh] *s.* red de sendas que usó el Vietcong para mover soldados y provisiones durante la guerra de Vietnam. (p. 436)

Holocaust [Holocausto] *s.* matanza sistemática en Alemania, durante la segunda guerra mundial, de unos seis millones de judíos así como millones de otros grupos étnicos. (p. 363)

homestead [residencia] *s.* tierra para asentarse y construir una casa. (p. 166)

Homestead Act [ley de Residencia] *s.* aprobada en 1862, esta ley ofrecía 160 acres de tierra gratis a cualquiera que acordara ocuparla y trabajarla por cinco años. (p. 172)

House of Burgesses [Cámara de los Burgueses] *s.* creada en 1619, la primera asamblea representativa de las colonias norteamericanas. (p. 33)

Hull House [Casa Hull] *s.* fundada en 1889, fue modelo para otras casas de acogida de la época. (p. 211)

Hundred Days [Cien Días] *s.* durante sus cien primeros días, del 9 de marzo a mediados de junio de 1933, Franklin Roosevelt mandó al Congreso muchos proyectos de ley nuevos. (p. 333)

Immigration Reform and Control Act of 1986 [ley de Reforma y Control de la Inmigración] *s.* ley pasada para reforzar las leyes de inmigración y las medidas para su cumplimiento. (p. 484)

imperialism [imperialismo] *s.* política por la cual las naciones más poderosas extienden su control económico, político o militar sobre territorios o naciones más débiles. (p. 257)

impressment [secuestro] *s.* el acto de capturar personas a la fuerza. (p. 116)

information revolution [revolución de la información] *s.* proceso tecnológico que ha cambiado radicalmente el volumen y el modo de transmitir información. (p. 479)

Indian Removal Act [ley del Traslado de los Indígenas] *s.* esta ley de 1830 requería que el gobierno negociara tratados para el traslado de los amerindios al oeste. (p. 119)

Industrial Revolution [revolución industrial] *s.* en la Inglaterra de fines del siglo XVIII, las maquinarias de fábrica empezaron a reemplazar las herramientas manuales, y la producción de bienes manufacturados reemplazó la agricultura como el principal modo de trabajo. (p. 123)

initiative [iniciativa] *s.* el procedimiento que permite a los votantes proponer una ley directamente. (p. 238)

installment buy [comprar a cuotas] *v.* comprar algo haciendo pequeños pagos mensuales. (p. 310)

Internet [Internet] *s.* interconexión mundial de redes informáticas. (p. 478)

Iran-Contra affair [asunto Irán-Contra] *s.* en 1986 el gobierno de Estados Unidos vendió armas a Irán a cambio de ayuda para liberar a los rehenes estadounidenses en el Oriente Medio y el dinero de la venta fue a los rebeldes Contra de El Salvador. (p. 472)

Iran hostage crisis [crisis de los rehenes de Irán] *s.* el 4 de noviembre de 1979 un grupo de iraníes invadieron la embajada de Estados Unidos en Teherán, capital de Irán, y tomaron de rehenes a 52 estadounidenses. (p. 463)

island hopping [brincar de isla a isla] *v.* estrategia usada durante la segunda guerra mundial según la cual los aliados invadían islas débilmente defendidas por los japoneses para así lanzar nuevos ataques. (p. 368)

isolationist [aislacionista] *s.* persona que creía que Estados Unidos debía mantenerse apartado de los asuntos de las otras naciones, excepto en defensa propia. (p. 309)

Jacksonian Democracy [democracia jacksoniana] *s.* idea de extender el poder político a toda la gente asegurando de ese modo el gobierno de la mayoría. (p. 118)

Jamestown. *s.* primer asentamiento inglés permanente en Norteamérica. (pp. 32–33)

jazz [jazz] *s.* tipo nuevo de música en los años veinte que capturó el despreocupado espíritu de la época. (p. 315)

Jim Crow [ley Jim Crow] *s.* ley que imponía la separación entre la gente blanca y la de piel negra en los lugares públicos del Sur. (p. 219)

Kellogg-Briand Pact [Pacto Kellogg-Briand] *s.* en 1928 firmaron este pacto muchas naciones que prometieron no declararse en guerra entre ellas excepto en defensa propia. (p. 309)

Knights of Labor [Caballeros del Trabajo] *s.* organización de obreros de oficios diferentes formada después de la guerra civil. (p. 199)

Korean War [guerra de Corea] *s.* conflicto entre Corea del Norte y Corea del Sur que duró desde 1950 a 1953; Estados Unidos, junto con otros países de las Naciones Unidas, luchó del lado de los coreanos del Sur y China luchó del lado de los coreanos del Norte. (p. 394)

Ku Klux Klan s. grupo constituido en 1866 que quería restaurar el control del Sur a los demócratas y mantener sumisos a los antiguos esclavos. (p. 146)

Laissez faire [dejad hacer] s. teoría que declaraba que el comercio no sujeto a regulaciones actuaría de manera beneficiosa a la nación. (p. 308)

League of Nations [Sociedad de Naciones] s. organización establecida después de la primera guerra mundial para resolver conflictos internacionales. (p. 293)

leisure s. tiempo libre. (p. 225)

Lend-Lease [ley de Préstamo y Arriendo] s. ley que le permitió a Estados Unidos mandar a las naciones que luchaban contra el Eje armas y suministros sin requerir pago inmediato. (p. 358)

liberal [liberal] s. persona que favorece acción por parte del gobierno para lograr la reforma social y económica. (p. 347)

lode [veta] s. mineral enterrado entre capas de roca. (p. 156)

long drive [largo arreo] s. arreo de ganado al ferrocarril. (p. 158)

Lost Generation [generación perdida] s. la generación de los años veinte, después de la primera guerra mundial cuando hombres y mujeres veían pocas esperanzas para el futuro. (p. 318)

Louisiana Purchase [Compra de Luisiana] s. en 1803, la compra a Francia del Territorio de Luisiana. (p. 115)

Loyalist [realista]. s. colono norteamericano que apoyaba a los británicos durante la Revolución norteamericana. (p. 39)

Mail-order catalog [catálogo de venta por correo] s. publicación que contenía fotografías y la descripción de los artículos para que la gente encargara por correo. (p. 225)

Manhattan Project [Proyecto Manhattan] s. programa ultrasecreto establecido en 1942 para construir una bomba atómica. (p. 369)

manifest destiny [destino manifiesto] s. creencia de que era el destino de Estados Unidos extenderse por todo el continente, desde al océano Atlántico al océano Pacífico. (p. 125)

Marbury v. Madison [Marbury contra Madison] s. caso de 1803 en que el Tribunal Supremo dictaminó que tenía el poder de invalidar leyes declarándolas inconstitucionales. (p. 115)

March on Washington [Marcha a Washington] s. enorme manifestación por los derechos civiles en Washington, D.C. en 1963. (p. 418)

Marshall Plan [Plan Marshall] s. aprobado en 1948, autorizó a Estados Unidos a dar más de trece mil millones de dólares para ayudar a la recuperación de las naciones de Europa después de la segunda guerra mundial. (p. 377)

mass culture [cultura de masas] s. cultura común compartida por grandes números de personas. (p. 224)

mass media [medios de comunicación de masas] s. comunicaciones que alcanzan a un público muy grande. (p. 316)

Mayflower Compact [Pacto del Mayflower] s. acuerdo firmado por los hombres que viajaron a América en el Mayflower, que requería leyes para el bien de la colonia y establecía el concepto de autogobierno. (p. 33)

melting pot [crisol de culturas] s. lugar donde las culturas se amalgaman. (p. 214)

Mexicano [mexicano] s. persona de ascendencia española cuyos antepasados habían venido de México y se habían establecido en el sudoeste. (p. 168)

militarism [militarismo] s. creencia de que una nación necesita una fuerza militar grande. (p. 277)

mission [misión] s. asentamiento creado por la Iglesia con el propósito de convertir a los amerindios al cristianismo. (p. 31)

monopoly [monopolio] s. compañía que elimina a sus competidores y controla una industria. (p. 193)

Monroe Doctrine [Doctrina Monroe] s. política de oposición estadounidense a cualquier interferencia europea en el hemisferio occidental, proclamada por el presidente Monroe en 1823. (p. 117)

Montgomery bus boycott [Boicoteo al transporte público de Montgomery] s. en 1955 los afroamericanos boicotearon el transporte público de Montgomery, Alabama, en respuesta al arresto de Rosa Parks, quien se había negado a dejar su asiento a una persona blanca. (p. 413)

Mound Builder [constructor de túmulos] s. amerindio primitivo que construía grandes estructuras de tierra. (p. 28)

muckraker [revuelve estiércol] s. hacia comienzos del siglo XX, periodista que exponía la corrupción dentro de la sociedad estadounidense. (p. 238)

Muslim [musulmán] s. adherente del islam. (p. 29)

NAACP s. constituida en 1909, la Asociación Nacional para el Progreso de la Gente de Color. (pp. 220, 313)

NAFTA [Tratado Norteamericano de Libre Comercio] s. aprobado en 1993, el Tratado Norteamericano de Libre Comercio o zona de libre comercio entre Estados Unidos, México y Canadá. (p. 473)

napalm [napalm] s. gasolina gelatinosa que arde violentamente. (p. 441)

NATO [OTAN] s. la Organización del Tratado del Atlántico Norte es una alianza militar constituida en 1949 por diez países de la Europa occidental, Estados Unidos y Canadá. (p. 391)

naturalization [naturalización] s. manera de darle ciudadanía completa a una persona nacida en otro país. (p. 43)

Nazi Party [Partido Nazi] s. partido Alemán Nacionalsocialista de los Trabajadores, llegó al poder bajo Adolfo Hitler en 1930. (p. 354)

NCAI s. Congreso Nacional de Amerindios, fundado en 1944 para promover el "bienestar común" de los amerindios. (p. 423)

neutral [neutral] adj. que no apoya ni a un país ni al otro. (p. 114)

neutrality [neutralidad] s. rechazo de la idea de apoyar a un país u otro durante una guerra. (p. 280)

New Deal [Nuevo Trato] s. programas de Franklin Roosevelt para luchar contra la depresión. (p. 333)

new immigrant [inmigrante nuevo] s. persona del sur y el este de Europa que entró a Estados Unidos después de 1900. (p. 212)

New Jersey Plan [Plan de Nueva Jersey] s. plan de gobierno propuesto en 1787 en la Convención Constitucional que proponía una cámara legislativa única en que cada estado tendría un solo voto. (p. 54)

Nineteenth Amendment [Enmienda Decimonovena] s. enmienda a la Constitución de Estados Unidos ratificada en 1920 que dio a las mujeres el derecho absoluto a votar. (p. 251)

Nisei [nisei] s. estadounidense japonés nacido en Estados Unidos. (p. 373)

NOW s. fundada en 1966, la Organización Nacional de la Mujer adelantó una campaña para que las mujeres consiguieran empleos con paga igual a la de los hombres. (p. 424)

nullification [invalidación] s. derecho de un estado a rechazar una ley federal que considerase inconstitucional. (p. 120)

Nuremberg Trials [Juicios de Nuremberg] s. procesos judiciales que tuvieron lugar en Nuremberg, Alemania, después de la segunda guerra mundial, en que se enjuició a líderes nazis por sus crímenes de guerra. (p. 378)

Open Door Policy [política de puertas abiertas] s. en 1899 Estados Unidos instó a las naciones que tenían intereses en China a que siguieran una política según la cual ningún país controlaría el comercio con China. (p. 267)

Oregon Trail [Camino de Oregón] s. camino hacia el oeste que iba de Independence, Missouri, al territorio de Oregón. (p. 125)

Palmer raids [allanamientos de Palmer] s. en 1920 agentes federales y la policía allanaron los hogares de personas que se sospechaba que eran radicales. (p. 295)

Panama Canal [canal de Panamá] s. atajo a través de Panamá que conecta los océanos Atlántico y Pacífico. (p. 268)

patent [patente] s. documento del gobierno que otorga a un inventor el derecho exclusivo a hacer o vender su invención durante un determinado número de años. (p. 184)

Patriot [patriota] s. colono norteamericano que durante la Revolución norteamericana estaba a favor de los rebeldes. (p. 39)

Pearl Harbor s. base naval en Hawai atacada de sorpresa por Japón el 7 de diciembre de 1941. (p. 358)

Persian Gulf War [guerra del Golfo Pérsico] s. en 1991 Estados Unidos y las Naciones Unidas echaron a Iraq de Kuwait, país que los iraquíes habían invadido en 1990. (p. 473)

petroleum [petróleo] s. líquido aceitoso e inflamable. (p. 183)

philanthropist [filántropo] s. persona que da grandes sumas de dinero a las organizaciones benéficas. (p. 194)

Pilgrim [peregrino] s. miembros del grupo que rechazó la Iglesia de Inglaterra, viajó a América y fundó la colonia de Plymouth en 1620. (p. 33)

Platt Amendment [Enmienda Platt] s. resultado de la guerra entre Estados Unidos y España, dio a Estados Unidos el derecho a intervenir en los asuntos de Cuba cuando existiera amenaza a la "vida, propiedad y libertad individual". (p. 264)

Plessy v. Ferguson [Plessy contra Ferguson] s. caso de 1896 en que el Tribunal Supremo dictaminó que la separación de las razas en las instalaciones públicas era legal. (p. 219)

political machine [maquinaria política] s. organización que logra votos suficientes para controlar un gobierno local. (p. 211)

popular culture [cultura popular] s. cosas como la música, la moda y las películas que son populares dentro de una cantidad grande de personas. (p. 316)

Populist Party [Partido Populista] s. también conocido como el Partido del Pueblo y constituido en 1890, este grupo quería una política que aumentara el precio de lo que cultivaban los granjeros. (p. 175)

progressivism [progresismo] s. movimiento reformista de principios del siglo XX que buscaba devolver el control del gobierno al pueblo, restablecer oportunidades económicas y corregir las injusticias de la vida estadounidense. (p. 237)

prohibition [prohibición] s. proscripción de la fábrica, venta y posesión de bebidas alcohólicas. (p. 313)

propaganda [propaganda] s. opinión expresada con el propósito de influir en las acciones de otras personas. (p. 290)

public works project [proyecto de obras públicas] s. proyecto patrocinado por el gobierno para construir recursos públicos, como caminos y diques. (p. 330)

Pullman Strike [huelga de Pullman] s. huelga nacional de ferrocarriles que se extendió por toda la industria ferroviaria en 1894. (p. 201)

Puritan [puritano] s. miembro de un grupo de Inglaterra que se asentó en la Colonia de la bahía de Massachusetts en 1630 y trató de reformar las prácticas de la Iglesia de Inglaterra. (pp. 33–34)

racial discrimination [discriminación racial] s. tratamiento diferente por motivos de raza. (p. 218)

ragtime s. mezcla de canciones afroamericanas y formas musicales europeas. (p. 227)

ration [racionar] v. distribuir una cantidad fija de cierto artículo. (p. 371)

recall [destituir] v. votar para sacar a un funcionario de su cargo. (p. 238)

Reconstruction [Reconstrucción] s. proceso que usó el gobierno de Estados Unidos para readmitir a los estados confederados a la Unión después de la guerra civil. (pp. 144–147)

Red Scare [Terror Rojo] s. entre 1919 y 1920, ola de pánico sobre una posible revolución comunista. (p. 295)

referendum [referéndum] *s.* cuando una ley que se ha propuesto se somete al voto del pueblo. (p. 238)

reservation [reserva] *s.* tierras destinadas por el gobierno de Estados Unidos para las tribus amerindias. (p. 160)

revenue sharing [reparto de las rentas públicas] *s.* la distribución de dinero federal a los estados y gobiernos locales con pocas o no restricciones en la manera cómo se gasta. (p. 454)

robber baron [capitalista inescrupuloso] *s.* líder industrial que se hizo acaudalado usando medios deshonestos. (p. 192)

rock 'n' roll *s.* tipo de música popular caracterizada por ritmos pesados y melodías simples que se desarrolló del rhythm and blues en los años cincuenta. (p. 401)

Roosevelt Corollary [Corolario de Roosevelt] *s.* la adición en 1904 a la Doctrina Monroe permitiendo a los Estados Unidos a actuar de "policía" en Latinoamérica. (p. 270)

Rosie the Riveter [Rosita la Remachadora] *s.* imagen de una mujer fuerte trabajando duro en una fábrica de armas durante la segunda guerra mundial. (p. 371)

Rough Rider *s.* miembro del Primer Regimiento Estadounidense de Voluntarios de Caballería que organizó Theodore Roosevelt y que luchó en la guerra entre España y Estados Unidos. (p. 263)

SALT *s.* Tratado sobre Limitación de Armas Estratégicas firmado en 1972 entre Estados Unidos y la Unión Soviética; limitaba las armas nucleares. (p. 456)

Sand Creek Massacre [masacre de Sand Creek] *s.* un ataque en 1864, en el que más de 150 hombres, mujeres y niños del pueblo cheyene murieron a manos de la milicia de Colorado. (p. 162)

SCLC *s.* Conferencia de Líderes Cristianos del Sur, grupo que coordinó por todo el sur las protestas para promover los derechos civiles. (p. 413)

secede [separarse] *v.* retirarse. (pp. 136, 137)

Second Battle of the Marne [segunda batalla del Marne] *s.* en 1918 esta batalla de la primera guerra mundial marcó el cambio decisivo en el curso de la guerra; las tropas aliadas junto con las estadounidenses detuvieron el avance alemán hacia el interior de Francia. (p. 287)

Second New Deal [segundo Nuevo Trato] *s.* conjunto de programas que se pasaron en 1935 para luchar contra la depresión. (p. 334)

Securities and Exchange Commission *s.* [Comisión de Valores y Bolsa] *s.* agencia que vigila la bolsa de valores y hace que las empresas sigan procedimientos honestos en la venta de acciones. (p. 346)

Sedition Act [ley de Sedición] *s.* ley aprobada en 1918 que hacía ilegal la crítica de la guerra. Imponía fuertes multas y largos períodos de encarcelamiento para los que participaran en actividades contra la guerra. (p. 290)

segregation [segregación] *s.* separación. (p. 219)

Seneca Falls Convention [convención de Seneca Falls] *s.* convención sobre los derechos de la mujer llevada a cabo en Seneca Falls, New York, en 1848. (p. 122)

service economy [economía de servicios] *s.* economía en que la mayoría de los empleos suministran servicios en lugar de producir mercancías. (p. 479)

Seventeenth Amendment [Enmienda Decimoséptima] *s.* enmienda a la Constitución estadounidense, ratificada en 1913, que autorizaba la elección directa de los senadores estadounidenses por el electorado de cada estado. (p. 246)

Sherman Antitrust Act [ley Antitrust Sherman] *s.* ley aprobada en 1890 que declaró ilegal que las corporaciones obtuvieran control de las industrias formandos trusts. (p. 239)

sit-down strike *s.* [huelga de brazos caídos] huelga en que los obreros permanecen dentro de la fábrica pero se niegan a trabajar. (p. 341)

Sixteenth Amendment [Enmienda Decimosexta] *s.* enmienda a la Constitución de Estados Unidos, ratificada en 1913, que dio al Congreso el poder de crear impuestos a las rentas. (p. 245)

slavery [esclavitud] *s.* sistema de servidumbre humana involuntaria. (p. 31)

slum [barrio bajo] *s.* barrio de casas abarrotadas de gente y peligrosas. (p. 210)

SNCC *s.* organizado en 1960, el Comité Coordinador No Violento de Estudiantes se creó para dar a los jóvenes un papel más importante en el movimiento por los derechos civiles. (p. 415)

social gospel [evangelio social] *s.* movimiento cuyo objetivo era mejorar la vida de los pobres. (p. 210)

socialism [socialismo] *s.* sistema económico en que todos los miembros de una sociedad son propietarios por igual de todas las empresas; los miembros comparten el trabajo y las ganancias (p. 200)

Social Security Act [ley de Seguridad Social] *s.* según esta ley aprobada en 1935, los empleados y los empresarios hacían pagos a un fondo especial, del cual podían recibir una jubilación después de retirarse. (p. 334)

sodbuster *s.* granjero de la frontera. (p. 173)

space race [carrera para conquistar el espacio] *s.* empezando en 1957, la Unión Soviética y Estados Unidos comenzaron a competir en la exploración del espacio. (p. 397)

Spanish-American War *s.* guerra de 1898 que comenzó cuando Estados Unidos demandó que España le concediera la independencia a Cuba. (p. 262)

speculation [especulación] *s.* comprar y vender acciones con la esperanza de obtener una ganancia rápida. (p. 328)

sphere of influence [esfera de influencia] *s.* región donde las naciones extranjeras demandan derechos especiales y privilegios económicos. (p. 267)

standard time [hora oficial] *s.* sistema adoptado en 1918 que dividió a Estados Unidos en cuatro zonas horarias. (p. 190)

suburb [barrio residencial] *s.* área residencial que rodea a una ciudad. (p. 398)

sunbelt *s.* estados más cálidos del sur y el suroeste. (p. 399)

supply-side economics [economía de la oferta] *s.* idea de que si se reducen los impuestos aumenta el número de empleos así como los ahorros y las inversiones, todo lo cual hace que aumenten las entradas del gobierno. (p. 471)

sweatshop *s.* lugar donde los obreros trabajaban largas horas en condiciones muy malas por salarios muy bajos. (p. 198)

T

Tammany Hall *s.* famosa maquinaria política de la ciudad de Nueva York de fines del siglo XIX. (p. 211)

tariff [arancel aduanero] *s.* impuesto a las mercancías importadas. (p. 113)

Teapot Dome Scandal [escándalo de Teapot Dome] *s.* episodio causado por el ministro del Interior Albert B. Fall quien arrendó ricas reservas públicas de petróleo a compañías privadas a cambio de dinero y tierras. (p. 308)

tenement [casa de vecindad] *s.* edificio de apartamentos generalmente en muy malas condiciones y atestado. (p. 209)

Tet offensive [ofensiva del Tet] *s.* en 1968, ataque sorpresa por las tropas del Vietcong contra las bases militares estadounidenses y más de 100 ciudades y pueblos de Vietnam del Sur durante el Tet, la celebración del año nuevo lunar vietnamita. (p. 442)

Thirteenth Amendment [Enmienda Decimotercera] *s.* enmienda a la Constitución de Estados Unidos adoptada en 1865 que abolía la esclavitud y la servidumbre involuntaria en Estados Unidos. (p. 143)

38th parallel *s.* la región al norte de esta latitud ocupada por las tropas soviéticas en 1945. (p. 393)

Three-Fifths Compromise [Acuerdo de los Tres Quintos] *s.* acuerdo de la Convención Constitucional que establecía que, para efectos de la representación y del cobro de impuestos, se contarían como parte de la población tres quintos de los esclavos de un estado. (p. 55)

Trail of Tears [Sendero de las Lágrimas] *s.* trágica marcha del pueblo cherokee desde sus tierras hasta el Territorio Indio, entre 1838 y 1839; miles de cherokees murieron. (p. 119)

transcontinental railroad [ferrocarril transcontinental] *s.* ferrocarril que se extendía por todo el continente. (p. 188)

Treaty of Guadalupe Hidalgo [Tratado de Guadalupe Hidalgo] *s.* tratado de 1848 que puso fin a la guerra estadounidense con México; México cedió California y Nuevo México a los Estados Unidos. (p. 126)

Treaty of Paris [Tratado de París] *s.* tratado de 1763 que puso fin a la guerra Francesa y Amerindia; Francia entregó toda norteamérica del este del río Mississippi. (p. 36)

Treaty of Paris of 1783 [Tratado de París de 1783] *s.* tratado que puso fin a la guerra Revolucionaria, confirmó la independencia de Estados Unidos y estableció los límites de la nueva nación. (p. 41)

Treaty of Versailles [Tratado de Versailles] *s.* tratado de 1919 que puso fin a la primera guerra mundial. (p. 294)

trench warfare [guerra de trincheras] *s.* clase de guerra durante la primera guerra mundial en que los combatientes se apiñaban en zanjas fortificadas y se disparaban artillería y fuego de ametralladora. (p. 278)

triangular trade [comercio triangular] *s.* sistema de comercio transatlántico en que se intercambiaban mercancías, incluso esclavos, entre África, Inglaterra, Europa, las Antillas y las colonias de Norte América. (p. 35)

Truman Doctrine [Doctrina Truman] *s.* política que prometía ayuda a la gente que luchaba por resistir las amenazas a la libertad democrática. (p. 391)

trust *s.* cuerpo legal creado para tener una cartera de acciones de varias empresas, con frecuencia en la misma industria. (p. 193)

Twenty-sixth Amendment [Enmienda Vigésima Sexta] *s.* enmienda a la Constitución de Estados Unidos, adoptada en 1971, redujo la edad del derecho a votar de los 21 a los 18 años. (p. 447)

U

United Nations [Naciones Unidas] *s.* organización internacional para mantener la paz a la que pertenecen la mayoría de las naciones del mundo, creada en 1945 para promover la paz, seguridad y desarrollo económico del mundo. (p. 379)

urbanization [urbanización] *s.* crecimiento de las ciudades como resultado de la industrialización. (p. 207)

U.S.S. *Maine* *s.* barco de guerra estadounidense que explotó misteriosamente y se hundió en el puerto de La Habana, Cuba, el 15 de febrero de 1898. (p. 261)

V

vaquero [vaquero] *s.* peón de ganado que vino de México con los españoles en el siglo XVI. (p. 158)

vaudeville [vodevil] *s.* tipo de espectáculo teatral en vivo con mezcla de canciones, baile y comedia. (p. 227)

Viet Cong *s.* comunista vietnamita. (p. 436)

Vietnamization [vietnamización] *s.* estrategia de la guerra de Vietnam de retirar las fuerzas estadounidenses gradualmente y dejar la lucha terrestre en manos de los vietnamitas del Sur. (p. 446)

vigilante [vigilante] *s.* persona dispuesta a tomar la ley en sus propias manos. (p. 159)

Virginia Plan *s.* plan presentado por Edmund Randolph, delegado a la Convención Constitucional de 1787, que proponía un gobierno de tres ramas y una legislatura bicameral en la que la representación se basaría en la población o la riqueza de un estado. (pp. 53–54)

Voting Rights Act of 1965 [ley de los Derechos al Voto] *s.* esta ley prohibía las pruebas de lectura y escritura y otras leyes que impedían que los afroamericanos se anotaran para votar. (p. 419)

W

war bond [bono de guerra] *s.* préstamo de interés bajo de la población civil al gobierno, que se pagaría dentro de un número de años. (p. 289)

War with Mexico [Guerra con México] *s.* conflicto de 1846 a 1848 entre los Estados Unidos y México. (p. 126)

War Powers Act [ley de Poderes de Guerra] *s.* aprobada en 1973, esta ley limita los poderes del presidente para declarar la guerra sin consultar el Congreso. (p. 447)

War Production Board [Junta de Producción Bélica] *s.* agencia establecida durante la segunda guerra mundial para coordinar la producción de suministros militares por las empresas estadounidenses. (p. 370)

Watergate scandal [escándalo de Watergate] *s.* escándalo que resultó de los esfuerzos del gobierno de Nixon por encubrir su participación en el allanamiento de la Sede Central del Partido Demócrata en el edificio de apartamentos Watergate. (p. 458)

Wounded Knee Massacre [masacre de Wounded Knee] *s.* masacre de 1890 por soldados estadounidenses de 300 amerindios desarmados, en Wounded Knee Creek, Dakota del Sur. (p. 164)

Y2K [año 2000] *s.* problema de computadora causado por programas de computadoras que usan sólo los dos últimos dígitos de un año; complicado por la llegada del año 2000. (p. 476)

Yalta Conference [Conferencia de Yalta] *s.* en 1945 Franklin Roosevelt, Winston Churchill y Joseph Stalin discutieron planes para el fin de la segunda guerra mundial y el futuro de Europa. (p. 363)

yellow journalism [periodismo amarillo] *s.* estilo de periodismo que usa la exageración y el sensacionalismo para presentar las noticias. (p. 261)

Zimmermann telegram [telegrama de Zimmerman] *s.* mensaje enviado en 1917 por el ministro de Relaciones Exteriores alemán al embajador alemán en México proponiendo una alianza entre México y Alemania y prometiendo ayudar a México a recuperar Texas, New Mexico y Arizona si Estados Unidos entraba en la guerra. (p. 280)

An *i* preceding a page reference in italics indicates that there is an illustration, and usually text information as well, on that page. An *m* or a *c* preceding an italic page reference indicates a map or a chart, as well as text information on that page.

ACKNOWLEDGMENTS

TEXT ACKNOWLEDGMENTS

Chapter 5, page 160: Excerpt from "Wahenee: An Indian Girl's Story Told by Herself to Gilbert L. Wilson," *North Dakota History,* Vol. 38, Nos. 1 & 2. Copyright © 1971 State Historical Society of North Dakota. Used by permission.

Chapter 7, pages 216–217: Excerpt from *Dragonwings* by Laurence Yep. Copyright © 1975 by Laurence Yep. Used by permission of HarperCollins Publishers.

pages 222–223: Excerpt from *Crusade for Justice: The Autobiography of Ida B. Wells,* edited by Alfreda M. Duster. Copyright © 1970 by The University of Chicago. Reprinted by permission of The University of Chicago Press. All rights reserved.

Chapter 11, page 311: "First Fig," from *Collected Poems* by Edna St. Vincent Millay. HarperCollins Publishers. Copyright © 1922, 1950 by Edna St. Vincent Millay. Reprinted by permission of Elizabeth Barnett, literary executor. All rights reserved.

page 323: "I, Too," from *Collected Poems* by Langston Hughes. Copyright © 1994 by the Estate of Langston Hughes. Reprinted by permission of Alfred A. Knopf, a division of Random House, Inc.

Chapter 12, pages 342–343: Excerpt from *Roll of Thunder, Hear My Cry* by Mildred D. Taylor. Copyright © 1976 by Mildred D. Taylor. Used by permission of Dial Books for Young Readers, a division of Penguin Putnam Inc.

Chapter 13, page 365: Excerpt from *Night* by Elie Wiesel, translated by Stella Rodway. Copyright © 1960 by MacGibbon & Kee, renewed 1988 by The Collins Publishing Group. Reprinted by permission of Hill and Wang, a division of Farrar, Straus & Giroux, Inc.

Chapter 14, page 398: Excerpt from "Remembering LaVern Baker, a strong-willed R&B original" by Steve Jones, *USA Today,* March 12, 1997. Copyright © 1997 by USA Today. Reprinted with permission.

Chapter 15, page 413: Excerpt from *Stride Toward Freedom: The Montgomery Story* by Martin Luther King, Jr. Copyright © 1958 by Martin Luther King, Jr., renewed 1986 by Coretta Scott King. Reprinted by arrangement with The Heirs to the Estate of Martin Luther King, Jr., c/o Writers House, Inc., as agent for the proprietor.

page 417: Excerpt from "Letter from Birmingham Jail" by Martin Luther King, Jr. Copyright © 1963 by Martin Luther King, Jr., renewed 1991 by Coretta Scott King. Reprinted by arrangement with The Heirs to the Estate of Martin Luther King, Jr., c/o Writers House, Inc., as agent for the proprietor.

pages 418, 426: Excerpts from "I Have a Dream" by Martin Luther King, Jr. Copyright © 1963 by Martin Luther King, Jr., renewed 1991 by Coretta Scott King. Reprinted by arrangement with The Heirs to the Estate of Martin Luther King, Jr., c/o Writers House, Inc., as agent for the proprietor.

Copyright © César E. Chávez Foundation. Reprinted by permission of the César E. Chávez Foundation.

Chapter 18, page 471: Excerpt from "Election No Surprise to Ordinary Folk" by Anne Keegan, *Chicago Tribune,* November 6, 1980. Copyright © 1980 by the Chicago Tribune Company. Used with permission. All rights reserved.

page 481: Excerpt from "Dominican Dominion" by Maximo Zeledon, *Frontera Magazine,* Issue 5. Reprinted by permission of Frontera Magazine.

Maps created by Mapping Specialists.

ART CREDITS

Cover and Frontispiece

cover background Copyright © Bob Gelberg/SharpShooters. *frontispiece background* The Granger Collection, New York. **Amelia Earhart:** Copyright © Albert L. Bresnik. **Maya Lin:** Copyright © 1999 Richard Howard/Black Star. **Juan Seguín:** Detail of *Juan Seguin* (1838), Jefferson Wright. Texas State Library and Archives Commission. **Harry S. Truman:** White House Collection. Copyright © White House Historical Association. Courtesy of the Harry S. Truman Library. **Ida Bell Wells:** The Granger Collection, New York. **Abigail Adams:** Portrait traditionally said to be Abigail Adams (about 1795), unknown artist. Oil on canvas, 30¼" x 26½", N-150.55. Photograph by Richard Walker. Copyright © New York State Historical Association, Cooperstown, New York. **Zitkala-Sa:** Negative no. Mss 299, Tom Perry Special Collections, Harold B. Lee Library, Brigham Young University, Provo, Utah. **Benjamin Franklin:** Copyright © Joseph-Siffrede Duplessis/Wood River Gallery/PNI. **Abraham Lincoln:** The Library of Congress. **Martin Luther King, Jr:** Photograph by Howard Sochrer/*Life* magazine. Copyright © Time Inc.

Table of Contents

viii–xvii *background* The Granger Collection, New York; **x** *top, Northern Pacific Railroad. The Pioneer Route to Fargo Moorhead Town Bismarck Dakota and Montana and the Famous Valley of the Yellowstone* (about 1885), Creator–Poole Brothers, Printers. Broadside. Chicago Historical Society; *bottom* The Granger Collection, New York; **xi** *top* Doubleday, Page and Company, New York, 1906, second issue; *center, Portrait of Queen Liliuokalani,* date and artist unknown. Bishop Museum; *bottom left* The Granger Collection, New York; *bottom right* Culver Pictures; **xii** *top* Copyright © Stock Montage; *center* The Granger Collection, New York; *bottom* Rob Boudreau/Stone Getty Images; **xiii** *top* Copyright © Bettmann/Corbis; *center* NASA; *bottom* Copyright © Charles Feil/Stock Boston/PNI.

Voices from the Past

xxi The Granger Collection, New York; **xviii** Copyright Hulton-Deutsch Collection/Corbis; **xix** Library of Congress; **xx** Survey Compass, accession number 1982–145. Colonial Williamsburg Foundation.

Themes of American History

xxiv *top* Copyright © 1999 PhotoDisc, Inc.; *center* Photograph by Howard Sochrer/*Life* magazine, Copyright © Time Inc.; *bottom* Michael S. Yamashita/Corbis; **xxv** *top* Library of Congress; *bottom* National Museum of American History/Smithsonian Institution, Washington, D.C.

Geography Handbook

2 *top right* Copyright © H. Abernathy/H. Armstrong Roberts; *center left* Copyright © Warren Morgan/H. Armstrong Roberts; *bottom* Copyright © 1996 Denver A. Bryan; **3** *top* Copyright © Nathan Benn/Stock Boston; *bottom right* Andy Sacks/Stone Getty Images; **4–5** The Granger Collection, New York; **4** *top* David Noble/FPG/Getty Images; **5** *top* Copyright © John Coletti/Stock Boston; *center* Copyright © Bill Horsman/Stock Boston; **6** *top* Copyright © George Mobley/NGS Image Collection; *center* Copyright © Lowell Georgia/NGS Image Collection; *bottom left* The Granger Collection, New York; **10** *top* Copyright © T. Algire/H. Armstrong Roberts; *bottom* Ken

Graham/Stone Getty Images; **11** *top* Copyright © SuperStock, Inc.; *bottom* Tom Dietrich/Stone Getty Images; **12** *top* Zane Williams/Stone Getty Images; *bottom* Eastcott/Momatiuk/Stone Getty Images; **13** *top* Copyright © SuperStock, Inc.; *bottom* Copyright © F. Sieb/H. Armstrong Roberts; **14–15** Illustration by Ken Goldammer; **16** *top* Copyright © M. Schneiders/H. Armstrong Roberts; *bottom* Copyright © D. Frazier/H. Armstrong Roberts; **17** *top left* Ron Levy/Getty News Services; *top right, center right, bottom right* Copyright © Steve Adams/NGS Image Collection; *bottom left* Cathlyn Melloan/Stone Getty Images; **18** *bottom* Copyright © J. Marshall/The Image Works; **19** *left* Culver Pictures; *right* Santi Visalli/The Image Bank/Getty Images.

Unit 1

Chapter 1, 22 Copyright © r. Kord/ H. Armstrong Roberts; **24, 25** The Granger Collection, New York; **27** Courtesy of Rock Art Foundation, San Antonio, Texas; **29** Benin *Horn-Blower* (about 1550–1680) unknown African artist. Nigeria, Court of Benin, Bini Tribe. Bronze, 24 ⅞" x 11 ⅝ x 6 ¾ "(63 cm x 29.4 cm x 17.2 cm). The Metropolitan Museum of Art, The Michael C. Rockefeller Memorial Collection, gift of Nelson A. Rockefeller, 1972 (1978.412.310). Photograph copyright © 1983 The Metropolitan Museum of Art; **30** *Portrait of a Man, Called Christopher Columbus* (1519), Sebastiano del Piombo. Oil on canvas, 42" x 34 ¾". The Metropolitan Museum of Art, gift of J. Pierpont Morgan, 1900; **31** The Newberry Library, Chicago; **32** British Museum; **34** Detail of Quaker Meeting (date unknown), Egbert Van Heemskerk. The Quaker Collection, Haverford (Pennsylvania) College Library; **36** Detail of *Braddock's Defeat* (1903), Edward Deming. State Historical Society of Wisconsin Museum Collection; **37** *James Otis Arguing Against the Writs of Assistance in the Old Towne Hall* (1901), Robert Reid. Courtesy of Commonwealth of Massachusetts Art Commission; **38, 39** The Granger Collection, New York; **41** *Surrender of Lord Cornwallis at Yorktown* (date unknown), John Trumball. Yale University Art Gallery, Trumball Collection; **42** The Granger Collection, New York.

Chapter 2, 48 The Granger Collection, New York; **49** *The Signing of the Constitution* (date unknown), H. C. Chandler. Art Resource, New York; **51** Copyright © Thad Samuels Abell II/ NGS Image Collection; **53** The Granger Collection, New York; **56** *bottom left* Copyright © John E. Fletcher & Arlan R. Wiler/ NGS Image Collection; *bottom right* William L. Clements Library, Map Division, University of Michigan; **57** *top* The Granger Collection, New York; *bottom* Courtesy of the Shelby County (Ohio) Historical Society **58** The Granger Collection, New York; **59** *left, Portrait of John Jay* (c. 1783, 1804–1805), Gilbert Stuart, believed to have been begun and finished by John Trumball. National Portrait Gallery, Smithsonian Institution/ Art Resource, New York; **235** *right,* **236** The Granger Collection, New York.

Constitution Handbook 64 *left* The Granger Collection, New York; *right* Copyright © Ivan Massar/Black Star; **65** *top* Copyright © Bob Daemmrich/The Image Works; *center* Copyright © Topham/The Image Works; *bottom* Courtesy of the *New York Times;* **66** *bottom* Copyright © J. L. Atlan/Corbis Sygma; **67** *top* Robert E. Daemmrich/Stone Getty Images; **69** *top* Copyright © 1973 Engelhardt in the *St. Louis Post-Dispatch.* Reprinted with permission; *bottom* Copyright © Patrick Forden/Corbis Sygma; **70** *background* The Granger Collection, New York; **70** *inset,* **79** AP/Wide World Photos; **80** *top right* Hulton/Archive/Getty Images; *top left* Culver Pictures; *center right* Copyright © 1972 Magnum Photos, Inc.; *center left* AP/Wide World Photos; *bottom right* Courtesy of Ronald Reagan Library; **86** AP/Wide World Photos; **87** Copyright © Collection of The New-York Historical Society; **89**

Baron Wolman/Stone Getty Images; **90** *left* Jean-Marc Giboux/Getty News Services; *right* Copyright © Bob Daemmrich/Corbis Sygma; **92** Ron Rovtar/FPG/Getty Images; **94** The Granger Collection, New York; **95** *left* FPG/Getty Images; *right* Cynthia Johnson/Getty News Services; **96** Franklin D. Roosevelt Library; **99** Copyright © Rock the Vote Inc.

Citizenship Handbook 102 AP/Wide World Photos; **103** *background* Copyright © Bob Daemmrich; *foreground* Copyright © 1994 Mark Harmel/FPG/Getty Images; **106** Copyright © Bob Daemmrich/The Image Works; **107** David Young-Wolff/Stone Getty Images; **108** AP/Wide World Photos.

Chapter 3, 110, 111 Copyright © Bettman/Corbis; **114** *George Washington in the Uniform of a British Colonial Colonel* (1772), Charles Wilson Peale. Washington-Custis-Lee Collection. Washington and Lee University, Lexington, Virginia; **116** Copyright © 1998 North Wind Pictures; **117** National Museum of American History, Smithsonian Institution; **118** Redwood Library and Athenaeum, Newport, Rhode Island; **120** Detail of *Plantation Burial* (1860), John Antrobus. Williams Research Center, The Historic New Orleans Collection. Photograph copyright © Jan White Brantley; **121** *from left to right* The Granger Collection, New York; The Granger Collection, New York; The Granger Collection. New York; The Granger Collection, New York; Copyright © Bettman/Corbis; **123** Copyright © Bettman/Corbis; **124** Illustration by Patrick Whelan; **129** From the collections of the Minnesota Historical Society.

Chapter 4, 130, 131 The Granger Collection, New York; **132** *top left, top right* Library of Congress; *bottom left, bottom right* The Granger Collection, New York; **133, 135** The Granger Collection, New York; **136** Lloyd Ostendorf Collection; **139** Culver Pictures; **140** The Lincoln Museum, Fort Wayne, Indiana. #0-43; **144** The Granger Collection, New York; **145** *His First Vote* (1868), Thomas Waterman Wood, Oil on board. Cheekwood Museum of Art, Nashville, Tennessee; **146** The Granger Collection, New York; **148** *left* Photograph copyright © High Impact Photograpy. Courtesy 103rd ENG; *center* Courtesy, Museum of the Confederacy; *bottom right* Fort Sumter National Park.

Unit 2

150–151 The Granger Collection, New York.

Chapter 5, 152 *Jerked Down* (1907), Charles M. Russell. Oil on canvas, 23" x 36 ¾", accession no. 0137.2246. From the Collection of Gilcrease Museum, Tulsa (Oklahoma); **153** Solomon D. Butcher Collection, Nebraska State Historical Society; **155** Denver Public Library; **157** *top* The Granger Collection, New York; *bottom* Copyright © Dan Suzio/Photo Researchers; **158** *California Vaqueros* (1875), James Walker. Oil on canvas, 31" x 46". Courtesy of The Anschutz Collection. Photograph by William J. O'Connor; **159** Culver Pictures; **160** *background* The Granger Collection, New York; *foreground* State Historical Society of North Dakota; **162** *Custer's Last Stand* (1899), Edgar S. Paxson. Oil on canvas, 70½" x 106". Buffalo Bill Historical Center, Cody, Wyoming; **163** *top* The Granger Collection, New York; *center* Culver Pictures; *bottom* Library of Congress; **164** Western History Collections, University of Oklahoma Libraries; **165** Library of Congress; **166** The Kansas State Historical Society, Topeka, Kansas; **167** *top, View of San Francisco [Formerly Yerba Buena]* (1847), attributed to Victor Prevost. Oil on canvas, 25" x 30". California Historical Society, gift of the Ohio Historical Society; *bottom* The Bancroft Library, University of California, Berkeley; **168** *top* The Granger Collection, New York; *center* Courtesy of The Arizona Historical Society/Tucson; *bottom* The Granger Collection, New York; **169** Photofest; **170–171** Wyoming Division of Cultural Resources; **171** *top* Library of Congress; **172**

R78 ACKNOWLEDGMENTS

foreground, Northern Pacific Railroad. The Pioneer Route to Fargo Moorhead Town Bismarck Dakota and Montana and the Famous Valley of the Yellowstone (about 1885), Creator–Poole Brothers, Printers. Broadside. Chicago Historical Society; **173** Solomon D. Butcher Collection, Nebraska State Historical Society; **175** The Granger Collection, New York; **176** Culver Pictures; **177** *Rush for the Oklahoma Land* (1894), John Steuart Curry. Department of the Interior.

Chapter 6, 180 Detail of *Forging the Shaft* (1874–1877), John Ferguson Weir. Oil on canvas, 52" x 73¼" (132.1 cm x 186.1 cm). Painted at West Point Foundry at Cold Spring, New York. The Metropolitan Museum of Art, New York. Purchase, Lyman G. Bloomingdale Gift, 1901 (01.7.1). Photograph copyright © 1983 The Metropolitan Museum of Art; **181** The Granger Collection, New York; **182** The Newberry Library, Chicago; **183** Copyright © Bettmann/Corbis; **185** Library of Congress; **186** *background* U.S. Dept. of Commerce—Patent & Trademark Office, Washington, D.C.; *left foreground* The Granger Collection, New York; *right foreground* Courtesy of AT&T; **187** *left background* U.S. Dept. of Commerce—Patent & Trademark Office, Washington, D.C.; *left foreground* First Church of Christ, Lynn, Massachusetts; **188** Special Collections Division, University of Washington Libraries. Negative no. 2315; **189** *top* Courtesy Colorado Historical Society; *bottom, The Last Spike* (1869). William T. Garrett Foundry, San Francisco. 17 6/10 carat gold, alloyed with copper. 5 9/16" x 7/16" x ½" (shaft including head), ½" x 1⅜" x 1¼". Iris & B. Gerald Cantor Center for Visual Arts at Stanford University. Gift of David Hewes, 1998.115; **191** Stamp Designs © United States Postal Service. Displayed with permission. All rights reserved. Written authorization from the postal service is required to use, reproduce, post, transmit, distribute, or publicly display these images; **192** Copyright © Bettmann/Corbis; **193** *left, John Davison Rockefeller* (1967), Adrian Lamb, after the 1917 oil by John Singer Sargent. Oil on canvas, 58¾" x 45¾". National Portrait Gallery, Smithsonian Institution, Washington, D.C./Art Resource, New York; *right* National Portrait Gallery, Smithsonian Institution, Washington, D. C./Art Resource, New York; **194** *left, The Hatch Family* (1871), Eastman Johnson. Oil on canvas, 48 x 73⅜". The Metropolitan Museum of Art, New York, Gift of Frederic H. Hatch, 1926 (26.97). Photograph copyright © 1999 The Metropolitan Museum of Art, New York; *right, Room in a Tenement Flat* (about 1910), photograph by Jessie Tarbox Beals. The Jacob A. Riis Collection, Museum of the City of New York; **196** *top right* Library of Congress; *center left* Chicago Historical Society; *bottom right* Library of Congress; **196** *bottom left,* **197** *center left* Copyright © Bettmann/Corbis; **197** *bottom* Chicago Historical Society; **198, 199** Copyright © Bettmann/Corbis; **200** Brown Brothers.

Chapter 7, 204 The Granger Collection New York; **205** Copyright © Bettmann/Corbis; **207** Copyright © Collection of The New-York Historical Society; **208** Illustration by Patrick Gnan; **209** The Granger Collection, New York; **211** Copyright © Bettmann/Corbis; **212** The Granger Collection, New York; **214** Brown Brothers; **215** Copyright © Michael S. Yamashita/Corbis; **216** Illustration by Ronald Himler. Copyright © 1995 HarperCollins Publishers; *bottom background* Copyright © Bill Pogue; **217** Copyright © Corbis; **218** Jacques Chenet/Getty News Services; **219** *top* Copyright © Joseph Schwartz Collection/Corbis; *bottom* Copyright © Corbis; **220** Library of Congress; **221** The Granger Collection, New York; **224, 225** Copyright © Bettmann/Corbis; **226** *top* Copyright © Lake County Museum/Corbis; *center, bottom* The Granger Collection, New York; **227** Copyright © Bettmann/Corbis; **229, 230** *top right* The Granger Collection, New York; **230** *bottom left* Culver Pictures; **231** Photographs by Sharon Hoogstraten.

Unit 3

232–233 Brown Brothers.

Chapter 8, 234 *top left, Street Arabs in Sleeping Quarters at Night* (date unknown), photograph by Jacob A. Riis. The Jacob A. Riis Collection, Museum of the City of New York; *top right* Library of Congress; *bottom left, Family Making Artificial Flowers* (about 1910), photograph by Jessie Tarbox Beals. The Jacob A. Riis Collection, Museum of the City of New York; *bottom right* Library of Congress; **235** Keystone-Mast Collection U.C.R./California Museum of Photography, University of California, Riverside; **236** Brown Brothers; **237, 238, 239** Library of Congress; **240** *bottom* Brown Brothers; *left inset* Doubleday, Page and Company, New York, 1906, second issue; **241** *Theodore Roosevelt* (date unknown), John Singer Sargent. White House Collection. Copyright © White House Historical Association; **242** *center* Culver Pictures; *bottom left* Copyright © F. Sieb/H. Armstrong Roberts; *bottom right* Copyright © W. Bertsch/H. Armstrong Roberts; **243** *bottom* Copyright © J. Blank/H. Armstrong Roberts; **244** Eugene V. Debs Collection/Tamiment Institute Library, New York University; **246, 247** Culver Pictures; **248** *top, Lillian Wald* 1867-1940, public health nurse, social worker. William Valentine Schevill, 1864-1951. Oil on cardboard, 71.7 x 71.7 cm (28¼ x 28¼ in.) feigned circle, 1919. NPG. 76.37 National Portrait Gallery, Smithsonian Institution, Washington, D. C. Gift of the Visiting Nurse Service of New York/Art Resource, New York; *bottom, A Short Cut over the Roofs of the Tenements; A Henry Street Visiting Nurse* (1908), photograph by Jessie Tarbox Beals. Museum of the City of New York. Lent by the Visiting Nurse Service of New York; **249** The Granger Collection, New York; **250** *left* FPG/Getty Images.

Chapter 9, 254 U.S. Naval Academy Museum; **255** Hawaii State Archives; **256** The Granger Collection, New York; **257** Copyright © Corbis; **259** *Portrait of Queen Liliuokalani,* date and artist unknown. Bishop Museum; **260** The Granger Collection, New York; **261** Chicago Historical Society; **262, 264** The Granger Collection, New York; **265** From *Puerto Rico: A Political and Cultural History,* Arturo Morales Carrion; **266** U.S. Naval Academy Museum; **269** Illustration by Nick Rotondo; *center left* Copyright © Bettmann/Corbis; **271** Copyright © Caren Firouz/Black Star/PNI; **272, 273** *bottom* The Granger Collection, New York.

Chapter 10, 274, 275, 277 The Granger Collection, New York; **279** *top center* Copyright © Mike Fizer/Check Six; *top right* Hulton Getty/Stone Getty Images; *bottom left* Copyright © Hulton-Deutsch Collection/Corbis; *bottom right* Hulton Getty/Stone Getty Images; **280** The Granger Collection, New York; **282–283** Illustration by Patrick Whelan; **282** *top right,* **284, 285** Copyright © Corbis; **287** *left* From *The Enormous Room* by E. E. Cummings, Penguin Twentieth Century Classics Edition. Cover painting *Prisoner's Round* (1890), Vincent van Gogh, after Dore. Pushkin Museum of Fine Arts, Moscow. Photograph courtesy Scala/Art Resource, New York; *right* Book cover from *A Farewell to Arms* by Ernest Hemingway. Cover illustration by Cathie Bleck. Reprinted by permission of Scribner, a Division of Simon & Schuster (New York: Scribner/Simon & Schuster, 1995); **289** Wyoming Division of Cultural Resources; **290** Culver Pictures; **291** Panel no. 1: "During the World War There Was a Great Migration North by Southern Negroes" from *The Migration of the Negro* mural series (1940–41), Jacob Lawrence. Tempera on masonite, 12" x 18". Acquired through Downtown Gallery, 1942. The Phillips Collection, Washington, D.C.; **293** Copyright © Corbis; **294** The Granger Collection, New York; **295** *right,* **299** *bottom* The Granger Collection, New York; **300** Culver Pictures; **301** Photographs by Sharon Hoogstraten.

Unit 4

302–303 Copyright © Morton Beebe/Corbis.

Chapter 11, 304 Copyright © Illustration House, Inc.; **305** *top right* Long Island Auto Museum, New York; *center* Smithsonian Institution, Washington, D.C.; *bottom left* Henry Ford Museum and Greenfield Village, Dearborn, Michigan; *bottom right* Public Domain; **306, 307** Brown Brothers; **308** Copyright © 1923 by The New York Times Co. Reprinted by permission; **309** *center right* Copyright © Stock Montage; **311** Copyright © Underwood & Underwood/Corbis; **312** Culver Pictures; **313** Brown Brothers; **314** Copyright © UPI/Copyright © Bettmann/Corbis; **315** Brown Brothers; **316** *from top to bottom* Movie Still Archives; Copyright © Blank Archives/Hulton/Archive/Getty Images; Copyright © Hulton/Archive/Getty Images; Photofest; **317** *left* Brown Brothers; *right* Copyright © Albert L. Bresnik; **318** *The Ascent of Ethiopia* (1932), Lois Mailou Jones. Oil on canvas, 23½" x 17¼". Accession no. M1993.191. Milwaukee Art Museum, Purchase, African-American Art Acquisition Fund, matching funds from Suzanne and Richard Pieper, with additional support from Arthur and Dorothy Nelle Sanders; **319** *top* Copyright © Stock Montage; *bottom* Book cover from first edition of *The Great Gatsby* by F. Scott Fitzgerald (New York: Charles Scribner's Sons, 1925). Used by permission of Scribner, a division of Simon & Schuster; **320, 321** *bottom* National Baseball Hall of Fame Library, Cooperstown, New York.

Chapter 12, 324 Museum of the City of New York; **325** The Granger Collection, New York; **326** From The Collection of Janice L. and David J. Frent; **327** Nebraska Historical Society; **329** Icon Comm./FPG/Getty Images; **330** From The Collections of the Minnesota Historical Society; **331** Copyright © Corbis; **332** Library of Congress; **333** Photograph by Margaret Suckley/Franklin D. Roosevelt Library; **334** *inset* Courtesy of The Tennessee Valley Authority; **336** F.D.R. Presidential Library; **337** Detail of *Mary McLeod Bethune* (1943–1944), Betsy Graves Reyneau. National Portrait Gallery, Smithsonian Institution, Washington, D. C./Art Resource, New York; **338** *inset* Copyright © Corbis; **339** *left* Photofest; *center, right* The Kobal Collection; **340** Copyright © Oscar White/Corbis; **341** Copyright © UPI/Copyright © Bettmann/Corbis; **342** Copyright © McDougal Littell Inc.; **343** Farm Security Administration—Office of War Information Photograph Collection; **344** Library of Congress; **346** *Construction of the Dam* (1937), William Gropper. Mural study, Department of the Interior, National Park Service. National Museum of American Art, Smithsonian Institution, Washington, D. C./Art Resource, New York; **347** Courtesy of Social Security Office; **348** *top* Icon Comm./FPG/Getty Images; *bottom* From The Collection of Janice L. and David J. Frent; **349** Photograph by Dorothea Lange/Library of Congress; **350** Details of *South Texas Panorama* (1939). Warren Hunter. Mural, Alice, Texas Post Office. National Museum of American Art, Smithsonian Institution, Washington, D. C./Art Resource, New York; **351** Photographs by Sharon Hoogstraten.

Chapter 13, 352 Copyright © UPI/Copyright © Bettmann/Corbis; **353** National Archives; **355** Photograph by Hugo Jaeger/*Life* magazine, copyright © Time Warner Inc.; **356** Copyright © Corbis; **357** The Granger Collection, New York; **359** Copyright © Corbis; **360** Copyright © 1999 Owen H. K./Black Star; **361** Copyright © The Mariner's Museum/Corbis; **362** *left,* **363** Copyright © Bettmann/Corbis; **364** *top* National Archives; **365** Copyright © Hulton-Deutsch Collection/Corbis; **366** Photograph by Margaret Bourke White/*Life* magazine, copyright © Time Inc.; **368** Copyright © Corbis; **370** National Archives; **371** The Granger Collection, New York; **372** U.S. Office of War Information, photo no. 208-LV-38BB-3 in the National Archives; **373** Copyright © Bettmann/Corbis; **374** Copyright © Wally McNamee/Corbis; **375**

Photograph by Dorothea Lange/National Archives; **376–377** *background* Copyright © Photolink/PhotoDisc, Inc.; **376** *bottom left* Copyright © Bettmann/Corbis; *bottom right* The Granger Collection, New York; **377** *top, Captain America™* and copyright © 1999 Marvel Characters, Inc. Used with permission; **378** Copyright © Bettmann/Corbis; **380, 381, 383** *bottom* The Granger Collection, New York.

Chapter 14, 384 *background* Photograph by Carl Iwasaki/*Life* magazine, copyright © Time Inc.; *foreground* Henry Ford Museum and Greenfield Village, Dearborn, Michigan; **385** Photograph by J. R. Eyerman/*Life* magazine, copyright © Time Warner Inc.; **386** *background* Copyright © R. Walker/H. Armstrong Roberts; *foreground* Cousley Historical Collections. Photograph by Stephen Mays, New York; **387** U.S. Army photographs; **389** Copyright © UPI/Bettmann/Corbis; **391** Photograph by Walter Sanders/*Life* magazine, copyright © 1972 Time Inc.; **392** Photofest; **393** AP/Wide World Photos; **395** Copyright © Bettmann/Corbis; **396** Photograph by Hank Walker/*Life* magazine. Copyright © Time Inc.; **397** Sovfoto/Eastfoto; **398** Courtesy of Brunswick Record Corporation; **399** Copyright © Frank Cezus/Stone Getty Images, Inc.; **400** *from top to bottom* Copyright © Hulton/Archive/Getty Images; Elvis Presley Enterprises, Inc. Used by permission; Harold Lloyd Trust/Hulton/Archive/Getty Images; The Kobal Collection; **402–403** *background* Illustration by Alexander Verbitsky; **402** *top* Copyright © Tom Bean/Stone Getty Images; *bottom left* Curt Teich Postcard Archives, Lake County Museum, Wauconda, Illinois; **402** *bottom right, center left* Copyright © 1996 Terrence Moore; **403** *center right* Copyright © Ferguson & Katzman/Stone Getty Images; *bottom* Copyright © Rob Boudreau/Stone Getty Images; **405** *bottom* Courtesy of Ross Lewis and the *Milwaukee Journal.*

Unit 5

406–407 Photograph by Francis Miller/*Life* magazine, copyright © Time Inc.

Chapter 15, 408 Copyright © James Blair/NGS Image Collection; **409** Photograph by John G. Moebes. Reprinted with permission of the *News & Record.* This reprint does not constitute or imply any endorsement or sponsorship of any product, service, company or organization; **410** Copyright © 1950 Elliott Erwitt/Magnum Photos, Inc.; **411** Copyright © Bettmann/Corbis; **412** AP/Wide World Photos; **413** Copyright © Black Star/Time Inc.; **414** Copyright © UPI/Copyright © Bettmann/Corbis; **416** Copyright © Bettmann/Corbis; **417** Copyright © 1963 Charles Moore/Black Star; **418** Photo no. KN-C30670 in the John F. Kennedy Library; **420** President Lyndon Baines Johnson Library and Museum; **421** AP/Wide World Photos; **422** Copyright © 1978 George Ballis/Take Stock; **423** Copyright © Robert Fried/Stock Boston/PNI; **424** Copyright © Bettmann/Corbis; **425** AP/Wide World Photos; **428** *top* Copyright © UPI/Copyright © Bettmann/Corbis; *center* Copyright © Black Star/Time Inc.; *bottom* Photograph by Sharon Hoogstraten; **429** *bottom, Freedom* (date unknown), Anthony Gauthier. Property of the Institute of American Indian Arts Museum, no. WIN14.

Chapter 16, 430 Copyright © Seny Norasingh/Light Sensitive; **431** *left* Copyright © Bettmann/Corbis; *right* Copyright © Wally McNamee/Corbis; **433** From *The Unquiet American* by Cecil B. Currey. Photograph courtesy of the author; **434** AP/Wide World Photos; **435** *right* Sovfoto/Eastfoto; **436** Copyright © Corbis; **437** Copyright © Bettmann/Corbis; **438** Copyright © Corbis; **439** Copyright © Bettmann/Corbis; **440** *left* Popperfoto/Hulton/ Archive/Getty Images; *center* PNI; *right* National Archives; **441** *left* Copyright © 1999 Jim Pickerell/Black Star; *right* Photograph by Larry Burrows/*Life* magazine, copyright © Time Inc. Courtesy of Larry Burrows Collection, New York; **443** Copyright © 1968 Herblock; **444** Copyright © John Paul Filo; **445** *inset* Copyright © UPI/Bettmann/Corbis; **446** Copyright © 1998 Nik Wheeler/Black Star; **447** Copyright © Dave G. Houser/Corbis.

Chapter 17, 450 *top left* Copyright © 1999 Robin Moyer/Black Star; *top right* Copyright © Philippe Ledru/Corbis Sygma; *center left* Jim Moore/Getty News Services; *center right* Copyright © 1997 Dennis Brack/Black Star; *bottom* Copyright © Hulton/Archive/Getty Images; **451** *top* Photograph by Harry Benson; *center left* Copyright © 1974, The Washington Post. Reprinted with permission; **452** *top left* AP/Wide World Photos; *center left* Copyright © Lary Voigt/Photo Researchers, Inc.; *center right* Copyright © Ted Thai/*Time* magazine; **453** Copyright © 1999 Dennis Brack/Black Star; **454** NASA; **456** AP/Wide World Photos; **457** Copyright © Penelope Breese/Getty News Services; **458** Cartoon by Paul Conrad. Copyright © Los Angeles Times Syndicate; **459** Copyright © 1974 Alex Webb/Magnum Photos, Inc.; **460** AP/Wide World Photos; **461** Copyright © R. Krubner/H. Armstrong Roberts; **462** Copyright © Dirk Halstead/Getty News Services; **464–465** *background* NASA; **464** *center left* Copyright © Ariel Skelley/Corbis Stock Market; **465** *top* Copyright © R. Krubner/H. Armstrong Roberts; *bottom right* Photograph by Vernon Merritt/*Life* magazine, copyright © Time Inc.; **466** From The Collection of David J. and Janice L. Frent.

Chapter 18, 468 Copyright © R. Ian Lloyd/Masterfile; **469** Copyright © 1999 USA Today. Reprinted with permission; **470** Copyright © 1993 Time Inc. Reprinted by permission; **471** From The Collection of Janice L. and David J. Frent; **472** Courtesy of Ronald Reagan Library; **473, 474** *top left* AP/Wide World Photos; **474** *top* Copyright © 1998 The Washington Post. Reprinted with permission; **475** Kevin Kallaugher, Cartoonists & Writers Syndicate/cartoonweb.com; **477** Copyright © Reuters NewMedia Inc./Corbis; **478** Copyright © Paul Soulders/Getty News Services; **479** Photograph by Donna McWilliam; **480** *top right* Copyright © Bettmann/Corbis; *center* Commodore Business Machines, Inc.; *center right* Copyright © Charles Feil/Stock Boston/PNI; *bottom left* Ted Kawalerski/The Image Bank/Getty Images/Chicago Core; **481** Copyright © Peter Charlesworth/ SABA; **482** Photograph by Doug Hoke; **483** Photograph copyright © Marion Ettlinger; **484** Copyright © Robert Brenner/PhotoEdit/PNI; **487** *bottom* Photograph by Kaku Kurita; **488** *top* Copyright © Peter Simon/ Stock Boston/PNI; *bottom left* Copyright © Lambert/Hulton/ Archive/Getty Images; *bottom center* Copyright © Henry/TSI Imaging/Stone Getty Images; **489** Photographs by Sharon Hoogstraten.

Special Report

491 *top, bottom* AP/Wide World Photos; **493** *top, bottom* AP/Wide World Photos; **494** AP/Wide World Photos; **495** *left* © Mario Tama/Getty Images; *right* © Reuters NewMedia Inc./Corbis.

Supreme Court

496 *top left* Copyright © Corbis; *bottom left* Copyright © 1994 North Wind Pictures; *bottom center* The Granger Collection, New York; *bottom right* Copyright © 1999 North Wind Pictures; **497** *top* Copyright © Corbis; *bottom left* Copyright © Bettmann/Corbis; *bottom right* AP/Wide World Photos; **498** *top left* Copyright © Corbis; *bottom right* The Granger Collection, New York; **499** Copyright © 1994 North Wind Pictures; **500** Copyright © Corbis; **501** *left* Culver Pictures; *right* The Granger Collection, New York; **502** Copyright © Corbis; *bottom right* The Granger Collection, New York; **503** Copyright © 1999 North Wind Pictures; **504** Copyright © Corbis; **505** *left* The Granger Collection, New York; *right* Lincoln University Archives, Langston

Hughes Memorial Library, Lincoln University, Penn.; **506** *top left* Copyright © Corbis; *bottom right* The Granger Collection, New York; **507** AP/Wide World Photos; **508** *top left* Copyright © Corbis; **509** Wally McNamee/Corbis; **510** *top left* Copyright © Corbis; *bottom right* AP/Wide World Photos; **511** Copyright © Corbis; **512** *top left* Copyright © Corbis; *bottom right* Copyright © Bettmann/Corbis; **514** *top left* Copyright © Owen Franken/Corbis; *bottom right* AP/Wide World Photos; **515** AP/Wide World Photos.

SkillBuilder Handbook

R15 Library of Congress; **R28** Courtesy of The Lloyd Ostendorf Collection.

Presidents of the United States

R40–R42 *all except Clinton* The Oval Office Collection™; *Clinton* AP/Wide World Photos.

McDougal Littell Inc. has made every effort to locate the copyright holders of all copyrighted material in this book and to make full acknowledgment for its use.